Two year olds of 2009

STEVE TAPLIN

Raceform

Published in 2009 by Raceform
Compton, Newbury, Berkshire, RG20 6NL

Copyright © Steve Taplin 2009

The right of Steve Taplin to be identified as the author of this work has been asserted by him in accordance with the Copyright, Designs and Patents Act 1988.

All rights reserved. No part of this publication may be reproduced, stored in a retrieval system, or transmitted in any form or by any means, electronic, mechanical, photocopying, recording, or otherwise, without the prior written permission of the publishers.

A catalogue record for this book is available from the British Library.

ISBN 978-1-906820-18-3

Designed by Fiona Pike

Printed by CPI William Clowes Beccles NR34 7TL

Contents

Foreword by William Haggas	4
Introduction	5
Fifty to Follow	7
Ten to Follow in Ireland	11
Star Two Year Olds	12
The Bloodstock Experts Mark Your Card	13
Two Year Olds	19
Stallion Reference	334
Racing Trends	346
Late Names	353
Index to Horses	355
Index to Dams	361

Foreword

It is hard to believe that this edition of Steve Taplin's "Two-Year-Olds" is the 25th.

This is the best book of its type available. It is comprehensively researched and developed during months of hard work and immense dedication. Steve takes the time and trouble to visit nearly all the trainers mentioned in the book as well as interrogating most of the leading bloodstock agents and breeders for their suggestions of horses to follow.

Steve then goes through each pedigree in meticulous detail therefore providing his readers with the opportunity to find winners galore in 2009 – and beyond that too.

Almost every trainer talks freely about the new intake of two-year-olds. This is a most exciting time and we all dream of finding the star which will propel our careers to new heights and with over 18,000 foals born in 2007 in England and Ireland the two-year-old crop for this year is large.

Many of them are covered in this excellent publication which I hope you will enjoy as much as me.

William Haggas

Introduction

Twenty five years old and still counting – the book that is, not the author! I've been privileged to have *Two-Year-Olds* endorsed by many of England's top trainers over the years. Visiting their yards has been a pleasure for me and hopefully a source of good information to those who have bought the book regularly. This year I'm delighted that Newmarket trainer William Haggas has kindly agreed to write the foreword. William's highly successful season in 2008 was one of the highlights of the racing year and his final tally of winners was easily a personal best. I must say it is always a pleasure for me to arrive at Somerville Lodge and interview him. His owners must be equally delighted at having their horses in his care.

Once again the majority of trainers have been extremely helpful to me, particularly throughout the first three weeks of April when the interviews took place. I managed to speak to no less than 68 of them. As always, their comments are in the book for my readers to dissect.

The various 'Horses to Follow' lists in the 2008 edition of *Two-Year-Olds* performed with credit, with almost 52% of selections winning at least once. Of particular merit was the section Bloodstock Experts Mark Your Card. Sixteen of the 'experts' were pleased to advise us and only one failed to pick a winner.

In response to many requests, I've re-introduced the Index to Dams. This will help you find the two-year-old sons and daughters of your favourite broodmares and it also helps when you're searching for a horse that's in the book as 'unnamed'.

Naturally, every year some horses fail to live up to the expectations of their connections, but you don't need to be a trainer to know that a thousand and one things can go wrong during a horse's development. Even those giants of the turf, Ballydoyle and Godolphin, have to go through an awful lot of sorting to separate the wheat from the chaff. So when a much smaller yard tastes success at the highest level they deserve every ounce of credit they can get. Ralph Beckett's Oaks win with Look Here, Robin Bastiman's Nunthorpe win with Borderlescott, John Best's excellent Royal Ascot victories with Kingsgate Native and Flashman's Papers, Rae Guest's filly Serious Attitude winning the Cheveley Park Stakes and Paul Blockley taking the Criterium International with Zafisio were some of the most notable examples in 2008. So the big prizes don't always go to the big yards.

Other notable performances in 2008 include Hayley Turner reaching the 100 winner mark. How sad she had to be stood down for a year after her bad fall in early March and I'm sure all racing fans wish her a full recovery and a successful return to the saddle. Richard Hannon's incredible tally of 95 two-year-old wins was another highlight of the season. Always kind and helpful when I visit his lovely yard and home at Herridge, Richard has developed a winner making machine for juveniles, although he did point out to me that this year his two-year-olds are "better types in general with the scope to improve even further and make good three-year-olds". Richard's partnership with bloodstock agent Peter Doyle is well-known and finding good horses at reasonable prices is something they manage to achieve year in, year out.

On a personal note as far as 2008 is concerned, the three horses racing under my Racing Partnership's banner hardly performed with any credit, but I console myself with the fact that most horses aren't very good and so my year was probably average in terms of what owners should expect!

The following is a rough guide to my description of the ability of family members mentioned in the pedigree assessment of every two-year-old, based upon professional ratings. Please note that these descriptions are standard throughout the book in the vast majority of cases, but there are instances where I rely upon my own judgement of the horse's rating.

Below 60 = moderate
60 – 69 = modest
70 – 79 = fair
80 – 89 = quite useful
90 – 99 = fairly useful
100 – 107 = useful
108 – 112 = very useful
113 – 117 = smart
118 – 122 = very smart
123 – 127 = high-class
128 – 134 = top-class
135 and above = outstanding

The two-year-olds in this book are listed under their trainers and I have carefully selected those horses most likely to perform well this year. There are several 'horses to follow' lists, such as the sections Fifty To Follow and Star Two-Year-Olds. These are always useful for those who want to follow a select number of horses. The Bloodstock Experts Mark Your Card, is a particularly fruitful section for pinpointing winners. Note also that many trainers suggest their Bargain Buy. My only stipulation is that the horse cannot have cost more than 30,000 guineas at the yearling sales.

My friends at Raceform have ensured that the book is comprehensively indexed.

The book is divided into the following sections:

- Fifty To Follow.
- Ten to Follow in Ireland.
- Star Two-Year-Olds. This system gives an instant appraisal of the regard in which a horse is held.
- The Bloodstock Experts Mark Your Card. Bloodstock agents and stud managers suggest potentially smart two-year-olds bought or raised by them.
- Two-Year-Olds of 2009. The main section of the book, with each two-year-old listed under the trainer. *Trainers' comments (when given) are in italics after the pedigree assessments.* Readers should bear in mind that all the trainers' comments come from my interviews, which took part in early April.
- Stallion Reference, detailing the racing and stud careers of sires with at least four two-year-olds in the book.
- Racing Trends. An analysis of some juvenile events that regularly highlight the stars of the future. It includes a list of three-year-olds to follow this season.
- Stop Press. Late Names.
- Index of Two-Year-Olds.
- Index of Dams.

There are inevitably some unnamed horses in the book, but please access my website www.stevetaplin.co.uk throughout the season for updates on those horses named after the book was published.

I must say a big thank you to Hilda Marshall for once again helping me out in the last few weeks in an effort to ensure the book is published in time. Thanks also to the racing and stud secretaries for being so helpful and, not least, the trainers for giving me their time so generously yet again.

Researched and compiled
by Steve Taplin BA (Hons).

Fifty to follow

Here is a choice selection of two year olds from the book for you to follow.

AATTASH
"Yes, he's a lovely horse. He could be really nice in the middle of the summer and I like him a lot".
Mick Channon

ABOVE LIMITS
"This is an interesting filly. I went to Goffs just to pick horses for Harry Findlay and I looked for ages and couldn't find one that I liked. Then late in the afternoon I saw this filly and I loved her. I'm very pleased we got her ... I think this filly is nice and she's got plenty of speed".
Tom Dascombe

AGE OF REFINEMENT
"She'll make her debut in July and I would say she looks much more like a sprinter than a stayer. A smallish filly, she should make a two-year-old, probably over six furlongs".
Sir Mark Prescott

ALRASM
"He's a big horse but very mature, he's going nicely and he looks like being one of our earlier runners. He's bred to be speedy and looks that way and although he's out of a Rainbow Quest mare he seems to take after the sire".
Michael Jarvis

AMNO DANCER
"He's showing me plenty and he's a big, strong, rangy horse and very similar to his sire in looks. He'll be out in May and the boys couldn't believe I bought him for only 12 Grand".
Mark Tompkins

BABYCAKES
"I like Marju fillies and this is a nice one. She won't be out early but she does everything asked of her easily".
Michael Bell

BLUE LYRIC
"She's nice and she's going well. She seems to have enough speed for six furlongs and I'd expect her out in June or July".
Luca Cumani

BOUGAINVILIA
"A lovely filly, she's gorgeous and you can see why she cost so much. I'll see how we go as regards distance and we'll start to do a bit more with her soon. A fine filly, she's medium-sized and particularly nice".
Richard Hannon

BUSINESS BAY
"He's the apple of my eye at the moment. A lovely horse and a week after we bought him the half-sister Saucey Evening was fourth in the Breeders Cup Juvenile Turf. This fellow will need a mile but he's a smashing physical specimen – there wouldn't be a better looking two-year-old in Newmarket".
Ed Vaughan

CANFORD CLIFFS
"He's a lovely horse that's done very well. A fine, big bay horse, Richard Hughes has ridden him already, so he's ready for action".
Richard Hannon

CHACHAMAIDEE
"This is a nice filly and an early foal that should make a two-year-old later on".
Henry Cecil

DARSHONIN
"He's an ideal size for a two-year-old, a very nice horse and one that goes along nicely with the Indian Ridge colt. He's full of quality".
Marcus Tregoning

DHERGHAAM
"He's a beautiful mover and a scopey individual that moves well. He looks a nice horse".
Ed Dunlop

DREAM OF GERONTIUS
"A sharp filly, she's working nicely and she'll be racing early on".
Richard Hannon

EJAAB
"A real strong two-year-old, he'll be out in May and we'll try and speed him up to see if he can make Ascot. A nice colt, he's all speed and a really well-made horse".
William Haggas

FLAMBEAU
"She's very big but she's strong and has good bone. You'd have to be careful in the next few weeks because of her size, but otherwise she's coming together nicely, she's doing some gentle half-speeds and looks a very nice filly for the middle of the year".
Henry Candy

FLY SILCA FLY
"She's very nice, she's all there and shows she's a nice two-year-old, so even though you wouldn't expect a Hawk Wing to be precocious she shows all the right signs. I haven't really got into her yet but she looks like being a really nice filly. She's certainly got ability and I think she'll need six or seven furlongs this year".
Mick Channon

FOOTSIE FOOTSIE
"A nice filly, she's very attractive and a good mover. She'll need a bit of time but she looks like she'll be a black type filly. A good 'goer' that floats along, she's done well".
Barry Hills

FOREST CROWN
"A half-sister to the Derby favourite Crowded House, I think this filly will be relatively forward. She's done well physically in the last month – she's really strengthened up a lot and I don't think she's finished yet. There's every chance she's a proper filly and she'd be one of my leading hopes".
Ralph Beckett

GHOSTWING
"A nice horse, it won't be long before he's out. He was small when we bought him but he's filled out over the winter and he really looks the part now. He's got some speed ... and he'd be one to watch out for".
Ann Duffield

HILL OF MILLER
"A nice horse, he's doing very well and he will be a two-year-old. He was a bit small when I bought him but he's fine now. Six furlongs should be his starting point".
Rae Guest

IN VIGO
"Hawk Wing isn't everyone's cup of tea but I think we've done well picking up this colt. He's done very well physically and has a good way of going, so I'd be surprised and disappointed if he didn't prove well worth his purchase price. I think he's a nice horse, solid, sound and a seven furlong type two-year-old".
William Jarvis

IQTINAA
"A very nice filly ... and hopefully she'll be one for the Albany Stakes – something like that. A filly with a lot of quality".
William Haggas

KONA COAST
"He's a beautiful mover and a scopey individual that moves well. He looks a nice horse".
John Gosden

LATANSAA
"I have the unraced three-year-old filly by Dalakhani and she's very nice. This Indian Ridge colt is too. He's a straightforward, good-tempered horse that knows his stuff and we just have to wait a bit with him because he could be a nice horse a bit later on ... He's the star of all

my two-year-olds at the moment".
Marcus Tregoning

LIFE AND SOUL
"There is a pedigree update because Mr Medici was recently placed in the Hong Kong Derby. This is a really nice, forward-going colt that should be a seven furlong type this year. I just have an idea that he may be a Chesham Stakes horse".
Amanda Perrett

LODEN
"He's a nice mover that goes well and he has a very good temperament. He'll be out in July and he'd be one of my nicest two-year-olds".
Luca Cumani

LOGOS ASTRA
"A smashing colt that goes very nicely A well-made horse, he's very easy to do anything with and he's my favourite at the moment. I wouldn't be surprised if he had the speed to go six furlongs but he'll probably be better over seven".
David Lanigan

MEEZAAN
"A very likeable horse and I'd like him the most of the ones we have from Sheikh Hamdan. He moves well and he's strong and purposeful. He's done a little work upsides and he goes well".
John Gosden

MOUNT JULIET
"I really like this filly, she's got a lot of class about her, has all the right attributes and is one for the middle part of the season. She's definitely got an engine, does everything right and you should hear a fair bit about her because she's the type that could be really good".
Simon Callaghan

NASHAMA
"This filly is athletic and has a lot of quality. A lovely prospect for this season and the next."
Saeed bin Suroor

ONE GOOD EMPEROR
"I think he's very classy. He finds everything easy and he's impressive in his slower paces. I'm hopeful he'll be one of our nicer two-year-olds. He should be out before June to see if he's good enough for Royal Ascot because I'd like to send as many there as possible".
John Best

PARADISE DREAM
"He's just coming into fast work now and he looks a speedy type. He has a great attitude and he's a lovely, laid-back colt that has the make and shape of a two-year-old sprinting type. I like the way he goes about things".
Jeremy Noseda

PARK TWILIGHT
"She's...been in fast work. She goes well, looks a two-year-old type, has a great attitude and a good action. She'll definitely be doing a job over six furlongs from May onwards. She's a filly that I like and she's nice, straightforward two-year-old".
Jeremy Noseda

PASTORAL PLAYER
"Yes, he's a racehorse all right. He's quite sharp but he's not small and he's on his toes – probably because he finds everything easy. I did a bit of work with him a couple of weeks ago and that was enough to show me he's got speed, so I'd be disappointed if he didn't win at two".
Hughie Morrison

PIN CUSHION
"A very smart filly, she's very forward in her work but not in her coat. So we're just waiting with her for a bit, but she looks a good filly".
Brian Meehan

PINK COAT
"A lovely horse, he shows all the right signs. He'll be a seven furlongs/mile colt for later on but he'll be really nice".
Mick Channon

QUALITY MOVER
"A lovely filly, I like her a lot. She's big and mature but I imagine she'll be running over six or seven furlongs in mid-summer".
David Simcock

RAINE'S CROSS
"He's done really well lately and I think he's a very nice horse. He's come to hand quickly for a Cape Cross and yet he's not just a two-year-old type because he does have scope".
Peter Winkworth

SATWA SON
"This is a nice horse. He came in late but he looks to go well. A strong, well-bred colt and he'll be a nice, mid-season two-year-old".
Ed Dunlop

SENT FROM HEAVEN
"A nice, quality filly, she's only done a few canters upsides but we're only taking our time with her. She's maturing and she's grown and put on condition. From the way she goes I'd have to say she could be really nice and she'll definitely be going for black type".
Barry Hills

SOMNIUM
"A real nice horse, when we bought him his dam hadn't bred a winner but since then both her first foals have won. He's one of our better horses, I'll kick start his season in May over six furlongs and aim him for the Tattersalls Sales race in Ireland. One to look out for".
Stan Moore

SWEET SONNET
"A beautifully bred filly who is doing very well and pleasing. We would hope to see her race in June."
Saeed bin Suroor

TARTAN TRIP
"This is a seriously nice horse. He's a typical Selkirk in many ways but his dam won over five furlongs at two and I think he'll win over six furlongs this year. He's got plenty of speed".
Andrew Balding

TELL HALAF
"He's improved leaps and bounds physically since he came here. We trained the mother and the half-brother and this colt is far more precocious than Topazes. I think he'll be one of the first of our two-year-olds to run and he's looking like a promising, early summer two-year-old".
Michael Bell

VIRGINIA HALL
"I see her being out around July time. It's a fast family and they all make two-year-olds"
Sir Mark Prescott

WALCOTT SQUARE
"I like him – he's a neat, strong, well-made horse and a good mover".
Roger Charlton

WALVIS BAY
"A very early-maturing colt that's showing early speed. I'll run him as soon as I can and I'd say he's quick in all departments!"
Tom Tate

WARLU WAY
"A May foal, he's a beautiful mover and a scopey individual that moves well. He looks a nice horse".
John Dunlop

WISECRAIC
"This could be our best horse. He should be ready in May and he's pretty smart. By a very good two-year-old sire and out of a Group One winner ... he's a big, strong, tall colt and he has scope ... he could be ready in May".
Tom Dascombe

Ten to follow in Ireland

ALSALWA
"She's a filly we like a lot and she'll be racing before the end of May. She's compact, has plenty of quality and will probably start off at six furlongs but she might well stay a mile by the end of the year".
Kevin Prendergast

FAMOUS WARRIOR
"I like him a lot, we haven't had him long but he's a good goer and a good galloper. I expect he'll want seven furlongs from mid-summer onwards".
Kevin Prendergast

JULIE'S JET
"She's a lovely filly out of a good mare I trained for Lady O'Reilly, hopefully she'll be out in late June or July. She'll probably want seven furlongs".
John Oxx

MARCUS GALERIUS (IRE)
"He goes nicely and he'll be out in May over six furlongs. His pedigree is very light but he's a good-looking colt".
Tommy Stack

MISTER TEE
"He's a cracking horse and he'll start in mid-April. You can't have too many Danehill Dancer's – I've had a few nice ones and this colt is every bit as good as they were. He'll be a smart horse if he delivers on the track what he does at home. He's ready to run and you'll be seeing him soon over five furlongs".
Ger Lyons

SHAREEN
"This is a particularly nice filly with a very fluent stride. She's quite strong and mature-looking and I'm hoping she'll be out in June. She's promising".
John Oxx

WALK ON BYE
"A nice filly, she seems to have a bit of toe and probably won't get much further than six or seven furlongs I should imagine. She goes nicely and she's a good-looking filly. We're getting quite excited about her and it won't be long before she's out".
Tommy Stack

WEALDMORE WAVE
"If I had a Royal Ascot horse I think it could be him. I think he's a very smart horse, he has a lovely attitude and hopefully he'll win next time out, over six furlongs. I like him a lot".
Ger Lyons

WRONG ANSWER (IRE)
"She's had a run and was only just touched off. She's not very big, but she's full of quality and she'll win all right".
Kevin Prendergast

UNNAMED
b.c. Shamardal – Mayenne (Nureyev)
"He's a thick-set colt and I would say you're looking at six furlongs with him in mid-summer. He looks like a real little two-year-old and he has the conformation of a sprinter".
Michael Grassick

Star Two Year Olds

Potential superstars to look out for!

The asterisks placed alongside the names of each two-year-old in the main section of the book give the reader an instant appraisal of the regard in which each horse is held. The highest rating a horse can attain is five stars.

All the five star two-year-olds of 2009 are listed below for quick reference.

AL MUTHANAA	William Haggas
ALTRUISTE	Sir Mark Prescott
BASS ROCK	John Oxx
BOYCOTT	John Gosden
COORDINATED CUT	Peter Chapple-Hyam
DORBACK	Henry Candy
EMIRATES DREAM	Saeed bin Suroor
FINE SIGHT	Richard Hannon
FREMONT	Richard Hannon
GALLIC STAR	Mick Channon
HOT PROSPECT	Michael Jarvis
KERALOUN	John Oxx
LATANSAA	Marcus Tregoning
MAWZOON	Michael Jarvis
MONSIEUR CHEVALIER	Richard Hannon
MONTPARNASSE	Brian Meehan
NEBULA STORM	Jeremy Noseda
RED JAZZ	Barry Hills
RUTHIE BABE	William Haggas
SENT FROM HEAVEN	Barry Hills
SIR PITT	John Gosden
SYRIAN	Michael Bell
TOWER	John Gosden
VIKING DANCER	Andrew Balding
YOUM JAMIL	Brian Meehan
b.c. Acclamation – Milly Fleur	Peter Chapple-Hyam

The Bloodstock Experts Mark Your Card

Each year I announce one of our experts as being "Top of the Class" but I don't recall the decision ever being as close as this one. Of the 62 selections from our experts last year, 52 ran with 28 winning 44 races between them. An admirable attempt at pointing us in the direction of winners – and not any old winners either! The selections included a Group One hero (well done Kirsten Rausing), the lucrative Goffs Million, Tattersalls Timeform Fillies' 800 and Tattersalls October Auction Stakes winners and four more Group/listed stakes winners including the highly-rated Finjaan. Only one of the 16 'experts' failed to tip a winner and he shall remain nameless in the expectation of redemption this time!

Now let's look at those who did particularly well with their 2008 'picks'. Angus Gold came four winners out of five including Finjaan – so narrowly beaten in the Dewhurst Stakes. In the "three out of four" category we have Will Edmeades (including the tough and consistent colt Bonnie Charlie) and Charlie Gordon-Watson (including Solario Stakes winner Sri Putra and the 106 rated Awinnersgame). Those with two winners apiece were Kirsten Rausing (most notably the Group 1 Criterium de Saint-Cloud winner Fame And Glory), Peter Doyle (Soul City won the Group 3 Prix La Rochette and the Goffs Million), Harry Herbert, Johnny McKeever, David Redvers and Anthony Stroud.

I think it's only fair to declare a tie for first place between **Kirsten Rausing** (the only one to select a Group 1 winner) and **Angus Gold** (who picked the most winners including the highest rated two-year-old of all the selections, Finjaan). Thanks once again to all our 'experts' for taking part and for trying their best to find us some nice winners.

Please note that most of the following two-year-olds are in the main section of the book listed under their trainers and are highlighted by the symbol ♠

PETER DOYLE

CANFORD CLIFFS. A colt by Tagula that cost 50,000 Guineas at Doncaster St Leger Sale, he's one of the nicest yearlings we bought. Trainer Richard Hannon.

DREAM OF GERONTIUS. A filly by Oratario, she cost 20,000 Guineas at Doncaster St. Leger. A lovely filly, she looks the part and I think the sire Oratorio could have a real future. Trainer Richard Hannon.

ELIZABELLE. A filly by Westerner out of Jus'chillen, she cost 35,000 Euros at Goffs' she's a half sister to the Group 2 winner Orizaba. This is a very nice filly with a great outlook and is enjoying her work. Trainer Richard Hannon.

SABII SANDS. A bay colt by Invincible Spirit that cost 120,000 Euros at Goffs, he's really matured early and could be anything. Trainer Richard Hannon.

ROSS DOYLE

BOUGAINVILIA. A gorgeous filly by Bahamian Bounty we bought at the Goffs Million Sale with a very good pedigree and plenty of size. She is a half sister to last years Queen Mary winner Langs Lash and looks like a lovely filly for the middle of the season. All these are with Richard Hannon.

HALF SISTER. A very racey filly by Oratario from the family of George Washington and she really looks the part. I would be a big fan of the stallion from what we bought as yearlings.

SUITED AND BOOTED. A lovely, big, strong colt by Tagula that walked around the sales like he owned the place. He is a half brother to Cake and the same people are involved in him so he is bound to be lucky.

LUCKY GENERAL. A medium sized, well-made colt by Hawk Wing from the family of Rag Top & Red Top. He looks like a very laid back, tough sort of individual that might just surprise a few people being by Hawk Wing.

TOM GOFF
b.c. Red Ransom – Sophielu. A relatively expensive Doncaster purchase at £67,000, this is a really lovely colt whom I've always had a soft spot for. He was sold by Highclere Stud and was beautifully prepared. Since then he went through a rather wooly stage through the winter but really looks marvelous now. Fingers crossed, he'll turn out to be a nice six to seven furlong two-year-old when the time comes for Peter Chapple-Hyam.

b.f. Sadler's Wells – Race The Wild Wind. This is a filly I bought for €520,000 at Deauville last year from Haras D'Etreham. She is owned by Andrew Black and is a really stunning filly. She is with Peter Chapple-Hyam who loves her and she's a half sister to King Charlemagne and Meshaheer, who were Group 1 and Group 2 winners respectively so she certainly has the pedigree to succeed. She won't be that precocious and is a pretty typical Sadler's Wells but I hope that she will be out over 7 furlongs to a mile later in the season. A very exciting prospect indeed whom I have always adored from the moment I clapped eyes on her.

b.c. Firebreak – Yanomami. A relatively precocious colt I picked up at Doncaster St Leger Sale for £32,000 from Fernham Farm. I was a big fan of Firebreak as a racehorse because he was so genuine. This colt is with Peter Chapple-Hyam who's happy with his progress so far. It's very early days but we're hoping he could be a fast sort in the high summer.

b.c. Konigstiger – Sylvette. A cracking two-year-old type I bought for €38,000 at the Baden-Baden Yearling Sale from Gestut Farhof. I loved him as a yearling as he looked a real runner. Although the sire is unproven, he was a pretty good two-year-old himself and the half-brother by Stravinsky won the Golden Peitsche so I'm hopeful this will make up into a decent horse in time with Dermot Weld.

b.c. North Light – Fifth Avenue Doll. Something of a gamble to say the least with the sire, although he had another lovely colt in Keeneland September. I paid 47,000gns for him at Tattersalls Part 2 from Pier House Stud, Ireland and he's with John Gosden. He won't be early but he's a real nice sort who moves well and they appear to be happy with him at the moment although he won't have done any fast work as such. Hopefully one to follow in seven furlong and mile races when the time comes.

ANGUS GOLD
ALRASM. Trainer Michael Jarvis likes him, he's got scope and is a nice sort. Richard Hills says he has a lovely action.

EJAAB. A Kyllachy colt, he looks a sharp two-year-old and is set and ready to go. William Haggas trains.

HABAAYIB. A speedy two-year-old, Richard Hills likes her, as does Keiren Fallon who has ridden her on the gallops. Hopefully not just a sharp two-year-old, she has scope and if she wins her maiden we might go to Ascot next. Trained by Ed Dunlop.

KHAJAALY. With Ed Dunlop, this Kheleyf colt was a favourite at Shadwell Stud where he was raised - everybody loved him. He has plenty of scope and is one for the second half of the season.

MEEZAAN. Trained by John Gosden, he's a Medicean colt and a very good-looking horse that carries himself well. One for the second half of the season.

CHARLIE GORDON-WATSON
Four horses I feel will be worth following this year.

MAGNETIC FORCE (IRE). A grey colt by Verglas in training with Sir Michael Stoute.

PARADISE DREAM. b.c. Kyllachy – Wunders Dream (Averti). Trained by Jeremy Noseda.

b.c. Johannesburg – Wise Investor (Belong To Me). Cost 80,000 at the recent Tattersalls Craven Breeze Up Sales. To be trained by Paul Cole.

b.c. Arch – Remediate (Miswaki). With Sir Michael Stoute.

HARRY HERBERT
DECORATIVE. This very well bred daughter of Danehill Dancer cost 130,000 Guineas. She is a faultless mover on the gallops and is a forward going filly who probably won't take too long to get ready once Michael Jarvis decides the timing is right. Having raved about Tiger Eye in last year's book hopefully Decorative will follow in her footsteps by winning the Tattersalls Fillies 800!

PLUME. John Warren bought this filly for us at the Goffs Million sale in Ireland and she cost Euros 100,000. She really is the most beautiful filly who has caught everyone's eye on Richard Hannon's Herridge Gallops. I suspect that she will be a mid summer filly and hopefully she will be good enough to compete in the Goffs Million in September.

POLTERGEIST. This is a strapping son of Invincible Spirit and a half brother to the Champagne Stakes (Gr 2) winner and 2000 Guineas second Vital Equine. He is a well-grown colt and is one of those that really catches the eye on the gallops and he is finding it all very easy so far. He should be ready to run during the second half of July or early August but it is just possible that his trainer will unleash him before then if he continues to impress at home. With Richard Hannon.

SYRIAN. This striking son of Hawk Wing cost only 30,000 guineas but he is already turning heads at Fitzroy Stables. He is a January foal out of the group winning daughter of Fraan, Lady Lahar, who has already produced the Montrose Stakes (Listed) winner Classic Legend. This colt has an arrogant air about him and he is one of those that really stretches up Warren Hill and he has an extremely precocious physique despite his size. I would expect him to be ready to run in early June and he just could be a Royal Ascot contender if good enough. Trained by Michael Bell.

LUKE LILLINGSTON
FARMER GILES. We purchased him at Doncaster and of the early ones this is the one Michael Bell seems to like most at present.

WALCOT SQUARE. Ed Sackville joined me last year and bought plenty of yearlings including this one for de La Warr Racing. Roger Charlton has already expressed himself well pleased.

b.f. Country Reel – Sister Celestine. We really enjoyed working with Tom Dascombe for the first time last year. We bought some lovely yearlings in Deauville the most precocious of which is this filly.

b.c. Shamardal – Yawl (Rainbow Quest). We raised this fine colt on behalf of Mark Dixon. Both parents were Group winning 2-y-o's and he looks the part. He will be trained by Walter Swinburn.

b.c. Marju – Zither (Zafonic). We sold some lovely yearlings from Mount Coote in 2008. Perhaps the one to make a high-class 2-y-o later on is this colt who I believe will be trained by Sir Michael Stoute for Hamdan Al Maktoum.

DAVID McGREAVY
KEYTA BONITA. Her dam is very closely related to Sir Percy. A really well balanced, hardy filly who looks as if she will improve and progress through the summer. Has got a good temperament so should enjoy her racing over 6 and 7 furlongs. (Michael.Quinlan)

JEHU. Struck me as a really good two year old sort and has gone to the best place to be educated. Very racey with plenty of quality. (M Channon).

YORKSTERS PRINCE. A really good-moving son of a sire who is much underrated. He has been gelded but shows plenty and will come into his own later in the year. (Michael.Quinlan).

JOHNNY McKEEVER

BEYOND DESIRE. This Invincible Spirit was my pick of all the Doncaster St Leger purchases (19 last year). She's in training with Michael Jarvis and should appear in late June or July.

CONTREDANSE. A beautiful filly, bought on behalf of the late Con Wilson at Tattersalls Book 1. She shows all the attributes of a group class filly. Trained by Brian Meehan

JACQUELINE QUEST. A really taking filly who I felt I got surprisingly cheaply at Goffs Millions. Henry Cecil tells me he's really pleased with her.

MOUNT JULIET. A filly by Danehill Dancer ex Stylist. A very good type we secured in Goffs. She is in training with Simon Callaghan who likes her very much.

b.c. Kyllachy – Talighta. A sharp, racey, quite early colt I spotted on Barton Stud early last year and then purchased when he came up at Doncaster St Leger. Brian Meehan thinks he's a "smasher" and there's even a share available in him!!!

DAVID REDVERS

ADMIN. A Namid colt that cost €22,000 at Fairyhouse and is now with Ralph Beckett. Looks to be very quick.

OIL STRIKE. Bought for £20,000 at Doncaster Festival Sale, this Lucky Story colt is a real 'man' of a colt with tremendous presence and ambitions to be a Royal Ascot two-year-old! Trained by Peter Winkworth.

ch.f. Camacho – Bailey's Cream. She cost £65,000 at the Doncaster St Leger Sales and goes to the Craven Breeze-Up. This is a gorgeous filly with remarkable 'paint' markings, we pinhooked her jointly with Cooneen Stud and she looks every inch a high class two-year-old. *She was subsequently purchased by Richard Frisby for 130,000 Guineas.*

b.f. Compton Place – Extrasensory. Cost 10,000 Guineas at Tattersalls and now with Stuart Williams. A small, cheap filly who has lots of speed and should be out very soon.

KIRSTEN RAUSING

ALLUVIUM. A colt by Selkirk out of Alouette, by Darshaan. He was purchased by Sheikh Mohammed for his new arrangement with Andre Fabre. This colt is a half-brother to multiple Group One winners Alborada and Albanova; also to stakes winner Alma Mater and a further 5 winners – in fact, all the Listed-winning, Group 1 placed dam's eight runners are winners, an unusual feat these days. ALLUVIUM's 380,000-guineas year-older half-brother Alanbrooke (by Hernando) won well in his second and final start at two and Albanova and Alborada were also two-year-old winners, the latter in the Group 3 Charlie Weld Park S at The Curragh. ALLUVIUM could be an interesting prospect, most likely from August onwards. (A. Fabre, France)

CHURCH OF ENGLAND. A colt by Selkirk out of Frosty Welcome, by With Approval. This is a very nice, athletic colt and a half-brother to the 2008 3-time winner Casual Garcia, out of a mare who won a Listed 12f race at Newmarket. This colt, purchased by Richard Frisby for Raymond Tooth, was forward as a yearling and could be seen out in the second half of the season. Michael Bell.

HEAR HEAR. A filly by With Approval out of Hertha, by Hernando. This filly is half-sister to a winner (Carefree, by Medicean) and the Lanwades-bred dam was useful in Scandinavia, winning the Danish Oaks. The second dam won in England at 2 and the family is that of Champion Stakes winner Storming Home and the good American filly It's In The Air. This homebred filly is moving sweetly on the gallops and should be seen out in July-August. (David Lanigan)

MOUNTAIN QUEST. A bay colt by Hernando out of Miss Katmandu, by Rainbow Quest. Homebred by Mr J.L.C. Pearce at Lanwades (as was this colt's dam). This is a classy colt, bred on the same lines as last year's Oaks winner, Look Here and himself a three-parts brother to Geoff Wragg's good horse, multiple Group winner Asian Heights. The dam is also a half-sister to multiple Group winner St Expedit. This good-looking colt is bred to go 12f but it would not surprise connections if he were to show his class in public towards the end of the season (Michael Bell).

ROBIN SHARP

BAOLI. A very racey filly with an attitude to race. In training with Richard Hannon.

GRITSTONE. A colt by Dansili out of Cape Trafalgar, he's the best moving yearling we've had and I'll be very disappointed if he is not very useful. With Richard Fahey.

WIGAN LANE. By Kheleyf out of Nesting, she's a lovely filly that I bought on behalf of a client. She's sure to be a two-year-old. With Richard Fahey.

AMANDA SKIFFINGTON

RUTHIE BABE. A bay filly by Exceed and Excel. A really attractive sort, she looked "the real deal" when I saw her earlier this month. Said to be looking good and she has a nice speedy pedigree. Trained by William Haggas.

ch.f. Bahamian Bounty – Zonic. This is a very sharp-looking filly, bought specifically to be a two-year-old, and I gather so far, so good! With Richard Hannon.

b.c. Camacho – Miss Indigo. He cost 14,000 Guineas at Tattersalls. A good-looking colt by a stallion whose progeny I really liked at the sales. With Roger Charlton.

LARRY STRATTON

GENTLE BEAT. A racey gelding by Whipper, he's a good-bodied second foal of an unraced mare from the family of Eltish, who should be out early. Trained by Tim Easterby.

THOUSANDKISSESDEEP. A bay filly by Night Shift out of Interim. This was a foal purchase who proved very popular at yearling sales. The first foal of a winner from the good Juddmonte Intermission family. Trained by John Gosden.

ch g. Bahamian Bounty – Petomi. A half-brother to four winners out of a full-sister to the good sprinter Andreyev. He's a good-moving, speedy sort and a tough cookie. Trained by Nick Littmoden.

b.f. Haafhd – Miss Adelaide. A quality filly, a second foal and a half-sister to the 2008 2-y-o winner Rebecca de Winter. Trained by Mick Quinlan.

WILL EDMEADES

AULTCHARN. A bay colt by Kyllachy, he was a smashing foal who I thought would be out of our range at the December Sales, so I was surprised to get him for 60,000 gns. He turned out to be a great pinhook, as he doubled that price when sold from Kirtlington Stud last year. Brian Meehan seems very happy with him.

DORBACK. A chestnut son of Kyllachy, I couldn't really fault him as a yearling at Doncaster, apart from the fact there is plenty of white on him. A powerful colt with a great outlook, he was also bought for Thurloe and is in training with Henry Candy, who knows more about the sire and his progeny than anyone.

GULF PUNCH. A bay filly by Dubawi, she was lovely as a foal, but she didn't really grow and lacked scope as a yearling. Failing to sell, she turned out to be a very disappointing pinhook. However, she is showing a good attitude in a workmanlike sort of a way at Richard Hannon's and should be the first of this list to run.

LEAN MACHINE. A bay colt by Exceed And Excel, this is a good-looking half-brother to the more than useful Whyome, which we also bought for Thurloe Thoroughbreds several years ago. This colt is an exceptional mover, also at Richard Hannon's, but he will need some time to allow his knees to mature fully.

Two Year Olds of 2009

ANDREW BALDING

1. BALDUCCI ★★★★
b.c. Dansili – Miss Meltemi (Miswaki Tern).
April 9. Fifth foal. 60,000Y. Tattersalls October 1. Not sold. Brother to the very useful 7f (at 2 yrs) and listed 1m winner and Group 3 Dahlia Stakes third Don't Dili Dali and to the fairly useful 1m winner Ada River and half-brother to the quite useful 2008 2-y-o 5f winner Haigh Hall (by Kyllachy) and the fair 7f to 8.7f winner Willie Ever (by Agnes World). The dam, a 7f and 1m 2-y-o winner in Italy, was third in the Group 1 Italian Oaks and is a half-sister to 2 winners. The second dam, Blu Meltemi (by Star Shareef), won 5 races at 2 and 3 yrs and was third in the Italian Oaks. (McMahon, Gorell, Russell).
"A very nice colt, he's very similar to his sister Ada River, he shows some speed and he's very much in the mould of a two-year-old. He'll probably want seven furlongs in June. I'm very pleased with the bunch of two-year-olds I have this year – I do seem to have a lot of nice horses".

2. BREAKHEART ★★★
b.c. Sakhee – Exorcet (Selkirk).
January 17. Half-brother to the very useful 6f winner of 4 races and Group 2 6f Diadem Stakes second Dark Missile and to the fair dual 6f winner Night Rocket (both by Night Shift). The dam, a fair 3-y-o 6f winner, is a half-sister to 2 winners including the useful UAE 7f and 1m winner Rock Music. The second dam, Stack Rock (by Ballad Rock), was a very useful winner of 9 races from 5f to 1m including the listed Hopeful Stakes and was second in the Group 1 Prix de l'Abbaye. (J C Smith).
"A big, backward colt – just like his half-sister Dark Missile was at this stage. Hopefully he'll emulate her by coming together and winning in the late summer because he's the spitting image of her".

3. CHINK OF LIGHT ★★★★
ch.c. Dr Fong – Isle Of Flame (Shirley Heights).
February 27. Eleventh foal. 65,000Y. Tattersalls October 2. Andrew Balding. Brother to the useful 9f, 12f and listed 2m winner Kindling and half-brother to the French listed 9f winner Thattinger (by Salse), to the 7f and 1m winner River Of Babylon (by Marju), the 2-y-o 7f winner Eden (by Polish Precedent), the 12f to 2m winner Dorothy's Friend (by Grand Lodge), the dual 3-y-o 1m winner Burning Impulse (by Cadeaux Genereux) – all 4 fairly useful, the fair 1m winner Pixie's Blue (by Hawk Wing) and a minor 3-y-o winner in France by Fairy King. The dam is an unraced daughter of the minor US stakes winner and Group 3 Irish 1,000 Guineas Trial second Burning Issue (by Persian Bold), herself a half-sister to the Middle Park Stakes winner Balla Cove. (D E Brownlow).
"A lovely horse, he's big, scopey and full of quality. I'm very pleased with him and I'd hope he'd be a seven furlong two-year-old".

4. COMPTON STREET ★★
ch.c. Compton Place – Balnaha (Lomond).
March 26. Half-brother to the Group 1 1m Coronation Stakes winner Balisada (by Kris) and to the quite useful 12f winner Talk To Mojo (by Deploy). The dam, a modest 3-y-o 1m winner, is a sister to Inchmurrin (a very useful winner of the Child Stakes and herself dam of the very smart and tough colt Inchinor), closely related to the very useful 1m winner Guest Artiste and a half-sister to the Mill Reef Stakes winner Welney. The second dam, On Show (by Welsh Pageant), won over 10f and was second in the November Handicap. (George Strawbridge).
"A good-looking colt, but he's only been with us a few weeks and we haven't done enough with him yet to know how good he is. But he moves very well and he's a medium-sized, attractive colt that should make a two-year-old by mid-season".

5. COOL VALENTINE ★★★
b.c. One Cool Cat – Miss Mirasol (Sheikh Albadou).
February 14. 13,000Y. Tattersalls October 2. M Mariscotti. Half-brother to the fair 10f winner Dark Prospect (by Nayef). The dam, a 2-y-o listed 6f winner, is a half-sister to 6 winners including the fairly useful 2-y-o dual 5f winner Let's Be Fair and the fairly useful 5f (at 2 yrs) and

6f winner Labrett. The second dam, Play The Game (by Mummy's Game), a fair 2-y-o 5f winner, is a half-sister to 6 winners including the Italian Group 1 winner Svelt, the Italian Group 3 winner and Group 1 placed Smageta and the dam of the Italian Group 1 winner Shulich. (M Mariscotti).
"A sharp colt, he'll be suited by six furlongs in May and he goes alright. He's certainly worth a mention".

6. DANGER MULALLY ★★★
b.c. Governor Brown – Glittering Image (Sadler's Wells).
January 29. Fifth foal. 16,000Y. Doncaster St Leger. Andrew Balding. Half-brother to Riptide, unplaced in one start at 2 yrs in 2008 and to the fair 2-y-o 1m winner and subsequent US stakes-placed winner Miss Josiey Wales (both by Val Royal). The dam is an unraced half-sister to one winner. The second dam, Noora Abu (by Ahonoora), won 12 races including the Group 2 Pretty Polly Stakes and is a half-sister to 6 winners. (J Dwyer).
"He goes nice enough, he's quite a good-looking horse and I like him. He'll probably end up a seven furlong/mile colt at the end of the year, but I think he'll have the speed for six at the end of May".

7. DREAM SPEED (IRE) ★★★
b.c. Barathea – Kapria (Simon du Desert).
March 12. Fourth foal. 62,000foal. Tattersalls December. Littleton Stud. Half-brother to the modest 2008 2-y-o 5f winner It's Toast (by Diktat), to the useful 2-y-o 6.5f St Leger Sales race winner Dream Eater (by Night Shift) and the modest 1m all-weather winner Tremelo Pointe (by Trempolino). The dam, a dual French 11f winner and third in the Group 3 Prix Penelope, is a half-sister to 2 winners out of the minor French 4-y-o winner Sheer Drop (by Kenmare), herself a half-sister to 5 winners. (J C Smith).
"Not as obvious a two-year-old type as his half-brother Dream Eater, but he's a thoroughly likeable horse nonetheless. A typical Barathea in looks, I'd expect him out in mid-summer over six/seven furlongs".

8. DROMORE ★★★★
ch.c. Traditionally – Try To Catch Me (Shareef Dancer).
February 17. Twelfth foal. 14,000Y. Tattersalls October 2. Andrew Balding. Closely related to the Group 1 10f Champion Stakes and US dual Grade 1 winner Storming Home (by Machiavellian) and half-brother to the fairly useful 12.3f winner Follow That Dream (by Darshaan), the fairly useful 11f to 13f winner Desert Frolic (by Persian Bold), the fair 2-y-o 7f winner Nawafell (by Kris) and the modest 1m winner Zulu Princess (by Hawk Wing). The dam, a French 3-y-o 1m winner, is closely related to the US stakes winner Air Dancer and a half-sister to the Group 2 Criterium de Maisons-Laffitte winner Bitooh and the listed Virginia Stakes winner Monaassabaat. The second dam, It's In The Air (by Mr Prospector), was a champion 2-y-o filly and winner of the Vanity Handicap (twice), the Ruffian Handicap, the Alabama Stakes and the Delaware Oaks (all Grade 1 events). (I G Burbridge).
"He's a really good-looking horse, he goes really well and he's a half-brother to a Champion Stakes winner – and all for just fourteen grand! It's interesting that he has Mr Prospector on both sides of his pedigree, I think he'll set off at seven furlongs in June and he looks every inch a racehorse". TRAINER'S BARGAIN BUY

9. EXTREME GREEN ★★★
ch.f. Motivator – Ventura (Spectrum).
February 20. Half-sister to the 11f to 14f winner and US Grade 2 second Cedar Mountain (by Galileo). The dam won twice over 1m at 3 yrs in Ireland. The second dam, Wedding Bouquet (by Kings Lake), a useful 5f to 7f winner in Ireland (including the Group 3 C L Weld Park Stakes), later won the Grade 3 6.5f Monrovia Handicap in the USA and is closely related to the outstanding Derby, Irish Derby and King George winner Generous. (George Strawbridge).
"Yes, I like her and she's more precocious than you would have thought on pedigree. A neat, athletic filly, not very big but more racey than I imagined she would be at this stage".

10. FIREBACK ★★★
b.c. Firebreak – So Discreet (Tragic Role).
May 9. Fourth foal. 15,000Y. Tattersalls October. G Howson. Half-brother to the quite useful 2008 2-y-o dual 5f winner Shes A Shaw Thing and to the fair 7f (at 2 yrs) and 1m winner Reel Buddy Star (by Reel Buddy). The dam is an unraced half-sister to 6 winners including the very smart triple Group 2 1m winner Gothenburg and the Group 3 placed Omaha City. The second dam, Be Discreet (by Junius), won 5 races in France at up to 7f and is a half-sister to 9 winners.

"We trained the sire as a two-year-old and this colt would be quite similar but probably not as precocious at this stage".

11. GUIDECCA TEN ★★
b.c. Peintre Celebre – Silver Rhapsody (Silver Hawk).
February 14. Fifth foal. 45,000Y. Tattersalls October 1. Andrew Balding. Half-brother to the Italian middle-distance winner Algernon Talmage (by Diesis). The dam won the Group 3 12f Princess Royal Stakes, was third in the Group 1 Yorkshire Oaks and is a half-sister to 5 winners out of the minor US winner Sister Chryss (by Fit To Fight), herself a half-sister to 8 winners including the dual US Grade 2 winner Coolawin. (D E Brownlow).

"He's very backward and will need plenty of time. One for the back-end of the season and next year".

12. IPSWICH LAD ★★★
ch.c. Halling – Poised (Rahy).
April 9. Fifth foal. €46,000Y. Tattersalls Ireland. Andrew Balding. Brother to the 2009 9f placed 3-y-o Hypnotist and to the very useful 2-y-o 6f and 7f winner Gothenburg. The dam, second over 9f at Chantilly at 3 yrs, is a sister to the Group 1 Sussex Stakes winner Noverre and closely related to the outstanding 2-y-o Arazi, winner of the Breeders Cup Juvenile, the Prix Robert Papin, the Prix Morny, the Prix de la Salamandre and the Ciga Grand Criterium (all Group 1 events between 5f and 8.5f). The second dam, Danseur Fabuleux (by Northern Dancer), was placed in the Group 3 12f Prix de Minerve and is closely related to the US Grade 1 winner Joyeux Danseur and the very useful 12f winner Fabulous Dancer. (M Evans).

"I really like this horse, he's done a lot of growing just recently so he's just going through a backward phase. He has a very good pedigree and he's a nice colt. A typical Halling in his looks, he's very similar to a good horse we had called Vanderlin but a slightly taller and scopier type. He'll make a two-year-old from mid-summer onwards, I do like him and he's owned by the Boss of Ipswich Football Club".

13. KATEHARI (IRE) ★★★
b.f. Noverre – Katariya (Barathea).
February 2. First foal. 38,000Y. Tattersalls October 2. Kern/Lillingston. The dam ran twice unplaced and is a half-sister to 3 winners including the Oaks third Katariya. The second dam, Katiykha (by Darshaan), a smart Irish listed 12f and 14f winner, is a half-sister to the fairly useful winners at up to 12f Kariniyd, Katiniyd and Katiymann. (The Toucan Syndicate).

"She's a nice filly – we really liked her at the Sales. She had a bit of a setback before Christmas but she's back cantering now and looks racey and nice".

14. LIQUID ASSET (FR) ★★
ch.g. Refuse To Bend – Lilyfoot (Sanglamore).
February 4. Fourth foal. 20,000Y. Tattersalls October 2. Andrew Balding. Half-brother to 2 winners over jumps by Poliglote and Smadoun. The dam won 2 minor races at 3 yrs in France and is a half-sister to 4 winners including the Group 1 Criterium de Saint-Cloud winner Linda's Lad. The second dam, Colza (by Alleged), a quite useful 2-y-o 1m winner, is a half-sister to 10 winners including the Group 3 6f July Stakes and listed 9f winner Wharf and the dam of the Arc winner Rail Link. (Mick & Janice Mariscotti).

"A nice, well-grown sort that looks every inch a two-year-old but one that will want seven furlongs or a mile. A solid, straightforward horse".

15. LORD ZENITH ★★★★
b.c. Zamindar – Lady Donatella (Last Tycoon).
January 29. Sixth foal. 30,000Y. Tattersalls October. Not sold. Half-brother to the quite useful 2-y-o 7f winner Maxwil (by Storming Home) and to the modest 6f and 7.6f winner Dark Moon (by Observatory). The dam, a modest 12f placed maiden, is a half-sister to 7 winners including the very useful Group 3 Earl of Sefton Stakes winner Right Wing. The second dam, Nekhbet (by Artaius), a fair 5f to 7f placed 2-y-o, is a half-sister to 7 winners including the Irish St Leger winner M-Lolshan. (M E Wates).
"A really nice horse, he's home-bred and I really like him. A big, scopey horse with a good engine, I trained the half-sister Dark Moon who won over seven furlongs at three. I'd say this colt has the speed for six furlongs but he'll probably end up a seven furlong horse later this year".

16. MECOX BAY (IRE) ★★★
b.c. Noverre – Birdsong (Dolphin Street).
May 19. Fifth foal. 40,000Y. Tattersalls October 2. Norris/Huntingdon. Brother to the fairly useful 2-y-o dual 5f winner Mubaashir and half-brother to the minor French winner of 4 races Filimeala (by Pennekamp). The dam, a fair dual 6f winner at 3 yrs, is a half-sister to 7 winners including the 2-y-o listed 6f Sweet Solera Stakes winner Lucayan Princess (herself the dam of four Group winners including the Group 1 winners Luso and Warrsan). The second dam, Gay France (by Sir Gaylord), a fairly useful 2-y-o 6f winner, is a half-sister to 10 winners including the dam of the Group 1 winner and sire Common Grounds. (E N Kronfeld).
"A nice horse that's done a lot of growing recently, he's a late foal, but he should be a mid-summer two-year-old. I like him, he's a good stamp of a horse with a good attitude and plenty of size and scope. He'll be a miler in time".

17. MON CADEAUX ★★★★
b.c. Cadeaux Genereux – Ushindi (Montjeu).
February 5. First foal. 37,000Y. Tattersalls October 2. Andrew Balding. The dam, a modest 12f winner, is a half-sister to 8 winners. The second dam, Fern (by Shirley Heights), a fairly useful 12f winner and third in the listed 10f Lupe Stakes, is a half-sister to 6 winners including the Group 1 Fillies Mile winner and Oaks second Shamshir. (Mick and Janice Mariscotti).
"He's very nice. More Montjeu than Cadeaux Genereux in many ways but he's still showing a bit of speed and he should start off at six furlongs at the end of May".

18. OPERA GAL (IRE) ★★★★
b.f. Galileo – Opera Glass (Barathea).
March 8. First foal. The dam, a quite useful 8.5f winner, is a sister to the very smart 2-y-o Group 3 7f Solario Stakes winner and Group 1 Dewhurst Stakes third Opera Cape and a half-sister to the high-class stayer Grey Shot and the smart sprint winner of 4 races Night Shot. The second dam, Optaria (by Song), was a quite useful 2-y-o 5f winner. (J C Smith).
"I like her and she looks like she'll be doing something this year. She's neat, forward-going and a good mover. We'll probably be starting her off over seven furlongs in June. A nice filly".

19. PIPETTE ★★★
b.f. Pivotal – Amaryllis (Sadler's Wells).
April 15. Half-sister to the French 10f and 12f winner and Group 2 10.5f Prix Greffuhle second Day Or Night (by Daylami). The dam, a fair 7f all-weather winner at 2 yrs, is closely related to the smart French/US 1m/9f winner Corrazona and a half-sister to the Breeders Cup Classic third Thirty Six Red. The second dam, Heartbreak (by Stage Door Johnny), won at up to 9f in the USA. (George Strawbridge).
"She's not with us yet, but I believe the same owner's top-class two-year-old filly Rainbow View didn't arrive at John Gosden's last year until mid-May, so I live in hope! I haven't seen her yet, but apparently she's very nice".

20. PITTODRIE STAR (IRE) ★★
ch.c. Choisir – Jupiter Inlet (Jupiter Island).
March 3. 12,000Y. Doncaster Festival. Andrew Balding. Half-brother to the fairly useful 2008 2-y-o 6f winner Kingship Spirit (by Invincible

Spirit), to the fair dual 7f winner Jonny Lesters Hair (by Danetime) and 3 minor winners in Italy by Alhaarth, Ashkalani and Common Grounds. The dam, a listed winner of 6 races from 2 to 5 yrs in Italy, is a half-sister to 5 winners. The second dam, Anegada (by Shirley Heights), won once at 4 yrs in Italy and is a half-sister to 4 winners including 3 listed winners in Italy. (Mr E M Sutherland).

"He's quite a nice horse and a half-brother to the Jeremy Noseda colt Kingship Spirit that won the big Sales race last year. He'll be worth putting in the book".

21. PORTMAN BOY ★★★
b.c. Exceed And Excel – Anqood (Elmaamul).
March 30. Third foal. 32,000Y. Tattersalls October 2. Andrew Balding. Half-brother to the fair 2008 1m placed 2-y-o Noordhoek Kid (by Dansili) and to the moderate 2-y-o 5f winner Echostar (by Observatory). The dam, a quite useful 7.6f winner, is a half-sister to 5 winners. The second dam, Mayaasa (by Lyphard), a fair 10f winner, is closely related to the Group 1 Queen Elizabeth II Stakes winner Maroof and a half-sister to the dam of Desert King. (M Evans).

"He looks every inch a two-year-old. Very athletic, he's a little bit keen at the moment but we won't hang around with him and he'll probably start at the beginning of May. He covers a lot of ground and has a good way of going, but he just needs to chill out. Apparently the dam was the same way".

22. ROYAL ASSENT ★★
b.f. Royal Applause – Brand (Shareef Dancer).
March 22. Sister to the useful 6f (at 2 yrs) and 1m all-weather winner Royal Warrant and half-sister to the unraced 2008 2-y-o Brandy Butter (by Domedriver), to the useful listed 1m winner of 7 races from 7f to 1m Banknote (by Zafonic), the 2-y-o 6f and 7f winner Captain Ginger (by Muhtarram) and the 6f to 1m winner Double Brandy (by Elmaamul) – both quite useful. The dam is an unraced half-sister to 5 winners out Beacon Hill (by Bustino), herself a half-sister to the dam of Height Of Fashion. (The Queen).

"She's just come in and is a little bit unfurnished.
She'll be a back-end two-year-old I would have thought, just like the other fillies we've had out of the family. The colts are generally better but having said that she is a full sister to Royal Warrant".

23. SIDE GLANCE ★★★
br.g. Passing Glance – Averami (Averti).
March 15. Second dam. Brother to the 2008 2-y-o 7f winner Advertise. The dam, a moderate 7f winner, is a sister to 2 winners. The second dam, Friend For Life (by Lahib), was unplaced. (Kingsclere Racing Club).

"He's a full brother to a two-year-old winner for us last year, Advertise but he looks even more of a two-year-old type, so I'd be fairly optimistic that he could win races this year".

24. SIMENON ★★★★
b.g. Marju – Epistoliere (Alzao).
February 25. Fourth foal. 60,000Y. Tattersalls October 2. Kern/Lillingston. The dam, placed once at 3 yrs in France, is a sister to the Group 2 Grand Prix de Deauville winner Epistolaire and a half-sister to the Group 2 Prix Hubert de Chaudenay winner Epitre. The second dam, Epistolienne (by Law Society), is a placed half-sister to 10 winners including the Group 2 Nassau Stakes winner Acclimatise. (Mr Greenwood, Ms James & Mr Cockburn).

"I like him, he's an easy-going sort and I would hope he'd be winning this year, probably over seven furlongs to start with".

25. SONG TO THE MOON (IRE) ★★★
b.f. Oratorio – Jojeema (Barathea).
February 10. Second foal. 26,000Y. Tattersalls October 1. G Howson. Half-sister to the modest 2008 2-y-o 1m winner Hum Cat (by One Cool Cat). The dam is an unraced half-sister to 5 winners including the high-class Group 2 12f Jockey Club Stakes and Group 3 12f Cumberland Lodge Stakes winner Riyadian. The second dam, Knight's Baroness (by Rainbow Quest), a smart filly, won over 7f (at 2 yrs) and the Irish Oaks and was placed in the Oaks, the Lingfield Oaks Trial, the Park Hill Stakes and the May Hill Stakes.

"She hasn't come to us yet but I have seen her and she's very scopey and a really nice filly. David Powell of Catridge Stud has kept a share in her which is probably a good sign because I think he's one of the best judges around".

26. STARGAZE (IRE) ★★★
b.c. Oasis Dream – Dafariyna (Nashwan).
January 26. 10,000Y. Tattersalls October. Not sold. Half-brother to the fair 7f (at 2 yrs) and 2m winner Bayonyx (by Montjeu). The dam, placed 3 times at up to 9f in Ireland, is a half-sister to 3 winners. The second dam, Dafayna (by Habitat), was a smart winner of the Group 3 Cork and Orrery Stakes and was placed in the July Cup and the Vernons Sprint Cup and is a half-sister to the 2,000 Guineas winner Doyoun. (D E Brownlow).
"A real nice horse, he's sharp and he'll run in April. A real two-year-old type, he's not very big but well put together. I hope he stays six furlongs because if he does he'll certainly win races - he has plenty of dash".

27. STRICTLY DANCING ★★★
b.f. Danehill Dancer – Lochangel (Night Shift).
March 28. Sixth foal. Half-sister to the modest 2008 6f placed 2-y-o Celestial Dream and to the quite useful 3-y-o 7f winner Star Pupil (by Selkirk). The dam, a very smart winner of the Group 1 5f Nunthorpe Stakes, is a half-sister to the champion sprinter Lochsong. The second dam, Peckitts Well (by Lochnager), was a fairly useful winner of five races at 2 and 3 yrs from 5f to 6f. (Mr J C Smith).
"She's nice enough, we haven't done a huge amount with her but she looks racey and her half-sister Celestial Dream will win this year too".

28. SUFFOLK PUNCH (IRE) ★★
ch.c. Barathea – Lamanka Lass (Woodman).
May 4. Fifth foal. €25,000Y. Tattersalls Ireland. Andrew Balding. Half-brother to the unplaced 2008 2-y-o Miss Mojito (by Lucky Story), to the 7f (at 2 yrs), 1m and subsequent US Grade 2 9f Oak Tree Derby winner Dark Islander (by Singspiel), the fair all-weather dual 12f winner Crocolat (by Croco Rouge) and a winner in Spain by Desert Prince. The dam, a fair 3-y-o 1m winner, is a half-sister to 5 winners including the Group 3 Darley Stakes winner Far Lane. The second dam, Pattimech (by Nureyev), won at up to 7f in the USA and is a sister to Annoconnor, winner of the Santa Ana Handicap, the Vanity Handicap and the Ramona Handicap (all Grade 1 9f events) and a half-sister to the Group 1 16f Grand Prix de Paris and the Grade 1 Melbourne Cup winner At Talaq. (M Evans).
"He's been disappointing physically since the Sales but he is a May foal so hopefully he'll improve. He should be a two-year-old type but we'll have to see how he progresses".

29. SWAN WINGS ★★★
b.f. Bahamian Bounty – Star Tulip (Night Shift).
March 24. Sister to the modest 2-y-o 7f winner Kamal and half-sister to the smart and consistent sprint winner of 14 races Texas Gold (by Cadeaux Genereux), to the fair 6f (at 2 yrs) to 11f and hurdles winner Indian Sun (by Indian Ridge), the fair 6f winner Kansas Gold (by Alhaarth), the modest dual 10f winner Choristar (by Inchinor) and a 4-y-o winner in Germany by Hector Protector. The dam was a useful winner of 3 races over 6f including the listed Sandy Lane Stakes and is a half-sister to 4 minor winners. The second dam, Silk Petal (by Petorius), a useful winner of 3 races over 7f including a German listed event, was third in the Group 3 Prix de Flore and is a half-sister to 5 winners. (N Jones).
"She has the make and shape of a sprinting two-year-old and I'd expect her out at the end of May".

30. TAPPANAPPA (IRE) ★★
b.c. High Chaparral – Itsibitsi (Brief Truce).
February 24. Fourth foal. 105,000Y. Tattersalls October 1. T Noonan. Half-brother to the quite useful 2-y-o 6f winner Baltimore Jack (by Night Shift), to the fair dual 5f winner (including at 2 yrs) Lyndalee (by Fasliyev) and the fair 2-y-o 7f winner Fits Of Giggles (by Cape Cross). The dam is an unraced half-sister to the UAE listed winner and Group 3 7f Hungerford Stakes third Siege.

The second dam, Above Water (by Reference Point), is an unplaced half-sister to 9 winners including the dam of Islington. (Mr P C McMahon).
"He's very backward and I wouldn't expect much from him until October".

31. TARTAN TRIP ★★★★
b.c. Selkirk – Marajuana (Robellino).
February 27. First foal. The dam, a quite useful 2-y-o 5f winner on her debut, is a half-sister to the useful 5f to 1m winner of 8 races (from 2-6 yrs) Border Music (by Selkirk). The second dam, Mara River (Efisio), a quite useful 6f to 1m winner, is a half-sister to several winners. (Kingsclere Racing Club).
"This is a seriously nice horse. He's a typical Selkirk in many ways but his dam won over five furlongs at two and I think he'll win over six furlongs this year. He's got plenty of speed".

32. THELADYINQUESTION ★★
b.f. Dubawi – Whazzat (Daylami).
April 26. First foal. 22,000Y. Tattersalls December. The dam, a useful 2-y-o listed 7f Chesham Stakes winner, is a half-sister to several winners including the useful 7f (at 2 yrs), listed 1m and Italian Group 3 1m winner Whazzis. The second dam, Wosaita (by Generous), a fair 12.3f placed maiden, is a half-sister to 9 winners including the very smart Group 1 10.5f Prix de Diane winner Rafha (herself the dam of 4 stakes winners including the Haydock Sprint Cup winner Invincible Spirit) and the Group 3 12f Blandford Stakes winner Chiang Mai. (J R Drew).
"A small filly, but she's racey looking and will hopefully be a two-year-old".

33. TREWARTHENICK ★★
br.c. Cape Cross – Play With Fire (Priolo).
March 9. Sixth foal. 48,000Y. Tattersalls October 1. Andrew Balding. Brother to the useful 5f (at 2 yrs) and listed 6f winner and Group 3 Horris Hill Stakes third Millbag and half-brother to the useful 5f and 6f winner and Group 3 Coventry Stakes fourth Coconut Penang (by Night Shift) and the fair Irish 9.5f winner My Dolly Madison (by In The Wings). The dam, a French 12f winner, is a half-sister to 6 winners including the French listed winners Play Around and Playact (subsequently Grade 2 placed in the USA). The second dam, Play Or Pay (by Play Fellow), won twice in France and was listed-placed and is a half-sister to 9 winners. (M Evans).
"He had a setback but he's cantering again now and we'll just have to feel our way with him. He had looked alright when he was in training earlier on".

34. VIKING DANCER ★★★★★
b.c. Danehill Dancer – Blue Siren (Bluebird).
April 12. Half-brother to the fair 2008 2-y-o 7f winner King's Siren (by King's Best), to the useful 2-y-o listed 5.2f winner and Group 2 Flying Childers Stakes third Speed Cop, the fairly useful dual 5f winner (including at 2 yrs) Siren's Gift (both by Cadeaux Genereux) and the fair 6f winner Indiana Blues (by Indian Ridge). The dam, a very useful winner of three races from 5f to 7f, was disqualified from first place in two more, notably the Group 1 5f Nunthorpe Stakes (the winner on merit) and is a half-sister to several winners including the quite useful 9f winner Northern Habit. The second dam, Manx Millennium (by Habitat), was placed over 1m and is a half-sister to several winners. (Mr J C Smith).
"A really good stamp of a horse. I haven't done a lot with him yet but he has a very good attitude which I'm pleased about because some of the family have been a bit quirky – notably Siren's Gift. He's been totally straightforward and is a very nice horse. Five and six furlongs should suit him well".

35. WHITE FINCH (USA) ★★
gr.f. Cozzene – Just A Bird (Storm Bird).
March 14. Half-sister to the quite useful 2008 2-y-o 7f winner Emirates Roadshow (by Distorted Humor) and to 2 minor winners in the USA by Conquistador Cielo and Dynaformer. The dam is an unraced half-sister to 5 winners including the US Grade 3 winner Recording. The second dam, Ratings (by Caveat), won 8 races in the USA including the Grade 2 Diana

Handicap and is a half-sister to 7 winners. (George Strawbridge).
"Yet to arrive at the yard".

36. YARRA RIVER ★★★★
b.br.c. Dr Fong – River Cara (Irish River).
April 2. Sixth foal. 20,000Y. Half-brother to the quite useful 2008 2-y-o 8.3f winner Warrior One (by Act One), to the fairly useful 1m winner Basque Beauty (by Nayef), the quite useful 2-y-o 1m winner Ciel (by Rainbow Quest), the fair 12f winner Rill (by Unfuwain), the fair 2-y-o all-weather 9.5f and hurdles winner Araglin (by Sadler's Wells) and the moderate 8.7f winner Beck (by Cadeaux Genereux). The dam, a French listed 2-y-o 1m winner, is a half-sister to 2 winners. The second dam, Mata Cara (by Storm Bird), a useful triple 7f winner, is a half-sister to 6 winners. (D E Brownlow).
"He's a very nice horse and he goes very well. He's neat, a very good mover, very athletic and looks every inch a seven furlong two-year-old, with the speed to start off at six. I'd be disappointed if he can't win races".

DAVID BARRON
37. DISPOL KEASHA ★★★
ch.f. Kheleyf – Easy Mover (Bluebird).
February 12. First foal. 16,000Y. Doncaster Festival. W B Imison. The dam, a fair 2-y-o 7f winner, is a half-sister to one winner. The second dam, Top Brex (by Top Ville), won once at 3 yrs in France and is a half-sister to 6 winners including the Italian Group 3 Premio Ambrosiano winner Charlo Mio. (W B Imison).
"She's forward, she'll be one of our first two-year-old runners and she goes quite well".

38. DIVINE CHOICE (IRE) ★★★★
b.c. Choisir – Arboreta (Charnwood Forest).
April 20. Second foal. 48,000Y. Doncaster St Leger. T D Barron. The dam, a minor Irish 1m winner, is a half-sister to 5 winners including the Irish listed winner and Group 3 placed Miss Childrey. The second dam, Blazing Glory (by Glow), won 3 races over 5f and is a full or half-sister to 6 winners. (Clive Washbourn).
"He wasn't a particularly early foal, so he'll be one to start in late May I should think. He's a good sort and a typical sprinter".

39. HOUSE OF FRILLS ★★★
b.f. Paris House – Frilly Front (Aragon).
March 15. The dam was a quite useful 5f winner of 6 races (including at 2 yrs). The second dam, So So (by Then Again), was a quite useful 6f, 7f (both at 2 yrs) and 1m winner. (J A Welsh).
"She looks quite early and will be an out-and-out sprinter. The mare has been very disappointing at stud but this filly could just be alright and the sire is still quite capable of throwing a nice horse".

40. PARBOLD HILL ★★★
br.f. Exceed And Excel – Let Alone (Warning).
January 25. Fifth foal. 41,000Y. Doncaster St Leger. Highfield Farm. Closely related to the modest 1m and 10f winner Tabulate (by Dansili) and half-sister to the US winner of 4 races and Italian listed-placed Mac Rhapsody (by Night Shift), to the quite useful 2-y-o 6f winner Rash Judgement (by Mark Of Esteem) and a bumpers winner by Tobougg. The dam, a fair 1m winner, is a half-sister to 4 minor winners. The second dam, Mettlesome (by Lomond), a French 1m (at 2 yrs) and 9f winner, is a half-sister to 5 winners including the Group 3 Rose Of Lancaster Stakes and subsequent Grade 1 Santa Anita Handicap winner Urgent Request. (D W Armstrong).
"A nice filly, she's fairly forward and I'd hope she'd be out sooner rather than later. She goes quite well at home so I'd be hopeful with her and you'd expect her to be a sprinter".

41. PEPPER LANE ★★★
ch.f. Exceed And Excel – Maid To Matter (Pivotal).
January 16. First foal. 15,000Y. Doncaster St Leger. Highfield Farm. The dam is an unraced sister to the useful 6f and 7f winner Polar Kingdom and a half-sister to 2 winners. The second dam, Scarlet Lake (by Reprimand), is an unplaced half-sister to 6 winners including the useful 2-y-o listed 6f winner Maid For The Hills and the useful 2-y-o 5f and 6f winner Maid For Walking (herself dam of the Grade 1 Turf Classic

winner Stroll) and to the placed dam of the Group 2 Sun Chariot Stakes winner Lady In Waiting. (D W Armstrong).

"A smaller filly than the other Exceed And Excel and perhaps not as forward at this stage, but for what we've asked of her we're quite happy. She'll be a sprinter".

RALPH BECKETT

42. ADMIN ★★★★
ch.c. Namid – Night Rhapsody (Mujtahid).
February 28. Fourth foal. €22,000Y. Tattersalls Ireland. David Redvers. Half-brother to the quite useful 2008 Irish 2-y-o 6f winner Monivea (by Fasliyev) and to the quite useful 6f and 7f 2-y-o winner Golan Knight (by Golan). The dam, a fair Irish 3-y-o 1m winner, is out of the Irish listed 1m and listed 10f winner Double On (by Doubletour), herself a half-sister to 3 winners. (The Anagram Partnership).

"A nice horse, he was a big yearling and so wasn't particularly forward – you didn't look at him and think 'two-year-old' but he was the only one I bought at Fairyhouse and I just really liked him. He has a good way about him, a good step to him and he's done everything I'd hoped he'd do so far. We'll be stepping up his work in the next few weeks and he looks a horse we can have plenty of sport with. He may just turn out to be a 'fun horse' but there's every chance he could be better than that". TRAINER'S BARGAIN BUY

43. AGONY AND ECSTACY ★★★
ch.f. Captain Rio – Agony Aunt (Formidable).
March 14. Seventh foal. Half-sister to the unplaced 2008 2-y-o Hesketh (by Nayef), to the fairly useful 6f winner of 4 races here and in the UAE winner Doctor Hilary (by Mujahid), the quite useful all-weather 6f winner Cool Tune (by Piccolo), the modest 5f to 7f winner of 7 races Only If I Laugh (by Piccolo), the moderate 1m all-weather winner Disabuse (by Fleetwood) and the moderate 10f and 11f winner Miss Havisham (by Josr Algharoud). The dam, a quite useful 10f winner, is a half-sister to one winner. The second dam, Loch Clair (by Lomond), is an unplaced half-sister to 6 winners including the Group 1 winner Wind In Her Hair (herself dam of the champion Japanese horse Deep Impact). (Miss R C Tregaskes).

"This is a sharp filly and I would think she'll be appearing before the end of May. She's a good moving filly, slightly quirky but we've done OK with Captain Rio's and I think she'll be up to winning a small race over five or six furlongs".

44. CEILIDH HOUSE ★★
ch.f. Selkirk – Villa Carlotta (Rainbow Quest).
March 10. Sister to the fairly useful 10f winner Shela House and half-sister to the quite useful 10f winner Villa Sonata (by Mozart) and to the quite useful 2008 1m placed 2-y-o (only start) Bothy (by Pivotal). The dam, a smart 12f listed winner of 4 races, is a half-sister to the fairly useful 10f winner Seeyaaj. The second dam, Subya (by Night Shift), was a very useful winner of 5 races from 5f (at 2 yrs) to 10f including the Lupe Stakes, the Masaka Stakes and the Milcars Star Stakes (all listed events). (J H Richmond-Watson).

"She'll be appearing in the autumn and is a typical Selkirk in that she's no oil painting. She's very similar to her half-brother, Bothy, who only appeared late on as a two-year-old last year, so in August or September we'll be finding out about her. A filly with plenty of size and scope and a good-moving filly with a straightforward attitude".

45. COUNTRY PRINCESS (FR) ★★★
b.f. Country Reel – Millefiori (Machiavellian).
February 12. Second foal. Deauville August. €55,000Y. David Redvers. The dam won 2 minor races in France and is a full or half-sister to 2 other minor winners. The second dam, Lovely Millie (by Bluebird), won the Group 3 Solario Stakes and is a half-sister to 5 winners. (Mr R J Roberts).

"A sharp, early sort and it's a family I know a bit about. She's French bred so if she was nice she might go over there to pick up the prize money and premiums on offer. She's tough and hopefully she'll be more than just an early two-year-old and she might get seven furlongs later on. It looks like she'll want quick ground and she's capable of winning a maiden".

46. DANNY'S CHOICE ★★★
ch.f. Compton Place – Pie High (Salse).
February 25. Third foal. 65,000Y. Doncaster St Leger. R Frisby. Half-sister to the unraced 2008 Irish 2-y-o Beauty Flash (by Oasis Dream) and to the fair 2-y-o 1m all-weather winner Crosstar (by Cape Cross). The dam, a fairly useful 7f winner of 4 races, is a half-sister to 5 winners including the Group 3 5f Premio Omenoni winner and Group 2 Diadem Stakes second Leap For Joy. The second dam, Humble Pie (by Known Fact), a fairly useful 2-y-o 6f winner, is a half-sister to 4 winners including the high-class sprinter College Chapel. (G B Partnership).

"She looks like a very solid filly and is quite laid-back. She looks all over a five/six furlong sprinter and it's a good family. She's still got a bit of maturing to do so she won't be ready until June time but I like her".

47. FOREST CROWN ★★★★
b.f. Royal Applause – Wiener Wald (Woodman).
April 1. Eleventh foal. Sister to the fairly useful dual 6f winner (including at 2 yrs) Riotous Applause and half-sister to the 2008 2-y-o Group 1 1m Racing Post Trophy winner Crowded House, the French listed 11f winner and Group 3 placed On Reflection (both by Rainbow Quest), the useful 12f winner Heron Bay (by Hernando), the quite useful 7.5f winner Woodland River (by Irish River), the New Zealand winner Bering Island (by Bering) and the placed dam of the US dual Grade 1 winner Ticker Tape. The dam is an unplaced half-sister to 6 minor winners abroad. The second dam, Chapel Of Dreams (by Northern Dancer), a dual Grade 2 winner in the USA, is a three-parts sister to the champion sire Storm Cat.

"A half-sister to the Derby favourite Crowded House, I think this filly will be relatively forward. She's done well physically in the last month – she's really strengthened up a lot and I don't think she's finished yet. There's every chance she's a proper filly and she'd be one of my leading hopes".

48. GLASS OF RED (IRE) ★★★
gr.f. Verglas – Embassy Belle (Marju).
March 20. First foal. €50,000Y. Goffs Million. David Redvers. The dam, a fair Irish 7f and 1m winner of 3 races at 4 yrs, was Grade 2 placed in the USA and is a half-sister to 6 winners. The second dam, Humble Mission (by Shack), is a placed half-sister to 3 winners. (R Morecombe & J Perryman).

"A sharp, forward-going filly with speed on both sides of her family. I haven't done a lot with her yet but I would think she'd be ready by the end of May. A tough, hardy filly, I like her but he may need a bit of cut in the ground".

49. GOOLAGONG (IRE) ★★★
b.f. Giant's Causeway – Maroochydore (Danehill).
March 23. Second foal. 105,000Y. Tattersalls October 1. D Redvers. The dam won the 2-y-o listed Silver Flash Stakes and is a half-sister to 6 winners including the Irish 2-y-o 7f and subsequent Hong Kong winner Bowman's Crossing. The second dam, Biraya (by Valiyar), is an unraced half-sister to 4 winners. (R A Pegum).

"A filly with a huge backside on her, but she isn't backward. David Redvers absolutely loved her and was adamant we should get her if the price was right. It's looking now that he was right because she's a nice filly that covers a lot of ground, but she's big and it's going to be a while before we ask her any proper questions".

50. INVINCIBLE PRINCE (IRE) ★★
b.c. Invincible Spirit – Forest Prize (Charnwood Forest).
February 10. Fourth foal. Doncaster St Leger. 45,000Y. David Redvers. Half-brother to the moderate 4-y-o 7f winner Polish Prize (by Polish Precedent). The dam, a fair 2-y-o dual 6f winner, is a half-sister to 6 winners including the triple Group 1 winner Somnus. The second dam, Midnight's Reward (by Night Shift), a quite useful 2-y-o 6f winner, is a half-sister to 11 winners. (Mr R J Roberts).

"A nice sort, he's a good-mover and I think a bit of him but he's got to show it. He hasn't really got it all together yet".

51. KENSEI ★★★
ch.c. Peintre Celebre – Journey Of Hope (Slew O'Gold).
April 29. Half-brother to the useful Irish 10f winner Dream To Dress (by Theatrical) and the fair Irish 12f winner Anticipated Move (by Silver Hawk). The dam, a quite useful Irish 2-y-o 6f winner, is a half-sister to numerous winners including the fairly useful 7f winner Military Option. The second dam, Comfort and Style (by Be My Guest), winner of the 2-y-o 5f listed Round Tower Stakes, is a half-sister to numerous winners including the Italian Group 2 10f winner My Franky and the US Grade 3 winner Strong Dollar. (J C Smith).
"This is a nice horse with a very good way of going and despite his foaling date and his pedigree, he's more forward than you'd expect. I think a bit of him and he ought to be worth watching out for".

52. MIRACLE WISH (IRE) ★★★
b.f. One Cool Cat – Bentley's Bush (Barathea).
February 19. First foal. €160,000Y. Goffs Million. Not sold. The dam, a quite useful 2-y-o 6f winner, was listed-placed and is a half-sister to 2 winners. The second dam, Veiled Threat (by Be My Guest), a French 10f winner and third in the Group 3 Prix de Sandringham, is a half-sister to 5 winners including the useful 12f to 14f winner Turtle Valley and the Italian listed winner and Group 2 6f Moet & Chandon Rennen third Prime Glade.
"A sharp filly and it's all speed on both sides of her family so as soon as she's ready we'll be cracking on. We'd like to hit hard and early but she's not quite ready to run yet. I like her, she has a good honest head on her and she looks tough".

53. MORORLESS ★★★
b.f. Exceed And Excel – Final Pursuit (Pursuit Of Love).
February 23. Fourth foal. 35,000Y. Tattersalls October 2. Will Edmeades. Half-sister to the modest triple 5f winner (including at 2 yrs) Choisette (by Choisir). The dam, a fairly useful 2-y-o 5.7f winner, is a half-sister to 9 winners including the very useful dual 6f winner and Group 3 Coventry Stakes second Sir Nicholas (subsequently very successful in Hong Kong), the smart sprint winner and Ayr Gold Cup second Double Action and the very useful 2-y-o listed 6f Sirenia Stakes winner Lipstick. The second dam, Final Shot (by Dalsaan), a quite useful winner of 3 races including the Ayr Gold Cup, is a half-sister to 2 winners. (MST Partnership).
"A filly with a bit of size and scope about her, she's going to be one for the mid-to-late summer. She's a good-moving filly and the family takes plenty of racing. I would hope that she's a nice filly and there's every chance that she'd be better than average".

54. NOTORIZE ★★★★
ch.c. Hernando – Hypnotize (Machiavellian).
February 17. Fifth foal. 33,000Y. Tattersalls October 2. David Redvers. Half-brother to the useful 2-y-o listed 8.3f winner of 6 races Hypnotic (by Lomitas), to the quite useful 2-y-o 6f winner Hip (by Pivotal) and the quite useful dual 7f winner Macedon (by Dansili). The dam, a useful 2-y-o dual 7f winner, is closely related to 2 winners including the Group 3 6f Cherry Hinton Stakes winner Dazzle and a half-sister to 5 winners including the useful 7f (at 2 yrs) and 1m listed winner Fantasize and to the placed dam of the Group 2 winning sprinter Danehurst. The second dam, Belle et Deluree (by The Minstrel), won over 1m (at 2 yrs) and 10f in France and is a half-sister to the very useful 6f and 1m winner and Cheveley Park Stakes second Dancing Tribute (herself dam of the Group/Grade 2 winners Souvenir Copy and Dance Sequence). (Mr R J Roberts).
"He's a lovely horse and despite the sire Hernando having a great year it's amazing that this was his highest priced yearling. I bought him on spec and he was an obvious one to get, given his sire was responsible for our Oaks winner! He's a big, tall, lengthy sort but he'll run this year and there's every chance he'll be nice. We'll campaign him with next year in mind but we'll still have a proper crack at races over seven furlongs or a mile later on this season".

55. OASIS DANCER ★★
br.gr.c. Oasis Dream – Good Enough (Mukaddamah).
April 30. Fifth foal. 52,000Y. Tattersalls October 1. David Redvers. Half-brother to the fair 2008 2-y-o 1m winner Bright Enough (by Fantastic Light), to the very useful 1m winner of 4 races and listed-placed Smart Enough (by Cadeaux Genereux) and the Japanese winner of 10 races Night School (by Machiavellian). The dam won once at 3 yrs in the USA and was third in the Group 1 Prix Saint-Alary and is a half-sister to 5 winners including the Group 3 Molecomb Stakes winner Classic Ruler. The second dam, Viceroy Princess (by Godswalk), a modest 2-y-o 7f seller winner, is a half-sister to 7 winners. (Mrs H I Slade).

"Although it's quite a speedy family, this is quite a big, long, scopey horse. He's got a lot of strengthening up to do and he'll be one for late summer. He's a good mover and he's just starting to do a bit better and I wasn't expecting him to progress just yet".

56. PRIMO DE VIDA (IRE) ★★
b.c. Trade Fair – Rampage (Pivotal).
February 21. First foal. 23,000Y. Doncaster St Leger. David Redvers. The dam, a fair 6f and 7f winner of 3 races, is a half-sister to 4 winners including the smart all-weather 5f and 6f winner J M W Turner. The second dam, Noor El Houdah (by Fayruz), a modest 5f to 7f winner of 6 races, is a sister to 2 winners and a half-sister to 3 winners including the useful 2-y-o listed 6f winner Smittenby. (Prime Of Life).

"An athletic sort of horse with quite a lot of the damsire Pivotal about him. He looks pretty straightforward and I'm hoping he'll progress. The sort of horse that should be capable of picking up a maiden auction and he might be better than that".

57. RADIO CITY ★★★
b.c. Intikhab – Red Shareef (Marju).
January 31. Fifth foal. 22,000Y. Tattersalls October 2. Ralph Beckett. Brother to the unplaced 2008 2-y-o Orangeleg and half-brother to the smart 6f and 1m winner of 4 races and listed placed Caesar Beware (by Daggers Drawn), the modest dual 6f winner (including at 2 yrs) Gainshare and the minor French 1m winner Zylig (both by Lend A Hand). The dam won 3 races at 2 and 3 yrs in Italy and is a half-sister to 5 winners. The second dam, Dash Of Red (by Red Sunset), won the listed Silver Flash Stakes in Ireland at 2 yrs and is a half-sister to 6 winners. (Clipper Group Holdings Ltd).

"He'll be out early and he's by a sire we've had a lot of luck with. It's a very quick family and he's done enough to show he's up to winning a maiden. He's solid and tough and I think he'll take plenty of racing, so we should have a lot of sport with him".

58. RIVER LANDING ★★★
b.c. Lucky Story – Beechnut (Mujadil).
April 29. Third foal. €22,000Y. Goffs Million. David Redvers. Brother to the modest 2008 2-y-o 1m winner Super Fourteen. The dam is an unraced sister to the winner and Group 3 Molecomb Stakes placed Connemara and to the listed-placed winner Presentation and a half-sister to 4 winners. The second dam, Beechwood (by Blushing Groom), won over 10.8f in France and is a half-sister to 5 winners. (Thurloe Thoroughbreds XXV).

"A nice horse, he was a very neat yearling but he's grown into a very scopey two-year-old. So I don't think he'll be appearing that early. I think he was well bought and I hope he'll be up to winning a maiden before going on. He'll be a good, fun horse and the sire did well with his first two-year-olds last year from a small crop".

59. SAN CASSIANO (IRE) ★★
b.g. Bertolini – Celtic Silhouette (Celtic Swing).
May 4. Third foal. 34,000Y. Tattersalls October 2. Not sold. Half-brother to the fair 2008 7f placed 2-y-o Dreamwalk (by Bahri) and to the very useful 7f (at 2 yrs) and Group 3 1m Premio Dormello winner and Group 2 May Hill Stakes third Celtic Slipper (by Anabaa). The dam, placed 4 times at 4 and 5 yrs in France, is a sister to the listed winner and Group 2 Dante Stakes second Celtic Silence and a half-sister to the

dual Group 3 winner Royal And Regal. The second dam, Smart 'n Noble (by Smarten), won the Group 2 Barbara Fritchie Handicap and is a half-sister to 7 winners. (P D Savill).

"He's going to need a bit of time, he's a May foal and a big, long, scopey horse. He's not unlike his half-sister Celtic Slipper in make, shape and character. I like the horse".

60. SEASIDE SIZZLER ★★
ch.c. Rahy – Via Borghese (Seattle Dancer).
February 23. Eleventh foal. 62,000Y. Tattersalls October 1. David Redvers. Half-brother to the fairly useful 2-y-o 6f winner Venetian Pride, to the quite useful 7f winner Pietro Siena (both by Gone West), the minor US 4-y-o winner Vespasian (by Woodman) and to two minor 2-y-o winners in Japan and the USA (both by Seeking The Gold). The dam, a winner of 11 races in Ireland and the USA including the Grade 2 9f Diana Handicap and the Group 3 1m Desmond Stakes, is a half-sister to 6 winners including the Grade 2 American Handicap winner El Angelo, the Group 2 Premio Ribot winner Miswaki Tern and the Group 3 Prix du Bois winner Porto Varas. The second dam, Angela Serra (by Arctic Tern), won the Group 2 12f Premio Legnano. (I J Heseltine).

"We think a bit of him and we'll give him plenty of time. He's been quite colty which I believe is not unlike Rahy's stock and he's a big, scopey sort of horse. I like him and his dam was an exceptional racemare- very tough - and it looks like he'll take plenty of graft as well".

61. ST IGNATIUS ★★★
b.c. Ishiguru – Branston Berry (Mukaddamah).
February 17. Fifth foal. 30,000Y. Tattersalls October 3. Kern/Lillingston. Half-brother to the modest 5f and 6f winner Briery Lane (by Tagula) and to a minor winner in Italy by Erhaab. The dam, a quite useful 5f and 6.5f winner, is a half-sister to 4 winners including the useful 6f (at 2 yrs) to 1m winner Tough Love. The second dam, Food Of Love (by Music Boy), a very useful sprint winner of 6 races, was second in the Group 3 King George Stakes and is a half-sister to 4 winners. (R A Pegum).

"A gorgeous individual and as good-looking a two-year-old as we have. I'm a fan of the sire and I think he's underrated. This horse is straightforward, I like him and he'll appear sometime in mid-summer".

62. TROPICAL TREAT ★★★
b.f. Bahamian Bounty – Notjustaprettyface (Red Ransom).
February 27. First foal. 28,000foal. Tattersalls December. Littleton Stud. The dam, a fairly useful 2-y-o 5f winner, was listed-placed and fourth in the Group 2 Lowther Stakes and is a half-sister to a winner in the UAE. The second dam, Maudie May (by Gilded Time), won over 8.5f in the USA and is a half-sister to Sri Pekan. (J C Smith).

"A very, very sharp filly. The family is all-speed and she's not going to take much getting ready. I like her and she has a good way about her. The dam barely got six furlongs and by the look of this filly she'll be the same".

63. UNNAMED ★★★
b.c. Bertolini – Princess Mood (Muhtarram).
March 28. Fifth foal. 31,000Y. Doncaster St Leger. David Redvers. Half-brother to the useful 2008 2-y-o listed 7f winner of 3 races Captain Ramius (by Kheleyf), to the very useful 6f and 7f listed winner Kingsgate Prince (by Desert Sun) and the fair 8.5f winner Smugglers Bay (by Celtic Swing). The dam, placed over 1m in Germany, is a half-sister to 4 winners in Germany. The second dam, Princess Nana (by Bellypha), won the Group 2 German 1,000 Guineas and is a half-sister to 6 winners. (Mrs I M Beckett).

"He looks sharp and I got lucky in that I bought him before his half-brother Captain Ramius showed how good he was. Some of the Bertolini's we've had have been quite fiery but he's laid-back and although there's a lot of speed there he's not very forward. So he'll be one for the second half of the year over five and six furlongs. There's a chance he might be quite a decent sort and he makes good use of himself".

MICHAEL BELL

64. ACTIVATE ★★
b.c. Motivator – Princess Manila (Manila).
April 16. Eleventh foal. 100,000Y. Tattersalls October 1. John Warren. Half-brother to the Group 1 Prix d'Ispahan winner Prince Kirk (by Selkirk), the Italian winners Prince Esteem (by Mark Of Esteem), Prince Honor (by Highest Honor) and Princer (by Irish River) and the French winner Platel (by Alysheba). The dam is an unplaced half-sister to 3 winners including the Group 1 Italian Derby winner Hailsham. The second dam, Halo's Princess (by Halo), won the Grade 1 Princess Elizabeth Stakes in Canada and is a half-sister to 6 winners and to the unraced dam of the Australian Grade 1 winners Curata Storm and Voile d'Or. (Highclere Thoroughbred Racing).
"From the first crop of Motivator and out of a Manila mare, he's a nice, well-made horse that will take a bit of time and is one for the second half of the season".

65. ADMISSION ★★★★
b.c. Azamour – Eve (Rainbow Quest).
February 7. Fourth living foal. 40,000Y. Tattersalls December. Not sold. Half-brother to the fairly useful 1m and 10f winner Dubai Twilight (by Alhaarth) and to the fairly useful 7f winner Charm School (by Dubai Destination). The dam, a quite useful winner of 3 races over 1m, is a half-sister to 7 winners including the 1m and listed 11.5f winner Birdie and the French middle-distance winner of 10 races (including 4 listed events) Faru. The second dam, Fade (by Persepolis), is an unraced half-sister to Tom Seymour, a winner of five Group 3 events in Italy. (Highclere Thoroughbred Racing).
"A very strong, imposing looking horse, I trained the mother who was a useful miler. I would say this horse is one for the second half of the season but he's a very impressive horse to look at as a physical specimen".

66. BABYCAKES (IRE) ★★★★
b.f. Marju – Dark Rosaleen (Darshaan).
February 2. Third foal. 90,000Y. Tattersalls October 1. B Grassick. Half-sister to the fairly useful 7f (at 2 yrs) and listed 1m winner Rosaleen (by Cadeaux Genereux) and to the quite useful 7f, 1m (both at 2 yrs) and 10f winner Rosbay (by Desert Prince). The dam is an unraced half-sister to 6 winners including the US stakes winner Tender Offer and the Hong Kong stakes winner Man Of Honour. The second dam, Santella Bell (by Ballad Rock), an Irish listed 10f winner, is a half-sister to the Group 3 Queens Vase winner Santella Man. (Mr J Acheson).
"I like Marju fillies and this is a nice one. She won't be out early but she does everything asked of her easily".

67. BLUE ZEALOT ★★★
b.f. Galileo – Massada (Most Welcome).
March 28. Seventh foal. 90,000Y. Tattersalls October 1. Kern/Lillingston. Half-sister to the German listed winner and Group 3 6f placed Miss Lips, to the minor German winner Moody Blues (both by Big Shuffle), the Italian listed winner Les Fazzani (by Intikhab) and a minor 2-y-o winner in Spain by King Charlemagne. The dam, a listed-placed 7f and 1m winner at 2 yrs in Germany, is a half-sister to 3 minor winners. The second dam, Maracuja (by Riverman), won over 1m at 2 yrs in France and is a half-sister to 3 minor winners. (Mrs O Hoare).
"She hasn't been with us that long and being a Galileo she's not going to be doing that much too soon, but she has a nice pedigree so we'll give her a bit of time. A good mover, I think she looks quite well-bought even though there is a recession on".

68. BOUNCY BOUNCY (IRE) ★★★
ch.f. Chineur – Wunderbra (Second Empire).
February 21. First foal. 27,000Y. Tattersalls October 3. Kern/Lillingston. The dam, a quite useful 5f and 6f winner, is a half-sister to 5 winners including the 5f winner of 3 races and Group 1 Phoenix Stakes fourth Galloway Boy and to the useful 5f and 6f winner and Group 3 Cornwallis Stakes third Grand Lad. The second dam, Supportive (by Nashamaa), won four races over 5f at 2 and 3 yrs in Ireland and is a half-sister to 3 winners. (A Scotney, D Asplin & Symonds).

"We trained the mother who was pretty speedy and this filly looks quite sharp. Bearing in mind she looks racey and is by a sprinter and out of a sprinter, she looks as though she should be able to do herself justice in sprints, although probably not early on".

69. CHURCH OF ENGLAND ★★★ ♠
gr.c. Selkirk – Frosty Welcome (With Approval).
April 30. Fourth foal. 30,000Y. Tattersalls October 2. R Frisby. Half-brother to Lipi (by Sadler's Wells), unplaced in one start at 2 yrs in 2008 and the fair 12f to 2m winner Casual Garcia (by Hernando). The dam, a useful 9f and 12f winner, is a half-sister to 5 minor winners. The second dam, Light Ice (by Arctic Tern), won 4 races at up to 10f in the USA and is a half-sister to 12 winners including the US Grade 1 winners Al Mamoon and La Gueriere. (R C Tooth).
"He's a backward horse, as both his pedigree and foaling date suggest, but he's a good mover and I'm hopeful we'll have some fun with him in the autumn".

70. CLEAR HILLS (IRE) ★★★
b.c. Marju – Rainbows For All (Rainbows For Life).
March 17. Third foal. 70,000Y. Tattersalls October 2. Kern/Lillingston. Half-brother to the unplaced Irish 2008 2-y-o Reach A Rainbow (by Royal Applause) and to the quite useful Irish 2-y-o 7f and subsequent French dual 3-y-o winner Rainbow Crossing (by Cape Cross). The dam, an Irish 2-y-o Group 3 7f Debutante Stakes winner, is a full or half-sister to 5 winners. The second dam, Maura's Guest (by Be My Guest), is an unraced half-sister to 7 winners including the Italian Group winners Conte Grimaldi and Bold Apparel. (R A Pegum).
"A big, strong, scopey horse. I hope he'll pull himself together in the second half of the season and he's probably our strongest, most well-made two-year-old. We won't be doing too much too soon with him though".

71. COLLECT ART (IRE) ★★★
b.c. Footstepsinthesand – Night Scent (Scenic).
March 27. Seventh foal. €60,000Y. Goffs Million. Kern/Lillingston. Half-brother to fair 2008 2-y-o 5f winner Night Seed (by Night Shift), to the useful dual 6f winner Burning Incense (by Namid), the Italian winner of 13 races and Group 2 second Fielding (by Ali-Royal) and the quite useful 2-y-o 6f and 7f winner Cartronageeraghlad (by Mujadil). The dam won over 1m and 9f in Ireland and is a half-sister to 5 winners including the Group 1 Phoenix Stakes winner Bradawn Breever. The second dam, Ozone (by Auction Ring), won 4 races at 2 and 3 yrs and is a half-sister to 8 winners. (R Green).
"Quite a sharp colt, he was bought at the Goffs Million sale so his season will be geared towards that. He's quite 'buzzy' mentally so we haven't done much with him yet. It doesn't look like he'd take much getting ready and he's a nice horse".

72. FARMER GILES (IRE) ★★★★ ♠
b.c. Danroad – Demeter (Diesis).
February 4. Fifth foal. 46,000Y. Doncaster St Leger. Kern/Lillingston. Half-brother to the quite useful 2008 2-y-o 6f winner Pyrrha (by Pyrus) and to the quite useful 12f winner Alrafidain (by Monsun). The dam, placed over 1m at 2 yrs on her only start, is a half-sister to 2 winners. The second dam, Nicer (by Pennine Walk), won the Irish 1,000 Guineas and is a half-sister to 9 winners. (R Green & M Bell).
"He's a nice, sharp colt with a good temperament and I think he has a great future".

73. FEARLESS FALCON ★★★★
b.c. Pivotal – Juno Madonna (Sadler's Wells).
February 2. Ninth foal. 350,000Y. Tattersalls October 1. Not sold. Half-brother to the smart Group 3 Sandown Classic Trial and Group 3 Mooresbridge Stakes winner Regime (by Golan), to the very useful 2-y-o 5f listed winner and Group 2 Cherry Hinton second Salut d'Amour (by Danehill Dancer), the quite useful 2-y-o 1m winner Wotchalike (by Spectrum), the quite useful Irish 12f and 17f winner Coquette Rouge (by Croco Rouge) and the minor French

winner Laureldean Lady (by Statue Of Liberty). The dam is an unraced half-sister to 5 winners including the Group 3 5f King George Stakes winner Title Roll and the Irish listed sprint winner Northern Express. The second dam, Tough Lady (by Bay Express), a fairly useful 2-y-o 6f winner, is a half-sister to 5 winners. (10-Up-Syndicate).

"There's quite a bit of speed in this pedigree and the half-brother Regime showed a good turn of foot for one by Golan. He's a promising, chunky two-year-old that should be racing by mid-summer".

74. GRAMMERCY (IRE) ★★★★
b.c. Whipper – Topiary (Selkirk).
March 17. Second foal. €52,000Y. Goffs Million. R Frisby. The dam, a minor winner in France at 3 yrs, is a half-sister to 4 winners including the Group 3 Prix d'Aumale winner Top Toss. The second dam, Tossup (by Gone West), won the listed Irish 1,000 Guineas Trial and is a full or half-sister to 5 winners. (Mr B Hawtin).

"A nice horse and a good advertisement for his sire, I'll be focusing his campaign around the Goffs Million, having him peaking for then rather than earlier. I like him".

75. GREEK KEY ★★★★
ch.c. Selkirk – Doohulla (Stravinsky).
January 31. First foal. €45,000Y. Goffs Million. Kern/Lillingston. The dam, a fairly useful dual 6f winner at 2 and 4 yrs, was listed-placed and is a half-sister to 7 winners. The second dam, Viva Zapata (by Affirmed), won the Group 2 Prix du Gros Chene and is a half-sister to 7 winners. (M B Hawtin).

"He looks to be quite speedy and quite mature for a Selkirk who is a sire that doesn't normally have early two-year-olds. He has an early foaling date and he definitely looks sharper than most Selkirk's that we've had. He'll be one of our earlier types and if he's good enough his season will be geared towards the Goffs Million".

76. JUICY PEAR (IRE) ★★★
b.c. Pyrus – Cappadoce (General Monash).
February 15. Third living foal. 45,000Y. Doncaster St Leger. Kern/Lillingston. Half-brother to the quite useful 1m and 9f winner Jewelled Dagger and to a winner in Spain (both by Daggers Drawn). The dam is an unplaced half-sister to 3 winners. The second dam, Urgent Liaison (by High Estate), is an unraced half-sister to 5 winners including the Group 2 winner Great Dane. (W Maguire).

"A strong, good-bodied, very healthy looking horse. I think he's a mid-summer type two-year-old".

77. KAIZAN (IRE) ★★
b.c. Azamour – Maid Of Killeen (Darshaan).
May 10. Sixth foal. Half-brother to the Group 1 6f Cheveley Park Stakes winner Indian Ink, to the quite useful 1m winner Navajo Joe (both by Indian Ridge) and the fairly useful 2-y-o 6f and 1m winner Unavailable (by Alzao). The dam, a fairly useful 2-y-o 9f winner, was listed-placed and is a half-sister to 3 winners. The second dam, Sovereign Touch (by Pennine Walk), is an unraced half-sister to 6 winners including the Group 2 winners Royal Touch and Foresee. (Lady Bamford).

"Hasn't arrived here yet".

78. LADY McGONAGALL (USA) ★★★
b.br.f. Malibu Moon – Bella Tusa (Sri Pekan).
March 4. Second foal. $70,000Y. Keeneland September. BBA (Ire). Half-sister to a minor winner at 2 yrs in Canada by Carson City. The dam, a 2-y-o dual listed 5f winner, was third in the Group 2 Criterium de Maisons-Laffitte and is a half-sister to the listed winner and Group 3 placed La Vita E Bella. The second dam, Coolrain Lady (by Common Grounds), was placed 12 times in Ireland from 1m to 10f and is a half-sister to 4 minor winners. (Mrs M Bryce).

"She has an engine but she needs to be channelled in the right direction because she's a bit of a 'Houdini character' in that she's escaped three times including once down Newmarket High Street! Fortunately she never has a scratch when she comes home. I think she'll be alright".

79. L'ENCHANTERESSE (IRE) ★★★
ch.f. *Kyllachy – Enchant (Lion Cavern).*
February 24. Sixth foal. 55,000Y. Tattersalls October 2. Kern/Lillingston. Half-sister to the useful 7f and 1m winner of 5 races Polar Magic (by Polar Falcon), to the fair 12f and hurdles winner Gandalf (by Sadler's Wells) and the modest 6f to 10f winner of 3 races Mobane Flyer (by Groom Dancer). The dam, a fairly useful 3-y-o 7f winner and third in the listed 10f Lupe Stakes, is closely related to the smart Group 3 6f Cherry Hinton Stakes winner Dazzle and the listed winner Hypnotize and a half-sister to 5 winners and to the placed dam of the Group 3 Cornwallis Stakes winner Danehurst. The second dam, Belle Et Deluree (by The Minstrel), won over 1m (at 2 yrs) and 10f in France and is a half-sister to the US Grade 2 winner Doneraile Court and to the dam of the Group/Graded stakes winners Dance Sequence and Souvenir Copy. (R Green).
"From a good fillies' family, she has a good pedigree although in my experience I don't think Kyllachy's are necessarily early so I'll give her a bit of time. Everyone who rides her likes her and I think she'll be nice in the second half of the season".

80. MADAME ROULIN (IRE) ★★★★
b.f. *Xaar – Cradle Rock (Desert Sun).*
January 24. Second foal. 17,000Y. Tattersalls October 3. Kern/Lillingston. The dam is an unraced sister to one winner and a half-sister to the listed winning 2-y-o and Group 2 placed Sir Xaar (by Xaar). The second dam, Cradle Brief (by Brief Truce), is an unraced half-sister to the Group 3 winner Tiger Royal. (Three To One Racing).
"She's a big, strong filly, very deep-girthed and a good mover. She'll be one of our earlier two-year-old fillies to run".

81. MISS CHAUMIERE ★★★
b.f. *Selkirk - Miss Corniche (Hernando).*
February 20. Sister to the very useful 1m winner Moyenne Corniche and half-sister to the quite useful 2008 2-y-o 6f winner Miss Eze (by Danehill Dancer). The dam, a 7f (at 2 yrs) and listed 10f winner, is a sister to 2 winners and a half-sister to numerous winners including the listed 1m winner Miss Riviera Golf. The second dam, Miss Beaulieu (by Northfields), was a useful 6f and 10f winner. (J L C Pierce).
"This filly looks quite useful, but the Selkirk-Hernando cross means we won't be doing anything too soon. A useful filly in the making".

82. MISS WHIPPY ★★★
b.f. *Whipper – Glorious (Nashwan).*
March 25. 38,000Y. Tattersalls October 2. R Frisby. Half-sister to the fairly useful triple 10f winner Closertobelieving (by Xaar), to the fairly useful 2-y-o 7f winner Abundant (by Zafonic), the fair all-weather 3-y-o 7f and 1m winner Athboy (by Entrepreneur), the fair 9f winner of 4 races Plush (by Medicean) and a winner in Greece by Danzero. The dam is an unraced half-sister to 7 winners including the smart 8.2f winner and Group 1 St James's Palace Stakes fourth Killer Instinct and the very useful 2-y-o 7f winner and Group 1 Hoover Fillies Mile second Pick of the Pops. The second dam, Rappa Tap Tap (by Tap On Wood), a useful 6f Blue Seal Stakes winner, is a half-sister to the Irish Oaks winner Colorspin (herself the dam of Opera House, Kayf Tara and Zee Zee Top), to the Group 2 Prix de l'Opera winner Bella Colora (dam of the high-class colt Stagecraft) and the Irish Champion Stakes winner Cezanne. (D W & L Y Payne).
"An attractive filly, she's quite neat and buzzes along but I would think that if we were to get stuck in there wouldn't be much left of her. So we'll take our time and she's a nice filly in the making".

83. MONT AGEL ★★★
b.c. *Danehill Dancer – Miss Riviera Golf (Hernando).*
March 5. Half-brother to the listed 7f winner Hotel Du Cap and the fairly useful 10f and 12f winner The Carlton Cannes (both by Grand Lodge). The dam won a listed event over 1m in France at 3 yrs and is a half-sister to several winners including the useful 2-y-o 6f winner and listed-placed Miss Riviera. The second dam,

Miss Beaulieu (by Northfields), was a useful 6f and 10f winner. (Mr J L Pearce).
"A nice colt and although we haven't done much with him yet he's a good mover and a strong colt that just needs a bit more time. We should be able to get on with him from June onwards".

84. MOTIRANI ★★★★
br.c. Motivator – Maharani (Red Ransom).
January 31. Eighth foal. 80,000Y. Tattersalls October 1. John Warren. Half-brother to the 1m and 10f winner and subsequent US Grade 1 Secretariat Stakes third Joe Bear (by Peintre Celebre), to the French listed-placed winner Bye Bye Love (by Sinndar), the fair 7f winner Lucefer (by Lycius) and 2 minor winners abroad by Nashwan and Desert Prince. The dam, placed once in Germany, is a half-sister to 7 winners including the Group 2 Laurent-Perrier Champagne Stakes winner Sri Pekan and the Group 3 Railway Stakes winner Daylight In Dubai. The second dam, Lady Godolphin (by Son Ange), won once in the USA and is a half-sister to 2 winners. (Miss Y M G Jacques).
"Of all our Motivator two-year-olds this colt is the most similar to his sire that we have. I'm hopeful that he'll be a very decent second half of the season two-year-old. He was an early foal and he should be one to go to war with this year".

85. MOUNTAIN QUEST ★★★ ♠
b.c. Hernando – Miss Katmandu (Rainbow Quest).
April 8. The dam, unplaced in one start, is a half-sister to the very smart 7f (at 2 yrs), Group 3 12f September Stakes and Group 3 13.4f Ormonde Stakes winner Asian Heights (by Hernando) and to the smart 10f winner St Expedit. The second dam, Miss Rinjani (by Shirley Heights), a fair 2-y-o 7f winner, was placed over 12f at 3 yrs and is a half-sister to several winners. (Mr J L C Pearce).
"You won't see too much of him early on as it's a family that improves with time, but all his riders like him and it looks like he should be able to do himself justice as a two-year-old. At this stage of the proceedings he gets up Warren Hill very well".

86. PROMPTER ★★★
b.c. Motivator – Penny Cross (Efisio).
April 6. Second foal. 70,000Y. Tattersalls October 2. John Warren. Half-brother to the unraced 2008 2-y-o Quinsman (by Singspiel). The dam, a useful 7f to 8.5f winner of 3 races, was listed placed twice and is a half-sister to 6 winners including the Group 2 Celebration Mile winner Priors Lodge. The second dam, Addaya (by Persian Bold), ran once unplaced and is a half-sister to 8 winners abroad. (Royal Ascot Racing Club).
"He's probably the sharpest of the three Motivators we have. He's an athletic colt and the signs are encouraging for the sire on the cross section we have here. This horse gets up Warren Hill with the minimum of fuss".

87. RED AMY ★★★
b.f. Hawk Wing – Ballet Ballon (Rahy).
March 24. First foal. 48,000Y. Tattersalls October 1. Kern/Lillingston. The dam, a fair 10f winner, is a half-sister to the useful 10f winner and 10f listed placed Design Perfection. The second dam, Bella Ballerina (by Sadler's Wells), a quite useful 3-y-o 9f winner, is a sister to the high-class Group 2 10f Prince of Wales's Stakes and Group 3 10f Brigadier Gerard Stakes winner Stagecraft and to the useful listed 9f winner Balalaika and a half-sister to the Group 3 Strensall Stakes winner Mullins Bay and the dual 1m listed stakes winner Hyabella. (T Neill).
"Quite a nice filly from a good middle-distance family. She's athletic and a good mover, we won't be doing much with her before midsummer, but she skips along well and is very light on her feet".

88. SALVATION ★★
b.f. Montjeu – Birdie (Alhaarth).
March 20. Third foal. 70,000Y. Tattersalls October 1. Bobby O'Ryan. Half-sister to Queens Flight (by King's Best), unplaced in 2 starts at 2 yrs in 2008. The dam, a 1m and listed 11.5f winner, is a half-sister to 7 winners

including the French middle-distance winner of 10 races (including 4 listed events) Faru. The second dam, Fade (by Persepolis), is an unraced half-sister to Tom Seymour, a winner of five Group 3 events in Italy. (Lady Carolyn Warren).
"She's a very scopey, well-made filly who will take time and I very much view her as a two year prospect, but she should be quite decent come the autumn hopefully".

89. SYRIAN ★★★★★ ♠
b.c. Hawk Wing – Lady Lahar (Fraam).
January 20. Fifth foal. 30,000Y. Tattersalls October 2. John Warren. Closely related to the unraced 2008 2-y-o Popmurphy (by Montjeu) and half-brother to the 2-y-o listed 1m winner Classic Legend (by Galileo) and the fairly useful 2-y-o 7f winner Kilburn (by Grand Lodge). The dam, a useful 2-y-o Group 3 7f Futurity Stakes and 3-y-o 8.3f winner, was third in the Group 2 Cherry Hinton Stakes and the Group 2 Falmouth Stakes and is a half-sister to 2 winners. The second dam, Brigadier's Bird (by Mujadil), is an unraced half-sister to 2 winners. (Highclere Thoroughbred Racing).
"This is a nice colt and the dam was quite a decent two-year-old. A strong, good-bodied, good-moving horse, he was well-bought and I'm looking forward to training him. I haven't done a lot with him yet but he's nice".
TRAINER'S BARGAIN BUY

90. TELL HALAF ★★★★
b.c. Oasis Dream – Topkamp (Pennekamp).
March 9. Second foal. 30,000Y. Tattersalls October 2. Not sold. Half-brother to the quite useful 7f and 1m winner of 5 races Topazes (by Cadeaux Genereux). The dam, a useful 5f (at 2 yrs) and 6f listed winner, is a half-sister to the listed winning sprinter Morinqua. The second dam, Victoria Regia (by Lomond), a stakes winner of 3 races from 6f to 1m here and in the USA, is a half-sister to 9 winners. (Baron Van Oppenheim).
"He's improved leaps and bounds physically since he came here. We trained the mother and the half-brother and this colt is far more precocious than Topazes. I think he'll be one of the first of our two-year-olds to run and he's looking like a promising, early summer two-year-old".

91. THELADYISATRAMP ★★
b.f. Bahamian Bounty – Affair Of State (Tate Gallery).
January 24. Thirteenth foal. Half-sister to the useful 2-y-o listed 6f and 7f winner Bibury Flyer, to the useful 10f and 11.8f winner Mojalid (both by Zafonic), the fairly useful 6f winner Diplomat (by Deploy), the quite useful 7f (at 2 yrs) and 9f winner Nordic Affair (by Halling), the quite useful 2005 2-y-o 7f winner Celestial Princess (by Observatory), the fair 2-y-o 5f winner Ice Maiden (by Polar Falcon), the fair 5f (at 2 yrs) and 6f winner Stately Princess (by Robellino), the modest 6f all-weather winner Gun Salute (by Mark Of Esteem) and the German and Swedish 5f to 1m winner Statesman (by Doyoun). The dam, a very useful Irish 2-y-o 6f winner, is a half-sister to 7 minor winners. The second dam, All Hat (by Double Form), won over 5f at 3 yrs and is a half-sister to 5 winners including the Cherry Hinton and Musidora Stakes winner Everything Nice – herself dam of the Irish 1,000 Guineas winner Nicer. (Mr Stephen Crown).
"The mare has produced some good ones and she was useful herself. This filly needs to strengthen before we really get on with her, but she could be alright".

92. THOMAS BAINES (USA) ★★★★
b.c. Johannesburg – Foofaraw (Cherokee Run).
February 2. Second foal. 55,000Y. Tattersalls October 1. Kern/Lillingston. The dam won 2 races at 2 and 3 yrs in North America and is a half-sister to 4 winners. The second dam, All The Rage (by Lyphard), is a placed daughter of the US Grade 1 winner Laugh And Be Merry. (R Green).
"A strong, well-made two-year-old type and an early foal, he's mature both physically and mentally and will be one of our first ones to run. He's a natural two-year-old type that wants to be a racehorse and he's getting there without us really getting after him".

93. TITIVATION ★★★
b.f. Montjeu – Flirtation (Pursuit Of Love).
April 8. Sixth foal. 200,000Y. Tattersalls December. Not sold. Half-sister to the modest 2008 2-y-o 1m winner Racketeer (by Cape Cross), to the high-class 1,000 Guineas, Irish 1,000 Guineas, Coronation Stakes, Matron Stakes and Sun Chariot Stakes winner Attraction (by Efisio) and the quite useful 2-y-o 5f winner Aunty Mary (by Common Grounds). The dam ran unplaced once over 7f at 3 yrs and is a half-sister to 4 winners including the French listed 12f winner and Group 2 placed Carmita. The second dam, Eastern Shore (by Sun Prince), is a placed half-sister to 7 winners including the listed winner and Group 2 placed Easy Landing. (Duchess Of Roxburghe).
"A half-sister to one of the best fillies of our generation in Attraction, she's bred slightly differently (being by Montjeu), but she's a very attractive, good-bodied filly that will probably have a spring break before coming back I again with a view to an autumn campaign".

94. WESTERNIZE ★★★
b.f. Gone West – Sleepytime (Royal Academy).
April 11. Seventh foal. 220,000Y. Tattersalls October 1. John Warren. Half-sister to the Group 3 Winter Derby winner of 9 races Gentleman's Deal and to the Irish 2-y-o 7f winner Spanish Harlem (both by Danehill). The dam, a very smart filly and winner of the 1,000 Guineas, is a sister to the Group 1 1m Sussex Stakes winner Ali Royal and a half-sister to the Group 1 12f Europa Preis and Group 1 10f Premio Roma winner Taipan. The second dam, Alidiva (by Chief Singer), was a useful winner of 3 races from 6f to 1m including a listed event and is a half-sister to 6 winners including the dual French Group 1 winner Croco Rouge. (Lady Carolyn Warren).
"Not yet in training but a very exciting filly on pedigree. I know she's much liked at the pre-training yard where she is, so we're very much looking forward to having her in the string".

95. WIGMORE HALL ★★★★
b.c. High Chaparral – Love And Laughter (Theatrical).
February 15. First foal. 60,000Y. Tattersalls October 2. Kern/Lillingston. The dam, a fair 2-y-o 7f winner, is a half-sister to 3 winners. The second dam, Hoh Dear (by Sri Pekan), won 4 races here and in North America including the 6f Empress Stakes (at 2 yrs) and the Grade 3 Natalma Stakes and was second in the Group 2 Cherry Hinton Stakes. (Mr B Hawtin).
"The sire has been slower to get going than some others but I think this is a nice colt. We know the family because we trained the second dam with a degree of success and he could be a Chesham Stakes horse although we haven't done much with him yet. For a High Chaparral he looks a very precocious two-year-old and he should do himself justice this year".

96. UNNAMED ★★★
b.f. Cape Cross – Badawi (Diesis).
April 23. Half-sister to the useful 2-y-o 7f winner and Group 3 7f Vintage Stakes third Fox, to the very useful 2-y-o 6f winner and Group 1 Cheveley Park Stakes third Badminton (by Zieten), the useful 6f and 7f winner and Group 3 Nell Gwyn Stakes second Cala (by Desert Prince), the useful all-weather 7f winner Rafferty (by Lion Cavern), the fairly useful 3-y-o 1m winner Badagara (by Warning), the quite useful all-weather 7f to 9f winner Saguaro, the fair dual winner at around 7f Balfour (both by Green Desert). The dam was a useful 1m and 9f winner of 4 races. The second dam, Begum (by Alydar), is an unraced half-sister to 7 winners including the US Grade 3 winner and good broodmare Old Goat. (Marwan Al Maktoum).
"We've trained a few out of this mare now and this is an athletic filly that gets up Warren Hill easily. Given her pedigree and her relatively late foaling date I doubt we'll see much of her before June but she's a nice filly".

97. UNNAMED ★★★
ch.c. Dr Fong – Farrfesheena (Rahy).
March 10. Half-brother to the fair 8.7f winner House Of Lords (by Donereile Court) and to the

modest 6f and 7f winner Blackmalkin (by Forest Wildcat). The dam, a fairly useful 1m placed maiden, is a sister to the fairly useful 12f winner Heavenly Bay and a half-sister 2 winners. The second dam, Bevel (by Mr Prospector), a French 1m winner, is out of a half-sister to Ajdal, Formidable and the dam of Arazi. (Marwan Al Maktoum).
"This is a big, strong horse with plenty of scope. He'll take a bit of time and won't be rushed but we like him".

98. UNNAMED ★★★★
b.f. Shamardal – Love Everlasting (Pursuit Of Love).
February 26. The dam, a very useful 2-y-o 7.5f and 3-y-o listed 12f winner, is a half-sister to 6 winners including the smart Group 3 10f Scottish Classic winner Baron Ferdinand. The second dam, In Perpetuity (by Great Nephew), a fairly useful 10f winner, is a half-sister to the Derby winner Shirley Heights and to Bempton (dam of the Group 2 winner Gull Nook and the Group 3 winners Mr Pintips and Banket). (Mr & Mrs G Middlebrook).
"A sweet filly and the dam was obviously very useful. I think she could be a good advertisement for her sire and she definitely looks promising. Very deep girthed with big eyes and big ears, she's a nice filly".

99. UNNAMED ★★★
b.f. Shamardal – Painted Moon (Gone West).
March 11. Second foal. The dam is an unplaced half-sister to numerous winners including the high-class Irish 1,000 Guineas, Coronation Stakes and Nassau Stakes winner Crimplene and the smart Group 3 12.3f Chester Vase winner Dutch Gold. The second dam, Crimson Conquest (by Diesis), a quite useful 2-y-o 6f winner, is a half-sister to the US stakes winner at around 1m Sword Blade. (Marwan Al-Maktoum).
"This filly skips along well and from the early signs of our two Shamardal two-year-olds you'd be encouraged for the sire. She looks quite speedy and hopefully she'll do herself justice over six and seven furlongs. She still looks quite wintry so we're taking our time with her, she's

not over-big but is definitely big enough and she's a two-year-old type to look at".

100. UNNAMED ★★
ch.f. Lomitas – Shadow Roll (Mark Of Esteem).
April 10. Third foal. Half-sister to the quite useful 2-y-o 6f winner Undertone (by Noverre). The dam, a fair 2-y-o 7f listed-placed maiden, is a half-sister to one winner and to the listed-placed Shadowless. The second dam, Warning Shadows (by Cadeaux Genereux), won the Group 2 10f Sun Chariot Stakes and was second in the Irish 1,000 Guineas. (Marwan Al Maktoum).
"Not yet in training".

ALAN BERRY

101. ANNA'S BOY ★★★
ch.c. Reel Buddy – Simianna (Bluegrass Prince).
March 20. 13,000Y. Doncaster St Leger. B Smart. The dam, a useful and tough listed sprint winner of 5 races, was Group 3 placed and is a half-sister to 2 winners. The second dam, Lowrianna (by Cyrano de Bergerac), a moderate 2-y-o 5f winner, is a half-sister to the smart hurdler Grinkov. (Mr A Underwood).

102. RED ROAR (IRE) ★★★
b.f. Chineur – Unfortunate (Komaite).
April 27. Fifth foal. 15,000Y. Half-sister to the Group 3 and dual listed 5f winner of 8 races Look Busy and to the modest 6f to 9f all-weather winner of 6 races The City Kid (both by Danetime) and half-sister to a winner in Greece by Raise A Grand. The dam, a 6f winner at 2 and 3 yrs, is out of the unplaced Honour And Glory (by Hotfoot), herself a half-sister to 6 winners including the dual Group 3 winning sprinter Singing Steven. (Sporting Kings).

103. UNNAMED ★★★
b.c. Avonbridge – Antonia's Folly (Music Boy).
February 22. Eleventh foal. 15,000Y. Doncaster St Leger. Alan Berry. Half-brother to the quite useful 2-y-o dual 5f winner Bond Domingo (by Mind Games), to the quite useful 3-y-o 6f winner Coranglais (by Piccolo), the fair 2-y-o 5f winners Antonia's Dilemma (by Primo Dominie) and Zaragossa (by Paris House), the modest

2-y-o 5f winner Billy Ruffian (by Kheleyf) and a winner in Denmark by Diktat. The dam, a modest 2-y-o 5f winner, stayed 6f and is a half-sister to 2 minor winners. The second dam, Royal Agnes (by Royal Palace), was a fair 14f winner and a half-sister to the smart 2-y-o All Systems Go.

104. UNNAMED ★★
b.f. Arakan – Columbine (Pivotal).
March 9. The dam, a fair 5f and 6f winner of 4 races, is a half-sister to the useful dual 5f winner and Group 3 5f Cornwallis Stakes third Fast Heart, to the fairly useful Irish 6f winner King Of Russia (by Common Grounds) and. The second dam, Heart Of India (by Try My Best), is an unraced half-sister to 9 winners including the very smart King's Stand Stakes and Temple Stakes winner Bolshoi and the useful sprinters Mariinsky, Great Chaddington and Tod.

105. UNNAMED ★★
b.f. Namid – Proud Myth (Mark Of Esteem).
February 5. Second foal. €3,000Y. Goffs October. A Berry. Half-sister to the fair 2008 2-y-o dual 5f winner Mythical Blue (by Acclamation). The dam an unraced half-sister to 2 winners in Australia. The second dam, Folklore (by Fairy King), won 3 races at 2 and 3 yrs in France including a listed event.

JOHN BEST
106. BOB GOES ELECTRIC (IRE) ★★★★
br.c. Camacho – Gracious Gretclo (Common Grounds).
February 11. Eighth foal. 19,000Y. Doncaster St Leger. J Best. Half-brother to the quite useful 7f (at 2 yrs) to 10f winner Granston, to the modest 7f (at 2 yrs) to 10f winner of 10 races Our Kes (both by Revoque), the modest 6f (at 2 yrs) and 5f winner Malahide Express (by Compton Place) and the modest 7f winner Grafton (by Desert Style). The dam was placed over 5f and 6f at 2 yrs and is a sister to the Group 3 July Stakes winner Rich Ground and a half-sister to 5 winners. The second dam, Gratclo (by Belfort), a modest winner of 5 races at 2 to 4 yrs over 6f and 7f, is a half-sister to 3 winners. (J Mayne).

"He's a sharp, early, stocky colt, not over-big but mentally he's 100%. Physically he just lacks a bit of scope for the long term, but I think he'll be one of my first two-year-old runners. He's sharp in every way and he handles everything you give him with no bother. He's one of a couple of horses I might be aiming at the Windsor Castle Stakes". TRAINER'S BARGAIN BUY

107. ECLIPSED (USA) ★★★
ch.c. Proud Citizen – Kamareyah (Hamas).
March 3. Third foal. €47,000Y. Goffs Million. John Best. Half-brother to 2 winners in the USA by Elusive Quality and Smooth Jazz. The dam, a quite useful 2-y-o 6f winner, is a half-sister to 6 minor winners here and abroad. The second dam, Nur (by Diesis), a fair 2-y-o 5f and 6f winner, is a sister to the useful sprinter Ra'a and to the listed Roses Stakes winner Janib and a half-sister to the very useful Group 2 6f Richmond Stakes winner Muqtarib. (Kent Bloodstock).

"He's a big, strong colt. He's unlikely to be that early and I haven't done a lot with him, but he does everything easily and he does look like being a two-year-old. Physically he's a really nice specimen and he should be out in June".

108. HILL TRIBE ★★★★
b.f. Tiger Hill – Morning Queen (Konigsstuhl).
March 12. Tenth foal. 47,000Y. Tattersalls October 1. John Best. Half-sister to the fair 10f to 18f winner Love Brothers (by Lomitas) and to 3 other minor winners abroad by Grand Lodge, Octagonal and Poliglote. The dam won once at 3 yrs in Germany and is a half-sister to 5 winners including the German triple Group 1 winner and champion sire Monsun. The second dam, Mosella (by Surumu), a German listed winner, is a half-sister to 5 winners. (Findlay & Bloom).

"Surprisingly, considering she's by Tiger Hill and you would think she'd need time, she really pleasing me at home. She's much sharper than you'd expect and I think a lot of her. I don't have a lot of fillies but at the moment she'd be the best of them. She's working well with faster bred horses and if she stays the sort of trip you'd expect I think she could be very nice".

109. INTERNET EXPRESS (USA) ★★★
ch.c. Freefourinternet – All My Yesterdays (Wild Again).
January 17. Second foal. $6,000foal. Ocala. John Best. The dam, a minor 2-y-o winner in the USA, is a half-sister to 4 other minor winners. The second dam, Rivery (by Riverman), is an unraced ahlf-sister to the US winner Sabona.
"Since we bought him his half-brother has won three races in America. This colt is quite mature, both physically and mentally, not over-big and he looks like being one of the early ones. He's pretty sharp and he's handling his work well".

110. KINGSGATE CHOICE (IRE) ★★★
b.c. Choisir – Kenema (Petardia).
March 4. Fifth foal. 60,000Y. Doncaster St Leger. John Best. Half-brother to a winner in Greece by Monashee Mountain. The dam won 6 races from 5f to 6f at 3 to 4 yrs and is a half-sister to 4 winners. The second dam, Burkina (by African Sky), won once at 2 yrs and is a half-sister to 3 winners. (J Mayne).
"Another very nice-looking colt, mentally he's very good and he's a tall colt with plenty of scope".

111. KUILSRIVER (IRE) ★★
b.c. Cape Cross – Ripple Of Pride (Sadler's Wells).
February 19. Fourth foal. €140,000Y. Goffs Million. John Best. Brother to the useful Irish 3-y-o dual 7f winner Award Ceremony and half-brother to the unraced 2008 2-y-o Perfectly Chilled (by Dalakhani). The dam, a fairly useful Irish 12f winner, is a sister to the top-class Refuse To Bend, a winner of four Group 1 races from 7f (at 2 yrs) to 10f and half-sister to the Melbourne Cup winner Media Puzzle. The second dam, Market Slide (by Gulch), an Irish 6f (at 2 yrs) and 6.5f winner, is a half-sister to the US Grade 1 winner Twilight Agenda. (Findlay & Bloom).
"He's going to need time, but he's started to shape up, he's laid-back but will want middle-distances next year. He's doing everything well and I'm pleased with him but he's one for much later on".

112. ONE GOOD EMPEROR (IRE) ★★★★
b.c. Antonius Pius – Break Of Day (Favorite Trick).
April 20. Third foal. 29,000Y. Doncaster St Leger. Not sold. Half-brother to the fairly useful 6f winner Laddies Poker Two (by Choisir). The dam is an unraced half-sister to the useful 2-y-o 5f winner and Group 2 Gimcrack Stakes second Ma Yoram. The second dam, Quelle Affaire (by Riverman), is a placed sister to the Group 3 Concorde Stakes winner and Queen Anne Stakes second Rami and a half-sister to the smart French sprinters Crack Regiment and La Grand Epoque. (S Malcolm, M Winwright, P Tindall).
"I think he's very classy. He finds everything easy and he's impressive in his slower paces. I'm hopeful he'll be one of our nicer two-year-olds. He should be out before June to see if he's good enough for Royal Ascot because I'd like to send as many there as possible".

113. UNNAMED ★★★
ch.c. Avonbridge – Calligraphy (Kris).
April 4. Second foal. 35,000foal. Tattersalls December. Intergalactic Bloodstock. The dam, a fair 3-y-o 7f winner, is a half-sister to 2 winners. The second dam, Inkpot (by Green Dancer), was placed twice over 1m at 2 yrs and is a half-sister to 6 winners including the fairly useful 2-y-o 7f winner Spurned (herself dam of the Group winners Hidden Meadow, Passing Glance and Scorned) and the German champion 2-y-o and subsequent US Grade 2 placed Winter Quarters. (Hucking Horses 3).
"A big, strong, impressive horse. I think the sire is going to do well. We'll start him in the middle of the summer".

114. UNNAMED ★★
ch.c. Johannesburg – Catsuit (Sir Cat).
February 26. First foal. $130,000Y. Keeneland September. John Best. The dam, a minor stakes-placed winner of 3 races in the USA, is a half-sister to 5 winners including the stakes winner and Grade 2 placed Egg Head. The second dam, Redding Ridge (by Screen King), a US stakes winner, is a half-sister to 4 winners.

(Kent Bloodstock).
"I've looked at Johannesburg's quite a lot but they've always been a little bit small and light for me. This guy is a bit bigger than that but he's just a bit 'buzzy'. I think we've got to grips with him now and as long as he stays OK mentally I think he'll have a great chance. He certainly has plenty of ability, it's just a case of keeping the lid on him. I'll start him off somewhere nice and quiet".

115. UNNAMED ★★★★
b.c. Smart Strike – Dans La Ville (Winning).
March 22. Sixth foal. $180,000Y. Keeneland September. John Best. Half-brother to 4 minor winners abroad. The dam won at 3 yrs in Chile and is a sister to the Grade 1 Chilean Oaks winner Santona (herself dam of the US Grade 3 winner Grand Hombre) and a half-sister to a Grade 2 winner in Chile. The second dam, Syracuse (by Sharp-Eyed Quillo), a minor winner in Chile, is a half-sister to 5 winners. (Dave Gorton).
"Owned by Dave Gorton who did so well with Square Eddie last year, he's a bit bigger than he was and I haven't pressed any buttons yet. At this stage I'd say he was a better specimen than Square Eddie and that whatever he does he finds easy".

116. UNNAMED ★★★
b.c. Wild Event – Golden Crown (Defensive Play).
January 28. Third foal. $20,000foal. Ocala. John Best. The dam won four minor races at 4 yrs in the USA and is a half-sister to 5 winners including one US stakes winner. The second dam, Joannie Banannie (by Executive Order), won 11 races in the USA including four minor stakes events.
"He's a big, strong horse that I thought would take a lot of time, but suddenly he started to blossom for me and he shocked me how good he looked when he worked properly for the first time. He'll be out by the end of May all being well".

117. UNNAMED ★★★
b.c. Grand Slam – Heart Lake (Unbridled).
February 17. Third foal. $115,000Y. Keeneland September. John Best. The dam is an unraced half-sister to the Canadian stakes winner South Bay Cove and to the winner and Group 3 Sirenia Stakes third Art Market. The second dam, Fantasy Lake (by Salt Lake), a champion 2-y-o filly in Canada, is a half-sister to 7 winners. (Kent Bloodstock).
"Probably one of the nicest-looking horses I've got in the yard. A strong, stocky well-developed horse that won't be very early and he should want a bit of a trip".

118. UNNAMED ★★★★
b.c. Western Pride – Majestical (Garthorn).
January 30. Tenth foal. $10,000foal. Ocala. John Best. Half-brother to 6 winners including the minor US stakes-placed Meandmyloveman (by Way West). The dam is a placed half-sister to 6 winners including a minor stakes winner in the USA. The second dam, Silken Glitter (by Kentucky Gold), is an unraced half-sister to 2 stakes winners. (Ian Beach, John Fletcher).
"He's a very fast individual, very well-balanced and a big, strong colt. He'll take a bit of time but he could be anything but I won't do too much, too early with him".

120. UNNAMED ★★★
gr.c. Starcraft – True Love (Robellino).
April 1. Seventh foal. €48,000foal. Goffs. Hungerford Park Stud. Half-sister to the fair 2-y-o 5f winner, listed-placed and subsequent US 1m winner Hucking Hot (by Desert Prince). The dam is an unraced half-sister to 7 winners including the Group 2 6f Coventry Stakes winner Hellvelyn. The second dam, Cumbrian Melody (by Petong), a quite useful 2-y-o 5f and 6f winner, is a half-sister to 5 winners. (Dave Gorton).
"I sold the half-sister Hucking Hot to America and they thought a lot of her but she didn't fulfil her potential. This colt is a much nicer horse than she ever was but I need to be patient with him. He's laid-back, he moves really well and I'm very happy with him".

JIM BOLGER

121. ATASARI (IRE) ★★★
b.f. *Whipper – Azra (Danehill).*
February 18. Half-sister to the Irish 2-y-o 7.5f winner Basra, to the fair 2-y-o 5f winner Russian General (both by Soviet Star), the fair Irish 7f and 10f winner Asafa (by King's Best and the Irish 3-y-o dual 1m winner Spectacular (by Spectrum). The dam, a useful Irish dual 6f listed winner (at 2 yrs), was third in both the Group 1 Moyglare Stud Stakes and the Group 1 National Stakes and is a half-sister to 3 minor winners. The second dam, Easy To Please (by What A Guest), a useful Irish 2-y-o 1m winner, trained on to win the Queen Alexandra Stakes and is a half-sister to 4 winners including the Group 3 Concorde Stakes winner Pernilla. (Mrs J S Bolger).

122. CAILOCHT (USA) ★★★
b.f. *Elusive Quality – Sumora (Danehill).*
February 5. First foal. $190,000foal. Keeneland November. Tom Gentry. The dam, a 2-y-o listed 5f St Hugh's Stakes winner, is a sister to the useful Irish 7f winner Fleeting Shadow and a half-sister to 2 winners. The second dam, Rain Flower (by Indian Ridge), is an unraced three-parts sister to the top-class Epsom Derby, Irish Champion Stakes and Dewhurst Stakes winner Dr Devious and a half-sister to 5 winners including the Japanese listed winner Shinko King and the Group 3 winners Royal Court and Archway. (Mrs J S Bolger).

123 CARRAIGLAWN (IRE) ★★★
b.c. *Rock Of Gibraltar – Affianced (Erins Isle).*
May 25. Fifth foal. Half-brother to the 1m (at 2 yrs) and Group 1 Irish Derby, Group 2 Prix Niel and Group 2 Prix Noailles winner Soldier Of Fortune, to the smart 7f (at 2 yrs) and Group 3 10f Meld Stakes winner Heliostatic (both by Galileo) and the quite useful Irish dual 10f winner Ard Fheis (by Lil's Boy). The dam, a useful 7f listed (at 2 yrs) and 10f winner in Ireland, is a half-sister to the Group 1 1m Gran Criterium winner Sholokhov and to 4 other stakes horses. The second dam, La Meillure (by Lord Gayle), a listed winner and Group 3 placed in Ireland, is a half-sister to 8 winners. (Mrs J S Bolger).

124. CHABAL (IRE) ★★★
b.c. *Galileo – Vagary (Zafonic).*
February 10. First foal. The dam is an unraced half-sister to the quite useful 2-y-o 7f winner and listed-placed Global Genius (by Galileo). The second dam, Vadsagreya (by Linamix), a French 7f (at 2 yrs) and 1m winner, was listed-placed and is a half-sister to 12 winners including the dams of the French 1,000 Guineas winner Vahorimix and the Breeders Cup Mile winner Val Royal. (Lady O'Reilly).

125. CITY VIEW (IRE) ★★★
b.c. *Bachelor Duke – Aeraíocht (Tenby).*
March 12. Half-brother to the fairly useful 2-y-o triple 7f winner Bunsen Burner (by Lil's Boy) and to the quite useful Irish 2-y-o 7f winner Chennai (by Mozart). The dam, a dual Irish 2-y-o 7f winner, is a half-sister to a winner. The second dam, Direct Lady (by Fools Holme), a winner of three races at 3 yrs over 11f and 12f and also three races over hurdles, is a half-sister to the Group 1 Heinz "57" Phoenix Stakes winner Eva Luna and the Group 3 Futurity Stakes winner Cois Na Tine. (D H W Dobson).

126. CRE NA COILLE (IRE) ★★
b.c. *Rock Of Gibraltar – National Swagger (Giant's Causeway).*
March 14. The dam, a fairly useful Irish 7f winner, was fourth in the 2-y-o Group 2 7f Debutante Stakes and is a half-sister to one winner. The second dam, Eva Luna (by Double Schwartz), a very useful winner of 5 races at up to 6f at 2 yrs including the Group 1 Heinz 57 Phoenix Stakes and the Group 3 6f Railway Stakes, is a sister to the Group 3 1m Futurity Stakes winner Cois Na Tine. (Mrs J S Bolger).

127. DEA MHEIN (IRE) ★★★
b.f. *Indian Ridge – Luminaria (Danehill).*
January 3. First foal. The dam is an unraced half-sister to 6 winners including the very useful 2-y-o listed 6f winner and dual Group 1 placed Luminata and the very useful dual 6f winner (including at 2 yrs) and Group 3 placed Aretha (both by Indian Ridge). The second dam, Smaoineamh (by Tap On Wood), an Irish 6f

winner at 2 yrs and useful at up to 14f, is a half-sister to the champion sprinter Double Form and the Lupe Stakes winner Scimitarra. (Mrs J S Bolger).

128. FIRINNE (IRE) ★★★
br.c. *Rock Of Gibraltar – Zavaleta (Kahyasi).*
April 20. €30,000Y. Tattersalls Ireland. BBA (Ire). Closely related to the Group 3 12f Noblesse Stakes winner Danelissima, to the Irish 2-y-o 7f winner and listed placed Daneleta (both by Danehill) and half-brother to the fairly useful Irish 2-y-o 1m winner and listed placed Simonetta (by Lil's Boy), the Irish 3-y-o 6.5f winner and listed-placed Benicio (by Spectrum) and a winner in Japan by Caerleon. The dam a useful dual listed 7f winner, is a half-sister to numerous winners including the 2-y-o Group 1 1m Gran Criterium winner Sholokov and the 2-y-o listed 7f winner Affianced (herself dam of the Irish Derby winner Soldier Of Fortune). The second dam, La Meilleure (by Lord Gayle), a listed winner in Ireland, was Group 3 placed. (Mrs J S Bolger).

129. FREE JUDGEMENT (USA) ★★★
b.br.c. *Vindication – South Bay Cove (Fusaichi Pegasus).*
February 25. First foal. €50,000Y. Goffs Million. Tracy Collins. The dam won 2 listed events in Canada at 2 yrs and is a half-sister to the winner and Group 3 placed Art Market. The second dam, Fantasy Lake (by Salt Lake), won 3 listed races and was a champion 2-y-o filly in Canada and is a half-sister to 7 winners. (Mrs June Judd).

130. GILE NA GREINE (IRE) ★★★★
b.f. *Galileo – Scribonia (Danehill).*
March 31. Second foal. Sister to the very useful 2008 2-y-o dual Group 3 6f winner Cuis Ghaire. The dam is an unraced half-sister to 6 winners including the very useful 2-y-o listed 6f winner and dual Group 1 placed Luminata and the very useful dual 6f winner (including at 2 yrs) and Group 3 placed Aretha. The second dam, Smaoineamh (by Tap On Wood), an Irish 6f winner at 2 yrs and useful at up to 14f, is a half-sister to the champion sprinter Double Form and the Lupe Stakes winner Scimitarra. (Mrs J S Bolger).

131. GIPSY COUNTESS (IRE) ★★★
b.f. *Sadler's Wells – Cozzene's Angel (Cozzene).*
May 16. Eighth foal. $600,000Y. Keeneland September. Tom Gentry. Half-sister to 3 winners including the US Grade 1 Champagne Stakes and Grade 1 Hollywood Futurity winner Toccet (by Awesome Again). The dam, a US stakes-placed winner of 3 races, is a half-sister to 2 stakes winners. The second dam, Charming Pan (by Trepan), won at 2 and 3 in France and is a half-sister to 2 stakes winners. (Mrs June Judd).

132. KITTY KIERNAN ★★★
b.f. *Pivotal – Alstemeria (Danehill).*
February 3. Second foal. 400,000Y. Tattersalls October 1. BBA (Ire). Half-sister to the unraced 2008 2-y-o Fernando Torres (by Giant's Causeway). The dam, a useful Irish 6f winner and fourth in the Group 1 Irish 1,000 Guineas, is a sister to the Group 1 1m Gran Criterium winner Spartacus and to the Group 2 10f Gallinule Stakes and Hong Kong Derby winner Johan Cruyff. The second dam, Teslemi (by Ogygian), a fair 3-y-o 1m winner, is a half-sister to 5 minor winners. (Ennistown Stud).

133. LUAN CINCISE (IRE) ★★
br.c. *Rock of Gibraltar – April Evening (Spectrum).*
March 31. The dam is an unraced sister to the Irish 3-y-o 6.5f winner and Group 3 Anglesey Stakes third Benicio and a half-sister to the very useful Group 3 12f Noblesse Stakes winner Danelissima. The second dam, Zavaleta (by Kahyasi), won the listed 7f Athasi Stakes and the listed 1m Derrinstown Stud 1,000 Guineas Trial and is a half-sister to 7 winners including the Group 1 Gran Criterium winner Sholokhov. (Mrs J S Bolger).

134. MARFACH (USA) ★★★
b.c. *Leroidesanimaux – Rhondaling (Welsh Pageant).*
February 17. Tenth foal. €105,000Y. Goffs Million. Jim Bolger. Half-brother to the US

champion older mare and triple Grade 1 winner Gourmet Girl (by Cee's Tizzy), to the US dual winner and Grade 1 placed Northern Mischief (by Yankee Victor) and 2 minor winners in the USA by Cee's Tizzy and Memo. The dam won twice at 2 yrs and was third in the Group 3 C L Weld Park Stakes and is a half-sister to 3 minor winners. The second dam, Touch Of Class (by Luthier), a minor winner at 4 yrs, is a half-sister to 3 winners including Kebir (Group 3 Prix Edmond Blanc). (Ennistown Stud).

135. REITERATION (USA) ★★★★
b.br.c. Vindication – For Dixie (Dixieland Band).
March 8. Seventh foal. $340,000Y. Keeneland September. Tom Gentry. Half-brother to 5 winners including the US Grade 1 Acorn Stakes winner Cotton Blossom (by Broken Vow) and the US Grade 3 winner Vicarage (by Vicar). The dam, a stakes winner of 3 races at 2 and 3 yrs in the USA, is out of the unraced Foain (by Forli). (Mrs J S Bolger).

136. ROCK MEDLEY (IRE) ★★★
ch.c. Rock Of Gibraltar – La Meillure (Lord Gayle).
April 4. Half-brother to numerous winners including the 2-y-o Group 1 1m Gran Criterium winner Sholokov (by Sadler's Wells), the fairly useful Irish 2-y-o dual 5f winner and dual Group 3 placed Raghida, the useful 6f to 7f winner and Group 3 placed Nordic Fox (both by Nordico), the very useful 6f (at 2 yrs) and listed 10f winner Napper Tandy (by Spectum), the useful dual listed 7f winner Zavaleta (by Kahyasi) and the 2-y-o listed 7f winner Affianced (by Erin's Isle). The dam was a quite useful listed 1m winner in Ireland at 3 yrs. (Mrs J S Bolger).

137. ROISE (IRE) ★★★
br.f. Rock Of Gibraltar – Ceirseach (Don't Forget Me).
May 10. Fifth foal. Half-brother to the fairly useful 2-y-o 5f winner and Group 3 7f Killavullan Stakes third Clash Of The Ash (by King Of Kings), to the 2-y-o 7f winner New Currency (by Touch Gold) and the Irish 7.5f (at 2 yrs) and 9.6f winner Laoch Na Mara (by Sea Hero) – both quite useful. The dam, a useful 7f (at 2 yrs) and 9.6f winner, is a half-sister to 5 winners including the smart listed 7f Tyros Stakes (at 2 yrs) and Group 2 10f Gallinule Stakes winner Project Manager. The second dam, Beparoejojo (by Lord Gayle), a useful Irish middle-distance performer, was also a leading juvenile hurdler. (Mrs J Bolger).

138. STAR POWER (IRE) ★★★
b.c. Galileo – Billet (Danehill).
April 9. First foal. €195,000Y. Goffs Million. Jim Bolger. The dam, placed second once over 6f at 2 yrs, is a half-sister to 2 winners. The second dam, Tathkara (by Alydar), is an unraced sister to the US Grade 1 winner Talinum and a half-sister to 7 winners. (Mrs J S Bolger).

139. STYLE QUEEN (IRE) ★★★
b.f. Galileo – Carson Dancer (Carson City).
May 4. Fifth foal. €70,000Y. Goffs Million. Jim Bolger. Half-sister to the fair 2008 2-y-o 7f and 1m winner Digger Derek (by Key Of Luck), to the Irish 2-y-o dual 7f winner Mistress Bailey (by Mister Baileys) and the French 2-y-o 6.5f winner Irish Heart (by Efisio). The dam is an unplaced half-sister to 8 winners including the Japan Cup winner Tap Dance City. The second dam, All Dance (by Northern Dancer), a minor French 3-y-o winner, is a half-sister to the Kentucky Derby winner Winning Colors. (Mrs J S Bolger).

140. SUPER HOOFER (IRE) ★★
b.f. Shamardal – Kelly Nicole (Rainbow Quest).
March 10. First foal. €145,000Y. Goffs Million. J Bolger. The dam, a fair 1m to 10f winner of 3 races, is a half-sister to 3 winners including the Irish dual 9f and subsequent US stakes winner Cold Cold Woman. The second dam, Banquise (by Last Tycoon), won over 2m in France and is a half-sister to 8 winners including the French dual Group 2 winner Modhish and the French Group 2 12.5f Prix de Royallieu winner and Irish Oaks second Russian Snows. (Mrs J S Bolger).

141. TIZ THE WHIZ (USA) ★★★
b.f. Tiznow – Troubling (Storm Cat).
April 27. $310,000Y. Keeneland September.

Tom Gentry. Half-sister to 2 winners including one in Japan by Gone West and to the unraced dam of the US stakes winner Tiz Now Tiz Then (by Tiznow). The dam is an unraced half-sister to 4 minor winners. The second dam, Dispute (by Danzig), won four Grade 1 events in the USA and is a half-sister to the US Grade 1 winners Adjudicating and Time For A Change. (Mrs June Judd).

142. VITA VENTURI (IRE) ★★★
ch.c. Galileo – Sateen (Barathea).
March 20. Third foal. €500,000Y. Goffs Million. Jim Bolger. Half-brother to the minor French 1m winner Sendora (by Kendor). The dam, a fairly useful 6f winner, is a half-sister to 9 winners including the listed 12f winner Puce (herself dam of the Group 2 Lancashire Oaks winner Pongee) and the dam of the Oaks, Irish Oaks and Yorkshire Oaks winner Alexandrova. The second dam, Souk (by Ahonoora), a fairly useful 7f winner, was listed placed over 1m and is a half-sister to 3 winners. (Mrs J S Bolger).

143. YES OH YES (USA) ★★★
b.f. Gone West – Diamonds For Lil (Summer Squall).
May 10. Third foal. $250,000Y. Keeneland September. BBA (Ire). Half-sister to the useful 2008 Irish 2-y-o 7.5f winner and Group 1 Moyglare Stud Stakes fourth Aaroness (by Distorted Humor). The dam, a minor US 2-y-o winner, is a half-sister to 5 winners including the US listed stakes winner Lovat's Lady. The second dam, Lady Lady (by Little Current), is an unraced half-sister to 5 stakes winners including the US Grade 1 winners Al Mamoon and La Gueriere. (Mrs J S Bolger).

MARCO BOTTI
144. AMBROGINA ★★★
b.f. Osorio – Oh Bej Oh Bej (Distinctly North).
February 28. Fourth foal. 22,000Y. Tattersalls October 3. A Brambilla. Half-sister to 2 winners in Italy by Cadeaux Genereux and Dr Fong. The dam won 8 races in Italy over 5f and 6f including at Group 3 event and is a half-sister to 7 winners including the Group 2 Italian 2,000 Guineas winner Alabama Jacks. The second dam, My Jemima (by Captain James), is a placed half-sister to 3 minor winners.
"A nice filly, she goes well and I think she definitely has the speed to cope with five furlongs, especially as the dam was quite fast. She shows quite a lot of speed and she has a very good character". TRAINER'S BARGAIN BUY

145. FINALMENT ★★★
ch.f. Selkirk – Selebela (Grand Lodge).
February 1. The dam, a useful 12f winner of 3 races and listed-placed, is a half-sister to a one winner. The second dam, Risarshana (by Darshaan), is an unplaced half-sister to one winner. (Scuteria Rencati Srl).
"A nice, good-looking filly, she goes well although we haven't done a lot with her yet. I expect she'll be one for seven furlongs or a mile, I'm quite positive about her and she definitely has ability".

146. FONTERUTOLI (IRE) ★★★
gr.c. Verglas – Goldendale (Ali-Royal).
April 22. Third foal. €45,000Y. Half-brother to the minor Italian winner Sogna (by Distant View). The dam was placed in the USA and is a half-sister to 5 winners including the dual US Grade 2 winner Sweet Ludy and Late Parade, a winner of 23 races in France and Italy including the Group 3 Gran Premio Citta di Napoli (3 times). The second dam, Skisette (by Malinowski), was placed in France and is a half-sister to 5 minor winners here and abroad. (Scuderia Rencati Srl).
"A small but very powerful colt, he goes well, he should be a sharp two-year-old and he's working nicely. We might start him off in the middle of May".

147. GRACIOUS MELANGE ★★
b.f. Medicean – Goodness Gracious (Green Desert).
February 20. Third foal. 58,000Y. Doncaster St Leger. Racing Factory. The dam, a fairly useful 7f winner at 2 yrs, is a half-sister to the listed winners Abbeyside and Flat Spin. The second dam, Trois Graces (by Alysheba), won once at

3 yrs in France and is a half-sister to 5 winners including Rami (Group 3 Concorde Stakes), Crack Regiment (Group 3 Prix Eclipse) and La Grand Epoque (second in the Group 1 Prix de l'Abbaye). The second dam, Ancient Regime (by Olden Times), won the Group 1 Prix Morny and is a sister to the Prix Maurice de Gheest winner Cricket Ball. (Newsells Park Stud Ltd).
"A nice filly from a good family, she looks racey but she won't be an early two-year-old. I could see her starting off at seven furlongs in the second half of the season".

148. ISOTIA ★★
b.f. Tiger Hill – Volvoreta (Suave Dancer).
March 27. Fourth foal. 35,000Y. Tattersalls October 2. A Brambilla. The dam won 4 races including the Group 1 Prix Vermeille, the Group 3 Prix des Reservoirs and the Group 3 Prix Penelope, was placed in the Prix de l'Arc de Triomphe and the French Oaks and is a half-sister to 4 winners including the Group 2 Prix Greffuhle second Egeo. The second dam, Robertiya (by Don Roberto), was a champion filly in Spain at 2 and 3 yrs and a winner of 10 races.
"A nice big, leggy filly, she's backward and will need time. She moves well but is one for the back end of the season and next year".

149. KAVAK ★★★★
ch.c. Dubawi – Kelang (Kris).
April 12. Eighth foal. 36,000Y. Tattersalls October 1. Not sold. Half-brother to the Italian listed winner Bukat Timah (by Inchinor), to the Italian listed-placed winners Daylang (by Daylami) and Kayak (by Singspiel) and 2 minor winners in Italy by Dansili and Dr Fong. The second dam, Ebbing Tide (by His Majesty), is an unplaced half-sister to 5 winners including the dam of Oh So Sharp. (Grundy Bloodstock Ltd).
"A very strong, compact horse and a good mover, I like him a lot and he'll make a two-year-old in mid-summer over seven furlongs. A lovely horse".

150. MASCAGNI (IRE) ★★★
b.c. Galileo – Takrice (Cadeaux Genereux).
May 1. Second foal. €105,000foal. Goffs. Rathbarry Stud. Half-brother to the fair 2008 2-y-o 6f winner Dynamo Dane (by Danehill Dancer). The dam, an Irish 2-y-o 7f winner, was third in the Group 3 Killavullen Stakes half-sister to 2 winners. The second dam, Hasanat (by Night Shift), won over 7f (at 2 yrs) and 9f in Ireland and was Group 3 placed. (Tenuta Dorna Di Montaltuzzo SRL).
"A lovely type of horse with a good temperament, he's another one who will start at seven furlongs and he'll be a ten furlong horse next year. A colt with a nice attitude and I like him a lot".

151. MAZAMMORRA (USA) ★★★
b.br.f. Orientate – Mumbo Jumbo (Kingmambo).
March 19. Fourth foal. $120,000Y. Keeneland September. Blandford Bloodstock. Half-sister to the US winner of 5 races and Grade 3 placed Crossword. The dam, a US stakes winner of 6 races, is a half-sister to 7 winners. The second dam, Dixie Accent (by Dixieland Band), was a US stakes winner of 5 races.
"A nice, straightforward filly, she definitely has ability and is quite smart but will need time. She looks like she'll need a trip and is one for the back-end of the season".

152. NUTELA ★★
br.f. Kheleyf – Uptown (Be My Guest).
April 24. First foal. €10,000Y. Tattersalls Ireland. M Botti. The dam, a modest Irish 10f placed maiden, is a half-sister to one winner. The second dam, Gild (by Caerleon), a minor Irish 12f winner at 3 yrs, is a sister to the smart Group 3 2m Jockey Club Cup winner Capal Garmon and a half-sister to 6 winners including the Group 3 Prix de Royaumont third Elite Guest.
"She's still growing so I'm not going to rush her and she's one for the second half of the season. She has ability though and is very straight-forward with a good temperament".

153. RAINBOW SIX ★★★
b.c. Tiger Hill – Birthday Suit (Daylami).
March 13. Second foal. 26,000Y. Tattersalls October 2. Marco Botti. Half-brother to the fair 2008 1m and 10f placed Excelsior Academy (by Montjeu). The dam, a useful 2-y-o dual 5f winner and third in the Group 2 Cherry Hinton Stakes, is a half-sister to 10 winners including the Irish 1,000 Guineas winner Classic Park and the US Grade 2 winner Rumpipumpy. The second dam, Wanton (by Kris), a useful 2-y-o 5f winner and third in the Group 2 Flying Childers Stakes, is a half-sister to 8 winners including the listed 5f winner and good broodmare Easy Option. (Op-Center).
"A lovely horse and good-looking, he goes well but I don't think he'll be that sharp and he's probably a six furlong horse in mid-summer. We've just started to do a bit more with him".

154. TIGRANES THE GREAT (IRE) ★★
b.c. Galileo – Aquila Oculus (Eagle Eyed).
April 30. Second foal. €60,000foal. Goffs. Emerald Bloodstock. The dam, a useful Irish 8.5f to 2m winner of 7 races, is a half-sister to 3 minor winners. The second dam, Out In The Sun (by It's Freezing), a 9f and hurdles winner, is a half-sister to 7 winners. (A Pettinari).
"When he first arrived I didn't really like him because he was backward and narrow, but he's definitely filled out, he's getting stronger and he's a very good mover. So he'll be a nice colt for the latter part of the season and next year".

155. TIRADITO (USA) ★★★
b.br.c. Tale Of The Cat – Saratoga Sugar (Gone West).
April 30. Third foal. $50,000Y. Keeneland September. Blandford Bloodstock. The dam is a placed sister to the US Grade 1 9f winner Link River. The second dam, Connecting Link (by Linkage), was placed once in the USA and is a half-sister to the US stakes winner Spectacular Bev (herself dam of a stakes winner) and the dam of the Queens Vase winner Stelvio. (El Caforce).
"Quite a nice colt and he should be one of our sharpest two-year-olds. We think a lot of him, he goes well and he's a stocky, compact colt. He's already done a few bits of work, he's going well and mentally he's quite a sharp two-year-old".

156. TOMODACHI (IRE) ★★★
b.f. Arakan – Ivory Bride (Domynsky).
February 21. Tenth foal. 32,000Y. Doncaster St Leger. McKeever St Lawrence. Half-sister to the very smart Ayr Gold Cup winner Funfair Wane (by Unfuwain), to the fairly useful 5f (at 2 yrs) to 9f winner Cabcharge Striker (by Rambo Dancer), the quite useful 5f and 6f winner Parkside Pursuit (by Pursuit Of Love), the quite useful 1m winner Bride's Answer (by Anshan), the fair 6f to 1m winner Pure Imagination (by Royal Academy) and the fair triple 6f winner Bold Argument (by Shinko Forest). The dam, winner of the listed 6f Rose Bowl Stakes, is a half-sister to numerous winners including the listed Ballymacoll Stud Stakes winner Putuna. The second dam, Ivoronica (by Targowice), was a fairly useful 2-y-o 5f winner. (Frontier Racing Club).
"She's a very good mover, I like her and she has some speed. She'll either start at six or seven furlongs and she's going well. Quite strong, she's medium-sized and isn't going to be huge but has enough scope".

157. VANILLA LOAN (IRE) ★★★
b.f. Invincible Spirit – Alexander Anapolis (Spectrum).
May 2. Third foal. 30,000Y. Tattersalls October 2. Not sold. Half-sister to the quite useful 2008 2-y-o dual 5f winner Cut The Cackle and to the fairly useful dual 6f winner Film Maker (both by Danetime). The dam, a quite useful 12f winner, is a full or half-sister to 3 winners. The second dam, Pirouette (by Sadler's Wells), winner of the listed 7f Athasi Stakes in Ireland and Group 3 placed, is a half-sister to 8 winners including the Irish listed 6f Greenlands Stakes winner and very useful sire Ballad Rock.
"A beautiful filly, she's quite strong and laid-back and looks like a colt actually. I like her, she goes well and has a good temperament, so I'm quite positive about her. I think she'll need seven

furlongs because she's quite tall and doesn't seem to have the speed for five".

158. UNNAMED ★★
b.f. Dansili – Aunt Flo (Royal Academy).
March 11. Fourth foal. 87,000Y. Tattersalls October 1. RBS Ltd. Half-sister to the minor French winner of 2 races at 3 and 4 yrs Sister Flo (by Mark Of Esteem). The dam, a useful 5f (at 2 yrs) to 7f winner of 3 races, was listed-placed and is a half-sister to 3 winners including the Australian Grade 3 winner Chester County. The second dam, Quinsigimond (by Formidable), a fair 6f and 7f winner of 4 races, is a half-sister to 2 winners.
"Still a bit weak, she's backward and we might struggle to get her out before the end of the season. She's very elegant but she will need time".

159. UNNAMED ★★★
br.f. Rakti – Cidaris (Persian Bold).
April 30. Seventh foal. 70,000Y. Tattersalls October 2. Not sold. Half-brother to the 5f Windsor Castle Stakes winner and Group 2 6f Mill Reef Stakes second Irony and to the fair Irish 2-y-o 6.5f winner District Six (both by Mujadil). The dam ran once unplaced and is a half-sister to 3 winners including the dam of the South African Grade 1 winner Rabiya. The second dam, Secret Sunday (by Secreto), a minor Irish 12f winner, is a sister to the 2,000 Guineas winner Mystiko and a half-sister to 6 winners.
"I like her, she's powerful, has a good temperament and goes well. One that should start off in mid-summer and we'll take it from there".

160. UNNAMED ★★
b.c. Oratorio – Kite Mark (Mark Of Esteem).
May 7. Fifth foal. 35,000Y. Tattersalls December. Not sold. Half-brother to the smart 2008 2-y-o Group 3 1m winner Kite Wood (by Galileo), to the quite useful 6f (at 2 yrs) and 10f winner Legislation (by Oasis Dream) and the quite useful 10f and 14.7f winner Daylami Dreams (by Daylami). The dam ran once unplaced and is a half-sister to 5 winners including the very smart Group 2 Park Hill Stakes and Group 2 Prix de Royallieu winner Madame Dubois (dam of the Group 1 winners Indian Haven and Count Dubois) and the 2-y-o 1m winner Sun and Shade (dam of the Richmond Stakes winner Daggers Drawn). The second dam, Shadywood (by Habitat), a useful 10f winner, was second in the Lancashire Oaks and is a half-sister to 8 winners.
"He's a fine, leggy horse but still a bit immature. One for seven furlongs in the second half of the season".

161. UNNAMED ★★
b.c. Cape Cross – Rasana (Royal Academy).
March 16. Half-brother to the quite useful 2009 3-y-o 10f winner Everynight (by Rock Of Gibraltar) and to the quite useful 5f and 6f winner of 4 races Rasaman (by Namid). The dam is an unplaced half-sister to the top-class colt Rakti, a winner of six Group events including the Champion Stakes, the Eclipse Stakes and the Queen Elizabeth II Stakes. The second dam, Ragera (by Rainbow Quest), was placed in Italy and is a half-sister to 8 winners.
"A nice, strong horse with a very good temperament, I can see him following the same pattern as his year older half-brother Everynight by having just the one run at the back-end".

162. UNNAMED ★★★
gr.c. Cape Cross – Success Story (Sharrood).
March 30. Tenth foal. 120,000Y. Tattersalls October 1. R MacNabb. Half-brother to Fisadara (by Nayef), unplaced in one start at 2 yrs in 2000, to the useful 10f and 12f listed winner Film Script (by Unfuwain), the fairly useful 6f and 7f and subsequent US stakes winner National Park (by Common Grounds), the fair 7f winner Barney McGrew (by Mark Of Esteem) and the fair 8.5f and 10f winner Champagne (by Efisio). The dam, a modest 10f winner, is a half-sister to 7 winners including the Group 2 13.5f Prix de Pomone winner Interlude. The second dam, Starlet, a smart 10f and 12f performer, won a Group 2 event in Germany

and is a half-sister to 8 winners including the US Grade 1 winner Unknown Quantity.
"A big, smart horse, he's very scopey and I like him a lot. He'll take his time and will be a better three-year-old, but he's a very good mover and has a good attitude".

CLIVE BRITTAIN
163. ALICE SARA (USA) ★★★
b.f. Kingmambo – Marisa (Swain).
February 9. Second foal. $100,000Y. Keeneland September. Rabbah Bloodstock. The dam is an unraced half-sister to 7 winners including the 1,000 Guineas, Coronation Stakes, Nassau Stakes and Lockinge Stakes winner Russian Rhythm (by Kingmambo) and the 2-y-o Group 2 1m Royal Lodge Stakes winner Perfectperformance. The second dam, Balistroika (by Nijinsky), is an unraced half-sister to numerous winners including Park Appeal (winner of the Cheveley Park Stakes and the Moyglare Stud Stakes and the dam of Cape Cross), Alydaress (Irish Oaks) and Desirable (winner of the Cheveley Park Stakes and the dam of Shadayid). (Saeed Manana).

164. SUPERSTITIOUS (USA) ★★★
b.f. Kingmambo – Zuri (Danzig).
April 12. Eighteenth foal. $150,000Y. Keeneland September. Rabbah Bloodstock. Sister to the US dual Grade 1 winner Voodoo Dancer and half-sister to 9 winners including the US stakes-placed Waycross (by Conquistador Cielo) and Gravette (by Demons Begone). The dam was placed at 3 yrs and is a half-sister to 6 winners. The second dam, Visibly Different (by Sir Ivor), won at 3 yrs in the USA. (Saeed Manana).

165. ZERO SEVEN ★★★
b.c. Halling – Tempting Fate (Persian Bold).
February 28. Half-brother to the quite useful Irish 6f winner Enigma Code (by Elusive Quality). The dam, a very smart dual 6f (at 2 yrs) and 7f listed winner, was third in the Group 1 1m Coronation Stakes and is a half-sister to the useful 1m (at 2 yrs) and Italian dual 10f listed winner Clapham Common and the fairly useful 5f winner of 5 races and listed-placed Cindora.

The second dam, West Of Eden (by Crofter), is an unraced half-sister to 9 winners, two of them listed-placed including the dam of the New Zealand Grade 1 winner Coberger. (Mr M Al Shafar).

166. UNNAMED ★★★
b.f. Oasis Dream – All For Laura (Cadeaux Genereux).
March 12. First foal. 70,000Y. Tattersalls October 2. Rabbah Bloodstock. The dam, a fairly useful 2-y-o 5f winner, was listed-placed and is a full or half-sister to 2 winners. The second dam, Lighthouse (by Warning), a fairly useful 3-y-o 8.3f winner, is a half-sister to 4 winners including the Group 1 Middle Park Stakes, Group 3 July Stakes and Group 3 Richmond Stakes winner First Trump. (Saeed Manana).

167. UNNAMED ★★★
b.f. Acclamation – Amistad (Winged Love).
February 2. Third foal. 65,000Y. Tattersalls October 2. Rabbah Bloodstock. The dam won once at 2 yrs in Germany and is a half-sister to 7 winners including the German Derby third Acamani. The second dam, Adjani (by Surumu), was placed in Germany and is a half-sister to 6 winners. (Saeed Manana).

168. UNNAMED ★★★
b.f. Dubawi – Avila (Ajdal).
March 26. Half-sister to the very smart Group 1 1m Racing Post Trophy and Group 2 10.4f Dante Stakes winner Dilshaan, to the fair all-weather staying winner of 6 races Aveiro (both by Darshaan), the smart 7f (at 2 yrs) and listed 10f winner and Group 1 1m Prix Marcel Boussac second Darrfonah (by Singspiel), the quite useful 12f winner Calakanga (by Dalakhani), the modest 10.5f winner Mama-San (by Doyoun) and a winner in Austria by Shirley Heights. The dam, a fair 7f placed maiden, is a half-sister to the smart middle-distance colts Alleging, Monastery and Nomrood. The second dam, Sweet Habit (by Habitat), is an unraced half-sister to the Group 2 Pretty Polly Stakes winner Fleur Royale. (Saeed Manana).

169. UNNAMED ★★★
ch.f. Pastoral Pursuits – Bint Al Hammour (Grand Lodge).
March 5. First foal. 40,000Y. Tattersalls October 2. Rabbah Bloodstock. The dam is an unplaced half-sister to 11 winners including the Group 3 Meld Stakes winner Muakaad. The second dam, Forest Lair (by Habitat), won once at 2 yrs and is a half-sister to the triple Group 3 winner Pampabird. (Saeed Manana).

170. UNNAMED ★★★
b.f. Kingmambo – Cloud Castle (In The Wings).
March 20. Closely related to the modest 9.7f winner Samdaniya (by Machiavellian) and half-sister to the smart Group 3 10f Winter Hill Stakes winner Queen's Best (by King's Best) and the French 12f winner and Group 3 Prix de Royaumont third Reverie Solitaire (by Nashwan). The dam was a very smart winner of the Group 3 Nell Gwyn Stakes and was placed in the Group 1 Yorkshire Oaks and the Group 1 Prix Vermeille. She is a half-sister to 5 winners including the high-class middle-distance horses and multiple Group 1 winners Warrsan and Luso. The second dam, Lucayan Princess (by High Line), a very useful winner of the listed 6f Sweet Solera Stakes at 2 yrs, was third in the 12.3f Cheshire Oaks and is a half-sister to 7 winners. (Saeed Manana).

171. UNNAMED ★★
b.c. Bahri – Easy Sunshine (Sadler's Wells).
April 21. Fourth foal. 32,000Y. Rabbah Bloodstock. The dam, an Irish 3-y-o 7f winner and third in the 2-y-o Group 3 7f C L Weld Park Stakes, is a sister to the Irish 6f (at 2 yrs) and 10f winner and listed-placed Unique Pose and a half-sister to 3 winners. The second dam, Desert Ease (by Green Desert), an Irish 2-y-o listed 6f winner, is a half-sister to 5 winners including the Group 3 Tetrarch Stakes and Group 3 7f Concorde Stakes winner Two-Twenty-Two. (Saeed Manana).

172. UNNAMED ★★★
b.f. Nayef – Emerald Fire (Pivotal).
February 17. Second foal. 65,000Y. Tattersalls October 2. Rabbah Bloodstock. The dam, a fair dual 6f winner (including at 2 yrs), is a half-sister to 5 winners. The second dam, Four-Legged-Friend (by Aragon), a useful 2-y-o listed 5f winner, is a half-sister to 7 winners including the dual US Grade 3 winner Superstrike and the dam of the Group 1 winning sprinters Goodricke and Pastoral Pursuits. (Saeed Manana).

173. UNNAMED ★★
ch.f. Gulch – Empress Anna (Imperial Ballet).
March 6. First foal. 34,000Y. Tattersalls October 2. Rabbah Bloodstock. The dam, a minor winner at 3 yrs in the USA, is a half-sister to 5 winners including the Irish listed winner and Group 3 placed Clean Cut. The second dam, Cutlers Corner (by Formidable), a very useful winner of the 5f Rous Stakes, was fourth in the Group 3 King George Stakes and is a half-sister to 6 winners. (Saeed Manana).

174. UNNAMED ★★★
b.f. King's Best – Injaaz (Sheikh Albadou).
February 21. Second foal. 28,000Y. Tattersalls October 2. Rabbah Bloodstock. Half-sister to the fair 2-y-o 6f winner, from 2 starts, Classic Fortune (by Royal Applause). The dam, a quite useful 6f winner, is a sister to the fairly useful 6f winner of 3 races Corndavon (herself dam of the smart 2-y-o Nevisian Lad). The second dam, Ferber's Follies (by Saratoga Six), a winning 2-y-o sprinter, was third in the Grade 2 6f Adirondack Stakes and is a half-sister to 11 winners including the US 2-y-o Grade 2 6f winner Blue Jean Baby. (Saeed Manana).

175. UNNAMED ★★★
b.f. Singspiel – Lady Zonda (Lion Cavern).
April 20. Fourth foal. Half-sister to the Irish 2-y-o 6f winner and listed 6f second (from 2 starts) May Meeting (by Diktat). The dam, a fairly useful 7f and 1m winner, is a half-sister to 6 winners. The second dam, Zonda (by Fabulous Dancer), was a useful 5f to 8.5f winner. (M Al Nabouda).

176. UNNAMED ★★★
b.br.f. Dixie Union – Low Tolerance (Proud Truth).
February 21. Eighth foal. Tattersalls October 1. Rabbah Bloodstock. Closely related to the US listed stakes winner and Grade 3 placed Saranac Jazz (by Dixieland Band) and half-sister to the US winner and Grade 3 placed Cat And The Hat (by Storm Cat) and 3 minor winners in the USA by Came Home, Deputy Minister and Storm Cat. The dam won 6 races including two Grade 3 stakes in the USA and is a half-sister to 6 winners. The second dam, Glorious Spring (by Hail To Reason), won 3 minor races in the USA and is a sister to Roberto. (Saeed Manana).

177. UNNAMED ★★★
b.f. Singspiel – Lunda (Soviet Star).
February 27 Tenth foal. Sister to the modest 7f and 1m winner Zamhrear and half-sister to the useful 10f winner and Group 3 placed Bazergan, to the fair 7f winner Jakarta (both by Machiavellian), the very useful 1m to 10f winner and Italian Derby third Lundy's Lane, the very smart 1m (at 2 yrs) and dual Group 3 middle-distance winner Blue Monday (both by Darshaan) and the 1m (all-weather) and 10f winner Dancing Tsar (by Salse). The dam ran three times unplaced at 3 yrs and is a half-sister to 6 winners including the high-class middle-distance horses Luso (winner of the Aral-Pokal, the Italian Derby and the Hong Kong International Vase) and Warrsan (Coronation Cup and Grosser Preis von Baden). The second dam, Lucayan Princess (by High Line), won the listed 6f Sweet Solera Stakes at 2 yrs, was third in the 12.3f Cheshire Oaks and is a half-sister to 7 winners. (Saeed Manana).

178. UNNAMED ★★★
ch.c. Exceed And Excel – Mantesera (In The Wings).
February 13. Second foal. 20,000Y. Tattersalls October 2. The dam is an unraced sister to the very smart Group 3 Nell Gwyn Stakes winner and Group 1 Yorkshire Oaks and Group 1 Prix Vermeille placed Cloud Castle and a half-sister to 5 winners including the high-class middle-distance horses and multiple Group 1 winners Warrsan and Luso and the Group 2 winner Needle Gun. The second dam, Lucayan Princess (by High Line), a very useful winner of the listed 6f Sweet Solera Stakes at 2 yrs, was third in the 12.3f Cheshire Oaks and is a half-sister to 7 winners. (Saeed Manana).

179. UNNAMED ★★
b.f. Dubawi – Mazuna (Cape Cross).
February 16. First foal. 15,000Y. Tattersalls October. Troy Steve. The dam, winner of the Group 3 12f Princess Royal Stakes, is a half-sister to the numerous minor winners. The second dam, Keswa (by King's Lake), a fairly useful 1m (at 2 yrs) and 12f winner, is a half-sister to 5 winners including the listed Zetland Stakes winner Matahif. (Saeed Manana).

180. UNNAMED ★★★
b.f. Bertolini – Mellow Jazz (Lycius).
January 24. Half-sister to the fairy useful 6f winner and listed placed Improvise (by Lend A Hand). The dam, a quite useful 6f (at 2 yrs) and 1m all-weather winner, is a half-sister to the Italian listed winner Mister Cavern. The second dam, Slow Jazz (by Chief's Crown), a French listed 1m winner, is a three-parts sister to the smart Group 1 6f Middle Park Stakes and Group 2 7f Challenge Stakes winner Zieten and to the Group 1 6f Cheveley Park Stakes and Group 3 5f Queen Mary Stakes winner Blue Duster. (S Ali).

181. UNNAMED ★★
b.br.f. Dubawi – Menhoubah (Dixieland Band).
April 14. Second foal. Half-sister to the modest 2009 9f fourth placed 3-y-o Morning Sir Alan (by Diktat). The dam won the Group 1 Italian Oaks and was third in the Group 1 Moyglare Stud Stakes. The second dam, Private Seductress (by Private Account), a US stakes-placed winner of 3 races, is a half-sister to 3 winners. (Saeed Manana).

182. UNNAMED ★★
ch.c. Motivator – Merewood (Woodman).
February 3. Third foal. 34,000Y. Tattersalls October 2. Rabbah Bloodstock. The dam, a fair

9f and 10f placed maiden, is a half-sister to 6 winners including to the high-class sprinter Reverence, winner of the Haydock Park Sprint Cup and the Nunthorpe Stakes and the very useful 2-y-o listed 6f Chesham Stakes winner Helm Bank. The second dam, Imperial Bailiwick (by Imperial Frontier), was a useful winner of 3 races at around 5f including the Group 2 Flying Childers Stakes, was Group 3 placed twice and is a half-sister to 3 winners in France. (Saeed Manana).

183. UNNAMED ★★★

ch.c. Sharmardal – Nasaieb (Fairy King).
May 22. Sixth foal. Half-brother to the useful 2-y-o 5f winner and Group 2 5f Flying Childers Stakes third Kissing Lights (by Machiavellian), to the fair 5f and 6f winner Best One (by Best Of The Bests), the fair 6f winner Luminous Gold (by Fantastic Light) and the minor French 2-y-o winner Nilassiba (by Daylami). The dam, a fairly useful 2-y-o 5f winner, was third in the listed 5f National Stakes and is a half-sister to 5 winners including the Group 3 7f Solario Stakes winner Raise A Grand. The second dam, Atyaaf (by Irish River), is an unplaced half-sister to 8 winners including the listed John Of Gaunt Stakes winner Weldnaas. (Saeed Manana).

184. UNNAMED ★★★

b.br.f. Dynaformer – Performing Arts (The Minstrel).
March 16. Thirteenth foal. $180,000Y. Keeneland September. Rabbah Bloodstock. Half-sister to the US Grade 2 winner Performing Magic (by Gone West), to the useful 2-y-o listed 6f winner Dance Trick, the fairly useful 2-y-o 6f winner Rehearsal Hall (both by Diesis), the very useful Group 3 Anglesey Stakes winner Woodborough (by Woodman) and the fairly useful 2-y-o 1m winner Choir Master (by Red Ransom). The dam, a useful 2-y-o 5f and 6f winner and third in the Irish 1,000 Guineas is a sister to the Heron Stakes winner and Group 1/Grade 1 placed The Noble Player and a half-sister to 9 winners. The second dam, Noble Mark (by On Your Mark), won the Group 3 6f Duke of York Stakes. (Saeed Manana).

185. UNNAMED ★★

b.f. Refuse To Bend – Raindancing (Tirol).
March 20. Eighth foal. 115,000Y. Tattersalls October 1. Rabbah Bloodstock. Half-sister to the unplaced 2008 2-y-o Eliza Griffith (by King's Best), to the fairly useful triple 5f winner and listed-placed Jack Spratt (by So Factual), the fair 3-y-o 7f winner Dash For Cover (by Sesaro), the fair 12f winner Yossi (by Montjeu) and the modest dual 1m winner Ballare (by Barathea). The dam, a fairly useful 2-y-o 6f winner, was third in the Group 3 6f Princess Margaret Stakes and is a sister to the smart 7f (at 2 yrs) to 10f winner and Group 1 placed Mountain Song and a half-sister to 6 winners including the Group 2 Cherry Hinton Stakes winner Please Sing. The second dam, Persian Song (by Persian Bold), is an unplaced sister to the Kentucky Derby second Bold Arrangement. (Saeed Manana).

186. UNNAMED ★★★

b.f. Dynaformer – Renowned Cat (Storm Cat).
January 21. Second foal. $350,000Y. Keeneland September. Rabbah Bloodstock. The dam is an unraced half-sister to 6 winners including the multiple US Grade 1 winner Escena, the Group 2 Blandford Stakes Humbel and the US Grade 3 winner Showlady. The second dam, Claxton's Slew (by Seattle Slew), a dual Irish listed winner, was Group 2 placed. (Saeed Manana).

187. UNNAMED ★★★

b.c. Exceed And Excel – Silent Heir (Sunday Silence).
April 4. Third foal. 40,000Y. Tattersalls October 1. Not sold. Half-brother to the 2-y-o Group 3 7f Prix La Rochette winner Young Pretender (by Oasis Dream). The dam, a quite useful 4-y-o 10f winner, is a half-sister to 4 winners. The second dam, Park Heiress (by Sunday Silence), is an unraced half-sister to 7 winners including the champion 2-y-o and Derby winner New Approach. (Saeed Manana).

188. UNNAMED ★★

b.c. Selkirk – Surval (Sadler's Wells).
February 1. Third foal. 85,000Y. Tattersalls

October 1. Rabbah Bloodstock. The dam, a fairly useful listed-placed 10.5f winner, is a half-sister to 4 winners including the dual Group 3 and subsequent US Grade 3 winner Delilah. The second dam, Courtesane (by Majestic Light), is a placed half-sister to 4 winners including the Group 3 5f Greenlands Stakes winner Drama (dam of the US Grade 3 winner Tycoon's Drama). (Saeed Manana).

189. UNNAMED ★★★
b.f. *Medicean – Time Saved (Green Desert)*.
April 13. Fifth foal. 110,000Y. Tattersalls October 1. Rabbah Bloodstock. Half-sister to the quite useful 2008 2-y-o 6f winner Emirates Sports (by King's Best), to the smart 7f (at 2 yrs) and Group 2 12f King Edward VII Stakes winner Plea Bargain (by Machiavellian), the useful 2-y-o 7f winner and Group 3 1m Prix des Chenes second Dubai Time (by Dubai Destination) and the modest 1m winner Tipsy Me (by Selkirk). The dam, a fairly useful 10f winner, is a sister to the useful 1m winner Illusion and a half-sister to 5 winners including Zinaad and Time Allowed, both winners of the Group 2 12f Jockey Club Stakes and the dams of the Group winners Anton Chekhov, First Charter, Plea Bargain and Time Away. The second dam, Time Charter (by Saritamer), was an exceptional filly and winner of the Oaks, the King George VI and Queen Elizabeth Diamond Stakes, the Champion Stakes, Coronation Cup, Prix Foy and Sun Chariot Stakes. (Saeed Manana).

190. UNNAMED ★★★
b.c. *Captain Rio – Valley Lights (Dance Of Life)*.
March 11. Ninth foal. 40,000Y. Tattersalls October 2. Rabbah Bloodstock. Half-brother to the useful triple 6f winner (including at 2 yrs) Masha-il (by Danehill), to the fairly useful dual 2-y-o 7f winner and subsequent US winner Il Colosseo (by Spectrum), the fairly useful 10f to 2m winner Mumbling (by Dr Devious) and a winner in Hong Kong by Bigstone. The dam was placed once (fourth of five) over 1m in Ireland and is a half-sister to 7 winners including the high-class miler Then Again. The second dam, New Light (by Reform), won over 10f and is a half-sister to the dam of the top-class Oaks and St Leger winner Sun Princess and the Coronation Cup winner Saddlers Hall. (Saeed Manana).

191. UNNAMED ★★★
br.f. *Doyen – Wimple (Kingmambo)*.
January 31. Third foal. Half-sister to the quite useful 2008 2-y-o 6f winner Master Rooney (by Cape Cross). The dam, a useful 5f and 6f winner at 2 yrs, was listed-placed and is a half-sister to 2 winners. The second dam, Tunicle (by Dixieland Band), won 4 minor races in the USA and is a half-sister to 5 winners. (Saeed Manana).

MEL BRITTAIN
192. HESLINGTON ★★★
ch.c. *Piccolo – Spice Island (Reprimand)*.
March 9. 3,500Y. Tattersalls October. M Brittain. Half-brother to the fair 2-y-o 5f winner Ginger Pickle (by Compton Place). The dam, a modest 2-y-o 6f winner, is a half-sister to 3 winners including the quite useful 5f and 6f winner Little Malvern (by Piccolo). The second dam, Little Emmeline (by Emarati), a 2-y-o 5f seller winner, is a half-sister to 3 winners including the listed Roses Stakes winner Dealers Wheels.
"I thought he'd run better than he has done in his first two starts, but I think we've made too much use of him. He's a big, heavy horse that wouldn't like it too firm and it's looking like he'll stay six without a problem. He's genuine and tough and is sure to win races".

193. LADY NAVARA (IRE) ★★
b.f. *Trans Island – Changari (Gulch)*.
April 21. Second foal. 3,500Y. Tattersalls October. M Brittain. Half-sister to the modest 2008 6f placed 2-y-o Danzadil (by Mujadil). The dam, a fairly useful 2-y-o 5f winner, is out of the French listed 6f 2-y-o winner Danzari (by Arazi). (David & Gwyn Joseph).
"She'll make her debut in mid-April and she's sharp and ready. I think she's one of those fillies that'll finish well, so I expect her to stay six furlongs alright".

194. MARCHIN STAR ★★★
ch.c. Chineur – March Star (Mac's Imp).
February 10. €8,500Y. Goffs Sportsman's. M Brittain. Half-brother to the fair 5f to 7f winner of 10 races Kensington (by Cape Cross) and to the modest 6f and 7f winner of 4 races Scuba (by Indian Danehill). The dam, a very useful winner of the Group 3 6f Phoenix Sprint Stakes, is a half-sister to 2 winners. The second dam, Grade A Star (by Alzao), an Irish 2-y-o 1m winner, stayed 11f and is a half-sister to 2 winners. (Northgate White).
"He makes his debut in mid-April, before your book comes out. He's a nice horse and he should be capable of winning races for us because he's showing promise".

195. TRADE SECRET ★★★
b.c. Trade Fair – Kastaway (Distant Relative).
April 7. Fifth foal. 2,500Y. Doncaster Festival. M Brittain. Half-brother to the fairly useful 2-y-o 5f winner Oro Verde (by Compton Place). The dam, a fairly useful dual 5f winner at 2 yrs, is a half-sister to 6 winners. The second dam, Flourishing (by Trojan Fen), a quite useful 2-y-o 7f winner, is a half-sister to 8 winners.
"This colt was fourth in the Brocklesbury which I think was a good race. He's a bit weak still, but he'll be a nice horse for us".

196. UNNAMED ★★
b.c. Xaar – Brigadiers Bird (Mujadil).
February 20. Ninth foal. 10,000Y. Tattersalls October 3. M Brittain. Half-brother to the modest 2008 6f placed 2-y-o Captain Carey, to the 2-y-o Group 3 Futurity Stakes winner and Group 2 Falmouth Stakes third Lady Lahar (herself dam of the listed winner Classic Legend), the moderate 12f all-weather winner Lord Lahar (all by Fraam) and the quite useful 1m all-weather 2-y-o winner Sri Pekan Two (by Montjeu). The dam is an unraced half-sister to 3 winners. The second dam, Brigadiers Nurse (by Brigadier Gerard), is an unraced half-sister to 4 minor winners. (Northgate Yellow).
"He's not going to be a sharp, early type, but he's a nice horse and I expect we'll see him when the six furlong races start.

197. UNNAMED ★★★
b.f. Royal Applause – First Musical (First Trump).
March 7. Fourth foal. 7,500Y. Tattersalls October. M Brittain. Half-sister to the quite useful 2-y-o dual 5f winner Avertuoso (by Averti) and to the modest 5.5f winner Casterossa (by Rossini). The dam, a fairly useful winner of 4 races from 5f to 6f at 2 yrs and second in the listed Firth Of Clyde Stakes and is a half-sister to 5 winners. The second dam, Musical Sally (by The Minstrel), is a half-sister to 5 winners.
"I was getting quite excited about her because I trained the dam and she was quite useful. But at the moment I'm giving her a bit of time because she was showing me she wasn't ready. I'd be disappointed if she wasn't any good though".

SIMON CALLAGHAN
198. AL KHIMIYA (IRE) ★★★
b.f. Johannesburg – Golden Flyer (Machiavellian).
January 27. Second foal. Sister to the fair 2008 6f placed 2-y-o Eagles Call. The dam is an unraced half-sister to 5 winners including the Irish Group 3 placed Gee Kel. The second dam, Shir Dar (by Lead On Time), won the US Grade 2 Palomar Handicap and is a half-sister to 9 winners. (Mr D O'Rourke).
"A filly that'll be out as soon as the six furlong races come out. She's done a few pieces of work already and she shows a very good attitude. A nice moving filly, we like her. She's the type of filly that'll start off relatively early because she's showing plenty but will get better and better as time goes on. She should train on to make a nice three-year-old as well".

199. DUBAWI HEIGHTS ★★★
b.f. Dubawi – Rosie's Posy (Suave Dancer).
February 11. Third foal. 72,000Y. Tattersalls October 1. N Callaghan. Half-sister to the useful 6f (at 2 yrs) and 1m winner Generous Thought (by Cadeaux Genereux). The dam, a quite useful 2-y-o 5.7f winner, is a half-sister to the Group 1 6f Haydock Sprint Cup winner Tante Rose and

the useful 2-y-o listed 7f winner Bay Tree. The second dam, My Branch (by Distant Relative), a very useful winner of the listed 6f Firth Of Clyde Stakes (at 2 yrs) and the listed 7f Sceptre Stakes, was second in the Group 1 Cheveley Park Stakes and third in the Irish 1,000 Guineas and is a half-sister to 5 winners. (Mr S Callaghan).

"This is a really racey filly from a very good, speedy family. It's Dubawi's first season so you don't really know, but she is a filly we really like and she has a bit of class about her. She's not small but she is very compact and really strong with a big back-end on her, so she's a real sprinter type".

200. FAITED TO PRETEND (IRE) ★★★★
b.f. Kheleyf – Lady Moranbon (Trempolino).
April 10. Thirteenth foal. 31,000Y. McKeever St Lawrence. Sister to the fair 2009 3-y-o 1m winner Muraweg and half-sister to the fairly useful 9.5f, 10f and hurdles winner Diego Cao (by Cape Cross), to the fairly useful 10f winner Space Cowboy (by Anabaa), the quite useful 5f and 6f 2-y-o winner Lady Le Quesne (by Alhaarth), the fair dual 7f winner Sweet Gale (by Soviet Star), 4 winners in France by Pistolet Bleu, Homme de Loi, Slip Anchor and Sillery and a winner of 6 races in Italy by Bering. The dam won twice over 9f and 10f at 4 yrs in France and is a half-sister to 6 winners. The second dam, Brigade Speciale (by Posse), won a listed event in France and is a half-sister to the Group 2 Royal Lodge Stakes winner Gairloch. (Frontier Racing).

"A very speedy, precocious filly, she'll be one of my first two-year-old fillies to run. She has lots of natural speed, isn't over-big but is all there physically – a real, early-season two-year-old and a typical sprinter. We really like her and you'll definitely be hearing about her early in the season".

201. GINGER GREY ★★★★
gr.c. Bertolini – Just In Love (Highest Honor).
April 3. Third foal. 52,000Y. Tattersalls October 1. Blandford Bloodstock. Half-brother to the quite useful 2-y-o 1m winner and listed-placed Dauberval (by Noverre) and to the fair 1m winner Nassmaan (by Alhaarth). The dam is an unraced sister to the French listed winner of 10 races Justful and a half-sister to 2 winners. The second dam, Just Class (by Dominion), a useful winner over 7f and 1m here, subsequently won three Grade 3 events in the USA at around 8.5f and is a half-sister to 5 winners including the Group 3 12f St Simon Stakes winner and smart broodmare Up Anchor. (Mr S Callaghan).

"This is a really nice horse, he's in full work and he goes particularly well. Very much the sort to make his mark at two and if I have got an Ascot horse this could well be him. He does everything really easily and he's definitely quite talented".

202. MOUNT JULIET (IRE) ★★★★ ♠
b.f. Danehill Dancer – Stylist (Sadler's Wells).
February 13. First foal. €80,000Y. Goffs Million. Not sold. The dam, a fair 8.5f winner, is a sister to French Ballerina (winner of four listed events in Ireland from 1m to 2m) and a half-sister to 4 winners including the Group 1 Fillies Mile winner and Irish Oaks second Sunspangled. The second dam, Filia Ardross (by Ardross), a very smart filly, won three Group 2 events in Germany and the Group 3 10f Select Stakes at Goodwood. (Frontier Racing Group).

"I really like this filly, she's got a lot of class about her, has all the right attributes and is one for the middle part of the season. She's definitely got an engine, does everything right and you should hear a fair bit about her because she's the type that could be really good".

203. TIGER HAWK ★★★★
b.c. Tale Of The Cat – Aura Of Glory (Halo).
February 2. Seventh foal. 60,000Y. Tattersalls October 2. Blandford Bloodstock. Half-brother to 2 minor winners in the USA by Honour And Glory and Honor Grades. The dam is an unraced half-sister to the Canadian stakes winner Fly North (herself dam of the champion US 3-y-o filly Farda Amiga). The second dam, Dry North (by Temperence Hill), won 3 races in the USA and is a half-sister to 4 stakes winners including the Irish Derby and King George winner St

Jovite. (Mr B Sangster & Mr S Callaghan).
"An incredibly tough horse that takes lots of work. He comes out full of himself every morning and he's a horse that I really like. Every bit of work you give him he seems to take in his stride and he's quite laid-back. We've done a couple of bits upsides with him and he definitely goes well. I'm really looking forward to him, he'll definitely make his mark as a two-year-old but he seems the sort to train on next year as well".

204. UNNAMED ★★
b.f. Rock Of Gibraltar – Blue Indigo
(Pistolet Bleu).
April 30. Fifth foal. 25,000Y. Tattersalls October. Not sold. Half-sister to the fair 2008 6f placed 2-y-o Layer Cake (by Monsieur Bond) and to the useful 1m (at 2 yrs) and subsequent US Grade 3 winner Genre (by Orpen). The dam was placed 5 times in France and is a half-sister to 5 winners. The second dam, Alcove (by Valdez), is an unplaced half-sister to 8 winners including the Breeders Cup Classic winner Arcangues. (Mr M Tabor).
"A really nice, big filly, she'll need time and is the type for the back-end of the season and for next year. She does everything right, she's a tall, rangy filly and we'll start her off at seven furlongs".

205. UNNAMED ★★★
b.c. Kyllachy – Entwine (Primo Dominie).
April 10. Sixth foal. 45,000Y. Tattersalls October 2. Simon Callaghan. Closely related to the fairly useful 7f (at 2 yrs) to 10f winner Lacework, to the fairly useful 6f (at 2 yrs) and 1m winner Envision and the fairly useful 2-y-o 5f and 6f winner Cyclical (all by Pivotal). The dam, a quite useful 2-y-o dual 5f winner, is a half-sister to 4 winners including the Group 2 Lowther Stakes winner Soar and the very smart 6f and 7f winner Feet So Fast (by Pivotal). The second dam, Splice (by Sharpo), a smart winner of the listed 6f Abernant Stakes, is a full or half-sister to 7 winners. (Mr Matthew Green).
"This is a really nice, strong, precocious sort and he'll be one of my first two-year-old runners. He goes really well and he has a bit of class about him. He looks pretty quick, we'll get on with him now and I can see him running sometime in May"..

206. UNNAMED ★★★
b.c. Noverre – Her Ladyship (Polish Precedent).
April 25. Tenth foal. 32,000Y. Tattersalls October 3. Blandford Bloodstock. Brother to the useful 2-y-o 6f winner Truly Royal and half-brother to the useful 2-y-o Group 3 1m Prix d'Aumale winner Dignify, the fairly useful Irish 12.7f winner House Of Bourbon (both by Rainbow Quest), the French winner and listed-placed Lady Bountiful (by Spectrum), the fairly useful 11f, 12f and hurdles winner Attorney General (by Sadler's Wells) and the quite useful 6f (at 2 yrs) and 7f winner Upper Class (by Fantastic Light). The dam, a smart French listed 10.5f winner and second in the Group 1 10.5f Prix de Diane, is a half-sister to 5 winners including the Group 1 7f Prix de la Salamandre winner Lord of Men. The second dam, Upper Strata (by Shirley Heights), was useful winner of the listed 10f Zetland Stakes at 2 yrs and the listed 2 mile George Stubbs Stakes at 4 yrs, is a half-sister to 5 winners. (Matthew Green).
"We bought him quite cheaply but I really like him and he'll start over six furlongs but will definitely be going seven. He's certainly got an engine and will be one of our better two-year-olds".

207. UNNAMED ★★
b.f. Bertolini – Ma N'ieme Biche
(Key To The Kingdom).
March 6. Tenth foal. 31,000Y. Doncaster St Leger. Blandford Bloodstock. Half-sister to the useful 3-y-o 6f and 7f winner A Very Good Year, to the German winner Ghost Of A Chance (both by Indian Ridge), the quite useful 6.5f winner Drifting Snow (by Danehill Dancer) and the fair 12f winner Mabel (by In The Wings). The dam was placed once in the USA and is a sister to the top-class filly Ma Biche (a winner of five Group 1 events including the 1,000 Guineas). The second dam, Madge (by Roi Dagobert), won once in France and is a half-sister to 8 winners

including the Cheveley Park Stakes winner Mige. (Matthew Green).
"She's quite a precocious type of filly that's done a few gentle pieces of work and she goes well. A sprinting type that will be out relatively early, she does everything right and has a bit of character about her – she's quite a livewire".

208. UNNAMED ★★★★
ch.c. Kyllachy – Mustique Dream
(Don't Forget Me).
March 7. Fifth foal. 130,000Y. Tattersalls October 1. **Tony Nerses.** Half-brother to the quite useful 2-y-o 5f winner Special Day (by Fasliyev), the fair dual 1m winner Marning Star (by Diktat) and the Italian winner of 2 races at 2 and 3 yrs and listed-placed Looking Back (by Stravinsky and herself dam of the Group 3 Tyros Stakes winner Rip Van Winkle). The dam, a quite useful dual 1m winner, is a half-sister to 5 winners. The second dam, Jamaican Punch (by Shareef Dancer), is an unplaced half-sister to 6 winners including the listed winners Tea House (dam of the Australian Grade 1 winner Danish) and Academic (also third in the Grade 1 San Juan Capistrano Handicap. (Saleh Al Homaizi & Imad Al Sagar).
"As nice a colt as I've got, he has a lot of quality about him. A really good-looking colt, he's going to need a bit of time, as a lot of Kyllachy's do, he does everything easily and has so much class. You wouldn't be surprised if he was a really good horse because he does everything really easily and he has an unbelievably good temperament".

209. UNNAMED ★★★
gr.f. Elusive City – Somaggia (Desert King).
February 10. First foal. €60,000Y. Goffs Million. **Blandford Bloodstock.** The dam is an unplaced half-sister to 8 winners including the listed winner and Group 1 Prix de la Salamandre third Speedfit Too. The second dam, Safka (by Irish River), a useful 2-y-o 5f winner, was third in the Group 3 5f Cornwallis Stakes and is a half-sister to 9 winners including the Group 2 7f Lockinge Stakes winner Safawan. (Mr M Tabor).
"A really good-looking filly, very strong and she's going to be relatively early. We won't rush her because she's got a bit of quality and she'll be starting as soon as the six furlong races start. A really speedy filly, we like her a lot and she'll start faster work in May".

210. UNNAMED ★★★
b.c. Compton Place – Westwood (Anabaa).
April 12. Fifth foal. 160,000Y. Tattersalls October 2. **Demi O'Byrne.** Half-brother to the unplaced 2008 2-y-o Gold Maha (by Compton Place) and to the quite useful 2-y-o 6f winner Silken Sky (by Septieme Ciel). The dam is a placed half-sister to 4 winners. The second dam, West Brooklyn (by Gone West), won 2 minor races at 2 and 3 yrs in France and is a half-sister to 10 winners including the French Group winners Prospect Wells and Prospect Park. (M Tabor).
"A middle to back-end type two-year-old, he's extremely good looking and has a lot of quality about him. He's not quite ready to do any faster work yet, but he's a great mover with a lot of quality about him".

JULIE CAMACHO

211. APPLEY BRIDGE ★★★
b.f. One Cool Cat – Coolrain Lady (Common Grounds).
February 16. Eleventh foal. 37,000Y. Doncaster St Leger. **Highfield Farm.** Half-sister to Mayorstone (by Exceed And Excel), unplaced in one start at 2 yrs in 2008, to the 2-y-o listed 1m winner and Group 3 Prix Saint-Roman second La Vita E Bella (by Definite Article), the 2-y-o dual listed 5f winner and Group 2 Criterium de Maisons-Laffitte third Bella Tusa (by Sri Pekan), the fairly useful 2-y-o dual 5f winner Light The Rocket (by Pips Pride) and the fair 2-y-o dual 7f winner Princess Petardia. The dam was placed 12 times in Ireland from 1m to 10f and is a half-sister to 4 minor winners. The second dam, Moneycashen (by Hook Money), won once at 3 yrs and over hurdles. (D A Armstrong).
"She looks a nice enough filly but we've only cantered her. We like everything she's done so far but she was just a bit immature when she started with her and when we x-rayed her

knees we could see they weren't quite mature enough. She looks a sharp enough filly though, she's strong and robust and is one for the middle of the season".

212. BEAT THE RUSH ★★
b.g. Tobougg – Rush Hour (Night Shift).
March 23. Fifth foal. 10,000Y. Brother to the modest 2m and hurdles winner Bouggler and half-brother to the unplaced 2008 2-y-o Short Cut (by Compton Place) and the quite useful 6f (at 2 yrs) and 7f winner of 4 races Lincolneurocruiser (by Spectrum). The dam is an unraced full or half-sister to 5 winners. The second dam, Hastening (by Shirley Heights), is an unraced sister to the Group 2 10f Prince of Wales's Stakes winner Perpendicular and a half-sister to the very useful Group 3 1m Juddmonte Stakes winner Prismatic. (Axom).

"He's backward, not surprising given that his brother is a hurdler. He's more athletic than Bouggler is and he should be a bit sharper, but he's definitely a back-end of the season horse and more of a three-year-old".

213. WALLGATE ★★★
b.f. Namid – Lay A Whisper (Night Shift).
January 19. First foal. The dam, a modest 1m placed 3-y-o, is a half-sister to numerous winners including the smart Group 3 7f Supreme Stakes winner Express Wish, the smart listed 7f winner Madid and the useful listed 7f winner Desert Alchemy. The second dam, Waffle On (by Chief Singer), a quite useful 3-y-o 6f winner here, subsequently won in France and is a half-sister to 5 winners including the Group 3 Premio Omenoni winner Leap For Joy. (D A Armstrong).

"She goes OK and she's likely to be out in April although she'll probably be better over six furlongs".

HENRY CANDY
214. BALLACHULISH ★★★
b.c. Kyllachy – Romantic Drama (Primo Dominie).
February 21. Second foal. 12,000Y. Doncaster St Leger. H Candy. Half-brother to the unraced 2008 2-y-o Romantic Bond (by Monsieur Bond). The dam was placed once at 2 yrs and is a half-sister to 2 winners. The second dam, Antonia's Choice (by Music Boy), a quite useful 5f winner, is a full or half-sister to 5 sprint winners. (Mr H Candy).

"He's going through a very backward stage at the moment which quite surprises me, because he looked quite sharp when I bought him and he has a sharp pedigree. He's grown a lot and I would imagine in the next few weeks he'll straighten up. He's a really good-moving horse, so I would hope he'll do the business. He's a five furlong colt, pure and simple".

215. BEAUCHAMP YORKER ★★★
ch.c. Compton Admiral – Compton Astoria (Lion Cavern).
February 6. Brother to the fairly useful dual 6f (at 2 yrs) and 7f winner Beauchamp Viceroy and the fair 3-y-o 7f winner Beauchamp Wizard. The dam is an unraced half-sister to one winner. The second dam, Perfolia (by Nodouble), a useful winner of 4 races over 7f, is a half-sister to the French 1,000 Guineas, Fillies Mile and Prix Marcel Boussac winner Culture Vulture. (E Penser).

"A big, strong horse with good bone, but he seems pretty mature and he has an early birthday. I see no reason why we shouldn't get on with him and I'd like to give him a run towards the end of May. He's a nice, big, strong, strapping colt".

216. DORBACK ★★★★★ ♠
ch.c. Kyllachy – Pink Supreme (Night Shift).
April 3. Second foal. 54,000Y. Doncaster St Leger. Will Edmeades. Half-brother to the modest 2008 2-y-o 6f winner Time For Old Time (by Olden Times). The dam, placed over 5f on her only start at 2 yrs, is a full or half-sister to 3 winners. The second dam, Bright Spells (by Salse), a 2-y-o 6f winner, was listed-placed. (Thurloe Thoroughbreds XXIV).

"A very strong, very mature horse that finds everything so easy it's a job to keep him in the string trotting – he just floats along. Because growth plates weren't quite as mature as I'd have liked I've not got on with him, otherwise I'd have been very tempted because he's a real strong 'He-Man' of a horse. If we can just hang on with him for a few weeks we'll aim to have him running in June. He looks a nice horse and he's a five/six furlong colt. The name comes from a grouse moor in Scotland".

217. FELSHAM ★★★
br.c. Kyllachy – Border Minstral (Sri Pekan).
March 19. Third foal. 26,000Y. Tattersalls October 2. H Candy. Half-brother to the smart 5f winner of 4 races Oldjoesaid (by Royal Applause). The dam, a fair 2-y-o 6f winner, is a sister to one winner and a half-sister to 6 winners including the Group 2 Cherry Hinton Stakes winner Please Sing and the very useful 7f (at 2 yrs) to 10f winner and Group 1 National Stakes third Mountain Song. The second dam, Persian Song (by Persian Bold), is an unplaced sister to the Solario Stakes winner Bold Arrangement (placed in seven Group/Grade 1 races including the Kentucky Derby). (Six Too Many).
"I obviously went to look at him because he's a half-brother to Oldjoesaid. It's a very fast pedigree and he's just starting to come to hand now. I should think by the look of him he'd be lucky to get five furlongs – he's that sort of build, with a massive muscle structure".

218. FINAL TURN ★★★
b.c. Kyllachy – Eveningperformance (Night Shift).
April 17. Half-brother to the quite useful 2-y-o 5f winner Dramatic Turn (by Pivotal) and to the fair 3-y-o 7f winner Evening Encore (by Kris). The dam was a very smart sprint winner of the Group 3 Flying Five and was second in the Group 1 Nunthorpe Stakes. The second dam, Classic Design (by Busted), is an unraced half-sister to the Two Thousand Guineas winner Tirol and to the unraced dams of the Group 1 Phoenix Stakes winner Lavery and the listed winners Sharp Point and High Target. (Mrs M J Blackburn).
"He was brought up as an orphan and had a fairly tricky upbringing. He was very weak when he arrived but he's making giant strides now and he could be OK. He's making up for lost time and changing by the week".

219. FLAMBEAU ★★★★
b.f. Oasis Dream – Flavian (Catrail).
March 2. Half-sister to the unplaced 2008 2-y-o Bended Knee (by Refuse To Bend) and to the moderate 2-y-o 6f and 7f winner Young Flavio (by Mark Of Esteem). The dam, a fairly useful 6f (at 2 yrs) and 7f winner, is a half-sister to 6 winners including the useful triple 7f winner Mata Cara (herself the dam of a French listed winner) and the fairly useful 10f winner Refugio. The second dam, Fatah Flare (by Alydar), won over 6f (at 2 yrs) and the Group 3 10.5f Musidora Stakes at 3 yrs. She is a half-sister to 8 winners including Sabin, a dual US Grade 1 winner over 9f and 10f. (Major M G Wyatt).
"She's very big but she's strong and has good bone. You'd have to be careful in the next few weeks because of her size, but otherwise she's coming together nicely, she's doing some gentle half-speeds and looks a very nice filly for the middle of the year".

220. HOOLIGAN SEAN ★★★
ch.g. Ishiguru – Sheesha (Shadeed).
April 26. Eighth foal. 23,000Y. St Leger Festival. H Candy. Brother to the 2008 6f placed 2-y-o (her only start) Shangani and half-brother to the quite useful 5f (at 2 yrs) and 6f winner of 4 races Seamus Shindig, to the fair 2-y-o 6f winner Shielaligh and the fair 7f winner Shebeen (all by Aragon). The dam, unplaced in one start, is a half-sister to 8 winners including the smart 12f King George V Handicap winner and St Leger fourth Samraan and the useful 6f (at 2 yrs) and 7f winner Star Talent. The second dam, Sedra (by Nebbiolo), a smart winner of 6 races from 6f (at 2 yrs) to 10f including the listed Ebbisham Handicap, was second in the Group 2 Sun Chariot Stakes and is a half-sister to 6 winners. (Mr H Candy).
"He's a relatively late foal and a bit tall and weak at the moment, but a fantastic mover that finds everything very easy. One for the second half of the year and I think he'll be nice".

221. IMPERIAL DELIGHT ★★
b.c. *Royal Applause – Playgirl (Caerleon).*
January 29. Third foal. 22,000Y. Tattersalls October 2. Not sold. The dam was placed over 10f and is a sister to the 10f winner and listed-placed Drama Class (herself dam of the listed 10f winner and Group 1 12f Irish Oaks second Scottish Stage) and a half-sister to 3 winners. The second dam, Stage Struck (by Sadler's Wells), a quite useful 12f winner, is a sister to the high-class Group 1 7f Dewhurst Stakes winner (in a dead-heat) Prince of Dance and to the useful middle-distance winners Ballet Prince and Golden Ball. (Mr A Solomons).
"He's only just arrived after having had an accident at his breaking yard. He's gone a bit backward but I loved him as a yearling and hopefully he can get back to the way he was. He has a good pedigree but I'm in the dark about him at the moment".

222. THE CONFESSOR ★★★★
b.c. *Piccolo – Twilight Mistress (Bin Ajwaad).*
March 12. Third foal. 14,000Y. Doncaster October. H Candy. Half-brother to Night Affair, a fair 6f winner on his only start at 2 yrs in 2008 and to the modest 6f and 7f winner of 3 races Shaded Edge (both by Bold Edge). The dam, a quite useful 5f to 7f winner of 3 races, is a half-sister to the useful 2-y-o 6f winner and listed 7f placed Romantic Evening. The second dam, By Candlelight (by Roi Danzig), was a quite useful 6f winner at 3 yrs. (Six Too Many).
"He's big and his knees have been a bit open so I'm just going steady, but it's a really quick pedigree and I thought the two-year-old last year, Night Affair, was very impressive when she won at Wolverhampton. This is a nice horse, he might get as far as six furlongs and he'll be out by mid-season". TRAINER'S BARGAIN BUY

223. TOY RAZOR ★★★
b.c. *Refuse To Bend – Child Prodigy (Ballad Rock).*
January 24. Seventh foal. 90,000Y. Tattersalls October 1. Anthony Stroud. Closely related to the fairly useful Irish 13f winner Road To Mandalay (by Galileo) and half-brother to the quite useful 2-y-o 8.5f all-weather and subsequent US winner Menuhin (by Royal Academy), to the fair 8.3f winner Du Pre (by Singspiel) and the modest 5f winner Heidi's Dash (by Green Desert). The dam, a quite useful 2-y-o 6f winner here, later won a minor race at 3 yrs in the USA and is a half-sister to 5 winners including the German and Italian Group 1 winner Kutub. The second dam, Minnie Habit (by Habitat), an Irish 4-y-o 9f winner, is closely related to the dual Group 3 sprint winner Bermuda Classic (herself dam of the Coronation Stakes winner Shake The Yoke). (Findlay & Bloom).
"A January foal and a big, strong horse, he looks like a three-year-old already. He seems to find everything very easy but because he's grown so much I'd be loath to put too much pressure on him for another month or two. I would say he'd win at two but would be a better three-year-old and seven furlongs in mid-season would probably be his starting point this year".

224. UNNAMED ★★★★
b.c. *Compton Place – Pretty Poppy (Song).*
February 10. Fourteenth foal. Doncaster St Leger. 20,000Y. H Candy. Half-brother to the top-class Group 1 5f Nunthorpe Stakes winner and sire Kyllachy, to the modest triple 6f winner Tadlil (both by Pivotal), the very useful triple 5f winner Borders (by Selkirk), the useful 5f winner of 4 races Speed On, the quite useful 2-y-o 5f winner Loving And Giving (both by Sharpo), the fairly useful dual 5f winner Follow Flanders, the quite useful 2-y-o 5f and 6f winner High Curragh (both by Pursuit Of Love), the quite useful 7f winner Ela Paparouna (by Vettori) and the fair dual 5f winners (including at 2 yrs) Pretty Miss (by Averti) and Poppy's Song (by Owington). The dam, a modest 2-y-o 5f winner, stayed 7.6f and is a half-sister to 4 winners including the Criterium de Maisons-Laffitte winner Corviglia. The second dam, Moonlight Serenade (by Crooner), is a placed sister to the winner and Group 3 5f Duke Of York Stakes third Blackbird. (Thurloe Thoroughbreds XVIII).
"Maybe people were put off buying him because the mare was twenty years old when

she had him, but he's making giant strides at the moment. He was small when we bought him but he's really growing now and developing a big front on him to match his 'Pretty Poppy' backside. All the mare's colts seem to have these colossal quarters on them. He's now levelling up, he's a tremendous mover and covers a huge amount of ground. As he was a February foal I would guess he'd catch up quite quickly now and hopefully he'll be out around June or July time. He's another one bred for five furlongs!"

HENRY CECIL

225. ALL WE KNOW ★★
b.c. Green Desert – Anniversary (Salse).
May 4. Fourth foal. 75,000Y. Tattersalls October 1. Henry Cecil. Half-brother to the fair 2m winner Swingkeel (by Singspiel). The dam, a fairly useful 12f winner, was listed placed over 2m and is a half-sister to 9 winners including the Group 2 12f Princess Of Wales's Stakes winner Craigsteel and the Group 1 20f Prix du Cadran winner Invermark. The second dam, Applecross (by Glint Of Gold), a smart winner of 3 races from 10f to 13.3f, was placed in the Park Hill Stakes and the Princess Royal Stakes and is a half-sister to 6 winners including the Park Hill Stakes winner Coigach. (J R May).
"A backward colt that's grown quite a bit".

226. CHACHAMAIDEE (IRE) ★★★
b.f. Footstepsinthesand – Canterbury Lace (Danehill).
January 29. Third foal. 135,000Y. Tattersalls October 1. Blandford Bloodstock. Half-sister to the fair 7f (at 2 yrs) and 1m winner of 4 races Maybe I Will (by Hawk Wing). The dam is an unraced sister to the Group 3 Gallinule Stakes winner and Irish Derby second Alexander Of Hales and to the Irish 2-y-o 1m winner and Group 1 1m Criterium International second Chevalier and a half-sister to the 1,000 Guineas winner Virginia Waters. The second dam, Legend Maker (by Sadler's Wells), won the Group 3 10.5f Prix de Royaumont, was third in the Group 2 13.5 Prix de Pomone and is a half-sister to 7 winners including the Group 2 12f King Edward VII Stakes winner Amfortas. (R A H Evans).
"This is a nice filly and an early foal that should make a two-year-old later on".

227. CHANNEL SQUADRON (IRE) ★★
b.c. Sadler's Wells – Caladira (Darshaan).
May 11. Eleventh foal. 50,000Y. Tattersalls December. Henry Cecil. Brother to the Beresford Stakes (at 2 yrs), Dante Stakes, Doncaster Cup and Lonsdale Stakes winner (all Group 2 events) Septimus and half-brother to the Irish 2-y-o 6.5f winner Hollow Hill (by Orpen) and the Italian winner Lady Poison (by Charnwood Forest). The dam won over 10f in Ireland at 3 yrs and is a half-sister to 8 winners. The second dam, Cape Race (by Northern Dancer), won at 3 yrs and is a half-sister to the Group/Grade 3 winners Never Return and Legal Case and to the smart sire Lord Gayle. (G Schoeningh).
"A late foal so he won't be ready for some time, but he's a nice colt".

228. DANUBE (IRE) ★★★
b.c. Montjeu – Darabela (Desert King).
January 24. Second foal. Half-brother to the quite useful 2008 2-y-o 1m and 9f winner of 3 races Doncosaque (by Xaar). The dam, an Irish 3-y-o 7f winner, is a half-sister to the smart Group 2 Goodwood Cup winner Darasim. The second dam, Dararita (by Halo), a winner in France over 12.5f at 3 yrs, is a half-sister to the Group 2 12.5f Prix Maurice de Neiuil winner Darazari, the listed 10.5f and 12f winner Dariyoun, the smart King Edward VII Stakes second Kilimanjaro and the 2-y-o 8.2f winner and French Derby third Rhagaas. (Ammerland).
"A sensible colt and a good mover that needs time".

229. DOLPHINA (USA) ★★
ch.f. Kingmambo – Sea Of Showers (Seattle Slew).
January 17. The dam won once over 1m and was third in the Group 2 1m Prix de Sandringham and is a half-sister to the triple US Grade 1 winner (over 7f and 1m) Aldebaran and

the Canadian Grade 1 Atto Mile winner Good Journey. The second dam, Chimes Of Freedom (by Private Account), won the Group 1 6f Moyglare Stud Stakes and the Group 3 6f Cherry Hinton Stakes at 2 yrs, prior to winning the Group 1 1m Coronation Stakes and the Group 2 1m Child Stakes in her second season. She is a half-sister to the very useful 2-y-o 6f listed Firth of Clyde Stakes winner and Cheveley Park Stakes second Imperfect Circle (herself dam of the top-class miler Spinning World). (Niarchos Family).
"Despite his early foaling date this is a backward colt for the late summer onwards".

230. FLORENTINE RULER (USA) ★★
b.c. Medicean – Follow That Dream (Darshaan).
April 3. Sixth foal. Half-brother to the fairly useful 6f and 7f winner of 13 races (including at 2 yrs) Desert Dreamer (by Green Desert). The dam, a fairly useful 12.3f winner, is a half-sister to 4 winners including the Group 1 10f Champion Stakes and triple US Grade 1 winner Storming Home. The second dam, Try To Catch Me (by Shareef Dancer), won once over 1m at 3 yrs in France and is a half-sister to 8 winners including the Group 2 Criterium de Maisons-Laffitte winner Bitooh. (Malih Al Basti).
"An active colt, he might make a two-year-old a bit later on".

231. JACQUELINE QUEST (IRE) ★★★ ♠
b.f. Rock Of Gibraltar – Coquette Rouge (Croco Rouge).
March 1. First foal. €60,000Y. Goffs Million. McKeever St Lawrence. The dam, a quite useful Irish 12f and 17f winner, is a half-sister to 4 winners including the Group 3 Classic Trial winner Regime and the 2-y-o 5f listed winner and Group 2 Cherry Hinton second Salut d'Amour. The second dam, Juno Madonna (by Sadler's Wells), is an unraced half-sister to 5 winners including the Group 3 5f King George Stakes winner Title Roll and the Irish listed sprint winner Northern Express. (N Martin).
"A nice filly, she should make up into a two-year-old".

232. KITHONIA ★★★★
b.f. Sadler's Wells – Ratukidul (Danehill).
January 1. First foal. The dam, a fair 2-y-o 7f winner, is a half-sister to the Group 1 Prix du Jockey Club and Group 1 10.5f Prix Lupin winner Hernando, to the Group 1 10.5f Prix Lupin and US Grade 2 1m winner Johann Quatz and the smart French 10.5f to 13.5f listed winner Walter Willy (both by Sadler's Wells). The second dam, Whakilyric (Miswaki), won over 5.5f and the Group 3 7f Prix du Calvados, was third in the Prix de la Salamandre (all at 2 yrs) and in the Group 1 7f Prix de la Foret and is a half-sister to the Prix Daphnis winner Bricassar. (Niarchos Family).
"A very early foal by Sadler's Wells and from a very good family, she's nice but she won't be ready for some time yet".

233. KLEIO ★★★
b.f. Sadler's Wells – Colza (Alleged).
April 2. Sister to the 2-y-o Group 1 10f Criterium de Saint-Cloud winner Linda's Lad and half-sister to useful French dual 1m winner and Group 3 placed Ulterior Motives (by Selkirk) and the minor French 1m winner Volantis (by Bluebird). The dam, a quite useful 2-y-o 1m winner, is a full or half-sister to 9 winners including the very useful Group 3 6f July Stakes and listed 3-y-o 9f winner Wharf. The second dam, Dockage (by Riverman), a winner over 1m at 2 yrs and a 9f listed event at 3 yrs in France, is a half-sister to 3 winners. (Khalid Abdulla).
"A nice filly but being a Sadler's Wells filly out of an Alleged mare she'll take time".

234. MOOSE MORAN (USA) ★★★★
gr.c. Lemon Drop Kid – After All (Desert Story).
January 26. Second foal. 75,000Y. Tattersalls October 2. Anthony Stroud. Half-brother to Just Mustard (by Johannesburg), unplaced in one start at 2 yrs in 2008. The dam, placed at 2 and 3 yrs, is a half-sister to the Hong Kong stakes winner and Grade 3 placed Right Way. The second dam, All Ashore (by Nureyev), was an unplaced half-sister to the champion 2-y-o El Prado and the Group 3 winner Entitled. (Raymond Tooth).

"A big colt, he moves well and will hopefully make a two-year-old in the second half of the season".

235. ON HER WAY ★★★
ch.f. Medicean – Singed (Zamindar).
February 9. Third foal. 65,000Y. Tattersalls October 2. Henry Cecil. Half-sister to the useful 2008 2-y-o dual 1m winner and Group 2 1m Royal Lodge Stakes third On Our Way (by Oasis Dream). The dam won once at around 1m in France and is a half-sister to the French listed winner and Group 3 placed Inhabitant. The second dam, Infringe (by Warning), won once at 3 yrs in France and is a half-sister to 7 winners including the Group 3 winners Ecologist, Green Reef and Infrasonic. (Malih L Al Basti).
"A flashy filly that will need time, she's a good mover".

236. PLUS ULTRA (IRE) ★★★
b.c. Rock Of Gibraltar – Tafseer (Grand Lodge).
May 10. First foal. 45,000Y. Tattersalls October 1. Henry Cecil. The dam is an unraced half-sister to 7 winners including the smart 2-y-o 7f winner and Group 2 1m Royal Lodge Stakes second Tholjanah. The second dam, Alkaffeyah (by Sadler's Wells), is an unraced half-sister to the listed 12f Galtres Stakes winner and Group 1 12f Prix Vermeille third Larrocha and a half-sister to the outstanding middle-distance stayer Ardross and the Pretty Polly Stakes winner Gesedeh. (Malih L. Al Basti).
"An active colt, he's a May foal but not a backward type".

237. PROTARAS (USA) ★★★
b.br.c. Lemon Drop Kid – Seven Moons (Sunday Silence).
March 10. Half-brother to Alpha Tauri (by Aldebaran), unplaced in 2 starts at 2 yrs in 2008. The dam is a half-sister to a 10f winner in France. The second dam, Moon Is Up (by Woodman), a listed 1m winner and Group 3 placed in France, is closely related to the French 2,000 Guineas, the St James's Palace Stakes and Prix du Moulin winner Kingmambo and the smart Group 3 6f Prix de Ris-Oranges winner Miesque's Son and a half-sister to the high-class French 1,000 Guineas, Prix de Diane and Prix Jacques le Marois winner East of the Moon. (Exors of the late Stavros Niarchos).
"A nice colt but he needs time".

238. RIGIDITY ★★★★
b.c. Indian Ridge – Alakananda (Hernando).
March 6. Fourth foal. 95,000Y. Tattersalls October 1. Sir M Prescott. Half-brother to the listed winner, Epsom Derby second and Irish Derby fourth Dragon Dancer, to the quite useful 10f winner Albarouche (both by Sadler's Wells) and the fairly useful 1m (at 2 yrs) to 14f winner of 5 races Ajaan (by Machiavellian). The dam, a fairly useful dual middle-distance winner, is a half-sister to 6 winners including the dual Champion Stakes winner Alborada and the triple German Group 1 winner Albanova. The second dam, Alouette (by Darshaan), a useful 1m (at 2 yrs) and listed 12f winner, is a sister to the listed winner and Irish Oaks third Arrikala and to the placed Jude (dam of the Group 1 winners Yesterday and Quarter Moon) and a half-sister to the dual Group 2 winner Last Second (dam of the French 2,000 Guineas winner Aussie Rules) and the Doncaster Cup winner Alleluia (dam of the Group 1 Prix Royal-Oak winner Allegretto). (Thomas Barr).
"An attractive colt and a nice mover".

239. SUBTEFUGE ★★★
b.f. Observatory – Artifice (Green Desert).
April 19. Fourth foal. Half-sister to Lady Trish (by Red Ransom), unplaced in one start at 2 yrs in 2008 and to the quite useful 7.5f winner Ramaad (by Dr Fong). The dam, a fair 3-y-o 6f winner, is a sister to 3 winners including the very useful Group 3 7f Jersey Stakes winner Ardkinglass and the useful dual 7f winner Darnaway and a half-sister to 5 winners including the useful 10f winners Kinlochewe and Jura. The second dam, Reuval (by Sharpen Up), a useful winner of 2 races over 1m at 3 yrs, is closely related to the dams of the Group 2 winners Ozone Friendly, Reprimand and Wiorno. (Dr Catherine Wills).
"An active colt, he could be alright".

240. TOMINTOUL SINGER (IRE) ★★★
ch.f. *Johannesburg – Shivaree (Rahy)*.
March 2. First foal. 25,000Y. Tattersalls December. Henry Cecil. The dam, a fair 2-y-o 6f winner, is a half-sister to one winner. The second dam, Shmoose (by Caerleon), a useful 6f winner at 2 yrs and listed-placed over 6f at 3 yrs, is a half-sister to 6 winners and to the good broodmare June Moon. (T Hillman).
"An active filly with a two-year-old pedigree".

241. TYMORA (USA) ★★
ch.f. *Giant's Causeway – Shiva (Hector Protector)*.
April 4. The dam, a high-class winner of the Group 2 10.5f Tattersalls Gold Cup and the Group 3 10f Brigadier Gerard Stakes, is a sister to the high-class Group 2 12f Prix Jean de Chaudennay and Group 3 12f Prix Foy winner Limnos and a half-sister to the useful 7f and listed 1m winner Burning Sunset. The second dam, Lingerie (by Shirley Heights), placed 7 times in France, is a half-sister to 4 winners including the French listed placed Evocatrice. (Niarchos Family).
"A nice filly that needs time".

242. VITA NOVA (IRE) ★★★
b.f. *Galileo – Treca (Darshaan)*.
February 8. First foal. 150,000Y. Tattersalls October 1. Blandford Bloodstock. The dam is an unraced half-sister to one winner. The second dam, Cortona (by Caerelon), winner of the listed Prix Imprudence and second in the French 1,000 Guineas, is a half-sister to 5 winners including the Group 3 winner and good broodmare Caprarola. (H E Sheikh Sultan).
"A nice, big filly that needs time, she's a good mover".

243. WHIRLY DANCER ★★
b.f. *Danehill Dancer – Whirly Bird (Nashwan)*.
May 1. First foal. 48,000Y. Tattersalls October 1. Not sold. The dam, a useful 9.5f to 11f winner, is a half-sister to the very useful 12f listed Galtres Stakes winner Inchiri and the very useful 2-y-o 8.3f winner and Oaks fourth Inchberry. The second dam, Inchyre (by Shirley Heights), a useful 1m winner and listed-placed over 12f, is a half-sister to 7 winners including the very smart and tough triple Group 3 7f winner Inchinor. (Woodcote Stud).
"She's very small and I haven't made an assessment of her yet".

244. UNNAMED ★★
b.c. *Montjeu – Be Glad (Selkirk)*.
February 8. Third foal. The dam, a French Group 3 placed 10f winner, is a half-sister to several winners including the Prix d'Aumale, the Prix Vanteaux and Prix de Malleret winner Bonash. The second dam, Sky Love (by Nijinsky), a fairly useful 10f winner, is a half-sister to the high-class Prix de la Cote Normande winner Raft. (Khalid Abdulla).
"This is a nice colt but although he was a February foal he'll need time".

245. UNNAMED ★★★★
b.f. *Zamindar – Clepsydra (Sadler's Wells)*.
February 3. Sixth foal. Half-sister to the 2008 2-y-o 1m winner (only start) Father Time, to the very smart Group 1 10f Criterium de Saint-Cloud (at 2 yrs) and Group 3 10.3f Musidora Stakes winner Passage Of Time (both by Dansili), the fairly useful 10f winner Sandglass (by Zafonic) and the quite useful 1m and 10f winner Timetable (by Observatory). The dam, a quite useful 12f winner, is a half-sister to several winners including the useful listed 10.5f winner Double Crossed. The second dam, Quandary (by Blushing Groom), a useful winner of 4 races from 9f to 10f including the listed James Seymour Stakes at Newmarket, is a half-sister to the Group 1 Prix du Moulin winner All At Sea. (Khalid Abdulla).
"A nice, active filly. She's very flashy, with four white legs".

246. UNNAMED ★★★
b.f. *Dansili – Emplane (Irish River)*.
February 24. Sister to the very useful 2008 2-y-o dual 7f winner Wingwalker and to the 2-y-o Group 3 7f Prix la Rochette winner and Group 1 placed Early March and half-sister to the fairly useful French 10f winner Itinerary (by

Dr Fong), the quite useful 7f winner Painted Sky (by Rainbow Quest) and the minor French 11f winner Coach Lane (by Barathea). The dam, a useful 3-y-o 1m winner, is a sister to the useful 2-y-o 1m winner Boatman and a half-sister to the quite useful 2-y-o 7f winner Palisade. The second dam, Peplum (by Nijinsky), a useful winner of the listed 11.3f Cheshire Oaks, is a half-sister to the top class filly Al Bahathri, winner of the 1,000 Guineas and the Coronation Stakes. (Khalid Abdulla).

"A nice filly by a good sire and a full sister to Wingwalker".

247. UNNAMED ★★★

b.c. Smart Strike – Honest Lady (Seattle Slew).

January 22. Half-brother to the useful 2008 2-y-o listed 7f winner Honest Quality (by Elusive Quality), to the US Grade 3 6f winner and dual Grade 1 placed First Defence (by Unbridled's Song), the French listed 1m winner Phantom Rose (by Danzig) and the French 2-y-o 5f winner Documentary (by Storm Cat). The dam, winner of the Grade 1 Santa Monica Handicap, is a half-sister to the US triple Grade 1 winner Empire Maker and the Grade 1 Arlington Million winner Chester House. The second dam, Toussaud (by El Gran Senor), a 6f and 7f winner here, subsequently won a Grade 1 in North America. (Khalid Abdulla).

"A nice colt and an early foal from a very good family".

248. UNNAMED ★★

b.c. Empire Maker – Imroz (Nureyev).

March 25. Half-brother to the fairly useful listed 10f winner Posteritas (by Lear Fan) and to the useful 2-y-o dual 7f winner Apex Star (by Diesis). The dam, a useful 6f (at 2 yrs) and 7f winner, was listed-placed and is a half-sister to 5 winners including the useful 3-y-o listed 1m winner Insinuate. The second dam, All At Sea (by Riverman), a high-class winner of 5 races from 1m to 10.4f including the Group 1 Prix du Moulin, is a half-sister to the Free Handicap winner Over the Ocean, the listed 10f winner Quandary and the US stakes winner Full Virtue. (Khalid Abdulla).

"It's too early to make a proper assessment but I quite like him".

249. UNNAMED ★★★

b.f. Empire Maker – Interim (Sadler's Wells).

January 26. Half-sister to the 6f (at 2 yrs), 10f and subsequent US Grade 1 10f placed Midships (by Mizzen Mast), to the very useful 10f and 12f winner and US Grade 1 placed Staging Post (by Pleasant Colony), to the fairly useful 1m and 9f winner Focus Group, the minor French 10.5f winner and Irish hurdles winner Indemnity (both by Kris S) the quite useful 9f winner Introducing (by Deputy Minister) and the quite useful dual 10f winner Interim Payment (by Red Ransom). The dam, a very useful 1m and 10f winner, is a half-sister to the high-class Interval, a sprinting winner of four races from 5f to 1m including the Group 2 Prix Maurice de Gheest and to the unraced dam of the Hoover Fillies Mile winner Invited Guest. The second dam, Intermission (by Stage Door Johnny), won the Cambridgeshire Handicap and is a half-sister to 7 winners including the high-class middle-distance colts Peacetime and Quiet Fling. (Khalid Abdulla).

"A nice filly and an early foal".

250. UNNAMED ★★

b.c. Cape Cross – Kalima (Kahyasi).

April 11. The dam is an unraced sister to the very useful 10f (at 2 yrs) and listed 13.8f winner Arrive and to the 2-y-o 5f winner and outstanding broodmare Hasili (dam of the top-class performers Banks Hill, Heat Haze, Intercontinental, Cacique, Champs Elysees and Dansili) and a half-sister to several winners. The second dam, Kerali (by High Line), a quite useful 3-y-o 7f winner, is a half-sister to numerous winners including the Group 3 6f July Stakes winner Bold Fact, the Group 1 Nunthorpe Stakes winner So Factual and the very useful Irish 7f to 1m winner Field Dancer. (Khalid Abdulla).

"Not yet in training (early April)".

251. UNNAMED ★★★
b.f. Dansili – Katrina (Ela-Mana-Mou).
May 2. Fourth foal. 230,000Y. Tattersalls October 1. Juddmonte Farms. Half-sister to the quite useful 12f winner Sri Lipis (by Cadeaux Genereux) and the moderate 14f winner Kritzia (by Daylami). The dam is an unraced half-sister to the Group 3 12f St Simon Stakes and listed 12f Galtres Stakes winner Kithanga (herself dam of the St Leger and Great Voltigeur winner Milan). The second dam, Kalata (by Assert), was unplaced on her only start and is a half-sister to 7 winners including the Italian Group 3 winner Karkisiya and to the dams of the Derby winner Kahyasi and the Yorkshire Oaks winner Key Change. (Khalid Abdulla).
"She's a nice filly but backward at present and one for later on".

252. UNNAMED ★★★
b.c. Sadler's Wells – Kind (Danehill).
January 28. First foal. The dam, a dual listed winner over 5f and 6f, was Group 3 placed and is a half-sister to the Arlington Million and Tattersalls Rogers Gold Cup winner Powerscourt (by Sadler's Wells) and to the smart 14f winner of 3 races Brimming. The second dam, Rainbow Lake (by Rainbow Quest), a smart winner of 3 races including the Group 3 12f Lancashire Oaks and the listed 10f Ballymacoll Stud Stakes, is a half-sister to several winners including the useful middle-distance winner Vertex. (Khalid Abdulla).
"A nice Sadler's Wells colt and an early foal that might make a two-year-old in the second half of the season".

253. UNNAMED ★★
b.f. Dansili – Spacecraft (Distant View).
February 27. The dam was placed twice over 6f and 7f at 3 yrs in France and is a half-sister to the Group 1 7f Prix de la Foret winner Etoile Montante and to the useful 6f winner and Group 1 Prix Marcel Boussac fourth Starfan. The second dam, Willstar (by Nureyev), won over 1m in France. (Khalid Abdulla).
"She's not very correct in front, so time will tell".

254. UNNAMED ★★★★
ch.f. Danehill Dancer – Verasina (Woodman).
April 17. Third foal. 30,000Y. Tattersalls October 2. Not sold. Half-sister to the quite useful 2-y-o 7f winner Farleigh House (by Lear Fan). The dam was placed second over 1m as a four-year-old from only two starts and is a sister to the listed-placed winner Compton Dragon and a half-sister to 6 winners including the US stakes winner Legend Of Russia. The second dam, Vilikaia (by Nureyev), won the Group 3 Prix de la Porte Maillot and is a sister to the Group 2 Prix d'Astarte winner Navratilovna and a half-sister to the good filly Maximova - herself dam of the Group 1 winners Septieme Ciel and Macoumba.
"Not an expensive purchase, but this is a very nice filly".

255. UNNAMED ★★★★
ch.c. Storm Cat – Wandesta (Nashwan).
February 10. Half-brother to the fair 3-y-o 7f winner Greek Dream (by Distant View) and to a number of disappointing horses. The dam, a smart 12f listed winner here and subsequently winner of the Grade 1 9f Santa Ana Handicap and Grade 1 10f Santa Barbara Handicap in the USA, is closely related to the Group 2 12f Prix du Conseil de Paris winner De Quest and a half-sister to the smart French 10f to 15f winner Turners Hill. The second dam, De Stael (by Nijinsky), a fairly useful dual 7f winner at 2 yrs, is a sister to the high-class middle-distance colts Peacetime and Quiet Fling and a half-sister to the Cambridgeshire winner Intermission – herself dam of the good sprinter Interval. (Khalid Abdulla).
"A very nice colt that might make a two-year-old later on".

256. UNNAMED ★★★★
b.c. Oasis Dream – Well Warned (Warning).
March 3. Brother to the quite useful 2-y-o 6f winner and listed-placed Prohibit and half-brother to the French 7f (at 2 yrs) and listed 6.5f winner Prior Warning (by Barathea). The dam, a useful 2-y-o 6f winner, was third in the Group 3 6f Cherry Hinton Stakes and is a sister to the

very useful listed 1m winner Out Of Reach. The second dam, Well Beyond (by Don't Forget Me), was a useful filly and winner of the listed 1m October Stakes. (Khalid Abdulla).
"A nice colt from a two-year-old family, he moves well".

MICK CHANNON
257. AATTASH (IRE) ★★★★
b.c. Clodovil – Mothers Footprints (Maelstrom Lake).
April 12. Seventh foal. 100,000Y. Tattersalls October 2. Gill Richardson. Half-brother to the quite useful 2-y-o 6f and 7f winner Lamh Eilh (by Lend A Hand). The dam is an unraced half-sister to 6 winners. The second dam, Daring Choice (by Daring Display), is a placed half-sister to 4 winners. (Sheikh Ahmed Al Maktoum).
"Yes, he's a lovely horse. He could be really nice in the middle of the summer and I like him a lot".

258. AYAM ZAINAH ★★★
ch.f. Pivotal – Ya Hajar (Lycius).
March 17. Fourth foal. Half-sister to the quite useful 3-y-o 6f winner Muhajaar (by Cape Cross) and to the fair 10f and 11f winner Laish Al Hajar (by Grand Lodge). The dam, a useful 2-y-o Group 3 7f Prix du Calvados winner, is a half-sister to the high-class Group 1 1m St James's Palace Stakes and Group 2 6f Mill Reef Stakes winner Zafeen. The second dam, Shy Lady (by Kaldoun), winner of a listed event over 6f in Germany, was fourth in the Group 2 6f Moet and Chandon Rennen. (Jaber Abdullah).
"A lovely filly, she was a bit later to come in than the others and I can't tell you a lot about her yet. Hopefully be ready for late May or June".

259. BASHIR BIL ZAIN ★★★
b.f. Cape Cross – Personal Love (Diesis).
February 1. Ninth foal. 80,000Y. Tattersalls October 2. Gill Richardson. Half-sister to the useful 10f winner and Group 3 Queens Vase third Helvetio (by Theatrical). The dam won 4 races over 6f and 7f at 2 and 3 yrs in Germany including two listed events and is a half-sister to the US Grade 2 Norfolk Stakes winner Supremo.

The second dam, Personal Glory (by Danzig), is an unraced half-sister to 9 winners including the US Grade 2 winner and sire Dynaformer. (Jaber Abdullah).
"I have two Cape Cross two-year-olds and they'll both be mid-summer horses. They're nice but they need a bit of time".

260. BITTER MAN (IRE) ★★★
b.c. Azamour – Savieres (Sadler's Wells).
March 25. Third foal. 30,000Y. Tattersalls October 2. Gill Richardson. The dam, a minor Irish 11f winner, is a sister to 5 winners including the Irish 9f winner and Group 1 National Stakes second Coliseum. The second dam, Gravieres (by Saint Estephe), won the Grade 1 Santa Ana Handicap and the Grade 3 California Jockey Club Handicap and is a half-sister to 9 winners. (Jaber Abdullah).
"A nice horse for the late summer onwards. He does everything nicely but he'll need at least seven furlongs".

261. BOGA ★★★
b.f. Invincible Spirit – Miznapp (Pennekamp).
April 10. Fourth foal. 24,000Y. Doncaster St Leger. Gill Richardson. The dam is an unraced half-sister to 2 winners including the Group 3 Ballycorus Stakes winner Al Tadh. The second dam, Titchcar (by Cadeaux Genereux), is a placed half-sister to the dual Group 2 winner Zindabad. (Findlay & Bloom).
"Yes, she's alright. A nice filly, she'll be running in May and she goes OK. I like her, she shows enough for five furlongs but she will be better at six".

262. DI STEFANO ★★★★
b.c. Bahamian Bounty – Marisa (Desert Sun).
March 4. Second foal. 60,000Y. Doncaster St Leger. Gil Richardson. Half-brother to the fairly useful 2008 2-y-o 5f and listed 6f winner Smokey Storm (by One Cool Cat). The dam is an unraced half-sister to 5 minor winners here and abroad. The second dam, Mithl Al Hawa (by Salse), a useful 2-y-o 6f winner, was listed placed is a half-sister to 9 winners. (Jon & Julia Aisbitt).
"He's sharp, he's ready to go and shows a bit of

263. DUTIFUL ★★★
ch.c. Dubawi – Pelagia (Lycius).
January 24. 30,000foal. Tattersalls December. Not sold. Half-brother to the useful 6f (at 2 yrs) and 1m winner and Group 2 6f Richmond Stakes second Upper Hand (by Mark Of Esteem), subsequently a winner over 1m in Hong Kong as Royal Prince. The dam is a 7f fourth-placed half-sister to 4 winners including the Group 1 1m Prix Marcel Boussac and Group 2 1m Prix d'Astarte winner Lady Of Chad (by Last Tycoon) and the dual Group 3 Sagaro Stakes winner Alcazar (by Alzao). The second dam, Sahara Breeze (by Ela-Mana-Mou), a quite useful 7f and 1m placed maiden, is a half-sister to 5 winners including the Group 1 Fillies Mile winner Ivanka. (Wood Street Syndicate II).

"He's a real nice horse. I don't think we'll see him until the back-end of the season because he's a big colt. He goes nicely now but he'll be better in a few months time for sure".

264. EXCELLENT DAY (IRE) ★★
b.f. Invincible Spirit – Tosca (Be My Guest).
April 15. Ninth foal. 50,000Y. Tattersalls October 2. Gill Richardson. Half-sister to the quite useful 2-y-o 5f winner Dalkey Girl (by Raise A Grand) and the fair 12f and 14f winner Tilla (by Bin Ajwaad). The dam is an unraced half-sister to 8 minor winners here and abroad. The second dam, Princess Eboli (by Brigadier Gerard), won the Group 3 12f Lancashire Oaks and is a half-sister to 6 winners. (Jaber Abdullah).

"She's fine but she's playing catch-up because she's a bit hairy in her coat and she's a fair bit behind some of the earlier ones. Needs six furlongs already".

265. FLY SILCA FLY (IRE) ★★★★
b.f. Hawk Wing – Nevis Peak (Danehill).
February 18. Second live foal. 30,000Y. Doncaster St Leger. Gill Richardson. The dam is an unraced sister to the New Zealand winner and Grade 3 placed Assafa. The second dam, Marigot Bay (by Fairy King), a dual 2-y-o winner in Ireland, was listed placed and is a half-sister to the Australian Group winners Langoustine and One World.

"She's very nice, she's all there and shows she's a nice two-year-old, so even though you wouldn't expect a Hawk Wing to be precocious she shows all the right signs. I haven't really got into her yet but she looks like being a really nice filly. She's certainly got ability and I think she'll need six or seven furlongs this year".

266. GALLIC STAR (IRE) ★★★★★
b.f. Galileo – Oman Sea (Rahy).
February 4. Second foal. €130,000Y. Goffs Million. Gill Richardson. The dam, a quite useful 2-y-o 6f winner, was listed-placed at 3 yrs and is a half-sister to 3 winners including the Group 3 Criterion Stakes winner Racer Forever. The second dam, Aneesati (by Kris), a quite useful 1m winner, was listed-placed 3 times and is a half-sister to several winners including the Prix de la Salamandre second Bin Nashwan and the 1m, 10f and subsequent US Grade 2 winner Magellan. (Jon & Julia Aisbitt).

"A very nice filly, she definitely needs six furlongs and I think she'll be good. She'll be ready in May and we'll see if she's good enough to go to Ascot. I think a fair bit of her and she shows all the right signs".

267. GOMRATH (IRE) ★★
b.c. Lomitas – Diner De Lune (Be My Guest).
January 28. Sixth foal. 110,000Y. Tattersalls October 2. Gill Richardson. Half-brother to the fair 12f and hurdles winner Tyrrells Wood (by Sinndar) and to the French 3-y-o 6.5f winner Sara Luna. The dam, a 2-y-o listed 7f winner in France, is a half-sister to 7 winners including the Irish Oaks winner Moonstone, the dual Grade 1 placed L'Ancresse and the Prix Saint-Alary winner Cerulean Sky. The second dam, Solo de Lune (by Law Society), a French 11f winner, is a half-sister to 6 winners including the Group/Grade 2 winners Truly A Dream and Wareed. (Jon & Julia Aisbitt).

"A lovely horse but he's definitely one for the end of the season and next year".

268. GRAND ZAFEEN ★★★★
ch.f. Zafeen – Majestic Desert (Fraam).
January 26. First foal. The dam was a smart 2-y-o 5f and 6f Tattersalls Breeders Stakes winner and was second in the Group 1 Cheveley Park Stakes. The second dam, Calcutta Queen (by Night Shift), was placed twice over 1m. (Mr A Jaber).
"She goes very well and she'll be out early. She's sharp and not very big – she's only a pony – but she goes like stink and she's a real two-year-old".

269. HAIRSPRAY ★★★
ch.f. Bahamian Bounty – Quickstyx (Night Shift).
February 21. Second foal. Half-sister to the modest 2008 2-y-o 7.5f winner Blusher (by Fraam). The dam, a fair 1m winner, is a half-sister to the smart 12f listed winner and US Grade 1 second Red Fort, to the useful 12f listed winner Red Carnation and the useful 12f November Handicap winner Red Wine. The second dam, Red Bouquet (by Reference Point), won 3 minor races from 12f to 13f at 4 yrs in Germany and is a half-sister to 4 winners including the Group 3 7f Prestige Stakes winner Red Camellia (herself dam of the Group 1 Fillies' Mile winner Red Bloom). (J Breslin).
"She's a very nice filly and she shows all the right signs. One for the mid-summer onwards and she's a two-year-old for sure. Ascot could be a bit soon for her".

270. IL PORTICO ★★
b.c. Zafeen – Diddymu (Revoque).
April 6. 12,000Y. Doncaster St Leger. G Howson. Half-brother to the fairly useful 1m winner of 3 races Summon Up Theblood (by Red Ransom) and to the moderate 5f winner Splendidio (by Zamindar). The dam, a modest 10f winner, is a half-sister to 6 winners including the listed winning sprinter and Group 2 placed Flanders. The second dam, Family At War (by Explodent), a fair 2-y-o 5f winner, is a half-sister to 4 minor winners in the USA. (Derek & Jean Clee).
"A big horse, he's just going to need a bit of time but he's nice".

271. JEHU ★★★ ♠
b.c. Antonius Pius – Chalosse (Doyoun).
March 28. Sixth foal. 24,000Y. Tattersalls October 3. David McGreavy. Half-brother to 2 minor winners in France by Barathea and Fasliyev. The dam is a placed half-sister to 5 winners including the French dual Group 1 winner Creator. The second dam, Chalon (by Habitat), won the Coronation Stakes and the Child Stakes and is a half-sister to 7 winners including the dual Group 3 winner Executive Perk. (Box 41).
"He's quite a nice horse that just needs a bit of time and he'll probably be better over six and seven furlongs. But he'll be alright".

272. JIBRRYA ★★★
b.c. Motivator – Takarna (Mark Of Esteem).
January 24. Fourth foal. 140,000Y. Tattersalls October 1. Gill Richardson. The dam is a placed half-sister to 5 winners including the Group 2 Royal Whip Stakes winner Takali and the Group 3 12f Meld Stakes winner Takarian, subsequently winner of the Bay Meadows Derby in the USA. The second dam, Takarouna (by Green Dancer), a very useful winner of the Group 2 12f Pretty Polly Stakes at the Curragh, is a sister to the smart Group 2 Dante Stakes winner Torjoun. (Sheikh Ahmed Al Maktoum).
"One for later on, but I like him and he'll make a two-year-old for sure".

273. KALAM DALEEL (IRE) ★★★
gr.c. Clodovil – Three Days In May (Cadeaux Genereux).
April 26. Second living foal. €65,000Y. Goffs Million. Gill Richardson. Half-brother to the unraced 2008 2-y-o Pete's Passion (by Rock Of Gibraltar). The dam, a fair 3-y-o 6f winner, is a half-sister to 6 winners including the very useful Crazee Mental - a winner over 6f and placed in the Cheveley Park Stakes, the Queen Mary Stakes and the Cherry Hinton Stakes. The second dam, Corn Futures (by Nomination), a fair 2-y-o 6f winner, is a half-sister to 7 winners. (Jaber Abdullah).
"A nice horse, I think he'll want six furlongs but he's shown me enough to say he's alright. A definite two-year-old".

274. LEITZU (IRE) ★★★
b.f. *Baratheo – Ann's Annie (Alzao).*
January 14. €28,000Y. Goffs Million. Not sold.
Closely related to the fairly useful 10f and 12f all-weather winner of 6 races Sgt Schultz (by In The Wings) and to the fair 12f winner Galianna (by Galileo) and half-sister to the modest 14f all-weather winner Red River Rock (by Spectrum). The dam, a quite useful 2-y-o 1m winner in Ireland, is a half-sister to 6 winners including the very smart Group 3 7f Criterion Stakes winner Pipe Major. The second dam, Annsfield Lady (by Red Sunset), a winner of 3 races in Ireland between 9f and 10f, is a half-sister to 4 winners including the Group 2 and dual Group 3 winner Insatiable. (Upsan Downs Racing).
"A lovely, big filly for a bit later in the year. She's fine and just needs a bit of time".

275. LELEYF (IRE) ★★★★
b.f. *Kheleyf – Titchwell Lass (Lead On Time).*
March 17. Half-sister to the fairly useful 2-y-o dual 5f winner Sundance (by Namid), to the modest 5f (at 2 yrs) to 8.7f winner of 11 races Louisade (by Tagula) and the modest 5-y-o 10f winner Denise Best (by Goldmark). The dam, a modest 10f winner, is a half-sister to numerous winners. The second dam, Bodham (by Bustino), won over 12f and 13.3f. (Box 341).
"A smashing little filly, she's a professional and although she won early I think there's a fair bit of improvement in her. It'll be interesting to see if she does improve when she runs in a Conditions or a Novice race".

276. LOFTHOUSE ★★★★
b.c. *Hunting Lion – Noble Destiny (Dancing Brave).*
February 14. Half-brother to the useful dual 5f winner Noble One, to the fair 3-y-o all-weather dual 6f winner Noble Lady (both by Primo Dominie), the fairly useful 10f winner Maiden Castle (by Darshaan), the 1m all-weather and German 10f winner Noble Investment (by Shirley Heights), the modest 6f (at 2 yrs) to 8.3f winner Noble Nova (by Fraam) and 2 minor winners abroad by Rainbow Quest and Lion Cavern. The dam was a fairly useful 2-y-o 7f winner. The second dam, Tender Loving Care (by Final Straw), a useful winner over 7f at 2 yrs, was second in the Group 3 1m May Hill Stakes and a half-sister to 9 winners including the May Hill Stakes winner Satinette.
"A colt that goes very well, he's an early type, he's very nice and definitely worth putting in the book".

277. MIZAYIN (IRE) ★★
gr.f. *Clodovil – Forest Storm (Woodman).*
March 18. Seventh foal. €42,000Y. Goffs Million. Gill Richardson. Half-sister to the useful 9f winner Fann and to the modest 9.5f winner Awaaser (both by Diesis). The dam is an unraced half-sister to the Grade 1 Hollywood Turf Handicap winner Strom Trooper and to the May Hill Stakes and Musidora Stakes winner Marillette (both by Diesis). The second dam, Stormette (by Assert), won over 12f in Ireland and is a half-sister to Storm Bird. (Jaber Abdullah).
"She's alright and she'll be a two-year-old. Probably needs six furlongs but she'll be running soon".

278. MUSIARA ★★★
b.f. *Hunting Lion – Search Party (Rainbow Quest).*
April 26. Half-sister to the quite useful 2-y-o triple 6f winner Bateleur (by Fraam) and to the fair 2-y-o 6f winner Evanesce (by Lujain). The dam, a fair 8.3f and 10f placed maiden, is a half-sister to the 6f (at 2 yrs) and subsequent Grade 1 10f Santa Barbara Handicap winner Bequest and to the useful 2-y-o 7f winner Fitzcarraldo. The second dam, Quest (by The Minstrel), won 3 races from 9f to 10f at 3 yrs, was third in the Group 3 Queen Mary Stakes, is a sister to the Group 1 Grand Criterium winner Treizieme and a half-sister to the Group 2 Yorkshire Cup winner Eastern Mystic. (Dave & Gill Hedley).
"Definitely a two-year-old type and she should win".

279. NADEEN (IRE) ★★★★
b.c. *Bahamian Bounty – Janayen (by Zafonic).*
May 2. The dam, a fairly useful dual 1m winner,

is a half-sister to the useful 2-y-o all-weather 7f winner Manntab. The second dam, Saafeya (by Sadler's Wells), a very useful listed 10f winner of 6 races, is a half-sister to one winner. (Jaber Abdullah).
"A sharp colt, he'll be running soon and he'll win over five furlongs because he shows plenty of boot".

280. NADINSKA ★★★
b.f. Doyen – Funny Girl (Darshaan).
April 7. Half-sister to the useful 6f (at 2 yrs), 10f and listed 12f winner Suzi's Decision (by Act One) and to the fairly useful 10f and 12f winner Pippa Greene (by Galileo). The dam was placed from 7f to 9f and is a daughter of the minor German winner Just For Fun (by Lead On Time), herself a sister to the Prix Herbager winner Judge Decision. (Norman Court Stud).
"She's one for the back-end of the season but she's very nice and I like her a lot. She could be a real nice filly one day and she'll be better next year than this".

281. PINK COAT ★★★
gr.c. Alhaarth – In The Pink (Indian Ridge).
March 8. First foal. 37,000Y. Tattersalls October 3. R Frisby. The dam, a quite useful 7f and 1m winner, is a half-sister to 3 winners including the useful 8.3f to 12f winner of 5 races Celtic Mission. The second dam, Norfolk Lavender (by Ascot Knight), a modest 1m all-weather winner here, subsequently won a stakes event in the USA and was Grade 3 placed and is a half-sister to 5 winners. (R A Keogh).
"A lovely horse, he shows all the right signs. He'll be a seven furlongs/mile colt for later on but he'll be really nice".

282. PINTURA ★★★★
ch.c. Efisio – Picolette (Piccolo).
April 21. Fifth foal. 30,000Y. Doncaster St Leger. Gill Richardson. Half-brother to the unplaced 2008 2-y-o Dancing Delta, to the 12f seller winner Ruby Dancer (both by Delta Dancer) and the quite useful 2-y-o 6f and 7f winner Pomme Frites (by Bertolini). The dam was placed once at 2 yrs and is a half-sister to one winner. The second dam, Poyle Jezebelle (by Sharpo), won once at 4 yrs and is a full or half-sister to 7 winners.
"He's a very nice horse and he goes well. He's almost ready to run now and he'll win early but he'll be even better at six furlongs".

283. RAINSBOROUGH ★★★★
b.c. Trans Island – Greeba (Fairy King).
April 30. The dam is an unplaced half-sister to numerous winners including the useful 5f and 6f winner and listed-placed Smart Ridge. The second dam, Guanhumara (by Caerleon), is an unplaced half-sister to the champion sprinter and high-class sire Cadeaux Genereux. (Mr Billy Parish).
"He'll be a nice horse later on and yet he shows a bit of speed now. He'll want six and seven furlongs".

284. ROYAL DESERT ★★★★
b.c. Pastoral Pursuits – Overcome (Belmez).
April 27. 17,000Y. Doncaster St Leger. Gill Richardson. Half-brother to the fair 6f (at 2 yrs) and 12f winner River Ardeche, to the modest 2-y-o 6f winner Bridget's Team (both by Elnadim) and the fair 1m winner of 3 races Brace Of Doves (by Bahamian Bounty). The dam won once over 10f in Germany and is a half-sister to 8 winners. The second dam, Olivana (by Sparkler), is an unraced half-sister to the German Derby winners Orofino and Ordos. (Ahmed Jaber).
"He goes like stink and he'll win. A five furlong horse for sure, he's a sharp colt".

285. SPECIALISING ★★
ch.c. Nayef – Spry (Suave Dancer).
February 6. Seventh foal. 75,000Y. Tattersalls October 1. R Frisby. Half-brother to the fair dual 1m winner Bajan Pride, to the fair 10f and hurdles winner Stow (both by Selkirk) and the modest 11f to 2m winner of 4 races Serramanna (by Grand Lodge). The dam, a quite useful 12f winner, is a half-sister to the Group 2 Hardwicke Stakes winner Sandmason, to the very useful 10f Newmarket Pretty Polly Stakes winner Sardegna and the smart triple 12f winner

Sebastian. The second dam, Sandy Island (by Mill Reef), a very useful winner of the Group 3 12f Lancashire Oaks and the 10f Pretty Polly Stakes, is closely related to Slip Anchor and a half-sister to the German 2,000 Guineas winner Swazi. (Mrs A C Black).
"A lovely filly but she won't be out until the end of the season".

286. STAR ZAFEEN ★★★
b.c. Zafeen – Beacon Silver (Belmez).
March 12. Sixth foal. 30,000Y. Tattersalls October 2. Gill Richardson. Half-brother to the fairly useful 7f, 1m (both at 2 yrs) and 8.6f winner Gramm (by Fraam). The dam won over hurdles and is a half-sister to 7 winners. The second dam, Nettle (by Kris), a useful listed 7f winner, is a half-sister to 5 winners. (Jaber Abdullah).
"He's quite nice, he won't be real early but he goes well now. When the seven furlong races come along he'll be perfect for the job".

287. TAWAABB ★★★★
ch.c. Kyllachy – Penmayne (Inchinor).
January 21. Sixth foal. 82,000Y. Tattersalls October 1. John Ferguson. Brother to the useful 2-y-o 5f and 6f winner and dual Group 3 placed Kylayne and half-brother to the Swedish winner of 3 races at 4 and 5 yrs Global Guardian (by Dr Fong) and to Penzena (by Tobougg), unplaced in one start at 2 yrs in 2008. The dam, a fairly useful 2-y-o 7f winner, was listed-placed and is a half-sister to 6 winners including the useful 6f, 6.5f (both at 2 yrs) and listed 1m winner Salamanca. The second dam, Salanka (by Persian Heights), a fair 3-y-o 10f winner, is a half-sister to one winner. (Sheikh Ahmed Al Maktoum).
"A very nice two-year-old. I think he'd win at five furlongs but he'll be better at six and in mid-May he'll hopefully be one of those I'll be looking at closely to see if he can be aimed at Royal Ascot".

288. TEXAS QUEEN ★★★
b.f. Shamardal – Min Asl Wafi (Octagonal).
April 21. The dam, a fair 7f placed 3-y-o, is a half-sister to the high-class Group 1 1m St James's Palace Stakes and Group 2 6f Mill Reef Stakes winner Zafeen to the very useful listed 7f winner Atlantic Sport and the useful 2-y-o Group 3 7f Prix du Calvados winner Ya Hajar. The second dam, Shy Lady (by Kaldoun), winner of a listed event over 6f in Germany, was fourth in the Group 2 6f Moet and Chandon Rennen and is a half-sister to 4 winners. (Jaber Abdullah).
"A sweet filly, she was a bit late starting, so she's a bit behind the others. She's a smashing filly and you couldn't knock her but she's just playing catch-up at the minute".

289. TISLAAM (IRE) ★★★★
ch.c. With Approval – Lady Angola (Lord At War).
February 25. €35,000Y. Goffs. Gill Richardson. Half-sister to the fair 2-y-o dual 6f winner Raiding Party (by Orpen). The dam, a quite useful 12f winner at 3 yrs, is a half-sister to 6 winners including the dam of the US Grade 1 winner Honor In War. The second dam, Benguela (by Little Current), won in the USA and is a half-sister to the US Grade 1 winners La Gueriere and Al Mamoon. (Jaber Abdullah).
"This could be the dark horse. He's a nice colt and I think he'll do well".

290. TOGA TIGER (IRE) ★★★★
b.c. Antonius Pius – Minerwa (Protektor).
March 29. Second foal. 13,000Y. Tattersalls October. Gill Richardson. The dam won 5 races from 5f to 7f at 3 and 4 yrs in Germany, was listed-placed and is a full or half-sister to 5 winners. The second dam, Marousskia (by Feenpark), won 4 races from 2 to 4 yrs in Germany and is a half-sister to 4 winners.
"He goes well. He's a nice horse and although I think he could win over five furlongs I think he'd be better over six". TRAINER'S BARGAIN BUY

291. TRELAWNY WELLS ★★
b.c. Pastoral Pursuits – Kythia (Kahyasi).
March 2. Second foal. 52,000Y. Tattersalls October 3. Gill Richardson. Half-brother to the fair 2008 8.3f placed 2-y-o Phoenix Enforcer (by Bahamian Bounty). The dam, a fair 2-y-o 8.5f

winner, is a half-sister to 2 minor winners. The second dam, Another Ranbow (by Rainbows For Life), is a placed half-sister to 8 winners including Reunion (Group 3 Nell Gwyn Stakes). (Box 41).
"A nice horse, I thought he was going to be early but he had a little setback. He's gone fat on us now, but he'll be alright later on".

292. YOUM AL MIZAYIN ★★
b.f. Cape Cross – Silent (Sunday Silence).
February 10. First foal. €130,000Y. Goffs Million. Gill Richardson. The dam, a minor winner at 3 yrs in France, is a half-sister to the Group 3 Sovereign Stakes and Group 3 Prix de Cabourg winner Layman. The second dam, Laiyl (by Nureyev), won over 10f and is a half-sister to 3 winners including the Group 3 Prix Cleopatre Allurement. (Jaber Abdullah).
"Just like my other Cape Cross two-year-old, she'll be alright later on but she's just ticking over at the minute".

293. UNNAMED ★★
b.c. Medicean – Armorique (Top Ville).
April 14. Eleventh living foal. €160,000Y. Goffs Million. Gill Richardson. Half-brother to the useful Irish 6f (at 2 yrs) and 7f winner Darwin, the fairly useful 7f winner Camaret (both by Danehill), the fair 1m and 10f winner Palmerin (by Oasis Dream), the modest 2-y-o 7f all-weather winner Tiger Dawn (by Anabaa) and the modest 10.2f winner Crozon (by Peintre Celebre). The dam, a minor winner and listed placed over 12f at 3 yrs in France, is a half-sister to 8 winners including the Group winners Modhish, Russian Snows and Truly Special (herself the dam of two Grade 2 winners). The second dam, Arctique Royale (by Royal And Regal), won the Irish 1,000 Guineas and the Moyglare Stud Stakes and is a half-sister to the dam of Ardross. (Findlay & Bloom).
"A lovely horse, but he's one for the back-end of the season. You won't see him for a while".

294. UNNAMED ★★★
b.c. Elusive City – Bonne Mere (Stepneyev).
February 10. First foal. €60,000Y. Goffs Sportsman's. **Bobby O'Ryan.** The dam, a listed-placed winner of 5 races, is a half-sister to 2 minor winners in France. The second dam, Gardine (by Fast Topaze), a listed-placed winner of 5 races, is a half-sister to 3 winners. (Liam Mulryan).
"He's only just come in but you should watch out for him, he should be a nice two-year-old".

295. UNNAMED ★★
b.br.c. Camacho – Clochette (Namaqualand).
March 20. Third foal. 40,000Y. Doncaster St Leger. Gill Richardson. Half-brother to the fair 2008 2-y-o 5f winner Calypso Girl (by Verglas) and the moderate 6f winner Time Share (by Danetime). The dam was placed twice over 6f at 3 yrs in Ireland and is a half-sister to 5 winners including the Group 1 Cheveley Park Stakes and Group 1 Moyglare Stud Stakes winner Capricciosa. The second dam, Clanjingle (by Tumble Wind), is a placed half-sister to 4 winners. (Findlay & Bloom).
"He's grown and he's a big, backward horse at the moment, so you'll not see him out for some time".

296. UNNAMED ★★★★
b.f. Galileo – Corrine (Spectrum).
April 12. Second foal. €130,000Y. Goffs Million. Gill Richardson. Sister to the 2008 Irish 2-y-o 1m winner Liszt. The dam won 4 races, including a listed event, in Norway and is a half-sister to 6 winners. The second dam, La Luna (by Lyphard), a winner over 9f at 3 yrs in France, is a sister to the Group 3 Prix Daphnis and Group 3 Prix Thomas Bryon winner Bellypha and a half-sister to the Prix Eugene Adam winner Bellman and the Peruvian Grade 1 winner Run And Deliver. (Findlay & Bloom).
"This is a very nice filly. She's going to be better next year obviously but she should hopefully do something as a two-year-old. Just a lovely type of filly".

297. UNNAMED ★★★
b.f. Oratorio – Edetana (Diesis).
May 3. Second foal. 62,000Y. Tattersalls October 2. Gill Richardson. The dam, placed

fourth 3 times from 1m to 10f, is a half-sister to one winner. The second dam, Edabiya (by Rainbow Quest), won the Group 1 7f Moyglare Stud Stakes and is a half-sister to the Irish Oaks and Prix Royal-Oak winner Ebadiyla and the Ascot Gold Cup winner Enzeli. (Mystery Partnership).
"A nice filly, I just think these Oratorio's are needing a bit of time. She'll make a two-year-old when she gets a bit more sun on her back".

298. UNNAMED ★★★★
b.c. *Rakti – Feather Boa (Sri Pekan).*
March 25. Third foal. 60,000Y. Tattersalls October 3. Gill Richardson. Half-brother to the quite useful 2-y-o 5f winner Mazzanti (by Pivotal). The dam, a quite useful 2-y-o dual 6f winner, is a half-sister to 3 winners including the listed winner Wagtail. The second dam, Dancing Feather (by Suave Dancer), a quite useful 1m winner, is a half-sister to 8 winners including the good broodmare Fragrant Hill (the dam of 4 stakes winners).
"He goes nicely, I think he'll be alright and he looks a very nice colt. Hopefully he could be a Chesham Stakes sort because he's not backward. One to watch out for".

299. UNNAMED ★★★
ch.c. *Compton Place – Locharia (Wolfhound).*
February 13. Fourth foal. 34,000Y. Tattersalls October 2. Gill Richardson. Half-brother to the fair 2008 5f placed 2-y-o Yanza (by Bahamian Bounty), the quite useful 6f winner Credit Swap (by Diktat) and the modest 6f winner Vivi Belle (by Cadeaux Genereux). The dam was a fairly useful 2-y-o 5f winner. The second dam, Lochbelle (by Robellino), a fair 10.2f winner, is a half-sister to 3 winners including the champion sprinter Lochsong (winner of the Prix de l'Abbaye (twice), the Kings Stand Stakes, the Nunthorpe Stakes, etc) and the Nunthorpe Stakes winner Lochangel. (Mystery Partnership).
"A nice horse, but he's a little bit behind the others. Both my Compton Place two-year-olds are nice but they won't be as early as you might expect".

300. UNNAMED ★★★
b.c. *Acclamation – Mystic Belle (Thatching).*
February 18. Fifth foal. 75,000Y. Tattersalls October 1. Not sold. Half-brother to the useful 7f, 1m (both at 2 yrs) to 2m winner Toldo (by Tagula) and to the Spanish 2-y-o 1m winner Muckabell (by Mukaddamah). The dam won twice over 7f at 4 yrs in Ireland and is a half-sister to 2 winners. The second dam, Mystic Reason (by Lyphard), won at 3 yrs in France, was listed-placed twice and is a half-sister to 9 winners. (Findlay & Bloom).
"A nice horse but he's had a few little setbacks so I haven't got him where I want. I thought he'd be really early but now he'll need time to mature, but he shows enough to let me know he'll be alright".

301. UNNAMED ★★★★
b.c. *Tobougg – Noble Desert (Green Desert).*
February 7. Second foal. 72,000Y. Doncaster St Leger. Angie Sykes. Half-brother to the modest 2008 2-y-o 1m winner Noble Dictator (by Diktat). The dam is an unplaced half-sister to 6 winners. The second dam, Sporades (by Vaguely Noble), won 3 races in France including the Group 3 10.5f Prix de Flore and is a half-sister to 9 winners including the high-class colts Mill Native (winner of the Grade 1 10f Arlington Million) and French Stress (winner of three Group 3 1m events in France and to the 2-y-o 5f Prix du Bois winner American Stress). (Findlay & Bloom).
"He's a really nice horse and he'll make a two-year-old alright. He'd want six, or possibly seven furlongs to be at his best but he's bit more forward than my other Tobouggs – more like his old man was as a two-year-old".

302. UNNAMED ★★★
b.c. *Danehill Dancer – Sabreon (Caerleon).*
February 28. Fifth foal. 72,000Y. Tattersalls October 1. Angie Sykes. Closely related to the quite useful 1m and hurdles winner Pillar Of Hercules (by Rock Of Gibraltar) and half-brother to the promising 2008 7f placed 2-y-o Moneycantbuymelove (by Pivotal), the fair 1m winner Moon Crystal (by Fasliyev) and a minor

winner in Japan by Mozart. The dam, a quite useful 10.2f winner, is a half-sister to 6 winners including the French 2,000 Guineas and Grade 1 Keeneland Turf Mile Stakes winner Landseer and the very smart listed 10f winner and Group 1 placed Ikhtyar. The second dam, Sabria (by Miswaki), is an unraced half-sister to 4 winners. (Findlay & Bloom).

"He goes quite nicely but he's just a little bit unfurnished. He's a nice horse and he shows speed but I still think he needs a bit more time".

303. UNNAMED ★★★
b.f. Vindication – Westerly Gale (Gone West).
January 29. First foal. €52,000Y. Goffs Million. Not sold. The dam, a minor winner at 3 yrs in the USA, is a half-sister to 4 winners including the US Grade 1 Jim Dandy Stakes winner Scorpion. The second dam, Petiteness by Chief's Crown), a winner of 3 races in the USA, was listed placed twice and is a half-sister to 11 winners including the dam of the US Grade 2 winner Imperfect World. (Liam Mulryan).

"She hasn't been in long but I like her – she's very nice".

304. UNNAMED ★★
b.c. King's Best – Zuleika Dobson (Cadeaux Genereux).
March 30. Fourth foal. 30,000Y. Tattersalls October 2. Gill Richardson. The dam, a useful 9f winner and third in the Group 3 9f Prix Chloe, is a half-sister to one winner. The second dam, Fresher (by Fabulous Dancer), won twice in France and was second in the Group 2 Prix d'Astarte and is a half-sister to 5 winners including the Group 2 Prix Niel winner Songlines. (J D Guest).

"A nice horse, but he's one for later in the season. There's a lot of the damsire Cadeaux Genereux about him".

PETER CHAPPLE-HYAM

305. ABU WATHAB ★★
b.c. Nayef – Fleeting Rainbow (Rainbow Quest).
April 15. Eleventh foal. 80,000Y. Tattersalls October 2. Andrew Sime. Half-brother to the high-class Group 1 10.5f Tattersalls Gold Cup and Group 2 10f Pretty Polly Stakes winner Rebelline, to the Group 2 Blandford Stakes and Group 3 Gallinule Stakes winner Quws (both by Robellino), the useful 2-y-o 6f and 7f winner Moonlight Man (by Night Shift), the fair Irish 1m and 10f winner Danzelline (by Danzero) and the French 1m winner Partly Sunny (by Alhaarth). The dam, a modest 10f placed 3-y-o, is a half-sister to 3 winners. The second dam, Taplow (by Tap On Wood), is an unraced half-sister to 7 winners including the dams of the Group winners Adam Smith, Braashee, Ghariba, Careafolie, Gouriev and Run And Gun. (Ziad A Galadari).

"Obviously given his pedigree he's quite backward and will take a bit of time. So he's more one for the autumn and next year but he goes along quite nicely at the moment and is doing everything he should be doing".

306. COORDINATED CUT (IRE) ★★★★★
b.c. Montjeu – Apache Star (Arazi).
February 14. Sixth living foal. 325,000Y. Tattersalls October 1. Blandford Bloodstock. Half-brother to the useful 2-y-o 6f and listed 1m winner New Mexican (by Dr Fong), to the useful Irish 6f (at 2 yrs) to 2m winner Sahara Desert, the fairly useful 1m (including at 2 yrs) and 10f winner Cactus King (both by Green Desert) and the useful 10f winner of 4 races and listed-placed Wild Savannah (by Singspiel). The dam, a fairly useful 7f (at 2 yrs) to 9f winner, was listed placed twice at up to 11.4f and is a half-sister to 6 winners. The second dam, Wild Pavane (by Dancing Brave), is an unraced half-sister to 6 winners including the listed winner Nuryana (dam of the Group 1 Coronation Stakes winner Rebecca Sharp). (Mr L J Inman).

"He would be my favourite at the moment but he's another one that will be better as a three-year-old. He'll be racing by August I would have thought and is a horse with definite ability. He's showing all the right signs".

307. CUNNING PLAN (IRE) ★★★
ch.c. Bachelor Duke – Madamaa (Alzao).
February 24. Fifth foal. €35,000Y. Tattersalls Ireland. Allan Bloodlines. Half-brother to the

fairly useful 2-y-o 5f and 6f winner Karayel (by Fasliyev) and to the fair 1m winner Methusaleh (by Mutamam). The dam, a quite useful Irish 10f winner, is a half-sister to 2 winners. The second dam, Leopardess (by Ela-Mana-Mou), a quite useful 10f winner, is a sister to the Irish listed 14f winner Na-Ammah and a half-sister to the dual Group 2 winner Alflora. (Mr A B S Webb & Partner).

"He came in a bit later than some of the others but he's beginning to catch up now. He's not the biggest horse in the world but he will be a two-year-old, probably around May time and he's definitely alright. I should think he'll be better over six furlongs than five".

308. FALAKEE ★★★
b.c. Sakhee – Sakhya (Barathea).
March 3. First foal. The dam was unplaced on her only start and is a half-sister to 4 winners including the useful 2-y-o 6f winner Mr Sandancer and the useful 2-y-o 7f winner Fantasy Island. The second dam, Um Lardaff (by Mill Reef), a winner over 11f and 12f at 3 yrs in France, is a sister to the Derby winner and high-class sire Shirley Heights and a half-sister to the good mare Bempton - dam of the Group 3 winners Mr Pintips and Banket and of the Group 2 winner Gull Nook (herself dam of the smart filly Spring). (Mr Ziad A Galadari).

"More of a three-year-old type than one for this year, but he'll still run this year and he'll be OK".

309. HAYZOOM ★★
b.c. Anabaa – Green Swallow (Green Tune).
March 6. Second foal. 80,000Y. Tattersalls October 2. Andrew Sime. The dam won the Group 3 Prix du Calvados at 2 yrs in France and is a half-sister to 4 winners including the French listed winner and US Grade 2 placed Green Girl. The second dam, Green Sails (by My Swallow), is a placed half-sister to 4 winners. (Ziad A Galadari).

"He had a few issues early on and was very sick so we've had to give him time but he'll get there. He was born to be a sharp two-year-old but he doesn't look it now".

310. SAKILE ★★★
ch.f. Johannesburg – Crooked Wood (Woodman).
April 20. Second foal. The dam, an Irish 2-y-o 7f and 1m winner and subsequently a minor 4-y-o winner in the USA, is a half-sister to 7 winners. The second dam, Crockadore (by Nijinsky), won 7 races in Ireland and the USA including the Grade 2 12f Orchid Handicap and the Grade 3 11f Sheepshead Bay Handicap (both on turf). She is closely related to the Group 3 Flying Five winner Flowing and a half-sister to 9 winners. (C G P Wyatt).

"She's small and is just starting to grow a bit fortunately. She'll be racing over six furlongs in May".

311. SAN JEMINIANO (IRE) ★★★
b.c. Bertolini – Kafayef (Secreto).
April 30. Tenth living foal. 47,000Y. Tattersalls October 2. Andrew Sime. Half-brother to the fairly useful 12f and 13f winner of 3 races Blimey O'Riley (by Kalanisi), to the Italian winner at 2 and 3 yrs and listed-placed Persian Filly (by Persian Bold), the French 2-y-o winner and listed-placed Ascot Dream (by Pennekamp), the fairly useful 2-y-o 7f winner Almaviva (by Grand Lodge), the modest 6f winner Gardrum (by Lycius) and a winner over hurdles by Spinning World. The dam is an unplaced half-sister to 10 winners including 3 stakes winners. The second dam, Sham Street (by Sham), a minor winner of 4 races in the USA, is a sister to the Italian Group 3 winner Stramusc and a half-sister to the dam of the Group 1 July Cup winner and champion sprinter Sakhee's Secret. (Ziad A Galadari).

"He goes along really nicely and I would have thought he'd be racing in May over six furlongs. He's a horse I like and he's very strong".

312. TAHER ★★★
b.c. Zamindar – Waafiah (Anabaa).
February 5. Half-brother to the fairly useful triple 1m winner Jaser and to the modest 6f and subsequent UAE 7f winner Ragad (both by Alhaarth). The dam, second over 7f at 3 yrs on her only start, is a half-sister to several winners including the very useful 1m and hurdles winner

Atlantic Rhapsody. The second dam, First Waltz (by Green Dancer), winner of the Group 1 6f Prix Morny and second in the Cheveley Park Stakes, is a half-sister to the dam of the Prix Lupin second Angel Falls. (Ziad A Galadari).

"He came in late and then took a bit of time to get going but he looks a two-year-old and he looks like making the racecourse around June time. He'll be alright".

313. UNNAMED ★★★★
ch.f. Pivotal – Aunt Pearl (Seattle Slew).
February 15. Twelfth foal. Sister to the fair 2008 2-y-o 7.5f winner Sri Kandi and half-sister to the smart 2-y-o Group 1 1m Gran Criterium and Group 2 7f Futurity Stakes winner Pearl Of Love (by Peintre Celebre), to the useful 7f winner and Group 3 May Hill Stakes second Kalidasa, the fairly useful 6f and 7f (at 2 yrs) and subsequent dual US Grade 3 winner Social Charter (both by Nureyev) and a minor 4-y-o winner in the USA by Sadler's Wells. The dam, a winner at up to 7f in the USA, is a half-sister to 7 winners including the US stakes winner Thunderdome (herself the dam of 2 listed winners). The second dam, Mr P's Girl (by Mr Prospector), won twice in the USA and is a sister to Prospector's Fire (dam of the Group 1 winners Fire The Groom and Dowsing) and a half-sister to the smart US colts Royal And Regal and Regal And Royal. (A W Black).

"She's a really nice filly and I've trained two from this family. I thought she was going to take plenty of time but I think she should be ready by July time and all being well she could be one for the fillies' maiden at the Newmarket July meeting. A lovely mover, she's a filly I like a lot".

314. UNNAMED ★★★★
b.c. Alhaarth – Blushing Barada (Blushing Groom).
February 5. Ninth foal. 95,000Y. Doncaster St Leger. C McCormack. Half-brother to the Group 3 Diomed Stakes winner of 9 races Blythe Knight (by Selkirk), to the quite useful staying winners High Topper (by Wolfhound) and Bid Me Welcome (by Alzao), the fair 9f and 10f winner Bubbling Fun (by Marju), the fair 2-y-o 1m winner Call Of Duty (by Storming Home), the modest 9f and 10f winner Barbirolli (by Machiavellian) and a 2-y-o winner in France by Anabaa. The dam is a placed full or half-sister to 5 winners including the Irish St Leger winner Authaal. The second dam, Galletto (by Nijinsky), was a smart listed Galtres Stakes winner.

"He'd be one of my nicer colts, more of a three-year-old type but he does everything really nicely. He shows that he's more than useful and I couldn't be happier with him. He'll be racing in July".

315. UNNAMED ★★★
ch.c. Monsieur Bond – Bond Shakira (Daggers Drawn).
March 12. Second foal. €20,000Y. Tattersalls Ireland. Allan Bloodlines. Brother to the fair 2008 2-y-o dual 5f winner Fangfoss Girls. The dam, a moderate 5f placed 2-y-o, is a half-sister to the dual winner and listed-placed Doric Charm. The second dam, Cinnamon Lady (by Emarati), a fair 7f winner at 3 yrs, is a half-sister to 5 minor winners.

"He goes along really nice and although he's more of a six furlong horse he'll be out in May. He's one I like a lot, he's not going to win at Royal Ascot but he's a nice horse".

316. UNNAMED ★★★
b.c. Bahamian Bounty – Branston Gem (So Factual).
February 26. Fifth foal. 48,000Y. Doncaster St Leger. Blandford Bloodstock. Half-brother to the modest 5f winner Braille and half-brother to the fair 2-y-o 5f winner The Terrier (by Foxhound). The dam, placed over 5f at 2 yrs, is a half-sister to the dual listed winner Falcon Hill. The second dam, Branston Jewel (by Prince Sabo), a fairly useful 2-y-o dual 5f winner, is a half-sister to 11 winners including the very useful and tough mare Branston Abby, a winner of 24 races at up to 7f including numerous listed events and the Group 2 winner Desert Deer. (The Comic Strip Heroes).

"He's quite sharp and I was trying to get him to Newbury in April but we won't quite make it. He's quite sharp and has done one piece of work already and I like him".

317. UNNAMED ★★
b.c. Selkirk – Epiphany (Zafonic).
February 13. First foal. The dam, a fair 2-y-o 6f winner, is a half-sister to one winner abroad. The second dam, Galette (Caerleon), a fairly useful 12f winner, is a half-sister to 6 winners including the Irish 2,000 Guineas winner Indian Haven, the smart Group 1 Gran Criterium winner Count Dubois and the dam of the Group winners Imperial Stride and High Pitched. (Saleh Al Homaizi).
"He's going to take a little bit of time and is more of a three-year-old type, but he should be running around August time and he's a horse I like".

318. UNNAMED ★★★
ch.c. Selkirk – Harmonist (Hennessy).
February 9. Second foal. 50,000Y. Tattersalls October 1. P Chapple-Hyam. The dam won twice at 3 yrs in the USA and was fourth in a Grade 3 stakes and is a half-sister to 4 winners including the US Grade 2 placed Country Store. The second dam, Geraldine's Store (by Exclusive Native), won 13 races including the Grade 2 Diana Handicap and is a half-sister to the Irish 1,000 Guineas and Coronation Stakes winner Al Bahathri (herself dam of the 2,000 Guineas and Champion Stakes winner Haafhd).
"He's quite sharp for a Selkirk and he could be the first one I've had that wins as a two-year-old. Seven furlongs would be his trip to start off with around July or August time and I like him".

319. UNNAMED ★★★
b.c. Bertolini – Ingeburg
(Hector Protector).
March 19. Fourth foal. 15,000Y. Doncaster St Leger. Blandford Bloodstock. Half-brother to the modest 13f winner Lios Tulcha (by Barathea). The dam won the 2-y-o listed 5.5f Prix la Fleche and is a half-sister to one winner. The second dam, Inchkeith (by Reference Point), a fair 9.4f and 10.2f winner, is a half-sister to 6 winners including the very smart and tough triple Group 3 7f winner Inchinor.
"He could be my first two-year-old runner, he's a nice horse and has done some work already. He goes along well and I can't fault him whatsoever. I like him and he should win early".
TRAINER'S BARGAIN BUY

320. UNNAMED ★★★
b.c. Kyllachy – Lowrianna
(Cyrano de Bergerac).
March 9. Eighth foal. 65,000Y. Tattersalls October 2. C McCormack. Half-brother to the useful and tough listed sprint winner of 5 races and Group 3 placed Simianna (by Bluegrass Prince), to the modest 6f to 7.6f winner of 5 races Bodfari Anna (by Casteddu) and the 5f seller winner Countess Bankes (by Son Pardo). The dam, a moderate 2-y-o 5f winner, is a half-sister to the smart hurdler Grinkov. The second dam, Tallow Hill (by Dunphy), is an unraced half-sister to 4 winners including the Cheveley Park Stakes winner Pass The Peace.
"He's very sharp and he should soon be doing some work. He might win over five furlongs but he'll be better over six I should think. I like him a lot and he's alright actually".

321. UNNAMED ★★★★★
b.c. Acclamation – Milly Fleur
(Primo Dominie).
March 17. Third foal. 130,000Y. Tattersalls October 1. Tony Nerses. Brother to the fairly useful 2-y-o 6f winner and listed-placed Bespoke Boy and half-brother to the unplaced 2008 2-y-o Milly Rose (by Diktat). The dam was a modest 6f winner at 3 yrs. The second dam, My Cadeaux (by Cadeaux Genereux), a fairly useful dual 6f winner, is a half-sister to 5 winners including the Group 2 5f Prix du Gros-Chene winner Millyant, the Group 2 5f Flying Childers Stakes and Group 3 5f Palace House Stakes winner Prince Sabo and the dam of the Gimcrack Stakes winner Abou Zouz. (Saleh Al Homaizi & Imad Al Sagar).
"He goes along really nice and I suppose if I'm going to win the Norfolk Stakes this will be the one. He'd be the best of my two-year-olds, he's done one piece of work and I was really pleased with him. He'll be running in May and I like him a lot. He'll win over five furlongs before going for the Norfolk".

322. UNNAMED ★★★ ♠
b.f. Sadler's Wells – Race The Wild Wind
(Sunny's Halo).
April 21. Tenth foal. Deauville August. €520,000Y. Blandford Bloodstock. Closely related to the very smart 2-y-o Group 3 6f July Stakes and 3-y-o listed 7f winner Meshaheer and to the high-class Group 1 6.5f Prix Maurice de Gheest winner King Charlemagne (both by Nureyev) and half-brother to 3 minor winners in the USA by Dayjur, Forty Niner and Rahy. The dam, winner of the Grade 1 8.5f Santa Maria Handicap and the Grade 2 Fantasy Stakes, is a half-sister to the dam of the US Grade 2 winner Mataji. The second dam, Redpath (by Indian Chief II), is a 2-y-o winning sister to the US stakes winner Bobby Murcer and a half-sister to the US Grade 3 winner and Kentucky Derby third Partez. (A W Black).
"She's had all sorts of problems and I haven't cantered her since January, just to give her plenty of time. But she's a really nice filly and she moves well. More of a three-year-old type but she could be quite nice".

323. UNNAMED ★★
b.c. Oasis Dream – Reasonably Devout
(St Jovite).
February 6. Seventh foal. 34,000Y. Doncaster St Leger. Blandford Bloodstock. Half-brother to the fair 13f to 2m winner of 4 races Atlantic Coast (by In The Wings) and to the modest 10f winner Extra Gold (by Grand Lodge). The dam, a 2-y-o turf winner in the USA, was listed placed and is a half-sister to 2 winners. The second dam, Castilla (by Bold Reason), won the Grade 1 Yellow Ribbon Stakes and four other graded stakes events and is a half-sister to 2 winners.
"He needs to grow a bit because he's quite small, so I've given him time and all being well he should be running in May time. I haven't cantered him enough yet to assess his ability".

324. UNNAMED ★★★
b.c. Red Ransom – Rise (Polar Falcon).
March 14. Second foal. 48,000Y. Doncaster St Leger. Frank Barry. Half-brother to the unplaced 2008 2-y-o Join Up (by Green Desert). The dam won 3 races from 6f to 7f at 2 and 3 yrs and is a half-sister to 4 winners including the smart 6f winner Feet So Fast and the Group 2 Lowther Stakes winner Soar. The second dam, Splice (by Sharpo), a smart winner of 7 races including the listed 6f Abernant Stakes, is a full or half-sister to 7 winners.
"He'll be one of the sharper ones. I think he'll win over five furlongs but he'll be better over six. I couldn't be happier with him and he could be quite decent".

325. UNNAMED ★★★★
b.c. Street Cry – Saint Boom
(Saint Ballado).
April 29. Fourth foal. 55,000Y. Tattersalls October 2. C McCormack. The dam is an unplaced half-sister to 2 winners. The second dam, Miner League (by Cherokee Colony), is an unplaced half-sister to 5 winners including the US Grade 2 winner Star Of Broadway. (Mrs Violet Mercer).
"He's never stopped growing but he's a lovely, big, strong horse and I like him a lot. He'll be alright from August onwards and he'd be one of my picks".

326. UNNAMED ★★★★ ♠
b.c. Red Ransom – Sophielu
(Rudimentary).
March 20. Fourth foal. 67,000Y. Doncaster St Leger. Blandford Bloodstock. Half-brother to the modest 1m winner Sophie's Dream (by Averti). The dam, a quite useful 3-y-o 7f winner, is a half-sister to 8 winners including the very useful 8.2f (at 2 yrs) and subsequent US stakes winner and Group 1 Italian Oaks second Attitre, the useful 3-y-o 7f and 1m winner and listed placed Alpenglow and the minor US stakes winner Silca Key Service. The second dam, Aquaglow (by Caerleon), a quite useful 7f and 1m winner, is a half-sister to 11 winners. (A W Black).
"I think he's got more ability than my other Red Ransom and he goes along really well. There are no problems at all with him, he'll be better over six furlongs than five and will make a better three-year-old but he's quite useful".

327. UNNAMED ★★★
ch.c. Kyllachy – Tatora (Selkirk).
April 24. Fifth foal. Brother to the Group 2 Betfair Cup and Group 3 Jersey Stakes winner Tariq. The dam is an unraced half-sister to 3 winners and to the placed dam of the Group 2 Flying Childers Stakes winner Wi Dud. The second dam, Tatouma (by The Minstrel), won twice at 2 yrs and is a half-sister to 4 winners. (Saleh Al Homaizi & Imad Al Sagar).

"He's a bit like his full brother Tariq in that he was a very slow to come to hand but he's getting there now and improving every week. So he might not be that backward. We'll try and get him out in May to see if he's good enough for Royal Ascot but to be honest I don't think he's that precocious and we might be better waiting for seven furlongs. The whole family look very similar but I don't he's quite got Tariq's ability".

328. UNNAMED ★★★ ♠
b.c. Firebreak – Yanomami (Slew O'Gold).
March 16. Eighth foal. 32,000Y. Doncaster St Leger. Blandford Bloodstock. Half-brother to the fairly useful 5f (at 2 yrs) and 6f winner of 7 races Mirasol Princess (by Ali-Royal), to the fair 6f and 7f winner (including at 2 yrs) Fractured Foxy (by Foxhound), the modest 6f and 7f winner Epitomise (by Mind Games) and the 2-y-o 5f seller winner Yarrita (by Tragic Role). The dam, a fair 3-y-o 6f winner, is a half-sister to 6 minor winners here and abroad. The second dam, Sunerta (by Roberto), won once at 2 yrs and is a half-sister to 8 winners including the champion US older horse Bates Motel, the Grade 1 winner Hatim and the Horris Hill Stakes winner Super Asset.

"I did his first bit of work on the all-weather the other day and he totally surprised me because previously he hadn't done much. He did really well and he could be more than useful. Six furlongs should suit him and he may not be a superstar but he's a nice horse".

329. UNNAMED ★★★
ch.c. Mr Greeley – Zabadani (Zafonic).
January 20. First foal. 135,000Y. Tattersalls October 1. C McCormack. The dam ran unplaced twice and is a half-sister to 6 winners including the Group 2 Prix Eugene Adam and Group 3 Prix La Force winner Radevore. The second dam, Bloudan (by Damascus), is an unraced half-sister to the Irish 1,000 Guineas and Coronation Stakes winner Al Bahathri (dam of the 2,000 Guineas and Champion Stakes winner Haafhd).

"He's huge, as Mr Greeley's normally are, so he'll be a back-end two-year-old. But he's really nice, he moves like a bird and I couldn't be happier with him".

ROGER CHARLTON

330. CENTURIO ★★
b.c. Pivotal – Grain Of Gold
(Mr Prospector).
March 30. Fourth foal. 90,000Y. Tattersalls October 1. Blandford Bloodstock. Half-brother to Golden Eagle (by Montjeu), unplaced in one start at 2 yrs in 2008 and to the quite useful dual 9f winner Gold Prospect (by Rainbow Quest). The dam, a fair 10.2f winner, is closely related to the smart 7f (at 2 yrs) and Group 3 10.5f Prix Fille de l'Air winner Goncharova. The second dam, Pure Grain (by Polish Precedent), won 5 races including the Group 1 12f Irish Oaks and the Group 1 12f Yorkshire Oaks and is a half-sister to 7 winners. (B E Nielsen).

"A very immature and rather leggy colt and we won't be seeing him until September time".

331. CLAYTON FLICK (IRE) ★★★
b.c. Kheleyf – Mambodorga
(Kingmambo).
May 9. Fourth foal. 33,000Y. Tattersalls December. Angie Sykes. Half-brother to the quite useful 5f and 6f winner (including at 2 yrs) Mambo Spirit (by Invincible Spirit). The dam is an unplaced half-sister to 11 winners including the French Group 2 and US Grade 2 winner Spring Star. The second dam, L'Irlandaise (by Irish River), won the listed Prix de Honfleur and is a half-sister to 2 winners. (Findlay & Bloom).

"He's done well since he was bought and he's a neat horse – typical of his sire. Hopefully he'll run by the end of May".

332. DIZZINESS ★★★
b.f. *Stormy Atlantic – Danzante (Danzig)*.
March 30. Tenth foal. Half-sister to the US Grade 1 9.5f Eddie Read Handicap winner Monzante (by Maria's Mon), to the useful French 2-y-o 7f winner Alpha Plus (by Mr Prospector), the fairly useful 2-y-o triple 5f winner and listed-placed Tentative (by Distant View), the 10f winner Roman Villa (by Chester House), the 7f winner Dance West (by Gone West) and the 2-y-o 5f winner Forante (by Forty Niner) – all quite useful. The dam, a sprint winner in France and in the USA, is a half-sister to the Breeders' Cup Classic winner Skywalker and to the French Group 3 7f winner Nidd. The second dam, Bold Captive (by Boldnesian), was a sprinter. (Khalid Abdulla).
"Quite an attractive filly, she should be a two-year-old and I see her as a six furlong type".

333. ELENORE ★★
b.f. *Rock Of Gibraltar – Top Forty (Rainbow Quest)*.
March 20. Second foal. 38,000Y. Tattersalls October 1. Not sold. The dam is an unraced half-sister to 5 winners including the French listed winner and triple Group 3 placed Self Defense. The second dam, Dansara (by Dancing Brave), is an unraced half-sister to 10 winners including the Irish Oaks winner Princess Pati and the Great Voltigeur Stakes winner Seymour Hicks. (Mr David Hardisty).
"A deep, strong filly, there's a lot of stamina in her pedigree and I should think she'll come along later in the year".

334. HUMIDOR (IRE) ★★★♠
b.c. *Camacho – Miss Indigo (Indian Ridge)*.
May 1. Fifth foal. 14,000Y. Tattersalls October 2. A Skiffington. Half-brother to the modest triple 12f winner Bluebell Ridge (by Distant Music) and to the moderate 5f winner Mickleberry (by Desert Style). The dam is a placed half-sister to 7 winners including the useful listed 10f Pretty Polly Stakes winner and Oaks fourth Musetta. The second dam, Monaiya (by Shareef Dancer), a French 7.5f and 1m winner, is a full or half-sister to 8 winners including the Canadian Grade 2 winner Vanderlin.
"A May foal, he's grown quite a lot since the sales and been troubled by a splint recently. He's an attractive horse and hopefully he'll be running in July".

335. KNOCKDOLIAN (IRE) ★★
b.c. *Montjeu – Doula (Gone West)*.
February 4. Fourth reported foal. Half-sister to the useful dual 7f (at 2 yrs) to 10f winner of 4 races Humungous (by Giant's Causeway) and to a minor 12f winner in France by Grand Lodge. The dam, a minor US 3-y-o turf winner, is a half-sister to the US Grade 2 winner sprint Cat Chat. The second dam, Phone Chatter (by Phone Trick), won 2 Grade 1 events in the USA and is a half-sister to 4 winners. (Lady R Wellesley).
"A big, scopey horse and typical of his sire, he won't seeing a racecourse until the end of the year".

336. LOVE MATCH ★★★★
b.f. *Danehill Dancer – Name Of Love (Petardia)*.
April 6. Half-sister to the US Grade 3 8.5f placed Perilous Pursuit and the fair all-weather 9.5f winner Almavara (both by Fusaichi Pegasus). The dam, a very useful 2-y-o Group 3 7f Rockfel Stakes and listed 7f Oh So Sharp Stakes winner, is a half-sister to 3 winners including the useful 7f winner (at 2 yrs) and 9f listed placed Annapurna. The second dam, National Ballet (by Shareef Dancer), is an unraced half-sister to 7 winners including the listed winners Broken Wave, Guarde Royale, Clifton Chapel and Saxon Maid. (Lady Rothschild).
"Very typical of the sire, this is a nice filly that looks a bit sharper than the other members of the family. I think she'll have the speed to begin over six furlongs from June onwards".

337. OLYMPIC MEDAL
b.f. *Nayef – Trying For Gold (Northern Baby)*.
April 9. Sister to the quite useful 2-y-o 1m winner Trianon and half-sister to the smart Group 2 12f Ribblesdale Stakes and Group 2 13.3f Geoffrey Freer Stakes winner Phantom Gold (herself dam of the Oaks second Flight Of

Fancy), the useful 10f listed winner Fictitious (by Machiavellian), the fairly useful 2-y-o 1m winner Tempting Prospect (by Shirley Heights) and the quite useful 10f winner Day Of Reckoning (by Daylami). The dam was a useful 12f and 12.5f winner at 3 yrs. The second dam, Expansive (by Exbury), won the Ribblesdale Stakes and is a sister to the Park Hill Stakes winner Example. (The Queen).

338. PERSONA NON GRATA (IRE) ★★
b.c. Azamour – Private Life (Bering).
March 16. Half-brother to the 7f (at 2 yrs) and dual German Group 3 10f winner Persian Storm (by Monsun). The dam won over 1m (at 2 yrs) and 12f and was listed-placed twice in France and is a half-sister to the French listed winner Parisienne. The second dam, Poughkeepsie (by Sadler's Wells), won once at 3 yrs in France and is a daughter of the King George and Oaks winner Pawneese. (B E Nielsen).
"A backward, tall horse and one for the autumn".

339. POLYPHEMUS (USA) ★★
ch.c. Giant's Causeway – Aqaarid (Nashwan).
March 11. Eighth foal. Half-brother to the quite useful 2-y-o 1m winner Elmonjed (by Gulch) and the to fair 7f winner Ladeena (by Dubai Millennium). The dam, a smart winner of the Group 1 Fillies Mile and the Group 3 7.3f Fred Darling Stakes, was second in the 1,000 Guineas and is a half-sister to 2 winners. The second dam, Ashayer (by Lomond), won the Group 1 1m Prix Marcel Boussac and the Group 3 10f Prix de Psyche. (B E Nielsen).
"A small horse, he's been troubled by splints but nonetheless he could come to hand by mid-season".

340. PORT OF TYNE ★★
b.c. Rock Of Gibraltar – Susun Kelapa (St Jovite).
February 14. Half-brother to the fairly useful 9f and 10f winner Military Power (by Dubai Destination), to the fair Irish 7f winner Monsusu (by Montjeu), the modest 5f winner Royal Composer (by Mozart) and the 1m seller winner Non Ultra (by Peintre Celebre). The dam won 2 races, over 7.8f (at 2 yrs) and 9f and is a half-sister to the US stakes winner Lac Dessert. The second dam, Tiramisu (by Roberto), a minor French 3-y-o winner, is a half-sister to the dam of the French 2,000 Guineas winner Green Tune and the Cheveley Park Stakes winner Pas de Reponse. (Mr P Hearson).
"A very backward horse and he's another one for just a couple of runs in the autumn".

341. SHIMANISHIKI ★★
ch.f. Shamardal – Tree Peony (Woodman).
February 11. Third foal. 38,000Y. Tattersalls October 2. Not sold. Half-sister to Molly The Witch (by Rock Of Gibraltar), unplaced in 2 starts at 2 yrs in 2008. The dam, a fair 3-y-o 7f winner, is a half-sister to 5 winners including the Group 3 placed Evening World. The second dam, Pivoine (by Nureyev), is an unraced half-sister to 7 winners including the dam of Peintre Celebre. (Mr A E Oppenheimer).
"Only just arrived, she's big and backward and I can't assess her as yet".

342. SPOKEN ★★★
ch.c. Medicean – Spout (Salse).
May 18. Third foal. Half-brother to the quite useful 12f winner Shout (by Halling), to the quite useful dual 12f and jumps winner Sea Wall (by Giant's Causeway) and the fair 11f and hurdles winner Reservoir (by Green Desert). The dam was a very smart winner of the Group 3 12f John Porter Stakes and the Group 3 Lancashire Oaks and is a half-sister to numerous winners including the French listed winner Mon Domino and the smart middle-distance performers Aldwych and Dombey. The second dam, Arderelle (by Pharly), a quite useful 3-y-o 10f winner, is a half-sister to 8 winners including the Group 2 Prix Greffulhe winner Arokar, the French listed winners Attirance and La Tirana and the dam of the Group 2 Derrinstown Stud Derby Trial winner Anvari. (Lady Rothschild).
"Probably a neater and more precocious horse than the dam has produced before. He's a May foal but he shows a bit of speed and I quite like him".

343. THEREAFTER (USA) ★★
ch.f. Lion Heart – Alvernia (Alydar).
February 16. Half-sister to the useful 9f and 10f winner and subsequent US Grade 2 placed Exterior (by Distant View), to the useful 10.5f listed winner of 5 races Acrobatic (by Storm Boot), the fairly useful listed-placed 1m winner Verbose (by Storm Bird) and the French 10f and 12f winner Safari Journey (by Johannesburg). The dam, a winner over 8.5f and 9f in the USA, is a half-sister to 5 winners and to the dam of the French 1,000 Guineas and US Grade 1 winner Matiara. The second dam, Miss Summer (by Luthier), won the listed 1m Prix de Saint-Cyr and is a half-sister to the Group 2 Prix Hocquart winner Mot d'Or, the Group 1 Gran Premio de Milano winner Lydian, the Group 2 Ribblesdale Stakes winner Ballinderry (herself the dam of Sanglamore) and the French 2,000 Guineas second Sharpman. (Khalid Abdulla).
"An attractive, nice filly and the stallion is doing well. She looks a filly for the second half of the year".

344. THE KIDNAPPER ★★
b.c. Red Ransom – Dolma (Marchand de Sable).
March 1. First foal. The dam won 6 races in France over 6f and 7f, including three listed events and was third in the Group 1 6.5f Prix Maurice de Gheest. The second dam, Young Manila (by Manila), was listed placed over 10f.
"A very small colt, about 14.2, he'll be out early and might be worth mentioning in the book".

345. TIGER BRIGHT ★★★
b.f. Seeking The Gold – Desert Tigress (Storm Cat).
April 8. First foal. The dam, a fair Irish 2-y-o 5f winner, is a sister to the 2-y-o Group 3 7f Horris Hill Stakes winner Hurricane Cat. The second dam, Sky Beauty (by Blushing Groom), a winner of nine Grade 1 events in the USA, is a half-sister to the quite useful 2-y-o 1m winner Ajayib. The second dam, Maplejinksy (by Nijinsky), won two Grade 1 events in the USA and is closely related to the brilliant sprinter Dayjur. (Lady Rothschild).
"A strong, good-topped filly with plenty of speed in her pedigree. She ought to make a two-year-old".

346. TOO PUTRA (IRE) ★★
b.c. Oratorio – Urgent Liaison (High Estate).
April 7. Seventh foal. 100,000Y. Tattersalls October 2. Charlie Gordon-Watson. Closely related to the fairly useful 10f winner and listed third Imoya (by Desert King) and half-brother to the fairly useful 12.3f winner Qudraat (by In The Wings) and the South African winner at 3 and 4 yrs Jahazi (by Green Desert). The dam is an unraced half-sister to 5 winners including the very smart Group 2 9f Budweiser International Stakes winner Great Dane. The second dam, Itching (by Thatching), is an unraced half-sister to 7 winners including the dual Group 1 winner Croco Rouge and Alidiva (dam of the Group 1 winners Sleepytime, Ali Royal and Taipan). (HRH Sultan Ahmad Shah).
"He's immature but he seems quite a nice colt for the second half of the year".

347. VISUAL ELEMENT (USA) ★★★
gr.f. Distant View – Kinetic Force (Holy Bull).
May 1. Half-sister to the smart listed 1m winner and Group 3 placed Enforce (by Kalanisi), to the fair 2-y-o 1m winner Sand Fairy (by Desert King). The dam was placed over 6f at 2 yrs in France and is a half-sister to numerous winners including the US Grade 1 7f winner Mizzen Mast. (Khalid Abdulla).
"Quite attractive, but a May foal and a rather big filly, she needs time".

348. WALCOT SQUARE (IRE) ★★★★♠
b.c. Marju – Lyrical Dance (Lear Fan).
February 7. Eighth foal. 70,000Y. Tattersalls October 2. Kern/Lillingston. Half-brother to the fairly useful 7f and 1m winner Furnace (by Green Desert), to the minor US stakes-placed winner of 3 races Jaha (by Diesis), the fair Irish 6f winner Lightwood Lady (by Anabaa) and the modest 1m winner Reballo (by King's Best). The dam, a minor winner at 4 yrs in the USA, is a sister to the French listed 10.5f winner Shaal and a half-sister to the Group/Grade 1 winners Black Minnaloushe, Pennekamp and Nasr El Arab and

the placed dam of the US dual Grade 1 winner Round Pond. The second dam, Coral Dance (by Green Dancer), was a very useful winner at up to 1m in France and the USA and was second in the Group 1 Prix Marcel Boussac. (De La Warr Racing).
"I like him – he's a neat, strong, well-made horse and a good mover. He could be out in May".

349. YABTREE (IRE) ★★★
b.c. Clodovil – Lorientaise (Xaar).
March 29. First foal. 52,000Y. Tattersalls October 2. Amanda Skiffington. The dam, placed once at 3 yrs in France, is a half-sister to 7 winners including the Group 3 Prix de Saint-Georges winner Pont-Aven (herself dam of the Group 2 winners Josr Algarhoud and Sainte Marine). The second dam, Basilea (by Frere Basile), is a placed half-sister to 7 winners. (J D Wolfensohn).
"A cheeky horse, he's been coughing and I haven't been able to do much with him, but he ought to make a two-year-old in May or June".

350. UNNAMED ★★
b.c. Dansili – Chaffinch (Lear Fan).
March 5. The dam, a quite useful 1m and 12f winner, is a half-sister to the useful 7f and subsequent US Grade 1 Yellow Ribbon Handicap winner Spanish Fern, to the fairly useful 2-y-o 1m winner Woodwardia and the useful triple 6f winner Dayville. The second dam, Chain Fern (by Blushing Groom), is an unraced sister to the Irish 1,000 Guineas and Coronation Stakes winner Al Bahathri and a half-sister to Geraldine's Store, an American stakes-winning filly at up to 10f. (Khalid Abdulla).
"Rather a weak and cheeky horse at the moment, I don't know a lot about him but he'll probably be a seven furlong two-year-old".

351. UNNAMED ★★★
b.f. Avonbridge – Jalissa (Mister Baileys).
January 28. First foal. 18,500foal. Tattersalls December. BBA (Ire). The dam, a quite useful 6f winner, is a half-sister to 3 winners including the smart 7f (at 2 yrs) to 10f winner of 7 races Vintage Premium. The second dam, Julia Domna (by Dominion), is an unplaced half-sister to the Hungerford Stakes winner Norwich.
"I trained the mare and this filly looks very much like the sire, Avonbridge. She looks to have a very nice temperament but she hasn't been here long".

352. UNNAMED ★★★
b.f. Oasis Dream – Marani (Ashkalani).
March 29. The dam, a useful 9f and listed 12f winner, is a half-sister to the useful French 2-y-o 1m winner Aquarelle. The second dam, Aquamarine (by Shardari), won the listed Cheshire Oaks and is a half-sister to the St Leger winner Toulon. (Khalid Abdulla).
"A small, typical Oasis Dream filly, she ought to be speedy even though the dam had stamina".

353. UNNAMED ★★
ch.f. Observatory – Quandary (Blushing Groom).
March 7. Half-sister to the useful listed 10.5f winner Double Crossed (by Caerleon), to the quite useful dual 12f and hurdles winner Political Intrigue (by Dansili), the quite useful 12f winner Clepsydra (by Sadler's Wells) and the fair 2m and hurdles winner Hue (by Peintre Celebre). The dam, a useful winner of 4 races from 9f to 10f including the listed James Seymour Stakes at Newmarket, is a half-sister to the high-class filly All At Sea (winner of the Group 1 Prix du Moulin and second in the Oaks and the Juddmonte International) and to the Free Handicap winner Over The Ocean. The second dam, Lost Virtue (by Cloudy Dawn), an unraced half-sister to the US Grade 2 Shuvee Handicap winner Anti-Lib, is out of a half-sister to Damascus. (Khalid Abdulla).
"A small, plain filly".

354. UNNAMED ★★
b.c. Motivator – Strike Lightly (Rainbow Quest).
February 2. Second foal. The dam is an unraced sister to the very smart middle-distance winner Ulundi and the French winner and Group 1 Prix Saint-Alary second Fleeting Glimpse (herself dam of the Group 3 May Hill Stakes winner Half Glance) and a half-sister to the 1,000 Guineas

winner Wince (dam of the Group 1 Yorkshire Oaks winner Quiff). The second dam, Flit (by Lyphard), a fair 3-y-o 10f winner, is a sister to the US Grade 2 winner Skimble (dam of the US Grade 1 winner Skimming) and closely related to the Grade 1 Washington Lassie Stakes winner Contredance and to the dam of the Lanson Champagne Stakes winner Eltish. (Khalid Abdulla).

"He hasn't been here very long and I don't know a lot about him, but keeping him sound may be an issue".

355. UNNAMED ★★★★
b.c. Dansili – Tantina (Distant View).
March 9. Third foal. Half-brother to the very smart 2008 2-y-o 1m winner and Group 2 1m Royal Lodge Stakes second and 2009 Greenham Stakes second Cityscape (by Selkirk) and to the useful triple 1m winner Scuffle (by Daylami). The dam, a smart winner of 4 races including two listed events over 7f, was Group 3 placed and is a half-sister to 2 winners. The second dam, Didina (by Nashwan), a winner over 6f at 2 yrs here, subsequently won the Grade 2 8.5f Dahlia Handicap in the USA and is a sister to one winner and a half-sister to 4 winners including the French listed 10f winner Espionage. (Khalid Abdulla).

"A very strong horse, I thought he was going to come to hand soon but he's growing and he's quite a heavy colt that will need a bit of time. He'll make up into quite a nice horse later on".

356. UNNAMED ★★★
gr.c. With Approval – Widescreen (Distant View).
March 25. Fifth foal. The dam is an unraced half-sister to the champion 2-y-o and 3-y-o Zafonic, winner of the 2,000 Guineas, the Dewhurst Stakes, the Prix de la Salamandre and the Prix Morny and to the smart Group 3 6f Prix de Cabourg winner Zamindar. The second dam, Zaizafon (by The Minstrel), won twice over 7f at 2 yrs and was placed in the Group 1 1m Queen Elizabeth II Stakes and the Group 3 1m Child Stakes. She is a half-sister to the unraced Modena, herself dam of the Eclipse Stakes and Phoenix Champion Stakes winner Elmaamul. (Khalid Abdulla).

"A small, quite athletic horse that could come to hand over six furlongs".

PAUL COLE

357. BANANA REPUBLIC (IRE) ★★★
ch.c. Danehill Dancer – Elite Guest (Be My Guest).
March 1. Tenth foal. €60,000Y. Goffs Million. Paul Cole. Brother to the 2008 Irish 5f and 7f placed 2-y-o Coat Of Arms, closely related to the 2005 Group 3 6.3f Anglesey Stakes winner Amigoni and to the Irish 2-y-o 5f listed and 3-y-o 7f listed winner Newton (both by Danehill) and half-brother to the French 9f (at 2 yrs) to 10.5f winner of 5 races and Group 2 placed Hesiode, the minor French winner of 5 races Bazbine (both by Highest Honor). The dam, a French 3-y-o winner and third in the Group 3 10.5f Prix de Royaumont, is a sister to Admire Lapis (a winner of 6 races in Japan) and a half-sister to 8 winners including the smart Group 3 2m Jockey Club Cup winner Capal Garmon. The second dam, Elevate (by Ela Mana Mou), a fairly useful dual 3-y-o 12f winner, was listed placed and is a half-sister to the top-class winners Sun Princess and Saddlers Hall. (J D Manley).

358. FANTASTIC PRINCE ★★★
ch.c. Cadeaux Genereux – Fantaisiste (Nashwan).
February 20. First foal. 50,000Y. Tattersalls October 1. Oliver Cole. The dam, a quite useful triple 6f all-weather winner (including at 2 yrs), is a half-sister to 2 winners. The second dam, Fantastic Belle (by Night Shift), a quite useful 6f winner, is a half-sister to 10 winners including the smart Group 3 10f Gordon Richards Stakes winner Germano, the listed 1m Prix de Saint-Cyr winner Fantastic Bid, the Canadian Grade 2 winner Moon Solitaire and the US stakes winner Fantastic Don. (Miss A Shaykhutdinova).

359. FERRIS WHEEL (IRE) ★★
b.f. Harlan's Holiday – Saraa Ree (Caro).
May 1. Half-sister to Chic Retreat (by Elusive

Quality), unplaced in 2 starts at 2 yrs in 2008, to the 2-y-o 6f to 1m winner and subsequent US Grade 1 Eddie Read Handicap winner Sarafan (by Lear Fan), the very useful 1m to 12f and dual listed winner Hagwah (by Dancing Brave), the quite useful 10f winner Swains Bridge (by Swain) and the fair 1m all-weather winner Shanghai Crab (by Manila). The dam, a useful 7f winner, is a half-sister to 3 winners. The second dam, Star River (by Riverman), won twice in France and is a sister to the top-class miler and sire Irish River. (Mr & Mrs C Wright).

360. GRAND MARY (IRE) ★★★
ch.f. *Kyllachy – Magic Sister (Cadeaux Genereux)*.
April 27. Fourth foal. 88,000Y. Tattersalls October 1. P Cole. Half-sister to the very smart listed 1m (at 2 yrs) and Group 1 1m Falmouth Stakes winner Rajeem (by Diktat). The dam, a modest 3-y-o 7f placed maiden, is a sister to the very smart 2-y-o Group 1 6f Prix Morny and Group 3 5f Molecomb Stakes winner Hoh Magic and a half-sister to 5 winners. The second dam, Gunner's Belle (by Gunner B), a modest 7f and 10f winner, is a half-sister to 8 winners including the very smart Group 2 Prince Of Wales's Stakes winner Crimson Beau. (Mrs F H Hay).

361. ISHTAR GATE (USA) ★★★
b.br.c. *Gone West – Sometime (Royal Academy)*.
March 30. Sixth foal. $230,000Y. Keeneland September. Hugo Merry. Half-brother to the Group 3 10.3f Dee Stakes winner Art Deco (by Peintre Celebre), to the very useful 7f (at 2 yrs) and listed 11f winner Manyana (by Alzao) and the fairly useful Irish 10f and 11f winner Vincenzio Galilei (by Galileo). The dam is an unraced sister to the 1,000 Guineas winner Sleepytime and the Group 1 1m Sussex Stakes winner Ali Royal and a half-sister to the Group 1 12f Europa Preis and Group 1 10f Premio Roma winner Taipan. The second dam, Alidiva (by Chief Singer), a useful listed winner of 3 races from 6f to 1m, is a half-sister to 6 winners including the dual Group 1 winner Croco Rouge. (Mr D S Lee).

362. KATE SKATE ★★★
ch.f. *Mark Of Esteem – Saristar (Starborough)*.
April 14. First foal. The dam, a fairly useful 5f (at 2 yrs) and dual 6f winner, is a half-sister to the fairly useful 2-y-o 6f and 1m winner Genari. The second dam, Sari (by Faustus), a quite useful 7f winner of 2 races (including at 2 yrs), is a half-sister to one winner. (R A Instone).

363. KYDATEE KILT ★★★
ch.c. *Kyllachy – Oatey (Master Willie)*.
April 12. Seventh living foal. 30,000Y. Doncaster St Leger. P Cole. Half-brother to the fair 2008 2-y-o dual 6f winner Spiritual Art (by Invincible Spirit), to the quite useful 2-y-o 5f winner Alternative (by Dr Fong) and the modest dual 1m winner Jomus (by Soviet Star). The dam, a modest dual 5f winner at 3 yrs, is a half-sister to 10 winners including the smart Group 3 Lingfield Derby Trial winner Munwar and the smart Irish middle-distance listed winner Hateel. The second dam, Oatfield (by Great Nephew), was placed at 2 yrs. (Mrs J M Haynes).

364. MISTIC MAGIC (IRE) ★★★
b.f. *Orpen – Mistic Sun (Dashing Blade)*.
April 12. Second foal. 45,000Y. Tattersalls October 3. P Cole. The dam, a listed-placed winner of 3 races from 2 to 5 yrs in Germany, is a half-sister to 5 winners. The second dam, Malatesta (by Persian Heights), a listed-placed winner in Germany, is a half-sister to 2 winners. (Mr S D Fisher).

365. NERVES OF STEEL (IRE) ★★★
b.c. *Oratorio – Spirit Of Tara (Sadler's Wells)*.
April 9. Eighth foal. €300,000Y. Goffs Million. Paul Cole. Half-brother to the high-class Group 2 1m and Group 3 1m and 9f winner Echo Of Light (by Dubai Millennium), the smart dual 12f listed winner Akarem and the Irish 3-y-o 1m and 9f winner and listed-placed Multazem (both by Kingmambo). The dam, a 12f winner at Galway and second in the Group 2 Blandford Stakes, is a sister to 3 winners including the 1,000 Guineas, Oaks, Irish Derby and Prix Vermeille winner Salsabil and a half-sister to 8

winners including the Group 1 St James's Palace Stakes winner Marju. The second dam, Flame Of Tara (by Artaius), won the Coronation Stakes. (Mrs F H Hay).

366. ORION THE HUNTER ★★★★
ch.c. Starcraft – Miss Universe (Warning).
April 12. Sixth living foal. 90,000Y. Tattersalls October 1. Not sold. Half-brother to the high-class 2008 2-y-o 6f, 7f and Grade 1 1m Breeders Cup Juvenile winner Donativum, to the useful 2-y-o 7f winner Tasdeed (both by Cadeaux Genereux), the 2-y-o 8.6f and subsequent dual US Grade 3 winner Worldly (by Selkirk), the fairly useful 8.3f, 10f and hurdles winner Day To Remember (by Daylami) and the quite useful 2-y-o 1m winner and listed-placed Comeback Queen (by Nayef). The dam, a useful 2-y-o 6f winner and third in the Group 3 Solario Stakes, is a half-sister to 5 winners including the useful German 7f (at 2 yrs) to 11f winner Silver Sign. The second dam, Reine d'Beaute (by Caerleon), a fairly useful 1m and 9f winner on her only starts, is a half-sister to 8 winners including the Group 3 May Hill Stakes winner Intimate Guest. (Mr & Mrs C Wright & The Hon Mrs J M Corbett).

367. PINK SYMPHONY ★★★★
b.f. Montjeu – Blue Symphony (Darshaan).
February 17. Third foal. 400,000Y. Tattersalls October 1. P Cole. Closely related to the very smart 2008 2-y-o Group 3 7f Prestige Stakes winner and 2009 Group 3 Nell Gwyn Stakes winner Fantasia (by Sadler's Wells) and half-sister to the fair 2-y-o 7f winner Blue Rhapsody (by Cape Cross). The dam, a fair 10f winner, is a half-sister to one winner. The second dam, Blue Duster (by Danzig), winner of the Group 1 6f Cheveley Park Stakes and the Group 3 5f Queen Mary Stakes, is a sister to the smart Group 1 6f Middle Park Stakes and Group 2 7f Challenge Stakes winner Zieten and a half-sister to 9 winners. (Mrs F H Hay).

368. RED AVALANCHE (IRE) ★★
gr.c. Verglas – Maura's Guest (Be My Guest).
March 9. Thirteenth foal. €45,000Y. Goffs Million. Paul Cole. Half-brother to the Irish 2-y-o listed 7f Debutante Stakes winner Rainbows For All, to the 6f and 7f winner and US Grade 3 placed Ray Of Sunshine, the Irish 7f (at 2 yrs) to 9f and hurdles winner Always Rainbows (all fairly useful and by Rainbows For Life), the modest 2-y-o 7f winner Rainbows Guest (by Indian Lodge) and 2 minor winners abroad by High Estate and Bob Back. The dam is an unraced half-sister to 7 winners including the Italian Group winners Conte Grimaldi and Bold Apparel. The second dam, Gay Apparel (by Up Spirits), was a stakes winner and Grade 1 placed in Canada. (Mr P de Cameret).

369. STATE FAIR ★★★★
b.c. Marju – Baralinka (Barathea).
February 20. The dam, a useful 5f (at 2 yrs) and triple 6f winner, is a half-sister to the Group 1 Fillies Mile, Falmouth Stakes, Sussex Stakes and Matron Stakes winner Soviet Song (by Marju). The second dam, Kalinka (by Soviet Star), a quite useful 2-y-o 7f winner, is a half-sister to 2 winners. (Elite Racing Club).

370. TIOMAN TWO ★★★
b.c. Red Ransom – Whole Grain (Polish Precedent).
January 24. First foal. 95,000Y. Tattersalls October 2. Charlie Gordon-Watson. The dam was last of 3 runners twice over 12f and 2m in France but is a sister to 2 winners including Pure Grain, winner of the Group 3 7f Prestige Stakes at 2 yrs and the Group 1 12f Irish Oaks and Group 1 12f Yorkshire Oaks at 3 yrs, and a half-sister to 6 winners. The second dam, Mill Line (by Mill Reef), a fair 14.6f winner at 3 yrs, is a half-sister to 6 winners. (HRH Sultan Ahmad Shah).

371. VELVET BAND ★★★
gr.f. Verglas – Applaud (Rahy).
February 12. Half-sister to the fairly useful listed 1m Masaka Stakes winner Jazz Jam (by Pivotal), to the quite useful 2-y-o 5f winner Reebal (by Danehill), the minor US winner of 8 races Pagliacci (by Gone West) and the minor French 3-y-o winner Framboise (by Diesis). The dam, a

smart 2-y-o winner of the Group 2 6f Cherry Hinton Stakes, is a sister to the useful 2-y-o 7f winner Houston Time and a half-sister to 4 winners including the listed winner Sauterne. The second dam, Band (by Northern Dancer), is a placed half-sister to 5 winners including the US Grade 3 9f New Orleans Handicap winner Festive. (Faisal Salman).

372. UNNAMED ★★★
b.c. Sadler's Wells – Frappe (Inchinor).
March 6. Seventh foal. 175,000Y. Tattersalls October 1. Charlie Gordon-Watson. Half-brother to Arabian Flame (by King's Best), placed twice over 7f on both his starts at 2 yrs in 2008, to the 7f (at 2 yrs) and Group 2 12f Ribblesdale Stakes winner Thakafaat (by Unfuwain), the fairly useful 10f winner Quantum (by Alhaarth) and the quite useful 2-y-o 7f all-weather winner Applauded (by Royal Applause). The dam, a fairly useful 2-y-o 6f winner, is a half-sister to the 2,000 Guineas winner Footstepsinthesand. The second dam, Glatisant (by Rainbow Quest), winner of the Group 3 7f Prestige Stakes, is a half-sister to 8 winners and to the placed dam of the very smart 2-y-o Superstar Leo. (HRH Sultan Ahmad Shah).

LUCA CUMANI
373. AFSARE ★★★
b.c. Dubawi – Jumaireyah (Fairy King).
April 15. Half-brother to the useful 8.6f to 10.4f winner and listed placed Reem Three (by Mark Of Esteem) and to the modest 12f and 14f winner Trip The Light (by Fantastic Light). The dam, a fairly useful 8.3f (at 2 yrs) and 10.3f winner, is a half-sister to numerous winners including the useful 10f to 14f winner Lost Soldier Three and the useful 10.5f and 12f winner Altaweelah. The second dam, Donya (by Mill Reef), was placed once over 10f from two outings and is a half-sister to the Rothmans International winner French Glory. (Sheikh Mohammed Obaid Al Maktoum).
"He's quite a nice, good-looking colt. It's early days but he should be racing in June or July".

374. AZITA ★★★
b.f. Tiger Hill – Zeeba (Barathea).
April 11. First foal. The dam, a fair 12f winner, is a sister to the useful listed 14f winner Lost Soldier Three and a half-sister to numerous winners including the useful 10.5f and 12f winner Altaweelah. The second dam, Donya (Mill Reef), was placed once over 10f from 2 outings and is a half-sister to the Rothmans International winner French Glory and the useful Irish winner at up to 12f Golden Isle. (Sheikh Mohammed Obaid).
"A big filly that won't be out until the second half of the season, but she's good-looking and seven furlongs will probably be her starting point. A nice filly".

375. BLUE LYRIC ★★★★
b.f. Refuse To Bend – Powder Blue (Daylami).
March 10. First foal. 58,000Y. Tattersalls October 2. Charlie Gordon-Watson. The dam, placed twice over 7f (both her starts), is a half-sister to 2 minor winners. The second dam, Blue Duster (by Danzig), won the Group 1 Cheveley Park Stakes and is a sister to the Group 1 Middle Park Stakes winner Zieten. (Fittocks Stud).
"She's nice and she's going well. She seems to have enough speed for six furlongs and I'd expect her out in June or July".

376. CHEETAH ★★
b.f. Tiger Hill – Kassiyra (Kendor).
May 4. Half-sister to the quite useful 10f winner Speed Ticket (by Galileo). The dam is a half-sister to several winners including the Group 2 15f Prix Kergorlay winner Kassani and the Group 3 12.5f Prix Minerve winner Kassana. The second dam, Kassiyda (by Mill Reef), a useful dual 10f winner, is a half-sister to the Epsom and Irish Derby winner Kahyasi and the St Simon Stakes winner Kaliana.
"Quite backward, she'll be one for the back-end of the season I should think. She's not developed physically yet".

377. DIAM QUEEN (GER) ★★★
b.f. Lando – Dance Solo (Sadler's Wells).
February 4. First foal. 80,000Y. Tattersalls October 2. Gill Richardson. The dam, placed 4 times from 7f to 11f here and in Germany, is a full or half-sister to 4 winners including the Group 1 St James's Palace Stakes winner Exclusive Art. The second dam, Obsessive (by Seeking The Gold), a useful 2-y-o 6f winner and third in the Group 3 10.4f Musidora Stakes, is a half-sister to 7 winners. (Jaber Abdullah).
"She's a nice filly, good-looking and a good mover, but she'll want seven furlongs or maybe even a mile to start with later on".

378. FALCUN ★★★
b.c. Danehill Dancer – Fanofadiga (Alzao).
April 3. The dam is a minor winning half-sister to numerous winners, notably the top-class Falbrav, winner of eight Group/Grade 1 events including the Hong Kong Cup, the Japan Cup, the Eclipse Stakes, the Queen Elizabeth II Stakes and the Juddmonte International Stakes. The second dam, Gift Of The Night, (by Alzao), won over 7.5f in France at 2 yrs.
"He moves well and is one for September time but he goes nicely".

379. GOLD RULES ★★
ch.c. Gold Away – Raphaela (Octagonal).
January 26. Third foal. 31,000Y. Doncaster St Leger. G Howson. The dam won once over 11f in France and is a half-sister to 6 winners. The second dam, Redden Queen (by Bering), won twice at 3 yrs in France and is a half-sister to 5 winners. (Mr L Marinopoulos).
"He's going to need seven furlongs or a mile later in the season but he seems to go OK".

380. KITTY WELLS ★★
b.f. Sadler's Wells – Kithanga (Darshaan).
March 4. Sister to the St Leger and Great Voltigeur Stakes winner Milan, to the fairly useful 12f winners Kahara and Kossack and the fair 11f winner Kibara and half-sister to the Irish 2-y-o 7f winner and Group 2 Great Voltigeur Stakes third Go For Gold (by Machiavellian). The dam was a smart winner of 3 races including the Group 3 12f St Simon Stakes and the listed 12f Galtres Stakes. The second dam, Kalata (by Assert), ran once unplaced in France and is a half-sister to the dams of the Derby winner Kahyasi, the Yorkshire Oaks winner Key Change, the St Simon Stakes winner Kaliana and the Group 3 10.5f Prix Cleopatre winner Kalajana. (Fittocks Stud Ltd).
"A very nice filly, but she's very big and very tall and if she does get to the racecourse this year it'll be right at the back-end".

381. LODEN ★★★★
b.c. Barathea – Tentpole (Rainbow Quest).
April 8. Fifth foal. Brother to the promising 2008 2-y-o 1m winner Too Much Trouble and half-brother to the modest 1m winner Bivouac (by Jade Robbery). The dam, an Irish 14f winner, is a half-sister to 3 winners. The second dam, Polent (by Polish Precedent), a minor French 13f and 15.5f winner, is a half-sister to 6 winners including the Oaks winner Snow Bride (herself dam of the Derby, King George and 'Arc' winner Lammtarra).
"He's a nice mover that goes well and he has a very good temperament. He'll be out in July and he'd be one of my nicest two-year-olds".

382. MEDIA HYPE ★★★
b.c. Tiger Hill – Hyperspectra (Rainbow Quest).
March 20. Seventh foal. 50,000Y. Tattersalls October 1. Not sold. Half-brother to the Group 3 7f Tetrarch Stakes winner and Irish 2,000 Guineas second France (by Desert Prince), to the fairly useful 11f and 12f winner Green Tabasco (by Green Desert) and the fair 11.8f winner Spectral Star (by Unfuwain). The dam, a fairly useful 10.2f winner, is a half-sister to 5 winners including the French winner and Group 3 Prix Eclipse second Hothaifah. The second dam, Hyabella (by Shirley Heights), a smart winner of the listed Ben Marshall and the listed Atalanta Stakes, is a half-sister to 6 winners including the Group 2 10f Prince of Wales's Stakes winner Stagecraft. (Castle Down Racing).
"He's a good-looking horse that moves well. He'll want seven furlongs in August or September".

383. MY MANIKATO ★★★
ch.c. Starcraft – Rainbow Queen (Spectrum).
February 19. Second foal. 28,000Y. Doncaster St Leger. Badgers Bloodstock. Half-brother to the unplaced 2008 2-y-o Sir Isaac (by Key Of Luck). The dam won 4 races from 6f to 1m at 3 and 4 yrs in Belgium and France and is a half-sister to the Group 3 Prix Miesque winner Stella Blue. The second dam, Libanoor (by Highest Honor), won 4 races at 3 yrs in France and is a sister to the French triple Group 3 winner Take Risks.
"He's a very good-looking horse that moves well. Probably one for September time".

384. NAJOOM ZAMAN (IRE) ★★★
b.f. Green Desert – North Sea (Selkirk).
January 26. The dam is an unplaced half-sister to one winner. The second dam, Sea Spray (by Royal Academy), a useful 7f (at 2 yrs) and listed 1m Masaka Stakes winner, is a half-sister to two other listed winners and to the dam of the French dual Group 2 winner Cut Quartz. (Jaber Abdullah).
"A big filly (unusually for a Green Desert) but she's going well and could be one for the midsummer as she's mentally quite alert".

385. PEDANTIC ★★
b.c. Danehill Dancer – High Reserve (Dr Fong).
March 13. First foal. The dam, a fairly useful 1m and 10f winner, is a half-sister to 5 winners including the useful Irish 1m winner and dual listed placed Poet and the French 2-y-o dual 6f winner and Group 3 6f Prix Eclipse second Hothaifah. The second dam, Hyabella (by Shirley Heights), won three races over 1m at 3 yrs including two listed events and is a half-sister to 6 winners including the Prince of Wales's Stakes winner Stagecraft. (Castle Down Racing).
"A backward horse, he won't be out until very late in the season, probably over seven furlongs".

386. QUEEN'S ENVOY ★★★
b.f. King's Best – Allied Cause (Giant's Causeway).
February 5. First foal. 35,000Y. Tattersalls December. Not sold. The dam, a fair 7f winner, is a half-sister to 3 winners including the Group 2 10f Sun Chariot Stakes winner Kissogram. The second dam, Alligram (by Alysheba), is an unplaced half-sister to 5 winners out of Queen Elizabeth II Stakes and Coronation Stakes winner Milligram. (Helena Springfield Ltd).
"A nice filly, she goes well and she has a good attitude – which is rare for a King's Best. Provided her temperament remains the same she'll be out in July or August".

387. SENSATIONALLY ★★
b.f. Montjeu – One So Wonderful (Nashwan).
April 21. Half-sister to the US Grade 2 8.5f winner Sun Boat and to the modest French 10f winner Alqaayid (both by Machiavellian). The dam won the Group 1 Juddmonte International Stakes and the Group 2 Sun Chariot Stakes and is a half-sister to 6 winners including the Rockfel Stakes winner Relatively Special and the Dante Stakes and Craven Stakes winner Alnasr Alwasheek. The second dam, Someone Special (by Habitat), won over 7f, was third in the Coronation Stakes and is a half-sister to the Queen Elizabeth II Stakes winner Milligram. (Helena Springfield Ltd).
"Still at the farm and I haven't seen her yet".

388. SORY ★★
b.c. Sakhee – Rule Britannia (Night Shift).
January 27. Second foal. 38,000Y. Tattersalls October 2. Charlie Gordon-Watson. The dam, a quite useful 10f and 12f winner, is a half-sister to 5 winners here and abroad. The second dam, Broken Wave (by Bustino), won 5 races including two listed events in France and is a half-sister to 6 winners. (Sheikh Mohammed Obaid Al Maktoum).
"A big horse, he will be a bit of a stayer and we'll probably see him out at the back-end. I don't expect him to do much as a two-year-old".

389. STARCRAFT REVIVAL ★★★
ch.c. Starcraft – Revival (Sadler's Wells).
March 13. Half-brother to the quite useful Irish 8.5f winner Uva Fragola (by Nashwan) and to the 10f seller winner Danalova (by Groom

Dancer). The dam, a quite useful 10f winner, is a half-sister to 3 winners including the Group 1 6f Nunthorpe Stakes winner and sire Pivotal. The second dam, Fearless Revival (by Cozzene), was a useful 2-y-o 6f and 7f winner and was listed-placed over 10f at 3 yrs.

"A good-looking colt that moves well, he'll make his first appearance some time in late summer".

390. START RIGHT ★★★★

b.c. Footstepsinthesand – Time Crystal (Sadler's Wells).
April 23. Third foal. €38,000Y. Goffs Million. Charlie Gordon-Watson. The dam, a 12f winner, is a half-sister to 4 winners. The second dam, State Crystal (by High Estate), was a very useful winner of the Group 3 12f Lancashire Oaks and was placed in the Yorkshire Oaks and the Prix Vermeille. She is a half-sister to 6 winners including the Group 1 Fillies' Mile winner Crystal Music, the Group 3 winners Dubai Success and Solar Crystal and the Irish Derby third Tchaikovsky. (Mr L Marinopoulos).

"He's a good-looking horse and he goes well. I expect he'll be out in June or July and he'll be one of our first colts to run. I think he may be alright over six furlongs".

391. SWIFTLY DONE (IRE) ★★

br.c. Whipper – Ziffany (Taufan).
March 28. Sixth foal. 200,000Y. Tattersalls October 1. Charlie Gordon-Watson. Half-brother to the very smart listed 7f winner of 6 races and Group 1 Lockinge Stakes second Major's Cast (by Victory Note) and to the very smart sprinter Jessica's Dream (by Desert Style), winner of the Group 3 Ballyogan Stakes and the Group 3 Premio Omenoni. The dam, a 2-y-o 7f seller winner, is a half-sister to one winner abroad. The second dam, Bonnie Banks (by Lomond), is an unplaced half-sister to 6 winners including the Group 3 Cornwallis Stakes winner Hanu. (Saeed Suhail).

"He has an injury at the moment so we'll have to see how he progresses".

392. YOUM MUTAMIEZ (USA) ★★★

b.br.c. Seeking The Gold – Shy Lady (Kaldoun).
April 24. Seventh foal. Closely related to the very useful listed 7f winner Atlantic Sport (by Machiavellian) and half-brother to the high-class Group 1 1m St James's Palace Stakes and Group 2 6f Mill Reef Stakes winner Zafeen (by Zafonic) and the useful 2-y-o Group 3 7f Prix du Calvados winner Ya Hajar (by Lycius). The dam, winner of a listed event over 6f in Germany, was fourth in the Group 2 6f Moet and Chandon Rennen and is a half-sister to 4 winners. The second dam, the minor French 3-y-o winner Shy Danceuse (by Groom Dancer), is a half-sister to the dual Group 3 winner Diffident. (Jaber Abdullah).

"He's a backward horse but one that could come right by September or October time. He's nice and good-looking, a bit on the leggy side and needs to strengthen up".

393. UNNAMED ★★

b.f. Shamardal – Autumn Melody (Kingmambo).
February 17. 85,000Y. Japan. The dam, unplaced in 3 starts at 2 yrs here, is a half-sister to the high-class Group 2 1m Queen Anne Stakes and Group 2 7f Challenge Stakes winner Charnwood Forest and to the smart Group 1 1m Racing Post Trophy winner Medaaly. The second dam, Dance Of Leaves (by Sadler's Wells), is an unraced sister to the Group 1 Grand Prix de Paris winner Fort Wood, closely related to the Group 1 July Cup winner Hamas, the Group 2 Prix de Pomone winner Colorado Dancer (herself the dam of Dubai Millennium) and the Group 1 Gamely Handicap winner Northern Aspen and a half-sister to the Group 3 Prix d'Astarte winner Elle Seule (herself dam of the Irish 1,000 Guineas winner Mehthaaf) and the champion US 2-y-o and Breeders Cup winner Timber Country. (Patinack Farm).

"She's a very big filly and she has a lot of developing to do, so she won't be out until much later on. But she's moves nicely and goes well".

394. UNNAMED ★★★
ch.f. Pivotal – Bombazine (Generous).
May 1. Seventh reported foal. Half-sister to the very useful dual 1m (at 2 yrs) and listed 11f and 12f winner Gravitas (by Mark Of Esteem), to the French 12f and listed 2m winner Affirmative Action, the fairly useful 10f winner Dubai Venture (both by Rainbow Quest), the fairly useful 11f and 12f winner of 3 races Armure (by Dalakhani) and the fairly useful 1m winner of 4 races Camelot (by Machiavellian). The dam, a useful 10f winner, is a half-sister to the Breeders Cup Mile and Irish 2,000 Guineas winner Barathea and to the Fillies Mile and Irish 1,000 Guineas winner Gossamer. The second dam, Brocade (by Habitat), a high-class filly at up to 1m, won five races including the Group 1 7f Prix de la Foret and is a half-sister to 7 winners. (Sarah J Leigh).
"A nice filly, she's quite tall and leggy so she needs to develop and mature, but she should be out in the second half of the season".

395. UNNAMED ★★
b.c. Galileo – Jabali (Shirley Heights).
March 31. Tenth foal. Half-brother to 6 minor winners in France by Caerleon, Grand Lodge, Green Desert, Linamix, Sanglamore and Vettori. The dam is an unplaced half-sister to 4 winners including the French Group winners Dadarissime and Floripedes (the dam of Montjeu). The second dam, Toute Cy (by Tennyson), is a placed full or half-sister to 4 winners including the Grade 1 Arlington Million winner Dear Doctor. (Tsega Horses and Mrs John Magnier).
"A good-looking horse, but he's a Galileo so you wouldn't rush him".

396. UNNAMED ★★★
b.c. Danehill Dancer – Landmark (Arch).
March 24. First foal. 140,000Y. Tattersalls October 1. Citywest Inc. The dam, a minor 2-y-o winner in the USA, is a half-sister to 2 winners including the Grade 1 Del Mar Oaks winner Arravale. The second dam, Kalosca (by Kaldoun), won 3 races in France and the USA, was Grade 2 placed and is a half-sister to the French stakes winners Mykonos and Crillon. (Mr Earle I Mack).
"He should make a two-year-old by August, probably over seven furlongs, he's a biggish sort but a good-looking horse that moves well".

397. UNNAMED ★★★★
b.c. Galileo – Miss Moses (Gulch).
April 19. First foal. 130,000Y. Tattersalls October 1. Citywest Inc. The dam won 3 races at 3 yrs in the USA including a listed stakes and is a half-sister to another minor US stakes winner in Lemonlime. The second dam, Prime Investor (by Deputy Minister), a minor US 3-y-o winner, is a half-sister to 6 winners including the Italian Group 2 winner Vers La Caisse. (Mr Earle I Mack).
"A big horse but strong, he should be racing in late summer and I think he's one you should look out for".

398. UNNAMED ★★★
b.c. Starcraft – Red Azalea (Shirley Heights).
March 11. Ninth foal. 72,000Y. Tattersalls October 2. Charlie Gordon-Watson. Half-brother to the useful 7f (at 2 yrs) and 12f winner and Group 3 7f Prestige Stakes third Red Peony (by Montjeu), to the quite useful 7f all-weather winner Grandalea (by Grand Lodge) and a winner at up to 10f in Spain by Polar Falcon. The dam, a fairly useful 7f (at 2 yrs) and 10f winner, is a half-sister to 4 winners including the Group 3 Prestige Stakes winner and French 1,000 Guineas third Red Camellia (herself dam of the Fillies Mile winner Red Bloom). The second dam, Cerise Bouquet (by Mummy's Pet), a fair 2-y-o 5f winner, is a half-sister to 6 winners including the Group 1 winners Ibn Bey and Roseate Tern. (Saeed Suhail).
"A big horse, he's good-looking but we won't see him out until the second half of the season over seven furlongs or a mile".

399. UNNAMED ★★
b.c. Azamour – Sagamartha (Rainbow Quest).
April 5. Fourth foal. 65,000Y. Tattersalls October 2. Charlie Gordon-Watson. Half-brother to the minor French 10f (including at 2

yrs) and 12f winner Sahara Lady (by Lomitas). The dam, a minor French 3-y-o winner, is a half-sister to 4 winners including the Group 2 Lowther Stakes and Group 2 Queen Mary Stakes winner Flashy Wings. The second dam, Lovealoch (by Lomond), a very useful 7f (at 2 yrs) and 9f winner here and placed in the Group 2 Falmouth Stakes and the Group 2 Premio Lydia Tesio, subsequently won once in the USA and is a half-sister to 7 winners. (Saeed Suhail).
"A good-looking horse but fairly big and backward. He'll take a bit of time but he'll make a two-year-old in the second half of the season".

400. UNNAMED ★★★
b.f. Alkaased – Velvet Queen (Singspiel).
February 24. The dam, the minor French 3-y-o winner, is a sister to the Group 1 Dubai World Cup, Group 2 10.5f Dante Stakes and Group 3 10f Select Stakes winner Moon Ballad and a half-sister to the useful 1m winner Velvet Lady (by Nashwan) and the quite useful 11f winner Eta Draconis (by Daylami). The second dam, Velvet Moon (by Shaadi), a very useful Group 2 6f Lowther Stakes and listed 10f winner, is a half-sister to the Group 1 12f Italian Derby, Group 2 7f Lanson Champagne Stakes and German Group 2 12f winner Central Park and to the Group 3 Lancashire Oaks winner Mellow Park. (Patinack Farm).
"She's tall but good-looking and will probably be out in September".

TOM DASCOMBE
401. ABOVE LIMITS ★★★★
b.f. Exceed And Excel – Cin Isa Luv (Private Account).
April 3. Eighth foal. €16,000Y. Goffs Million. Angie Sykes. Half-sister to the quite useful 1m and subsequent Australian winner Bugatti Royale (by Dynaformer) and to 3 minor winners in the USA by Meadowlake, Charismatic and Honor Grades and to the unraced dam of a stakes winner. The dam won once at 3 yrs in the USA and is a half-sister to 8 winners including the US Grade 1 winner Script Ohio and the US Grade 3 winner Young Daniel. The second dam, Grandma Lind (by Never Bend), won 4 races in

the USA. (Findlay & Bloom).
"We have 41 two-year-olds and I think we've got some nice ones, so despite the good year we had in 2008 I'd rather be where we are now than at this time last year. This is an interesting filly. I went to Goffs just to pick horses for Harry Findlay and I looked for ages and couldn't find one that I liked. Then late in the afternoon I saw this filly and I loved her. I'm very pleased we got her, Exceed And Excel did so well with his first crop last year and this is the first horse I've had by him. I think this filly is nice and she's got plenty of speed. She may have won by the time the book is published".

402. BAHAMIAN SUN ★★★
ch.c. Bahamian Bounty – Firesteed (Common Grounds).
March 12. Third foal. €35,000Y. Goffs Million. Oneway. Half-brother to the quite useful dual 10f winner Going To Work (by Night Shift). The dam, a 1m winner and listed-placed in France at 3 yrs, is a half-sister to 2 winners. The second dam, Power take Off (by Aragon), won twice over 1m and was listed-placed several times and is a half-sister to the smart sprinter Governor General and to the dam of the Canadian Grade 2 winner Youmadeyourpoint. (Findlay & Bloom).
"A big, gross two-year-old that I thought would take ages but in actual fact he was galloping in March. He got a touch of a sore shin so I've backed off him but he could be out in May. A big colt, but not weak, he's a nice strong horse".

403. BARZAN ★★★
ch.c. Danehill Dancer – Le Montrachet (Nashwan).
March 12. Third foal. £58,000 2-y-o. Goffs Kempton Breeze Up. Kern/Lillingston. Closely related to a minor winner in New Zealand by Green Desert and half-brother to the quite useful 12f winner Baba Ganouge (by Desert Prince). The dam is an unraced sister to one minor winner and a half-sister to the Group 1 Coronation Stakes and Group 1 Prix Marcel Boussac winner Gold Splash and the good broodmare Born Gold (the dam of three Group

3 winners). The second dam, Riviere d'Or (by Lyphard), winner of the Group 1 10f Prix Saint-Alary, is closely related to the Group 3 winner Chercheur d'Or and the French 2,000 Guineas second Goldneyev.

"A nice colt, he's being given a bit of time but he'll be a six furlong two-year-old to start with and we'll step him up from there. He breezed very well at the sale".

404. CLASSIC COLORI (IRE) ★★★
b.c. Le Vie Dei Colori – Beryl (Bering).
March 23. Sixth foal. €55,000Y. Tattersalls Ireland. Kern/Lillingston. Half-brother to the fair 2008 2-y-o 7f winner Spinning Sound (by Spinning World), to the US stakes winner and Grade 3 placed Vauquelin (by Xaar), the quite useful 5f (at 2 yrs) and 1m winner Glenmuir (by Josr Algarhoud) and the 4-y-o 6f seller winner Juniper Banks (by Night Shift). The dam was a fair 12f at 3 yrs and is a daughter of the 2-y-o winner Fayrooz (by Gulch), herself a half-sister to 4 winners. (The Classic Strollers Partnership).

"He was bought as a replacement for Classic Blade – he's owned by the same people. He's a nice colt and was definitely the pick of the sale. A beautiful-looking colt, he's just gone a bit weak now and he probably needs a bit more time, but he's a good-moving, straightforward horse with a good attitude. I'm happy with him".

405. CLIFTON ENCORE (USA) ★★★
b.f. War Chant – Theatrical Pause (Theatrical).
February 14. The dam is a half-sister to the smart Group 2 6f Gimcrack Stakes winner Country Reel. The second dam, Country Belle (by Seattle Slew), won twice over 1m at 3 yrs in France including a listed event, was third in the Group 3 Prix de la Grotte and is a half-sister to several winners including the the top-class sprinter Anabaa and the French 1,000 Guineas winner Always Loyal. (Clifton Parners).

"She's got plenty of size and you wouldn't think she'd be ready to canter yet but she's almost ready for working. She has a good attitude and she's a good eater".

406. DON'T TELL MARY (IRE) ★★★
b.f. Starcraft – Only In Dreams (Polar Falcon).
March 15. Eighth foal. 32,000Y. Doncaster Festival. David Redvers. Half-sister to the fairly useful 2008 2-y-o 6f winner Exceptional Art (by Exceed And Excel), to the very useful 2-y-o 5f and 6f winner and Group 2 July Stakes second Cape Fear (by Cape Cross) and the moderate 3-y-o 1m seller winner If I Can Dream (by Brief Truce). The dam, a fair 2-y-o 7f winner, is a half-sister to 4 other minor winners. The second dam, Dream Baby (by Master Willie), was unplaced on her only start and is a half-sister to 9 winners. (K P Trowbridge).

"She's quite 'buzzy' and just needs to chill out a bit. She's quite sharp and will start off at five furlongs in May but will definitely get further. I like her a lot".

407. PRINCESS AURORA (USA) ★★★
ch.f. Mr Greeley – My Reem (Chief's Crown).
February 1. Seventh foal. $500,000Y. Saratoga August. Blandford Bloodstock. Sister to the quite useful 2-y-o 6f winner Mistress Greeley and half-sister to 4 winners including the minor US stakes winners Jesse's Justice (by Lear Fan) and Willard Straight (by Lion Cavern). The dam is an unraced half-sister to 4 winners including the listed winner and Group 1 Oaks fourth Knoosh. The second dam, Fabulous Salt (by Le Fabuleux), a winner at 3 here and 4 in the USA, was listed-placed and is a half-sister to the US stakes winner and good broodmare Ballare. (A W Black).

"She's currently got a problem and I would think the earliest we could hope to get her out would be July. She's a beautiful looking filly with a nice pedigree and is the most expensive one I have. She was small but she's done nothing but grow".

408. QUAESTOR (IRE) ★★★★
b.c. Antonius Pius – Lucky Oakwood (Elmaamul).
February 14. Sixth foal. €15,000Y. Tattersalls Ireland. Kern/Lillingston. Half-brother to a winner in Japan by Grand Lodge. The dam, a fair 2-y-o 7f all-weather winner, is a half-sister to 11 winners including the listed 1m Cecil Frail

Handicap winner Incisive and the listed 10f Lupe Stakes winner Gisarne and to the unraced dam of the Australian Grade 1 winner Bezeal Bay. The second dam, Fair Sousanne (by Busted), a fair 6f and 10f placed maiden, is a half-sister to 5 minor winners. (Mr J D Brown).
"He won't take long. He's a big, strong, forward two-year-old and he was inexpensive but he looks like a racehorse and a two-year-old type".

409. RAKTIMAN (IRE) ★★★
ch.c. Rakti – Wish List (Mujadil).
April 8. Seventh foal. €25,000Y. Tattersalls Ireland. Kern/Lillingston. Half-brother to the 2008 Group 2 7f Superlative Stakes winner Firth Of Fifth (by Traditionally) and to the dual 2-y-o 7f seller winner Sunstroke and a winner in Greece (both by Raphane). The dam won twice over 5f at 2 yrs in Ireland and is a half-sister to the dam of the Group 3 Greenlands Stakes winner Final Exam. The second dam, Final Moment (by Nishapour), won the listed Athasi Stakes, was fourth in the Irish 1,000 Guineas and is a half-sister to 4 winners. (Mr D E Perchard).
"He won't be early but he's a big, strong, imposing horse that will take a bit of time".

410. SOCCER (USA) ★★★★
ch.c. Van Nistelrooy – Bonita Gail (Geiger Counter).
February 21. Fifth foal. €40,000Y. Goffs Million. Not sold. Half-brother to the US stakes-placed winner Class N Charm (by Lure). The dam was placed at 2 yrs in the USA and is a half-sister to 3 minor winners there. The second dam, Artic Anna (by Briartic), won 6 minor races in the USA and is a half-sister to 9 winners including the US Grade 2 winners Miss Indy Anna and Time Limit. (Findlay & Bloom).
"I was really impressed with his debut win, because taking into account the lad's claim he gave ten pounds to the second horse who had already had a run. I thought he'd run well but be caught out for experience and now he might go to Ascot in late April. We were second in that race last year with a horse that was nowhere near as forward as Soccer is. The dream would be to go to the Coventry Stakes with him, but we'll have to see how he progresses. He's a big, strong colt, very straightforward and easy-going".

411. WALKINGONTHEMOON ★★★★
ch.c. Footstepsinthesand – Bendis (Danehill).
April 15. Fourth foal. 26,000Y. Doncaster St Leger. Kern/Lillingston. Half-brother to the 2008 modest 5f fourth placed 2-y-o Monaco Mistress, to the quite useful dual 6f winner (including at 2 yrs) Rubirosa (both by Acclamation) and a winner over hurdles by Golan. The dam, a 7f winner at 3 yrs in Germany, is a half-sister to 5 winners. The second dam, Berenice (by Groom Dancer), a fair 10f winner, was listed-placed and is a half-sister to 3 winners. (The Tipperary Partners).
"He's very forward, he's very lean and he'll make his debut at Newbury in mid-April. He's galloped with Soccer who won on his debut and he should be a nice, sharp two-year-old. His pedigree doesn't really suggest that he'd be an early two-year-old, but he is".

412. WISECRAIC ★★★★
b.c. Kheleyf – Belle Genius (Beau Genius).
March 21. €14,000Y. Tattersalls Ireland. Kern/Lillingston. Brother to the fair 2008 2-y-o 7f winner Zelloof and half-brother to the quite useful 6f and 7f winner Birjand, the quite useful 2-y-o 6f winner Dellini (both by Green Desert), to the quite useful 1m winner Bin Rahy (by Rahy), the fair Irish 1m and 9f winner Fereeji (by Cape Cross) and the minor Irish 12f winner Battish (by Pennekamp). The dam won the Group 1 7f Moyglare Stud Stakes. The second dam, Time And Tide (by Mr Leader), a minor US 4-y-o winner, is a half-sister to the Brigadier Gerard Stakes winner Hibernian Gold. (L Mann, S Briddon & N Attenborough).
"This could be our best horse. He should be ready in May and he's pretty smart. By a very good two-year-old sire and out of a Group One winner, he was very cheap. He's a big, strong, tall colt and he has scope. Earlier on he was looking quicker than my winning two-year-old, Soccer".

413. UNNAMED ★★★★
b.f. Orpen – Morale (Bluebird).
March 11. Sixth foal. 30,000Y. Doncaster St Leger. Kern/Lillingston. Sister to the listed Hilary Needler Trophy winner Clare Hills and half-sister to the quite useful 2-y-o 6f winner Weet A Head (by Foxhound) and the fair Irish 9.5f winner Hoffman (by Dr Devious). The dam is an unraced sister to the Scandinavian listed winner Bluebeard and a half-sister to 3 winners including the useful 1m and 10f winner Sheba Spring. The second dam, Shebasis (by General Holme), is an unraced half-sister to 6 minor winners in the USA.
"A very nice filly, she's got a touch of a sore shin but that's basically because she's growing a lot. I'd like to think she'll be ready to go in May and I'm hoping she'll be an Ascot filly. She's got speed, size and scope. She's very straightforward and genuine and she just needs a clear run".

414. UNNAMED ★★★
b.c. Oratorio – Novelette (Darshaan).
May 13. €7,000Y. Tattersalls Ireland. Kern/Lillingston. Half-brother to the very useful 7f (at 2 yrs), 10f and subsequent UAE 12f winner Book Of Music (by Sadler's Wells) and to the fair dual 12f winner Calzaghe (by Galileo). The dam won once at 3 yrs in France and is a sister to the very useful Group 3 7.3f Fred Darling Stakes winner and Group 2 10f Nassau Stakes third Sueboog (herself dam of the Group 1 Prix Jean Prat winner Best Of The Bests) and a half-sister to 5 winners including the useful 1m winner Marika. The second dam, Nordica (by Northfields), a useful 6f and 1m winner, is a half-sister to the dam of the useful listed winner Recondite. (Mr C McHale).
"I was willing to pay 40,000 for him and I got him for 7,000. A beautiful looking horse, he'll need a bit of time but he's not going to be a five or six furlong sprinter. He was an absolute steal". TRAINER'S BARGAIN BUY

415. UNNAMED ★★★
b.f. Marchand de Sable – Plead (Bering).
March 31. Fourth foal. €22,000Y. Deauville August. Kern/Lillingston. Half-sister to a minor winner in France by Hernando. The dam won once at 3 yrs and is a half-sister to 6 winners including the French listed winners Play Around and Playact (subsequently Grade 2 placed in the USA). The second dam, Play Or Pay (by Play Fellow), won twice in France and was listed-placed and is a half-sister to 9 winners.
"If it was a beauty contest she'd be a Group One horse and I think she can shift as well. She'll be given time but she should be out in mid-season. I own a bit of her because I like her so much, she wasn't expensive and I think she could be very nice".

416. UNNAMED ★★★
ch.c. Proud Citizen – Sejm's Lunar Star (Sejm).
May 18. Fifth foal. $57,000Y. Keeneland September. M O'Toole. £24,000 2-y-o. Goffs Kempton Breeze Up. Half-brother to a minor US winner by Dixie Union. The dam, a US stakes winner of 4 races at 2 and 3 yrs, is a half-sister to 4 winners. The second dam, Sitting Duck (by Quack), a minor US dual 3-y-o winner, is a full or half-sister to 7 winners.
"He's a late foal so he'll take a bit of time. But he's very smart-looking and he breezed well at the sale, especially for a horse who was three months off his second birthday".

ANN DUFFIELD
417. CIAN ROONEY ★★★
b.c. Camacho – Exponent (Exbourne).
April 25. Sixth living foal. €47,000Y. Goffs Million. De Burgh/Farrington. Closely related to the smart Irish dual listed 2-y-o 5f winner and Group 2 Railway Stakes second Drayton and to the unplaced 2008 2-y-o Serious Times (both by Danetime) and half-brother to the quite useful 5f (at 2 yrs) and 6f winner Exponential (by Namid) and a winner over jumps by Desert King. The dam is an unraced half-sister to 6 minor winners here and abroad. The second dam, Water Angel (by Halo), is an unraced half-sister to 2 winners. (Findlay & Bloom).
"We like him, he's quite tall and has grown a lot. He's one for late May over five furlongs to start with, but he'll stay six".

418. COOLMINX (IRE) ★★★
b.f. *One Cool Cat – Greta d'Argent (Great Commotion).*
March 25. Second foal. €25,000Y. Goffs Million. Ann Duffield. Sister to the useful 2008 2-y-o dual 5f winner Baycat. The dam, a fairly useful 1m (at 2 yrs) to 12f winner of 4 races, is a half-sister to 4 winners including the listed winner and Group 2 placed Winged d'Argent. The second dam, Petite-D-Argent (by Noalto), won over 6f (at 2 yrs) and 7f and is a half-sister to one winner. (Mrs H Steel).
"A nice filly, she's not over-big but big enough and she's got a bit of ability. She'll be out in May over five furlongs and I think she's quite capable".

419. DIVORCEFROMREALITY ★★
b.br.c. *Key Of Luck – Golden Anthem (Lion Cavern).*
February 10. First foal. €18,000Y. Goffs Million. De Burgh/Farringdon. The dam, a fairly useful 2-y-o 5f winner, was listed-placed over 6f and is a sister to the very useful US 2-y-o and subsequent 1m listed Goodwood winner Fong's Thong. The second dam, Bacinella (by El Gran Senor), is an unraced sister to the dual Italian winner and listed -placed Mandarina and is a three-parts sister to the listed winner Xtra. (Findlay & Bloom).
"More of a three-year-old type, so he won't be out until much later in the year. Very impressive to look at, he's a big horse without being a giant".

420. FIREFLASH ★★★
b.c. *Noverre – Miss Langkawi (Daylami).*
March 15. Second foal. €66,000Y. Tattersalls Ireland. Gill Richardson. The dam, a fair 2-y-o 6f winner, is a half-sister to one winner abroad. The second dam, Miss Amanpuri (by Alzao), a fairly useful 2-y-o 7f winner, is a half-sister to the very smart Ormonde Stakes winners Asian Heights and St Expedit.
"A very nice horse with a good attitude and plenty of bone. He's a stocky, two-year-old type and he goes well". TRAINER'S BARGAIN BUY

421. GHOSTWING ★★★★
gr.c. *Kheleyf – Someone's Angel (Runaway Groom).*
March 19. Second foal. 75,000Y. Doncaster St Leger. Gill Richardson. The dam is an unplaced half-sister to 6 minor winners. The second dam, Yazeanhaa (by Zilzal), fourth over 6f at 2 yrs on her only outing, is closely related to the useful 2-y-o triple 6f winner Anjiz and a half-sister to the Group 2 5f Prix du Gros-Chene winner and Group 1 Prix de l'Abbaye third Nabeel Dancer. (Mrs H Steel).
"A nice horse, it won't be long before he's out. He was small when we bought him but he's filled out over the winter and he really looks the part now. He's got some speed, he'll start in late April and he'd be one to watch out for".

422. ROYAL CHEER ★★★
b.f. *Royal Applause – Rise 'N Shine (Night Shift).*
March 15. Sixth living foal. 36,000Y. Doncaster St Leger. G Lyons. Half-sister to the quite useful 5f and 6f winner of 4 races Total Impact (by Pivotal), to the fair 2-y-o 6f winner Then 'n Now (by Dansili) and the modest 6f winner of 3 races Scarlet Secret (by Piccolo). The dam won over 5f at 4 yrs and is a half-sister to 8 winners including the Group 2 Prix du Gros Chene second Touch And Love. The second dam, Clunk Click (by Star Appeal), is a placed half-sister to 9 winners including the triple Group 2 winner Sure Blade. (Mrs D G Garrity).
"A very nice filly, she's nicely bred, quite close-coupled and compact, not over-big but very strong. She has plenty of bone and a good attitude. We'd have hopes for her".

423. SHARP SHOES ★★★
br.c. *Needwood Blade – Mary Jane (Tina's Pet).*
April 29. Fourth foal. 26,000Y. Doncaster St Leger. Gill Richardson. Half-brother to the fair 2-y-o 6f winner Maryolini (by Bertolini). The dam, a fair winner of 12 races from 5f to 6f at 2 to 8 yrs, is a half-sister to 2 winners. The second dam, Fair Attempt (by Try My Best), is an unraced half-sister to 6 winners. (Mr T P & Mr D McMahon).
"A gorgeous horse, he's very tall and strong but

very 'up behind' and we've never pushed the button with him because he'll be one for much later on. He'll be a sprinter when he is ready to run".

424. SHEILING (IRE) ★★
b.f. Halling – Mystery Play (Sadler's Wells).
March 17. Thirteenth foal. €40,000Y. Goffs Million. Ann Duffield. Half-sister to 7 winners including the very useful UAE 5f to 7f winner of 11 races Conceal (by Cadeaux Genereux), the useful 1m winner Playacting (by Forty Niner), the fairly useful Irish 1m winners Inspector Powell and Clouseau (both by Selkirk) and the fairly useful 1m winner Crown Of Thorns (by Diesis). The dam, a useful 7f (at 2 yrs) and 11.5f winner, is a half-sister to numerous winners including the Queen's Vase winner Arden, the French listed winner Kerulen and the dam of the US Grade 1 winner Kiri's Clown. The second dam, Kereolle (by Riverman), is a placed half-sister to the top-class broodmare Miss Manon (dam of the Group winners Mot D'Or, Lydian and Ballinderry). (Mrs H Steel).
"A nice filly, she's quite tall and a bit 'on the leg'. She's a mid-season type and if she's ready early enough we might start her off at six furlongs and then step her up in distance".

425. SILKENVEIL (IRE) ★★
b.f. Indian Ridge – Line Ahead (Sadler's Wells).
May 5. Second foal. €95,000foal. Goffs. Gill Richardson. The dam was unplaced on her only start and is a half-sister to 2 winners. The dam was placed 3 times including when second in the Group 3 Prestige Stakes and is a half-sister to 4 winners including the Group 2 Great Voltigeur winner Bonny Scot and the dam of the King George and 2,000 Guineas winner Golan. The second dam, Scots Lass (by Shirley Heights), won over 13f. (Mrs H Steel).
"A very nice sort but she's very tall and definitely one for the back-end".

426. SPYING ★★★
ch.c. Observatory – Mint Royale (Cadeaux Genereux).
March 16. Third foal. Half-brother to the useful 2-y-o 5f winner and Group 3 6f Sirenia Stakes second La Neige (by Royal Applause) and to the fair 5f to 8.5f 3-y-o winner of 3 races Ten Shun (by Pivotal). The dam is an unplaced sister to the very smart Group 1 6f Prix Morny and Group 1 6f Middle Park Stakes winner and sire Bahamian Bounty and a half-sister to 2 winners. The second dam, Clarentia (by Ballad Rock), a very useful winner of 5 races at up to 6f, was third in the Group 3 Cornwallis Stakes. (The Duchess of Sutherland).
"We're not in a hurry with him because although physically he's quite mature, mentally he's taking a bit of time. He's a superb mover and he'll be pretty quick when his time comes".

427. SUMMA CUM LAUDE ★★★
gr.f. With Approval – Sulitelma (The Minstrel).
April 19. Half-sister to the modest 2-y-o 6f winner Seta Pura (by Domedriver), to the quite useful 2-y-o 5f winner Ice Mountain (by Kyllachy), to the quite useful 10f to 12f winner Tromp, the fair 7f and 1m winner Robinzal (both by Zilzal), the fair 2-y-o 1m winner Min Mirri, the modest 6f and 1m winner Border Glen (both by Selkirk), the fair Irish 5f winner Neeze (by Cadeaux Genereux) and the modest 9.4f all-weather winner Semiramis (by Darshaan). The dam, a modest 2-y-o 5f all-weather winner, is a half-sister to 3 winners including the German listed winner El Supremo. The second dam, Sharmila (by Blakeney), ran once unplaced and is a half-sister to the King George VI and Queen Elizabeth Diamond Stakes winner Petoski. (Kirsten Rausing).
"She'll be out quite soon and she has a bit of pace. She's not very big but she's strong. A nice filly and very, very game, the dam barely got five furlongs but the sire might help this filly stay a bit further".

428. THISTLESTAR ★★
b.f. Lion Heart – Katiba (Gulch).
February 19. Tenth foal. €66,000Y. Goffs Million. Ann Duffield. Half-sister to 7 winners including the useful 1m and 10f winner and listed-placed Badaayer, the minor US winner Rahilah (both by Silver Hawk), the useful 7f

winner and listed-placed Meadaaar (by Diesis), the fairly useful 1m winner Kariyh (by Shadeed) and the quite useful triple 1m winner Blonde Streak (by Dumaani). The dam, a useful 6f and 7f winner, was listed-placed and is a sister to the dual US stakes winner Remember Ike and a half-sister to 5 winners. The second dam, Schematic (by Upper Nile), a US stakes winner of 7 races, is a half-sister to the triple US Grade 1 winner Very Subtle. (Mrs H Steel).

"She's a mid-summer onwards two-year-old and a nice, quality filly. A three-year-old in the making".

429. UNNAMED ★★
b.f. Domedriver – Alter Ego (Alzao).
March 31. Third foal. €4,500Y. Tattersalls Ireland. Ann Duffield. The dam, a quite useful 2-y-o 7f winner here, was listed placed in Germany and is a half-sister to 5 winners including the listed winner Marakabei. The second dam, Kirsten (by Kris), won at 3 yrs and is a half-sister to 5 winners including the King George winner Petoski.

"There are shares in her available if anyone's interested. She'll make a nice two-year-old and you ought to keep an eye on her. She's from one of Kirsten Rausing's families".

430. UNNAMED ★★★
b.g. Firebreak – Amber Mill (Doulab).
May 12. Half-brother to the very useful Group 3 6f Ballyogan Stakes winner Golden Nun (by Bishop Of Cashel), to the fairly useful 2-y-o 5f winner and Group 3 6f third Amber Valley (by Foxhound), the fairly useful 6f (at 2 yrs) and 1m winner Iskander (by Danzero), the quite useful 2-y-o 6f winner Cheap n Chic (by Primo Valentino), the quite useful 2-y-o dual 5f winner Salamanca (by Paris House), the quite useful 3-y-o 6f winner Amber's Bluff (by Mind Games) and the modest 5f and 6f all-weather winner of 5 races Mr Pertemps (by Primo Dominie). The dam, a useful winner over 5f (twice) and 6f, is a half-sister to 4 winners. The second dam, Millaine (by Formidable), a half-sister to the Italian dual Group 1 winner Svelt, was placed once and stayed 12f.

"A nice horse, he was gelded as a yearling because he was very naughty but I'm very happy with him now, he's going nicely and he'll be out in May".

431. UNNAMED ★★★
b.f. Kyllachy – Swift Baba (Deerhound).
March 1. Half-sister to the fair 2-y-o 5f winner Swallow Star (by Observatory). The dam is an unplaced half-sister to the useful 2-y-o 6f winner and listed-placed Rudik and to numerous winners abroad. The second dam, Nervous Baba (Raja Baba), was a Grade 2 6f winner in the USA.

"A backward filly, she's lovely but quite tall and still growing. One for July onwards and it's quite a speedy two-year-old family".

ED DUNLOP

432. AKAMON ★★★
ch.f. Monsun – Akanta (Wolfhound).
March 22. Fourth foal. 85,000Y. Tattersalls October 1. Not sold. Sister to a minor German 4-y-o winner. The dam won once at 2 yrs in Germany and is a half-sister to 7 winners including the Group 2 German 2,000 Guineas winner Aviso and the dam of the Group 1 German Oaks winner Amarette. The second dam, Akasma (by Windwurf), won 3 races at 3 yrs in Germany, is a half-sister to 5 winners including the German Group 2 winner Ajano. (Mrs J Ellis & Lord Derby).

"A very attractive filly, she's a good mover. Being by Monsun she's not going to be early but she goes well".

433. ALMADAAR ★★★
b.c. Exceed And Excel – Masaader (Wild Again).
February 1. First foal. The dam, a fairly useful dual 6f winner (including at 2 yrs), is a half-sister to the smart 2-y-o Group 1 6f Middle Park Stakes winner Hayil and the useful 2-y-o winners Mizhar, Farqad and Elnahaar. The second dam, Futuh (by Diesis), a fairly useful 2-y-o 6f winner, is a half-sister to the Canadian Selene Stakes winner Rose Park (herself the dam of the smart US Grade 2 winner Wild Rush). (Hamdan Al-Maktoum).

"I trained the mare and this is her first foal. A strong, neat, attractive colt and typical of the sire, he looks racey and he'll be an early type. So far he's done everything I've want him to do".

434. ANGIE'S NAP (USA) ★★★
ch.f. Lion Heart – Magick Top (Topsider).
April 27. Sixth foal. 25,000Y. Doncaster St Leger. Blandford Bloodstock. Half-sister to the US listed-placed winner Brocco's Magick (by Brocco) and 3 minor winners in the USA by Afternoon Deelites, Scarlet Ibis and Silver Ghost. The dam, a minor winner of 3 races at 2 and 3 yrs in the USA, is a half-sister to 4 winners. The second dam, Coming Spring (by Graustark), won twice in the USA and is a half-sister to Roberto. (Findlay & Bloom).
"This is the first horse we bought for Harry Findlay who kindly sent us three horses. I bought her on spec and Harry liked her. She's neat and strong but her foaling date is quite late. She moves well, looks to have some speed and should be earlyish". TRAINER'S BARGAIN BUY

435. ATHWAAB ★★★
b.f. Cadeaux Genereux – Ahdaaf (by Bahri).
March 2. First foal. The dam, a quite useful 7f winner, is a half-sister to 2 winners. The second dam, Ashrakaat (by Danzig), a very useful 6f and 7f listed winner, is a sister to the July Cup winner Elnadim and is closely related to the Irish 1,000 Guineas winner Mehthaaf. (Hamdan Al-Maktoum).
"She's a little bit backward but she moves well and looks a bit more mature than I thought. She looks a nice filly but she'll need a bit of time".

436. BALSHA (USA) ★★★
ch.f. Mr Greeley – Carefree Cheetah (Trempolino).
February 23. Fifth foal. $375,000Y. Keeneland September. Shadwell Estate Co. Half-sister to the US winner of 3 races, Grade 3 placed and smart miler Warrior Girl (by War Chant). The dam, placed over 10f at 3 yrs, is a half-sister to 6 winners including the Group 2 Mill Reef Stakes, Group 3 Hungerford Stakes and Group 3 Criterion Stakes winner Arkadian Hero. The second dam, Careless Kitten (by Caro), won once at 3 yrs in the USA and is a half-sister to 7 winners including the US Grade 1 winner Field Cat and the dams of the Group/Grade 1 winners Hold That Tiger, Editor's Note, Hennessy, Pearl City, Family Style and Lost Kitty. (Hamdan Al Maktoum).
"Still in Dubai and I haven't seen her, but I'm led to believe they like her".

437. DHERGHAAM (IRE) ★★★★
b.c. Exceed And Excel – Alnasreya (Machiavellian).
May 9. Half-brother to the fair 2008 7f placed 2-y-o Aathaar (by Marju). The dam, a quite useful 3-y-o 1m winner, is a half-sister to the Chilean Group 1 11f winner Fontanella Borghese. The second dam, Littlewick (by Green Desert), is a placed half-sister to 6 winners including the dam of the high-class Group 1 1m Coronation Stakes winner Rebecca Sharp (by Machiavellian) and the smart Group 3 11.5f Lingfield Derby Trial winner Mystic Knight. (Hamdan Al Maktoum).
"A May foal, he's a beautiful mover and a scopey individual that moves well. He looks a nice horse".

438. FAITHFUL DUCHESS (IRE) ★★★
b.f. Bachelor Duke – Portelet (Night Shift).
April 22. Ninth foal. 60,000Y. Tattersalls October 1. Vefa Ibrahim Araci. Half-sister to the Splendorinthegrass, unplaced in 2 starts at 2 yrs in 2008, to the very smart 2-y-o Group 2 7f Champagne Stakes winner Etlaala, the useful 7f and 1m winner and listed-placed Selective, the modest 5f winner Come What May (all by Selkirk), the useful 6f and 7f winner Overspect (by Spectrum) and the fair dual 7f winner Marmooq (by Cadeaux Genereux). The dam, a fairly useful 5f winner of 4 races, is a half-sister to 4 winners. The second dam, Noirmont (by Dominion), is an unraced half-sister to the Group winners Braashee, Adam Smith and Ghariba. (Mr V I Araci).

102 TWO YEAR OLDS OF 2009

"A nice filly and I would expect her to have some speed. She's a fairly late April foal so she'll need a bit of time but is definitely a two-year-old".

439. FREQUENCY ★★★
b.c. Starcraft – Soundwave (Prince Sabo).
May 16. Second foal. 13,000Y. Tattersalls October. Will Edmeades. Half-brother to the fair 2008 2-y-o 5f winner Sloop Johnb (by Bahamian Bounty). The dam is an unraced half-sister to 5 winners including the 2-y-o Group 1 6f Cheveley Park Stakes winner Airwave. The second dam, Kangra Valley (by Indian Ridge), a moderate 2-y-o 5f winner, is a half-sister to 7 minor winners. (Thurloe Thoroughbreds XXV).

"A late foal but an interesting colt as I thought he was going to be early. He's got some speed on the dam's side and he looks OK. He's grown a little bit and is strengthening up and doing well".

440. HABAAYIB ★★★★ ♠
b.f. Royal Applause – Silver Kestrel (Silver Hawk).
March 4. Second foal. 130,000Y. Tattersalls October 1. Shadwell Estate Co. Half-sister to the unraced 2008 2-y-o Lady Asha (by Mr Greeley). The dam, a minor winner of 2 races at 3 and 4 yrs in the USA, is a half-sister to 4 winners. The second dam, Salty Perfume (by Salt Lake), won the Grade 2 Adirondack Stakes in the USA and is a half-sister to 6 winners including the German Group 2 winner Green Perfume. (Hamdan Al Maktoum).

"She looks a nice, early filly and has the pedigree to suit. She was expensive for a Royal Applause, but she's attractive and will shortly begin fast work. Nice".

441. HUWAAYA ★★
b.f. Acclamation – Sometime Never (College Chapel).
February 14. Fourth foal. 86,000Y. Doncaster St Leger. Shadwell Estate Co. Half-sister to Rosa Rossa (by Opening Verse), a winner of 5 races at 3 and 4 yrs and from 1m to 10f. The dam is an unraced half-sister to 5 winners including the Italian Group 3 winner Su Tirolesu. The second dam, Glenross (by Warning), is an unraced half-sister to 8 winners. (Hamdan Al Maktoum).

"A backward filly, she's gone home for a break".

442. IJAAZA (USA) ★★
b.f. Storm Cat – Sierra Madre (Baillamont).
March 10. Sister to the high-class Group 1 7f Prix de la Salamandre and Group 1 1m Sussex Stakes winner Aljabr and half-sister to the useful 10f winner Jabaar (by Silver Hawk) and the useful French 2-y-o winner and 3-y-o listed 7f fourth Makaarem (by Danzig). The dam, a very smart winner of the Group 1 1m Prix Marcel Boussac and the Group 1 12f Prix Vermeille, is a half-sister to several minor winners. The second dam, Marie d'Irlande (by Kalamoun), a modest French 1m winner, is a sister to the very smart French 9f and 10f winner Dom Racine.

"She's in Dubai and I haven't seen her".

443. INVITEE ★★★
ch.f. Medicean – Party Doll (Be My Guest).
May 17. Fifteenth foal. 55,000Y. Tattersalls October 2. Cheveley Park Stud. Half-sister to the fairly useful 2008 2-y-o 5f winner Effort (by Dr Fong), to the German 2-y-o 7f and Group 2 German 1,000 Guineas winner Briseida (by Pivotal), the Group 2 6.5f Criterium des 2 Ans and Group 2 5f Prix du Gros-Chene winner and sire Titus Livius, the French and North American winner of 4 races Bahama Dream, the UAE 5f winner Zadalrakib (all by Machiavellian), the 2-y-o winner and listed-placed Party Zane (by Zafonic), the fairly useful 2-y-o 5f and subsequent US winner Shegardi (by Primo Dominie) and the minor French 3-y-o winner Doliouchka (by Saumarez). The dam, a very useful winner of 4 races in France including 3 listed events from 5f to 1m, was fourth in two Group 3 events and is a half-sister to 10 winners. The second dam, Midnight Lady (by Mill Reef), won once at 2 yrs and is a half-sister to 5 winners including the US Grade 2 winner Regal Bearing. (Cheveley Park Stud).

"A late foal, so not an obvious two-year-old. She was small but she's grown hugely and although she moves well she won't be rushed".

444. KANAF (IRE) ★★★★
b.c. Elnadim – Catcher Applause
(Royal Applause).
February 9. Third foal. 50,000Y. Doncaster St Leger. Shadwell Estate Co. The dam ran twice unplaced and is a half-sister to 2 minor winners. The second dam, Pfalz (by Pharly), a useful listed 1m winner, was third in the Group 3 Diomed Stakes and is a half-sister to 4 winners. (Hamdan Al Maktoum).
"A nice, uncomplicated colt that I like. A strong, mature colt that you hardly notice but he goes well and has some speed. He'll be starting faster work soon and could be OK".

445. KHAJALLY (IRE) ★★★ ♠
b.c. Kheleyf – Joyfullness (Dixieland Band).
March 16. Fifth foal. 140,000Y. Tattersalls October 2. Shadwell Estate Co. Half-brother to the Italian 2-y-o winner and listed-placed Flying Teapot (by King Charlemagne), to the quite useful Irish 1m winner Song In My Heart (by Spartacus) and the modest 6f and 7f winner Contented (by Orpen). The dam is an unraced half-sister to 11 winners including the dam of the Group 2 Royal Lodge Stakes winner Mons. The second dam, Arewehavingfunyet (by Sham), won the Grade 1 Oak Leaf Stakes and is a half-sister to 6 winners. (Hamdan Al Maktoum).
"A fine, big, good-looking horse that's only recently arrived, he had a slight setback after the Sales. He's cantering and moves well and he's a bit behind the others but seems to be coping well".

446. LANIZZA ★★
ch.c. Alhaarth – Cerulean Sky (Darshaan).
March 26. Half-brother to Mooteeah (by Sakhee), unplaced in 2 starts at 2 yrs in 2008 and to the very smart Group 2 2m 2f Doncaster Cup winner Honolulu (by Montjeu). The dam, a 1m (at 2 yrs) and Group 1 10f Prix Saint-Alary winner, is a sister to the smart 10f winner Qaatef and to the 7f (at 2 yrs) and listed 12f winner and Breeders Cup Filly & Mare second L'Ancresse and a half-sister to the useful French 2-y-o listed 7f winner Diner de Lune. The second dam, Solo de Lune (by Law Society), a French 11f winner, is a half-sister to the Grade 2 E P Taylor Stakes winner Truly A Dream and the French Group 2 winner Wareed. (Hamdan Al Maktoum).
"He's in Dubai so I don't know about him".

447. LITTLE OZ (IRE) ★★★
br.f. Red Ransom – Australie (Danehill).
April 7. First foal. The dam, a Group 3 Prix de Flore winner, is a sister to the Irish listed-placed 2-y-o and 5f 3-y-o winner Keepers Hill. The second dam, Asnieres (by Spend A Buck), a minor winner in France at 4 yrs, is a half-sister to the Breeders Cup Classic and 9.3f Prix d'Ispahan winner Arcangues, to the Prix de Psyche winner and French 1,000 Guineas second Agathe (dam of the triple Group 1 winner Alexandrie) and the dam of the 1,000 Guineas winner Cape Verdi. (Ballygallon Stud Ltd).
"She's in pre-training and arrives with me soon. A strong filly that looks to have some speed even though on pedigree I expected her to have some stamina. She looks mature and looks a two-year-old type".

448. LORD ARATAN (GER) ★★★
b.c. Tiger Hill – Luce (Sadler's Wells).
February 10. First foal. The dam is an unplaced half-sister to the 7f and subsequent US Grade 2 9f winner Aragorn and the useful French 2-y-o 5.5 winner Sashimi. The second dam, Onaga (by Mr Prospector), is a placed sister to the US Grade 2 All Along Stakes winner Sha Tha (herself dam of Group 2 10f Prix Dollar winner State Shinto) and a half-sister to the Group 3 Henry II Stakes winner Briar Creek and the dam of the Group 1 Phoenix Stakes winner One Cool Cat.
"Being by Tiger Hill I would expect him to take some time but he's a good-bodied, good-looking horse. I have three Tiger Hill two-year-olds and they all appear to want a bit of time. He'll be a good stallion with the produce of better mares coming through, but they won't be sharp, early two-year-olds".

449. MONTELISSIMA (IRE) ★★★
b.f. Montjeu – Issa (Pursuit Of Love).
February 4. First foal. The dam, unplaced in 3

starts, is a half-sister to numerous winners including the high-class Group 1 12f Yorkshire Oaks and Group 3 12f Lancashire Oaks winner Catchascatchcan (herself dam of the very smart miler Antonius Pius) and the listed 10f winner Licorne. The second dam, Catawba (by Mill Reef), a useful 10.5f winner, is a half-sister to 7 winners including the Ribblesdale Stakes winner Strigida. (Mrs G A Rupert).
"A nice filly but she'll need a bit of time. She's very racey and a typical Montjeu".

450. REZWAAN ★★★
b.c. Alhaarth – Nasij (Elusive Quality).
March 22. Third foal. The dam, a useful 6f (at 2 yrs) and listed 1m winner, was Group 3 placed twice and is a half-sister to 3 winners. The second dam, Hachiyah (by Generous), a fairly useful 10f winner, is closely related to the Italian Derby third Mutawwaj and a half-sister to the Peruvian champion Faaz. (Hamdan Al Maktoum).
"The first foal of a mare I trained to win a Guineas trial at Kempton. He's strong and powerful and looks to move well but he's an Alhaarth with a bit of a temperament".

451. SAARY ★★★
b.c. Green Desert – Jeed (Mujtahid).
May 15. Half-brother to the very useful 2-y-o listed 6f winner and Group 3 6f Princess Margaret Stakes second Nidhaal (by Observatory), to the fairly useful 12f winner of 5 races on the Flat and dual hurdles winner Maslak (by In The Wings) and the fair 9f winner Riqaab (by Peintre Celebre). The dam, a quite useful 2-y-o 6f winner, is a half-sister to 2 winners. The second dam, Secretary Bird (by Kris), is an unraced half-sister to the classic winners Assert (French and Irish Derby), Bikala (French Derby) and Eurobird (Irish St Leger). (Hamdan Al Maktoum).
"In Dubai but I'm told they like this colt. He's going to take some time though as he's a late foal".

452. SAGGIATORE ★★★
b.f. Galileo – Madame Dubois (Legend Of France).
April 24. Thirteenth foal. Closely related to the useful dual 12f winner Place de l'Opera (by Sadler's Wells and herself the dam of 3 stakes winners) and half-sister to the Irish 2,000 Guineas winner Indian Haven (by Indian Ridge), to the smart Group 1 Gran Criterium winner Count Dubois (by Zafonic), the useful dual 12f winner Massif Centrale (by Selkirk), the fairly useful 10f all-weather winner Paragon Of Virtue (by Cadeaux Genereux), the fairly useful 12f winner Galette (by Caerleon) and the quite useful 12f winner Richelieu (by Kris). The dam, a very smart filly, won 5 races from 9f to 14.6f including the Group 2 Park Hill Stakes and the Group 2 Prix de Royallieu and is a half-sister to 4 winners including the dam of the very smart 2-y-o Daggers Drawn. The second dam, Shadywood (by Habitat), a useful 10f winner, was second in the Lancashire Oaks and is a half-sister to 8 winners. (Cliveden Stud Ltd).
"The best bred of them all but she's a late foal and she's going to need some time. Not an obvious two-year-old type".

453. SATWA EXCEL ★★★
b.f. Exceed And Excel – Pericardia (Petong).
March 14. Ninth foal. €65,000Y. Goffs Million. D Metcalfe. Half-sister to the useful listed 10f Lupe Stakes winner Halicardia (by Halling), to the fairly useful 5f and 6f winner Card Games (by First Trump), the fairly useful 7f winner Noble Nick (by Primo Dominie), the quite useful 7f and 1m winner Dansa Queen (by Dansili) and the Italian winner of 9 races Bonheur de Chat (by Deploy). The dam is an unplaced half-sister to 4 winners including Prince Ferdinand, winner of the Group 3 7f Jersey Stakes. The second dam, Greensward Blaze (by Sagaro), won a 1m seller and is a half-sister to 2 minor winners. (The Lamprell Partnership).
"A filly I bought, she's very good-looking, looks to have some speed and goes well. I like her"

454. SATWA ROYAL ★★★
b.c. Royal Applause – Dance For Fun (Anabaa).
April 4. Third foal. 50,000Y. Tattersalls October 1. Not sold. Half-brother to the Group 1 Coronation Stakes, Group 1 Yorkshire Oaks and

Group 1 Matron Stakes winner Lush Lashes (by Galileo). The dam, a fair 1m all-weather winner, is out of the unraced Hilaris (by Arazi), herself a half-sister to 5 winners including the Group 3 Gallinule Stakes winner Exaltation. (The Lamprell Partnership).
"A big colt that will need some time. He moves well and he's fine".

455 SATWA SON ★★★★
b.c. Oasis Dream – Cozy Maria (Cozzene).
March 11. Third foal. 50,000Y. Tattersalls October 1. David Metcalfe. Half-brother to Albaasha (by Lemon Drop Kid), unplaced in one start at 2 yrs in 2008. The dam, a useful 10f winner, was listed-placed twice and is a half-sister to 6 winners in the USA. The second dam, Mariamme (by Verbatim), won twice at 3 yrs in the USA and is a half-sister to 7 winners including the Grade 1 Breeders Cup Turf winner Miss Alleged. (The Lamprell Partnership).
"This is a nice horse. He came in late but he looks to go well. A strong, well-bred colt and he'll be a nice, mid-season two-year-old".

456. SCARCITY (IRE) ★★
b.f. Invincible Spirit – Sanpa Fan (Sikeston).
March 16. Fourth foal. 62,000Y. Tattersalls October 1. John Warren. Half-sister to the Italian winner of 7 races from 2 to 4 yrs Wanix (by Wixim). The dam won 6 races at 2 to 5 yrs in Italy and is a half-sister to 3 other minor winners. The second dam, Ramk (by Riverman), ran twice unplaced and is a half-sister to 2 winners. (Highclere Thoroughbred Racing).
"She's had a problem and won't be seen until later on".

457. TIGER COURT ★★
b.f. Tiger Hill – Cruinn A Bhord (Inchinor).
May 6. Half-sister to the quite useful 1m and 10f winner Viva Vettori and to the modest 12f and hurdles winner Chess Board (both by Vettori). The dam, a fairly useful 7f winner, is a half-sister to 6 winners including the top-class filly Ouija Board (by Cape Cross), a winner of 10 races from 7f (at 2 yrs) to 12f including 7 Group/Grade 1 races. The second dam, Selection Board (by Welsh Pageant), was placed over 7f at 2 yrs and is a sister to the top class Queen Elizabeth II Stakes and Budweiser Arlington Million winner Teleprompter. (Lord Derby).
"A nice filly but she's not going to be an early type. She moves well and has just come in after having had a bit of a holiday".

458. VARACHI ★★★
b.c. Kyllachy – Miss Rimex (Ezzoud).
March 13. Sixth foal. 80,000Y. Tattersalls October 1. Vefa Ibrahim Araci. Half-brother to the Hong Kong Group 3 7f winner Flaming Lamborghini (formally a dual 7f winner under the name Warden Complex), to the modest 2008 2-y-o 6f winner Newlyn Art (both by Compton Place) and the fair Irish 1m winner Baileys Best (by Mister Baileys). The dam, a quite useful 6f (at 2 yrs) and 1m winner, is a half-sister to 6 winners including the dam of the stakes winners Guys And Dolls and Pawnbroker. The second dam, Blue Guitar (by Cure The Blues), a fairly useful winner of 2 races over 1m and 8.3f, is a half-sister to 2 listed winners including the smart broodmare Melody. (Mr V I Araci).
"A colt I bought, he looks nice and is a strong, mature, typical Kyllachy. He's out of an Ezzoud mare which may be a slight concern but he moves well".

459. UNNAMED ★★★
b.c. Alhaarth – Headrest (Habitat).
March 7. 12,500Y. Tattersalls October 2. Highflyer Bloodstock. Half-brother to the Group 2 10f Pretty Polly Stakes winner and Grade 1 Beverly Hills Handicap third Polaire (by Polish Patriot), to the fairly useful Irish 5f and 6f winner Southern Bound (by Fasliyev), the fair 11f and 12f winner Bramantino (by Perugino), the fair 10f winner Lurdi (by Lure) and two minor winners by Kalaglow and Caerleon. The dam is an unplaced sister to the Group 3 Princess Royal Stakes winner One Way Street (herself dam of the Group winners Grape Tree Road, Red Route and Windsor Castle) and to the dam of the May Hill Stakes and Hungerford Stakes winner Ever Genial. (The Serendipity Partnership).

"A little, neat, sharp Alhaarth that I bought cheaply. He's strong, mature, moves well and goes OK".

460. UNNAMED ★★★★
b.f. Night Shift – Photo Flash (Bahamian Bounty).
January 22. Fourth foal. 115,000Y. Doncaster St Leger. Blandford Bloodstock. Sister to the fairly useful 2-y-o 5f winner and listed placed Deal Breaker and half-sister to the Group 2 6f Richmond Stakes winner Prolific (by Compton Place). The dam, a fair 1m winner, is a half-sister to 6 winners including the smart 2-y-o Group 2 1m Royal Lodge Stakes winner Atlantis Prince. The second dam, Zoom Lens (by Caerleon), placed once over 7f at 2 yrs, is a half-sister to 4 winners. (St Albans Bloodstock).
"A strong, mature filly that's done everything right so far. She was bought to be a two-year-old and she looks like it".

461. UNNAMED ★★★★
b.c. Compton Place – Superlove (Hector Protector).
February 13. Fourth foal. 50,000Y. Tattersalls October 1. Angie Sykes. Half-brother to 2 winners in Germany by Surako and Auenadier. The dam is an unraced half-sister to 6 winners including the Irish listed winner Villa Carlotta. The second dam, Subya (by Night Shift), was a very useful winner of 5 races from 5f (at 2 yrs) to 10f including the Lupe Stakes, the Masaka Stakes and the Milcars Star Stakes (all listed events). (Findlay & Bloom).
"I like him, he's a nice horse that looks racey. He's a good moving horse, a good size and certainly a two-year-old type".

462. UNNAMED ★★★
ch.f. El Corredor – Ten Carats (Capote).
March 8. Third foal. 130,000Y. Tattersalls October 2. John Warren. Half-sister to 2 minor winners in the USA by Siphon and Medaglia d'Oro. The dam, a stakes-placed winner of 3 races in the USA, is a half-sister to 8 winners. The second dam, Miss Waikiki (by Miswaki), a stakes-placed winner at 2 yrs in the USA, is a half-sister to 4 winners. (St Albans Bloodstock).
"Her sister ran in the Breeders Cup Juvenile. She's a tall, very good-looking filly but won't be early and is one for later in the year".

HARRY DUNLOP

463. AVERROES (IRE) ★★★
ch.c. Galileo – Shapely (Alleged).
May 1. Eighth foal. 100,000Y. Tattersalls October 1. Blandford Bloodstock. Half-brother to the quite useful 1m and all-weather 10f winner Persuade (by Lure), to the fair 10f to 12f winner Dan Tucker (by Dansili), the minor French 3-y-o winner Darkshape (by Zamindar) and a winner in Greece by Sanglamore. The dam, a quite useful 2-y-o 7f winner, is a full or half-sister to 10 winners including the Group 3 6f July Stakes winner Wharf and the dams of Rail Link (Prix de l'Arc de Triomphe) and Linda's Lad (Criterium de Saint-Cloud). The second dam, Dockage (by Riverman), a winner over 1m at 2 yrs and a 9f listed event at 3 yrs in France, is a half-sister to 3 winners. (HE Sheikh Sultan Bin Khalifa Al Nehayan).
"For a Galileo he's not the biggest and I actually think he'll make a two-year-old by mid-season, probably over seven furlongs. I like him, he's a nice, easy-moving two-year-old and he could just be alright".

464. GREEN MOON (IRE) ★★
b.c. Montjeu – Green Noon (Green Tune).
February 16. First foal. The dam won 3 races at 2 yrs including the Group 3 1m Prix d'Aumale and was second in the Group 1 Prix Marcel Boussac. The second dam, Terring (by Bering), ran twice in France. (Mrs Ben Goldsmith).
"He's a lovely, big horse from a very nice female family but he's very much one for later in the year. A good mover and a good, quality colt. I like him a lot".

465. LADY SLIPPERS (IRE) ★★★
ch.f. Royal Academy – Woodland Orchid (Woodman).
March 11. Full sister to the 2-y-o Group 3 6f Coventry Stakes winner CD Europe and half-sister to the French 1m winner and listed Prix

Yacowlef second Cedar Sea (by Persian Bold), the quite useful UAE 7f winner Cover Drive (by Giant's Causeway) and the modest 10f winner African Pursuits (by Johannesburg). The dam is an unplaced half-sister to the Group 3 Derrinstown Stud Derby Trial winner Truth Or Dare, the UAE Group3 winner D'Anjou and the listed winner Sandstone. The second dam, Rose de Thai (by Lear Fan), won twice in France, was third in the Group 3 Prix Thomas Bryon and is a half-sister to 8 winners. (Airlie Stud).

"She's literally just arrived here from Ireland, so I don't know much about her but she looks to me like a mid-season two-year-old. I would imagine she'd be a six furlong two-year-old".

466. LIEBELEI (USA) ★★★
b.br.f. Royal Academy – Part With Pride (Executive Pride).
February 11. Eighth reported foal. $85,000Y. Fasig-Tipton Kentucky July. Blandford Bloodstock. Half-sister to 5 winners including the US Grade 3 winner Happy Trails (by Peaks And Valleys). The dam won 7 races and was Grade 3 placed in the USA and is out of the minor US winner Bye Bye Cy (by Cyane). (W J Armitage).

"She's quite an immature filly. We did a little bit with her a month ago and she clearly showed me she needed time. I would imagine she'll be a seven furlong two-year-old and she's an attractive filly".

467. LISTELLO (USA) ★★★
ch.c. More Than Ready – Dowry (Belong To Me).
February 20. First foal. £24,000 2-y-o. Goffs Kempton Breeze Up. Blandford Bloodstock. The dam won 4 minor races in the USA and is a half-sister to 4 winners, including one stakes winner. The second dam, Sea Jamie Win (by Dixieland Band), a minor winner in the USA, is a half-sister to 9 winners.

"A nice, big, strong-topped colt. He'll start off at six furlongs and I like him".

468. OLD MONEY ★★★
ch.f. Medicean – Nouveau Riche (Entrepreneur).
February 1. First foal. The dam, a fair 3-y-o 1m winner, is a half-sister to the smart Group 3 Prix La Rochette winner Guys And Dolls, to the smart 1m (at 2 yrs) to 11f listed winner Pawn Broker and the useful dual 7f 2-y-o winner and Group 3 placed Blushing Bride. The second dam, Dime Bag (by High Line), a quite useful winner of 4 races at up to 2m (including on the all-weather), is a half-sister to 7 minor winners. (Normandie Stud).

"She looked very immature a month ago but she's suddenly started to do well and I wouldn't be surprised if she does turn into a mid-season two-year-old. But the owner tends to prefer to take time with the two-year-olds, so she could take a bit longer. I would presume seven furlongs would be her starting point".

469. PROFESSOR BOLLINI ★★★
b.c. Bertolini – Nofa's Magic (Rainbow Quest).
April 10. Second foal. 3,000Y. Tattersalls October. Harry Dunlop. The dam, placed over 10f and 12f, is a half-sister to 5 winners including the Group 1 9f Prix Jean Prat winner Olden Times. The second dam, Garah (by Ajdal), a very useful winner of 4 races over 6f, was second in the Group 3 5f Duke Of York Stakes and is a half-sister to 6 winners. (Be Hopeful 2 Partnership).

"Quite a nice little horse, he'll be one of our first two-year-olds to run and should prove well worth the money he cost". TRAINER'S BARGAIN BUY

470. ROYAL ETIQUETTE ★★
b.c. Royal Applause – Alpine Gold (Montjeu).
March 9. First foal. The dam, a quite useful 2-y-o dual 1m winner, is closely related to the quite useful 2-y-o 1m winner Ski For Me and a half-sister to 2 winners. The second dam, Ski For Gold (by Shirley Heights), a fair 2-y-o 7f winner, stayed 2m and is a half-sister to the very useful 6f (at 2 yrs) and subsequent Grade 1 10f Santa Barbara Handicap winner Bequest and the useful 2-y-o 7f winner Fitzcarraldo. (Anamoine Ltd).

"A big horse that will take time. He'll want seven

furlongs or a mile, but he's a nice colt and he may surprise us".

471. SOUNDS OF THUNDER ★★★
b.f. Tobougg – Distant Music (Darshaan).
February 6. 11,000Y. Tattersalls October. Highflyer Bloodstock. Half-sister to the fair 1m (at 2 yrs) and 10f winner Rock Lobster (by Desert Sun), to the fair 11f to 2m winner of 11 races Desert Island Disc (by Turtle Island), the fair 10f winner Musical Echo (by Distant Music) and the moderate 10f and 11f winner Toccata Aria (by Unfuwain). The dam is an unraced half-sister to 5 winners. The second dam, Dancing Vaguely (by Vaguely Noble), won the listed 12f Prix Belle de Nuit and is a daughter of the French 1,000 Guineas and Prix Vermeille winner Dancing Maid. (Tessona Racing, F Mosselmans & Partners).
"She's doing some faster work and I'm very pleased with her progress. I'd like to start her in May over six furlongs because she's got some speed and I like her. She doesn't look a typical two-year-old but she needs getting on with and I think she'll be a nicer individual as the season goes on".

472. STATUESQUE ★★★
b.f. Red Ransom – Blue Icon (Peintre Celebre).
March 26. Third foal. Half-sister to Blue Nymph (by Selkirk), unplaced in one start at 2 yrs in 2008. The dam, a winner over 11f in France, is a half-sister to several winners including the Group 1 10f Prix de l'Opera winner Bright Sky. The second dam, Bright Moon (by Alysheba), won three Group 2 races over middle-distances in France. (Mr J Richmond-Watson).
"She's quite an interesting filly. She's quite big and her mother died leaving her an orphan unfortunately. I would imagine she'll be a seven furlong filly and she's a good mover".

JOHN DUNLOP
473. AALYA (IRE) ★★★
b.f. Peintre Celebre – Weqaar (Red Ransom).
March 8. Third foal. Half-sister to the unplaced 2008 2-y-o Jumaana (by Selkirk). The dam, a quite useful 10.2f winner, is a half-sister to several winners including the Prix de l'Arc de Triomphe and Juddmonte International winner Sakhee. The second dam, Thawakib (by Sadler's Wells), won twice over 7f (at 2 yrs) and the Group 2 12f Ribblesdale Stakes. She is a half-sister to numerous winners including the top-class middle-distance colt Celestial Storm (winner of the Group 2 Princess of Wales's Stakes) and to the placed dam of the Group 1 Rothmans International winner River Memories. (Hamdan Al Maktoum).
"A nice, attractive filly, but currently in Dubai (mid-April)".

474. ALBEED ★★★
b.f. Tiger Hill – Ayun (Swain).
March 7. Second foal. Half-sister to the unplaced 2008 2-y-o Akmal (by Selkirk). The dam, a useful 1m and 10f winner, is a half-sister to the smart 7f (at 2 yrs) and Group 3 1m Desmond Stakes winner Haami and the fairly useful 2-y-o 1m winner Asas. The dam, a very useful filly, won over 7f at 2yrs and the Group 2 10f Premio Lydia Tesio and listed 10f Lupe Stakes at 3 yrs. She is a half-sister to 6 winners including the Derby winner Erhaab out of the French 10.5f winner Histoire (by Riverman). (Hamdan Al Maktoum).
"A strong, quality filly, currently in Dubai".

475. ALMUTHAM (USA) ★★★
b.br.c. Dynaformer – Forest Lady (Woodman).
May 1. Third foal. $260,000Y. Keeneland September. Shadwell Estate Co. The dam is an unraced sister to the Group 1 Grand Criterium and Grade 1 Secretariat Stakes winner and Irish Derby third Ciro and to the US stakes-placed winner Woodyousmileforme and a half-sister to 4 winners. The second dam, Gioconda (by Nijinsky), a 1m winner at 3 yrs in France, is a half-sister to the classic winners Hector Protector, Bosra Sham and Shanghai. (Hamdan Al Maktoum).
"A big, quality colt, still in Dubai".

476. ALNASEEM (USA) ★★★
b.f. Nayef – Elrehaan (Sadler's Wells).
January 1. Second foal. Half-sister to the fairly

useful 1m (including at 2 yrs) and 7f winner Tarteel (by Bahri). The dam, a fairly useful 2-y-o 7f winner, was third in the listed Cheshire Oaks and is a half-sister to 3 winners including the useful 2-y-o 7f winner Wahsheeq. The second dam, Moss (by Woodman), ran once unplaced in the USA and is a half-sister to the William Hill Sprint Championship and Prix de l'Abbaye winner Committed (herself dam of the US Grade 1 winner Pharma). (Hamdan Al-Maktoum).
"A lovely filly, she's yet to arrive from Dubai".

477. BERLING ★★★★
gr.c. Montjeu – Danaskaya (Danehill).
March 27. Third foal. 650,000Y. Tattersalls October 1. Peter Doyle. Half-brother to the fair Irish 2-y-o 7f winner Kayd Kodaun (by Traditionally). The dam, a useful Irish 2-y-o 6f winner and third in the Group 1 6f Cheveley Park Stakes, is a half-sister to 5 winners including the triple listed 7f winner Modeeroch and the 2-y-o 8.5f winner and Group 1 1m Gran Criterium third Chinese Whisper (by Montjeu). The second dam, Majinskaya (by Marignan), winner of the listed 12f Prix des Tuileries, is a half-sister to 6 winners including the dam of the Group 1 5f Prix de l'Abbaye winner Kistena. (Benny Anderson).
"A very attractive colt and a very good mover, he's probably one for the second half of the season".

478. CAUCUS ★★
b.c. Cape Cross – Maid To Perfection (Sadler's Wells).
February 19. Fourth foal. Half-brother to the fair 11.6f winner Perfect Reward (by Cadeaux Genereux). The dam, a useful 7f (at 2 yrs) and 10f winner, is a half-sister to 3 winners including the useful 2-y-o 7f winner Artistic Lad. The second dam, Maid For The Hills (by Indian Ridge), was a useful 2-y-o and won twice over 6f including the listed Empress Stakes. She is a half-sister to the dams of the Group winners Stroll, Lady In Waiting and Savannah Bay. (Normandie Stud Ltd).
"A well-made, well-balanced colt but relatively backward".

479. CLARIETTA ★★★★
b.br.f. Shamardal – Claxon (Caerleon).
April 6. Sixth foal. 290,000Y. Tattersalls October 1. Not sold. Half-sister to the fair 2008 7f and 1m fourth placed 2-y-o Al Tamooh (by Dalakhani), to the useful 7f (at 2 yrs) and listed Lingfield Oaks Trial and subsequent US Grade 3 winner and Group 1 Nassau Stakes second Cassydora (by Darshaan), to listed 10f winner Classic Remark (by Dr Fong) and the quite useful 10f winner Circle Of Love (by Sakhee). The dam, a very useful 1m (at 2 yrs) and Group 2 10f Premio Lydia Tesio winner, is a half-sister to 3 winners including the Group 2 placed Bulwark. The second dam, Bulaxie (Bustino), a very useful winner of the Group 3 7.3f Fred Darling Stakes, was second in the Group 2 Premio Lydia Tesio and is a half-sister to 6 winners including the Group 3 10f Prix de la Nonette winner and smart broodmare Dust Dancer. (Bluehills Racing Ltd).
"An attractive, good-moving filly. Probably one for the second half of the season".

480. DREAM SPINNER ★★★
b.c. Royal Applause – Dream Quest (Rainbow Quest).
April 29. Fifth foal. 20,000Y. Tattersalls October 2. Not sold. Half-brother to the quite useful all-weather 12f and 13f winner Nando's Dream (by Hernando) and to a winning hurdler by Sinndar. The dam, a useful 10f winner and listed-placed, is a sister to the smart German Group 2 12f winner Baroon and a half-sister to the Group 2 Goldene Peitsche and Group 3 6f Prix de Meautry winner Vision Of Night and to the smart Group 3 5f Prix de Saint-Georges winner Struggler. The second dam, Dreamawhile (by Known Fact), a quite useful 3-y-o 7f winner, is a half-sister to 5 winners including the Group 1 Italian Derby winner My Top. (Bluehills Racing Ltd).
"A good-looking, well-made colt, he'll be relatively early but the dam stayed well".

481. ELTHEEB ★★★
b.c. Red Ransom – Snowdrops (Gulch).
April 14. First foal. 150,000Y. Tattersalls

October 1. Shadwell Estate Co. The dam won 10 races from 3 to 6 yrs in the USA including three Grade 3 stakes. The second dam, Roses In The Snow (by Be My Guest), a useful 1m winner and listed-placed here, subsequently won in the USA and is a half-sister to 6 winners. (Hamdan Al Maktoum).
"A big, tall colt but a good mover – one for the second half of the season".

482. GOODWOOD DIVA ★★★★
ch.f. *Kyllachy – Donna Vita (Vettori)*.
March 11. Second foal. 17,000Y. Tattersalls October 2. R Frisby. Half-sister to the unplaced 2008 2-y-o Siciliando (by Bertolini). The dam, a fairly useful 2-y-o 7f winner, was fourth in a listed event over 11f at 3 yrs and is a half-sister to 3 winners including the Group 1 placed Reduit. The second dam, Soolaimon (by Shareef Dancer), is a placed half-sister to 4 winners including the French Group 3 winner Audacieuse. (Goodwood Racehorse Owners Group (16) Ltd).
"One of the more forward two-year-olds at Arundel. She's a good mover and is showing potential for the future".

483. GUNDAROO ★★★★
b.f. *Oasis Dream – Encore My Love (Royal Applause)*.
February 22. Fourth foal. Half-sister to the unplaced 2008 2-y-o Harry Raffle (by Observatory) and to the quite useful 2-y-o 5f and 6f winner Prospect Place (by Compton Place). The dam, a modest 6f placed 2-y-o, is a half-sister to 6 winners including the Group 1 Racing Post Trophy winner Be My Chief. The second dam, Lady Be Mine (by Sir Ivor), a minor 3-y-o 1m winner at Yarmouth, is a half-sister to 6 winners including Mixed Applause (dam of both the high-class miler Shavian and the Ascot Gold Cup winner Paean). (Mrs M Burrell).
"A very good-looking, good-moving filly that should make a two-year-old".

484. HAATHEQ (USA) ★★
b.c. *Seeking The Gold – Alshadiyah (Danzig)*.
April 30. Closely related to the fair 6f and 7f winner Badweia (by Kingmambo) and half-brother to the useful 2-y-o dual 6f winner and dual listed-placed Wid (by Elusive Quality). The dam, a useful 2-y-o 6f winner, is a half-sister to 7 winners including the smart 7f (at 2 yrs) and 10f listed winner Imtiyaz and the very useful Bint Shadayid, winner of the Group 3 7f Prestige Stakes and placed in the 1,000 Guineas and the Fillies Mile. The second dam, Shadayid (by Shadeed), a very smart filly, won the 1,000 Guineas and the Prix Marcel Boussac. (Hamdan Al Maktoum).
"A big, backward colt and one for the second half of the season".

485. HAJJAN (USA) ★★★★
b.c. *Mr Greeley – Danzig Island (Danzig)*.
March 21. Twelfth foal. $400,000Y. Keeneland September. Shadwell Estate Co. Half-brother to 7 winners including the US Grade 3 winner of 13 races High Strike Zone (by Smart Strike) and the minor US stakes winner Secret Beauty (by Mt Livermore). The dam is an unraced half-sister to the Group 2 Waterford Crystal Mile and Grade 2 Eddie Reid Handicap winner Sharrood and the US stakes winners Island Escape and Our Reverie. The second dam, Angel Island (by Cougar II), won the Grade 2 8.5f Alcibiades Stakes at 2 yrs in the USA. (Hamdan Al Maktoum).
"A very attractive, racey colt that should make a two-year-old. Currently still in Dubai".

486. LATHAAT ★★★
b.br.f. *Dubai Destination – Khulood (Storm Cat)*.
January 17. Third foal. Half-sister to the fair 2008 7f placed 2-y-o Imaam (by Pivotal) and to the quite useful 2-y-o 5f winner Kashoof (by Green Desert). The dam, a useful listed 7f (at 2 yrs) and Group 3 7f Nell Gwyn Stakes winner, is a half-sister to numerous winners including the Irish 1,000 Guineas winner Mehthaaf and the July Cup winner Elnadim. The second dam, Elle Seule (by Exclusive Native), a very smart winner of the Group 3 1m Prix d'Astarte, also won over 10.5f and is a half-sister to the Group/Grade 1 winners Fort Wood, Hamas and Timber Country and to the Group winners Northern Aspen,

Colorado Dancer and Mazzacano. (Hamdan Al Maktoum).
"A good-looking, quality filly but she'll take some time to develop".

487. MINIYAMBA (IRE) ★★★
b.f. Sadler's Wells – Atlantide (Southern Halo).
March 8. Third foal. 230,000Y. Tattersalls October 1. Peter Doyle. The dam won once over 10f in France and is a half-sister to 7 winners including the Group 3 Prix de la Jonchere winner Android and the listed winners and smart broodmares Airline and Astorg. The second dam, Action Francaise (by Nureyev), won the Group 3 Prix de Sandringham and is out of the outstanding filly Allez France. (Benny Anderson).
"A good-looking, good-moving filly but relatively backward".

488. MUDAARAAH ★★★
b.f. Cape Cross – Wissal (Woodman).
February 27. Closely related to the useful listed 6f winner Ethaara (by Green Desert) and half-sister to the useful 2-y-o listed 7f winner Sudoor (by Fantastic Light). The dam is an unraced sister to the high-class 2-y-o Group 2 7f Laurent Perrier Champagne Stakes Bahhare and a half-sister to the Group 1 1m St James's Palace Stakes and Group 1 1m Queen Elizabeth II Stakes winner Bahri. The second dam, Wasnah (by Nijinsky), a fairly useful maiden, was placed at up to 10.5f and is a half-sister to the Group/Graded stakes winners Dance Bid, Northern Plain and Winglet. (Hamdan Al Maktoum).
"An attractive filly and a good mover but still relatively immature".

489. MUFARRH (IRE) ★★
b.c. Marju – What A Picture (Peintre Celebre).
March 8. Second foal. 170,000Y. Tattersalls October 2. Shadwell Estate Co. Half-brother to Partner Shift (by Night Shift), placed once over 7f at 2 yrs in 2008 from 2 starts. The dam is an unplaced half-sister to 6 winners including the Group 1 Gran Criterium winner Night Style and the listed Prix d'Automne winner Maid Of Dawkins. The second dam, Style For Life (by Law Society), won 2 races in France over middle-distances, was listed-placed and is a half-sister to 7 winners including the Irish Derby winner Grey Swallow. (Hamdan Al Maktoum).
"A big, strong colt and a good mover but he's bred for middle-distances".

490. MUNSARIM ★★★
b.c. Shamardal – Etizaaz (Diesis).
March 25. Sixth foal. Half-brother to the fairly useful 2008 2-y-o 1m winner Almiqdaad (by Haafhd) and to the smart 6f (including at 2 yrs) and listed 7f winner of 6 races Munaddam (by Aljabr). The dam, a listed 1m winner and second in the Group 1 12f Prix Vermeille, is a half-sister to the listed 6f Sirenia Stakes winner Santolina and the US Grade 3 7f Lafayette Stakes winner Trafalger. The second dam, Alamosa (by Alydar), is an unraced half-sister to the King George VI and Queen Elizabeth Diamond Stakes winner Swain out of the US Grade 1 winner Love Smitten. (Hamdan Al Maktoum).
"A big, powerful colt but will need some time. Currently in Dubai".

491. NAASEF ★★★
b.c. Pivotal – Hathrah (Linamix).
April 23. Second foal. Half-brother to the unplaced 2008 2-y-o Itlaak (by Alhaarth). The dam, winner of the listed 1m Masaka Stakes and third in the 1,000 Guineas, is a half-sister to 5 winners including the smart Group 2 12f Premio Ellington winner Ivan Luis and the French/German listed winners Amathia and Zero Problemo. The second dam, Zivania (by Shernazar), a useful Irish winner of 4 races from 1m to 9.5f, is a half-sister to the Group 3 Prix Gontaut Biron winner Muroto. (Hamdan Al Maktoum).
"A very good-looking colt but a relatively late foal and he'll need some time".

492. PAINSWICK (USA) ★★★★
ch.c. Elusive Quality – Pleine Lune (Alzao).
February 19. Half-brother to the quite useful 11f and 13f winner Fear To Tread (by Peintre Celebre) and to the fair Irish 10f winner

Wilderness Bay (by Fasliyev). The dam, a French 2-y-o 6f and 1m winner, is a half-sister to 6 winners including the Group 1 Criterium de Saint-Cloud (at 2 yrs) and Group 1 Grand Prix de Saint-Cloud winner Pistolet Bleu and the Group 3 10.5f Prix de Flore winner Palme d'Or. The second dam, Pampa Bella (by Armos), a very useful filly, won 3 races including the Group 3 10.5f Prix Penelope, was third in both the Prix de Diane and the Prix Saint Alary and is a half-sister to 8 winners. (R Scully).
"A well-bred individual and a very good mover. A mid-season two-year-old".

493. PERSIAN HEROINE (IRE) ★★★★
b.f. Intikhab – Persian Fantasy (Persian Bold).
February 16. Half-sister to the very useful listed 1m to 12f winner Persian Lightning (by Sri Pekan), the fairly useful 14f and 2m winner Height Of Fantasy (by Shirley Heights), the quite useful 12f winner Pershaan (by Darshaan) and the modest 1m winner Pairumani Princess (by Pairumani Star). The dam, a fairly useful dual 12f winner, is a half-sister to numerous winners including Group 2 winner Lucky Guest. (Windflower Overseas Holdings Inc).
"A strong, compact filly and a good mover who shows some speed".

494. QUEEN OF WANDS ★★
b.f. Sakhee – Maid To Treasure (Rainbow Quest).
February 18. Second foal. Half-sister to the fair 2008 9f placed 2-y-o King Of Wands (by Galileo). The dam, a fair 7f (at 2 yrs) and 10f placed maiden, is a half-sister to numerous winners including the useful 7f (at 2 yrs) and 10f winner Maid To Perfection and the useful 2-y-o 7f winner Artistic Lad. The second dam, Maid For The Hills (by Indian Ridge), was a useful 2-y-o and won twice over 6f including the listed Empress Stakes and is a half-sister to 5 winners including the Group 3 6f Princess Margaret Stakes second Maid For Walking. (Normandie Stud).
"A good mover but bred for middle-distances and unlikely to run in the first half of the season".

495. ROSE ALBA (IRE) ★★★
gr.f. Verglas – Green Rosy (Green Dancer).
May 11. Fifteenth foal. 72,000Y. Tattersalls October 1. Not sold. Half-sister to the 2008 Irish 7f placed 2-y-o Rockhampton (by Galileo) and to 8 winners including the French Group 2 12f winners America (by Arazi) and Majorien (by Machiavellian), the listed 6f Hopeful Stakes winner Rose Indien (by Crystal Glitters) and the 7f (at 2 yrs in France) and dual 9.5f winner Royal Racer (by Danehill). The dam, a French 10f winner and listed-placed, is a sister to the French listed winner Big Sink Hope and a half-sister to 9 winners including the good broodmare Rensaler (dam of the US Grade 1 winner Jovial). The second dam, Round The Rosie (by Cornish Prince), won once at 2 yrs in the USA and is a half-sister to 2 stakes winners. (Susan Abbott Racing).
"A well-made, good-moving filly but a late foal and immature".

496. SADERAAT (USA) ★★
ch.f. Aljabr – Teeba (Seeking The Gold).
March 12. First foal. The dam, a fairly useful 3-y-o 1m winner, was listed placed twice and is closely related to 2 winners including the smart 7f (at 2 yrs) and 10f listed winner Imtiyaz and a half-sister to numerous winners including Bint Shadayid, winner of the Group 3 7f Prestige Stakes and placed in the 1,000 Guineas and the Fillies Mile. The second dam, Shadayid (by Shadeed), won the 1,000 Guineas, the Prix Marcel Boussac and the Fred Darling Stakes and was placed in the Oaks, the Coronation Stakes, the Queen Elizabeth II Stakes, the Sussex Stakes and the Haydock Park Ladbroke Sprint Cup. She is a half-sister to several winners including the very useful dual 7f winner and Jersey Stakes third Dumaani. (Hamdan Al-Maktoum).
"A lengthy, immature filly currently still in Dubai".

497. SPRING HEATHER (IRE) ★★★★
b.f. Montjeu – Spotlight (Dr Fong).
March 12. First foal. 105,000Y. Tattersalls October 1. Not sold. The dam, a listed 1m and subsequent US Grade 2 Lake Placid Handicap

winner, is a full or half-sister to 3 winners including the listed placed Dusty Answer. The second dam, Dust Dancer (by Suave Dancer), won 4 races including the Group 3 10f Prix de la Nonette and is a half-sister to 6 winners including the Group 3 7.3f Fred Darling Stakes winner Bulaxie (herself dam of the Group 2 winner Claxon). (Bluehills Racing Ltd).
"A small, strongly built filly and a good mover".

498. SUROOH (USA) ★★
b.f. Pivotal – Alabaq (Riverman).
March 28. Half-sister to the fairly useful 7f winner Aamaaq (by Danehill) and to the fair dual 10f winner Asaateel (by Unfuwain). The dam, a smart winner of the Group 3 1m Premio Bagutta and listed 10f Pretty Polly Stakes, is a half-sister to the Group 3 Rockfel Stakes winner Bint Salsabil and to the very useful 2-y-o 6f and 7f winner Sahm. The second dam, Salsabil (by Sadler's Wells), won the Prix Marcel Boussac, the 1,000 Guineas, the Irish Derby, the Epsom Oaks and the Prix Vermeille - all Group 1 events. She is a half-sister to the high-class colt Marju, winner of the St James's Palace Stakes. (Hamdan Al Maktoum).
"Still in Dubai and has suffered a minor injury".

499. WARLU WAY ★★★★
b.c. Sakhee – Conspiracy (Rudimentary).
March 16. Half-brother to the quite useful 2007 2-y-o 7f winner Presbyterian Nun (by Daylami), to the useful 10f to 11.6f winner In Disguise (by Nashwan), the fairly useful 2-y-o triple 7f winner Jedburgh (by Selkirk) and the fairly useful 2-y-o 7f winner Impersonator (by Zafonic). The dam, a useful 2-y-o listed 5f winner, is a half-sister to 7 winners including the Group 2 10f Sun Chariot Stakes winner Ristna and the dual listed winner Gayane. The second dam, Roussalka (by Habitat), won 7 races at up to 10f including the Coronation Stakes and the Nassau Stakes (twice) and is a half-sister to the Fillies Triple Crown winner Oh So Sharp (herself dam of the Prix Saint Alary winner Rosefinch). (The Earl Cadogan).
"An attractive, good-looking colt and a very good mover".

500. WASEET ★★★
ch.c. Nayef – Najayeb (Silver Hawk).
February 22. Third foal. Half-brother to the quite useful 2-y-o 1m winner Mutadarrej (by Fantastic Light). The dam is an unraced half-sister to the high-class Prix de l'Arc de Triomphe and Juddmonte International winner Sakhee and is closely related to the useful 7f (at 2 yrs) and 10f winner Nasheed. The second dam, Thawakib (by Sadler's Wells), a useful dual 7f (at 2 yrs) and Group 2 12f Ribblesdale Stakes winner, is a half-sister to numerous winners including the top-class middle-distance colt Celestial Storm (winner of the Group 2 Princess of Wales's Stakes). (Hamdan Al Maktoum).
"A backward colt but a good walker who is still in Dubai".

501. ZAHOO (IRE) ★★★
b.f. Nayef – Tanaghum (Darshaan).
May 12. Third foal. Half-sister to the fair 2008 1m placed 2-y-o Tactic (by Sadler's Wells) and to the quite useful 1m winner Taaresh (by Sakhee). The dam, a useful listed-placed 10f winner, is a half-sister to 4 winners including the smart Group 2 10f Premio Lydia Tesio winner Najah. The second dam, Mehthaaf (by Nureyev), won the Irish 1,000 Guineas, the Tripleprint Celebration Mile and the Nell Gwyn Stakes and is closely related to the Diadem Stakes winner Elnadim and to the French 2-y-o 7.5f winner Only Seule (herself dam of the Group 1 7f Prix de la Foret and Group 1 6.5f Prix Maurice de Gheest winner Occupandiste). (Hamdan Al Maktoum).
"An attractive, strong filly. Still in Dubai".

502. UNNAMED ★★★
b.c. Hawk Wing – Divine Grace
(Definite Article).
February 20. Fourth foal. 40,000Y. **Tattersalls October 1. John Dunlop.** Half-brother to the German Group 2 6f Goldene Peitsche winner of 5 races Electric Beat (by Shinko Forest) and the modest 5.2f winner Divalini (by Bertolini). The dam ran unplaced twice and is a half-sister to 2 winners. The second dam, Grey Patience (by Common Grounds), is an unraced half-sister to

8 winners including the listed winners Cape Town and Regiment. (The Blue Bar Partnership). "A big, immature colt but a very good mover".

PAT EDDERY
503. CONTRACT CATERER (IRE) ★★
b.c. Azamour – Nawaji (Trempolino).
March 18. Seventh foal. €28,000Y. Goffs Million. Not sold. Half-brother to the useful 2-y-o 7f winner Ahmedy (by Polish Precedent), to the quite useful 9.5f winner Noticeable (by Night Shift) and fair 7f (at 2 yrs) to 10f winner Press Express (by Entrepreneur). The dam, a poor placed maiden at up to 13f, is a sister to the Group 3 10f Select Stakes winner Triarius and a half-sister to the listed Fred Archer Stakes winner Sharp Noble and the unraced dam of the Group 3 Prix des Reservoirs winner Bint Alnasr. The second dam, Noble Decretum (by Noble Decree), is an unplaced half-sister to 12 winners.
"He's a nice colt that's very stoutly bred and although he will run at two and he's doing everything right he won't be out until the seven furlong races at least. He's not over-big, he has a good attitude, he's done one or two bits of work and he's OK". Pat's Assistant, Simon Double, was once again kind enough to talk about their horses with me.

504. HEARTS OF FIRE ★★★★
b.c. Firebreak – Alexander Ballet (Mind Games).
April 22. Third foal. 13,000Y. Doncaster St Leger. Pat Eddery. Half-brother to Django Reinhardt (by Tobougg), unplaced in one start at 2 yrs in 2008. The dam, an Irish 3-y-o 5f winner, is a half-sister to 3 winners including the fairly useful listed placed Day By Day. The second dam, Dayville (by Dayjur), a quite useful triple 6f winner, is a half-sister to 4 winners including the Grade 1 Yellow Ribbon Handicap winner Spanish Fern. (Pat Eddery Racing (Detroit)).
"Winner of the Brocklesbury Stakes in March, I think this is a serious horse and we'll have to look at Royal Ascot with him. I think it was an above average Brocklesbury and Pat has always thought a lot of him. At the Sales we never thought he'd be this early and the thing about him is not just his precocity but his temperament – he takes everything in his stride. That'll stand him in good stead because he's got a bit of scope and we never saw him as a whiz-bang two-year-old. He came to hand himself very early".

505. KENSWICK ★★★
b.f. Avonbridge – The Jotter (Night Shift).
January 14. 14,000Y. Tattersalls October 3. Pat Eddery. Half-sister to the useful 6f (at 2yrs) and subsequent US stakes-placed winner Final Row (by Indian Ridge), to the fair 7f and 1m winner of 12 races Out For A Stroll (by Zamindar) and the fair 8.5f winner Ice Prince (by Polar Falcon). The dam, a useful 2-y-o 5f and 6.5f winner, was second in three listed events, fourth in the Group 3 7f Prestige Stakes and is closely related to the Group 1 Gran Criterium second Line Dancer. The second dam, Note-Book (by Mummy's Pet), a fairly useful 6f winner, is a sister to the Norfolk Stakes winner Colmore Row and a half-sister to the smart miler Long Row out of the Irish 1,000 Guineas winner Front Row. (The Hill Top Partnership).
"A neat filly, she's nice and she'll be out quite soon. Nicely-bought, she's got speed and ability and she looks a two-year-old type".

506. UNNAMED ★★★
ch.f. Danehill Dancer – Easter Heroine (Exactly Sharp).
February 16. Seventh foal. 230,000Y. Tattersalls October 1. Pat Eddery. Half-sister to the 2-y-o 5f and 6f winner, Group 1 Middle Park Stakes third and subsequent US Grade 3 winner Doc Holiday (by Dr Devious) and the 7f to 1m winner Greek Easter (by Namid). The dam was placed over 7f (at 2 yrs) and 10f in Ireland and is a half-sister to 4 winners including the useful 5f and 6f winner Ocker. The second dam, Violet Somers (by Will Somers), is an unraced sister to the smart sprinters Balidar (winner of the Prix de l'Abbaye) and Balliol (winner of the Cork and Orrery Stakes). (Derek Smith).
"A very nice filly, we haven't done much with her yet but you'd expect her to be out at two

and Pat likes her quite a bit. Obviously we'll take our time with her because she was an expensive filly".

507. UNNAMED ★★★
gr.f. Verglas – Jinx Johnson (Desert King).
February 24. First foal. 20,000Y. **Doncaster St Leger Festival. Pat Eddery.** The dam, a modest Irish 1m winner, is a half-sister to the Italian listed winner and Group 2 placed Morena Park (by Pivotal). The second dam, Peace In The Park (by Ahonoora), was unplaced twice and is a half-sister to 6 winners including the Irish 2-y-o listed winner and Group 1 Phoenix Stakes third Buffalo Berry.
"She's suddenly come to hand over the last few weeks and we might send her for a Fillies' maiden at Warwick in early May. We know she's got ability because of a yardstick we have with Hearts Of Fire. She'll be out over five or six furlongs and there's plenty of speed in the pedigree. She's always active – always on the go – and she's definitely got 'two-year-old' written all over her".

508. UNNAMED ★★★★
b.g. Mujahid – Leominda (Lion Cavern).
February 5. Second foal. 26,000Y. **Doncaster Festival. Pat Eddery.** Half-brother to the minor French 3-y-o 1m winner Athara (by Forzando). The dam, a modest 5f and 6f placed 2-y-o maiden, is a half-sister to 8 winners including the dam of the Group winners Franklins Gardens and Polar Ben. The second dam, Arminda (by Blakeney), is an unraced half-sister to 4 winners including the French Oaks winner Madam Gay. (Pat Eddery Racing (Reel Buddy)).
"This could be very nice and I put him on a par with Hearts Of Fire. He was a bit of a Playboy so we gelded him. Paul Eddery rides him a lot, he's got bags of ability but has a very different temperament from Hearts Of Fire and even now he isn't a girl's ride. We haven't really put a gun to his head yet but everything he's done has pleased us and he'll probably be out at the end of May over six furlongs. He's a big horse with bags of scope and he was easily the best-looker on his day of the Sales".

509. UNNAMED ★★★
b.c. Oratorio – Willowbridge (Entrepreneur).
April 6. Fourth foal. 200,000Y. **Tattersalls October 1. Pat Eddery.** Closely related to the quite useful triple 1m winner Willow Dancer (by Danehill Dancer). The dam is an unraced half-sister to 6 winners including the Breeders Cup Turf winner Northern Spur and the Doncaster Cup winners Great Marquess and Kneller. The second dam, Fruition (by Rheingold), was second in the 12f Lupe Stakes and is a half-sister to 9 winners including the top-class broodmare Flame of Tara (the dam of Salsabil and Marju). (Derek Smith).
"She's lovely and she'll make a two-year-old with the scope to go on. I think she'll probably be out before our other Danehill Dancer filly and she's already shown us that she's got what it takes. I would think it's too early to get her out in time for Ascot, but I'd expect her to be making her debut in a maiden around that time. Pat likes her a lot".

DAVID ELSWORTH
510. ALL MY HEART ★★★
ch.f. With Approval – All Is Fair (Selkirk).
March 9. Sixth foal. The dam, a quite useful 2-y-o 6f winner, is a sister to the Italian 2-y-o winner Mia Robino. The second dam, Allegra (by Niniski), a fair 12f winner at 3 yrs, is a half-sister to 4 winners including the Nassau Stakes and Sun Chariot Stakes winner Last Second, the Irish Oaks third Arrikala and the Moyglare Stud Stakes third Alouette (herself dam of the Champion Stakes winner Alborada). (Miss K Rausing).
"I think she'll be running in mid-season and she looks a two-year-old type. She's doing well".

511. DASHING DOC (IRE) ★★★★
ch.c. Dr Fong – Dashiba (Dashing Blade).
February 7. Half-brother to the smart 7f (at 2 yrs) and listed 1m and 10f winner Barsheba (by Barathea) and to the useful 2-y-o listed 1m winner Doctor Dash (by Dr Devious). The dam, a useful 9f and 10f winner, is a half-sister to several winners including the fairly useful 10f and 12f winner Smart Blade (by Elegant Air) and

the hurdles winner Sharriba (by Sharrood). The second dam, Alsiba (by Northfields), a modest winner of one race at 4 yrs, was a staying half-sister to several winners and to the dam of the Irish St Leger winner Oscar Schindler. (J C Smith).
"A relatively early type, I think he'll start off at six furlongs and both his half-sister Barsheba and his half-brother Doctor Dash won as a two-year-olds. So I expect he'll do the same".

512. DUTY DRIVEN ★★★★
b.c. Motivator – Duty Paid (Barathea).
February 10. Third foal. Half-brother to the modest 7f and 1m winner Duty Doctor (by Dr Fong). The dam, a useful 2-y-o listed 6f winner, is a sister to the useful 1m winner and listed-placed Lady Miletrian and a half-sister to 3 winners. The second dam, Local Custom (by Be My Native), was placed at up to 7f at 2 yrs and is a sister to the listed winner Tribal Rite and a half-sister to the Middle Park Stakes winner Balla Cove. (J C Smith).
"The dam won at Royal Ascot as a two-year-old but being by Motivator I'm expecting this colt to be one for the second half of the season. He's a very nice colt".

513. FAIR TRADE ★★★★
ch.c. Trade Fair – Ballet (Sharrood).
February 2. Eleventh foal. 80,000Y. Tattersalls October 2. Suzanne Roberts. Half-brother to the smart 1m (at 2 yrs) and listed 10f winner Island Sound (by Turtle Island), to the useful 10f and 11.6f winner Serge Lifar (by Shirley Heights), the fairly useful Irish 10f winner Ballyhaunis (by Daylami), the quite useful 10f winner Quintoto (by Mtoto), the German 7f winner Batanga (by Primo Dominie) and the modest 14.8f all-weather winner Charlie's Gold (by Shalford). The dam, a moderate 5f and 6f placed maiden, is a half-sister to 10 winners including the May Hill Stakes winner Satinette. The second dam, Silk Stocking (by Pardao), won 3 races including the listed 9f Strensall Stakes and is a half-sister to 5 winners including the smart sprinter Shiny Tenth. (R C Tooth).
"He'll benefit from being given a bit of time, but having said that I don't think he'll take that long.

He should be out by mid-summer, possibly over seven furlongs. I'm hoping he'll be a Royal Lodge Stakes type because he's a fine, big horse".

514. GIFT OF LOVE (IRE) ★★
b.f. Azamour – Spot Prize (Seattle Dancer).
April 8. Half-sister to the useful 7f (at 2 yrs) and listed 10f winner Premier Prize (by Selkirk), to the Group 2 15f Prix Kergorlay winner Gold Medallist (by Zilzal), the fairly useful 12f winner Stage Right (by In The Wings), the quite useful 14f winner Prize Dancer (by Suave Dancer) and the modest 12f and hurdles winner Prize Ring (by Bering). The dam, a useful filly, won over 5f at 2 yrs and was fourth in the Oaks. The second dam, Lucky Break (by What Luck), won 4 races in the USA. (J C Smith).
"The family are all good three-year-olds. They train on and although this is a quality filly and I like her a lot realistically I think she'll be a middle-distance three-year-old".

515. HIDDEN FIRE ★★★
b.f. Alhaarth – Premier Prize (Selkirk).
May 3. Third foal. The dam, a useful 7f (at 2 yrs) and listed 10f winner, was third in the Group 2 Sandown Mile and is a half-sister to 4 winners including the Group 2 15f Prix Kergorlay winner Gold Medallist. The second dam, Spot Prize (by Seattle Dancer), a useful filly, won over 5f at 2 yrs and was fourth in the Oaks. (J C Smith).
"A nice, quality filly that should make a two-year-old in the second half of the season".

516. HIGHLAND QUAICH ★★★
ch.c. Compton Place – Bee One (Catrail).
April 8. Half-brother to the modest 2008 2-y-o 1m winner Highland River (by Indian Creek) and to the fair triple 1m winner Highland Harvest (by Averti). The dam was placed over 5f and 6f and is a half-sister to several winners. The second dam, Ruwy (by Soviet Star) won over 1m. (J Wotherspoon).
"This is a nice colt by a sire that gets two-year-olds so I'd expect him to be racing by the summer. I entered his half-brother Highland River for the Derby because I thought he was better than he's proved so far".

517. SNOQUALMIE STAR ★★★
ch.f. Galileo – Seattle Ribbon (Seattle Dancer).
February 22. Closely related to the useful 2008 2-y-o listed 1m winner Snoqualmie Girl and to the smart listed 10f winner and Group 2 Dante Stakes third Snoqualmie Boy (both by Montjeu) and half-sister to the quite useful 2-y-o 6f winner Robocop, the modest 9f and 10f winner Seattle Robber, the fair 10f winner Seattle Storm (all by Robellino) and the fair 7f and 10f winner Seattle Express (by Salse). The dam, placed over 9f and 10f at 3 yrs, is a sister to the 2-y-o Group 1 1m winner Seattle Dancer. The second dam, Golden Rhyme (by Dom Racine), was a quite useful 3-y-o 7f winner. (J C Smith).
"You'd expect this filly to be a two-year-old and we're hopeful she can keep up the standard of the other two progeny, Snoqualmie Girl and Snoqualmie Boy, because she's by a very good stallion. You'd expect her to be suited by a mile in the late summer and early autumn".

518. SONG OF THE DESERT ★★★
b.f. Desert Sun – Blue Lullaby (Fasliyev).
March 2. First foal. The dam was a fair 3-y-o 7f winner. The second dam, Whispering (by Royal Academy), a quite useful maiden, was placed three times over 10f and is a half-sister to the dual Group 1 winner Croco Rouge and to the listed winner Alidiva (herself dam of the very smart 1,000 Guineas winner Sleepytime, the high-class Group 1 1m Sussex Stakes winner Ali Royal and the high-class Group 1 12f Europa Preis and Group 1 10f Premio Roma winner Taipan). (The Oh So Soba Partnership).
"The sire was good in the southern hemisphere but he didn't really get the mares he deserved here. This filly will make a two-year-old over six or seven furlongs".

519. THREE'S A CROWD ★★★
b.f. Royal Applause – Thracian (Green Desert).
April 18. Half-sister to the quite useful dual 2m winner Trilemma (by Slip Anchor), to the fair 2-y-o 7f winner Thrasher (by Hector Protector), the fair 2-y-o 5f winner Sunley Gift (by Cadeaux Genereux) and a winner in Japan by Zafonic. The dam, a fairly useful 2-y-o 6f and 7f winner, is a half-sister to 12 winners including the Group 2 12f Ribblesdale Stakes winner Third Watch, the Group 3 Prix Foy winner Richard of York, the Group 2 Premio Dormello winner Three Tails (herself dam of the high-class colts Tamure and Sea Wave), the Group 3 Fred Darling Stakes winner Maysoon and the dams of the Group winners Lend A Hand and Talented. The second dam, Triple First (by High Top), won 7 races including the Sun Chariot Stakes, the Nassau Stakes and the Musidora Stakes. (Whitsbury Manor Stud).
"She's doing everything right at the moment and certainly could be a two-year-old but she's physically immature and needs a bit of time. One for the middle of the season onwards".

520. UNNAMED ★★★
ch.f. Compton Place – Anthyllis (Night Shift).
February 16. Third foal. £20,000 2-y-o. Goffs Kempton Breeze Up. D Elsworth. Half-sister to a 3-y-o winner in France by Acclamation. The dam is an unraced sister to the US Grade 2 Sunset Handicap winner Plicck. The second dam, Anthis (by Ela-Mana-Mou), is a placed half-sister to 5 winners including the dam of the Group 2 Queen Anne Stakes winner Waajib.
"He's one of my early ones. Bought at the breeze ups, he's going nicely now after the short break I gave him since the Sales. He should prove to be worth what I paid for him".
TRAINER'S BARGAIN BUY

521. UNNAMED ★★★
b.c. Cape Cross – Aunty Rose (Caerleon).
March 18. Fourth foal. 24,000Y. Tattersalls October 2. Not sold. Half-brother to the quite useful 3-y-o dual 7f winner Mr Macattack (by Machiavellian). The dam, a useful 2-y-o 7f winner, was third in both the Group 3 1m May Hill Stakes and the Group 3 7f Nell Gwyn Stakes and is a half-sister to the Group 3 Gordon Richards Stakes winner Generous Rosi, the listed Marshall Stakes winner Generous Libra and the Group 3 Hungerford Stakes winner Bin Rosie. The second dam, Come On Rosi (by Valiyar), won over 6f at 3 yrs and is a half-sister to 8 winners. (Gordon Li).

"He hasn't grown a lot and it looks like he might be early. A neat little horse and he's quite precocious".

522. UNNAMED ★★★
b.c. Titus Livius – Honey Storm (Mujadil).
April 18. Fourth foal. 40,000Y. Tattersalls October 3. D Elsworth. Brother to the fair 7f and 1m winner of 3 races Coalpark and half-brother to the fair 2008 6f to 8.7f 2-y-o Rumble Of Thunder (by Fath). The dam won over 1m and is a half-sister to 9 winners including the Group 3 winner and Group 2 placed Compton Bolter. The second dam, Milk And Honey (by So Blessed), won twice at 2 yrs and is a half-sister to 9 winners including the Group 3 winner Beeshi. (M R Green).

"This is a nice colt, he's neat and well-balanced and I expect him to be a fairly early two-year-old".

523. UNNAMED ★★
ch.c. Halling – Sadie Thompson (King's Best).
March 11. First foal. 8,000Y. Tattersalls October 1. Suzanne Roberts. The dam was a fair 2-y-o 7f winner. The second dam, Femme Fatale (by Fairy King), a useful dual 6f winner of 2 races (including a listed event at 2 yrs), was second in the Group 2 Sun Chariot Stakes and is a half-sister to the 6f (at 2 yrs) and smart dual listed 10f winner Foodbroker Fancy.

"For a Halling he looks quite precocious and he was cheap. I love the sire because I've had some good horses by him".

524. UNNAMED ★★★
b.c. Namid – Tashyra (Tagula).
April 6. Second foal. £14,000 2-y-o. Goffs Kempton Breeze Up. D Elsworth. The dam was placed fourth once and is a sister to 2 winners including the German 2-y-o Group 2 winner Tagshira and a half-sister to one winner. The second dam, Shiyra (by Darshaan), a minor Irish 1m and 10f winner, is a half-sister to 3 winners.

"He's quite a nice colt and probably one of our earlier ones. A precocious type, I gave him a short break but now I'm beginning to bring him on".

525. UNNAMED ★★
b.c. Grand Slam – Tobaranama (Sadler's Wells).
May 9. Fifth foal. 10,000Y. Tattersalls October 2. Suzanne Roberts. Half-brother to the quite useful 2-y-o 6f winner Winged Flight (by Fusaichi Pegasus). The dam, a 9f winner in Ireland, was listed-placed and is a half-sister to 8 winners including the Group 1 5f Heinz "57" Phoenix Stakes winner Pharaoh's Delight. The second dam, Ridge The Times (by Riva Ridge), a fair 2-y-o 5f winner, is a half-sister to 6 winners in the USA. (D Elsworth).

"A nice, quality colt but he was a late foal and he'll take a bit of time. He cost very little JAMES EUSTACE

526. DOYENNE DREAM ★★
b.f. Doyen – Cribella (Robellino).
April 18. Half-sister to the listed 10f winner Ruby Wine (by Kayf Tara). The dam was a modest dual 12f winner. The second dam, Crinoline (by Blakeney), a fair 12f winner, stayed 2m. (Hockham Lodge Stud).

Physically she's very nice and very similar to Ruby Wine who was a lovely filly we had. If anything she's an even stronger type at this age than Ruby Wine was. I think this was quite a good mating. We've got her cantering and then turned her out for some spring grass and the owner tells me she's done even better for it".

527. IRON CONDOR ★★★
b.c. Tobougg – Coh Sho No (Old Vic).
February 26. 7,000Y. Tatersalls October. Not sold. Half-brother to the modest 14f, 2m and hurdles winner At The Money (by Robellino). The dam was a modest 15.4f and hurdles winner. The second dam, Castle Peak (by Darshaan), a fairly useful 12f winner, is a half-sister to the Prix du Cadran winner Sought Out and to the listed winners Queen Helen and Greektown (herself dam of the Geoffrey Freer Stakes winner Multicolored) and the dam of the Great Voltigeur Stakes winner Bonny Scot. (H D Ness).

"He's a nice type of horse and I think he'll end up going through the dual purpose route but he could just be more forward than his half-brother At The Money who was placed over a mile as a two-year-old. I think this horse is more precocious and he just might be a dark horse as a two-year-old". TRAINER'S BARGAIN BUY

528. MARKSBURY ★★★
b.f. Mark Of Esteem – Penelewey (Groom Dancer).
March 8. Third foal. Half-sister to the modest 2008 dual 1m placed (both her starts) Penperth (by Xaar) and to the useful 1m (at 2 yrs) and 10f winner Jedediah (by Hernando). The dam, a useful 6f and 7f winner of 3 races, is a half-sister to 5 winners here and abroad. The second dam, Peryllys (by Warning), is a placed half-sister to 6 winners. (Major M G Wyatt).
"She's quite forward and has literally thrived since she went onto the heath cantering. Her half-brother Jedediah was precocious enough to win as a two-year-old and he was by Hernando. I trained the half-sister Penperth and this filly would be a lot more forward than her. She's not very tall but she's getting stronger by the day and I'll start her over five furlongs but am expecting her to stay further".

529. MEDALIA ★★★
ch.f. Medicean – Alegria (Night Shift).
March 30. Fourth foal. Half-sister to the modest 2008 7f. placed 2-y-o Integria and to the quite useful dual 6f winner (including at 2 yrs) Fast Bowler (both by Intikhab). The dam, a fairly useful dual 6f winner (including at 2 yrs), is out of the fair middle-distance placed maiden High Habit (by Slip Anchor), herself a half-sister to the smart sprinter Blue Siren. (J C Smith).
"A half-sister to Fast Bowler who I thought would be half decent but he ended up being a bleeder. This is quite a big filly and she probably won't be that early but she has a great attitude and has been incredibly straightforward and I like her for that reason! I think she'll be starting off at six or seven furlongs and she'll probably stay a mile".

530. TIGER STAR ★★★
b.c. Tiger Hill – Rosy Outlook (Trempolino).
February 25. Half-brother to the very useful 2-y-o 6f and Group 3 7f Horris Hill Stakes winner Rapscallion (by Robellino) and to the useful 2-y-o 6f winner and listed-placed Orcadian (by Kirkwall). The dam, a quite useful 6f winner, is out of Rosyphard (by Lyphard), herself a sister to the dual French Group 3 winner Tenue de Soiree and a half-sister to the European champion 2-y-o filly Baiser Vole. (Mr J C Smith).
"All the members of the family have got a bit of a kink about them, but this is probably the best-looking of them all. He's been quite tricky to break in and now we've got him cantering I hope that's his kink out of the way! He does look like being a two-year-old, he's a good mover and an athlete and not too backward I hope".

531. TORRAN SOUND ★★
b.c. Tobougg – Velvet Waters (Unfuwain).
February 10. First foal. 25,000Y. Tattersalls October 2. James Eustace. The dam, a fair 11.7f winner, is a half-sister to 6 winners including the 10f, 12f and subsequent UAE Group 3 12f winner Gower Song. The second dam, Gleaming Water (by Kalaglow), a quite useful 2-y-o 6f winner, is a sister to the Group 3 Solario Stakes winner Shining Water (herself dam of the Group 1 Grand Criterium winner Tenby) and a half-sister to 8 winners. (The MacDougall Partnership 2).
"I bought him because I like the family and I didn't feel he was expensive. He'll want seven furlongs and a mile towards the end of the season and might well make up into a dual purpose horse".

RICHARD FAHEY
532. BAHAMIAN MUSIC (IRE) ★★
b.c. Bahamian Bounty – Strings (Unfuwain).
February 20. Second foal. 32,000Y. Tattersalls October 1. Bobby O'Ryan. Half-brother to the unplaced 2008 2-y-o Super Flight (by Exceed And Excel). The dam is an unraced half-sister to 5 winners including the French 2,000 Guineas winner Victory Note. The second dam, Three Piece (by Jaazeiro), an Irish placed 2-y-o, is a half-sister to 8 winners including Orchestration (Group 2 Coronation Stakes) and Welsh Term (Group 2 Prix d'Harcourt).

533. DAREDEVIL DANCER (USA) ★★
b.c. Johannesburg – Amybdancing (Diablo).
February 14. Fourth foal. 62,000Y. Tattersalls October 2. Charlie Gordon-Watson. The dam, a stakes-placed winner of 3 races at 2 to 4 yrs, is a half-sister to 4 winners. The second dam, Whenourshipcomesin (by General Assembly), won 10 races in the USA and is a half-sister to 7 winners including 3 stakes winners.

534. GRITSTONE ★★★♠
b.c. Dansili – Cape Trafalgar (Cape Cross).
March 15. Second foal. 70,000Y. Tattersalls October 1. Not sold. The dam, a fair 5f and 6f 2-y-o winner of 4 races, was subsequently stakes-placed in the USA and is a half-sister to 3 winners. The second dam, West Escape (by Gone West), a fairly useful 1m winner at 3 yrs, is a half-sister to 6 winners.

535. MIGHTY CLARETS (IRE) ★★★
br.c. Whipper – Collected (Taufan).
Tenth foal. €25,000Y. Goffs February. Emerald Bloodstock. Half-sister to the useful 2-y-o German Group 2 6f winner and Group 1 Gran Criterium second Checkit (by Mukaddamah), to the fair 9.5f all-weather (at 2 yrs) and 12f winner Mr Excel (by Orpen) and the fair 6f (at 2 yrs) and 10f winner Witney Royale (by Royal Abjar). The dam is an unraced half-sister to 4 minor winners abroad. The second dam, Crosmieres (by Lyphard), was placed at 3 yrs in France.

536. OLYMPIC CEREMONY ★★★
br.c. Kyllachy – Opening Ceremony (Quest For Fame).
May 7. Second foal. 50,000Y. Doncaster St Leger. Robin O'Ryan. Brother to the 2008 6f placed 2-y-o Olympic Dream. The dam, a fair 7f (at 2 yrs) and 10f winner of 6 races, is a half-sister to 4 winners including the Group 2 Park Stakes winner Arabian Gleam. The second dam, Gleam Of Light (by Danehill), won over 7f and is a full or half-sister to 4 winners.

537. PERFECT ENDING (IRE) ★★
b.c. Lucky Story – Wheeler's Wonder (Sure Blade).
March 13. Ninth foal. 48,000Y. Tattersalls October 1. Bobby O'Ryan. Half-brother to the Group 2 Lancashire Oaks and Group 2 Prix de Royallieu winner Anna Pavlova (by Danehill Dancer) and to the modest 1m and 9f winner Cyclonic Storm (by Catrail). The dam, a moderate 12f, 2m and jumps winner, is a half-sister to 9 winners including the US Grade 3 winner Kirov Premiere (herself dam of the US Grade 1 winner and champion Japanese filly Cesario) and the dam of the dual Group 2 winner Gothenburg. The second dam, Querida (by Habitat), won once at 2 yrs in Ireland and is a half-sister to the top-class sprinter-miler Chief Singer.

538. SHE'S A CHARACTER ★★★
b.f. Invincible Spirit – Cavernista (Lion Cavern).
January 30. Fifth foal. 28,000Y. Tattersalls October 2. R O'Ryan. Half-sister to the fairly useful 1m to 12f winner of 4 races Celtic Spirit (by Pivotal), to the fair 6f winner Capetown Girl (by Danzero) and the Italian 9f to 11f winner Keycavern (by Key Of Luck). The dam is a placed half-sister to 9 winners including the Group 1 Prix du Cadran winner Give Notice and the 1m listed winner Sovinista. The second dam, Princess Genista (by Ile de Bourbon), a very useful 1m and 8.5f winner, was third in the Musidora Stakes and is a half-sister to 11 winners.

539. VENTURA COVE (IRE) ★★★★
ch.c. Bahamian Bounty – Baby Bunting (Wolfhound).
February 11. Fifth foal. 80,000Y. Doncaster St Leger. Robin O'Ryan. Brother to the 2008 2-y-o listed 5f winner of 3 races Bahamian Babe and to the fairly useful 5f and 6f winner Victorian Bounty. The dam, a modest sprint-placed maiden, is a half-sister to 7 winners including the smart Group 3 Cork And Orrery Stakes and Grade 3 Jaipur Stakes winner Atraf, the useful Group 2 Richmond Stakes winner Son Pardo and the useful 6f winner Emerging

Market. The second dam, Flitteriss Park (by Beldale Flutter), a modest 1m winner, is a half-sister to 5 winners including the South African Grade 3 winner Lady Of Habits and the 2-y-o listed winner Snipe Hall.

540. WIGAN LANE ★★★★♠
b.f. *Kheleyf – Nesting (Thatching).*
April 21. Fifth foal. 45,000Y. Doncaster St Leger. Gill Richardson. 28,000Y. Tattersalls December. Highfield Farm. Half-sister to the useful 5f and 6f winner of 4 races from 2 to 6 yrs Hoh Hoh Hoh (by Piccolo) and to the fair 2-y-o 5f winner Miss Otis (by Danetime). The dam is an unplaced full or half-sister to 3 winners and to the dams of the Group 2 winners Tariq and Wi Dud. The second dam, Tatouma (by The Minstrel), a quite useful 2-y-o 5f and 6f winner, is a half-sister to 4 winners including the dams of 2 listed winners.

541. WILLIAM MORGAN (IRE) ★★★
ch.c. *Arakan – Dry Lightning (Shareef Dancer).*
March 31. Fifth foal. €10,000Y. Goffs Million. R O'Ryan. Half-brother to the quite useful 2008 2-y-o 7f winner Confucius Captain (by Captain Rio), to the fairly useful 6f and 7f winner Harrison George (by Danetime), the quite useful 2-y-o 6f winner Asian Tiger (by Rossini), the quite useful 1m, 11f and hurdles winner Harper Valley (by Val Royal) and two 2-y-o winners at around 7f in Italy by Victory Note and Russian Revival. The dam, a modest 10f winner, is a half-sister to 4 winners. The second dam, Valkyrie (by Bold Lad, Ire), won once at 2 yrs and is a half-sister to 4 winners including the Prince Of Wales's Stakes second Sabre Dance.

542. UNNAMED ★★★
b.c. *Bahamian Bounty – Dark Eyed Lady (Exhibitioner).*
April 7. Ninth foal. €16,000Y. Doncaster October. Crown Select. Half-brother to quite useful 2-y-o 6f winner Vision Of Dreams (by Efisio), to the quite useful 2-y-o 5f winner Oh So Dusty, the modest dual 6f winner Piccleyes (both by Piccolo), the quite useful 2-y-o 7.5f winner Bridge Place (by Polar Falcon), the fair 8.5f winner Leptis Magna (by Danehill Dancer), the fair 2-y-o dual 5f and subsequent minor US stakes winner Green Eyed Lady (by Greensmith). The dam, a quite useful 2-y-o 5f and 6f winner, is out of the minor 6f winner of 6 races Tribal Eye (by Tribal Chief).

543. UNNAMED ★★★★
br.f. *Whipper – Mise (Indian Ridge).*
March 16. Third foal. €150,000Y. Goffs Million. F.R. Racing. Half-sister to the quite useful 2008 2-y-o 7f winner Silver Games (by Verglas) and to the Group 1 1m Falmouth Stakes and Group 2 6f Lowther Stakes winner Nahoodh (by Clodovil). The dam is an unraced half-sister to 6 winners including the French Group 3 winner Not Just Swing and the French listed winner Minoa. The second dam, Misbegotten (by Baillamont), a French listed 1m Prix Finlande winner, was second in the Group 2 Prix de l'Opera and is a half-sister to 4 winners.

JEREMY GASK
I interviewed Assistant Trainer (and ex-Timeform man) Kevin Blake about the Jeremy Gask trained two-year-olds, which are based at Sutton Veny in Wiltshire.

544. UNNAMED ★★★
b.c. *Bertolini – Buckle (Common Grounds).*
April 8. Sixth foal. Half-brother to the 2-y-o listed 5f winner and Group 3 placed Waterways (by Alhaarth) and a minor winner in France by Cadeaux Genereux. The dam, a fair dual 1m winner at 3 yrs, subsequently won in France and is a half-sister to 8 winners. The second dam, Maratona (by Be My Guest), ran unplaced twice in France and is a half-sister to the Fillies Triple Crown winner Oh So Sharp and the Nassau Stakes winner Roussalka.
"He'll be one of the earlier two-year-old we have and he's a well-made, forward type that has the scope to go on".

545. UNNAMED ★★
b.f. *Noverre – Golden Opinion (Slew O'Gold).*
May 13. Closely related to the useful 7f and 1m winner Excellento and to the French 7f winner

Dareen (both by Rahy) and half-sister to the useful 3-y-o 7f winner Meiosis, the modest 5f and 6f winner Conjecture (both by Danzig), the quite useful 2-y-o 5f winner Straw Poll (by Dixieland Band), the French 2-y-o 1m winner Sun Music and the fairly useful French 1m winner Goddess Of Wisdom (both by Sadler's Wells). The dam, a top class miler, ran only at 3 yrs when she won four races including the Group 1 Coronation Stakes and the Group 3 Prix du Rond Point, was second in the July Cup to Cadeaux Genereux and third in the French 1,000 Guineas to Pearl Bracelet. The second dam, Optimistic Lass (by Mr Prospector), was a smart winner of the Group 2 10f Nassau Stakes and the Group 3 10.5f Musidora Stakes.

"Still in pre-training and I personally haven't seen her yet. She's a late foal and I should imagine she'd stay a mile later on".

546. UNNAMED ★★★
b.f. Rock Of Gibraltar – Karsiyaka (Kahyasi).
May 1. Seventh foal. 48,000foal. Tattersalls December. Blandford Bloodstock. Half-sister to the quite useful 2008 2-y-o 6f winner Isabella Grey (by Choisir), to the useful dual 7f winner (including on the all-weather at 2 yrs) Contractor (by Spectrum), the quite useful 10f winner Planetarium (by Fantastic Light), the fair 1m winner Pearl's Girl (by King's Best) and the modest dual 11f winner Altos Reales (by Mark Of Esteem). The dam is an unraced half-sister to 3 winners including the dam of the May Hill Stakes winner Karasta. The second dam, Karlafsha (by Top Ville), won twice in France including the listed 1m Prix des Lilas and is a half-sister to the 5 winners.

"She's a small filly but is looking more like a racehorse as the weeks go by. She's got a fair bit of attitude about her and she'll be one for the mid-summer onwards. She's coping with everything fine now and settling down now".

547. UNNAMED ★★★
b.f. Danehill Dancer – Labrusca (Grand Lodge).
February 27. Fourth foal. €42,000Y. Goffs Million. De Burgh/Farrington. Sister to the quite useful 2008 6f placed Irish 2-y-o Akrisrun. The dam was third over 10f on her only start and is a half-sister to 7 winners including the high-class Group 1 12f Yorkshire Oaks and Group 3 12f Lancashire Oaks winner Catchascatchcan (herself dam of the very smart miler Antonius Pius) and the listed 10f winner Licorne. The second dam, Catawba (by Mill Reef), a useful 10.5f winner, is a half-sister to 7 winners including the Ribblesdale Stakes winner Strigida.

"A very nice filly, she's athletic and racey looking. We've backed off her a bit now and she's having a bit of a break. One for the back-end of the season and I think she'll be a seven furlong/mile filly. One of the nicer types for sure".

548. UNNAMED ★★
b.f. Footstepsinthesand – Rubies From Burma (Forty Niner).
March 16. Sixth foal. 60,000Y. Tattersalls October 1. John Warren. Half-sister to the unraced 2008 2-y-o Hatta Stream (by Oasis Dream), to the useful 11.8f winner and listed 12f second Ivory Gala (by Galileo) and the quite useful 2-y-o 1m and subsequent UAE winner Alo Pura (by Anabaa). The dam, a winner of 3 races from 5f to 6f and listed placed over 5.5f in Ireland, is a half-sister to 9 winners including the French 1,000 Guineas, Fillies Mile and Prix Marcel Boussac winner Culture Vulture. The second dam, Perfect Example (by Far North), is an unraced half-sister to the dams of the Grade/Group 1 winners Awe Inspiring, Polish Precedent and Zilzal.

"She's only recently arrived from pre-training and she's very big, good-looking filly. Definitely one for the back-end and much more of a three-year-old but she's very nice and has loads of scope".

549. UNNAMED ★★★
b.c. Barathea – Shannon Dore (Turtle Island).
April 19. Fifth foal. 16,000Y. Tattersalls October 2. DeBurgh/Farringdon. Half-brother to the fairly useful 2008 2-y-o 6f winner Frognal (by Kheleyf) and to the useful 2-y-o 6f winner and listed placed Borthwick Girl (by Cape Cross). The dam, a quite useful 2-y-o 6f winner, is a

half-sister to one winner. The second dam, Solas Abu (by Red Sunset), a quite useful 9f and 10f winner in Ireland, is a half-sister to 2 winners.

"He's a bit sharper than his pedigree would suggest – he's quite strong and forward physically. He should progress as well – he's not just going to be a two-year-old. One for around June time and he should have the speed to start at six furlongs".

550. UNNAMED ★★★
b.c. E Dubai – Sudenlylastsummer (Rinka Das).
February 6. Fifth foal. Goffs Million. Half-brother to 2 minor winners in the USA, including a 2-y-o, by Allen's Prospect. The dam won 3 races at 2 and 3 yrs in the USA and is a half-sister to 13 winners. The second dam, Sally Lunn (by Cyane), a US stakes-placed winner, is a half-sister to 4 winners including the US Grade 2 winner Batna.

"A very attractive individual and one of our better quality two-year-olds. One for the mid-season onwards, he'll start at six furlongs and should stay a mile later on".

JAMES GIVEN
551. CAOL ILA ★★★
b.f. Invincible Spirit – Pink Cashmere (Polar Falcon).
April 24. Ninth foal. 40,000Y. Tattersalls October 2. James Given. Sister to the quite useful 2-y-o 6f winner Naayla and half-sister to the German 2-y-o 6f winner and Group 3 placed Medina (by Pennekamp), the useful 2-y-o dual 5f winner Pike Bishop (by Namid), the fairly useful 2-y-o 5f winner and Group 3 Firth Of Clyde Stakes second Broken Applause (by Acclamation), the fairly useful Irish 2-y-o 6f winner Contact (by Grand Lodge) and the fair 6f (at 2 yrs) to 7f winner of 5 races Motu (by Desert Style). The dam is an unraced three-parts sister to the Group 1 6f July Cup winner Owington and a half-sister to 8 winners. The second dam, Old Domesday Book (by High Top), a fairly useful 10.4f winner, was third in the listed 10f Sir Charles Clore Memorial Stakes. (Danethorpe Racing Partnership).

"I'm sure she'll be a two-year-old but she's still growing and she wasn't an early foal. Bred on the same lines as Owington, she shows a bit of speed but she's still a bit 'up behind' and needs to level up. She's got a sprinter's backside on her and we'll get there I'm sure. Incidentally she's named after an Irish malt whisky".

552. DANCING FREDDY (IRE) ★★★
b.c. Chineur – Majesty's Dancer (Danehill Dancer).
April 12. 12,000 2-y-o. Goffs Breeze-Up Sales. J Given. Half-brother to Fathtastic (by Fath), unplaced in two starts at 2 yrs in 2008. The dam is an unplaced half-sister to numerous winners including the South African dual Grade 3 winner of 11 races Dancal. The second dam, Majesty's Nurse (by Indian King), won 3 races over 5f and 6f in Ireland and is a half-sister to 2 winners.

"He's very forward, strong and level-headed and will be running in April. He's everything you'd expect from a Breeze Up horse as he's precocious and ready to go. He shows a lot of speed at home and will be a five furlong sprinter – plain and simple".

553. DIXIE BRIGHT (USA) ★★★
b.br.c. Dixie Union – Tell Me Now (A P Indy).
April 8. $105,000Y. Fasig Tipton July. Mky/Ent Heatherway. Half-brother to the fairly useful Irish 2-y-o 6f winner Greek Mythology (by Mr Greeley). The dam is an unraced half-sister to 6 winners including the Group 3 7f Solario Stakes winner White Crown and the US stakes winner and Grade 1 placed Dr Caton. The second dam, Won't She Tell (by Banner Sport), a minor stakes winner of 9 races in the USA at up to 9f, is a half-sister to the American Triple Crown winner Affirmed. (Brighton Farm Ltd).

"He's very forward and will be out early. I think he'll be better over six furlongs than five but he still shows plenty of zip. Not very big, but very much a typical two-year-old".

554. FOOTSIE (IRE) ★★★
b.f. Footstepsinthesand – Marlene-D (Selkirk).
April 16. Sixth foal. 45,000Y. Tattersalls October 1. Not sold. Half-sister to the very useful dual 1m winner (including at 2 yrs) and listed-placed

General Eliott (by Rock Of Gibraltar), to the very useful 6f and 7f 2-y-o winner Shanghai Lily (by King's Best) and the useful 7f (at 2 yrs) and 1m winner Eden Rock (by Danehill). The dam, a minor Irish 3-y-o 9f winner, is a half-sister to 7 winners including the useful Queen's Vase winner Arden and the French listed winner Kerulen and to the placed dam of the US Grade 1 winner Kiri's Clown. The second dam, Kereolle (by Riverman), is a placed half-sister to the dam of the Group 1 winners Lydian and Ballinderry. (Linda Fish).

"A nice, elegant filly that covers the ground. Not surprisngly she's growing at the moment and with the Selkirk influence I don't think she'll be a sprinting type two-year-old, but she shows speed and a bit of class as well. One for the middle of the season".

555. GREELEY BRIGHT (USA) ★★★
b.f. Mr Greeley – Lady Nicholas (Nicholas).
May 3. Seventh foal. 55,000Y. Tattersalls October 1. Brighton Farm. Sister to the Canadian listed stakes winner of 13 races Pants And Kisses and half-sister to 4 minor winners in the USA by Smart Strike, Cherokee Run, Mt Livermore and Strategic Mission. The dam is an unplaced half-sister to 5 winners including the US Grade 1 winners Auntie Mame and Star de Lady Ann. The second dam, Lady Vixen (by Sir Ivor), is an unplaced half-sister to 5 winners. (Brighton Farms Ltd).

"She's done quite a lot of work, she knows her job quite well and is quite forward. She shows speed and is probably a six furlong type".

556. ITSTHURSDAY ALREADY ★★★
b.c. Exceed And Excel – Succinct (Hector Protector).
April 5. Second foal. 18,000Y. Tattersalls October 2. James Given. Half-brother to the fair 2008 2-y-o 7f winner Starry Sky (by Oasis Dream). The dam, a useful listed 10f winner, is a half-sister to the German listed winner Succession. The second dam, Pitcroy (by Unfuwain), a useful 10f winner, is a half-sister to 8 winners including the Group 3 7f Jersey Stakes winner Ardkinglass. (Danethorpe Racing Partnership).

"He's a nice horse, he's quite well-bred and being by Exceed And Excel he was quite well-bought. He's a scopey horse but he'll probably start at six furlongs".

557. LULAWIN ★★★
br.f. Kyllachy – Obsessive (Seeking The Gold).
April 15. Tenth foal. 38,000Y. Tattersalls October 1. Not sold. Closely related to the Group 1 St James's Palace Stakes and Group 2 Mill Reef Stakes winner and Grade 1 Breeders Cup Mile second Excellent Art (by Pivotal) and half-sister to the smart 7f (at 2 yrs), 12f and 2m 4f Ascot Stakes winner Double Obsession (by Sadler's Wells), the fairly useful 1m winner Medallist (by Danehill), the quite useful 2-y-o 6f winner Spy Master (by Green Desert) and the fair 2-y-o all-weather 8.6f winner Possessed (by Desert Prince). The dam, a useful 2-y-o 6f winner and third in the Group 3 10.4f Musidora Stakes, is a half-sister to 7 winners. The second dam, Secret Obsession (by Secretariat), a fairly useful 10f winner, is a half-sister to 7 winners including the Group 2 12f King Edward VII Stakes winner Beyton. (Living Legend Racing Partnership).

"A three-parts sister to Excellent Art and she's all there physically but just needs to mature a bit. She's doing fast canters at the moment but needs a bit of time. Being by Kyllachy you'd have to think she'd have a bit of speed, so I'd be thinking along the lines of starting her at six furlongs, but she might even be seven furlong two-year-old".

558. TARTUFO DOLCE ★★★★
b.f. Key Of Luck – Corn Futures (Nomination).
February 27. Eleventh foal. 26,000Y. Doncaster St Leger. James Given. Sister to the modest 2008 5.3f placed 2-y-o Entrancer and to the useful 2-y-o 5f Weatherbys Supersprint winner Siena Gold and half-sister to the very useful 2-y-o Crazee Mental – a winner over 6f and placed in the Cheveley Park Stakes, the Queen Mary Stakes and the Cherry Hinton Stakes, the modest 7f all-weather winner Futuristic (both by Magic Ring), the fair 6f (at 2 yrs) and 7f winner Trading Aces (by Be My Chief), the fair

all-weather 9.4f winner Reap (by Emperor Jones), the fair 6f winner Three Days In May (by Cadeaux Genereux) and a winner in Germany by Bold Fact. The dam, a fair 2-y-o 6f winner, is a half-sister to 7 winners including the dam of the March Stakes and Glorious Stakes winner Midnight Legend. The second dam, Hay Reef (by Mill Reef), won once at 3 yrs and is a half-sister to the dam of the Irish 2,000 Guineas winner Wassl. (Danethorpe Racing Partnership).
"A precocious two-year-old, she knows her job and is nice and fast. She looks similar to her sister Siena Gold and we have high hopes that she'll emulate her. She's quick and five furlongs will be fine for her". TRAINER'S BARGAIN BUY

559. TOBERMORY BOY ★★
ch.c. Tobougg – The In-Laws (Be My Guest).
April 16. Eighth foal. Half-brother to the 2008 7f fourth placed 2-y-o Myttons Maid, to the dual 3-y-o winner abroad Better Believe (both by Bertolini), the quite useful 2-y-o 1m winner Lady Mytton (by Lake Coniston), the fair 10f winner Prince Vector (by Vettori) and the French 10f winner Risky Nizzy (by Cape Cross). The dam, a fairly useful 2-y-o 7f winner, is closely related to the fairly useful 7f winner Mrs Fisher and a half-sister to 6 winners including the dam of the listed winner and Irish 1,000 Guineas second Dimenticata. The second dam, Amboselli (by Raga Navarro), was placed over 5f at 2 yrs and is a half-sister to 9 winners. (Living Legend Racing Partnership II).
"He's going to take a bit of time as he's developing into a big, strong horse that'll make a nice three-year-old. His pedigree doesn't suggest he'll be anything other than a later developing two-year-old and that's what he is. He's not a horse to rush and seven furlongs or a mile will be his trip later this year".

560. YANKEE BRIGHT ★★★★
b.f. Elusive Quality – Sharp Minister
(Deputy Minister).
March 26. Fifth foal. Half-sister to the 2-y-o Group 3 7f Horris Hill Stakes and dual 3-y-o 1m winner Dijeer, to the fairly useful UAE dual 1m winner Plavius (both by Danzig) and the US stakes-placed winner Sharp Writer (by Capote). The dam is an unplaced sister to the US Grade 2 and French Group 3 winner Flag Down. The second dam, Sharp Call (by Sharpen Up), a stakes-placed winner in Canada, is a half-sister to 7 winners. (Brighton Farm Ltd).
"A very nice filly with a lot of class about her, she has a very nice way of going. She'd already done plenty before she arrived here, so she knows her job and all we have to do now is keep her ticking along. She's got speed but I'm sure she'll stay seven furlongs this year. A classy horse".

561. UNNAMED ★★★
b.c. Cadeaux Genereux – Bibi Karam
(Persian Bold).
April 10. Fourth foal. 16,000Y. Doncaster Breeze Up Sale. J Given. Brother to the quite useful 2-y-o 7f winner Lord Peter Flint and half-brother to the fairly useful Irish 10f and 11f winner Bold Bibi (by Hernando). The dam, a winner over 1m in Ireland and listed-placed, is a sister to the Group 3 Royal Whip Stakes winner Baba Karam and a half-sister to 7 winners. The second dam, Lady Pavlova (by Ballymore), won 3 races and was second in the Group 2 Park Hill Stakes and is a half-sister to 3 winners.
"I've only just bought him at the Breeze Up sales, so I don't know much about him. He's a nice specimen and he breezed well, he's a good-topped colt and looks a two-year-old in the making".

562. UNNAMED ★★★
b.f. Compton Place – Gleam Of Light (Danehill).
April 11. Ninth foal. Half-sister to the very smart dual Group 2 7f Park Stakes winner Arabian Gleam (by Kyllachy), to the fairly useful 12f winner and listed-placed Bumptious (by Mister Baileys), the fairly useful 2-y-o 7f winners Gleaming Blade (by Diesis) and Opening Ceremony (by Quest For Fame) and the French winner of 3 races Light Quest (by Quest For Fame). The dam, a quite useful dual 7.5f winner at 3 yrs, is a half-sister to 4 minor winners. The second dam, Gold Runner (by Runnett), is a

placed half-sister to 6 winners including the dual Guineas winner Don't Forget Me. (Baileys Horse Feed).

"A nice filly, she's quite 'butty' and strong. She didn't arrive here until after some of the others so she's just learning her job now and I'd expect her to be a six furlong filly. She needs a bit of time but she's learning all the time".

563. UNNAMED ★★
ch.c. Refuse To Bend – Supersonic (Shirley Heights).
April 10. 2,000Y. Tattersalls October 3. Tom Ryan. Half-brother to the unplaced 2008 2-y-o Beat Faster (by Beat Hollow) and to the modest 12f seller and hurdles winner Whirling (by Groom Dancer). The dam was placed 7 times and stayed 10.5f and is a sister to the listed 2-y-o 10f Zetland Stakes and listed 2 mile George Stubbs Stakes winner Upper Strata (herself dam of the Prix de la Salamandre winner Lord Of Men and the French Oaks second Her Ladyship). The second dam, Bright Landing (by Sun Prince), was placed four times over 5f at 2 yrs and is a half-sister to the very useful 2-y-o Easy Landing. (C G Rowles Nicholson).

"He's got a nice way of going but on pedigree you'd expect him to stay middle-distances. We haven't asked him any questions yet but he does look nice because he's quite forward already and is looking like a seven furlong two-year-old".

JOHN GOSDEN
564. AMERICAN SPIRIT (IRE) ★★★
b.f. Rock Of Gibraltar – Funsie (Saumarez).
February 26. Fourth foal. 435,000Y. Tattersalls October 1. London Thoroughbred Services. Half-sister to the quite useful 2008 Irish 2-y-o 1m winner Sirgarfieldsobers, to the Epsom Derby, Juddmonte International Stakes and Racing Post Trophy winner Authorized (both by Montjeu) and the quite useful 10f winner Empowered (by Fasliyev). The dam is an unraced half-sister to 8 winners including the Group 3 10.5f Prix Cleopatre winner Brooklyn's Dance (herself the dam of 5 stakes winners) and the dam of the Group 1 winners Okawango and Quijano. The second dam, Valle Dansante (by Lyphard), won once in France and is a full or half-sister to 12 winners including the French 2,000 Guineas winner and sire Green Dancer. (George Strawbridge).

"She's still in pre-training but she's coming to me and is worth mentioning. A strong filly that's done well, it would be nice to have her on the track in the second half of the year".

565. ARDENT ★★★
b.f. Pivotal – Polish Romance (Danzig).
May 21. Ninth foal. Half-sister to the fairly useful 5f (at 2 yrs) and listed 6f winner Irresistible (by Cadeaux Genereux) and the fair all-weather dual 8.7f winner Italian Romance (by Medicean). The dam, a minor 7f winner in the USA, is a sister to the US stakes winner Polish Love and a half-sister to 3 minor winners. The second dam, Some Romance (by Fappiano), won the Grade 1 1m Frizette Stakes and the Grade 1 7f Matron Stakes and is a half-sister to the Grade 1 Hollywood Turf Cup winner Vilzak and the US Grade 2 winner Jane's Dilemma. (Cheveley Park Stud).

"A three-parts sister to Infallible (by Pivotal out of Irresistible), she's growing a lot at the moment but has a good action and a good attitude. One for September/October time, she's a nice type of filly".

566. BAZARUTO ★★★★
ch.c. Pivotal – Isla Azul (Machiavellian).
February 19. Third foal. Half-brother to the unplaced (in 2 starts) 2008 2-y-o Grey Ghost (by Linamix) and to the moderate 1m winner Blue Savannah (by Anabaa). The dam is a placed sister to the high-class Group 1 1m Coronation Stakes winner Rebecca Sharp and a half-sister to 8 winners including the smart Group 3 11.5f Lingfield Derby Trial winner Mystic Knight, the useful listed 11.4f Cheshire Oaks winner Hidden Hope, the useful dual 7f winner Rosse and the useful 10f winner Mayo. The second dam, Nuryana (by Nureyev), was a useful winner of the listed 1m Grand Metropolitan Stakes and is a half-sister to 5 winners.

"I like him, he goes alright and is a nice sort of

horse. Medium–sized, I'd hope to have him out by July time and he has a good action".

567. BEACHFIRE (IRE) ★★★
ch.c. Indian Haven – Maine Lobster (Woodman).
February 15. Fifth foal. 100,000Y. Tattersalls October 2. John Ferguson. Brother to Lord Of The Dance, unplaced in one start at 2 yrs in 2008 and half-brother to the very smart Group 2 Sandown Mile and dual Group 3 winner Major Cadeaux (by Cadeaux Genereux). The dam, a fair 7f placed 2-y-o, is a half-sister to the US stakes winner Cap Beino. The second dam, Capades (by Overskate), won 11 races including the Grade 1 Selima Stakes and is a half-sister to 3 winners.
"Like his brother Major Cadeaux he's a little bit delicate. He's a nice mover and everything else about him is fine. He just wouldn't want someone pushing him".

568. BEGGAR'S OPERA (IRE) ★★★
b.c. Singspiel – Hannda (Dr Devious).
March 3. First foal. 80,000Y. Tattersalls October 1. John Ferguson. The dam, a winner over 10f in Ireland from 2 starts, is a half-sister to the Irish Group 3 7.5f Concorde Stakes winner Hamairi and to the Irish 5f (at 2 yrs) and 3-y-o listed 6f winner Hanabad. The second dam, Handaza (by Be My Guest), won over 1m winner at 3 yrs in Ireland and is a half-sister to 5 winners including the Irish Group 3 winners Hazariya and Hazarista.
"I like him a lot, he's light on his feet but he's not a precocious sort and more the sort we'll see around September time. He'll be a nice horse in time".

569. BOYCOTT (IRE) ★★★★★
b.c. Refuse To Bend – Withorwithoutyou (Danehill).
April 6. Second foal. 160,000Y. Tattersalls October 2. John Ferguson. Half-brother to the 2008 2-y-o Group 2 6f Coventry Stakes winner and Group 1 6f Phoenix Stakes second Art Connoisseur (by Lucky Story). The dam, a quite useful 2-y-o 7f winner, is a half-sister to one winner. The second dam, Morningsurprice (by Future Storm), is an unraced half-sister to 5 winners including the high-class broodmare Morning Devotion (dam of the Oaks and Irish Derby winner Balanchine and the Group 2 winners Romanov and Red Slippers).
"He goes well and he'd be one of my better two-year-olds. A neat, well-balanced colt, he's a good mover that should be suited by six furlongs like his half-brother Art Connoisseur".

570. BRISBANE (IRE) ★★★★
b.c. Kheleyf – Waroonga (Brief Truce).
February 14. Sixth foal. 45,000Y. Doncaster St Leger. R O'Gorman. Half-brother to the 2008 6f placed 2-y-o Veroon (by Noverre), to the fairly useful dual 5f winner (including at 2 yrs) Foursquare (by Fayruz) and the quite useful 5f and 6f winner of 7 races at 3 and 4 yrs Lord Of The Reins (by Imperial Ballet). The dam is an unraced half-sister to 5 winners. The second dam, Water Spirit (by Riverman), is an unraced half-sister to 9 winners.
"He's doing a bit of work, he looks above average and he'll be happy over six furlongs".

571. CHOIR SOLO ★★★★
b.f. Medicean – Choirgirl (Unfuwain).
February 27. Fifth foal. Half-sister to the fair 2008 7f and 1m placed Choral Festival and to the quite useful dual 12f winner Chord (both by Pivotal). The dam, a very useful 2-y-o 7f winner and second in the Group 3 7f Prestige Stakes, was listed-placed twice over 10f and is a half-sister to numerous winners including the Group 1 10f Curragh Pretty Polly Stakes winner Chorist. The second dam, Choir Mistress (by Chief Singer), is an unraced half-sister to 6 winners including the smart Group 2 11.9f Great Voltigeur Stakes winner Sacrament. (Cheveley Park Stud).
"We trained the dam and I like this filly. She has a very good action and a good level of ability. A little bit on the weak side at the moment but a very likeable filly".

572. CLAN PIPER ★★★
b.c. Exceed And Excel – Song Of Skye (Warning).
April 25. Fifth foal. 100,000Y. Tattersalls October 2. John Ferguson. Half-brother to the quite useful 2008 2-y-o 1m and 8.7f winner Stevie Junior (by Monsieur Bond) and to the quite useful 5f (at 2 yrs) and 7f winner and listed-placed Skyelady (by Dansili). The dam, a quite useful 5f (at 2 yrs) and 7f winner, is a half-sister to 5 winners. The second dam, Song Of Hope (by Chief Singer), a useful 2-y-o 5f winner, was second in the listed Firth of Clyde Stakes and is a half-sister to 10 winners.
"He did a bit of work this morning and looked to have some speed. He wouldn't want revving up and although he'll be OK over five furlongs he'd be happier over six. I like him".

573. COLOURBEARER (IRE) ★★★
ch.c. Pivotal – Centifolia (Kendor).
January 22. First foal. 140,000Y. Tattersalls October 1. John Ferguson. The dam won 4 races at 2 yrs in France including the Group 2 Criterium de Maisons-Laffitte and is a half-sister to one winner. The second dam, Djayapura (by Fabulous Dancer), won once at 3 yrs in France and is a half-sister to 4 winners.
"A neat colt, he goes well but we'll wait for the six furlong events with him".

574. COMMISSIONAIRE ★★
b.c. Medicean – Appointed One (Danzig).
April 20. Brother to the fair triple 1m winner Officer and half-brother to the smart 7f and 1m winner (at 2 yrs) and Group 3 10f Select Stakes second Battle Chant (by Coronado's Quest), to the fairly useful 7f winner Matoaka (by A P Indy) and the quite useful 1m winner Constitute (by Gone West). The dam, a minor US stakes winner, is a sister to the Group 2 1m Lockinge Stakes winner Emperor Jones and the listed 6f Sirenia Stakes winner and Group 1 Middle Park Stakes third Majlood and a half-sister to the Group 1 1m William Hill Futurity Stakes winner Bakharoff. The second dam, Qui Royalty (by Native Royalty), a winner of 5 races at up to 1m in the USA, was second in the Grade 3 Boiling Springs Handicap and is a half-sister to 8 winners including the US Grade 3 winner Qui Native. (Cheveley Park Stud).
"A nice, big horse, he's immature at this stage and he's going to be one for latter part of the season".

575. COTTON KING ★★★★
b.c. Dubawi – Spinning The Yarn (Barathea).
April 13. Seventh foal. 240,000Y. Tattersalls October 1. John Ferguson. Half-brother to the 2-y-o Group 1 7f Moyglare Stud Stakes winner and US Grade 1 placed Necklace (by Darshaan). The dam ran once unplaced and is closely related to the top-class King George VI and Queen Elizabeth Diamond Stakes winner Opera House and the Ascot Gold Cup and Irish St Leger winner Kayf Tara and a half-sister to the Group 1 Prix de l'Opera winner Zee Zee Top. The second dam, Colorspin (by High Top), won the Irish Oaks and is a half-sister to 8 winners including the Irish Champion Stakes winner Cezanne and the Group 2 Prix de l'Opera winner Bella Colora (herself dam of the high class colt Stagecraft).
"A nice, promising sort for August/September time and a good mover that covers a lot of ground".

576. DEIRDRE ★★★
b.f. Dubawi – Dolores (Danehill).
March 5. Third foal. Half-sister to the listed 14f winner Samuel (by Sakhee) and to the useful 10f winner Duncan (by Dalakhani). The dam, a listed 1m winner and second in the Group 2 1m Sun Chariot Stakes, is a half-sister to one winner. The second dam, Agnus (by In The Wings), a winner twice in Belgium, is a half-sister to 4 other winners abroad including Wavy Run, a winner of 13 races in Spain, France and the USA including the US Grade 2 San Francisco Mile Handicap. (Normandie Stud).
"An active filly, she's improved and strengthened a lot and I'm happy with her at this stage".

577. DHAAMER (IRE) ★★
ch.c. Dubai Destination – Arjuzah (Ahonoora).
March 22. Brother to the quite useful 3-y-o 1m

winner Aflaam, closely related to the smart 2-y-o 7f and 3-y-o listed 7f winner Malhub (by Kingmambo) and half-brother to the very useful 6f winner (including at 2 yrs) Mutaakkid (by Dayjur) and the modest 6f to 8.5f all-weather winner Burhaan (by Green Desert). The dam, a useful winner of the listed 7f Sceptre Stakes, is a half-sister to the Irish listed winner Ormsby out of the useful 1m Lincoln Handicap winner Saving Mercy (by Lord Gayle). (Hamdan Al Maktoum).

"He's a strong boy. He was late to break in and he's just doing ordinary canters at this stage".

578. FALLEN IDOL ★★★★
b.c. Pivotal – Fallen Star (Brief Truce).
March 18. Fourth foal. Half-brother to the fair 2008 2-y-o 1m winner Fallen In Love (by Galileo) and to the useful 12f winner Star Of Gibraltar (by Rock Of Gibraltar). The dam, a listed 7f winner and Group 3 placed twice, is a half-sister to 6 winners including the Group 1 7f Lockinge Stakes winner Fly To The Stars. The second dam, Rise And Fall (by Mill Reef), is an unplaced full or half-sister to 7 winners including the listed winners Special Leave, Spring To Action and Laughter. (Normandie Stud).

"He's shown me a natural level of ability and has a good action and a good stride. He's quite full of himself and I've done a couple of half-speeds with him – more to occupy his mind than to think I want to run him soon. I just need to focus him a bit. I like the way he goes and he looks quite a nice colt".

579. HABBAH ★★★
b.f. Pastoral Pursuits – Preference (Efisio).
March 24. Fifth foal. 45,000Y. Doncaster St Leger. Shadwell Estate Co. Half-sister to the unraced 2008 2-y-o Best Start (by Medicean), to the fairly useful 5f and 6f winner of 4 races Ice Planet (by Polar Falcon) and the modest dual 6f winner Maia (by Observatory). The dam is an unraced sister to the Group 3 Beeswing Stakes winner Casteddu and to the listed winner Barbaroja and a half-sister to 3 winners. The second dam, Bias (by Royal Prerogative), won 6 races at 2 and 3 yrs.

"She's just cantering at this stage and she's gone through a growing stage, but she's going the right way".

580. HEAVENLY QUEST (IRE) ★★★
ch.f. Dubawi – Cephalonie (Kris S).
February 9. Fifth foal. Half-sister to the useful 6f (at 2 yrs) and listed 1m winner Festivale (by Invincible Spirit) and to the useful 6f (at 2 yrs) and 1m winner and listed-placed Tell (by Green Desert). The dam, a French 12f winner, is a half-sister to the Japanese stakes winner Fifty Oner. The second dam, Heraklia (by Irish River), is an unraced half-sister to 4 winners from the family of Machiavellian.

"A solid sort of filly and it looks like she'd want to start over seven furlongs. A strong filly for the middle of the season".

581. ISDAAR (IRE) ★★
b.c. Invincible Spirit – Kildare Lady (Indian Ridge).
February 2. Second foal. 240,000Y. Tattersalls October 1. Shadwell Estate Co. Half-brother to the fair 9.5f winner Barliffey (by Bahri). The dam is an unraced half-sister to 5 winners including the very useful listed Doncaster Stakes winner and Group 3 placed Shaard. The second dam, Braari (by Gulch), a fairly useful 2-y-o listed 6f winner, is a sister to the US stakes winner Special Alert and a half-sister to 8 winners.

"I've had to geld him because he's been quite tricky to deal with. He's doing work right now and he'd need to step up a notch".

582. JAZZ AGE (IRE) ★★★
b.c. Shamardal – Tender Is Thenight (Barathea).
May 15. Seventh foal. 85,000Y. Tattersalls October 2. John Ferguson. Half-brother to the unplaced 2008 French 2-y-o All Night Blues (by Night Shift), to the French 1,000 Guineas winner Tie Black (by Machiavellian), the modest 1m winner Zaarmit and the minor Irish 7f winner Midnight Folk (both by Xaar). The dam won once at 3 yrs in France and is a half-sister to 10 winners including the Breeders Cup Mile and William Hill Sprint Championship winner Last Tycoon, the Group 2 6f Premio Melton and

Group 3 6f Goldene Peitsche winner Astronef and the French winner Save Me The Waltz (herself dam of the French 1,000 Guineas winner Valentine Waltz). The second dam, Mill Princess (by Mill Reef), won over 10f at 2 yrs in France and is a half-sister to the Irish Derby winner Irish Ball and the top-class broodmare Irish Bird (dam of the classic winners Assert, Bikala and Eurobird).

"He did a little bit of half-speed upsides today and I like the way he went. He's strengthened a lot and has a good action".

583. KONA COAST ★★★★
b.c. Oasis Dream – Macadamia (Classic Cliche).
January 24. Second foal. 85,000Y. Tattersalls October 1. John Gosden. The dam, a smart winner of 5 races including the Group 2 1m Falmouth Stakes, is a half-sister to 6 winners including the very useful winner and listed-placed Azarole and the useful 2-y-o 5f and 6f winner Pistachio – subsequently a Group 3 winner in Scandinavia. The second dam, Cashew (by Sharrood), a quite useful 1m winner, is a half-sister to 6 winners here and abroad.

"A nice horse, strong and a good mover, he's strengthened well and is a businesslike colt. He's named after the place in Hawaii where they grow Macadamia nuts".

584. LAAZEM (IRE) ★★
b.c. Piccolo – Untimely (Inchinor).
February 26. First foal. 100,000Y. Doncaster St Leger. Shadwell Estate Co. The dam, a modest 3-y-o 1m winner, is a half-sister to one winner. The second dam, All The Time (by Dancing Brave), is an unplaced half-sister to numerous winners including the very smart Group 2 9.7f Prix Dollar winner Wiorno and the very smart Trusthouse Forte Mile, Gimcrack Stakes and Earl of Sefton Stakes winner Reprimand. (Hamdan Al Maktoum).

"He's a good-looking horse and I'm doing a bit with him right now but he hasn't shown me much. He's very idle and is improving gradually but only inch by inch rather than anything more".

585. LADY OF AKITA (USA) ★★★
ch.f. Fantastic Light – Chancey Squaw (Chief's Crown).
April 25. Sixth foal. Half-brother to the high-class Japanese stakes winner of 7 races from 1m to 10f Agnes Digital (by Crafty Prospector) and to the 2002 Irish 2-y-o 6f winner and Group 1 Fillies Mile third Reach For The Moon (by Pulpit). The dam, a minor winner in the USA, is a half-sister to 6 winners including the Royal Lodge Stakes winner Royal Kingdom and the French listed winners Beaute Dangereuse and Matador. The second dam, Alliance (by Alleged), won over 10.5f in France, was second in the Group 3 10.5f Prix de Flore and is a half-sister to Blushing Groom.

"A nice filly and fortunately she's grown – she was a bit too neat. I'm happy with her as she's a good mover with a good positive attitude".

586. MAAREK ★★★
b.c. Pivotal – Ruby Rocket (Indian Rocket).
January 30. First foal. 130,000Y. Tattersalls October 1. Shadwell Estate Co. The dam, a listed 5f and 6f winner, was Group 3 placed twice and is a half-sister to 7 winners including the Irish 2-y-o 6f listed winner Alexander Alliance and the German listed winner and Group 3 6.5f Prix Eclipse second Inzar's Best. The second dam, Geht Schnell (by Fairy King), is a placed half-sister to one winner abroad.

"A neat little guy when he came in, he's gone through a growing phase and has gone a little weak with it but he is a nice moving horse. An early foal, I'd be hoping when he levels off I'd be kicking on with him. A mid-season two-year-old".

587. MAID TO DREAM ★★★
b.f. Oasis Dream – Maid For The Hills (Indian Ridge).
April 17. Tenth foal. Sister to the fairly useful 2008 2-y-o 6f winner Run For The Hills, closely related to the quite useful 2-y-o 6f winner Green Tambourine (by Green Desert) and half-sister to the useful 7f (at 2 yrs) and 10f winner Maid To Perfection (by Sadler's Wells), the useful 2-y-o 7f winner Artistic Lad (by Peintre Celebre),

the fairly useful 1m to 12f winner of 4 races Maid To Believe (by Galileo), the quite useful 8.6f winner King's Kama (by King's Best). The dam was a useful 2-y-o and won twice over 6f including the listed Empress Stakes. She is a half-sister to 5 winners including the Group 3 6f Princess Margaret Stakes second Maid For Walking. The second dam, Stinging Nettle (by Sharpen Up), a fairly useful 2-y-o listed 6f winner, is a half-sister to 4 winners including the Group 2 1m Royal Lodge Stakes winner Gairloch.
"A nice filly, she's strengthened and gone the right way. Coming in her coat now, she's done nothing other than canter but she's a likeable filly".

588. MASS RALLY ★★★
b.c. Kheleyf – Reunion (Be My Guest).
March 10. Seventh foal. €75,000Y. Goffs Million. John Ferguson. Half-brother to the fair 2008 2-y-o 7f winner Test Match (by Exceed And Excel), to the quite useful 4-y-o 6f and 7f winner Gunfighter (by Machiavellian) and a winner in Japan by Giant's Causeway. The dam, a very useful 6f (at 2 yrs) and Group 3 7f Nell Gwyn Stakes winner, is a half-sister to 7 winners. The second dam, Phylella (by Persian Bold), won in France (over 10f) and in the USA, is a sister to the US stakes winner Karman Girl and a half-sister to 4 winners.
"He moves well, but he's only been with me two days so I don't know a lot about him. He's worth a mention though and he carries himself well".

589. MEEZAAN (IRE) ★★★★ ♠
b.c. Medicean – Varenka (Fasliyev).
February 6. First foal. 200,000Y. Tattersalls October 1. Shadwell Estate Co. The dam, a fairly useful 2-y-o 7.5f winner, was listed-placed in Italy. The second dam, Castara Beach (by Danehill), placed fourth once over 7f at 2 yrs, is a sister to the useful Group 3 7f Criterion Stakes winner Hill Hopper (herself dam of the dual Group 1 winner Nannina) and a half-sister to 5 winners including the Australian Grade 1 winner Water Boatman.
"A very likeable horse and I'd like him the most of the ones we have from Sheikh Hamdan. He moves well and he's strong and purposeful. He's done a little work upsides and he goes well".

590. MIDFIELDER (USA) ★★
ch.c. Smart Strike – Quiet Weekend (Quiet American).
March 4. Fourth foal. $500,000Y. Keeneland September. Blandford Bloodstock. Half-brother to the quite useful 7f winner Step In Line (by Giant's Causeway). The dam, a minor French 2-y-o 5f winner, is a half-sister to 4 winners (2 of them stakes-placed). The second dam, Amirati (by Danzig), a quite useful 2-y-o 5f winner, is a half-sister to the US Grade 1 winners and sires A P Indy and Summer Squall.
"Like a lot of them he's gone through a growing phase and has gone weak with it. He's just doing one easy canter a day and he's most likely a horse for the autumn".

591. ORIENTAL CAT ★★★★
b.c. Tiger Hill – Sentimental Value (Diesis).
January 17. Second foal. 100,000Y. Tattersalls October 2. John Ferguson. Half-brother to the fair 10f winner Barwell Bridge (by Red Ransom). The dam, a winner of 2 stakes events in the USA and Grade 3 placed, is a half-sister to 3 winners in Japan. The second dam, Stately Star (by Deputy Minister), a stakes winner of 6 races in the USA, is a half-sister to 7 winners.
"He should be a bit earlier than most Tiger Hill's. Hopefully he should be racing in July at Newmarket and he's a nice, strong colt that I like".

592. OUTSHINE ★★★
ch.f. Exceed And Excel – Sunny Davis (Alydar).
March 1. Twelfth foal. 32,000Y. Doncaster St Leger. R O'Gorman. Half-sister to the useful 6f (at 2 yrs) to 1m (in Sweden) winner Warming Trends, to the Italian winner of 6 races Dawing (both by Warning), the quite useful 12f winner Sunny Chief (by Be My Chief), the quite useful 10f winners Roborant (by Robellino) and Dance In The Sun (by Halling), the fair 6f (at 2 yrs) to 1m winner Davis Rock (by Rock City), the fair 10f winner Shesha Bear (by Tobougg) and the Italian 2-y-o winner Golden Aviance (by

Generous). The dam, a fair 2-y-o 7f winner, is out of the minor US winner Goldie Hawn (by Northern Dancer), herself a sister to the Grade 2 winner Larida (dam of the Coronation Stakes winner Magic Of Life) and a half-sister to the champion US filly Miss Oceana.
"She just needs to strengthen and I'm moving along with her a bit. She's got a good way of going".

593. POUNCED ★★★
b.c. Rahy – Golden Cat (Storm Cat).
Half-brother to the quite useful 2009 3-y-o 10f winner Big Bound (by Grans Slam), to the useful dual 10f winner and listed-placed Pampas Cat (by Seeking The Gold), the useful Irish 5f winner and listed 7f Acomb Stakes second Celtic Cat (by Danehill) and the modest 8.7f winner Mozie Cat (by Mozart). The dam won over 1m at 3 yrs in Ireland and was listed-placed and is a half-sister to 7 winners including the very useful Irish listed 1m and 10f winner and subsequent US winner Eurostorm, the useful 10.3f winner Tamiami Trail and the useful 12f winner Garden Society. The second dam, Eurobird (by Ela-Mana-Mou), a smart winner of 4 races including the Irish St Leger and the Blandford Stakes, is a half-sister to the French Derby winner Bikala and to the Irish Derby and French Derby winner Assert.
"He's not very big but he's active and looks like making a two-year-old".

594. SENATE ★★★
ch.c. Pivotal – Sauterne (Rainbow Quest).
March 11. Fourth foal. 160,000Y. Tattersalls October 1. John Ferguson. Half-brother to the fair 2-y-o 7f winner Determined Stand (by Elusive Quality). The dam, a listed winner of 3 races from 7f to 10f, is a half-sister to 5 winners including the smart 2-y-o Group 2 6f Cherry Hinton Stakes winner Applaud. The second dam, Band (by Northern Dancer), is a placed half-sister to 5 winners including the US Grade 3 9f New Orleans Handicap winner Festive.
"A tall horse and a good mover that's quite full of himself. I like him but he's not going to be an early sort at all".

595. SIR PITT ★★★★★
b.c. Tiger Hill – Rebecca Sharp (Machiavellian).
February 15. Half-brother to the smart 7f (at 2 yrs) and 10f winner and Group 2 10f Irish Derby Trial third Grand Central, to the quite useful 10f and hurdles winner Farringdon (both by Sadler's Wells), the useful 6f (at 2 yrs) and 1m listed winner Miss Pinkerton (by Danehill) and the fair 10f to 12f winner of 5 races Rawdon (by Singspiel). The dam, a high-class winner of the Group 1 1m Coronation Stakes, is a half-sister to numerous winners including the smart Group 3 11.5f Lingfield Derby Trial winner Mystic Knight. The second dam, Nuryana (by Nureyev), was a useful winner of 2 races over 1m including the listed Grand Metropolitan Stakes and is a half-sister to 5 winners.
"I like him. I know he's a Tiger Hill out of a mare that was a good miler, so I'd be aware of not doing too much too soon, but he's a very nice horse. He came in a little bit behind the others but he caught up very quickly. A colt with a good, big stride to him".

596. SPACE WAR ★★★
b.c. Elusive City – Princess Luna (Grand Lodge).
February 15. First foal. 80,000Y. Tattersalls October 2. John Ferguson. The dam, a minor German 3-y-o winner, is a half-sister to 4 winners. The second dam, Princess Nana (by Bellypha), won the Group 2 German 1,000 Guineas and is a half-sister to 6 winners.
"Yes, I like him and he's showed me a nice level of ability. At the moment he has a sore shin so he's on the easy list but he's a nice, active horse".

597. THAT'S MY STYLE ★★★★
gr.f. Dalakhani – Pearl Dance (Nureyev).
March 20. Half-sister to the useful 2008 2-y-o dual 7f winner and Group 2 1m Royal Lodge Stakes fourth Ridge Dance (by Selkirk). The dam, a useful 2-y-o 6f winner and third in the Group 1 Moyglare Stud Stakes, is a half-sister to the German listed winner and Group 1 German Derby fourth Ocean Sea and the US winner and Grade 3 third Dixie Splash. The second dam, Ocean Jewel (by Alleged), is an unraced half-sister to 6 minor winners. (George Strawbridge).

"She's only just arrived in the yard, but she goes OK and she's a nice-moving filly".

598. THRILL ★★★★
ch.f. Pivotal – Irresistible (Cadeaux Genereux).
February 28. Sister to the very smart 7f (at 2 yrs) and Group 3 7f Nell Gwyn Stakes winner and Coronation Stakes and Falmouth Stakes second Infallible. The dam was a fairly useful 5f (at 2 yrs) and listed 6f winner and is a half-sister to one winner. The second dam, Polish Romance (by Danzig), a minor 7f winner in the USA, is a sister to the US stakes winner Polish Love and a half-sister to 3 minor winners. (Cheveley Park Stud).
"A nice filly, she's big and strong. As a sister to Infallible she'll probably be similar in that she wouldn't want me rushing her and she's likely to appreciate a bit of cut in the ground, but she's nice".

599. TOWER ★★★★★
b.c. Nayef – Palatial (Green Desert).
April 12. Brother to the smart 2-y-o Group 2 1m May Hill Stakes winner and 1,000 Guineas second Spacious and half-brother to the useful 7f (at 2 yrs) and 1m winner Artimino (by Medicean). The dam, a useful winner of 4 races over 7f (including at 2 yrs), is a half-sister to the useful listed 10f winner Ice Palace. The second dam, White Palace (by Shirley Heights), was a quite useful 3-y-o 8.2f winner.
"A big boy, he goes well, has a big action and is a grand looking horse. A little plain around his head perhaps, but he's a very likeable horse in the string".

600. TRUST DEED ★★★
b.c. Singspiel – Confidante (Dayjur).
May 2. Eighth foal. Brother to the Group 3 7f (at 2 yrs) and Group 1 10.5f Prix de Diane winner Confidential Lady and half-brother to the fairly useful 7f winner Crown Counsel and the fair 5f and 7f winner Registrar (both by Machiavellian) and the quite useful 1m winner Censored (by Pivotal). The dam, a fairly useful 3-y-o dual 7f winner, is a half-sister to 6 winners including the 2-y-o 6f winner Wind Cheetah, the Group 3 7f Solario Stakes winner White Crown and the 11.8f winner Zuboon – all useful. The second dam, Won't She Tell (by Banner Sport), a minor stakes winner of 9 races in the USA at up to 9f, is a half-sister to the American Triple Crown winner Affirmed. (Cheveley Park Stud).
"He's just a little immature at the moment but he's a nice type of colt. Certainly a horse more for September time than anything else".

601. VALENZANI ★★★
b.c. Royal Applause – Frascati (Emarati).
February 5. First foal. Doncaster St Leger. 115,000Y. Blandford Bloodstock. The dam, a quite useful 5f winner of 7 races from 2 to 4 yrs, was listed placed twice and is a half-sister to 3 winners. The second dam, Fizzy Fiona (by Efisio), is an unraced half-sister to one winner.
"A nice, solid type of colt with some speed about him. He has a relaxed attitude and I like him at this stage".

602. WEATHERVANE ★★★
b.c. Red Ransom – Westerly Air (Gone West).
March 12. Third foal. Half-brother to the fair 2008 2-y-o 7f winner (on her only start at 2 yrs) Floodlit (by Fantastic Light). The dam, a fair 9.3f winner, is a half-sister to 4 winners including the Grade 2 Long Island Handicap, the Group 3 May Hill Stakes and Group 3 Prestige Stakes winner Midnight Line. The second dam, Midnight Air (by Green Dancer), won the Group 3 1m May Hill Stakes at 2 yrs and is a half-sister to 5 minor winners and to the dam of the Group 1 5f Prix de l'Abbaye winner Imperial Beauty.
"A big boy, he's come together well. He's going to be one for much later on but he'll be a nice horse to watch come the autumn".

603. WEEPING WILLOW (IRE) ★★★
b.f. Kheleyf – Bezant (Zamindar).
April 29. Second foal. 65,000Y. Doncaster St Leger. Blandford Bloodstock. Sister to the fairly useful 2008 2-y-o 6f winner Deposer. The dam, placed once at 3 yrs over 1m, is a half-sister to 3 winners including the Group 2 Beresford Stakes third Sant Jordi. The second dam, Foresta Verde (by Green Forest), is a placed half-sister to 8 winners.

"A nice type of filly, she's had a bit of a cough and lost a bit of time but she has a good action and a good attitude".

604. WHISTLE BLOWER ★★★★
b.c. Exceed And Excel – Song Of Hope (Chief Singer).
February 17. Thirteenth foal. 32,000Y. Doncaster St Leger. R O'Gorman. Half-brother to Praise Of Folly (by Selkirk), unplaced in two start at 2 yrs in 2008, to the fairly useful 2-y-o 6f winner Xtrasensory, the quite useful 5.2f (at 2 yrs) and 7f winner Song Of Skye (by Warning), the fair 2-y-o 6f winner Stolen Melody (by Robellino), the fair 7f and 1m all-weather winner Kingdom Princess, the modest dual 5f winner Miriam (both by Forzando) and a winner in Denmark by Primo Dominie. The dam, a useful 2-y-o 5f winner and second in the listed Firth of Clyde Stakes, is a half-sister to 10 minor winners. The second dam, Penny Blessing (by So Blessed), won twice at 2 yrs, was fourth in the Cheveley Park Stakes and is a half-sister to 8 winners.
"A nice colt, he goes well doing a bit of work upsides and looks to have some quality".

605. ZIGATO ★★★
b.c. Azamour – Maycocks Bay (Muhtarram).
March 12. Fifth foal. 22,000Y. Tattersalls October 1. John Gosden. Half-brother to the quite useful 2008 2-y-o 7f winner Sariska (by Pivotal) and to the 8.7f (at 2 yrs), 10f and listed 14f winner Gull Wing (by In The Wings). The dam, a useful 14f listed winner, is a half-sister to several winners including the useful 7f and 1m winner (at 2 yrs) and listed 10.3f placed 3-y-o Indian Light. The second dam, Beacon (by High Top), is an unraced half-sister to 6 winners including the Group 3 10f Gordon Richards Stakes winner Compton Ace.
"He arrives next week and he goes quite nicely. Being by Azamour he was largely ignored at the Sales but his half-sister Sariska is currently working nicely for Michael Bell".

606. UNNAMED ★★★
ch.c. Smart Strike – Allencat (Storm Cat).
April 1. Second foal. $500,000Y. Keeneland September. Blandford Bloodstock. The dam is an unraced half-sister to 2 winners. The second dam, Pharma (by Theatrical), won 7 races in the USA including the Grade 1 Santa Ana Handicap and is a half-sister to the US multiple Grade 2 winner Hap and to the unraced dam of the multiple Grade 1 winner English Channel.
"A big, rangy colt, he won't be early so he's typical of the sire in that respect. He's the kind of horse you'd see in the autumn but he looks promising at this stage".

607. UNNAMED ★★★★
b.c. Oasis Dream – Arabesque (Zafonic).
March 31. Fifth foal. Brother to the quite useful 2008 2-y-o 6f winner Bouvardia and half-brother to the very smart listed 6f winner Camacho (by Danehill). The dam, a useful listed 6f winner, is a sister to 2 winners including the useful 5f and 6f winner Threat. The second dam, Prophecy (by Warning), was a very useful winner of the Group 1 6f Cheveley Park Stakes and was second in the Group 3 7f Nell Gwyn Stakes. (Khalid Abdulla).
"He's working at the moment, doing some nice 'upsides' and he goes well. He's a strong colt and I like the way he travels".

608. UNNAMED ★★★
b.br.f. Dixie Union – Belterra (Unbridled).
March 13. Third foal. $400,000Y. Keeneland September. Blandford Bloodstock. The dam won 4 races at 2 and 3 yrs in the USA including the Grade 2 Golden Rod Stakes, was third in the Grade 1 Ashland Stakes and is a half-sister to 6 winners including the triple Grade 2 winner Royal Haven. The second dam, Cruising Haven (by Shelter Half), is an unraced half-sister to a US Grade 3 winner.
"She's not precocious but she's a nice filly. She's a good mover and has a good attitude but she's only cantering at present".

609. UNNAMED ★★
b.br.c. Smart Strike – Bienandanza (Bien Bien).
February 24. Fourth foal. $240,000Y. Keeneland September. Blandford Bloodstock. The dam, a stakes winner of 3 races at 4 yrs in the USA, is a half-sister to one winner. The second dam, Fit n Fappy (by Fappiano), a 2-y-o winner and Grade 2 placed in the USA, is a half-sister to 6 winners.
"He's a bit of a lad and not the most helpful of characters. He's going to be the type for a mile maiden come September. I'd just like to see his attitude be a little bit more positive".

610. UNNAMED ★★★
b.f. Dansili – Bonash (Rainbow Quest).
February 12. Half-sister to the multiple Group 3 middle-distance winner and French Derby fourth Day Flight (by Sadler's Wells) and to the very useful 2-y-o 7f winner Bionic (by Zafonic). The dam, a very useful filly, won 4 races in France from 1m to 12f including the Prix d'Aumale, the Prix Vanteaux and the Prix de Malleret and is a full or half-sister to 4 winners. The second dam, Sky Love (by Nijinsky), a fairly useful 10f winner, is a half-sister to the high-class Prix de la Cote Normande winner Raft. (Khalid Abdulla).
"She's like the family and is a filly with quality that wouldn't want to be rushed. She'll appreciate a bit of cut in the ground in September and I like the way she goes".

611. UNNAMED ★★★★
b.c. Shamardal – Bush Cat (Kingmambo).
April 9. Third foal. 95,000Y. Tattersalls October 2. Hugo Lascelles. Half-brother to the modest 2008 fourth placed 2-y-o Ask Dan (by Refuse To Bend) and to the quite useful 2-y-o 1m winner and subsequent US Grade 3 placed Meer Kat (by Red Ransom). The dam, a quite useful 2-y-o 7f winner, is a half-sister to 3 winners. The second dam, Arbusha (by Danzig), won the listed 1m Schwarzgold Rennen, was third in the Group 3 Royal Whip Stakes and is a sister to the Group 2 6f Goldene Peitsche winner Nicholas and a half-sister to 9 winners.
"He wasn't the easiest to break in but he's going strong in his work right now and he's improved a lot. I'm happy enough with him, I like the way he goes, he's businesslike and strong. They look hardy, tough horses these Shamardal's, like their father".

612. UNNAMED ★★★
b.f. Distorted Humor – Caressing (Honour And Glory).
February 7. Second foal. $625,000Y. Keeneland September. Blandford Bloodstock. Half-sister to a minor US 3-y-o winner by Storm Cat. The dam, a champion 2-y-o filly and winner of the Grade 1 Breeders Cup Juvenile Fillies, is a half-sister to numerous winners including the stakes winner Platinum Blonde. The second dam, Lovin Touch (by Majestic Prince). A US stakes winner of 4 races at 2 and 3 yrs, was Grade 2 placed.
"An immature filly, very 'ribby' and long at this stage but she's got quality about her".

613. UNNAMED ★★
b.f. Redoute's Choice – Catnipped (Rory's Jester).
January 17. Sixth foal. 160,000Y. Tattersalls October 1. John Ferguson. Closely related to the Australian stakes-placed winner Fangio (by Danehill) and to 2 minor winners in Australia by Danzero and Giant's Causeway and half-sister to a minor Australian winner by King's Best. The dam, a Grade 2 winner of 3 races at 2 yrs in Australia, is a half-sister to 3 winners. The second dam, Final Claus (by Christmas Tree), won once in Australia and is a half-sister to 7 winners.
"She was born in the Southern Hemisphere but to our time - I don't know how many have tried this before. She's a nice filly, she's growing and she's a bit wrong in her coat but I think that's because the seasons are confused in her system. So I'll go gently with her. My experience with the ones from South America in the old days in California was that you always had to give them extra time".

614. UNNAMED ★★★★
b.c. Exceed And Excel – Cayman Sound (Turtle Island).
March 15. Third foal. 52,000Y. Doncaster St Leger. Blandford Bloodstock. Half-brother to

the fair 1m and 9f winner Charlevoix (by King Charlemagne). The dam, a minor 12f winner, is a half-sister to 6 winners. The second dam, Kukri (by Kris), is an unraced half-sister to 3 winners.
"He's working right now and he shows me a good level of ability. Five and six furlongs will suit him fine".

615. UNNAMED ★★★
b.f. Shamardal – Crystal View (Imperial Ballet).
February 18. First foal. 80,000Y. Doncaster St Leger. Blandford Bloodstock. The dam won 4 races in Ireland at 2 yrs from 7f to 1m including the Group 3 1,000 Guineas Trial and is a half-sister to 3 winners including the Group 2 placed Miss Trish. The second dam, Fey Rouge (by Fayruz), is an unplaced half-sister to 9 winners.
"She's a quick-actioned filly and she goes fine. At this stage I'd expect her to be out quite early, probably around May time".

616. UNNAMED ★★★
b.c. Oasis Dream – Delta (Zafonic).
March 1. Second foal. Half-brother to the quite useful 2008 2-y-o 1m winner Sampi (by Beat Hollow). The dam was a French 3-y-o dual 1m winner. The second dam, Fleet River (by Riverman), a fairly useful 2-y-o 7f winner, is a half-sister to the very smart Eltish, winner of the 7f Lanson Champagne Stakes and the 1m Royal Lodge Stakes and runner-up in the Grade 1 8.5f Breeders Cup Juvenile, to the useful 8.3f winner Yamuna, the useful 5f and 6f winner Forest Gazelle and the French listed 10f winner Souplesse. (Khalid Abdulla).
"A nice, big horse, he's shown some immaturities but he's got a little bit about him".

617. UNNAMED ★★
gr.c. Empire Maker – Diese (Diesis).
February 27. Half-brother to the useful French 6f (at 2 yrs) and 1m winner Speak In Passing (by Danzig), to the useful 7f (at 2 yrs) and 10f winner Senure, the useful winner at up to 15f in France Terrazzo (both by Nureyev), the quite useful 4-y-o 8.2f winner Dexterity (by Kingmambo) and the fair 10f winner Five Fields (by Chester House). The dam, winner of the Group 3 10.5f Prix Corrida and a listed event over 10f in France, is a half-sister to numerous good winners including the champion European 2-y-o Xaar, winner of the Group 1 Dewhurst Stakes and the Group 1 Prix de la Salamandre and the Group 3 1m Prix Quincey winner Masterclass. The second dam, Monroe (by Sir Ivor), a useful Irish 5f and 6f winner, is a sister to the good 2-y-o Gielgud and to the very smart Malinowski and a half-sister to the dual Grade 1 winner Blush With Pride and to Sex Appeal – the dam of El Gran Senor and Try My Best. (Khalid Abdulla).
"He's a big boy and he's going to take time. You'd be looking at the mile maidens into October with him".

618. UNNAMED ★★
b.c. Proud Citizen – Fair Settlement (Easy Goer).
May 5. Ninth foal. $525,000Y. Keeneland September. Blandford Bloodstock. Half-brother to 4 winners including the minor US stakes-placed Mustang Jock (by Wild Again). The dam is an unraced half-sister to the US Grade 3 winner Party Manners. The second dam, Duty Dance (by Nijinsky), a US Grade 2 and Grade 3 winner, is a half-sister to the US Grade 1 winner Squander.
"A strong colt, he's tall and rangy and a little bit immature of his joints at the moment (that comes from him being out of an Easy Goer mare). He's just doing easy canters and is a horse to wait with".

619. UNNAMED ★★★
b.c. Motivator – Fickle (Danehill).
January 29. Fourth foal. 100,000Y. Tattersalls October 1. John Gosden. Half-brother to the useful Tarfah (by Kingmambo), a winner of 5 races over 1m and 9f including the Group 3 Dahlia Stakes. The dam, a fairly useful 1m and listed 10f winner, is a half-sister to 7 winners including the useful 11.5f listed winner Birdie and to the French middle-distance winner of 10 races (including 4 listed events) Faru. The second dam, Fade (by Persepolis), is an unraced half-sister to Tom Seymour, a winner of five Group 3 events in Italy and fourth in the Queen's Vase.

"He's a tall boy that carries his head a bit awkwardly at times. He needs to just strengthen and 'do' and I'd be hopeful I could have him out in August or September".

620. UNNAMED ★★★
b.c. Whipper – Flaming Song (Darshaan).
March 5. Eighth foal. Deauville August. €340,000Y. John Ferguson. Half-brother to 4 winners including the German Group winners Fight Club (by Lavirco) and Flambo (by Platini). The dam, a minor French 2-y-o winner, is out of the listed placed Pale Blue (by Kris), herself a half-sister to 7 winners.
"He's a strong boy and he goes well. He should be sharp being by Whipper and that's how he looks. A five/six furlong horse".

621. UNNAMED ★★★
ch.c. Dubawi – Friendlier (Zafonic).
February 15. Third foal. 110,000Y. Tattersalls October 1. John Gosden. Half-brother to the quite useful 2-y-o 7f winner Foolin Myself (by Montjeu). The dam is an unraced half-sister to 3 winners including the top-class filly User Friendly, winner of the Oaks, the St Leger, the Irish Oaks and the Yorkshire Oaks and second in the Prix de l'Arc de Triomphe. The second dam, Rostova (by Blakeney), a fairly useful winner of 4 races from 12f to 14f, is a half-sister to 7 winners including the very successful Italian filly Judd.
"A big, rugged colt, he's solid and strong. A colt with a good way of going, he'll be one for the seven furlong/mile races around September".

622. UNNAMED ★★★
b.f. Exceed And Excel – Global Trend (Bluebird).
February 5. Second foal. Half-sister to Bawaardi (by Acclamation), a fair second over 6f on his only start at 2 yrs in 2008. The dam is an unraced half-sister to 3 winners including the French and US stakes winners Night Chapter. The second dam, Context (by Zafonic), is a placed half-sister to 5 winners including the US Grade 2 winner Bon Point.
"A strong filly with a good action. She looks like she's quite speedy".

623. UNNAMED ★★★
ch.f. Shamardal – Golden Silca (Inchinor).
April 10. Fourth foal. 170,000Y. Tattersalls October 2. John Gosden. Half-sister to Silca Meydan (by Diktat), unplaced in one start at 2 yrs in 2008 and to the modest 7f and 1m winner Silca Destination (by Dubai Destination). The dam, a smart Group 2 6f Mill Reef Stakes and German Group 2 winner, was second in the Group 1 Coronation Stakes and the Group 1 Irish 1,000 Guineas and is a half-sister to 6 winners including the smart 2-y-o Group 1 6f Prix Morny winner Silca's Sister and the very useful 5f and 6f winner of 12 races (including at 2 yrs) Green Manalishi. The second dam, Silca-Cisa (by Hallgate), a fairly useful dual 5f winner, was listed placed over 5f at 4 yrs and is a half-sister to one winner.
"A nice type of filly, she's important now her dam has died and I hope she does well. I like her and she's a very strong two-year-old".

624. UNNAMED ★★★
b.c. Galileo – Guignol (Anita's Prince).
March 5. Fourth foal. 85,000Y. Tattersalls October 1. Blandford Bloodstock. The dam, a minor Irish 3-y-o 5f winner, is a half-sister to 8 winners including the US Grade 3 winner Down Again and to the dam of the Irish and French 2,000 Guineas winner Bachir. The second dam, Dawn Is Breaking (by Import), won twice over 5f at 2 yrs in Ireland at 2 yrs and is a half-sister to 6 winners.
"He's not with me yet but I've seen him and he goes nicely".

625. UNNAMED ★★★
b.c. Dubawi – Hasten (Lear Fan).
January 23. Fourth foal. 220,000Y. Doncaster St Leger. Malih Al Basti. Half-brother to the 7f seller winner Gassal (by Oasis Dream), to the fair 1m winner Hasty Lady (by Dubai Destination) and a minor winner abroad by Johannesburg. The dam was placed twice in the USA and is a half-sister to 6 winners including the 2-y-o Group 3 Autumn Stakes winner and Group 1 Racing Post Trophy second Fantastic View. The second dam, Promptly (by Lead On Time), a

quite useful 6f winner here, subsequently won a minor stakes event over 1m in the USA and is a half-sister to 6 winners.

"He's a solid citizen and I like the way he does everything. He hasn't arrived here yet but I've just been down to see him at Malcolm Bastard's place and he looks a nice horse".

626. UNNAMED ★★★★
b.c. Acclamation – It Takes Two (Alzao).
February 22. Ninth living foal. 180,000Y. Doncaster St Leger. R O'Gorman. Half-brother to the Group 3 6f Greenlands Stakes winner Final Exam, to the dual French winner El Bosco (both by College Chapel), the 2-y-o Group 2 6f Lowther Stakes third Spirit Of Chester (by Lend A Hand) and the Irish dual 13f winner Final Opinion (by King's Theatre). The dam is an unplaced half-sister to 2 minor winners out of the listed 7f Athasi Stakes winner and Irish 1,000 Guineas fourth Final Moment (by Nishapour).

"A nice horse, he's working well and he's very laid-back. I like the way he goes".

627. UNNAMED ★★★
b.c. Speightstown – Lunar Colony (A P Indy).
April 8. Third foal. $350,000Y. Keeneland September. Juddmonte Farms. Half-brother to a minor winner in Canada by Pine Bluff. The dam, a fair 10f winner, is a sister to the US winner and Grade 1 placed Soul Search and a half-sister to the US stakes winner and Grade 2 placed Reform Act. The second dam, Solar Colony (by Pleasant Colony), won twice at 3 yrs and is a sister to the US Grade 1 winner Pleasant Stage and to the US Graded stakes winners Colonial Play and Stage Colony.

"I trained the mother and this is a tall, rangy colt. I think speed onto this mare will be a good thing, I like the way he moves but he's not going to be precocious".

628. UNNAMED ★★★★
b.f. Dansili – Namaste (Alzao).
February 6. The dam, a moderate 12f placed maiden, is closely related to the very smart Wemyss Bight, a winner of five races from 9f (at 2 yrs) to 12f including the Group 1 Irish Oaks and the Group 2 Prix de Malleret and a half-sister to several other stakes horses. The second dam, Bahamian (by Mill Reef), was a very useful winner of the Group 3 12f Lingfield Oaks Trial and was placed in the Prix de l'Esperance (disqualified from first place), Prix de Pomone, Park Hill Stakes and Princess Royal Stakes. She is a half-sister to the very useful winners Captivator, Eileen Jenny and Kasmayo. (Khalid Abdulla).

"I like her and I think she's one of those it would be easy push too soon. She has a lovely action, covers the ground well and is a nice type of filly, but you'd want to be waiting for the seven furlong maidens for her".

629. UNNAMED ★★★
b.f. Dubawi – Regina Maria (Unbridled).
January 15. Sixth foal. $300,000Y. Keeneland September. M Johnston. Half-sister to a minor winner in the USA by Cozzene. The dam is an unraced half-sister to 3 winners including the US Grade 2 winner and Grade 1 placed Tejano Run and the US Grade 2 winner and Group 2 Royal Lodge Stakes second More Royal. The second dam, Royal Run (by Wavering Monarch), is an unraced half-sister to 3 US Graded stakes winners.

"A strong filly, she's a nice type with a very, very good attitude. Just a nice filly to be around, she'll start off in a seven furlong maiden and will make a nice mile type".

630. UNNAMED ★★
b.c. Elusive Quality – Sahara Star (Green Desert).
February 1. Twelfth foal. 145,000Y. Doncaster St Leger. R O'Gorman. Half-brother to the smart Group 2 5f Flying Childers Stakes and Group 3 5f King George V Stakes winner Land Of Dreams, to the fair 2-y-o 6f winner Starchy (both by Cadeaux Genereux), the quite useful 7.6f and 1m winner Star Invader (by Nashwan), the quite useful 12f winner Edraak (by Shirley Heights), the French 2-y-o 1m winner Just A Poser (by Darshaan) and the French 3-y-o winner Tan Tan (by King's Best). The dam won the Group 3 5f Molecomb Stakes, was third in the Lowther Stakes and is a half-sister to 6

winners including the Group 3 7f Greenham Stakes winner and Irish 2,000 Guineas fourth Yalaietanee. The second dam, Vaigly Star (by Star Appeal), was a smart sprinter and a half-sister to the high-class sprinter Vaigly Great.

"A backward colt at this stage, he's a perfectly pleasant horse that's doing his canters but he wouldn't want any more at the moment".

631. UNNAMED ★★★
b.f. Dynaformer – Santolina (Boundary).
March 19. Third foal. Keeneland September. 320,000Y. Blandford Bloodstock. The dam, a listed 6f Sirenia Stakes winner, is a half-sister to the listed 1m winner and Group 1 12f Prix Vermeille second Etizaaz and to the US Grade 3 7f Lafayette Stakes winner Trafalger. The second dam, Alamosa (by Alydar), is an unraced half-sister to the King George VI and Queen Elizabeth Diamond Stakes winner Swain out of the US Grade 1 winner Love Smitten.

"A backward filly, she's very elegant and a good mover but is very much one I could see running in a mile maiden at Doncaster in September".

632. UNNAMED ★★★
b.c. Oratorio – Saxon Maid (Sadler's Wells).
April 27. Eleventh foal. €60,000Y. Goffs Million. Angie Sykes Bloodstock. Half-brother to the fair 6f to 12f winner Saxe-Coburg (by Warning) and to 2 minor winners abroad by Nashwan and Doyoun. The dam won 5 races including 2 listed events over 12f and 14f and is a half-sister to 6 winners including the listed winners Broken Wave, Guarde Royale and Clifton Chapel. The second dam, Britannia's Rule (by Blakeney), won the Lupe Stakes and was third in the Oaks.

"He canters nicely and moves well. Looks a nice type of colt".

633. UNNAMED ★★
ch.f. Gone West – Shoogle (A P Indy).
February 11. Sister to the quite useful 2008 2-y-o 1m winner (on his only start at 2 yrs) Close Alliance and half-sister to the fair 2-y-o 6f winner Moral Duty (by Silver Deputy) and to the quite useful French 1m winner Cross Purposes (by Distant View). The dam, a quite useful 2-y-o 7f winner, is closely related to the US Grade 1 winner Sleep Easy and a half-sister to the US Grade 1 winner Aptitude and the smart 6f (at 2 yrs) to 8.5f (in the USA) winner Electrify. The second dam, Dokki (by Northern Dancer), is an unraced half-sister to the US Grade 1 winners Coastal and Slew O'Gold. (Khalid Abdulla).

"She's backward. I had the mother and this is a very likeable filly but she'll want top of the ground. Her mother didn't really race much early on and this filly is one for September time".

634. UNNAMED ★★
b.br.f. Mr Greeley – So Spirited (Favorite Trick).
April 17. Fourth foal. $350,000Y. Keeneland September. Blandford Bloodstock. The dam is an unraced half-sister to the US Grade 1 winners El Corredor and Roman Ruler and to the US Grade 3 winner Silver Tornado. The second dam, Silvery Swan (by Silver Deputy), is an unraced half-sister to 7 winners.

"She's just gone a little bit weak – that can happen to them at this time of the year. I just think she's a filly for much later on".

635. UNNAMED ★★
b.c. Empire Maker – Zenda (Zamindar).
February 9. Half-brother to Rio Carnival (by Storm Cat), unplaced in one start at 2 yrs in 2008. The dam won the French 1,000 Guineas and is a half-sister to the July Cup and Nunthorpe Stakes winner Oasis Dream and the very useful dual listed 1m winner Hopeful Light. The second dam, Hope (by Dancing Brave), is an unraced sister to the very smart filly Wemyss Bight, a winner of five races from 9f (at 2 yrs) to 12f including the Group 1 Irish Oaks and the Group 2 Prix de Malleret. (Khalid Abdulla).

"He's very tall and very backward, so he'll take a lot of time".

MICHAEL GRASSICK

636. AMBER NECTAR (IRE) ★★
b.f. Barathea – Nishan (Nashwan).
February 5. Tenth foal. 20,000Y. Tattersalls October 2. Not sold. Sister to Netta (unplaced in one start at 2 yrs in 2008), to the Irish 1m and

9f winner and listed-placed Pepperwood and the Irish 12f winner and Group 2 10f Pretty Polly Stakes and Group 2 10f Royal Whip Stakes second Molomo and half-sister to the Irish 7f winner Shoshana (by Perugino) and a 4-y-o winner in Germany by Marju. The dam is an unraced half-sister to 3 winners including the Group 3 Prix de Sandringham winner Orford Ness. The second dam, Nesaah (by Topsider), a fairly useful 10f and 10.5f winner, is a half-sister to 8 winners including the very useful Group winners Privity and Zindari.

"A big, backward filly and you're looking at the back-end of the season and next year with her. She's only been here about a month and it took her a while to settle in. She's a nice, big, rangy filly with plenty of scope".

637. TWINKLING ICE (USA) ★★★
ch.f. *Elusive Quality – Starry Ice (Ice Age).*
March 18. Seventh foal. $260,000Y. Keeneland September. B Grassick. Half-sister to the US Grade 1 Carter Handicap winner Forest Danger (by Forestry), to the US stakes-placed winner Skipping Stars (by Skip Away) and a minor US winner by Orientate. The dam won 5 races in the USA including the Grade 2 Landaluce Stakes and is a half-sister to 6 winners including 2 US stakes winners. The second dam, Forumstar (by Inherent Star), won 6 minor races in the USA from 2 to 5 yrs.

"Only just arrived in the yard".

638. UNNAMED ★★★
b.f. *Hawk Wing – Flames Last (Montjeu).*
January 30. First foal. The dam, a moderate 14f winner, is closely related to 5 winners including the 1,000 Guineas, Oaks, Irish Derby and Prix Vermeille winner Salsabil and a half-sister to numerous winners including the Group 1 St James's Palace Stakes winner Marju. The second dam, Flame Of Tara (by Artaius), won the Coronation Stakes. (Miss P F O'Kelly).

"A nice filly, she's only been here about six weeks and even though she was an early foal I don't expect her out before August/September, probably over seven furlongs. She has a nice attitude and a good action. The dam was only small but this filly has a bit of scope and size to her and I like her".

639. UNNAMED ★★★
b.c. *Shamardal – Mayenne (Nureyev).*
February 27. Closely related to the quite useful Irish 10f winner Carnbridge (by Giant's Causeway) and half-brother to the useful 2-y-o 6f to 7f winner of 3 races Sutter's Fort (by Seeking The Gold), to the very useful 12f listed winner My Renee (by Kris S), the quite useful 1m winner Menaggio (by Danehill) and the fair 12f winner Dalaval (by Dalakhani). The dam is an unraced three-parts sister to the top-class colt Carnegie, winner of the Prix de l'Arc de Triomphe and the Grand Prix de Saint-Cloud, to the smart Group 2 10f Prix Guillaume d'Ornano winner Antisaar, the useful 10f and 12f winner Wayne County and the useful listed 13.5f winner Honfleur and a half-sister to the smart Group 3 St Simon Stakes winner Lake Erie. The second dam, Detroit (by Riverman), won the Prix de l'Arc de Triomphe and is a half-sister to 5 winners including the Cheveley Park Stakes winner Durtal (herself dam of the Ascot Gold Cup winner Gildoran). (Miss P F O'Kelly).

"He's not been broken long but he looks relatively sharp for the family. He's a thick set colt and I would say you're looking at six furlongs with him in mid-summer. He looks like a real little two-year-old and he has the conformation of a sprinter".

RAE GUEST
640. CONCILIATORY ★★★
gr.f. *Medicean – Condoleezza (Cozzene).*
February 9. Third foal. Half-sister to the fair 1m and 9f placed Indy Driver (by Domedriver). The dam, a fair 14f winner, is out of the French 1m (at 2 yrs) to 11.5f listed winner Rosabella (by Niniski), herself a half-sister to 6 winners. (Miss K Rausing).

"A big, backward filly, but she'll be alright from mid-summer onwards over seven furlongs plus. She does everything nicely and although she's not a typical two-year-old type we'll be hoping she'll be one of the better ones at the end of the season".

641. HILL OF MILLER ★★★★
b.c. Indian Ridge – Roshani (Kris).
April 28. Fifth foal. €17,000Y. Tattersalls Ireland. Rae Guest. Half-brother to the useful 1m listed winner of 3 races Zayn Zen and to the fairly useful 1m, 10f and UAE winner Zaafran (both by Singspiel). The dam, a fair 1m and 10f winner at 3 yrs, is a half-sister to 8 minor winners here and in the USA. The second dam, Maratona (by Be My Guest), ran twice unplaced in France and is a half-sister to the Fillies Triple Crown winner Oh So Sharp (dam of the Prix Saint-Alary winner Rosefinch and the US Grade 2 winner Shaima) and the Nassau Stakes winner Roussalka (dam of the Group winners Ristna and Shahid).

"He's been bought to run in the Irish Sales race. I bought one for this owner before that finished second in the race, so we're hoping to go one better! A nice horse, he's doing very well and he will be a two-year-old. He was a bit small when I bought him but he's fine now. Six furlongs should be his starting point".

642. LUCKY DIVA ★★
ch.f. Lucky Story – Cosmic Countess (Lahib).
April 20. 2,000Y. Tattersalls October 4. Not sold. Half-sister to the modest 1m winner Miss Madame (by Cape Cross). The dam, a fair 2-y-o 6f winner, is a half-sister to several winners including the fairly useful dual 7f winner Cosmic Prince. The second dam, Windmill Princess (by Gorytus), a poor 1m and 11f placed maiden, is a half-sister to 4 winners and to the unraced dam of the September Stakes winner Spartan Shareef. (Gracelands Stud).

"Tall and well behaved, she's doing nicely. We haven't done enough with her to tell yet but she should make a two-year-old because she seems to be doing OK".

643. LUCKY FLYER ★★
br.f. Lucky Story – Fly Like The Wind (Cyrano de Bergerac).
March 27. Fifth foal. 1,000Y. Tattersalls October 3. Not sold. The dam, a fair 3-y-o 5f winner, is a half-sister to 6 other minor winners. The second dam, Thulium (by Mansingh), is an unplaced sister to the high-class sprinter and useful sire Petong and a half-sister to 5 winners. (Gracelands Stud).

"Other than her physique she's very similar to Lucky Diva in that she's a home-bred from a family that gets plenty of minor winners and is doing nothing wrong at the moment. A small and stocky type".

644. MELINOISE ★★
b.f. Tobougg – Carollan (Marju).
March 22. Half-sister to the fair dual 6f winner Lady Carollina (by Bertolini). The dam, a modest 10f placed maiden, is a half-sister to 3 winners. The second dam, Caroline Lady (Caro), a French 12f winner, is a half-sister to 5 winners including the US Grade 3 winner Lord Sreva. (Mr L Vaessen).

"We had the half-sister and she was nice but wasn't a two-year-old type. This one is much the same in that she'll be very nice but probably not this year. She'll probably want further than Lady Carollina who only wanted six furlongs. A lovely, big filly and a good type".

645. MIGHTY APHRODITE ★★★
b.f. Observatory – Sahara Rose (Green Desert).
February 12. 5,000Y. Tattersalls October. Rae Guest. Half-sister to the fair 2008 2-y-o 6f winner Oriental Rose (by Dr Fong), to the quite useful 1m and 10f winner Nelsons Column (by Benny The Dip) and a minor 9f winner abroad by Xaar. The dam ran once unplaced and is a half-sister to 6 winners including the Group 1 6f Cheveley Park Stakes winner Regal Rose. The second dam, Ruthless Rose (by Conquistador Cielo), ran twice unplaced and is a half-sister to 9 winners including the high-class miler Shaadi. (Mrs P Smith).

"A nice, big filly, we'll be looking to her being one of our better ones at the end of the year and she should be a nice three-year-old".

646. PATACHOU ★★
b.f. Domedriver – Pat Or Else (Alzao).
May 5. Eighth foal. Sister to the moderate 2009 3-y-o 1m winner Patronne and half-sister to the 2-y-o listed 7f Silver Flash Stakes winner Triskel

(by Hawk Wing), the fairly useful 7f and 1m winner Trafalgar Square (by King's Best), to the quite useful 2-y-o 10f winner Dumfies (by Selkirk), the quite useful 12f winner Saluem (by Salse) and the 2-y-o 6f and 7f seller winner Run Lucy Run (by Risk Me). The dam is a placed half-sister to 6 winners including the Group 1 12f Prix Vermeille winner My Emma and the Group 1 St Leger and Group 1 Ascot Gold Cup winner Classic Cliché. The second dam, Pato (by High Top), a fairly useful 2-y-o 7f and triple 4-y-o 10f winner, is a sister to the very smart sprinter Crews Hill. (Miss K Rausing).

"A light filly, we'll be getting on with her early because we don't expect a lot of her. It's a good family but there's not a lot of her so although the family generally gets better with age she hasn't much scope. Six or seven furlongs should suit her".

647. SCILLY BREEZE ★★★
gr.g. Linamix – Mitraillette (Miswaki).
January 22. First foal. 3,000Y. Tattersalls October. Not sold. The dam, a quite useful 2-y-o 7f winner, is closely related to 2 winners by Woodman and to another by Forty Niner and a half-sister to 2 winners. The second dam, Crockadore (by Nijinsky), won 7 races in Ireland and the USA including the Grade 2 12f Orchid Handicap and the Grade 3 11f Sheepshead Bay Handicap (both on turf) and is closely related to the Group 3 Flying Five winner Flowing.

"He's not very big and he's been gelded so we're going to get on with him and make him into a two-year-old. He's not bred to be one but he's doing well and he should be a tough, fun horse for his owners. Hopefully we'll get him out over five furlongs because he seems sharp enough".

648. SERIOUS SPIRIT ★★
b.f. Pastoral Pursuits – Motto (Mtoto).
January 27. €4,000Y. Tattersalls Ireland. Rae Guest. The dam, a fairly useful 12f winner, is a half-sister to 3 winners including the quite useful 2-y-o 7f winner Aston Mara. The second dam, Coigach (by Niniski), a very useful 1m (at 2 yrs) and Group 3 Park Hill Stakes winner, is a half-sister to the listed Cheshire Oaks winner Kyle Rhea and to the Park Hill Stakes second Applecross (herself dam of the Group winners Invermark, Craigsteel and Inchrory). (Mr D Willis).

"She was bought cheaply in Ireland for the Sales race. She's grown into a nice filly but she's gone a bit weak on us so we're just giving her an easy time. Hopefully she'll come out in the midsummer".

649. SHIPWRECKED ★★
b.c. Kyllachy – Council Rock (General Assembly).
April 30. Half-brother to the very smart Group 2 5f Flying Childers Stakes and Weatherbys Super Sprint winner Superstar Leo, to the quite useful 5f and 6f winner Chiquita (both by College Chapel), the fairly useful 6f to 8.5f winner Royal Artist (by Royal Academy), the quite useful 2-y-o 5f winner Rocking (by Oasis Dream), the quite useful 2-y-o 5f winner Horoscope (by Eagle Eyed), the fair 7f (at 2 yrs) to 8.3f winner Starship (by Galileo), the modest dual 1m winner Phi Phi (by Fasliyev) and minor winners abroad by Keen, Anshan and Royal Academy. The dam, a fair 9f and 10f placed 3-y-o, is a half-sister to 6 winners including the Group 3 Prestige Stakes winner Glatisant and the listed Virginia Stakes winner Gai Bulga. The second dam, Dancing Rocks (by Green Dancer), was a very smart filly and winner of the Group 2 10f Nassau Stakes.

"He's a bit small and he was late coming in, but he's a good mover, he's done well and is as good as gold. Just doing easy work at the moment so we don't know much about him yet".

650. ZELOS SPIRIT ★★★★
b.f. Tiger Hill – Good Mood (Devil's Bag).
April 24. Eleventh living foal. 7,000Y. Tattersalls October 3. Rae Guest. Half-sister to the minor US stakes winner Grand Royle (by Danzig), to the UAE 9f and 10f winner and listed-placed Dubai World (by Deputy Minister), the fair UAE 6f winner Keep Faith (by Storm Cat), 2 minor winners in the USA by Capote and Deputy Minister and a winner in Greece by Noverre. The dam, a US Grade 3 winner, is a half-sister to the

US Grade 2 10f winner Academy Award and to the Grade 3 8.5f Nijana Stakes winner Statuette (herself dam of the Irish 5f (at 2 yrs) and 7f winner and Group 1 7f Dewhurst Stakes second Tomahawk) and to the placed dam of the US Grade 1 winner Well Chosen. The second dam, Mine Only (by Mr Prospector), a minor US 3-y-o winner, is a full or half-sister to 3 stakes winners. (Beadle, Booth, Davies & Jennings).
"A very nice filly and hopefully by the end of the season she'll be one of our better ones, despite the cheap price tag. A bigger type than our other Tiger Hill filly but they'll share the same training regime".

651. UNNAMED ★★★
ch.f. Redback – Endless Peace (Russian Revival).
April 6. 2,000Y. Tattersalls October 3. Rae Guest. The dam, a modest 6f (at 2 yrs) to 8.7f placed maiden, is a half-sister to several winners including the smart Group 3 winning sprinter and 2-y-o Group 2 placed Hoh Mike and the very useful sprinter Hogmaneigh. The second dam, Magical Peace (by Magical Wonder), a quite useful Irish 6f winner, is a half-sister to one winner. (Beadle Booth Bloodstock Ltd).
"She looks like being a sharp filly, she looked small at the Sales but it's because she's so close-coupled everyone thought she was tiny but she's not – she's a good size. She should prove to be bargain for what she cost". TRAINER'S BARGAIN BUY

652. UNNAMED ★★★
b.f. Tiger Hill – Eternity Ring (Alzao).
February 28. Second foal. 12,000Y. Tattersalls October 2. Rae Guest. The dam is an unraced half-sister to 7 winners including the Group 3 winners Baron Ferdinand and Love Everlasting. The second dam, In Perpetuity (by Great Nephew), a fairly useful 10f winner, is a half-sister to 6 winners including the Derby winner and high-class sire Shirley Heights and to the placed Bempton (herself dam of the Group winners Gull Nook, Mr Pintips and Banket).
"A nice little Tiger Hill filly, she's not going to be early but she's doing very well and we'd be hopeful for her towards the end of the season.

We have two by the same sire and I like them both although they're two different types. I think they'll both be better as three-year-olds".

653. UNNAMED ★★
b.f. Pearl Of Love – Latest Chapter (Ahonoora).
March 1. Tenth foal. Half-sister to the very useful Irish Group 3 7f Boland Stakes winner Social Harmony (by Polish Precedent), to the fairly useful Irish 1m winner Artist's Tale (by Singspiel), the fair 7f winner Syrinx (by One Cool Cat) and the Irish winners Lady Luck (over 1m by Kris), God Speed (over 6f by Be My Guest), Discreet Option (over 5f by Night Shift) and Bounce Back (over 7f by Alzao). The dam is an unraced half-sister to the Grade 1 Belmont Stakes winner Go And Go. The second dam, Irish Edition (by Alleged), won at 3 yrs and is a half-sister to the US Grade 1 winner Twilight Agenda and the dam of the Group 1 winners Refuse To Bend and Media Puzzle.
"She's only just arrived in the yard but you shouldn't leave her out because she looks to be quite a nice type".

654. UNNAMED ★★★
b.f. Green Desert – Midnight Shift (Night Shift).
March 15. Closely related to the fair 2008 6f placed 2-y-o Midnight Oasis (by Oasis Dream) and half-sister to the Group 3 5f Ballyogan Stakes winner Miss Anabaa (by Anabaa), the smart 5f and 6f winner of 6 races (including the Portland Handicap) Out After Dark, the useful 5f and 6f winner of 5 races Move It (both Cadeaux Genereux), the modest 6f winner Mina (by Selkirk) and the moderate 5f winner Midnight Sky (by Desert Prince). The dam, a fair dual 6f winner at 3 yrs, is a half-sister to 8 winners including the high-class Group 1 6f July Cup winner Owington. The second dam, Old Domesday Book (by High Top), a fairly useful 3-y-o 10.4f winner, was third in the listed 10f Sir Charles Clore Memorial Stakes. (C J Mills).
"She came in late but we know the family well and she seems to be a nice filly. I couldn't say any more than that because she's just doing steady canters twice a day but she's very typical of all the family. Not as big as Miss Anabaa

655. UNNAMED ★★
b.c. Oasis Dream – Millyant (Primo Dominie).
April 1. Ninth foal. 40,000Y. Tattersalls October 2. Not sold. Half-brother to the useful 6f winner and listed 6f placed Millybaa (by Anabaa), to the fairly useful 2-y-o 5f winner Juantorena (by Miswaki) and the quite useful 5f winner of 4 races Millinsky (by Stravinsky). The dam, winner of the Group 2 5f Prix du Gros-Chene, is a half-sister to the Group 2 5f Flying Childers winner and very useful sire Prince Sabo and to the Irish listed winner Bold Jessie (herself dam of the Gimcrack Stakes winner Abou Zouz). The second dam, Jubilee Song (by Song), won once at 3 yrs and is a sister to the dual winner and Nell Gwyn Stakes second Shark Song and to the winner of 10 races and listed-placed Band On The Run. (C J Mills).
"A nice colt, he's just a bit backward at the moment but he's doing everything well. Horses from this family often do better as they get older so we're not pushing him at the moment. It's a fast family but not always as two-year-olds. A decent sized horse, he will be nice next year".

WILLIAM HAGGAS

656. ABRASIVE (IRE) ★★
b.c. Rock Of Gibraltar – Independence (Selkirk).
April 17. Fifth foal. 100,000Y. Tattersalls October 1. W Haggas. Brother to the Group 1 1m Criterium International and Group 1 Eclipse Stakes winner Mount Nelson and half-brother to the fairly useful 2-y-o 1m winner Monitor Closely (by Oasis Dream), the quite useful 1m winner Stone Of Scone (by Pivotal) and the quite useful 9.5f winner Off Message (by In The Wings). The dam won four races at 3 yrs from 7f to 1m including the Group 2 Sun Chariot Stakes and the Group 3 Matron Stakes and is a half-sister to one winner. The second dam, Yukon Hope (by Forty Niner), a fair maiden, is out of a half-sister to Reference Point. (Findlay & Bloom).
"He's backward and 16 hands plus already, so he's a back-end of the season type. But he has a beautiful pedigree and although 100,000 guineas is a lot of money in anyone's language I think he was still relatively inexpensive. Very much a three-year-old type though".

657. AL MUTHANAA ★★★★★
ch.c. Pivotal – Mail The Desert (Desert Prince).
March 11. Third foal. 300,000Y. Tattersalls October 1. Shadwell Estate Co. Half-brother to the modest 2008 6f fourth placed 2-y-o Postman (by Dr Fong). The dam, winner of the Group 1 7f Moyglare Stud Stakes and third in the Coronation Stakes, is a half-sister to 2 winners. The second dam, Mail Boat (by Formidable), is an unraced half-sister to 4 winners including the Group 3 Chester Vase winner and St Leger third Dry Dock. (Hamdan Al Maktoum).
"He was one of my favourite yearlings and I was thrilled to get him sent to me. If he's good enough his race will be the Middle Park and it would be wrong of me to try and get him ready for Royal Ascot. I'm going to train him as if he's a good horse and hope that he is. He's a beautiful looking colt and a good mover. This year I think I've got the nicest bunch of two-year-olds I've ever had because I've got horses that are much more racey".

658. ATTESTATION ★★★
b.f. Carnival Dancer – Testament (Darshaan).
January 29. Second foal. The dam, unplaced on her only start, is closely related to 2 winners including the smart Group 2 11.9f Great Voltigeur Stakes winner Sacrament and a half-sister to 5 winners and to the dam of the Group 1 Pretty Polly Stakes winner Chorist. The second dam, Blessed Event (by Kings Lake), a very useful winner of the listed 10f Ballymacoll Stud Stakes and placed in 5 Group races including the Yorkshire Oaks and the Champion Stakes, is a half-sister to 4 minor winners. (Cheveley Park Stud).
"She's a backward filly. We don't know enough about Carnival Dancer and yet everyone suspects he's not a very good stallion, but if I told you this filly was by Sadler's Wells you'd believe me. She a very good looking filly, she's a

nice mover and she's having a break at the moment. An August two-year-old I would think and seven furlongs would be a minimum for her".

659. AZIZI ★★★
b.c. Haafhd – Harayir (Gulch).
January 30. Half-brother to the smart listed 10f winner Izdiham, to the useful 12f winner Moonjaz (both by Nashwan) and the quite useful 10.5f winner Mulaazem (by King's Best). The dam was a very smart winner of the Lowther Stakes (at 2 yrs), the 1,000 Guineas, the Tripleprint Celebration Mile and the Hungerford Stakes. She is a sister to the useful 10f to 12f winner Ahraar and a half-sister to the useful 7f (at 2 yrs) to 10f winner Min Alhawa. The second dam, Saffaanh (by Shareef Dancer), a quite useful 12.2f winner, is out of the Irish Oaks winner Give Thanks. (Hamdan Al Maktoum).

"I don't think I've ever had a colt that's by a Guineas winner and out of a Guineas winner. The mare has been disappointing, this horse is really idle and he has quite a plain head but there is something about him. He doesn't sweat much and I'm hoping he's saving something for the track. He'll be a summer two-year-old".

660. BLANCMANGE ★★★★
b.f. Montjeu – Blue Dream (Cadeaux Genereux).
April 27. The dam, a useful 6f winner, was listed-placed and is a half-sister to 4 winners including the 1m (at 2 yrs) and 9.2f winner and listed-placed Equity Princess. The second dam, Hawait Al Barr (by Green Desert), a useful 12f to 2m winner, is a half-sister to 3 winners. (J B Haggas).

"I like her very much. She was bred by my father and in my opinion she's quite similar to a Montjeu filly that won the Ribblesdale for us called Mont Etoile – she's quite rangy but she also has speed. She'll stay seven furlongs and probably a mile, she isn't backward at all and is a nice filly to look out for".

661. BLITZING ★★★
b.f. Bertolini – Blinding (High Top).
January 31. 6,000Y. Doncaster St Leger.
Highflyer Bloodstock. Half-sister to the 2-y-o 5f winner and listed-placed High Priority (by Marju), to the 8.5f winner Fools Rush In (by Entrepreneur), the 1m all-weather winner Doc Watson (by Dr Devious) – all 3 fairly useful, the fair 7f winner Blindspin (by Intikhab) and a winner in Denmark by Caerleon. The dam, unplaced on both her efforts at 3 yrs, is a half-sister to the Group 3 7.3f Hungerford Stakes, Group 3 7f Kiveton Park Stakes and Group 3 7f Beeswing Stakes winner Hadeer. The second dam, Glinting (by Crepello), won over 6f at 2 yrs, was placed in the Nell Gwyn Stakes and is a half-sister to 11 winners. (Rutland Thoroughbred Racing).

"A filly from a very fast family although the mare is quite old now. She's quite racey, a good mover and quite strong. She'll be a two-year-old".

662. CHURCH MELODY ★★
b.f. Oasis Dream – Chorist (Pivotal).
March 19. Half-sister to the moderate 2008 8.7f placed 2-y-o King's Chorister (by King's Best). The dam won the Group 1 10f Curragh Pretty Polly Stakes and two Group 3 events and is a half-sister to the very useful 2-y-o 7f winner and Group 3 7f Prestige Stakes second Choirgirl. The second dam, Choir Mistress (Chief Singer), is an unraced half-sister to 6 winners including the smart Group 2 11.9f Great Voltigeur Stakes winner Sacrament. (Cheveley Park Stud).

"She's a lovely filly that's just started work but I have reservations about her staying sound".

663. CLOUD'S END ★★★
b.f. Dubawi – Kangra Valley (Indian Ridge).
April 13. Ninth foal. Half-sister to the champion 2-y-o filly and Group 1 6f Cheveley Park Stakes winner Airwave (by Air Express), to the fairly useful 2-y-o 6f winner Reqqa (by Royal Applause), the quite useful dual 5f winner Kangarilla Road (by Magic Ring), the fair 5f winner of 4 races Beverley Macca (by Piccolo) and the modest dual 6f winner Danakim (by Emarati). The dam, a moderate 2-y-o 5f winner, is a half-sister to 7 minor winners. The second dam, Thorner Lane (by Tina's Pet), a quite useful

sprint winner of 2 races, is a full or half-sister to 7 winners. (Manor Farm Stud, Rutland).

"She's a home-bred by the Watsons who kindly sent her here, she did everything right when she was broken and she's quite a tall filly that isn't going to be immediately early but is bred to be a two-year-old. I have three Dubawi's and their all quite different but none of them are particularly attractive. They're all quite tall and workmanlike. This filly will make a two-year-old by June or July".

664. CORONARIA ★★
b.f. Starcraft – Anthos (Big Shuffle).
March 15. Second foal. Half-sister to the fair 2008 6f and 7f placed 2-y-o Nemorosa (by Pivotal). The dam was a quite useful 2-y-o 6f winner. The second dam, Anemone (by Motley), won 5 races in Germany from 2-5 yrs. (Cheveley Park Stud).

"She's OK at the moment without being special and she should be a back-end two-year-old. Being out of a Big Shuffle mare she'll probably want some cut in the ground".

665. DALALAAT (GER) ★★★
b.f. Oasis Dream – Denice (Night Shift).
April 1. Fifth foal. 55,000Y. Doncaster St Leger. Shadwell Estate Co. The dam, a winner over 5f at 2 yrs in Germany and second in the Group 2 German 1,000 Guineas, is a half-sister to 2 winners. The second dam, Despoina (by Aspros), won in Germany and is a full or half-sister to 6 winners. (Hamdan Al Maktoum).

"She's very lazy and so is a bit difficult to assess. She has quite an ugly head but having said all that she's not bad. She's quite strong, moves alright and has grown a lot since the Sales. A midsummer type two-year-old".

666. DHAAFER ★★
b.c. Nayef – Almurooj (Zafonic).
April 22. Eighth foal. Half-brother to the quite useful 2008 7f placed 2-y-o Sayyaaf, to the useful listed 6f winner Judhoor (by Alhaarth), to the fairly useful 7f and 1m winner Muzher (by Indian Ridge) and the quite useful 2-y-o 6f winner Al Sifaat (by Unfuwain). The dam, a moderate 5f and 6f placed maiden, is a half-sister to 7 winners including the smart 6f (at 2 yrs), Group 2 7f Challenge Stakes and Group 3 7f Greenham Stakes winner Munir and the very useful Irish 1m listed stakes winner and Group 1 Coronation Stakes second Hasbah. The second dam, Al Bahathri (by Blushing Groom), was a high-class winner of 6 races from 6f to 1m, notably the Irish 1,000 Guineas and the Coronation Stakes. (Hamdan Al Maktoum).

"He's had a problem and has gone home for a while but he's quite nice and he has a nice pedigree. A back-end two-year-old and more of a three-year-old. A beautiful looking horse though".

667. DHAN DHANA (IRE) ★★
b.f. Dubawi – Kylemore (Sadler's Wells).
April 12. Sixth foal. 52,000Y. Tattersalls October 1. BBA Germany. Half-sister to the fairly useful 2008 2-y-o 7f winner Purple Sage (by Danehill Dancer) and to the fair 10f winner Annabelle's Charm (by Indian Ridge). The dam ran twice unplaced and is a sister to the Group 1 Criterium de Saint-Cloud and Grade 1 Canadian International Stakes winner Ballingarry and to the Group 1 1m Racing Post Trophy winner Aristotle and a half-sister to the Group 1 St James's Palace Stakes and Prix Jean Prat winner Starborough. The second dam, Flamenco Wave (by Desert Wine), won the Group 1 6f Moyglare Stud Stakes and is a half-sister to 3 winners. (Mohammed Jaber).

"A quite tall, backward filly out of a Sadler's Wells mare, she's one for the back-end of the season. She's quite narrow behind and needs to furnish but she's quite willing and a very genuine looking filly so she could be alright as a three-year-old".

668. DIVINE CALL ★★★
b.c. Pivotal – Pious (Bishop Of Cashel).
February 11. Fourth foal. Brother to the fairly useful 2-y-o 7f winner Blithe and to the unraced 2008 2-y-o Penitent. The dam, a fair dual 6f winner (including at 2 yrs), is a half-sister to 3 winners including the fair 6f, 8.5f and hurdles winner Mister RM. The second dam, La Cabrilla

(by Carwhite), a fairly useful 2-y-o 5f and 6f winner, was third in the Group 3 Princess Margaret Stakes and is a half-sister to 6 winners including the Group 1 Nunthorpe Stakes winner Ya Malak. (Cheveley Park Stud).

"A nicely-bred horse. We've had both the mare's first two foals including the unraced three-year-old Penitent who is improving all the time. They were all backward (in keeping with the sire) but this one has got nice, mature knees on him and he's quite a well-made horse. Blithe showed me absolutely nothing at home and just got better and better. Penitent showed me nothing last year and I'm just getting into him now. I suspect this fellow will be idle as well and we'll just have to get stuck into him when he's ready!"

669. EJAAB ★★★★ ♠
b.br.c. Kyllachy – Whittle Woods Girl (Emarati).
February 24. Tenth foal. 60,000Y. Doncaster St Leger. Shadwell Estate Co. Half-brother to the modest 6f winner Twitch Hill (by Piccolo), to the modest 7f winner Zagala (by Polar Falcon), the moderate 5f and 6f winner of 6 races High Esteem (by Common Grounds) and the moderate 7f winner Make It Happen Now (by Octagonal). The dam, a quite useful winner of 5 races over 6f at 3 yrs, is a sister to the Wokingham Handicap winner Emerging Market and a half-sister to the Group 2 Richmond Stakes winner Son Pardo and the Group 3 Cork and Orrery Stakes winner Atraf. The second dam, Flitteriss Park (by Beldale Flutter), a modest 1m winner, is a half-sister to 5 winners and to the dam of the South African Grade 1 winner Lord Shirldor.

"A real strong two-year-old, he'll be out in May and we'll try and speed him up to see if he can make Ascot. A nice colt, he's all speed and a really well-made, 'butty' horse".

670. ENGULF (IRE) ★★★
b.c. Danehill Dancer – All Embracing (Night Shift).
March 2. Second foal. €260,000Y. Goffs Million. Angie Sykes. The dam, a quite useful 7f winner, is a half-sister to numerous winners including the very smart 6f and 7f (at 2 yrs) and Group 2 10f Prix Guillaume d'Ornano winner Highdown and the Group 2 12f King Edward VII Stakes second Elshadi. The second dam, Rispoto (by Mtoto), a modest 12f winner, is a half-sister to 7 winners including the Group 3 10f Royal Whip Stakes winner Jahafil. (Findlay & Bloom).

"A nice, well-made horse, he'll hopefully be the type to start at the Newmarket July meeting, he moves well, has a good temperament and has a chance of being good one. The owners have been very kind to me, they've sent me some lovely horses and I hope for their sake they get a good one. They adopted the policy that the market would be down and that horses would be better value and they went for it. Good luck to them – we need people like that".

671. FABULOSITY ★★
ch.f. Kyllachy – Sheppard's Cross (Soviet Star).
February 7. Half-sister to the very useful 6f (at 2 yrs), Group 3 7.5f Concorde Stakes and dual listed winner Sheppard's Watch, to the fair 2-y-o 5.2f winner Fovant (both by Night Shift) and the useful 2-y-o 7f winner Torcross (by Vettori). The dam, a quite useful 7f winner, is a half-sister to the Irish listed sprint winner Clean Cut. The second dam, Cutler's Corner (by Sharpen Up), was a smart sprint winner of 3 races. (J B Haggas).

"She's only ordinary at the moment, it looks like she'll want fast ground and let's hope she can sprint because that's what she's bred for. A genuine filly, but not showing much at the moment".

672. FLOUNCING (IRE) ★★★
b.f. Barathea – Man Eater (Mark Of Esteem).
February 21. Third foal. €22,000Y. Goffs Million. Amanda Skiffington. Half-sister to Al Wujood (by Orpen), unplaced in two starts at 2 yrs in 2008. The dam, a modest maiden, was placed 5 times over 5f and is a half-sister to several winners including the South African listed winner L'Passionata and to the Italian listed winner Firebelly. The second dam, Desert Delight (by Green Desert), is an unraced half-sister to 9 winners including the Group 3 May Hill Stakes winner Intimate Guest. (Gibson,

Goddard, Hamer, Hawkes).
"A strong, well-made, nice-moving filly that should be a mid-summer two-year-old".

673. HAMLOOLA ★★★
b.f. Red Ransom – Dusty Answer (Zafonic).
April 29. Fourth foal. 210,000Y. Tattersalls October 1. Shadwell Estate Co. Half-sister to Halliwell House (by Selkirk), unplaced in one start at 2 yrs in 2008 and to the French 3-y-o winner and Group 2 Italian Oaks second Counterclaim (by Pivotal). The dam, a quite useful 2-y-o 7f winner, was listed placed over 1m and is a half-sister to 3 winners including the listed 1m and subsequent US Grade 2 winner Spotlight. The second dam, Dust Dancer (by Suave Dancer), won 4 races including the Group 3 10f Prix de la Nonette and is a half-sister to 6 winners including the Group 3 7.3f Fred Darling Stakes winner Bulaxie (herself dam of the Group 2 winner Claxon). (Hamdan Al Maktoum).
"A filly from a good family, she's quite plain but looks a nice filly. A fairly late foal, she's one for mid-summer onwards and she's bred to be good".

674. HERCULEAN ★★★
b.c. Sakhee – Someone Special (Habitat).
April 21. Fifteenth foal. 80,000Y. Tattersalls October 1. John Warren. Half-brother to the Group 1 10.4f Juddmonte International Stakes winner One So Wonderful, to the quite useful 10f winner One So Marvellous (both by Nashwan), the Group 2 10.4f Dante Stakes and Group 3 1m Craven Stakes winner Alnasr Alwasheek (by Sadler's Wells), the very useful 7f Rockfel Stakes winner and Relatively Special (by Alzao), the French listed winner Raucous Lad (by Warning), the quite useful 1m winner You Are The One (by Unfuwain), the quite useful 6f winner All Time Great (by Night Shift) and the hurdles winner Someone Brave (by Commanche Run). The dam, a useful 7f winner and third in the Group 1 1m Coronation Stakes, is a half-sister to the top-class miler Milligram. The second dam, One in a Million (by Rarity), won the 1,000 Guineas and the Coronation Stakes and is out of an unraced half-sister to Deep Run. (Highclere Thoroughbred Racing).
"I like this horse, he's quite narrow and unfurnished and the mare is quite old but he doesn't look like an old mare's foal. He's one for the back-end of the season but I can see him winning a Newmarket maiden in October – he's that sort - and he's got a chance of being a nice horse. I think Sakhee is an underrated sire".

675. IQTINAA ★★★★
b.f. Royal Applause – Chanterelle (Indian Ridge).
March 9. Second foal. 80,000Y. Doncaster St Leger. Shadwell Estate Co. Half-sister to Zelos Diktator (unplaced in one start at 2 yrs in 2008. The dam, a fair 2-y-o 6f winner, is a half-sister to 2 winners. The second dam, Chantereine (by Trempolino), a minor winner at 3 yrs in France, is a half-sister to 3 winners including the dam of the Kentucky Derby and Belmont Stakes winner Thunder Gulch.
"A very nice filly with lots of quality. She's the same as every other Royal Applause I've had in that she has bad knees - but they still all run like smoke. This is a lovely filly and hopefully she'll be one for the Albany Stakes – something like that. A filly with a lot of quality".

676. JEAN JEANNIE ★★★
b.f. Giant's Causeway – Moon Dazzle (Kingmambo).
April 4. First foal. 70,000Y. Tattersalls October 1. A Stroud. The dam, a useful 1m and UAE 9f winner, is a half-sister to 7 winners including the Group 2 German 2,000 Guineas winners Dupont and Pacino. The second dam, June Moon (by Sadler's Wells), is an unraced half-sister to 6 winners including the French 1,000 Guineas second Firth Of Lorne. (Mr B Kantor).
"Yes, she's alright – the first foal out of a decent mare from a family we've had a lot of luck with. The mother was quite good and this filly has done very well. She was a bit small when she came in but she's fine now. There's still not a lot of her but I'd hope she'd be a mid-season onwards two-year-old. All the family have shown a bit at home so hopefully she will too at some stage".

677. JEMIMA NICHOLAS ★★★
b.f. Compton Place – Spritzeria (Bigstone).
February 9. Second living foal. 38,000Y. Tattersalls October 2. Not sold. Half-sister to the unplaced 2008 2-y-o Esprit De Midas (by Namid). The dam, a quite useful 2-y-o 6f winner, is a half-sister to 2 winners including the smart 2-y-o 6f winner and Group 1 1m Racing Post Trophy third Henrik. The second dam, Clincher Club (by Polish Patriot), a fair 5f (at 2 yrs) and 7.5f winner, is a half-sister to 8 winners. (Mr Nick Hughes).
"We trained the mare who wasn't a bad two-year-old at all and it's a real, winning family. I like her and although she's shown a bit of a temperament she's getting better and better as the weeks go on so I don't think that'll be an issue. She'll make a two-year-old in mid summer".

678. KALK BAY ★★★
b.c. Hawk Wing – Politesse (Barathea).
March 14. Third foal. 15,000Y. Tattersalls October 2. W Haggas. Half-brother to the smart Group 2 6f Diadem Stakes winner of 6 races King's Apostle (by King's Best). The dam is an unraced half-sister to one winner out of the Group 1 6f Cheveley Park Stakes and Group 3 6f Princess Margaret Stakes winner Embassy (by Cadeaux Genereux), herself a half-sister to 5 winners including the Group 2 Pretty Polly Stakes winner Tarfshi. (Mr B Kantor).
"He was an inexpensive yearling but he'll win an auction plate in the second half of the season. He needs a bit of time but he's a nice horse". TRAINER'S BARGAIN BUY.

679. KAYAAN ★★
br.c. Marju – Raheefa (Riverman).
March 28. Sixth foal. Half-brother to the smart 1m (at 2 yrs) and listed 10f winner Rawyaan, to the useful 7f and subsequent UAE 9f and 10f winner Muthaaber (both by Machiavellian), the fairly useful dual 10f winner Maraakeb (by Linamix) and the fair 10f and 2m winner Zuwaar (by Nayef). The dam was a fair 3-y-o 10f winner. The second dam, Oogie Poogie (by Storm Bird), was placed at up to 10f here before winning in the USA and is a daughter of the champion mare Cascapedia. (Hamdan Al Maktoum).
"Quite backward and a great big horse, but he's not unattractive and he's quite solid. A nice horse for much later on".

680. LADY MCBETH (IRE) ★★★★
b.f. Avonbridge – Scottish Exile (Ashkalani).
March 22. Second foal. Half-sister to the smart 2008 5f and 6f 2-y-o winner and dual Group 3 second Bonnie Charlie (by Intikhab). The dam, a fair triple 5f winner, is a sister to the fairly useful 6f winner of 5 races and listed-placed Million Percent and a half-sister to 3 winners. The second dam, Royal Jade (by Last Tycoon), a fairly useful 7f winner, is a half-sister to 6 winners including the Group 3 5f King George Stakes winner Averti. (Mrs M Bryce).
"She done really well, she's a very sweet filly and wants to get with it, so she'll be a nice two-year-old".

681. MADLOOL (IRE) ★★★
b.c. Oasis Dream – Bourbonella (Rainbow Quest).
March 11. Fourth foal. Deauville August. €300,000Y. Peter Doyle. Brother to the very smart Group 3 Jersey Stakes winner Aqlaam. The dam is an unraced half-sister to 8 winners including the high-class and multiple winning stayer Persian Punch and the Group 3 7f Solario Stakes winner Island Magic. The second dam, Rum Cay (by Our Native), a fair 14.6f winner, is a half-sister to the listed winner of 10 races Gymcrak Premiere. (Hamdan Al Maktoum).
"A brother to our stable star, Aqlaam, he hasn't got his quality unfortunately. Sheikh Hamdan bought him in Deauville privately, I think he's a two-year-old and I'll try and train him for the Coventry Stakes. Whether he's that good I don't know but he hasn't got the scope that Aqlaam had and I can't see him being better as a three-year-old. We'll press on with him".

682. MAKE IT BIG ★★
b.c. Singspiel – High Straits (Bering).
March 12. Third foal. Brother to the 2008 Irish 7f placed 2-y-o (on only start) Soul Train and

half-brother to the modest 10f winner Royal Straight (by Halling). The dam, a fair 8.2f winner, is out of the very useful dual 7f winner High Summer (by Nureyev), herself a sister to the 2-y-o listed 1m winner and Group 1 placed Most Precious (dam of the dual Group 1 winner Matiara) and a half-sister to the useful 7f (at 2 yrs) and listed 1m winner Private Line. (Sentinel Bloodstock Ltd).

"A big, backward, lengthy, three-year-old type. But he's a very nice mover and is one of the few horses I have that's bred to stay the Derby trip. I see him being a nice, staying three-year-old".

683. MUBARERAAT ★★★
ch.f. Singspiel – La Belga (Roy).
January 29. Fourth foal. 100,000Y. Tattersalls October 2. Shadwell Estate Co. Half-sister to a minor German 4-y-o winner by Giant's Causeway. The dam, a Grade 1 winner in Argentina and Grade 1 placed 3 times, is a half-sister to one winner. The second dam, La Baraca (by Mariache), a Grade 1 winner in Argentina, is a half-sister to 6 winners including the Argentinian Grade 1 winner Leyden. (Hamdan Al Maktoum).

"She'll take a bit of time but she's not that big and not that backward. Hopefully an August/September filly, she's a nice mover".

684. PEBBLE BEECH (IRE) ★★★
b.f. Footstepsinthesand – Brigids Cross (Sadler's Wells).
February 13. First foal. 105,000foal. Tattersalls December. Cheval Court Stud. The dam is an unraced sister to the Group 1 7f Moyglare Stud Stakes winner Sequoyah (the dam of Henrythenavigator) and to the 2-y-o Group 1 Fillies' Mile winner Listen and a half-sister to the Irish listed 5.6f winner and Group 3 7f placed Oyster Catcher. The second dam, Brigid (by Irish River), a minor French 3-y-o 1m winner, is a sister to the French listed 7f winner Or Vision (herself dam of the Group/Grade 1 winners Dolphin Street, Insight and Saffron Walden) and a half-sister to 6 winners. (T Hirschfield, D Scott, L Piggott).

"She's well-bred but isn't bred to be early and she also has quite a weak second thigh – also suggesting she won't be that early. She has a bit of a temperament – not nasty, just hot and I hope we can channel her in the right direction".

685. PRAESEPE ★★★
b.f. Pivotal – Superstar Leo (College Chapel).
January 31. Sister to the very smart Group 3 5f Molecomb Stakes and Group 3 5f King George Stakes winner Enticing and half-sister to the quite useful dual 5f winner (including at 2 yrs) Speed Song (by Fasliyev). The dam, a very smart 2-y-o, won 5 races including the Group 2 5f Flying Childers Stakes and the Weatherbys Super Sprint and is a full or half-sister to numerous winners. The second dam, Council Rock (by General Assembly), a fair 9f and 10f placed 3-y-o, is a half-sister to 6 winners including the Group 3 Prestige Stakes winner Glatisant and the listed Virginia Stakes winner Gai Bulga. (Lael Stable).

"She hasn't got the quality of either Enticing or Speed Song but she's got a good backside. She's quite 'up behind' and needs to grow in front. I think she'll be fast but I suspect she won't be out before July at the earliest. So despite her early foaling date I think she could be a late developing two-year-old".

686. PRISONER ★★
b.c. Indian Ridge – Limanora (Machiavellian).
March 2. First foal. Tattersalls October 2. 160,000Y. Not sold. The dam is an unplaced half-sister to 4 winners including the Grade 1 Breeders Cup Mile winner Domedriver, the French Group 3 winner Tau Ceti and the dam of the Group 2 winner Freedonia. The second dam, Napoli (by Baillamont), won 3 listed races in France and is a sister to the French Group 3 winner D'Arros. (Highclere Thoroughbred Racing).

"Too backward at present to make a sensible judgement, but all that could change as the season progresses".

687. QANOON ★★
ch.c. Afleet Alex – Solvig (Caerleon).
February 17. Fourth foal. $600,000Y. Keeneland September. Shadwell Estate Co. Half-brother to a minor winner in the USA by War Chant. The dam won two Grade 3 races in the USA and is a half-sister to 3 winners. The second dam, Incha (by Nashwan), was placed over 1m and 11f. (Hamdan Al Maktoum).
"Still in Dubai, so I can't tell you anything about him, but his price tag suggests he might be a bit useful!"

688. REDDEN ★★★
b.c. Pivotal – Coy (Danehill).
February 11. Second foal. Half-brother to the unplaced 2008 2-y-o Demand (by Red Ransom). The dam won over 6f (at 2 yrs) and the listed 1m Valiant Stakes and is a sister to the fairly useful triple 7f winner Presumptive. The second dam, Demure (by Machiavellian), is an unraced half-sister to the very smart colt Diffident, winner of the Group 3 6f Diadem Stakes, the Group 3 6f Prix de Ris-Orangis and the listed 7f European Free Handicap. (Cheveley Park Stud).
"Another nicely bred two-year-old, he's got open knees and I don't think he's going to be that early but he's a strong horse and he'll make up into a back-end two-year-old. A nice, well-made horse".

689. RUTHIE BABE ★★★★★ ♠
b.f. Exceed And Excel – Lady Oriande (Makbul).
February 17. First foal. 90,000Y. Doncaster St Leger. A Skiffington. The dam is a placed sister to the Group 2 6f Goldene Peitsche and Group 3 6f Prix de Ris-Oranges winner Striking Ambition. The second dam, Lady Roxanne (by Cyrano de Bergerac), a moderate 5f seller and 6f all-weather winner, is a sister to the US Grade 3 Hollywood Turf Express Handicap winner Cyrano Storme and a half-sister to 6 minor winners. (Exors of the late F C T Wilson).
"This is my favourite. She's one I'll be aiming for the Queen Mary, she's got a great temperament and is a good mover. She's very nice and definitely a five star job. A small, neat filly that will run in April. The only reservation I'd have is that she'll probably want top of the ground".

690. SAFWAAN ★★★★
b.c. Selkirk – Kawn (Cadeaux Genereux).
January 28. First foal. The dam, unplaced in one start, is a half-sister to the Group 2 1m Prix du Rond-Point and Group 3 8.5f Diomed Stakes winner Trans Island, to the Italian Group 3 winner Welsh Diva and the useful 2-y-o 7f winner Nothing Daunted (all by Selkirk). The second dam, Khubza (by Green Desert), a quite useful 3-y-o 7f winner, is a half-sister to 7 winners including the Group 2 winners Barrow Creek and Last Resort and the listed winners Arctic Char and Heard A Whisper. (Hamdan Al Maktoum).
"A nice horse, he's a little bit heavy but I like him. A good-looking horse and an early foal, he could be anything. He's all Cadeaux Genereux and not Selkirk, he looks fast and will be a nice horse".

691. SIX WIVES ★★★
b.f. Kingsalsa – Regina (Green Desert).
February 16. First foal. The dam, a fairly useful 2-y-o dual 5f winner, is a half-sister to the fairly useful dual 1m winner Dubois, the fairly useful 2-y-o 7f winner Rainbow Queen and the quite useful 2-y-o 6f winner Wish. The second dam, Dazzle (by Gone West), a smart winner of the Group 3 6f Cherry Hinton Stakes and placed in both the Cheveley Park Stakes and the 1,000 Guineas, is a half-sister to the listed winners Fantasize and Hypnotize. (Cheveley Park Stud).
"She'll be our first runner and she shows a bit. She'll start off in April, I think she'll want top of the ground and although there's not a lot of her, she's a natural and she's done a bit of work with older horses".

692. SOORAAH ★★
b.f. Dubawi – Al Persian (Persian Bold).
April 3. 20,000Y. Tattersalls October 1. Rabbah Bloodstock. Half-sister to the fairly useful 1m winner Dicharachera (by Mark Of Esteem), to the quite useful 7f winner Dowlleh (by Noverre) and a Spanish 1m to 10.5f winner by Suave

Dancer. The dam won 3 races in Spain at 3 and 4 yrs and is a half-sister to 5 winners including the useful 10f winner and Lancashire Oaks second La Sky (herself dam of the Oaks winner Love Divine) and the Champion Stakes winner Legal Case. The second dam, Maryinsky (by Northern Dancer), won twice at up to 9f in the USA and is a half-sister to 10 winners including the US Grade 3 winners Bold Place and Card Table.

"A big, tall, backward filly, she's sixteen hands plus. Not a bad filly, she has a good temperament but she'll take a bit of time".

693. TAAJUB (IRE) ★★★★
b.c. Exceed And Excel – Purple Tiger (Rainbow Quest).
March 11. Second foal. 80,000Y. Tattersalls October 2. Shadwell Estate Co. Half-brother to the quite useful 5f and 6f winner Polish Pride (Polish Precedent). The dam is an unraced half-sister to 4 winners including the German Group 2 winner and Italian Group 1 second Notability. The second dam, Noble Rose(by Caerleon), won the Group 3 Park Hill Stakes and the listed Galtres Stakes and is a half-sister to 4 winners. (Hamdan Al Maktoum).

"This is quite a nice horse. He's out of a Rainbow Quest mare but he looks an all-out two-year-old. He'll probably wait for six furlongs, he's a nice horse with a good temperament and he was bought to run a two-year-old and that's what he'll do. A nice horse".

694. TADHKEER ★★★
ch.g. Refuse To Bend – Shuruk (Cadeaux Genereux).
April 25. Fifth foal. Half-brother to the fairly useful 5f and 6f winner Maimoona (by Pivotal). The dam, a fair 2-y-o 6f winner, is a half-sister to the very smart 6f (at 2 yrs) to 10f winner and Grade 1 Rothmans International and Group 1 Prix de la Salamandre placed Volochine, the stayer Mawared, the 1m (at 2 yrs) and listed 14.8f winner Kahtan and the middle-distance winner Ghataas – all very useful. The second dam, Harmless Albatross (by Pas de Seul), won the Group 3 1m Prix des Chenes at 2 yrs and a 1m listed event at 3 yrs and is a half-sister to the Group 2 10f Prix d'Harcourt winner Fortune's Wheel. (Hamdan Al Maktoum).

"He's been gelded recently because he was quite colty but he's strong and there's nothing wrong with him. A nice, well-made horse".

695. THE ONLY BOSS (IRE) ★★★
ch.c. Exceed And Excel – Aljafliyah (Halling).
February 14. Second foal. 42,000Y. Tattersalls October 1. Blandford Bloodstock. Half-brother to the unplaced 2008 2-y-o Ennovy (by Tobougg). The dam is an unplaced half-sister to 3 winners including the US Grade 3 winner Sohgol. The second dam, Arruhan (by Mujtahid), a quite useful 5f (at 2 yrs) and 7f winner, is a half-sister to 5 winners including the smart listed 7f winner Royal Storm. (Mohammed Jaber).

"He's done very well because he was very "light-middled" when he came in. I guess he'll run up quite light because he's quite shallow. He'll be a two-year-old but he's out of a Halling mare so he might need a bit of time and he might need a bit of cut. Not a bad sort and one for the mid-season".

696. UP AT LAST ★★
b.f. Cape Cross – Upend (Main Reef).
March 13. Sister to the smart listed 1m winner of 4 races and Group 1 placed Musicanna and half-sister to the useful 10f and 10.5f winner Shortfall (by Last Tycoon), the useful 1m (at 2 yrs) and 12f winner Al Azhar (by Alzao), the quite useful 2-y-o 6f and 7f winner Runswick Bay (by Intikhab), the fair 10f winner of 4 races Silvaline (b Linamix), the fair 14.8f winner Up And About (by Barathea) and the fair 2m winner Ashnaya (by Ashkalani). The dam, a smart winner of 3 races from 10f to 12f including the Group 3 St Simon Stakes and the listed Galtres Stakes, was second in the Group 3 Princess Royal Stakes and is a half-sister to 6 winners (3 of them over hurdles) including the dam of the high-class stayer and champion hurdler Royal Gait. The second dam, Gay Charlotte (by Charlottown), a winner over 7.5f at 2 yrs in Ireland and over 1m at 3 yrs in the USA, is out of the Irish Oaks winner Merry Mate. (Mr Peter Player).

"She's very backward and has gone home for a break. A very nice, kind filly but she needs time – as her pedigree would suggest".

697. WHAT AN ISSUE ★★★
ch.f. Strong Hope – Radioactivity
(Dixieland Band).
March 18. Tenth foal. 65,000Y. Tattersalls October 1. BBA (Ire). Half-sister to 6 winners including Champali, a winner of four Grade 3 stakes in the USA, the US listed stakes winner Drexel Monorail (both by Glitterman) and two minor winners in the USA by Aptitude and Formal Gold. The dam won 2 minor races at 3 yrs in the USA and is a half-sister to 6 winners. The second dam, Geiger Countess (by Mr Prospector), won 2 races in the USA and is a full or half-sister to 7 winners. (Laundry Cottage Stud).
"She should make a two-year-old although she's a bit 'hit and miss' at the moment with one problem or another. So I haven't been able to crack on with her, but she's quite a well-made filly so she should be a two-year-old and she goes OK".

698. WRIGGLE (IRE) ★★★
b.g. Refuse To Bend – Isana (Sunday Silence).
March 16. Second foal. €55,000Y. Goffs Million. McNabb Brothers. Half-brother to the quite useful 2008 2-y-o 6f winner Guertino (by Choisir). The dam, placed over 6.45f at 3 yrs in France, is a sister to the French winner and listed-placed Celestial Lagoon (herself dam of the listed winner and Group 3 placed Maria Gabriella). The second dam, Metaphor (by Woodman), a listed-placed winner at 2 yrs in France, is a half-sister to 5 winners including the dual Group 3 winner King Of Happiness. (Findlay & Bloom).
"He's a nice horse. I've just cut him because he wasn't going the right way but he'll be OK and looks a two-year-old type".

699. UNNAMED ★★★
b.c. Exceed And Excel – China Beauty
(Slip Anchor).
March 26. The dam is a placed half-sister to the US Grade 3 Golden Gate Handicap winner Deploy Venture. The second dam, Tasseled (Tate Gallery), is an unplaced half-sister to the Irish listed winner Outside Pressure and to the dam of Rock Of Gibraltar. (Y C Mak).
"He's big and quite strong and he'll be a nice two-year-old. When we get into him I think he'll come to hand quite quickly".

700. UNNAMED ★★★★
b.c. Green Desert – Imperial Bailiwick
(Imperial Frontier).
April 6. Closely related to the modest 2008 2-y-o 6f winner Impressible (by Oasis Dream) and half-brother to the high-class sprinter Reverence (by Mark Of Esteem), winner of the Haydock Park Sprint Cup and the Nunthorpe Stakes, the very useful 2-y-o listed 6f Chesham Stakes winner and 1m Britannia Handicap second Helm Bank (by Wild Again), the fairly useful 5f (at 2 yrs) and 6f winner Quiet Elegance (by Fantastic Light), the modest 6f winner Fortress (by Generous), the modest 10f winner Sedgwick (by Nashwan) and a winner at up to 7.5f in Italy by Efisio. The dam was a useful winner of 3 races at around 5f including the Group 2 Flying Childers Stakes, was placed in the Molecomb Stakes and the Prix du Petit-Couvert and is a half-sister to 3 winners in France (all over 1m+). The second dam, Syndikos (by Nashua) was second 6 times in the USA and is a half-sister to 5 minor winners. (Mr & Mrs G Middlebrook).
"He's a nice horse and although his knees are still quite open he's a two-year-old and the race I want to win with him is the Gimcrack. So if he's good enough that's what we'll try for. He was broken by Malcolm Bastard who liked him a lot and he's usually quite a good barometer. We had him in for bit, then turned him away for a break and to allow his knees to mature. He'll come back in soon, we'll try and win a maiden with him in June and hopefully aim him for a decent race. He has a stallion's pedigree, he's a good mover and six furlongs should suit him well".

701. UNNAMED ★★★★
b.c. Marju – Mubkera (Nashwan)
March 2. 70,000foal. Tattersalls December. A O

Nerses. Half-brother to the fair 2008 2-y-o 1m winner Aqwaal (by Red Ransom) and to the minor French 12f winner Manjam (by Almutawakel). The dam, a quite useful 1m winner (at 2 yrs) and listed 10f placed, is a half-sister to several winners. The second dam, Na Ayim (by Shirley Heights), a modest 2-y-o 6f winner, is a half-sister to several winners out of a half-sister to the dam of Rainbow Quest and Slightly Dangerous. (Saleh Al Homaizi & Imad Al Sagar).

"The first horse I've had for these new owners, he's got a bit of furnishing to do but he's got a nice temperament and a nice action. He just needs to grow a bit but he has the makings of a very smart looking horse".

702. UNNAMED ★★★
b.f. Cape Cross – Patacake Patacake (Bahri).
March 17. Half-sister to the 2008 Irish 2-y-o 7.5f winner Fremantle (by Galileo) and the smart dual listed 10f winner Mashaahed (by In The Wings). The dam, a modest 6f and 1m placed 2-y-o, is a half-sister to 8 winners including the Group 2 Champagne Stakes winner Bog Trotter and the US stakes winner and 2,000 Guineas second Poteen. The second dam, Chaleur (by Rouge Sang), a stakes winner in Canada and Grade 3 placed, is a half-sister to 4 winners. (Netherfield House Stud).

"A backward filly, but she has a lot of quality and is certainly worth mentioning".

703. UNNAMED ★★★
b.br.f. Shamardal – Sena Desert
(Green Desert).
February 28. Fifth foal. Half-sister to the quite useful 7f winner Sydney Star (by Machiavellian) and to the modest 11f winner Sounds Of Jupiter (by Galileo). The dam, a fairly useful 10.2f winner, is a half-sister to the smart Group 3 7f Solario Stakes (at 2 yrs) and Group 2 10f Prix Guillaume d'Ornano winner Best Of The Bests. The second dam, Sueboog (by Darshaan), a very useful winner of the Group 3 7.3f Fred Darling Stakes, was third in the Group 2 Nassau Stakes and is a half-sister to 6 winners. (Mohammed Obaida).

"Yes, I like this filly. She's tall, well-grown and well-made. A nice mover with a pretty good temperament, she's one for the second half of the season and I quite like her".

704. UNNAMED ★★★
b.f. Motivator – Wosaita (Generous).
January 18. Eighth foal. 52,000Y. Tattersalls October 1. Not sold. Half-sister to the useful 7f (at 2 yrs), listed 1m and Italian Group 3 1m winner Whazzis (by Desert Prince), to the useful 2-y-o listed 7f Chesham Stakes winner Whazzat (by Daylami), to the quite useful 2-y-o 7f and 1m winner Special Envoy (by Barathea), the quite useful 2-y-o all-weather 8.6f winner Whatizzit (by Galileo) and a hurdles winner by Selkirk. The dam, a fair 12.3f placed maiden, is a half-sister to 9 winners including the very smart Group 1 10.5f Prix de Diane winner Rafha (herself the dam of 4 stakes winners including the Haydock Sprint Cup winner Invincible Spirit) and the Group 3 12f Blandford Stakes winner Chiang Mai. The second dam, Eljazzi (by Artaius), a fairly useful 2-y-o 7f winner, is a half-sister to 8 winners including the high-class miler Pitcairn (the sire of Ela-Mana-Mou). (St Albans Bloodstock).

"There have been plenty of stakes winners in the family and hopefully she can do well because she was bought for her career in the paddocks. She looks nice but is quite backward at the moment".

RICHARD HANNON
705. ALWAYS IN FASHION (IRE) ★★★
ch.f. Alhaarth – Always Mine
(Daylami).
February 1. First foal. €40,000Y. Goffs Million. Peter Doyle. The dam is an unplaced half-sister to 5 winners including the Group 2 12.5f Prix de Royallieu winner Mouramara. The second dam, Mamoura (by Lomond), won over 10f and 12f in Ireland and is a half-sister to 5 winners. (James Peyton).

"Not a bad little filly, I don't know enough about her at the moment but she's a good mover, she's cantering and has a good pedigree".

706. BANKS AND BRAES ★★★
b.c. Red Ransom – Bonnie Doon (Grand Lodge).
February 26. First foal. The dam is an unraced half-sister to 6 winners including the French listed and US stakes winner Calista and the US stakes-placed winner Earthrise. The second dam, Proskona (by Mr Prospector), a high-class 3-y-o winner of the Group 3 6f Prix de Seine et Oise and the Group 2 6f Premio Umbria, is a half-sister to 10 winners including the top-class broodmare Korveya (dam of the classic winners Hector Protector, Shanghai and Bosra Sham). (H M The Queen).
"A nice, decent-sized colt and he's a good mover but he hasn't been with me long".

707. BAOLI ★★★ ♠
b.f. Dansili – Thorntoun Piccolo (Groom Dancer).
April 25. First foal. 55,000Y. Tattersalls October 1. Peter Doyle. The dam is a placed half-sister to 10 winners including the listed Doncaster Mile, listed City Of York Handicap and subsequent Canadian Grade 2 winner Vanderlin. The second dam, Massorah (by Habitat), won the Group 3 5f Premio Omenoni and was second in the Group 3 Prix du Gros Chene and is a half-sister to 4 winners. (A P Patey).
"A lovely bay filly, medium sized and a good looker. There's nothing wrong with her at all and she's by a very good stallion".

708. BEYOND THE CITY (USA) ★★
b.c. Elusive Quality – Whats Doin (Relaunch).
March 6. Seventh foal. €75,000Y. Goffs Million. Peter Doyle. Half-brother to a listed winner in Panama and to 3 minor winners in the USA by Silver Deputy, Dehere and Grand Slam. The dam, a minor dual winner in the USA, is a half-sister to 7 winners including the US Grade 3 winner Miss Ra He Ra. (Byerley Thoroughbred Racing).

709. BIG AUDIO (IRE) ★★★
b.c. Oratorio – Tarbela (Grand Lodge).
February 15. Second foal. 87,000Y. Doncaster St Leger. Peter Doyle. The dam, a moderate 7f placed 2-y-o in Ireland, is a half-sister to 2 winners. The second dam, Tarwiya (by Dominion), won the Group 3 7f C L Weld Park Stakes, was third in the Irish 1,000 Guineas and is a half-sister to 5 winners including the Group 3 Norfolk Stakes winner Blue Dakota. (M Pescod).
"A lovely horse – or he will be one day I hope. A good-looking colt, I have four Oratorio's that are all doing well and are no bother".

710. BLUE ANGEL (IRE) ★★
b.f. Oratorio – Blue Cloud (Nashwan).
February 27. Seventh foal. 32,000Y. Tattersalls October 2. Peter Doyle. Half-sister to the French 1m and 9f winner Bank Guard (by Peintre Celebre), the French 9f winner Bomber Pilot (by Numerous) and another minor French winner by Polish Precedent. The dam, winner of the listed 7f Prix Imprudence at 3 yrs, is a half-sister to the top-class miler Bigstone and the French listed winner Bague Bleue. The second dam, Batave (by Posse), a 3-y-o 6f winner here, subsequently won in France and was placed in both the Group 3 6f Prix de Meautry and the Group 3 5f Prix de Saint-Georges. (G Howard-Spink).
"A nice filly, she looks like she could be fairly sharp but we haven't done that much with her yet because there are no two-year-old races for them early on".

711. BOUGAINVILIA (IRE) ★★★★ ♠
b.f. Bahamian Bounty – Temple Street (Machiavellian).
February 5. Third foal. €240,000Y. Goffs Million. Peter Doyle. Half-sister to the 2008 2-y-o Group 2 5f Queen Mary Stakes winner Langs Lash (by Noverre) and to a winner in Greece by Danehill Dancer. The dam is an unraced half-sister to 4 winners. The second dam, Echoes (by Niniski), won the Group 3 Prix Corrida and is a half-sister to 5 winners. (W Durkan).
"A lovely filly, she's gorgeous and you can see why she cost so much. I'll see how we go as regards distance and we'll start to do a bit more with her soon. A fine filly, she's medium-sized and particularly nice".

712. BRUNETTE (IRE) ★★★
br.f. Camacho – Hidden Agenda
(Machiavellian).
February 27. Seventh foal. 30,000Y. Tattersalls October 2. Kern/Lillingston. Half-sister to the useful 9f winner Regal Agenda, to the modest 9f and 9.4f winner Sting Like A Bee (both by Ali-Royal) and the modest 7f winner of 4 races Government (by Great Dane). The dam, placed once over 11f at 3 yrs, is a half-sister to 5 winners. The second dam, Ever Genial (by Brigadier Gerard), won the Group 3 7f Hungerford Stakes and the Group 3 1m May Hill Stakes and is a half-sister to 3 winners. (Mrs J Wood).
"A lovely, big, fine-looking filly. She's just cantering away and the sire has had a winner already".

713. CALYPSO STAR (IRE) ★★★★
ch.c. Exceed And Excel – Reematna
(Sabrehill).
February 26. Sixth foal. 27,000Y. Tattersalls October 1. Peter Doyle. Half-brother to the fairly useful dual 6f winner (including at 2 yrs) Ebn Reem (by Mark Of Esteem), to the fairly useful 2-y-o dual 6f winner Dahteer (by Bachir) and the fair UAE 7f winner Fire Two (by Cape Cross). The dam, a fair 7f placed 3-y-o, is a full or half-sister to 2 winners including the Italian Derby winner and Irish Derby second Morshdi. The second dam, Reem Albaraari (by Sadler's Wells), was a fair dual 6f placed 2-y-o. (N A Woodcock & A C Pickford).
"A lovely horse, he's classy looking and a chestnut with a lot of white about him. He goes well and is more of a six/seven furlong type. A big, strong horse by a good stallion".

714. CANDLESHOE (IRE) ★★★
b.f. Danehill Dancer – Keepers Dawn (Alzao).
April 15. Sixth foal. 50,000Y. Tattersalls October 2. Peter Doyle. Half-sister to the modest 10f winner Keepers Knight (by Sri Pekan). The dam, a useful 2-y-o 6f winner and second in the Group 3 7.3f Fred Darling Stakes, is a half-sister to 2 winners. The second dam, Keepers Lock (by Sunny's Halo), is an unraced half-sister to 4 minor winners. (Mrs J Wood).
"A really lovely filly, she could be anything but she needs a bit of time. She has a good pedigree and being by Danehill Dancer would give her a bit of a chance too".

715. CANFORD CLIFFS ★★★★ ♠
b.c. Tagula – Mrs Marsh (Marju).
February 8. Second foal. 50,000Y. Doncaster St Leger. Peter Doyle. The dam is an unraced half-sister to 5 winners including the US Grade 2 and Grade 3 winner Pina Colada. The second dam, Drei (by Lyphard), placed fourth over 1m at 3 yrs on her only outing, is a half-sister to 3 winners. (Robin Heffer).
"He's a lovely horse that's done very well. A fine, big bay horse, Richard Hughes has ridden him already, so he's ready for action". I spoke to Richard Hughes who confirmed he thought a fair bit about this colt.

716. CARNABY STREET (IRE) ★★★★
b.c. Le Vie Dei Colori – Prodigal Daughter
(Alhaarth).
February 3. First foal. 50,000Y. Doncaster St Leger. Peter Doyle. The dam is an unraced daughter of the Irish 6f winner and listed-placed Shallow Ground (by Common Grounds), herself a half-sister to the US Grade 2 winner Shanawi. (Noodles Racing).
"A lovely, big horse that goes very well. He won't be a five furlong horse but he looks like being a nice two-year-old".

717. CAVIAR ★★★
ch.f. Thunder Gulch – Cozzene'saffair
(Black Tie Affair).
January 26. Fourth foal. 45,000Y. Tattersalls October 2. John Warren. Half-sister to two minor 3-y-o winners in the USA by Open Forum and Valid Expectations. The dam, a winner of 8 races in the USA including a minor stakes event, is a half-sister to 4 winners. The second dam, Cozzene's Flite (by Stage Flite), a US stakes winner and listed-placed, is a half-sister to 5 winners. (Highclere Thoroughbred Racing).
"A small filly, she's a lovely mover and she looks sharp".

718. CITY OF ROME (IRE) ★★
b.c. *Elusive City – Marain (Marju).*
April 4. Third foal. €55,000Y. Tattersalls Ireland. Peter Doyle. The dam is an unplaced sister to the useful 2-y-o 5f and 6f winner and Group 3 6f Princess Margaret Stakes second Gipsy Rose Lee and a half-sister to 5 winners. The second dam, Rainstone (by Rainbow Quest), was placed twice over 1m on the all-weather, won once in Belgium and is a half-sister to 5 winners including the Group 3 5f Cornwallis Stakes and Group 3 5f Norfolk Stakes winner Magic Ring. (Cunningham Family).
"A good-looking horse and I like him a lot but I haven't done much with him yet. I won't be rattling his cage for a bit".

719. COUNT OF ANJOU (USA) ★★★★
b.c. *Lion Heart – Woodmaven (Woodman).*
February 8. Third foal. Deauville August. €140,000Y. Peter Doyle. The dam, placed once at 3 yrs in the USA, is a half-sister to 2 winners including the dual Group 3 winner and 1,000 Guineas second Arch Trial. The second dam, Gold Pattern (by Slew O'Gold), a minor US winner of 4 races, is a half-sister to 5 winners. (J A Lazzari).
"He's a really nice colt. We paid a lot of money for him and when his owner comes back from America we'll start to do more with him. A lovely colt and one to look out for".

720. CROWN (IRE) ★★★
b.f. *Royal Applause – Bolivia (Distant View).*
March 14. Second foal. 50,000foal. Catridge Farm Stud. The dam is an unraced half-sister to 10 winners including the smart dual 12f winner Bequeath and the listed winners Bal Harbour and Binary. The second dam, Balabina (by Nijinsky), a very useful 10f winner and fourth in the Sun Chariot Stakes, is a sister to the Coronation Cup winner Quiet Fling and the Guardian Classic Trial winner Peacetime. (Mrs Julie Wood).
"She ran very green on her debut and didn't get the run of the race. She's not over-big, but a typical two-year-old type".

721. CULTURED PRIDE (IRE) ★★
ch.f. *King's Best – Cultured Pearl (Lammtarra).*
April 5. Fifth foal. 18,000Y. Tattersalls October 2. Peter Doyle. Sister to the quite useful 2-y-o 6f winner Culture Queen and half-sister to the fair 2-y-o 5f winner Piece Of My Heart (by Fasliyev) and the fair 12f and 13.8f winner Pearl's A Singer (by Spectrum). The dam was placed once over 8.2f at 3 yrs and is a half-sister to one winner. The second dam, Culture Vulture (by Timeless Moment), won the Fillies Mile, the Prix Marcel Boussac and the French 1,000 Guineas (all Group 1 events) and is a half-sister to 9 winners. (R E Greaterex and D G Churston).
"She's quite big and not one to be racing over five furlongs. A lovely looking filly and very strong, we'll hang on with her for a bit".

722. DEAL ★★★
b.f. *Invincible Spirit – Desert Order (Desert King).*
April 25. Fourth foal. 16,000Y. Tattersalls December. Not sold. The dam is an unraced half-sister to 3 winners including the Group 1 National Stakes winner Beckett. The second dam, Groom Order (by American Order), is an unraced half-sister to 2 winners. (Mrs Madeleine Mangan).
"A small filly, she looks sharp and if she'll be a two-year-old if anything".

723. DEELY PLAZA ★★★★
b.c. *Compton Place – Anchorage (Slip Anchor).*
April 18. Twelfth foal. 40,000Y. Tattersalls October 2. Peter Doyle. Half-brother to the quite useful 2-y-o 7f winner Red Leggings (by Shareef Dancer), to the quite useful 2m winner of 4 races Lord Alaska (by Sir Harry Lewis), the fair all-weather 10.5f and 11f winner Eagle's Landing (by Eagle Eyed), two bumper winners by Hernando and Efisio and to the placed dam of the Group 3 Cornwallis Stakes winner Hunter Street. The dam, a quite useful dual 12.3f winner, is a half-sister to 6 winners including the Ormonde Stakes winner Brunico. The second dam, Cartridge (by Jim French), was a useful 6f and 7f winner and a half-sister to 3 winners. (Mrs J Wood).

"A smashing colt and a real chip off the old block – a real Compton Place. He'll be pretty sharp and he's ready to do some work now".

724. DREAM OF GERONTIUS (IRE) ★★★★ ♠
b.f. Oratorio – Shades Of Rosegold (Bluebird).
April 9. Fourth foal. 21,000Y. Doncaster St Leger. Peter Doyle. The dam was placed twice at 3 yrs in Germany and is a half-sister to 6 winners including the US Grade 3 winner Alexis. The second dam, Sister Golden Hair (by Glint Of Gold), a listed placed 2-y-o winner in Germany, is a half-sister to 2 winners abroad. (Mrs J Wood).
"A sharp filly, she's working nicely and she'll be racing early on".

725. DREAM VENTURE ★★★
b.f. Tiger Hill – Dream Lady (Benny The Dip).
January 23. Half-sister to the modest 2008 2-y-o 8.7f winner Dream Huntress (by Dubai Destination). The dam is an unraced half-sister to the useful 12f, 13f and German listed winner Elusive Dream. The second dam, Dance A Dream (by Sadler's Wells), a smart winner of the Cheshire Oaks and second in the Epsom Oaks, is a sister to the 2,000 Guineas winner Entrepreneur and to the very useful middle-distance listed winner Sadler's Image and a half-sister to 7 winners including the Coronation Stakes winner Exclusive.
"She's only doing strong canters at the moment because she's not going to be early. She's a nice filly but a bit nervy. A fine, strong filly though".

726. ESSEXBRIDGE ★★
b.c. Avonbridge – Aonach Mor (Anabaa).
February 1. Fifth foal. 22,000Y. Doncaster St Leger. Peter Doyle. Half-brother to the 1m seller winner Mercari (by Bahamian Bounty). The dam is an unraced half-sister to 7 minor winners. The second dam, Rechanit (by Local Suitor), won 4 races at 3 yrs in Italy and is a half-sister to 7 winners including the dual Group 2 winner Sapience. (R H W Morecombe & Partners).
"He's ready for a bit of work now, he's a nice colt and we'll probably get him to the races early on".

We've got a few Avonbridge two-year-olds and I like them. They're strong and good movers".

727. FINE SIGHT ★★★★★
b.c. Cape Cross – Daring Aim (Daylami).
February 13. Second foal. Half-brother to Highland Glen (by Montjeu), unplaced in one start at 2 yrs in 2008. The dam, a fairly useful 12f winner, is a half-sister to 4 winners including the smart 2-y-o 6f winner and Group 1 12f Oaks second Flight Of Fancy. The second dam, Phantom Gold (by Sadler's Wells), a very useful filly, won from 1m (at 2 yrs) to 12f including the Group 2 Ribblesdale Stakes and the Group 3 St Simon Stakes. (The Queen).
"He has a middle-distance pedigree and yet I don't know whether to go early with him or wait, but he certainly goes very well and I like him a lot. He can certainly gallop and there's a bit of class about him".

728. FIRST CAT ★★
b.g. One Cool Cat – Zina La Belle (Mark Of Esteem).
March 5. First foal. The dam, a listed-placed Italian 1m winner of 3 races, is a half-sister to the Group 3 6f Railway Stakes winner and Group 1 7f Prix de la Salamandre second Honours List. The second dam, Gold Script (by Script Ohio), a French 5.5f (at 2 yrs) and listed 12f Prix de Thiberville winner, is a half-sister to 5 winners. (R Barnett).
"A one-eyed horse, he's done nothing wrong and he did a bit upsides the other day but he was green and needed it. He's doing OK though".

729. FLAPJACK ★★
b.f. Trade Fair – Inya Lake (Whittingham).
April 28. 10,000Y. Doncaster St Leger. Peter Doyle. Half-sister to the fairly useful triple 6f winner Jimmy Styles (by Inchinr), to the fair 2-y-o dual 5f winner Lake Hero (by Arkadian Hero) and the modest triple 5f winner Special Gold (by Josr Algarhoud). The dam, a useful 2-y-o winner of 4 races over 5f including the Group 3 Molecomb Stakes, subsequently won a listed 5f event at 3 yrs and is a half-sister to one winner. The second dam, Special One (by

Aragon), was a modest 2-y-o 5f winner and a half-sister to 7 winners. (S Leech).
"He wants six furlongs now and he did have one run to get him going but he'll improve for that".

730. FOOTSTEPSOFSPRING (FR) ★★★
b.c. *Footstepsinthesand – Moon West (Gone West).*
February 27. First foal. 72,000foal. Tattersalls December. Catridge Farm Stud. The dam, a French 7f winner at 3 yrs, is a half-sister to 7 winners including the Group 2 German 2,000 Guineas winners Dupont and Pacino. The second dam, June Moon (by Sadler's Wells), is an unraced half-sister to 6 winners including the French 1,000 Guineas second Firth Of Lorne. (Mrs J Wood).
"A nice, good, strong horse. He's a lovely mover but we've settled him back a bit because he was a bit 'free' early on. He won't be a very early two-year-old".

731. FREMONT (IRE) ★★★★★
b.c. *Marju – Snow Peak (Arazi).*
February 25. 48,000foal. Tattersalls December. Catridge Farm Stud. Brother to the smart listed 6f and listed 1m winner and Group 1 Golden Jubilee Stakes third Asset. The dam won twice in France at 3 yrs including over 1m and is a half-sister to 6 winners including the useful French 7f winner and listed-placed Flurry. The second dam, Snowtop (by Thatching), an Irish sprint winner of 3 races including a listed event, is a half-sister to 9 winners including the Group 1 1m William Hill Futurity Stakes winner Al Hareb. (Mrs Julie Wood).
"A lovely horse, but we'll put a bit of time on him. A full-brother to Asset, he's a lovely two-year-old and one of the stars of the show hopefully. We'll start him at six furlongs I should think. I asked the owner to sell me a quarter share but she wasn't having any!" Stable jockey Richard Hughes added how much he liked this colt.

732. FULL MANDATE (IRE) ★★★★
b.f. *Acclamation – Dani Ridge (Indian Ridge).*
April 7. Third foal. €60,000Y. Goffs Million. Peter Doyle. Half-sister to the fairly useful 2008 2-y-o 6f winner and Group 3 Albany Stakes third Danidh Dubai (by Noverre) and to the quite useful 6f (at 2 yrs) and 5f winner Ridge Wood Dani (by Invincible Spirit). The dam, a quite useful triple 6f winner, is a sister to the Group 3 Diomed Stakes winner Blomberg and a half-sister to 2 winners. The second dam, Daniella Drive (by Shelter Half), won 12 minor races at 2 to 5 yrs in the USA and is a half-sister to 4 winners. (Mrs A M Doyle & Partners).
"A good-looking filly, she's very nice and I like her a lot. A lovely mover, she's sharp and should be one for the pot!"

733. GLAMOUR PROFESSION (IRE) ★★★
ch.f. *Captain Rio – Kriva (Reference Point).*
April 28. Seventh foal. €28,000Y. Tattersalls Ireland. Peter Doyle. Sister to the fairly useful 2008 2-y-o 7f winner Midnight Cruiser and half-sister to the Scandinavian winner of 10 races and listed-placed Peruginos Flyer (by Perugino), the fair 10f, 11f and hurdles winner Shrivar (by Sri Pekan), the fair all-weather 12f and 14f winner Rickety Bridge (by Elnadim), the dual US 4-y-o winner Bourgeoisie (by Royal Academy) and a minor 2-y-o winner abroad by Marju. The dam, a fair 17.2f winner at 3 yrs, is a half-sister to 4 winners including the dam of the good Hong Kong horse Housemaster. The second dam, Kraemer (by Lyphard), won 4 races in France and the USA including the listed 8.5f Bay Meadows Oaks, was second in the Grade 2 Del Mar Oaks and is a half-sister to 5 winners including the high-class Prix du Rond-Point and Prix d'Astarte winner Shaanxi. (Justin Dowley & Michael Prescod).
"She'll be working soon, we're waiting for a bit of rain so we can work them on the grass. It won't be long before we see her racing". I recognise the name as the title of a Steely Dan song – not unusual for owner Michael Pescod who apparently is a big jazz fan. ST.

734. GULF PUNCH ★★★ ♠
b.f. *Dubawi – Fruit Punch (Barathea).*
January 23. 10,000Y. Tattersalls October 2. Not sold. The dam won once at 3 yrs in France and is a half-sister to 6 winners including the

Japanese stakes winner Kei Woman. The second dam, Friendly Finance (by Auction Ring), is an unraced half-sister to 7 winners including Riverman. (R Barnett).
"She's a nice filly and there's plenty of speed in the damline. She's a smallish, stocky filly and strong. She's going to be alright. She did a bit of work up the hill the other day and did well".

735. HALF SISTER (IRE) ★★★★ ♠
b.f. Oratorio – Fifty Five (Lake Coniston).
May 14. Sixth foal. 48,000Y. Tattersalls October 2. Peter Doyle. Half-sister to a minor winner in France by Orpen. The dam, a minor French 3-y-o winner, is a half-sister to the muliple Group 1 winners George Washington and Grandera. The second dam, Bordighera (by Alysheba), won once over 13f in France, was second in the listed 12f Prix des Tuileries and is a half-sister to 7 winners. (Mr Richard Morecombe & Mrs Anne Ferguson).
"A cracking filly, we wouldn't be rushing with her but she's got every chance".

736. HELAKU (IRE) ★★★★
b.c. Rakti – Saibhreas (Last Tycoon).
April 10. Eighth foal. 85,000Y. Tattersalls October 2. J Brummitt. 75,000Y. Tattersalls December. Peter Doyle. Half-brother to the unplaced 2008 2-y-o Reigning In Rio, to the French 1m, 10f (both at 2 yrs) and listed 12f winner Hopes And Fears (both by Captain Rio), to the fairly useful dual 7f winner (including at 2 yrs) Dancing Guest (by Danehill Dancer), the fair 7f all-weather winner Desert Lightning (by Desert Prince) and a winner over hurdles by King's Theatre. The dam, an Irish 10f winner, is a half-sister to 7 winners including the Irish listed winner and Group 3 placed Nordic Soprano. The second dam Angor (by Lorenzaccio), won at 3 yrs and is a half-sister to 6 winners including the dual Group 1 winning sprinter Double Form. (Mr Michael Pescod & Mr Justin Dowley).
"A smashing colt, he's not over-big but he's very active. Unlike his Dad he's a well-behaved horse and he's a lovely colt to watch out for".

737. HELIOCENTRIC ★★
ch.c. Galileo – Yding (Danehill).
March 27. First living foal. 48,000Y. Tattersalls October 3. D R Tucker. The dam is an unraced half-sister to one winner. The second dam, Ship's Twine (by Slip Anchor), is a placed half-sister to 9 winners including the Group winners Alderbrook and Restructure. (D D Clee).
"He hasn't been in very long, he's a nice horse but he's not going to be early".

738. HIGGY'S RAGAZZO (FR) ★★
b.c. Sinndar – Super Crusty (Namid).
March 21. First foal. Deauville August. €44,000Y. Will Edmeades. The dam, a minor winner in France, is out of the unraced Shawana (by Turtle Island), herself a half-sister to the Irish and French Oaks winner Shawanda. (I Higginson).
"He's a bit 'on the leg' and he'll take a bit of time but he's alright".

739. INVINCIBLE SOUL (IRE) ★★
b.c. Invincible Spirit – Licorne (Sadler's Wells).
May 7. Eleventh foal. €160,000Y. Goffs Million. Peter Doyle. Half-brother to the fairly useful 10f and hurdles winner Dabus (by Kris). The dam, a fairly useful 10f and 12f winner, is a half-sister to 6 winners including the Group 1 Yorkshire Oaks winner Catchascatchcan (herself dam of the Group 2 winner Antonius Pius). The second dam, Catawba (by Reform), a fairly useful 10.5f winner, is a half-sister to 7 winners including the Ribblesdale Stakes winner Strigida. (Mr P Fahey).
"A lovely, tall, good-looking horse. I'm in no rush with him and he wouldn't be a five furlong horse anyway".

740. KAJIMA ★★
b.c. Oasis Dream – Mambo Mistress (Kingmambo).
April 2. Third foal. 82,000Y. Tattersalls October 1. John Warren. Half-brother to the quite useful French 8.5f winner Bestofthem (by Stormin Fever). The dam is an unraced half-sister to 5 winners. The second dam, Mistress S (by Kris S), a US listed winner and Grade 2 placed, is a full or half-sister to 6 winners. (Miss Y M G Jacques).

"A very nice horse, but he's quite big and probably on the backward side, so he's one we wouldn't be in a rush with really".

741. KING'S APPROACH (IRE) ★★★
gr.c. Fasliyev – Lady Georgina (Linamix).
February 12. First foal. €40,000Y. Goffs Million. Peter Doyle. The dam, a fair dual 7f winner at 3 yrs, is out of the fair 14f and 2m winner Georgia Venture (by Shirley Heights), herself a half-sister to 10 winners. (David & Gwyn Joseph).
"He's ready to run and he goes well. He's alright and he'll win early".

742. LILLY VALENTINE (IRE) ★★★★
b.f. Rock Of Gibraltar – Liska (Bigstone).
February 13. Second foal. €70,000Y. Goffs Million. Peter Doyle. The dam, a French 3-y-o 9f winner, was third in the Group 3 Prix Vanteaux and is a half-sister to 5 winners including the Irish and US winner of 9 races and Group 1 Livadiya and the dam of the dual Group 1 winner Linngari. The dam, a French 9f and 10.5f winner, is a half-sister to 5 winners including the Group 3 12f Prix Minerve winner Linnga. (Brian Dolan).
"She's really nice. A lovely, strong filly that moves very well, I'm very happy with her and she's a great natured filly. She has a lovely temperament and she could be a really nice one".

743. LOST HORIZON (IRE) ★★★
b.f. Elusive City – Souvenir Souvenir (Highest Honor).
April 3. Fifth foal. Deauville August. €70,000Y. Peter Doyle. Half-sister to the minor French winner Sing Faraway (by Galileo). The dam, a minor French 3-y-o winner, is a half-sister to 6 winners including the French Group 3 winner Comillas. The second dam, Rive du Sud (by Nureyev), was a minor 2-y-o winner. (Mrs J Wood).
"She'd be sharp enough to go six furlongs and she's a nice enough filly".

744. LOVE ACTION (IRE) ★★★
b.f. Motivator – Speciale (War Chant).
March 2. Second foal. 100,000Y. Tattersalls October 1. Peter Doyle. The dam won 2 races including the 2-y-o listed 6f Prix Yacowlef and is a half-sister to the Group 3 Gladness Stakes and German Group 3 winner Common World. The second dam, Spenderella (by Common Grounds), won once at 3 yrs in France and is a half-sister to 7 winners including the US Grade 1 Yellow Ribbon Invitational winner Aube Indienne. (Mrs R Ablett).
"One for later in the season, she's nice enough but being by Motivator although we might start her over six furlongs but you'd expect her to need seven in the end".

745. LOYALISTE (FR) ★★★
ch.c. Green Tune – Whitby (Gold Away).
February 21. Second foal. Deauville August. €210,000Y. Peter Doyle. The dam was placed 13 times in France and is a half-sister to 7 winners including the dam of the US Beverly D Handicap winner Gorella. The second dam, Eloura (by Top Ville), won twice in France. (Mrs S A F Brendish).
"A beautiful horse, he won't be going early but he's a smasher. We might start him at six furlongs but seven would be more his trip and he'd probably go further. We won't be rushing him".

746. LUCKY GENERAL (IRE) ★★★ ♠
b.c. Hawk Wing – Dress Code (Barathea).
March 4. Fourth foal. €50,000Y. Goffs Million. Peter Doyle. Half-brother to the unplaced 2008 2-y-o Luvmedo (by One Cool Cat), to the quite useful Irish 2-y-o 7f winner Slaney Rock (by Rock Of Gibraltar) and the fair 2-y-o 5f winner and listed 5f placed Dress To Impress (by Fasliyev). The dam, a quite useful 2-y-o 5f winner, is a sister to the useful 2-y-o Group 3 7f C L Weld Park Stakes winner Rag Top and a half-sister to 6 winners. The second dam, Petite Epaulette (by Night Shift), a fair 5f winner at 2 yrs, is a half-sister to the Group 1 1m Gran Criterium second Line Dancer. (Mrs J Wood).
"Another good-looking horse, but being by

Hawk Wing he wouldn't be starting at five furlongs. He's a fine, big, good-looking colt".

747. MAGIC LANTERN ★★
ch.f. Halling – Papabile (Chief's Crown).
March 7. Third foal. 25,000Y. Tattersalls October 3. Peter Doyle. Half-sister to the fair 10f winner Papality (by Giant's Causeway). The dam, a useful winner of 3 races over 1m including 2 listed events, is a sister to the champion 2-y-o Grand Lodge and a half-sister to 5 winners including the dual listed winner La Persiana. The second dam, La Papagena (by Habitat), is an unraced half-sister to 7 winners including the very useful 3-y-o 7f and 1m winner Pamina, the very useful 11f and 12.5f winner Lost Chord. (J D Manley).
"She's going to need six, or more likely seven furlongs and considering she's out of a sister to Grand Lodge we didn't give a lot for her".

748. MAGNUS THRAX (USA) ★★★
b.c. Roman Ruler – Wild Catseye
(Forest Wildcat).
February 21. Second foal. 45,000Y. Tattersalls October 1. Peter Doyle. The dam, a stakes winner of 3 races at 2 and 3 yrs in the USA, is a half-sister to 6 minor winners. The second dam, A Real Eye Opener (by Cutlass), a winner and Grade 3 placed in the USA, is a half-sister to 4 winners. (M Pescod).
"He's a smashing looking colt, I don't know anything about the sire but this colt is quite big and we're not going to be getting him out early".

749. MASTER OF DANCE (IRE) ★★★★
ch.c. Noverre – Shambodia (Petardia).
May 4. Fourth foal. 30,000Y. Doncaster St Leger. Peter Doyle. Half-brother to the fairly useful triple 7f winner Bettalatethannever (by Titus Livius). The dam is an unraced half-sister to 5 winners. The second dam, Lucky Fountain (by Lafontaine), is an unraced sister to the Group 2 Geoffrey Freer Stakes winner Shambo. (Mr P D Merritt).
"A sharp colt, he'll be fairly early and he's working now. He might be a May foal but he can go". TRAINER'S BARGAIN BUY

750. MONSIEUR CHEVALIER (IRE) ★★★★★
b.c. Chevalier – Blue Holly (Blues Traveller).
January 23. Third foal. 17,000Y. Tattersalls October. Peter Doyle. Brother to the quite useful 2008 2-y-o 5f winner Mister Fips and half-brother to the modest 2-y-o 5f seller winner Suzieblue (by Redback). The dam, a quite useful 5f (including at 2 yrs) and 6f winner, is a half-sister to numerous winners. The second dam, Holly Bird (Runnet), won over 12f in Ireland and was listed-placed. (Mrs V Hubbard & Mr I Higginson).
"Quite an impressive winner of the Newmarket Conditions race won last year by Art Connoisseur prior to that colt winning the Coventry Stakes. Royal Ascot is beckoning this colt now too".

751. MOONLINE DANCER (FR) ★★★
b.f. Royal Academy – Tulipe Noire (Alleged).
January 26. Seventh foal. Deauville August. €160,000Y. Will Edmeades. Sister to a minor winner in France and half-sister to 3 minor winners in France (by Diesis), the USA (by Grand Slam) and Canada (by Nureyev). The dam is an unraced sister to the Group 2 Prix de Royallieu, Group 2 Ribblesdale Stakes and Group 2 Premio Legnano winner Tulipa and a half-sister to the Italian Group 1 and German triple Group 3 winner Devil River Peek. The second dam, Black Tulip (by Fabulous Dancer), won 7 races in France (including 2 listed events) from 10f to 12f, was Grade 2 placed over 12f in the USA and is a half-sister to 7 winners. (Malih L Al Basti).
"A very classy filly, I won't do too much too soon with her because she's not bred to go early. But I won't be that long in starting to warm her up, she knows what to do and is very relaxed in herself".

752. MOONRAKER'S CHOICE (IRE) ★★★
ch.f. Choisir – Staploy (Deploy).
February 24. Third foal. €30,000Y. Goffs Sportsman's. Peter Doyle. Half-sister to a minor winner abroad by Tendulkar. The dam, a fair 1m to 11f maiden, is a half-sister to 3 winners. The second dam, Balliasta (by Lyphard), is an unplaced half-sister to the Group 1 Prix 'Ispahan

winner Sanglamore. (The Moonrakers).
"A good, big filly, she's a lovely mover and will start off at six furlongs".

753. OUR BOY BARRINGTON (IRE) ★★★
b.c. Catcher In The Rye – Daily Double
(Unfuwain).
April 12. Fifth foal. 32,000Y. Doncaster St Leger. Peter Doyle. Half-brother to the fair 2008 2-y-o 5f winner Sharpener (by Invincible Spirit), to the fair 9f and 10f winner of 4 races from 3 to 5 yrs Princess Cocoa (by Desert Sun), the fair Irish 4-y-o dual 6f winner Lady Power (by Almutawakel) and the minor Italian winner of 3 races from 2 to 4 yrs Live To Run (by Intikhab). The dam is an unraced half-sister to 3 minor winners in France and Germany. The second dam, Double Line (by What A Guest), is a placed half-sister to 5 winners including the Group 3 winner and good broodmare Perlee. (Mrs J Wood).
"We've done nothing with him yet, he's a nice horse but he's just cantering away".

754. PALEO (IRE) ★★★
ch.f. Indian Ridge – Crossbreeze (Red Ransom).
May 3. Third foal. €50,000Y. Goffs Million. Peter Doyle. Half-sister to the minor 2008 Italian 2-y-o winner Super Nancy (by Refuse To Bend). The dam, a fair 6f placed 2-y-o, is a half-sister to the Group 1 St Leger winner Rule Of Law. The second dam, Crystal Crossing (by Royal Academy), winner of the listed 6f Doncaster Bloodstock Rose Bowl Stakes, is a sister to the very useful 2-y-o Group 3 7f Prestige Stakes winner and US Grade 2 placed Circle Of Gold and a half-sister to 4 winners. (Knockalney Stud and Partners).
"A filly with a decent pedigree, I won't be rushing her because she hasn't come in her coat yet".

755. PALISADES PARK ★★★
b.c. Compton Place – Brooklyn's Sky
(Septime Ciel).
May 1. Third living foal. 26,000Y. Tattersalls October 2. G Howson. Half-brother to the fair 2008 7f placed 2-y-o Spit And Polish (by Polish Precedent). The dam won once at 2 yrs in France and is a half-sister to 3 winners. The second dam, West Brooklyn (by Gone West), won 2 races at 2 and 3 yrs in France and is a half-sister to 9 winners including the Group 2 Prix Greffuhle winner Prospect Wells. (David Powell & Partners).
"He's alright, he's sharp and he goes well. He's just got a bit of a sore shin so we've backed off him a bit".

756. PLANET RED ★★★
ch.c. Bahamian Bounty – Aries (Big Shuffle).
February 25. Third foal. 14,000Y. Tatersalls October. Peter Doyle. The dam, a fair 2-y-o 7f winner, is a full or half-sister to 6 winners in Germany. The second dam, Auenlust (by Surumu), won 3 races over 1m in Germany and is a full or half-sister to 11 winners. (Mr F Perryman & Mr R Morecombe).

Jockey Richard Hughes told me this colt is a nice type and it should be worth keeping an eye out for him.

757. PLUME ★★★★ ♠
b.f. Pastoral Pursuits – Polar Storm
(Law Society).
March 6. Tenth foal. €100,000Y. Goffs Million. John Warren. Half-sister to the fair 2-y-o dual 5f winner Chilly Cracker, the 10f seller winner By Storm (both by Largesse), the modest dual 6f winner Run On and the modest 9f and hurdles winner Lawnett (both by Runnett). The dam, a fair 6f (at 2 yrs) to 1m winner, is a full or half-sister to 6 winners including the very useful 2-y-o Group 3 5f Debutante Stakes and 3-y-o 6f winner Polar Bird (herself the dam of 3 stakes winners including the Group 2 Prix Robert Papin winner Ocean Ridge). The second dam, Arctic Winter (by Briartic), a winner at 2 yrs in Germany, is a sister to the Canadian Grade 1 winner Son Of Briartic and a half-sister to 9 winners including the dam of the Canadian Grade 1 winner Halo's Princess. (Highclere Thoroughbred Racing).
"A lovely filly and one of the nicest movers you've ever seen, but unfortunately she slipped up crossing the road and ended up with a long

cut on her backside. It held her up for four weeks but she's getting over it now. It's healing but taking it's time. She'll be a six furlong filly".

758. POLTERGEIST ★★★★ ♠
b.c. Invincible Spirit – Bayalika (Selkirk).
March 28. Fourth foal. 75,000Y. Tattersalls October 1. Not sold. Half-brother to the Group 2 7f Champagne Stakes winner and 2,000 Guineas second Vital Equine (by Danetime) and to the quite useful 1m winner Bramaputra (by Choisir). The dam is an unraced half-sister to 4 winners including an Italian listed winner. The second dam, Bayrika (by Selkirk), won the Group 3 Prix Berteux and is a half-sister to 7 winners out of the Prix Saint-Alary winner Behera. (Highclere Thoroughbred Racing).
"A big, backward horse, he's fine and good-looking apart from a bit of a plain head. He's got a very good frame and he'll make up into a lovely horse one day. It's a very good pedigree".

759. POSE (IRE) ★★★
b.f. Acclamation – Lyca Ballerina (Marju).
April 11. Second foal. 58,000Y. Doncaster St Leger. Peter Doyle. Half-sister to the modest 2008 8.7f placed 2-y-o Jobekani (by Tagula). The dam, a fair 7f winner at 3 yrs, is a half-sister to 4 winners. The second dam, Lovely Lyca (by Night Shift), a fair 1m and 11.8f winner, is a sister to the listed 1m winners Barboukh (herself dam of the Group 3 10f Prix Exbury winner Barbola) and a half-sister to 6 winners. (Highclere Thoroughbred Racing).
"She's growing but she'll be out before mid-summer. A nice filly".

760. QUADRILLE ★★★★
b.c. Danehill Dancer – Fictitious (Machiavellian).
February 7. Half-brother to the quite useful dual 1m winner Hunting Tower (by Sadler's Wells). The dam, a useful 10f listed winner, is a sister to the smart Group 2 12f Ribblesdale Stakes and Group 2 13.3f Geoffrey Freer Stakes winner Phantom Gold (herself dam of the Oaks second Flight Of Fancy). The second dam, Trying For Gold (by Northern Baby), was a useful 12f and 12.5f winner at 3 yrs. (The Queen).
"Another big, fine galloping horse. He's a lovely mover but I won't be going early with him".

761. QUICK REACTION ★★★
b.c. Elusive Quality – Arutua (Riverman).
February 22. Half-brother to the 7f (at 2 yrs) and listed 12f winner Juliette (by Sadler's Wells), to the useful Irish 6f (at 2 yrs) and 1m winner and subsequent US Grade 2 placed Plato (by Lure), the fairly useful 6f winner (including at 2 yrs) Farha (by Nureyev), the quite useful 2-y-o 7.5f winner Lost In Wonder (by Galileo) and the fair 2-y-o 7f winner Naval Review (by Storm Cat). The dam is an unraced half-sister to the Group 2 Prix Greffuhle Stakes winner Along All and the French Group 3 placed Arnaqueur. The second dam, All Along (by Targowice), was a top-class middle-distance filly and winner of the Prix de l'Arc de Triomphe, Prix Vermeille, Turf Classic, Washington D C International and Rothmans International (all Group or Grade 1 events). (The Queen).
"A fine, big, good-looking horse but he hasn't done a lot yet and he'll be working upsides soon. Everything's fine with him".

762. RAGSTA (IRE) ★★★
b.f. Key Of Luck – Rag Top (Barathea).
February 25. The dam, a useful 2-y-o Group 3 7f C L Weld Park Stakes winner, is a half-sister to several winners including the fairly useful 7.6f and subsequent US 1m winner Red Top. The second dam, Petite Epaulette (by Night Shift), a fair 5f winner at 2 yrs, is a half-sister to the Group 1 1m Gran Criterium second Line Dancer. (F Jones).
"A nice filly with a good pedigree, I haven't done much with her yet but we'll be stepping her up from mid-April onwards. She has a good temperament for a Key Of Luck, it's a good family and they all have ability".

763. RED BADGE (IRE) ★★★
ch.c. Captain Rio – Red Fuschia (Polish Precedent).
March 1. Second foal. 46,000Y. Doncaster St

Leger. Peter Doyle. The dam is an unraced half-sister to 3 winners including the Group 3 placed Red Peony. The second dam, Red Azalea (by Shirley Heights), a fairly useful 7f (at 2 yrs) and 10f winner, is a half-sister to 4 winners including the smart Group 3 Prestige Stakes winner and French 1,000 Guineas third Red Camellia (herself dam of the Fillies Mile winner Red Bloom). (M Pescod).
"A good-looking colt that's ready for work now and I'll be getting on with him soon. He's done plenty of cantering".

764. ROYAL BOX ★★★
b.c. Royal Applause – Diamond Lodge
(Grand Lodge).
February 15. First foal. The dam, a fairly useful 1m and 9f winner of 4 races at 3 yrs, is a half-sister to numerous minor winners. The second dam, Movieland (by Nureyev), won the Group 3 1m Prix des Reservoirs and is a half-sister to the Group 3 Prix de Sandringham winner Only Star. (The Queen).
"He's a bit cheeky so we're going to get him working on the grass once we get some rain. A well-made horse, he's bit small, but nice".

765. SABII SANDS (IRE) ★★★ ♠
b.c. Invincible Spirit – Miriana (Bluebird).
February 25. Third foal. €120,000Y. Goffs Million. Peter Doyle. The dam is an unplaced sister to the Group 3 Prix de la Rochette winner Fine Fellow and a half-sister to 8 winners. The second dam, Majieda (by Kashmir II), is a placed half-sister to 3 winners including the dam of the Group 1 National Stakes winner Manntari. (Mr A T J Russell).
"A lovely horse, but he's got a bit of size to him so we won't be rushing him. I think my owners have spent a bit more this year and got horses that have a bit more scope, so I have some better quality horses".

766. SEA DUBAI ★★★
b.c. Mark Of Esteem – Royal Flame
(Royal Academy).
March 23. Fifth foal. 23,000Y. Tattersalls October 3. Peter Doyle. Half-brother to the quite useful 2008 Irish 7f placed 2-y-o Egypt (by Dansili), to the fairly useful 7f and 1m winner Arabian Spirit (by Oasis Dream) and a winner over hurdles by Germany. The dam, a modest 10f all-weather winner, is a half-sister to one winner. The second dam, Samnaun (by Stop The Music), is an unraced half-sister to 8 winners including the Group 2 German 1,000 Guineas winner Quebrada and to the placed dam of the Group 1 German Oaks winner Silvester Lady. (Malih L Al Basti).
"A good-looking horse that won't be early but I expect he'll be out by the end of May. A lovely mover".

767. STAGS LEAP (IRE) ★★★
b.c. Refuse To Bend – Swingsky
(Indian Ridge).
March 26. First foal. €110,000Y. Goffs February. Wessex Bloodstock. The dam, unplaced on her only start, is a sister to the French listed 1m winner Indianski. The second dam, Plissetskaia (by Caerleon), won in France at 2 yrs and was listed-placed and is a half-sister to numerous winners. (Mrs Julie Wood).
"A very nice horse but he's not a five furlong type. Looking at him he'll need every bit of six furlongs".

768. SUITED AND BOOTED ★★★ ♠
ch.c. Tagula – Carpet Lady
(Night Shift).
February 24. Fifth foal. 48,000Y. Tattersalls October 1. Peter Doyle. Brother to Tagula Night, a fair second over 6f at 2 yrs in 2008 and half-brother to the 2-y-o listed 5f winner of 3 races Cake (by Acclamation), the modest 2-y-o 6f winner Wachiwi (by Namid) and the German 6f winner Nadal (by Shinko Forest). The dam, a fair dual 6f placed 2-y-o, is a half-sister to 5 winners including the Hong Kong stakes winner Classic Fountain. The second dam, Lucky Fountain (by Lafontaine), is an unraced sister to the Group 2 Geoffrey Freer Stakes winner Shambo. (Des Anderson & Simon Leech).
"A fine horse, he's good-looking and a good mover. He won't be that early and he wouldn't be a five furlong horse either".

769. SUNARISE (IRE) ★★★
b.f. Galileo – Sun Silk (Gone West).
March 17. Fourth foal. 22,000Y. Tattersalls October 1. Peter Doyle. Half-sister to the fairly useful Irish 2-y-o 7.5f winner Sakkara Star (by Mozart) and to the quite useful 9f winner Victory Design (by Danehill). The dam is an unplaced half-sister to 2 winners including the dam of 2 minor US stakes winners. The second dam, Silk Slippers (by Nureyev), won the Group 2 Hoover Fillies Mile. (Mrs Julie Wood).
"She hasn't been in very long but I think she bought her cheap! She's a very nice filly with a decent pedigree and I wouldn't mind her myself!"

770. TARITA (IRE) ★★★♠
ch.f. Bahamian Bounty – Zonic (Zafonic).
January 25. First foal. 32,000Y. Tattersalls October 1. Amanda Skiffington. The dam is a placed half-sister to 3 winners including the dam of the Group 2 July Stakes winner Nevisian Lad. The second dam, Ferber's Follies (by Saratoga Six), a winning 2-y-o sprinter, was third in the Grade 2 6f Adirondack Stakes and is a half-sister to 11 winners including the US 2-y-o Grade 2 6f winner Blue Jean Baby. (De La Warr Racing).
"She's going to take a bit of time and she'll be one for six and seven furlongs. I do like the Bahamian Bounty's – they're nice horses".

771. TWICE AS NICE ★★★
b.c. Compton Place – Sunley Stars (Sallust).
April 6. 28,000foal. Tattersalls December. Catridge Farm Stud. Brother to the useful listed 5f and Weatherbys Supersprint winner If Paradise, closely related to the fairly useful 1m in UAE) and 9.4f winner Don Sebastian (by Indian Ridge) and half-brother to the 2-y-o 5f winner All She Surveys (by Mazilier). The dam is an unplaced half-sister to 5 winners. The second dam, Russeting (by Mummy's Pet), won once at 2 yrs and is a sister to the Group 2 Vernons Sprint Cup winner Runnett. (Mrs J Wood).
"He's done very well since he came in and he's a full brother to the owner's decent horse If Paradise, so I should think he'd be one to look out for".

772. VALIANT KNIGHT (FR) ★★★★
ch.c. Night Shift – Pilgrim Of Grace (Bering).
February 12. First foal. Deauville August. €115,000Y. Peter Doyle. The dam, a listed winner of 5 races in France, is a half-sister to one winner. The second dam, Vagabond Chanteuse (by Sanglamore), won once at 2 yrs and was second in the Group 3 Musidora Stakes. (Mrs S A F Brendish).
"He's a very good-looking horse, he'd want six furlongs at least but he's a lovely type and strong. I can't say enough about him, I think he's lovely".

773. UNNAMED ★★★
gr.c. Indian Ridge – Dundel (Machiavellian).
March 21. Eighth foal. €260,000Y. Goffs Million. Ridge Manor Stables. Brother to the smart 2-y-o 6f winner and Group 2 6f Coventry Stakes second Luck Money and half-brother to the 2-y-o Group 3 7f Prix du Calvados winner Charlotte O'Fraise (by Beat Hollow), the modest 2m 1f and hurdles winner Lodgician (by Grand Lodge), the Irish 1m and hurdles winner River Nurey (by Fasliyev) and the French 3-y-o winner Wing And Wing (by Singspiel). The dam, a quite useful 7f winner, is a half-sister to 6 winners including the Group 3 6f Prix de Seine-et-Oise winner Seltitude. The second dam, Dunoof (by Shirley Heights), a fairly useful 2-y-o 7f winner, is a sister to the Premio Roma, Park Hill Stakes and Ribblesdale Stakes winner High Hawk (the dam of In the Wings) and to the winning dams of the Derby winner High-Rise and the Grade 1 Rothmans International winner Infamy. (C F Harrington).
"He had a slight problem just after the Sales but he arrives back in training today. Obviously his price tag tells you he's a lovely colt but I don't know anything much him just yet".

774. UNNAMED ★★★
b.c. Intikhab – Handsome Anna (Bigstone).
March 14. Fourth living foal. 70,000Y. Doncaster St Leger. Malih Al Basti. Half-brother to the quite useful 6f, 7f (both at 2 yrs) and 1m winner Hansomelle and the modest 5f and 6f winner of 6 races (including at 2 yrs) The History

Man (both by Titus Livius). The dam was placed 6 times at around 7f in Ireland and is a half-sister to 6 winners including the useful 10f to 12.3f winner Jehol. The second dam, Buz Kashi (by Bold Lad, Ire), a 6f 2-y-o winner, was disqualified after winning the Coronation Stakes and is a half-sister to the Lingfield Derby Trial winner Caporello. (Malih L Al Basti).

"He was doing very well until his shins started to warm up so we gave him a little break. He looks to me like being a runner and I think he'd have enough speed for five furlongs but he'd be better over further. A nice horse, he's got speed".

775. UNNAMED ★★★★
b.c. Elusive City – Rouge Noir (Saint Ballado).
March 7. Third foal. €110,000Y. Goffs Million. Peter Doyle. Half-brother to the 2008 2-y-o listed 5f winner Light The Fire (by Invincible Spirit). The dam, a minor winner at 3 yrs in the USA, is a half-sister to a winner in Japan. The second dam, Ardana (by Danehill), won the Group 3 Premio Bagutta and is a half-sister to 5 winners. (J R May).

"A good-looking horse that cost a lot of money. A lot of my two-year-olds this year look like they need further than five furlongs. This colt is a case in point and he looks as if he has a bit of quality about him".

776. UNNAMED ★★★★
b.c. Marju – Zanna (Soviet Star).
February 4. First foal. 42,000Y. Tattersalls October 1. Peter Doyle. The dam was placed 4 times in France at 2 and 3 yrs and is a half-sister to 5 winners including the French listed winner Zandiyka (dam of the French 1,000 Guineas winner Zalaiyka). The second dam, Zanata (by African Sky), is a winning half-sister to 5 winners. (Mrs Rita McArdle).

"He's not over-big, he's a nice, robust colt and strong. He did a bit of work the other morning and did particularly well. He certainly knew what to do!"

PATRICK HASLAM
777. BATEAU BLEU ★★★
b.c. Auction House – Fresh Look (Alzao).
February 28. 5,000Y. Tattersalls October 3. Not sold. Brother to the fair 2-y-o dual 6f winner Estimator and half-brother to the quite useful 2-y-o 6f winner Euro Route (by Desert Style), the fair 2-y-o dual 6f winner Lady Benjamin (by Spinning World) and the modest 6f to 1m winner of 9 races Tuscarora (by Revoque). The dam, a modest 11.5f winner, is a half-sister to 6 minor winners here and abroad. The second dam, Bag Lady (by Be My Guest), a quite useful placed maiden, stayed 1m and is a half-sister to 3 winners. (S A B Dinsmore).

"He'll be racing from mid-April onwards over five furlongs but he'll be better over six. He's scopey, well-balanced with a good attitude and for me he's certainly a good five grand's worth. If you follow him you won't go far wrong, he's a nice colt".

778. DANCE FOR JULIE (IRE) ★★★★
b.f. Redback – Dancing Steps (Zafonic).
February 17. Third foal. 14,000Y. Doncaster St Leger. Ben Haslam. The dam is an unraced sister to the winner and UAE Group 3 placed Seeking The Prize and a half-sister to numerous winners including the useful 10f winner Dancing Phantom. The second dam, Dancing Prize (by Sadler's Wells), a useful maiden, was third in the listed Lingfield Oaks Trial and is a sister to the Group 1 Fillies Mile second Dance To The Top. (Mr M J James).

"I like her quite a lot, she'll make a two-year-old, she's forward and has been working well. One for mid-May probably and she's one I'd be hopeful for".

779. DESTINY'S DANCER ★★
b.f. Dubai Destination – Cybinka (Selkirk).
April 2. Sixth foal. 7,000Y. Doncaster St Leger. Ben Haslam. Half-sister to the fair 6f winner Young Ivanhoe (by Oasis Dream). The dam, a fairly useful listed 7f winner, is a half-sister to 2 minor winners. The second dam, Sarmatia (by Danzig), was unraced and is closely related to the smart Group 2 Forte Mile winner Rudimentary and a half-sister to the champion miler and sire Kris and the champion 2-y-o and high-class sire Diesis. (Mr M J James).

"She goes well and is quite sharp. I expect she'll run in May, she's a workmanlike filly and she'll be OK".

780. KEENES ROYALE ★★★★
b.f. *Red Ransom – Kinnaird (Dr Devious)*.
April 15. First foal. 140,000Y. Tattersalls October 1. Not sold. The dam won 6 races including the Group 1 Prix de l'Opera and the Group 3 May Hill Stakes and is a half-sister to one winner. The second dam, Ribot's Guest (by Be My Guest), is an unplaced half-sister to 6 winners. (Newsells Park Stud Ltd).
"Yes, she's a nice filly out of a good mare we trained. I'm pleased with her, she has scope and a good attitude. She'll probably be racing in June over six furlongs before stepping up to seven. The dam won five races as a two-year-old".

781. MISS DREAMY ★★★
b.f. *Whipper – Highest Dream (Highest Honor)*.
April 20. 10,000Y. Tattersalls October 2. Not sold. Half-sister to the German 6f winner of 5 races Smarten Die (by Diesis), to the fair 1m winner Swainsworld (by Swain) and a winner in France by Distant Music. The dam won 3 races from 2 to 4 yrs in Fance and the USA and was listed placed and is a half-sister to 7 winners including the French listed winner and Group 3 placed Special Ring and the French listed winner Celebrissime. The second dam, Ring Beaune (by Bering), won twice in France and is a half-sister to 10 winners including the Group 1 Criterium de Saint-Cloud winner Poliglote and the Group 2 Prix de Malleret winner Animatrice. (Blue Lion Racing).
"A small, sharp filly, there's nothing wrong with her and I see her being out in late April or early May. Certainly one we'll be getting on with".

782. UNNAMED ★★★
b.c. *Choisir – Cut The Red Tape (Sure Blade)*.
April 29. €4,500Y. Tattersalls Ireland. A Oliver. Half-brother to the Irish listed 6f winner and Group 3 7f Ballycorus Stakes third Poco A Poco (by Imperial Frontier), to the Irish 2-y-o 6f winner and listed placed Gallito Castao (by Fumo di Londra) and the modest 6f winner Cookie Cutter (by Fasliyev). The dam, a fair 2-y-o 7f winner, is a half-sister to 4 winners including the smart Group 2 Beefeater Gin Celebration Mile and Group 3 7f Beeswing Stakes winner Bold Russian and the fairly useful 9f winner Axe. The second dam, Russian Ribbon (by Nijinsky), a quite useful 1m winner, is a half-sister to 4 winners including the dam of the triple South African Grade 1 winner Teal. (Mr John Maguire).
"He's quite a nice colt and I like the sire. He wasn't expensive but he's workmanlike and has a sensible head on him. Fingers crossed he'll be alright and he's probably a mid-season type two-year-old. I expect he'll be best at seven furlongs and then a mile this year".

783. UNNAMED ★★★
b.g. *Cape Cross – Lady Salsa (Gone West)*.
January 10. 19,000Y. Tattersalls October 1. Not sold. Half-brother to the unplaced 2008 2-y-o Royal Salsa (by Royal Applause) and to the quite useful 2-y-o 8.2f winner Cuban Missile (by Danehill Dancer). The dam won once at 3 yrs in France and is a half-sister to 3 winners. The second dam, Chicarica (by The Minstrel), won the Group 3 Cherry Hinton Stakes and is a half-sister to 5 winners. (Widdop Wanderers).
"He's an interesting horse. He's quite a big, scopey horse but he handles himself well and he has an economic, smooth action. You do get the odd big horse that does OK as a two-year-old and hopefully he looks like being one of them. The type for August/September over seven furlongs".

BARRY HILLS

I'm indebted to Barry's assistant, Kevin Mooney, for talking through these two-year-olds with me.

784. ALWARQAA ★★★
b.f. *Oasis Dream – Al Sifaat (Unfuwain)*.
April 1. Second foal. The dam, a quite useful 2-y-o 6f winner, is a half-sister to the useful listed 6f winner Judhoor (by Alhaarth). The second dam, Almurooj (by Zafonic), a moderate 5f and 6f placed maiden, is a half-sister to

7 winners including the smart 6f (at 2 yrs), Group 2 7f Challenge Stakes and Group 3 7f Greenham Stakes winner Munir and the very useful Irish 1m listed stakes winner and Group 1 Coronation Stakes second Hasbah. (Hamdan Al Maktoum).

"Probably not as forward in her coat as some of the other two-year-olds, but she's had two bits of work and has gone through the stalls OK and the boys are happy with her. She shows a bit of speed and she'll start off at five furlongs before stepping up".

785. ANGEL OF FASHION ★★★★
b.f. Invincible Spirit – Vanitycase (Editor's Note).
February 4. First foal. 16,000Y. Doncaster St Leger. BBA (Ire). The dam is an unplaced half-sister to one winner in Japan. The second dam, Like My Style (by Alzao), is an unraced half-sister to 6 winners including Scorpion (St Leger, Coranation Cup, Grand Prix de Saint-Cloud) and Memories (US Grade 2 winner).

"This filly has done well lately, she goes well and she'll definitely win. She's sharp but she's got a bit of scope a well".

786. ATACAMA CROSSING (IRE) ★★★★
b.c. Footstepsinthesand – Endure (Green Desert).
March 25. First foal. 38,000Y. Tattersalls October 2. BBA (Ire). The dam ran twice unplaced and is a half-sister to 6 winners including the Canadian Grade 3 winner Alexis and the Irish listed winner Freshwater Pearl. The second dam, Sister Golden Hair (by Glint Of Gold), a listed-placed winner at 2 yrs in Germany, is a half-sister to 2 winners.

"A nice horse that shows a lot of speed, he's got a good engine and he's probably a six furlong type to start with. A nice horse".

787. BEBOPALULA (IRE) ★★★
gr.f. Galileo – Pearl Bright (Kaldoun).
April 8. Fourth foal. €80,000Y. Goffs Million. BBA (Ire). Half-sister to the modest 2008 5f placed 2-y-o Gemini Jive (by Namid) and to the useful 2-y-o 6f winner and Group 2 6f Mill Reef Stakes third Berbice (by Acclamation). The dam,

a quite useful 2-y-o 7f winner, is a half-sister to 4 winners. The second dam, Coastal Jewel (by Kris), is an unraced half-sister to 5 winners.

"She's growing and she's going to need seven furlongs in the second half of the year. A nice, quality filly".

788. BE INVINCIBLE (IRE) ★★★
b.c. Invincible Spirit – Lupulina (Saratoga Six).
March 17. Tenth foal. €80,000Y. Goffs Million. BBA (Ire). Half-brother to the quite useful 2-y-o 6f winner Legal Eagle and to 4 winners in Germany by Platini, Wolfhound and Suave Dancer. The dam, a listed-placed 3-y-o winner in Germany, is a half-sister to 6 winners. The second dam, La Polonaise (by Danzig), a US stakes winner, is a half-sister to the US Grade 1 winner Prismatical.

"He's done plenty of long canters and he's a very good mover. A bit babyish at the minute, he's not very forward in his coat but I would think he's a horse that would need a race to make him grow up, but he's not done anything wrong, so I'd give him a chance".

789. CASH QUEEN ANNA (IRE) ★★★
b.f. Dr Fong – Cashel Queen (Kingmambo).
February 26. Second foal. €50,000Y. Goffs Million. BBA (Ire). The dam was placed over 1m and 9.5f and is a half-sister to 5 winners including the French 1,000 Guineas third La Nuit Rose (herself dam of the Group 3 Winter Hill Stakes winner Tam Lin). The second dam, Caerlina (by Caerleon), won the Group 1 Prix de Diane and is a half-sister to 8 winners.

"She's a little bit 'hot' at the minute but she's done very well and although she looks forward in her coat you'd have to hang on to her for a bit because of her pedigree. She's done nothing wrong and is one for the second half of the season".

790. CHAIN OF EVENTS ★★
ch.c. Nayef – Ermine (Cadeaux Genereux).
April 28. Sixth foal. 85,000Y. Tattersalls October 1. BBA (Ire). Brother to the smart 10f winner, Group 1 German Derby third and Group 2 King Edward VII Stakes third Top Lock and

half-brother to the fairly useful 5.7f (to 2 yrs) to 7f winner Hoh Bleu Dee (by Desert Style) and the quite useful 7f winner of 4 races at 4 and 5 yrs Carnivore (by Zafonic). The dam, a quite useful 3-y-o 1m winner, is a half-sister to 6 winners including the very smart 1m (at 2 yrs) and Group 3 10f Brigadier Gerard Stakes winner and 2,000 Guineas and Derby third Border Arrow. The second dam, Nibbs Point (by Sure Blade), a useful winner of the listed 12f Galtres Stakes, was second in the Group 3 Park Hill Stakes and is a half-sister to 9 winners.

"He's grown a lot, but he hasn't missed a day's work. He has a good action and a good attitude but he'll be one for the late summer onwards and next year".

791. CHAMPAGNELIFESTYLE ★★★★
b.f. Montjeu – White Rose (Platini).
January 26. Third foal. 78,000Y. Tattersalls October 1. Not sold. The dam won the Group 3 7f Prix Miesque at 2 yrs, was placed in the German 1,000 Guineas and German Oaks and is a half-sister to 4 winners including the German Group 2 winners Wild Side and Win For Us. The second dam, Wild Romance (by Alkalde), a champion 2-y-o filly in Germany, is a half-sister to 4 winners.

"She's going to need a bit of time but she's done well and grown. The Guvnor likes her but she's only ticking away for now".

792. CHELSEA MORNING (USA) ★★★
ch.f. Giant's Causeway – Binya (Royal Solo).
February 8. Second foal. $200,000Y. Keeneland September. Crispin de Moubray. The dam, a US Grade 3 winner, was Group 3 placed in France and is a half-sister to 8 winners including the dual US Grade 1 winning filly Sabin and the smart 10.5f Musidora Stakes winner Fatah Flare. The second dam, Beaconaire (by Vaguely Noble), a stakes winner of 3 races at up to 10f in France, is a half-sister to the high-class filly Kittiwake (herself dam of the Prix Jean Prat winner Kitwood and the excellent American filly Miss Oceana).

"A big, attractve filly, she's a good mover but she'll want some time and is one for the second half of the season. She's only cantered upsides but she's done nothing wrong as yet". Remember the Joni Mitchell record of the same name? I'm showing my age, I know! ST.

793. COMPTON WAY ★★★
b.c. Compton Place – Never Away (Royal Applause).
February 28. First foal. 26,000Y. Doncaster St Leger. BBA (Ire). The dam, a moderate 1m and 10f placed maiden, is a half-sister to 3 winners including the 2-y-o Group 2 5.5f Prix Robert Papin winner Never A Doubt. The second dam, Waypoint (by Cadeaux Genereux), a fairly useful 6f and 7f winner (including on the all-weather), is a half-sister to 5 winners including the Group 2 6f Diadem Stakes winner and high-class sire Acclamation.

"When he came here from the sales he looked as plain as anything, but in the last few weeks he's really thrived and strengthened. He'll be alright, he has no problems at all and I think he'll have a bit of speed".

794. ERFAAN ★★★
b.c. Forest Camp – Look For Good (Unbridled's Song).
January 13. Third foal. 150,000Y. Tattersalls October 2. Shadwell Estate Co. Half-brother to Ascot Hall (by Aldebaron), a winner of 2 races at 2 and 3 yrs in the USA. The dam, a minor US 3-y-o winner, is a half-sister to 5 winners including the US Grade 1 placed Nonproductiveasset. The second dam, Flowers Kris S (by Kris S), was stakes-placed and is a half-sister to 4 winners including the US Grade 1 winner Stocks Up.

"In three months time you won't recognise this horse. He's pulled himself together really well because when he came in he was 'up behind' and he had no action at all. He's getting going now and he'll be a nice, seven furlong horse and a tough one too".

795. ESAAR (USA) ★★
b.c. Mr Greeley – Al Desima (Emperor Jones).
March 24. Fifth foal. $500,000Y. Keeneland September. Shadwell Estate Co. Half-brother to the fair 7f (at 2 yrs), 10f and hurdles winner

Altilhar and to the South African stakes-placed winner Distance Done (both by Dynaformer). The dam, a fairly useful 2-y-o 7f winner, subsequently won in the USA, was third in the Grade 1 Yellow Ribbon Stakes and is a half-sister to 8 winners. The second dam, Miss Up N Go (by Gorytus), is an unraced half-sister to Ribblesdale Stakes winner Miss Petard (herself dam of the Park Hill Stakes winner Rejuvenate) and to the dam of the Derby winner Oath and the triple Group 1 winner Pelder.
"Currently in Dubai (mid-April). We have thirteen two-year-olds over there".

796. FANCY STAR ★★★
b.c. Starcraft - Lorien Hill (Danehill).
March 23. Second foal. Half-brother to Kyllorien (by Kyllachy), unplaced in one start at 2 yrs in 2008. The dam, a fair 7.5f winner, is a half-sister to 2 winners. The second dam, Lothlorien (by Woodman), a quite useful 1m winner, is a sister to the useful 1m (at 2 yrs) to 10f winner Monsajem and to the US 2-y-o winner Mellifont and a half-sister to 6 winners.
"He came in late so we're taking our time with him, but he's a very good mover and he's got a good way of going. He'll be alright and he'll make a two-year-old a bit later on".

797. FOOTSIE FOOTSIE (IRE) ★★★★
b.f. Footstepsinthesand – Change Partners (Hernando).
February 25. Second foal. Half-sister to the unplaced 2008 2-y-o Heaven Knows When (by Dansili). The dam, a fair 12f winner, is a half-sister to 7 winners including the useful 2-y-o 6f winner and Group 3 7f Rockfel Stakes third Total Love and the useful middle-distance winner Shonara's Way. The second dam, Favorable Exchange (by Exceller), won 3 races in France from 10f to 12f and is a half-sister to 6 winners including the Group 1 Grosser Preis von Baden winner Valour.
"A nice filly, she's very attractive and a good mover. She'll need a bit of time but she looks like she'll be a black type filly. A good 'goer' that floats along, she's done well".

798. GHOST (IRE) ★★★
b.c. Invincible Spirit – Alexander Phantom (Soviet Star).
February 11. First foal. 52,000Y. Tattersalls October 2. BBA (Ire). The dam is an unraced half-sister to 3 minor winners. The second dam, Phantom Waters (by Pharly), won twice at 3 yrs and is a half-sister to 9 winners including the Group 3 Solario Stakes winner Shining Water (herself dam of the Grand Criterium and Dante Stakes winner Tenby).
"He's only trotting at the moment after having his shins blistered, but the bigger lads ride him because he's quite excitable and they like him. He does move nicely and he's going to be a nice horse in time".

799. GREY BUNTING ★★
b.c. Oasis Dream – Ribbons And Bows (Dr Devious).
May 7. Second foal. 70,000Y. Tattersalls October 2. BBA (Ire). Half-brother to Time Medican (by Medicean), placed third over 7f on his only start at 2 yrs in 2008. The dam, a fairly useful 6f (at 2 yrs), and 9.5f winner, was listed-placed and is a half-sister to 5 winners. The second dam, Nichodoula (by Doulab), a modest 3-y-o 7f and 1m winner, is a half-sister to 8 winners including the Group 1 Juddmonte International Stakes winner Terimon.
"He's very backward at the moment, he hasn't grown much and has had a few niggling problems. A fairly late foal, I think he just needs time to grow and mature".

800. HOUSE RED (IRE) ★★★★
b.c. Antonius Pius – Cindy's Star (Dancing Dissident).
April 11. Tenth foal. €50,000Y. Goffs Million. BBA (Ire). Half-brother to the modest 1m winner Faith Healer (by Key Of Luck), to the Irish 2-y-o 7f and subsequent Hong Kong winner Ducky Divey (by Elbio) and 3 minor winners abroad by Elbio, Desert Story and Woods Of Windsor. The dam, a modest 1m winner at 3 yrs, is a half-sister to one winner. The second dam, La Duse (by Junius), is a placed half-sister to 3 winners.

"He's a bit better than a House Red! A real nice type, the Guvnor thought he was a bit too forward for is own good so he backed off him a bit. He's just stepped him back up into work now and he feels like a goer. A nice horse to sit on, not over-big but a nice mover and he's one to look forward to".

801. HOVERING HAWK (IRE) ★★
b.f. *Hawk Wing – Aurelia (Rainbow Quest)*.
January 25. Second foal. 38,000Y. Tattersalls October 2. BBA (Ire). Half-sister to the fairly useful 2008 2-y-o 7f winner Aurorian (by Fantastic Light). The dam, a fair 2-y-o 10f winner, is a half-sister to 8 winners. The second dam, Fern (by Shirley Heights), a fairly useful 12f winner and third in the listed 10f Lupe Stakes, is a half-sister to 6 winners including the Group 1 Fillies Mile winner and Oaks second Shamshir.
"She's done well lately and she's quite nice but she's grown and will need some time".

802. MARIGOLD MISS (IRE) ★★★
b.f. *Marju – Pure Gold (Dilum)*.
March 25. Fifth foal. 40,000Y. Tattersalls October 2. BBA (Ire). Half-sister to the useful 6f (at 2 yrs), 1m listed and UAE 9f listed winner and Group 2 placed Royal Alchemist (by Kingsinger), the fair 1m and 10f winner Swift Alchemist (by Fleetwood) and a winner over hurdles by Fleetwood. The dam, a quite useful 7f winner, is a half-sister to 4 winners. The second dam, Gold Runner (by Runnett), is a placed half-sister to 6 winners including the English and Irish ,000 Guineas winner Don't Forget Me.
"She's had a few niggling problems and she's never stopped growing. We're taking our time with her, she's a nice, quality filly but probably one for July or August time".

803. MAROON ★★★
b.f. *Rainbow Quest – Mamounia (Green Desert)*.
January 22. The dam, a useful winner of 4 races from 7f to 9f including the listed Sceptre Stakes, is a sister to the fairly useful 1m to 10f winner Clipperdown and a half-sister to the very useful French Group 3 13f winner Maroussie's Wings. The second dam, Maroussie (by Saumarez), won 3 races including the Group 3 10f Prix Fille de l'Air and is a half-sister to 7 winners.
"The dam was tough and this filly looks the same. She had a little problem in February but she's fine now. She's not very big and I don't think she'd take much getting ready. Even though she's by Rainbow Quest she shows a bit already and we'll crack on with her".

804. NIZAA (USA) ★★★★
b.br.c. *Dixieland Band – Star Queen (Kingmambo)*.
February 16. Fifth foal. 100,000Y. Doncaster St Leger. Shadwell Estate Co. Half-brother to Incandescent Star (by Cozzene), a minor winner of 6 races abroad. The dam, a minor US stakes winner, is a half-sister to the US Grade 3 winner Patience Game. The second dam, Starboard Tack (by Seattle Slew), is an unraced half-sister to 2 stakes winners.
"A really nice horse, he has a good way of going and you wouldn't recognise him from when he first came in. He wasn't very big but he's grown up now. Everyone who rides him likes him but he's not going to be a five furlong horse and he'll be a nice horse for the middle part of the year".

805. OUR DREAM QUEEN ★★★
b.f. *Oasis Dream – Our Queen Of Kings (Arazi)*.
February 20. Fourth foal. Half-sister to the fair 2008 2-y-o 5f and 7f winner Changing The Guard (by King's Best), to the Group 3 Brownstown Stakes winner and Group 2 Cherry Hinton Stakes third Spinning Queen (by Spinning World), the useful 10f and 12f winner and 2-y-o 7f listed-placed Shannon Springs (by Darshaan), the fairly useful dual 7f winner Amber Queen (by Cadeaux Genereux) and the Italian 3-y-o 5f winner Jekill (by Royal Academy). The dam is an unraced half-sister to 7 winners including the Grade 1 9f Hollywood Derby winner Labeeb, the Grade 2 Arlington Handicap winner Fanmore and the Group 2 9f Budweiser International Stakes winner Alsassam. The second dam, Lady Blackfoot

(Prince Tenderfoot), a very useful Irish listed winning sprinter, is a half-sister to 3 winners.
"She's been working and is due to start at Newmarket's Craven meeting in the race in which her dam finished second. She probably doesn't have the scope of her dam but she'll do her winning in the first half of the season".

806. RASHAAD (IRE) ★★
b.br.c. Smart Strike – Martinique
(Pleasant Colony).
March 28. Third foal. $650,000Y. Keeneland September. Shadwell Estate Co. Brother to the US Grade 3 winner Communique. The dam, a stakes-placed winner in the USA, is a half-sister to the Group 1 Irish Champion Stakes winner and sire Muhtarram and the US Grade 3 winner Profit Column. The second dam, Ballet de France (by Northern Dancer), won the Group 3 C L Weld Park Stakes and is a half-sister to the Group 1 Gran Premio d'Italia winner St Hilarion and the US triple Grade 2 winner Savinio.
"Currently still in Dubai".

807. RASSELAS (IRE) ★★★★
b.c. Danehill Dancer – Regal Darcey
(Darshaan).
April 28. Fourth foal. 120,000Y. Tattersalls October 1. BBA (Ire). Half-brother to Pagan Flight (by Hawk Wing), unplaced in 2 starts at 2 yrs in 2008. The dam, placed fourth once over 13f in Ireland at 4 yrs, is a sister to the listed winner Talaash and a half-sister to 2 winners. The second dam, Royal Ballet (by Sadler's Wells), ran unplaced twice over 10f at 3 yrs and is a sister to the Group 1 Racing Post Trophy and the Group 1 King George VI and Queen Elizabeth Diamond Stakes winner King's Theatre and a half-sister to the champion 2-y-o colt High Estate.
"This colt will make a two-year-old, he's a nice, compact little horse and a bit babyish at the moment. He's not as far forward as some of them but he wants to be and we'll step him up now. I think he'll come to hand pretty quick and when you ride him he feels like he's got plenty of speed. I like him, he's a real nice horse and he'll want six furlongs to start with I should think. Being a late April foal out of a Darshaan mare you'd think he'd need a bit more time but he's a willing partner".

808. RED JAZZ (USA) ★★★★★
b.c. Johannesburg – Now That's Jazz
(Sword Dancer).
February 9. Third foal. €95,000Y. Goffs Million. BBA (Ire). Half-brother to Rhapsodysfootsteps (by Halo), a minor US winner of 4 races at 2 and 3 yrs. The dam, a minor winner in the USA at 3 yrs, is a half-sister to 8 winners including two US listed stakes winners. The second dam, Mardi Gras Mombo (by Tampa Trouble), a winner of 5 minor races in the USA, is a half-sister to 7 winners.
"He goes really well and we almost ran him in the Brocklesbury. He goes very well in the stalls, he's a good mover and he'll win his races alright. He'll definitely stay six furlongs and he's a nice horse".

809. RESOLUTE ROAD ★★★
b.c. Medicean – Madam Ninette
(Mark Of Esteem).
February 2. Third foal. 38,000Y. Tattersalls October 2. Highflyer Bloodstock. Half-brother to the unplaced 2008 2-y-o Waahej (by Haafhd). The dam is an unraced half-sister to 9 winners including the very smart King's Stand Stakes and Temple Stakes winner Bolshoi and the useful sprinters Mariinsky, Great Chaddington and Tod. The second dam, Mainly Dry (by The Brianstan), is an unraced half-sister to 4 winners.
"He'll make a two-year-old, he's a nice horse that seems to have done his growing and is now starting to do OK. You wouldn't know you'd got him, he won't be a five furlong horse but he'll be nice".

810. ROCKABILLY REBEL ★★★
b.c. Reel Buddy – Its All Relative
(Distant Relative).
April 28. €18,000foal. Goffs. A & B Bloodstock. Half-brother to the fair 2-y-o 7f and 7.5f winner King Alfie (by Foxhound). The dam, a fairly useful 2-y-o dual 5f winner, is a half-sister

to 2 winners. The second dam, Sharp Anne (by Belfort), won 7 races over 5f and 6f at 2 and 3 yrs.

"He's done really well but I think he's going to want time. Royal Ascot was even mentioned but the Guvnor feels that will come too soon for him. He's a good goer and a good mover that's grown and matured". TRAINER'S BARGAIN BUY

811. SENT FROM HEAVEN (IRE) ★★★★★
b.f. Footstepsinthesand – Crystal Valkyrie (Danehill).
April 7. Fourth foal. Half-sister to the modest 2-y-o 6f winner Spinning Crystal (by Spinning World). The dam, a fair 10f winner, is a half-sister to 3 minor winners. The second dam, Crystal Cross (by Roberto), a quite useful winner of 4 races at up to 14f, is a half-sister to the Group 1 Haydock Park Sprint Cup winner Iktamal , the French Group 2 winner First Magnitude and the US Grade 2 winner Rockamundo.

"A nice, quality filly, she's only done a few canters upsides but we're only taking our time with her. She's maturing and she's grown and put on condition. From the way she goes I'd have to say she could be really nice and she'll definitely be going for black type".

812. SEYAAQ (USA) ★★
ch.c. Aljabr – Muwakleh (Machiavellian).
May 7. Half-brother to the quite useful 7f (at 2 yrs) and 1m winner Manaal (by Bahri). The dam, winner of the UAE 1,000 Guineas and second in the Newmarket 1,000 Guineas, is a sister to the high-class Dubai World Cup and Prix Jean Prat winner Almutawakel and to the useful 10f winner Elmustanser and a half-sister to the smart 10f winner Inaaq. The second dam, Elfaslah (by Green Desert), a useful winner of three races from 10f to 10.4f at 3 yrs including a listed event at the Curragh, is a half-sister to the Group 1 12f Italian Derby winner and 'King George" second White Muzzle. (Hamdan Al Maktoum).

"Still in Dubai".

813. SHARAAYEEN ★★★
br.c. Singspiel – Corinium (Turtle Island).
March 24. Third foal. 85,000Y. Tattersalls October 2. Shadwell Estate Co. Half-brother to the fair 2008 1m placed 2-y-o Decision (by Royal Applause) and to the useful 2-y-o 6f winner Dramaticus (by Indian Ridge). The dam, a smart listed 7.3f and 1m winner, is a half-sister to 6 winners including the smart 1m winner and Irish 2,000 Guineas second Fa-Eq. The second dam, Searching Star (by Rainbow Quest), a modest 6f (at 2 yrs) to 11.3f placed maiden, is a half-sister to 8 winners including the smart listed Blue Riband Trial winner Beldale Star and the listed winner and useful broodmare Moon Drop.

"A lovely looking horse, he's only cantering at present but he's shaped up really well. He was a bit boisterous when he first came in but we've settled him down and everyone who rides him likes him. He'll be a seven furlong two-year-old".

814. SUN RAIDER (IRE) ★★★
b.c. Namid – Doctrine (Barathea).
March 6. Second foal. 25,000Y. Tattersalls October 2. BBA (Ire). Half-brother to the unraced 2008 2-y-o Always Be True (by Danehill Dancer). The dam, a fairly useful 2-y-o 7f and 1m winner, is a half-sister 2 minor winners. The second dam, Auspicious (by Shirley Heights), a fairly useful 10.2f winner, is a sister to the smart Group 2 11.9f Great Voltigeur Stakes winner Sacrament and a half-sister to 5 winners and to the dam of the Group 1 winner Chorist.

"He's a big two-year-old and he'll probably need a bit of cut in the ground but he's a very good-looking horse. One for the middle of the season over seven furlongs".

815. SWEET CAROLINE (IRE) ★★
b.f. Footstepsinthesand – Dame Alicia (Sadler's Wells).
May 5. €30,000Y. Goffs Million. Brian Grassick. Half-sister to Captain Algren (by Cape Cross), unplaced in one start at 2 yrs in 2008 and to the fair Irish 12f winner Lady Alicia (by Hawk Wing). The dam, fourth in the Group 3 7f C L Weld Park Stakes at 2 yrs, won over 9f at 3 yrs and is a half-sister to the Irish Group 2 1m and US Grade 2 9f

winner Century City. The second dam, Alywow (by Alysheba), a champion filly in Canada, won 7 races including the Grade 3 8.5f Nijana Stakes and was second in the Grade 1 Rothmans International and the Grade 1 Flower Bowl Invitational.
"She's quite a nice filly but she didn't come in till late so she's just ticking over. She's got a lot of filling out to do, so she won't be out for some time".

816. SWILLY FERRY (USA) ★★★★
b.c. Wiseman's Ferry – Keepers Hill (Danehill).
February 23. Second foal. 58,000Y. Doncaster St Leger. BBA (Ire). The dam, an Irish listed-placed 2-y-o and 5f 3-y-o winner, is a half-sister to 4 winners including the Group 3 winner Prix de Flore winner Australie. The second dam, Asnieres (by Spend A Buck), a minor winner in France at 4 yrs, is a half-sister to 8 winners including the Breeders Cup Classic and 9.3f Prix d'Ispahan winner Arcangues, the Prix de Psyche winner and French 1,000 Guineas second Agathe (dam of the Group 1 winners Aquarelliste and Artiste Royal) and the dams of the 1,000 Guineas winner Cape Verdi and the dual Grade 1 winner Angara.
"He ran in the Brocklesbury at Doncaster and he picked up as if he was going to win, but he'd only done two pieces of work so he probably needed the experience. He's a nice horse, very laid-back and a lovely horse to deal with. He's a winner waiting to happen and I think he's crying out for six furlongs".

817. TAMAATHUL ★★
gr.c. Tiger Hill – Tahrir (Linamix).
February 8. First foal. The dam, a useful dual 7f winner, is a sister to the listed 7f Prix Djebel winner and dual Group 3 placed Mister Charm and to the French listed 7f winner Green Channel and a half-sister to the Group 3 Prix de Guiche winner Mister Sacha (by Tiger Hill). The second dam, Miss Scaha (by Last Tycoon), won the listed Topaz Sprint Stakes in Ireland at 3 yrs and is a half-sister to 6 winners including the Italian listed 7.5f winner Pinta.
"Currently still in Dubai".

818. TASMEEM (IRE) ★★
gr.c. Acclamation – Park Approach (Indian Ridge).
April 1. First foal. 135,000Y. Tattersalls October 2. Shadwell Estate Co. The dam, a fair 5f to 7f placed maiden (including at 2 yrs), is a half-sister to 4 winners. The second dam, Abyat (by Shadeed), is an unraced half-sister to 8 winners including the Group 1 Middle Park Stakes winner Hayil.
"He's a very backward horse and all he's done is a few canters upsides. He hasn't shown us anything as yet".

819. TIPPERARY BOUTIQUE (IRE) ★★
b.f. Danehill Dancer – Moselle (Mtoto).
April 1. Fifth foal. €90,000Y. Goffs Million. BBA (Ire). Half-sister to the dual French winner (including over 9f at 2yrs) and listed-placed Leitmotiv and to the minor French winner Commedia dell'arte (both by Sadler's Wells). The dam won 3 races including the listed 10.4f Middleton Stakes and the listed 10.2f Virginia Stakes and is a half-sister to 6 winners. The second dam, Miquette (by Fabulous Dancer), won over 12f and 13.5f in France including a listed event and is a half-sister to 6 winners including the Group 3 Prix de Pomone winner Moquerie (herself the dam of 4 listed winners).
"A nice filly that's well put together and she carries quite a lot of condition. She came in late so she's miles behind the rest, but everyone likes her and she's got a bit of spirit too. One for the second half of the season".

820. TRANQUIL WATERS (IRE) ★★
b.c. Sadler's Wells – Belle Of Honour (Honour And Glory).
March 3. Second living foal. €100,000Y. Goffs Million. BBA (Ire). The dam is an unraced half-sister to 6 winners including the Japanese 2-y-o winner and listed placed Shinko Nobby. The second dam, Christabelle (by Northern Dancer), was placed once at 2 yrs in Ireland and is a half-sister to the Group 3 Prix de Minerve winner I Will Follow (the dam of Rainbow Quest), to the Group 3 Fred Darling Stakes winner Slightly Dangerous (the dam of

Commander in Chief, Warning, Deploy, Dushyantor and Yashmak) and to the unraced Idyllic (the dam of Scenic).
"A lovely horse and a lovely mover, but much more of a three-year-old type".

821. WEST LEAKE STAR (IRE) ★★
b.c. Antonius Pius – Red Beach (Turtle Island).
February 20. First foal. 44,000Y. Doncaster St Leger. BBA (Ire). The dam is an unraced half-sister to 5 minor winners here and abroad. The second dam, Velinowski (by Malinowksi), is an unraced half-sister to 7 winners including the Group 3 Princess Of Wales's Stakes winner Lord Helpus.
"He's not very big but he's actually growing now and it's about time he did. He's yet to show us anything, but sometimes all they need is a bit of time".

822. WINGED ★★★
b.f. Hawk Wing – Aurelia (Rainbow Quest).
January 25. Second foal. 38,000Y. Tattersalls October 2. BBA (Ire). Half-sister to the fairly useful 2008 2-y-o 7f winner Aurorian (by Fantastic Light). The dam, a fair 2-y-o 10f winner, is a half-sister to 8 winners. The second dam, Fern (by Shirley Heights), a fairly useful 12f winner and third in the listed 10f Lupe Stakes, is a half-sister to 6 winners including the Group 1 Fillies Mile winner and Oaks second Shamshir.
"She's a nice filly, she's grown and has done really well. Seven furlongs will suit her and she'll be really nice".

823. UNNAMED ★★
b.f. Acclamation – Anneliina (Cadeaux Genereux).
April 23. Fourth living foal. 90,000Y. Doncaster St Leger. BBA (Ire). Half-sister to the quite useful 2008 2-y-o 5.8f winner Rioliina (by Captain Rio), to the quite useful 2-y-o triple 6f winner Cheap Street (by Compton Place) and the moderate 5f and 6f winner of 4 races Piccostar (by Piccolo). The dam is a placed half-sister to 5 minor winners. The second dam, Blasted Heath (by Thatching), a useful winner of 2 listed events over 5f (at 2 yrs) and 1m, is a half-sister to 5 winners including the Group 1 Middle Park Stakes winner Balla Cove.
"Unfortunately she had an accident when being broken so she's needed plenty of time off. She's only just got going, so although she's lengthened and done quite well in herself we've done nothing with her yet".

824. UNNAMED ★★
b.f. Le Vie Dei Colori – Emma's Star (Darshaan).
January 30. Sixth foal. 28,000Y. Doncaster St Leger. BBA (Ire). Half-sister to the useful 6f winner of four races Genki (by Shinko Forest) and to the fair 6f winner Hazelrigg (by Namid). The dam, a winner over 8.5f in Italy at 3 yrs, is a half-sister to 4 other winners in Italy. The second dam, Notte Chiara (by Artaius), won the listed Premio Minerva and is a half-sister to 8 winners.
"He's growing like mad and is 'up behind' so he's on the back burner at the moment. The Guvnor didn't like him when he first arrived from the sales but he does now. He moves OK but how good he is we don't know because he's doing nothing yet".

825. UNNAMED ★★★★
b.f. Zamindar – Esplanade (Danehill).
April 3. Sister to the quite useful 2-y-o 6f winner Seasider. The dam, a fair 10f winner, is a sister to the French listed 1m winner Kithira and a half-sister to the Group 3 Prix de Psyche winner Tenuous. The second dam, Atropa (by Vaguely Noble), was placed over 12f and is a half-sister to 4 winners. (Khalid Abdulla).
"She's a very attractive filly and has done well considering the time she's had off. It took her a little time to get used to the surroundings but she's settled down now. She's grown and filled out, she's a good mover and she just might be a really nice filly".

826. UNNAMED ★★
ch.c. Shamardal – Lonely Ahead (Rahy).
April 7. The dam, a useful 2-y-o 6f winner, is a half-sister to the smart 2-y-o Group 2 7f Champagne Stakes winner Almushahar. The second dam, Sayyedati (by Shadeed), won the Group 1 7f Moyglare Stud Stakes and the Group

1 6f Cheveley Park Stakes at 2 yrs, the 1,000 Guineas and Prix Jacques le Marois at 3 yrs and the Sussex Stakes at 5 yrs. She is a full or half-sister to numerous winners including the very smart multiple Group 1 winner Golden Snake.
"He's on the back burner at the minute, he didn't do well to start with but he's improving now. Just a plain horse, he's got a lot of growing to do and he's immature. It'll be a while before we see him out".

827. UNNAMED ★★★
b.c. Xaar – New Orchid (Quest For Fame).
March 9. Half-brother to the Group 1 6f Haydock Sprint Cup winner African Rose (by Observatory). The dam, a useful 10f winner and third in the Group 3 Lancashire Oaks, is a half-sister to 3 winners including the champion 2-y-o Distant Music, winner of the Group 1 7f Dewhurst Stakes, the Group 2 7f Champagne Stakes and the Group 2 9f Goffs International Stakes. The second dam, Musicanti (by Nijinsky), a French 14.5f winner, is a half-sister to the top-class American middle-distance colt Vanlandingham, winner of the Washington D.C. International, the Jockey Club Gold Cup and the Suburban Handicap. (Khalid Abdulla).
"He's a great big horse but he's a good mover and light on his feet. He reminds me of Distant Music. Although he's big he's not too heavy and he's a good goer, so I'd say he'll be alright".

828. UNNAMED ★★★
b.c. Aptitude – Rouwaki (Miswaki).
March 1. Third foal. Half-brother to the quite useful 1m winner Rattan (by Royal Anthem). The dam is an unplaced half-sister to the Grade 1 Kentucky Oaks winner Flute. The second dam, Rougeur (by Blushing Groom), won over 10f and 12f in the USA. (K Abdulla).
"He's quite a nice horse that's well put together. He isn't going to be that quick but he'll be a nice horse for six furlongs plus. He's took all his work well and nothing bothers him".

829. UNNAMED ★★★★
b.f. Invincible Spirit – Saramacca (Kahyasi).
April 12. Sixth foal. €95,000Y. Goffs Million.

BBA (Ire). Sister to the unplaced 2008 2-y-o Invincible Miss and half-sister to the fairly useful 12f to 15f and hurdles winner Rajeh (by Key Of Luck). The dam, a 12f winner at 4 yrs, is a half-sister to 6 winners. The second dam, Herila (by Bold Lad), won at 3 yrs in France and is a half-sister to 8 winners.
"This is a quality filly and she hasn't got an owner yet. She's really nice and she's going to be a second half of the season two-year-old. Seven furlongs plus will suit her".

830. UNNAMED ★★
b.f. Storm Cat – Sayyedati (Shadeed).
February 22. Half-sister to the smart 2-y-o Group 2 7f Champagne Stakes winner Almushahar (by Silver Hawk), to the useful 2-y-o 6f winner Lonely Ahead (by Rahy), the quite useful 8.3f winner Cunas (by Irish River) and the US 1m winner Djebel Amour (by Mt Livermore). The dam won the Group 1 7f Moyglare Stud Stakes and the Group 1 6f Cheveley Park Stakes at 2 yrs, the 1,000 Guineas and Prix Jacques le Marois at 3 yrs and the Sussex Stakes at 5 yrs. She is a full or half-sister to numerous winners including the very smart multiple Group 1 winner Golden Snake. The second dam, Dubian (by High Line), won 4 races including the Group 1 10f Premio Lydia Tesio, was third in the Oaks and the Irish Oaks and is a half-sister to the triple champion hurdler See You Then. (Mohammed Obaida).
"She very 'up behind' at the minute, immature physically and quite a quirky character. She'll take a bit of time".

831. UNNAMED ★★
b.f. Oasis Dream – Serene View (Distant View).
February 1. Half-sister to Tranquil Tiger (by Selkirk), a winner of 6 races from 10f to 14f including 4 listed events. The dam, a French 1m winner, was listed placed twice and is a half-sister to several winners. (Khalid Abdulla).
"Not yet in training in mid-April".

832. UNNAMED ★★★
b.br.f. Chapel Royal – Storm Dove (Storm Bird).
April 7. Fifth foal. Half-sister to the fairly useful

2-y-o 1m winner and 3-y-o listed placed Cruel Sea (by Mizzen Mast) and to the fairly useful 2-y-o 7f winner Good Standing (by Distant View). The dam, a 2-y-o 6f and useful 3-y-o listed 7f winner at Goodwood, was placed in the Group 3 Kiveton Park Stakes and is a half-sister to a minor stakes-placed winner. The second dam, Daeltown (by Dictus), a smart French filly, won at up to 10f. (Khalid Abdulla).

"She's a nice filly but she's just ticking along gently at present. She's grown and matured after being a very slight filly when she came in. A good mover, she's one for the second half of the season but she's quite a nice filly".

833. UNNAMED ★★
ch.c. Danehill Dancer – Waratah
(Entrepreneur).
March 23. Third foal. €150,000Y. Goffs Million. BBA (Ire). Half-brother to the unplaced 2008 2-y-o Aigle de Mer (by Hawk Wing) and to a minor winner abroad by Spartacus. The dam won over 10f in Italy and is a half-sister to 6 winners including the very useful 2-y-o 7f winner and Group 3 Musidora Stakes third Etoile. The second dam, La Luna (by Lyphard), a winner over 9f at 3 yrs in France, is a sister to the Group 3 Prix Daphnis and Group 3 Prix Thomas Bryon winner Bellypha and a half-sister to the Prix Eugene Adam winner Bellman and the Peruvian Grade 1 winner Run And Deliver.

"We haven't sold him yet but he goes well and he's a good goer. He's grown and we're not doing much with him just yet".

834. UNNAMED ★★
b.f. Mizzen Mast – Zaghruta
(Gone West).
May 8. Fifth foal. The dam is an unraced sister to the champion 2-y-o and 3-y-o Zafonic, winner of the 2,000 Guineas, the Dewhurst Stakes, the Prix de la Salamandre and the Prix Morny and to the smart Group 3 6f Prix de Cabourg winner Zamindar. The second dam, Zaizafon (by The Minstrel), won twice over 7f at 2 yrs and was placed in the Group 1 1m Queen Elizabeth II Stakes and the Group 3 1m Child Stakes. She is a half-sister to the unraced Modena, herself dam of the Eclipse Stakes and Phoenix Champion Stakes winner Elmaamul. (Khalid Abdulla).

"A nice filly with a lovely temperament, she's just ticking away at the minute but she's a good mover and one for the second half of the season".

JOHN HILLS
835. AFFIRMABLE ★★
b.f. Doyen – Bella Bellisimo (Alzao).
April 1. Third foal. Half-sister to the unplaced 2008 2-y-o Against The Rules (by Diktat) and to the fair 7f winner Scroll (by Mark Of Esteem). The dam, a 2-y-o 6f winner, is a half-sister to the 1m winner Ros The Boss – both quite useful. The second dam, Bella Vitessa (by Thatching), is unplaced half-sister to 6 winners including the German Group 1 12f Aral-Pokal and listed Pretty Polly Stakes winner Wind In Her Hair and the Grade 3 Vineland Handicap and Pretty Polly Stakes winner Capo di Monte. (Longview Stud & Bloodstock Ltd).

"She came in late, she's very attractive and has a bit of quality about her but she needs to get some strength".

836. BOMBARDINO (IRE) ★★★
b.c. Pivotal – Magnolia Lane
(Sadler's Wells).
January 24. First foal. 45,000Y. Tattersalls October 1. Not sold. The dam is a placed sister to the Group 1 Ascot Gold Cup and Coronation Cup winner Yeats and a half-sister to the Group 2 Royal Whip Stakes winner Solskjaer and the Japanese stakes winner and Grade 1 fourth Tsukuba Symphony. The second dam, Lyndonville (by Top Ville), a minor Irish 3-y-o 14f winner, is a half-sister to 4 winners including the Group 1 Fillies Mile winner Ivanka. (Gary & Linnet Woodward).

"He's a very nice, solid horse and he has an interesting pedigree being by Pivotal and out of a full-sister to Yeats. He's not going to be ready until the second half of the year but he's a lovely mover and the breeder pointed out to me that Yeats actually won as a two-year-old. So this is another horse with a chance to be a good one".

837. CELTIC RANSOM ★★★★
b.c. Red Ransom – Welsh Valley (Irish River).
February 10. Third foal. 30,000Y. Doncaster St Leger. A Skiffington. Half-brother to the fairly useful 2-y-o 7f winner Brecon (by Unfuwain) and the fair 2-y-o 9.5f winner Man Of Gwent (by In The Wings). The dam, a modest 6f placed maiden, is a half-sister to 8 winners including the Group 2 6f Gimcrack Stakes winner Chilly Billy and the US Grade 3 placed Mister Approval. The second dam, Sweet Snow (by Lyphard), won over an extended 10f in France and is a half-sister to 9 winners including the US stakes winners Windansea and Sing And Swing. (Mrs Kingham & Partners).
"Bred by Kevin Mercer at Usk Valley Stud, this colt is really nice. The sire is decent for a start and I think the colt has a really good future. He's well-balanced, he's got speed and he's going to make a two-year-old. He's not quite ready to press buttons with yet and he'll be one for June onwards. A very likeable colt".

838. ITWASONLYAKISS ★★★
b.f. Exceed And Excel – Reem One (Rainbow Quest).
April 13. Second foal. €26,000Y. Goffs Sportsman's. Amanda Skiffington. The dam, a fair 9f winner, was placed over 12f. The second dam, Felona (by Caerleon), a useful 9f and 10f winner, is a half-sister to the listed 1m winner and St James's Palace Stakes third Aramram. (Gary Woodward & Donald Kerr).
"As soon as the sun comes she'll be out there. The sire has done very well and although she's out of a Rainbow Quest mare this filly looks like an early two-year-old. I don't see her as necessarily a five furlong sprinter but she has got natural speed".

839. KEY LIGHT (IRE) ★★★
b.f. Acclamation – Eva Luna (Double Schwartz).
January 28. Ninth foal. €47,000Y. Goffs Million. A Skiffington. Half-sister to the quite useful Irish 2-y-o Group 2 7f Debutante Stakes fourth National Swagger (by Giant's Causeway) and to the Irish 3-y-o 5f winner Burma Tiger (by Indian Ridge). The dam, a very useful winner of 5 races at up to 6f at 2 yrs including the Group 1 Heinz 57 Phoenix Stakes and the Group 3 6f Railway Stakes, is a sister to the Group 3 1m Futurity Stakes winner Cois Na Tine. The second dam, Guess Again (by Stradavinsky), won over 1m at 3 yrs and is a half-sister to 4 winners. (Mrs P de W Johnson).
"She's a nice filly, she has a bit of natural speed and she wants a bit of sunshine on her to pull herself together a bit. The sire has been very successful and the dam won a Group One but she has been a bit disappointing at stud. This filly looks like she'll be quite fast and she'll be a two-year-old".

840. LETSPLAYBALL ★★★★
b.c. Dansili – Rosapenna (Spectrum).
March 27. First foal. 35,000Y. Tattersalls October 2. Not sold. The dam, a half winner of 4 races at 3 and 4 yrs, is a half-sister to 6 winners. The second dam, Blaine (by Lyphard's Wish), is a placed half-sister to 7 winners including Alligatrix (dam of the dual Group 1 winner Croco Rouge and the top-class broodmare Alidiva).
"He's nice and he's going very well right now. He's not one of those big, backward Dansili's, he's very 'together' and collected. He's got quality, he's slightly close coupled and I'm on the verge of giving him some work. He's one of my most forward ones, which you wouldn't necessarily expect from Dansili, top-class stallion though he is".

841. MONOGRAPH ★★
b.g. Kyllachy – Beading (Polish Precedent).
April 16. Fourth foal. Half-brother to the fair 2008 2-y-o 7f winner Glowing Praise (by Fantastic Light), to the quite useful dual 7f winner Cindertrack (by Singspiel) and the modest 1m winner Satin Braid (by Diktat). The dam, a quite useful 3-y-o 1m winner, is a half-sister to 3 winners including the listed Atalanta Stakes winner Intrepidous. The second dam, Silver Braid (by Miswaki), a useful 2-y-o 7f winner, was second in the Group 3 7.3f Fred Darling Stakes and is a half-sister to 5 winners here and abroad. (Longview Stud & Bloodstock Ltd).

"He's only just come to me but I trained the dam and she was very capable. We had a bit of fun with her and she won on the July course at Newmarket. This horse was gelded before he arrived and he should make a two-year-old but not just yet. A horse with a nice action".

842. PEEBLESONTHEBEACH ★★★
b.c. Footstepsinthesand – Peep Show
(In The Wings).
February 15. Second foal. 30,000Y. Tattersalls October 1. A Skiffington. The dam ran once unplaced and is a sister to one winner and a half-sister to 5 winners including the Group 3 John Porter Stakes and Group 3 Lancashire Oaks winner Spout. The second dam, Arderelle (by Pharly), a quite useful 3-y-o 10f winner, is a half-sister to 8 winners including the Group 2 Prix Greffuhle winner Arokar.
"The family doesn't look like it's that fast, but this colt does look to have some speed. I've got two by this stallion and I like them both. He'll want a minimum of six and more likely seven furlongs as a two-year-old, so his season will start then. He's got what it takes, he's very well-balanced and once the distances come right for him I think he'll be up and running".

843. SILK RUNNER (IRE) ★★★
ch.f. Barathea – Sao Gabriel
(Persian Bold).
May 9. Fifth foal. €85,000Y. Goffs Million. Not sold. Half-sister to the quite useful Irish 3-y-o 7f winner Spring Snowdrop (by Danehill Dancer). The dam is an unraced half-sister to 6 winners including the Champion Stakes winner Legal Case and the dam of the Oaks winner Love Divine. The second dam, Maryinsky (by Northern Dancer), won twice in the USA and is a half-sister to 10 winners. (Tony Waspe Partnership).
"She came in very late but she's going to make a two-year-old even though she's behind some of the others. She's a real, scopey filly and she's got some natural speed. I'm looking forward to her in the second half of the season".

844. VOLATILIS ★★★
b.c. Antonius Pius – Fire Flower (Sri Pekan).
March 22. Fourth foal. €10,000Y. Tattersalls Ireland. Not sold. The dam is an unraced half-sister to 3 minor winners. The second dam, Dimant Rose (by Tromos), is an unraced half-sister to Rainbow Quest.
"A cracking little colt, he's a bonny, well-balanced, early two-year-old and he's doing nicely now".

845. UNNAMED ★★★
b.c. Hernando – First Fantasy (Be My Chief).
March 7. Fifth foal. 30,000Y. Tattersalls October 2. Amanda Skiffington. Half-brother to Sitwell (by Dr Fong), unplaced in one start at 2 yrs in 2008 and to the quite useful 1m winner Infatuate (by Inchinor). The dam, a fairly useful listed winner of 6 races from 9.7f to 10.5f, is a half-sister to 3 winners. The second dam, Dreams (by Rainbow Quest), a quite useful 10.3f winner, is a half-sister to 4 winners including Jeune (winner of the Melbourne Cup and the Group 2 12f Hardwicke Stakes) and the Group 2 12f King Edward VII Stakes winner Beneficial.
"A lovely horse, the dam was pretty good and the sire can really get a good horse, even though his foals are not commercial at the sales. I think this is a lot of horse for what he cost and he's going to be one for the second half of the season. His real future lies as a three-year-old over ten furlongs and maybe more, he has a Derby entry and he's a beauty".

846. UNNAMED ★★★
ch.f. Singspiel – Fragrant Oasis (Rahy).
April 15. Fifth foal. 11,000Y. Tattersalls October 2. Amanda Skiffington. Sister to the modest 8.7f winner Forbidden and half-sister to the fair 10f winner Carpet Ride (by Unfuwain) and the fair 7f and 1m winner of 5 races Hazewind (by Daylami). The dam, a listed 7f winner, is closely related to the modest 7f winner Mithi Al Gamar and a half-sister to the quite useful winners Wakeel and Top Guide. The second dam, Raahia (by Vice Regent), a fairly useful 2-y-o 6f winner, was third in the Group 3 7f Nell Gwyn Stakes.
"She's a little cracker and perhaps a little bit more forward than you'd expect for a Singspiel.

The dam was pretty quick though and this is a tough, hardy, cheeky filly that will want fast ground. She's not tall, but she's got a bit of substance about her and I really like her. She'll make a two-year-old".

847. UNNAMED ★★★
b.c. Montjeu – Ionian Sea (Slip Anchor).
April 19. Ninth foal. Closely related to the 2-y-o 1m winner and Derby second The Great Gatsby and to the 2-y-o 7f winner and Group 1 Racing Post Trophy third Magritte (both by Sadler's Wells) and half-brother to the quite useful 12f and 13f winner Marigold (by Marju) and the French winner and Group 3 second Ithaca (by Groom Dancer). The dam, a listed 12f winner in France, is a half-sister to 4 winners including the Derby second Blue Stag. The second dam, Snow Day (by Reliance II), won the Group 3 Prix de Royaumont and the Group 3 Prix Fille de l'Air and is a half-sister to the Royal Lodge Stakes winner Made Of Gold.
"He's a lovely colt, I've leased him from Coolmore and he's a big baby at present. He's just got something about him – he's a beautiful walker and a very smooth mover. So all you can say about him is that the raw material is there and he's got a chance. He's a dream rather than a known quantity. It's interesting to note that I used to ride out Snow Day (the second dam) for John Gosden in California".

848. UNNAMED ★★★★
b.c. Oasis Dream – Night Mirage (Silver Hawk).
February 19. 30,000Y. Tattersalls October. Not sold. Half-brother to the quite useful 2-y-o 6f to 8.7f winner and listed-placed Dream Fantasy (by Barathea), to the quite useful 2-y-o 1m winner Night Mist, the modest 12f winner Kirkstone (both by Alzao)and the modest 10f winner Borrowdale (by Royal Applause). The dam won twice over 9f at 3 yrs and is a half-sister to 6 winners including the US stakes winner and Grade 1 placed Jack Of Clubs. The second dam, Colony Club (by Tom Rolfe), won 6 minor races in the USA and is a half-sister to the US Grade 2 winner Pass The Glass. (Mr & Mrs G Middlebrook).

"The first horse I've had for the Middlebrooks who are successful breeders and this horse is very, very nice. He's high up on my list but he's in separate parts as we speak, so he's going to need a bit of time. I would say he'd make a two-year-old in the second half of the year and he shows natural speed".

849. UNNAMED ★★
ch.c. Giant's Causeway – Stark Passage (Woodman).
April 20. Fifth foal. $60,000Y. Keeneland September. James Delahooke. Half-brother to 2 minor winners. The dam, a minor US 4-y-o winner, is a half-sister to the US dual Grade 2 winner and Grade 1 placed Nasty Storm. The second dam, A Stark Is Born (by Graustark), won 4 minor races in the USA and is a half-sister to 2 stakes winners. (Gary Woodward & Donald Kerr).
"I admire the stallion Giant's Causeway and this filly has settled in well. She doesn't look an early sort but she's a good mover and thoroughly likeable although I don't know much about her yet. One for the back-end of the season".

850. UNNAMED ★★★
ch.f. Motivator – Subya (Night Shift).
March 8. Eleventh foal. 30,000Y. Tattersalls October 2. J Hills. Half-sister to the 2008 2-y-o 7f and 1m winner and subsequent US 3-y-o Grade 3 6.5f winner Battle Of Hastings (by Royal Applause), to the smart 12f listed winner Villa Carlotta (by Rainbow Quest), the fairly useful 7f winner and listed-placed Subyan Dreams (by Spectrum), the fairly useful 10f winner Seeyaaj (by Darshaan), the moderate 10f winner Jemima's Art (by Fantastic Light), the moderate 1m and jumps winner Ohana (by Mark Of Esteem) and the moderate 14f and hurdles winner Color Man (by Rainbow Quest). The dam was a very useful winner of 5 races from 5f (at 2 yrs) to 10f including the Lupe Stakes, the Masaka Stakes and the Milcars Star Stakes (all listed events). The second dam, Ashshama (by Arctic Tern), a quite useful 10f winner, is a half-sister to 4 winners including the German listed winner and Group 3 placed Shine Share.

"She's interesting because there's a big pedigree update with Battle of Hastings winning a Grade 3 6.5 furlong event the other day at Santa Anita. So the filly has a lot going for her, she's quite light framed and you couldn't say she'd be early, but she goes well. She just needs to find her strength and I like her".

851. UNNAMED ★★★
ch.f. Footstepsinthesand – Susi Wong (Selkirk).
March 9. 24,000Y. Tattersalls October 2. Not sold. Half-sister to the smart 7f (at 2 yrs) to 12f winner of 7 races including the Group 3 St Simon Stakes Buccellati (by Soviet Star), to the Italian listed 2-y-o winner and Group 3 6f Premio Primi Passi second Golden Stud (by In The Wings), to the Scandinavian listed winner La Petite Chinoise (by Dr Fong) and the quite useful 10.2f winner Hope An Glory (by Nashwan). The dam won once at 3 yrs in Germany, was listed-placed and is a half-sister to 4 winners. The second dam, Stay That Way (by Be My Guest), is an unraced half-sister to the Coronation Stakes winner Chalon (dam of the Prix Ganay and Prix d'Ispahan winner Creator) and to the Irish listed winner Elegance In Design (dam of the Irish Oaks winner Dance Design).

"She's similar to my Motivator filly in that she's another one who goes quite nicely but is a bit light framed. By all accounts her dam was just the same. There's been a pedigree update with Buccellati winning the St Simon Stakes and this filly just needs a bit of time to mature, she's a bit weak at the moment".

852. UNNAMED ★★
b.f. Acclamation – Truly Generous (Generous).
March 26. Tenth foal. 20,000Y. Tattersalls October 1. Not sold. Half-sister to the French listed 1m winner and Group 3 Prix de Psyche third Antique (by Dubai Millennium), to the fair 10f, 12f and hurdles winner Nawamees (by Darshaan) and the minor French dual 11f winner Trouble Fete (by Fantastic Light). The dam won the listed Prix Petite Etoile, is closely related to the very smart Truly Special (winner of the Group 3 10.5f Prix de Royaumont and herself dam of the E.P. Taylor Stakes winner Truly A Dream) and a half-sister to 7 winners including the Group 2 13.5f Grand Prix de Deauville winner Modhish and the Group 2 12.5f Prix de Royallieu winner Russian Snows. The second dam, Arctique Royale (by Royal and Regal), won the Irish 1,000 Guineas and the Moyglare Stud Stakes and is a half-sister to the dam of Ardross.

"She's a likeable filly that's going through a growth spell right now. Even though the sire is good with two-year-olds, this one is up at the back end like a dragster. It's a nice family but this filly is going to need a bit of time".

853. UNNAMED ★★★
b.f. Montjeu – Velouette (Darshaan).
January 9. Second foal. The dam is an unraced half-sister to the Group 2 10.5f Dante Stakes and Group 3 10f Select Stakes winner Moon Ballad. The second dam, Velvet Moon (by Shaadi), a very useful Group 2 6f Lowther Stakes and listed 10f winner, is a half-sister to the dual Group 1 winner Central Park.

"This is a gorgeous filly bred by Barronstown Stud. A lovely, big, scopey filly from a proper family. They do say that a lot of Montjeu fillies can be very tricky, but so far her temperament has been exemplary. I know that Montjeu sires many more good colts than fillies but William Haggas's Mont Etoile was very good so it can happen. This filly has got the frame and the pedigree to make it".

854. UNNAMED ★★★★
b.c. Kheleyf – Victoria Lodge (Grand Lodge).
January 31. First foal. 40,000Y. Doncaster St Leger. A Skiffington. The dam is an unraced daughter of the Irish listed-placed Lake Victoria (by Lake Coniston), herself a half-sister to 5 winners including the US Grade 1 winner Delighter and the Oaks third Oakmead.

"He's a very nice colt but he's due to go to the breeze up sales. I just hope I can keep him because I think he's my nicest two-year-old. He's no five furlong horse but he can really go and he's a very nice horse. Out of a Grand Lodge mare, he's just got a bit of length across his back and he should start his career at six furlongs". This colt was sold to Wessex Bloodstock for 60,000 Guineas at the Doncaster Breeze up Sale but returned to the John Hills yard.

MICHAEL JARVIS

855. ALRASM (IRE) ★★★★ ♠
b.c. Acclamation – New Deal (Rainbow Quest).
March 29. Second foal. 150,000Y. Doncaster St Leger. Shadwell Estate Co. The dam, a minor 3-y-o 1m winner in France, is a half-sister to 3 winners including the Group 2 Lowther Stakes third Dunloskin. The second dam, Dalinda (by Nureyev), won 5 races including a Grade 3 event in the USA and is a half-sister to 4 winners. (Hamdan Al Maktoum).
"He's a big horse but very mature, he's going nicely and he looks like being one of our earlier runners. He's bred to be speedy and looks that way and although he's out of a Rainbow Quest mare he seems to take after the sire".

856. BEST INTENT ★★★
ch.f. King's Best – Hydro Calido (Nureyev).
April 8. Half-sister to the French listed 7f winner Esperero (by Forty Niner). The dam, a very useful filly and winner of the Group 2 1m Prix d'Astarte, was second in the French 1,000 Guineas and is a half-sister to the champion European 2-y-o and 2,000 Guineas second Machiavellian, to the smart Group 1 Prix Morny and Group 1 Prix de la Salamandre winner and 1,000 Guineas third Coup de Genie and the very smart Group 1 Prix Jacques le Marois winner Exit to Nowhere (by Irish River). The second dam, Coup de Folie (by Halo), won four races from 6f to 10f including the Group 3 1m Prix d'Aumale and was stakes-placed in the USA. The third dam, Raise the Standard (by Hoist the Flag), is an unraced half-sister to Northern Dancer. (Lordship Stud).
"She's a nicely balanced filly and looks like being a mid-summer two-year-old. A filly with a good action and she's a nice, forward going type with a good temperament, which is important for a King's Best. She looks like she could have some speed".

857. BEYOND DESIRE ★★★ ♠
b.f. Invincible Spirit – Compradore (Mujtahid).
April 11. Fourth foal. 55,000Y. Doncaster St Leger. McKeever St Lawrence. Half-sister to the fair 6f (at 2 yrs) to 10f winner of 6 races Cherri Fosfate (by Mujahid). The dam, a quite useful 5f to 7f winner of 4 races, is a half-sister to 6 winners including the Group 3 Princess Royal Stakes winner Mazuna. The second dam, the fairly useful 1m (at 2 yrs) and 12f winner Keswa (by Kings Lake), was listed placed and is a half-sister to 5 winners including the listed Zetland Stakes winner Matahif.
"She hasn't been with us long but she's doing well and it looks like she'll come through the summer. She has grown a bit and has gone 'up behind' but physically she's going the right way".

858. CANSILI STAR ★★★
b.c. Dansili – Canis Star (Wolfhound).
May 6. Fourth living foal. 105,000Y. Tattersalls October 1. M Jarvis. Half-brother to the unraced 2008 2-y-o Cavallo Da Corsa (by Galileo) and to the dual 1m winner Jawaab (by King's Best). The dam is an unraced half-sister to 8 winners including the very useful triple 2-y-o 5f and Group 3 1m Child Stakes winner Inchmurrin (dam of the good 7f colt and sire Inchinor), the very useful 1m winner Guest Artiste and the Group 2 6f Mill Reef Stakes winner Welney and the dam of the Coronation Stakes winner Balisada. The second dam, On Show (by Welsh Pageant), won over 10f, was second in the November Handicap and is a half-sister to 5 winners. (A D Spence).
"He looks very wintry at the moment but he's nicely balanced horse from a good, speedy family on the dam's side. Not many Dansili's are early but he looks like having the speed for six or seven furlongs and he should be nice. I like him".

859. DECORATIVE ★★★★ ♠
b.f. Danehill Dancer – Source Of Life (Fasliyev).
February 16. First foal. 130,000Y. Tattersalls October 1. John Warren. The dam is an unraced half-sister to 5 winners including the

Group 3 Prix de Flore winner Australie. The second dam, Asnieres (by Spend A Buck), a minor winner in France at 4 yrs, is a half-sister to 8 winners including the Breeders Cup Classic and 9.3f Prix d'Ispahan winner Arcangues, the Prix de Psyche winner and French 1,000 Guineas second Agathe (dam of the Group 1 winners Aquarelliste and Artiste Royal) and the dams of the 1,000 Guineas winner Cape Verdi and the dual Grade 1 winner Angara. (Highclere Thoroughbred Racing).

"Slightly 'on-the-leg' but a very active, athletic type and she goes nicely. Hopefully she'll have the speed for six furlongs and I think she'll be one of our nicer fillies. She won't be rushed because I think she just could get a little bit buzzy, but she looks racey and she's a nice filly".

860. DOROOJE (IRE) ★★★

b.c. Green Desert – Tarfshi (Mtoto).
March 26. The dam, a winner of 5 races from 7f (at 2 yrs) to 10f including the Group 2 Pretty Polly Stakes, is a full or half-sister to 4 winners including the champion 2-y-o filly and Cheveley Park Stakes winner Embassy. The second dam, Pass The Peace (by Alzao), won the Cheveley Park Stakes, was second in the French 1,000 Guineas and is a half-sister to 3 winners. (Sheikh Ahmed Al Maktoum).

"Tarfshi was a good racemare but she's been disappointing at stud. This colt is quite typical of Green Desert in that he's good-bodied and well-balanced but you'd like the mare to have a better record".

861. DYLANESQUE ★★★

b.f. Royal Applause – Ventura Highway (Machiavellian).
March 3. Third foal. Half-sister to the modest 2008 7f placed 2-y-o Venture Capitalist (by Diktat) and to the smart listed 9f (at 2 yrs) and Group 3 Derby Trial winner Alessandro Volta (by Montjeu). The dam is an unraced half-sister to 6 winners including the dam of the Group 3 winner and Irish 2,000 Guineas second France. The second dam, Hyabella (by Shirley Heights), won three races over 1m at 3 yrs including the listed Atalanta Stakes and the listed Ben Marshall Stakes and is a half-sister to 6 winners including the high-class Prince of Wales's Stakes winner Stagecraft. (Helena Springfield Ltd).

"A nice-looking, neat filly with a particularly good action and although she hasn't been with me long she certainly looks like a two-year-old".

862. ELLBEEDEE (IRE) ★★

b.f. Dalakhani – Tochar Ban (Assert).
February 20. Tenth foal. €75,000Y. Goffs Million. M Jarvis. Half-sister to the French 2-y-o 1m winner and subsequent US Grade 2 San Clemente Handicap and Grade 2 San Gorgonio Handicap winner Uncharted Haven (by Turtle Island), to the fairly useful 12f and 14f winner Albany (by Alhaarth), the fairly useful 2-y-o 7f winner Torinmoor (by Intikhab), the quite useful 12f winner Tioman (by Dr Devious), the minor US 3-y-o winner Chocolate Reef (by Wild Again) and the placed dam of the Irish Group 3 winner Ferneley. The dam, a quite useful 10f winner, is a half-sister to 6 winners including the listed Italian winner Isticanna (herself dam of the Group 2 Royal Whip Stakes winner Chancellor). The second dam, Guest Night (by Sir Ivor), a very useful 7f and 9f winner, was third in the Group 3 Fred Darling Stakes and is a half-sister to 4 winners. (S Dartnell).

"She looks very much a staying type, but she's not over big and is quite well-balanced. One for the seven furlong plus races from late summer onwards".

863. ERTIKAAN ★★

b.c. Oasis Dream – Aunty Mary (Common Grounds).
April 9. Fourth foal. 60,000Y. Doncaster St Leger. Shadwell Estate Co. Half-brother to the fair 2008 2-y-o 7f winner Pride Of Kings (by King's Best) and to the quite useful 5f (at 2 yrs) to 7f winner King's Bastion (by Royal Applause). The dam, a quite useful 2-y-o 5f winner, is a half-sister to the 1,000 Guineas, Irish 1,000 Guineas, Coronation Stakes, Matron Stakes and Sun Chariot Stakes winner Attraction. The second dam, Flirtation (by Pursuit Of Love), ran unplaced once over 7f at 3 yrs and is a half-

sister to 4 winners including the French listed 12f winner and Group 2 placed Carmita.

"He's met with a setback and we haven't seen him for a while. Obviously his pedigree is nice and it's disappointing because he did look a sharp sort, but I can't assess him properly at the moment".

864. FERDOOS ★★
b.f. *Dansili – Blaze Of Colour (Rainbow Quest).*
March 29. Second foal. 200,000Y. Tattersalls October 1. M Jarvis. The dam, a quite useful dual 12f winner, was listed-placed and is a half-sister to 5 winners including the Group 3 placed Equity Princess. The second dam, Hawait Al Barr (by Green Desert), a useful 12f to 2m winner, is out of a half-sister to the dams of the Kentucky Derby and Preakness Stakes winner Real Quiet and the high-class miler Allied Forces. (Sheikh Ahmed Al Maktoum).

"She looks very much a staying filly and is one for the autumn and next year. Quite a nice filly though".

865. GOJERI (IRE) ★★★
ch.c. *Choisir – Lady Elysees (Royal Academy).*
April 7. Second foal. 26,000Y. Tattersalls October 2. M Jarvis. The dam is an unraced half-sister to 8 winners including the US Grade 3 winner Gone For Real and the dam of the US Grade 2 winner Josh's Madelyn. The second dam, Intently (by Drone), a US stakes winner of 8 races and Grade 3 placed, is a half-sister to 7 winners. (G Moss, J Sims, R Marchant).

"Very much in the make and shape of a sprinter, he's a very strong quartered horse. He has grown a bit so although I did think he'd be particularly early I've reviewed that now and he looks more like one for the mid-summer".
TRAINER'S BARGAIN BUY

866. HIGH RANSOM ★★★★
b.f. *Red Ransom – Shortfall (Last Tycoon).*
March 15. Fifth foal. 52,000Y. Tattersalls October 2. Will Edmeades. Half-sister to the useful 9f, 12f and jumps winner Contraband (by Red Ransom), to the quite useful 10f to 13f winner Fall In Line (by Linamix) and the fair 12f and 13f winner Parachute (by Hector Protector). The dam, a useful 10f and 10.5f winner, was fourth in the Group 3 12f Princess Royal Stakes and subsequently won once in the USA. She is a half-sister to 6 winners including the useful 2-y-o dual 1m winner Al Azhar. The second dam, Upend (by Main Reef), a smart winner of 3 races from 10f to 12f including the Group 3 St Simon Stakes and the listed Galtres Stakes, is a half-sister to 6 winners including the dam of the high-class stayer and champion hurdler Royal Gait. (Thurloe Thoroughbreds XXIV).

"She's a well-grown and good-moving filly. I like her and I think she'll be a summer two-year-old, probably over seven furlongs. A nice, forward going filly with a good action".

867. HOT PROSPECT ★★★★★
b.c. *Motivator – Model Queen (Kingmambo).*
March 12. Fifth foal. 230,000Y. Tattersalls October 1. M Jarvis. Closely related to the useful French 11f and 12f winner and Group 2 Prix Noailles fourth Mount Helicon and half-brother to the very useful 6f and 7f winner Regal Parade (by Pivotal) and the minor French 10f winner Sister Sylvia (by Fantastic Light). The dam, a fair 3-y-o 7f winner, is a half-sister to 5 winners including the French listed 1m winner Arabride. The second dam, Model Bride (by Blushing Groom), is an unraced half-sister to 6 winners including the smart Queen Elizabeth II Stakes third Zaizafon (herself the dam of Zafonic) and to the unraced Modena (the dam of Elmaamul and Reams Of Verse). (A D Spence).

"A horse we like very much and by the first-season sire Motivator, he's quite like his sire and has a lovely action. A horse with a quality head, he's athletic and hopefully he'll be a late summer two-year-old".

868. MARRAYAH ★★★
b.f. *Fraam – Mania (Danehill).*
January 23. Fourth foal. 57,000Y. Tattersalls October 2. Shadwell Estate Co. Half-sister to the quite useful 2008 2-y-o 6f winner Gower Valentine (by Primo Valentino) and to the fairly useful 2-y-o 6f winner Fanatical (by Mind Games). The dam is an unraced half-sister to

4 winners including the dam of the Group 1 winners Youmzain and Creachadoir. The second dam, Anima (by Ajdal), is a placed half-sister to 8 winners including the multiple Group 1 winner Pilsudski. (Hamdan Al Maktoum).

"A small, neat filly, she looks a bit immature at the moment, distinctly wintry and backward, she has a fair bit to go but she should make a two-year-old in the second half of the season".

869. MAWZOON (IRE) ★★★★★
ch.c. Pivotal – Two Clubs (First Trump).
March 26. Sixth foal. 200,000Y. Tattersalls October 1. Shadwell Estate Co. Half-sister to the unplaced 2008 2-y-o Dance Club (by Fasliyev), to the Group 1 Haydock Park Sprint Cup, Group 2 6f Coventry Stakes and Group 2 Diadem Stakes winner Red Clubs (by Red Ransom) and the fair dual 6f winner Elusive Hawk (by Noverre). The dam won 5 races over 6f including the listed Doncaster Stakes and the listed Prix Contessina and is a half-sister to 7 winners including the 5f Windsor Castle Stakes winner and Group 1 Phoenix Stakes third Gipsy Fiddler. The second dam, Miss Cindy (by Mansingh), a fairly useful 5f to 7f winner of 6 races, is a sister to the Vernons Sprint Cup winner and useful sire Petong. (Hamdan Al Maktoum).

"He's a nice, scopey horse. A good-sized colt with a good attitude and with his pedigree you'd expect speed. At the moment I'd be looking at June or July for him. A nice horse".

870. MUSAAFER (IRE) ★★★★
b.c. Marju – Alexander Icequeen (Soviet Star).
January 17. First foal. €300,000Y. Goffs Million. Shadwell Estate Co. The dam, a useful 2-y-o 6f winner and Group 3 placed twice, is a half-sister to 2 winners including the Italian listed winner Dock Chicks. The second dam, Regal Revolution (by Hamas), a useful 2-y-o winner of 5 races including the listed 6f Firth Of Clyde Stakes, is a half-sister to one winner. (Hamdan Al Maktoum).

"He's quite a rangy, lengthy horse with a good action and I'd be looking for him to start in July. A nice sort of colt, we like him".

871. NOAFAL (IRE) ★★★
ch.c. Bahamian Bounty – Miss Party Line (Phone Trick).
April 18. Fifth foal. 60,000Y. Tattersalls October 2. Shadwell Estate Co. Half-brother to the unplaced 2008 2-y-o Sister Clement (by Oasis Dream), to the French 2-y-o listed 6f winner Corsario (by Zafonic) and the very useful 7f (at 2 yrs) and 6f winner of 4 races Bentong (by Anabaa). The dam won once at 3 yrs in France and is a sister to the US Grade 2 winner All Chatter and a half-sister to 5 winners. The second dam, La Mimosa (by Bold Forbes), a stakes winner of 5 races in the USA, is a half-sister to 4 winners including the US Grade 1 winner Caline. (Hamdan Al Maktoum).

"He's quite a nice horse, good-bodied with a plain head on him but he's good-actioned and he looks a two-year-old. He should be racing in May or June".

872. ON THE CUSP (IRE) ★★★
b.c. Footstepsinthesand – Roman Love (Perugino).
March 25. Second foal. €45,000Y. Goffs Million. M Jarvis. The dam ran once unplaced and is a half-sister to the Irish Champion Stakes, Prince Of Wales's Stakes and Singapore Airlines International Cup winner Grandera and to the 2,000 Guineas, Phoenix Stakes and National Stakes winner George Washington. The second dam, Bordighera (by Alysheba), won once over 13f in France, was second in the listed 12f Prix des Tuileries and is a half-sister to 7 winners. (S Dartnell).

"He was quite a sharp, neat-looking horse but he has grown in the last two months and has really gone 'on the leg' a bit. So from looking an early type he doesn't look anything like that now. We'll be looking for him to start during the summer".

873. PARVAAZ (IRE) ★★★
ch.c. Rahy – Saabga (Woodman).
February 1. Sixth foal. Half-brother to the quite useful 7f (at 2 yrs) and 8.5f winner Jazmeer (by Sabrehill), to the quite useful 3-y-o 1m all-weather winner Sabbaag (by Mark Of Esteem)

and the fair 9.7f winner Wasalat (by Bahri). The dam was second over 7f at 2 yrs on her only outing and is half-sister to the Irish Group 3 Futurity Stakes second and subsequent US stakes winner Newton's Law and to the Group 1 Gran Premio d'Italia winner Close Conflict. The second dam, Catopetl (by Northern Dancer), is an unraced sister to the Derby winner Secreto. (Sheikh Ahmed Al-Maktoum).

"Rather a chunky, solid horse and very typical of Rahy horses. We quite like him and he should be a summer two-year-old".

874. QUDWAH (IRE) ★★★

b.f. Acclamation – Almond Flower (Alzao).
February 21. Twelfth foal. 42,000Y. Tattersalls October 2. Shadwell Estate Co. Half-sister to the useful 2-y-o 7f and listed 7.5f winner Bakewell Tart, to the useful listed 7f winner Macaroon, the fair 2-y-o 5f all-weather winner Babeth (by Indian Lodge), the modest 5f winner Sweet Namibia (by Namid) and 3 minor winners abroad by Mujtahid, Namaqualand and Taufan. The dam won over 5f in Ireland at 2 yrs and was second in the listed Oral B Marble Hill Stakes. The second dam, Pretty Peach (by Gorytus), won over 7f in Ireland at 3 yrs and is a half-sister to 6 winners. (Hamdan Al Maktoum).

"Quite a smallish filly, but she could come to hand around June time. At the moment she looks a bit wintry and backward but she's the make and shape of a two-year-old and she should be alright a bit later on".

875. RIDE A RAINBOW ★★★

b.f. Rainbow Quest – Celtic Heroine (Hernando).
March 29. The dam, a smart 7f (at 2 yrs) and 1m listed winner, is a half-sister to 2 winners. The second dam, Celtic Fling (Lion Cavern), a fair 3-y-o 8.3f winner, is a half-sister to the outstanding champion 2-y-o Celtic Swing, winner of the French Derby and the Racing Post Trophy. (P D Savill).

"I trained the dam who was useful. This filly is tiny, but having said that the mare was too as a two-year-old but she did develop and grow. She's very likeable this filly, very busy with quite a bit of 'go' about her. I can see her being one for the back-end and for next year but as I say, she's likeable".

876. ROBINSON CRUSO ★★★

b.c. Footstepsinthesand – Miss Hawai (Peintre Celebre).
January 23. Third foal. 100,000Y. Tattersalls October 1. Demi O'Byrne. Half-brother to the Irish listed 9f winner and Group 3 Noblesse Stakes third Beach Bunny (by High Chaparral). The dam is an unraced half-sister to 3 winners including the French listed winner Mer de Corail. The second dam, Miss Tahiti (by Tirol), won the Group 1 Prix Marcel Boussac and is a half-sister to 3 winners. (M A Jarvis).

"A nice, early foal and the mare sold for quite a bit of money at the December Sales. He looks like being one of our early two-year-olds, he's sharp and should have the pace for five furlongs – or certainly six. It's a bit of a shame that to get the name we had to drop the 'E' off the end!"

877. SARBOLA ★★★★

b.c. Dubai Destination – Compose (Anabaa).
January 26. First foal. 92,000Y. Tattersalls October 2. M Jarvis. The dam, placed once at 3 yrs in France, is a half-sister to 2 minor winners. The second dam, Totality (by Dancing Brave), a quite useful 14f winner from just 2 outings, is a sister to the Epsom and Irish Derby winner Commander in Chief and a half-sister to numerous winners including the champion 2-y-o and miler Warning, the Irish Derby second Deploy, the Great Voltigeur Stakes winner Dushyantor and the Flower Bowl Handicap and Ribblesdale Stakes winner Yashmak. (Sheikh Ahmed Al Maktoum).

"A nice colt and an early foal, he's quite well-balanced and a good moving horse. I think he should make a summer two-year-old and we like him".

878. SUPER COLLIDER ★★★★

b.c. Montjeu – Astorg (Lear Fan).
February 5. Seventh foal. 230,000Y. Tattersalls October 1. J Brummitt. Closely related to the US listed stakes winner and Group 1 Prix Saint-

Alary second Asti (by Sadler's Wells) and half-brother to the French winner and Group 3 Prix de Seine-et-Oise third Amazon Beauty (by Wolfhound). The dam won the listed 1m Prix de la Calonne and is a half-sister to 7 winners including the Group 3 Prix de la Jonchere winner Android. The second dam, Action Francaise (by Nureyev), won the Group 3 Prix de Sandringham and is out of the outstanding filly Allez France. (B E Nielsen).

"He's a tall horse and really active. As his pedigree suggests we'll wait for the seven furlong races because he was bought with his three-year-old career in mind. But he's a nice, free-going sort and he should make a runner in the autumn".

879. TESSLAM ★★★
ch.c. Singspiel – Rowaasi (Green Desert).
March 21. Half-brother to the modest 2008 5f placed 2-y-o Mesyaal (by Alhaarth). The dam, a very useful 2-y-o listed 5f National Stakes winner, is a half-sister to several winners including the fairly useful 2-y-o 5.2f winner Marl. The second dam, Pamela Peach (by Habitat), a half-sister to the Jersey Stakes second Dawson Place, was a sprint winner at 4 yrs in the USA. (Sheikh Ahmed Al Maktoum).

"He's a nice, forward-going horse that looks a little bit more mature than most of the Singspiels at this stage. He certainly looks like being a summer two-year-old and he's a nice horse".

880. WAABEL ★★★
b.br.c. Green Desert – Najah (Nashwan).
March 9. The dam, a smart Group 2 10f Premio Lydia Tesio winner, is a sister to 3 winners and a half-sister to the useful 10f winner and listed-placed Tanaghum. The second dam, Mehthaaf (by Nureyev), won the Irish 1,000 Guineas, the Tripleprint Celebration Mile and the Nell Gwyn Stakes and is closely related to the Diadem Stakes winner Elnadim and to the French 2-y-o 7.5f winner Only Seule (herself dam of the Group 1 7f Prix de la Foret and Group 1 6.5f Prix Maurice de Gheest winner Occupandiste). (Hamdan Al Maktoum).

"He's a medium-sized horse, not very typical of the sire in appearance actually but he has a nice action. It may be that he takes more after the mare and I would think he's going to be a mid-summer type two-year-old"

881. YAA WAYL (IRE) ★★★
b.c. Whipper – Lidanna (Nicholas).
April 8. Sixth foal. 38,000Y. Tattersalls October 1. M Jarvis. Half-brother to the fair 2008 5f to 7f placed 2-y-o Dreams Forever (by Bachelor Duke), to the Irish 2-y-o 5f and subsequent Hong Kong listed winner Prince Monalulu (by Intikhab), the fairly useful Irish 7f winner and listed-placed Lidanski (by Soviet Star) and the quite useful Irish dual 6f winner Capall An Ibre (by Traditionally). The dam, a very useful winner of the Group 3 6f Greenlands Stakes, is a half-sister to 5 winners including the Czech 1,000 Guineas winner Shapely Star. The second dam, Shapely Test (by Elocutionist), won over 1m in Ireland and is a half-sister to a listed winner in Australia and to 4 minor winners in the USA. (Sheikh Ahmed Al Maktoum).

"He wasn't that expensive and he looks the type for the first half of the season. We've just started to do a bit with him and he goes quite nicely. Hopefully he'll be fast enough for five furlongs and he should be a speed horse".

882. UNNAMED ★★
b.c. Shamardal – Akrmina (Zafonic).
April 17. Third foal. Half-brother to the fair 2008 7f placed 2-y-o Beraimi (by Alhaarth). The dam, the fair 7f winner, is a sister to the high-class triple Group 2 7f winner Iffraaj and to the useful 2-y-o Group 3 7f Prix du Calvados winner Kareymah and a half-sister to several winners including the useful dual 1m winner Jathaabeh. The second dam, Pastorale (by Nureyev), a fairly useful 3-y-o 7f winner, is a half-sister to 7 winners including the high-class miler and sire Cape Cross. (Sheikh Ahmed Al Maktoum).

"He's a little bit plain, but quite a solid horse with good bone. He doesn't look particularly early and that's typical of the family. We don't know about Shamardal's yet but the ones I have seen to be good-boned horses that need a bit of time to develop – they don't look sharp to me. It looks like a sort of seven furlong/mile pedigree".

883. UNNAMED ★★★
b.f. *King's Best – Anaamil (Darshaan).*
February 23. The dam, a quite useful 11f winner, is a half-sister to 2 winners. The second dam, Nouskey (by Polish Precedent), a winner over 7f (at 2 yrs) and the Group 3 12f Lancashire Oaks, is a half-sister to 9 winners including the Group 1 2m 2f Prix du Cadran winner San Sebastian and the German listed winner and Group 1 placed Chesa Plana (herself dam of the Japan Cup and Grand Prix de Saint-Cloud winner Alkaased). (Sheikh Ahmed Al Maktoum).
"She's a nice, big filly, very active and a good mover. She could easily be a filly that will come to hand in August and she's a nice goer".

884. UNNAMED ★★
b.c. *Shamardal – Bahr (Generous).*
January 29. Fifth foal. Closely related to the fairly useful 2-y-o 1m winner In Dubai (by Giant's Causeway) and half-brother to the quite useful 2008 2-y-o 7f winner Raaeidd (by King's Best), the very useful dual listed 1m winner Baharah (by Elusive Quality), the fairly useful 7.5f (at 2 yrs) and UAE 7f winner Naaddey (by Seeking The Gold). The dam, winner of the listed 7f Washington Singer Stakes (at 2 yrs), the Group 3 12f Ribblesdale Stakes and the Group 3 10.4f Musidora Stakes, is a half-sister to numerous winners. (Sheikh Ahmed Al Maktoum).
"It's a late-developing family and this colt looks very similar. He's solid, good-boned and very laid-back and it looks as though he won't show us anything until the autumn".

885. UNNAMED ★★★
b.f. *Shamardal – Belle Argentine (Fijar Tango).*
April 25. Ninth foal. Half-sister to the smart 2-y-o Group 3 5f Cornwallis Stakes winner Alzerra (by Pivotal), to the useful 3-y-o 6f and 7f winner and Group 3 7f Solario Stakes third Matloob (by Halling), the quite useful 3-y-o 1m winner Saaryeh (by Royal Academy) and the modest UAE 7f and 1m winner For Once (by Green Desert). The dam won the listed 1m Prix La Camargo in France, was third in the French 1,000 Guineas and fourth in the 10.5f Prix de Diane. The second dam, Jarlina (by Pharly), is an unraced half-sister to the Group 2 Prix d'Harcourt winner Lovely Dancer. (Sheikh Ahmed Al-Maktoum).
"She's actually quite a nice-bodied horse. She doesn't have the best of forelegs but she's quite active and not a bad mover. She won't be too early and if you forgave her forelegs she's quite a nice filly".

886. UNNAMED ★★
b.f. *Alhaarth – Beraysim (Lion Cavern).*
March 1. Half-sister to the useful 6f to 1m UAE winner of 5 races Almaram (by A P Indy), to the quite useful 2-y-o 7f winner Jadaara (by Red Ransom) and the fair 9.5f winner Noubian (by Diesis). The dam, a very useful winner of the listed 7f Oak Tree Stakes, is a half-sister to the useful 2-y-o 7f winner Velour. The second dam, Silk Braid (by Danzig), was a useful winner of a 3-y-o 9f York maiden and a 12f Italian listed event and is a half-sister to the Belmont and Preakness Stakes winner and champion 3-y-o colt Risen Star. (Sheikh Ahmed Al Maktoum).
"A tall, leggy filly and in appearance she takes after her dam, but she's on the weak side at the moment and she's going to be a filly for August onwards I should think".

887. UNNAMED ★★
b.f. *Bahamian Bounty – Clincher Club (Polish Patriot).*
March 14. Eighth foal. 80,000Y. Tattersalls October 1. Angie Sykes. Half-sister to the smart 2-y-o 6f winner and Group 1 1m Racing Post Trophy third Henrik (by Primo Dominie) and to the quite useful 2-y-o 6f winners Bishop's Lake (by Lake Coniston) and Spritzeria (by Bigstone). The dam, a fair 5f (at 2 yrs) and 7.5f winner, is a half-sister to 8 winners. The second dam, Merry Rous (by Rousillon), won once at 2 yrs and is a half-sister to 5 winners including the dual Group 3 winning sprinter Tina's Pet. (Findlay & Bloom).
"She's a little bit 'on the leg' at the moment and needs to strengthen and develop. One for later in the year as she's a bit weak at the moment".

888. UNNAMED ★★
b.c. Montjeu – Delicieuse Lady (Trempolino).
March 23. Sixth foal. 220,000Y. Tattersalls October 1. Charlie Gordon-Watson. Half-brother to the Group 1 French Derby winner Blue Canari (by Acatenango), to the listed winner Blue Ksar (by Anabaa) the French winner and Group 3 placed Crabapple (by Unfuwain) and the French 2-y-o winner Ballerina Blue (by High Chaparral). The dam won 4 minor races abroad and is a half-sister to 4 winners including the US stakes winner and smart broodmare Quest For Ladies. The second dam, Savoureuse Lady (by Caerleon), winner of the Group 3 10.5f Prix Fille de l'Air and placed in four other Group events, is a full or half-sister to 14 winners including the top-class colt Mtoto and to the dam of the Group 1winner Mutamam. (HRH Sultan Ahmad Shah).
"Quite a tall horse and a bit 'on the leg' at the moment but he has a good action and we'll wait for the seven furlong races with him. The sort of two-year-old that should hopefully be nice in the autumn".

889. UNNAMED ★★★
ch.c. Bertolini – Dorrati (Dubai Millennium).
February 22. First foal. The dam is an unraced half-sister to 4 winners including the 7f (at 2 yrs) and dual listed 1m winner Baharah and the fairly useful 2-y-o winners In Dubai and Naaddey. The second dam, Bahr (Generous), winner of the listed 7f Washington Singer Stakes (at 2 yrs), the Group 3 12f Ribblesdale Stakes and the Group 3 10.4f Musidora Stakes, is a half-sister to numerous winners. (Sheikh Ahmed Al-Maktoum).
"Hopefully he's more forward than the majority of our horses, he's quite a chunky, solid sort and looks to be a speed horse. We're just starting to do a bit with him and I'm hoping he'll be one to start off in the second half of May".

890. UNNAMED ★★
b.f. Highest Honor – Geminiani (King Of Kings).
April 3. Half-sister to the fairly useful 11f and 14f winner and Group 3 2m second Amerigo (by Daylami). The dam, winner of the Group 3 7f Prestige Stakes and second in the Group 3 Musidora Stakes, is a half-sister to the 2-y-o Group 1 6f Phoenix Stakes and Group 2 5f Queen Mary Stakes winner Damson. The second dam, Tadkiyra (by Darshaan), won over 10f at 3 yrs in France and is a half-sister to 8 winners including the Group 3 winners Tashtiya, Tassmoun and Tashkourgan. (B E Nielsen).
"She hasn't been in very long and is very much a three-year-old type but she's a nice sort of filly".

891. UNNAMED ★★★
b.c. Danehill Dancer – Humble Fifteen (Feather Ridge).
February 18. Seventh foal. 130,000Y. Tattersalls October 2. Charlie Gordon-Watson. Half-brother to the minor US 3-y-o winner Nossenko (by Stravinsky). The dam, a minor US 2-y-o stakes-placed winner, is a half-sister to 7 winners including the US Grade 3 8.5f Honeybee Stakes winner Humble Eight and the Irish listed winners Royal Devotion, Thady Quill and April Starlight. The second dam, Alleged Devotion (by Alleged), is an unraced half-sister to the top-class Irish Derby and Epsom Oaks winner Balanchine and to the Group 2 winners Romanov and Red Slippers. (HRH Sultan Ahmad Shah).
"A nice enough horse but I wouldn't say he was a typical Danehill Dancer. He's a rather more solid horse with big, strong quarters. We've done very little with him because he had a bit of a setback but he's OK now and he's a very active, cheeky sort at the moment, so perhaps we should be doing a bit more with him. A nice horse that should make a summer two-year-old and he is strong".

892. UNNAMED ★★
ch.f. Pivotal – My Dubai (Dubai Millennium).
February 17. First foal. The dam, placed over 7f on her only start, is a half-sister to 7 winners including the very smart triple Group 2 7f winner Iffraaj, the useful 2-y-o Group 3 7f Prix du Calvados winner Kareymah and the useful dual 1m winner Jathaabeh. The second dam, Pastorale (by Nureyev), a fairly useful 3-y-o 7f winner, ran only twice more including in a walk-

over. (Sheikh Ahmed Al-Maktoum).
"A medium-sized filly, she's distinctly immature and has a long way to go at the moment".

893. UNNAMED ★★★
b.c. Oratorio – True Joy (Zilzal).
February 12. Eighth foal. 200,000Y. Tattersalls October 1. Charlie Gordon-Watson. Half-sister to the German listed winner Nans Joy (by In The Wings), to the US stakes-placed winner Referral (by Silver Hawk) and a minor French 4-y-o 6.5f and 7.6f winner Torbato (by Machiavellian). The dam, unplaced in one start, is a half-sister to 9 winners including the high-class July Cup winner and sire Green Desert and the US 5.5f stakes winner Yousefia (herself dam of the Group 3 Princess Margaret Stakes winner Mythical Girl). The second dam, Foreign Courier (by Sir Ivor), is an unraced half-sister to 15 winners, notably the Grade 1 winners Althea (dam of the champion Japanese 2-y-o filly Yamanin Paradise), Ali Oop and Ketoh and the dams of the Grade 1 winners Aldiza and Azaam. (HRH Sultan Ahmad Shah).
"He's a stocky, muscular sort of horse, quite short-backed. He had a bit of a setback in the winter but he's back on track now and he looks like being a summer two-year-old. He goes quite nicely, he's full of muscle and he will be a strong horse".

WILLIAM JARVIS
894. ADMIRAL COCHRANE (IRE) ★★★
b.c. Noverre – Michelle Hicks (Ballad Rock).
March 5. Half-brother to the fairly useful 2-y-o 6f winner Malvern Light (by Zieten) and to 2 minor winners abroad by Night Shift. The dam, a fairly useful Italian listed 2-y-o 7.5f winner, is a half-sister to 7 winners including the useful Group 2 1m Premio Regina Elena winner Ancestral Dancer. The second dam, Exuberine (by Be My Guest), a quite useful 1m winner, is a half-sister to 5 winners. (Dr J Walker).
"He reminds me of another Noverre colt we had for Dr Walker called Admiral Dundas. A likeable little horse, he was late coming in but he's fine now and so far so good. He's a neat colt and he'll be sharp enough".

895. CUTHBERT (IRE) ★★★
b.c. Bertolini – Tequise (Victory Note).
March 29. Second foal. 11,000Y. Tattersalls October 2. Blandford Bloodstock. The dam, a quite useful Irish 1m and 10f winner, is a half-sister to 4 minor winners. The second dam, Tameeza (by Shahrastani), ran once unplaced and is a half-sister to 5 winners. (Mr J Bowditch).
"He wasn't expensive but he's very well-balanced and has a good way of going. Quite a striking horse, I like him and I think he has ability".

896. GUESSWORK ★★★★
ch.f. Rock Of Gibraltar – Show Off (Efisio).
February 6. Fifth reported foal. Half-sister to the fairly useful 2-y-o 6f winner Bling (by Mark Of Esteem), to the fair 7f winner Bluff (by Bluebird) and the modest 6f and 7f winner Excessive (by Cadeaux Generaux). The dam, placed fourth once over 6f at 2 yrs, is a half-sister to 9 winners including the listed 5f winner and Group 2 5f second Easy Option (dam of the Group 1 Prix de la Foret winner Court Masterpiece and the Group 3 winner Maybe Forever) and the 2-y-o 5f winner and Group 2 5f third Wanton (dam of the Irish 1,000 Guineas winner Classic Park). The second dam, Brazen Faced (by Bold And Free), a quite useful 2-y-o 5f winner, is a half-sister to 8 winners. (Mrs S J Davis).
"Yes, she's a pretty nice filly. I've had most of the family and I would think this is the nicest the mare has thrown. She's very athletic and is an enthusiastic worker. I need to keep the lid on her temperament but the pedigree is strong and I'd be extremely surprised if she didn't win as a two-year-old and it's a case of whether or not she gets any black type".

897. HAYEK ★★★★
b.c. Royal Applause – Salagama (Alzao).
January 30. Second foal. 30,000Y. Tattersalls October 2. W Jarvis. The dam, a fairly useful 7f winner, is a half-sister to 5 winners including the smart listed 7f winner Madid and the useful listed 7f winner Desert Alchemy. The second dam, Waffle On (by Chief Singer), a quite useful

3-y-o 6f winner here, subsequently won in France and is a half-sister to 5 winners including the Group 3 Premio Omenoni winner Leap For Joy. (Dr J Walker)
"He's done nothing but improve physically since we bought him and he's developed into a very good-looking colt. Still a little bit on the weak side, but he's a very well-grown horse now and we think he can go a bit. He's got a good way of going and a good temperament so I'd be surprised if he didn't show some useful form".
TRAINER'S BARGAIN BUY

898. IN VIGO ★★★★
b.c. *Hawk Wing - Marie de Blois (Barathea)*.
March 12. Third foal. 57,000Y. Tattersalls October 1. John McCormack. Half-brother to the French listed 10f and 11f winner and Group 2 Prix Hocquart third Shujoon (by Sakhee) and to the fair 2-y-o 7f winner Maryqueenofscots (by Fantastic Light). The dam won twice at 3 yrs in Germany and was listed-placed and is a half-sister to one winner. The second dam, Mary Astor (by Groom Dancer), won 5 races at 3 yrs in France and is a half-sister to 11 winners including the Group 3 winner and high-class broodmare Kanmary. The dam won twice at 3 yrs in Germany, was listed-placed and is a half-sister to 2 winners. The second dam, Mary Astor (by Groom Dancer), won 5 races at 3 yrs in France and is a half-sister to 11 winners including the Group 3 winner and high-class broodmare Kanmary. (A Foster).
"Hawk Wing isn't everyone's cup of tea but I think we've done well picking up this colt. He's done very well physically and has a good way of going, so I'd be surprised and disappointed if he didn't prove well worth his purchase price. I think he's a nice horse, solid, sound and a seven furlong type two-year-old".

899. KERCHAK (USA) ★★
b.c. *Royal Academy - Traude (River Special)*.
February 22. Fourth foal. 32,000Y. Tattersalls October 2. Blandford Bloodstock. Half-brother to a minor 4-y-o winner in the USA by Real Quiet. The dam ran once unplaced in the USA and is a half-sister to 9 winners. The second dam, Pucheca (by Tom Rolfe), is an unraced half-sister to the US triple Grade 1 winner Royal Glint and to the dam of Caerleon. (The Silverback Partnership).
"Not a bad type, he's a very eye-catching horse to look at. He's training well and everything is fine with him at the moment. He hasn't shown me that much just yet but he's a very good-looking colt".

900. PERSE ★★★★
br.f. *Rock Of Gibraltar - La Persiana (Daylami)*.
February 5. First foal. The dam, a very useful dual listed 10f winner, is a half-sister to the champion 2-y-o Grand Lodge (Group 1 7f Dewhurst Stakes and Group 1 1m St James's Palace Stakes winner), to the useful 1m listed winner Papabile and the useful 10f winner Savannah. The second dam, La Papagena (by Habitat), is an unraced half-sister to 7 winners including the very useful 7f and 1m winner Pamina and the very useful 11f and 12.5f winner Lost Chord. (Gillian, Lady Howard de Walden).
"Without any shadow of a doubt if I've got one good one this is her. Everything about her is just beautiful, she's very good-looking and has a good temperament. It's more likely that she'll be better as a three-year-old, especially as the dam improved with age and it's not a two-year-old family. You won't see her out before mid-season but I love her".

901. ROCK A DOODLE DOO (IRE) ★★★
b.c. *Oratorio - Nousaiyra (Be My Guest)*.
April 27. Seventh living foal. €42,000Y. Goffs Million. Blandford Bloodstock. Half-brother to the fair 9.5f all-weather winner Lytham (by Spectrum). The dam is a placed half-sister to 4 winners including the Group 3 Princess Royal Stakes winner Narwala (herself dam of the French Group 2 winner Affadavit and 3 listed winners). The second dam, Noufiyla (by Top Ville), a middle-distance maiden, is a half-sister to 5 winners including the Cherry Hinton Stakes winner Nasseem. (Doodle Doo Partnership).
"Yes, I like him and he'll be fine. He's a sharp colt and although he was a late April foal he looks a two-year-old for certain. A strong, neat

To achieve success you should ...read between the lines:

HERNANDO
NORTHERN DANCER Sire Line

Classic Winner and Triple Champion Triple Classic Sire

The leading sire – winners to runners (**52.5%**) – in Europe in 2008 incl. Gr.1 Oaks winner and Champion UK Filly **LOOK HERE** and Gr.2 winner **CASUAL CONQUEST** (also dual Gr.1 Classic placed)

SIR PERCY
NEVER BEND Sire Line

Gr.1 winning unbeaten Champion 2-y-o and Derby winning Champion 3-y-o

The **ONLY** horse in the last 15 years to have had the speed to win over 6f as a 2-y-o and the class to win the Derby at 3

First crop are foals in 2009

PICCOLO
IN REALITY Sire Line

The most successful stallion son of **WARNING**

Gr.1 winning sprinter and a dual Gr.1 sire

Sire of over 134 ind. 2-y-o winners, incl. exciting Australian 2-y-o **TEMPLE OF BOOM**

Yearlings made up to £100,000 in 2008

VITA ROSA *NEW for 2009*
HAIL TO REASON Sire Line

First and Only Son of World Class Sire **SUNDAY SILENCE** (the sire of the winners of over 3,600 races and approximately $750 million) to stand in the UK

Classic French family of **RIVERQUEEN**

SELKIRK
NATIVE DANCER Sire Line

Dual European Champion Miler

Champion and Classic Sire of 10 ind. Gr.1 winners

Sire of 71 individual Group/Stakes winners incl. 2008 Gr.2 winners **PIPEDREAMER** and **TAM LIN**

Successful broodmare sire of **MOUNT NELSON** (Gr.1), **QUIFF** (Gr.1), **SIMPLY PERFECT** (Gr.1), etc.

WITH APPROVAL
GREY SOVEREIGN Sire Line

Triple Crown winner and Horse of the Year

Multiple Group sire of the winners of over 1600 races and $43m worldwide, including 2008 Black Type winners **SILVERFOOT, MISSION APPROVED, BROKE SHARPLY** and **INDIAN CHOICE** *(in France)*.

First European crop are 2yo's in 2009

---

info@lanwades.com • www.lanwades.com
Tel: +44 (0)1638 750222 • Fax: +44 (0)1638 751186

≡ LANWADES   The independent option™

THE LIVING LEGEND RACING PARTNERSHIP

For an inexpensive way to enjoy the benefits of being a racehorse owner, join us in 2009.

Call Steve Taplin on 07754 094204
or e-mail stevetaplin@blueyonder.co.uk

In the winner's enclosure at Chester (top picture) and Pontefract.

THE ONLY ITEM YOU'LL NEED
THIS SUMMER

The Summer Festivals Betting Guide 2009 includes in-depth analysis of over 30 of the Flat season's major betting heats including major races from France and Ireland, plus a preview of the top two-year-old races.

Now in its seventh year, the Summer Festivals Betting Guide has proven itself to be a valuable weapon in the arsenal of any serious punter.

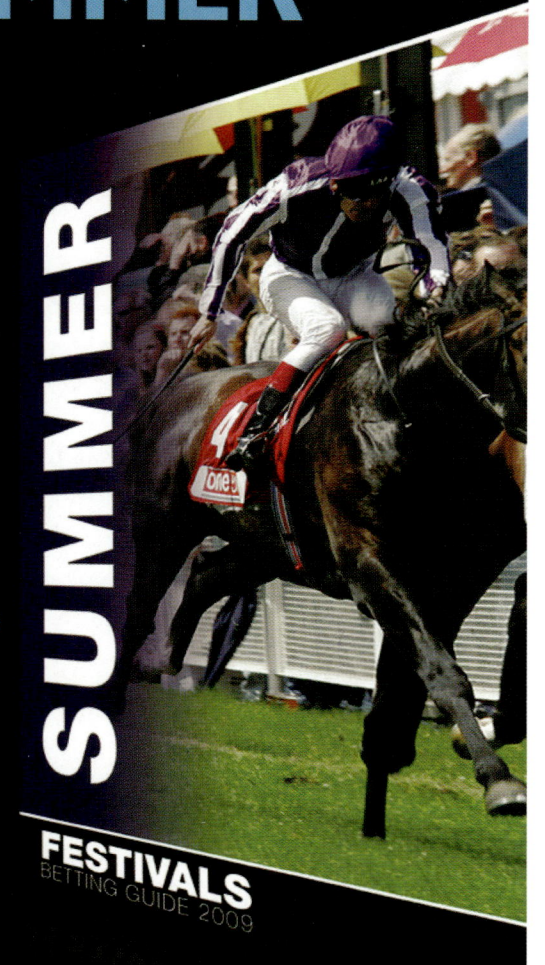

THE ULTIMATE SUMMER ACCESSORY

THE SUMMER FESTIVALS BETTING GUIDE 09

ON SALE NOW FROM WWW.WEATHERBYSSHOP.CO.UK

NAYEF

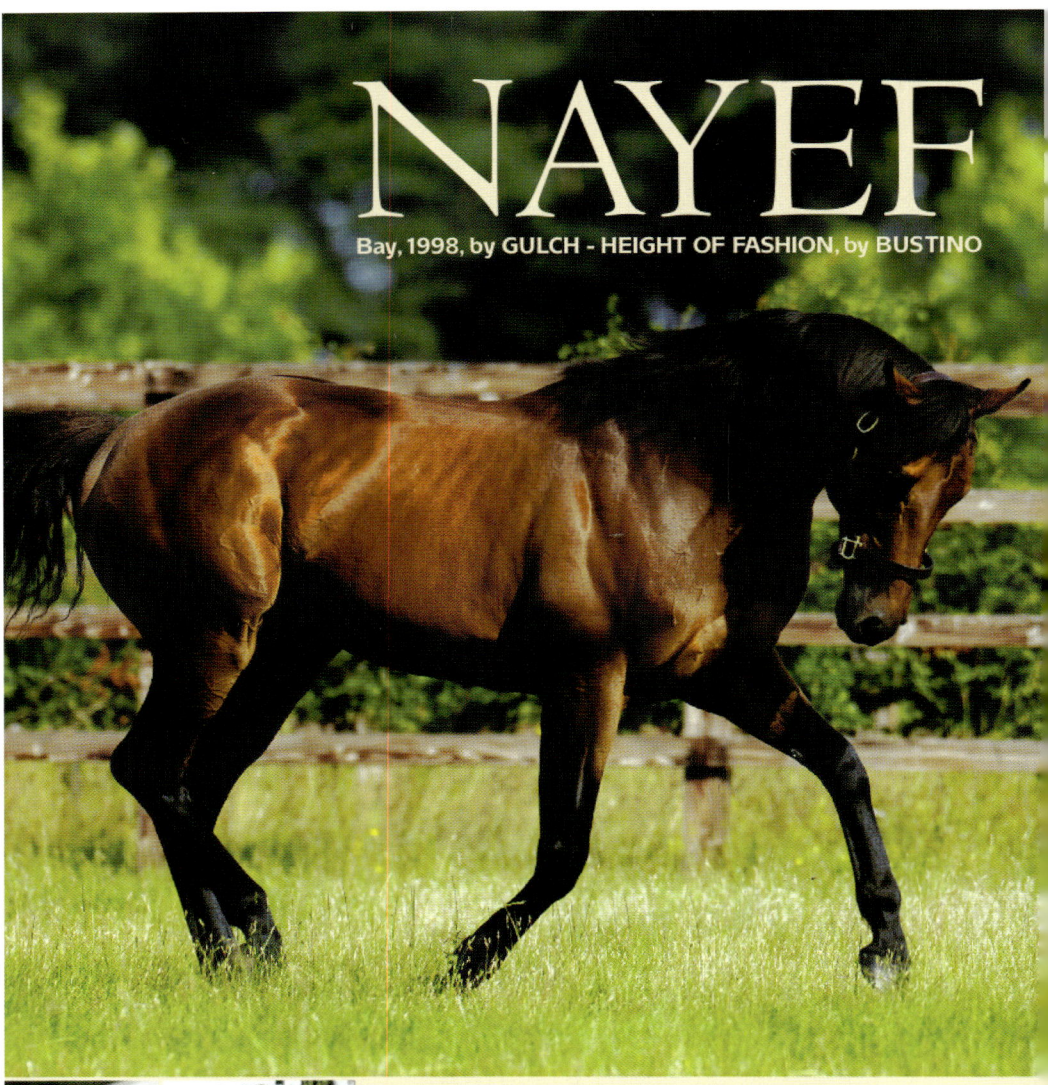

Bay, 1998, by GULCH - HEIGHT OF FASHION, by BUSTINO

THE ULTIMATE RACEHORSE.

Leading 2nd Season Sire 2008.*

FROM HIS FIRST CROP Dual **Group 1** winner **TAMAYUZ**, Prix de l'Opera (**G.1**) winner **LADY MARIAN** and the Classic placed duo: **TOP LOCK** & **SPACIOUS**. Plus Dual Listed winner **MAGIC EYE**.

*Racing Post website November 2008

Contact: RICHARD LANCASTER, JOHNNY PETER-HOBLYN or LOUISE CHANDLER
on +44 (0)1842 755913
e-mail: enquiries@shadwellstud.co.uk
www.shadwellstud.co.uk

SHADWELL
STANDING FOR SUCCESS

colt that goes well and he's as early a two-year-old as I've got. We'll probably start him off in May".

902. TELESCOPIC ★★
b.f. *Galileo – Orlena (Gone West)*.
March 31. Fourth foal. Closely related to the fairly useful Irish 1m and hurdles winner and 9f listed placed Hovering (by In The Wings) and half-sister to the fairly useful 9.5f winner Pelican Waters (by Key Of Luck) and the modest 2-y-o 7f all-weather winner Limit (by Barathea). The dam, a minor 2-y-o 7f winner in France, is a half-sister to the listed winner and 1,000 Guineas third Vista Bella. The second dam, Cox Orange (by Trempolino), won 10 races in France and the USA including the Group 3 Prix du Calvados and four US Grade 3 events and is a half-sister to 7 winners including the Group 1 Prix Marcel Boussac winner Amonita. (Mrs S J Davis).
"She's very weak and backward at the moment, so it looks like she'll take a bit of time and it's a bit too early to assess her".

903. TIGERS CHARM ★★★
b.c. *Tiger Hill – Amazing Dream (Thatching)*.
January 29. Fourth living foal. 8,000Y. Tattersalls October 3. Blandford Bloodstock. Half-brother to the minor French 2-y-o winner Unimix (by Linamix). The dam, a fairly useful 5.2f listed and 6f Tattersalls Breeders Stakes winner, is a half-sister to 6 winners including the useful 2-y-o dual 5f winner and Group 3 Cornwallis Stakes second The Tatling. The second dam, Aunty Eileen (by Ahonoora), is an unraced half-sister to 6 winners including the smart sprinter Lugana Beach. (A N Verrier).
"A nice, big, rangy horse, he's backward and will take a bit of time but there's no reason why he won't make a two-year-old in the second half of the season".

904. UNNAMED ★★★
b.c. *Tiger Hill – Dunloskin (Selkirk)*.
March 24. Half-brother to Cairnsmore (by Singspiel), unplaced in one start at 2 yrs in 2008. The dam was third in the Group 2 6f Lowther Stakes at 2 yrs. The second dam, Dalinda (by Nureyev), won once at 4 yrs in France and is a half-sister to 2 minor winners. (A S Belhab).
"I've got a lot of time for this horse. Michael Jarvis trained the mare and she was pretty useful. He's a very active colt with a good disposition and he's well-balanced and a good-mover. There's no reason why he won't be OK and despite the Tiger Hill – Selkirk cross he doesn't look slow, so hopefully we'll start him at six furlongs. I like him".

905. UNNAMED ★★
b.f. *Invincible Spirit – Final Favour (Unblest)*.
March 30. Third foal. 30,000Y. Tattersalls October 1. Not sold. Half-sister to the fair triple 5f winner (including at 2 yrs) Sister Etienne (by Lend A Hand) and to the fair 2-y-o 5f winner Sinead Of Aglish (by Captain Rio). The dam is an unraced half-sister to 9 winners including the Irish Group 3 winner Shindella. The second dam, Antipol (by Polyfoto), is an unraced half-sister to 6 minor winners. (A Partnership).
"I had hoped she'd be showing a bit more at this stage. She's out of a fast family and by a good two-year-old sire but she's taking her time at the moment. An attractive filly with a good temperament".

906. UNNAMED ★★
b.c. *Tiger Hill – Mill Line (Mill Reef)*.
May 24. 10,000Y. Tattersalls December. W Jarvis. Half-brother to numerous winners including the high-class filly Pure Grain, winner of the Group 3 7f Prestige Stakes at 2 yrs and the Group 1 12f Irish Oaks and Group 1 12f Yorkshire Oaks at 3 yrs (by Polish Precedent). The dam, a fair 14.6f winner at 3 yrs, is a half-sister to 6 winners. (Ali Saeed).
"A late foal out of an old mare and he looks like he'll need a lot of time, but having said that he looks a very cheap horse. One that could develop into a high-class middle-distance horse one day because he's rangy and will be a good stamp of a horse when he grows into himself. He reminds me of a good staying horse I had a few years ago called Blown Away".

907. UNNAMED ★★
b.f. *Shamardal – Three Wishes (Sadler's Wells)*.
March 15. Fifth foal. 40,000Y. Tattersalls October 1. Rabbah Bloodstock. Half-sister to Age of Couture (by Hold That Tiger), unplaced in 2 starts at 2 yrs in 2008, to the minor French 2-y-o winner Todman Avenue (by Lear Fan) and to a minor Italian 3-y-o winner by Diesis. The dam was placed third over 1m in Ireland and is a sister to the winner and Irish Oaks third Sister Bella and a half-sister to 4 winners. The second dam, Valley Of Hope (by Riverman), is an unraced half-sister to 5 winners including the Group 1 Prix Jacques le Marois winner Vin de France and the Group 2 Mill Reef Stakes winner Vacarme. (Mr A S Belhab).
"We need to watch this filly's temperament but she's a medium-sized, good-moving filly and if she goes the right way we certainly wouldn't be without hope".

908. UNNAMED ★★
b.f. *Doyen – Total Aloof (Groom Dancer)*.
March 14. Ninth foal. 56,000Y. Tattersalls October 1. Rabbah Bloodstock. Half-sister to Tout Seul (by Ali-Royal), a winner of 6 races including the Group 1 7f Dewhurst Stakes, to the quite useful 2-y-o 6f winner Totally Yours (by Desert Sun), the Irish 2-y-o 6f winner Soaring Eagle (by Eagle Eyed) and a winner in Greece by Fantastic Light. The dam, a fair dual 5f winner at 3 yrs, is a half-sister to 2 winners in Japan. The second dam, Bashoosh (by Danzig), is a placed full or half-sister to 6 winners. (Mr A Belhab).
"She's a small filly but she's a half-sister to a Group 1 winner so if we can win with her she'll be a nice broodmare".

EVE JOHNSON HOUGHTON

909. BRAVO BRAVO ★★
b.c. *Sadler's Wells – Top Table (Shirley Heights)*.
April 10. Eleventh foal. 110,000Y. Tattersalls October 1. BBA (Ire). Half-brother to the useful 2-y-o 5.3f, 6f and listed 7f winner Zato (by Zafonic), to the useful 6f (at 2 yrs) and listed 1m winner Krispy Knight, the fairly useful 12.3f winner and listed-placed Manama Rose (both by Kris), the fair 7f all-weather winner Parable (by Midyan), the Irish 7f winner Amaranda (by Fasliyev), the modest 7f winner Moonmaiden (by Selkirk) and a 2-y-o winner in Denmark by Bering. The dam, a modest 12f placed maiden, is a half-sister to 5 winners including the very smart 1m listed winner and Group 1 Juddmonte Lockinge Stakes third Centre Stalls. The second dam, Lora's Guest (by Be My Guest), a useful 7f winner, is a sister to the 1,000 Guineas and Sussex Stakes winner On The House. (D D Clee).
"A big, beautiful, backward beast! He does everything very easily but he won't be out until the back-end".

910. GOLDEN WATERS ★★★
b.f. *Dubai Destination – Faraway Waters (Pharly)*.
March 24. Seventh foal. Half-sister to the 1m and listed 10f winner of four races and Epsom Oaks second Something Exciting (by Halling). The dam, a useful 6f winner (at 2 yrs) and listed 10f Pretty Polly Stakes second, is a half-sister to 6 winners including the very useful 1m to 10.4f winner and Group-placed Prince Of Denial. The second dam, Gleaming Water (by Kalaglow), a quite useful 2-y-o 6f winner, is a sister to the Group 3 Solario Stakes winner Shining Water (herself dam of the Group 1 1m Grand Criterium winner Tenby) and a half-sister to 8 winners. (Mr R Crutchley).
"She's only just arrived so I don't know a lot about her, but the family all get better with age. She's a very well-made filly, won't be out very early and I would imagine that she'd be a better three-year-old, but having said that we have won some nice two-year-old races with the family".

911. HOUNDS DITCH ★★★
b.c. *Avonbridge – Pudding Lane (College Chapel)*.
March 30. Fourth foal. 8,000Y. Tattersalls October 3. Not sold. Half-brother to the very useful listed 5f winner of 6 races Judd Street (by Compton Place). The dam, a modest maiden, ran only at 2 yrs and stayed 7f and is a half-sister to 2 winners. The second dam, Fire Of London

(by Shirley Heights), was placed over 10f and is a full or half-sister to 9 winners. (Fight the Ban).
"A backward type, he's so like Judd Street was at this age and he didn't win as a two-year-old until December. I would imagine he'd be one for the back-end as well because every time we do a bit with him he grows. He has a big back-end on him and he'll have plenty of toe when we do get him to the racecourse".

912. LAUBERHORN ★★
b.c. *Dubai Destination – Ski Run (Petoski).*
April 4. Second foal. 5,000Y. Tattersalls October 2. R F Johnson-Houghton. The dam, a very useful 12f and 2m winner, was third in the Group 3 Lonsdale Stakes and in the Group 3 Park Hill Stakes and is a half-sister to 3 winners. The second dam, Cut And Run (by Slip Anchor), is an unplaced sister to the Italian middle-distance listed winner Hesperia and a half-sister to the French listed winners Wavey and Rebuff.
"He was very cheap but he's a lovely, big, lengthy horse that won't be out until the back-end".

913. ROODLE ★★★★
b.f. *Xaar – Roodeye (Inchinor).*
March 10. First foal. The dam, a useful 5f (at 2 yrs) and 7f winner, was listed-placed and is a half-brother to the quite useful 2006 2-y-o 7f winner Roodolph. The second dam, Roo (by Rudimentary), a quite useful 2-y-o 5f and 6f winner, is a half-sister to 4 winners including the Group 2 6f Gimcrack Stakes winner Bannister (by Inchinor). (Mrs F M Johnson Houghton).
"She's racey and she's very nice – but I am biased because I've seen her since she was a foal! I like her a lot and she's done everything we've asked. She just growing at the moment but she does everything easily and I'm really pleased with her. She's quite a rangy filly and we'll be aiming for similar distances to her dam, starting her over five furlongs in late May perhaps and then stepping her up".

914. SLICE (IRE) ★★★
b.c. *Daggers Drawn – Windomen (Forest Wind).*
March 19. €12,500Y. Tattersalls Ireland. Eve Johnson Houghton. Brother to the fairly useful 6f (at 2 yrs) and 10f winner and listed-placed Harvest Joy and half-brother to the modest 7f to 10f and hurdles winner Touch Of Ivory (by Rossini). The dam is an unraced half-sister to 3 winners. The second dam, Lucky Coin (by Hadeer), won at 3 yrs and is a half-sister to the Group 1 Prix Jean Prat winner Lapierre. (Eden Racing III).
"A sharp, typical two-year-old, he'll start off at five furlongs in late April or early May".

915. XAARA STAR (IRE) ★★★
b.f. *Xaar – Bint Kaldoun (Kaldoun).*
February 6. €4,500Y. Tattersalls Ireland. Eve Johnson Houghton. Half-sister to the quite useful dual 6f 2-y-o winner Kaldoun Kingdom (by King's Best), to the fair 10f to 12f winner of 6 races Shape Up (by Octagonal) and the fair 7f to 10f winner of 7 races Zabeel Tower (by Anabaa). The dam, a quite useful 7f (at 2 yrs) to 12f placed maiden, is a sister to the German listed sprint winner Shy Lady (herself dam of the St James's Palace Stakes winner Zabeel) and a half-sister to 5 winners. The second dam, Shy Danceuse (by Groom Dancer), a minor French 1m winner, is a half-sister to 7 winners including the dual Group 3 winning sprinter Diffident. (Betfair Club ROA).
"She's a bit of a madam and she was cheap but she's racey and she should be early. A good-topped filly that goes very nicely".

916. UNNAMED ★★★★
b.c. *Royal Applause – Corndavon (Sheikh Albadou).*
April 12. Sixth living foal. 62,000Y. Tattersalls October 1. Eve Johnson Houghton. Brother to the smart 2-y-o Group 2 6f July Stakes winner Nevisian Lad, to the fairly useful 5f (at 2 yrs) and 6f winner and listed-placed Woodnook and the quite useful dual 7f winner Windermere Island (both by Cadeaux Genereux). The dam, a fairly useful 6f winner of 3 races, is a sister to the listed-placed winner Injaaz and a half-sister to the US sprint winner of 13 races and listed-placed Hardball. The second dam, Ferber's

Follies (by Saratoga Six), a winning 2-y-o sprinter, was third in the Grade 2 6f Adirondack Stakes and is a half-sister to 11 winners including the US 2-y-o Grade 2 6f winner Blue Jean Baby. (Anthony Pye-Jeary & Mel Smith).

"He's very nice, I really like him a lot and he'll probably start off at six furlongs. He looks the real deal for a two-year-old and although we haven't done much fast work yet with our two-year-olds he does everything nicely. We bought him to be a two-year-old that might make either Royal Ascot or Newmarket's July meeting and he hasn't put me off yet. He's very well-made and he looks like he has the scope to train on as a three-year-old".

917. UNNAMED ★★
b.f. Sadler's Wells – Horatia (Machiavellian).
March 26. Fifth foal. 38,000Y. Tattersalls October 1. Not sold. Closely related to the quite useful 7f, 1m and subsequent UAE winner Muzdaher (by Danzig). The dam, a 10f winner here, subsequently won the Grade 3 Matchmaker Stakes in the USA and is a half-sister to 4 winners including Smart Alec, a smart winner of 5 races here and in France (including over 7f at 2 yrs) and second in the Group 3 9f Earl Of Sefton Stakes. The second dam, Ahead (by Shirley Heights), a very useful 12f winner and third in the Group 3 12f Princess Royal Stakes, is a sister to the listed winner Criquette and a half-sister to the top-class miler Markofdistinction. (Mrs V D Neale).

"She'll take plenty of time and is one for the back-end of the season. She's nicely made and was bought to be a foundation mare, so we're hoping we can win with her and get some black type – but I think that will be next year".

MARK JOHNSTON
918. AVONROSE ★★★
b.f. Avonbridge – Loveleaves (Polar Falcon).
April 3. Fourth foal. 20,000Y. Tattersalls October 2. Mark Johnston. Half-sister to the very smart Group 2 1m Oettingen Rennen and Group 3 7f Supreme Stakes winner of 7 races Lovelace (by Royal Applause). The dam, a fairly useful 8.3f winner, is a half-sister to 4 winners. The second dam, Rash (by Pursuit Of Love), is an unraced half-sister to 6 winners including the useful 2-y-o dual 6f winner Maid For The Hills and the useful 2-y-o 5f and 6f winner Maid For Walking (herself dam of the US Grade 1 winner Stroll). (Around The World Partnership)

919. AWZAAN ★★★
b.c. Alhaarth – Nufoos (Zafonic).
February 8. First foal. The dam, a useful 5f, 6f (both at 2 yrs) and listed 7f winner, is a half-sister to the 5 winners including the fairly useful 2-y-o sprint winner of 3 races Valiant Romeo. The second dam, Desert Lynx (by Green Desert), a fair dual 6f winner, is a half-sister to the very smart dual listed 5f winner Watching. (Hamdan Al Maktoum).

920. CHERRY BEE ★★★
b.f. Acclamation – Norfolk Lavender (Ascot Knight).
January 31. Eighth foal. €35,000Y. Goffs Million. M Johnston. Half-sister to the useful 8.3f to 12f winner of 5 races Celtic Mission (by Cozzene), to the quite useful 7f and 1m winner In The Pink (by Indian Ridge), the quite useful Irish 10f winner Takween (by Nayef) and the fair 2-y-o 6f winner Fragrant Star (by Soviet Star). The dam, a modest 1m all-weather winner here, subsequently won a stakes event in the USA and was Grade 3 placed. She is a half-sister to 5 winners including the US stakes winner Concordene out of the 1,000 Guineas winner Nocturnal Spree (by Supreme Sovereign), herself a half-sister to the Prix Saint-Alary winner Tootens and to the dam of the St Leger winner Moonax. (Favourites Racing Ltd)

921. CLOUDY CITY (USA) ★★★
b.br.c. Giant's Causeway – Mambo Slew (Kingmambo).
February 20. First foal. $50,000Y. Keeneland September. M Johnston. The dam won two Grade 3 events in the USA and is a half-sister to 7 winners including the US Grade 3 winner Awesome Time. The second dam, Slew Boyera (by Seattle Slew), won one at 2 yrs in France and is a half-sister to 6 winners including the US and

Argentinian Grade 1 winner Mat-Boy. (A D Spence)

922. DANCING DUDE (IRE) ★★★
ch.c. Danehill Dancer – Wadud (Nashwan).
February 6. Third foal. Deauville August. €280,000Y. Mark Johnston. Brother to the fair 2008 1m placed 2-y-o Sussex Dancer and to the Group 3 Noblesse Stakes winner Ice Queen. The dam, placed fourth once over 12f, is a sister to 3 winners including the very smart 7f (at 2 yrs) and Group 3 12f Gordon Stakes winner Rabah and the useful 2-y-o 6f winner and Group 1 Cheveley Park Stakes third Najiya and a half-sister to 2 winners. The second dam, The Perfect Life (by Try My Best), won the Group 3 5f Prix du Bois, was second in the Group 2 Prix Robert Papin and is a sister to the top-class colt Last Tycoon (winner of the Breeders Cup Mile, the Kings Stand Stakes and the William Hill Sprint Championship) and a half-sister to 9 winners.

923. ELATION ★★★★
b.f. Cape Cross – Attraction (Efisio).
March 1. First foal. The dam, a high-class 1,000 Guineas, Irish 1,000 Guineas, Coronation Stakes, Matron Stakes and Sun Chariot Stakes winner, is a half-sister to the quite useful 2-y-o 5f winner Aunty Mary. The second dam, Flirtation (by Pursuit Of Love), ran unplaced once over 7f at 3 yrs and is a half-sister to 4 winners including the French listed 12f winner and Group 2 placed Carmita. (The Duke of Roxburghe)

924. FLORIDITA ★★★
ch.f. Fusaichi Pegasus – Rose Of Zollern (Seattle Dancer).
March 21. Fourth foal. €42,000Y. Goffs Million. Not sold. Sister to the fairly useful 2-y-o dual 7f all-weather winner and subsequent German dual listed placed Flor Y Nata and half-sister to the unraced 2008 2-y-o Tarooq (by War Chant) and to the fair all-weather 6f and 7f winner Rosa De Mi Corazon (by Cozzene). The dam won 9 races including the German 1,000 Guineas and a stakes event in the USA and is a half-sister to 3 winners. The second dam, Kalisha (by Rainbow Quest), is an unraced half-sister to the Dewhurst Stakes winner Kala Dancer. (Miss K Rausing)

925. GREEN LIGHTNING ★★★
b.c. Montjeu – Angelic Song (Halo).
January 19. Fourteenth foal. 70,000Y. Tattersalls December. M Johnston. Closely related to the Irish 2-y-o 1m and subsequent US Grade 1 Hollywood Turf Cup winner Sligo Bay, to the smart 8.5f (at 2 yrs) and listed 13.3f winner Wolfe Tone and 2 winners in Japan including the stakes winner Millennium Wing (both by Sadler's Wells) and half-brother to the Japanese winner of 5 races Lady Ballade (by Unbridled) and a minor US winner by Gone West. The dam is an unraced sister to Glorious Song (a winner of 17 races including four Grade 1 events and herself the dam of Singspiel and Rahy), to the champion 2-y-o colt Devils Bag and the Grade 2 Arlington Classic winner Saint Ballado. The second dam, Ballade (by Herbager), won over 5f and 6f in the USA. (The Green Dot Partnership)

926. LE VOLCAN D'OR ★★★
ch.c. Giant's Causeway – Twenty Eight Carat (Alydar).
April 9. Ninth foal. $75,000Y. Keeneland September. M Johnston. Closely related to the useful Irish 2-y-o listed 5f winner Heart Shaped and to the fairly useful Irish 2-y-o 5f winner and listed-placed Facchetti (both by Storm Bird) and half-brother to the US Grade 1 Champagne Stakes winner and Preakness Stakes second A P Valentine (by A P Indy) and the minor US stakes winner of 10 races Summer Bet (by Summer Squall). The dam, a minor winner of 2 races over 6f and 1m at 4 yrs in the USA, is a half-sister to 6 winners including the stakes winner Pulling Punches. The second dam, Voo Doo Dance (by Stage Door Johnny), was a stakes winner of 8 races. (Syndicate 2008)

927. LICENCE TO KILL ★★
b.c. War Chant – With A Wink (Clever Trick).
February 12. Ninth foal. $130,000Y. Saratoga August. Mark Johnston. Brother to the minor US stakes winner Up Like Thunder and half-

brother to two US stakes winners by Dixieland Band including the Grade 3 placed Jena Jena. The dam won 6 races in the USA including the Grade 2 Delaware Handicap and is a half-sister to 4 winners including the US dual Grade 3 winner and Grade 1 placed Raja's Shark. The second dam, Shark's Jaws (by Mitey Prince), won 11 races and was Grade 3 placed. (The Vine Accord)

928. NAVE (USA) ★★★
b.c. Pulpit – Lakabi (Nureyev).
April 30. Sixth foal. $300,000Y. Keeneland September. M Johnston. Brother to the fairly useful 7f and 1m winner Throne Of Power and half-brother to the triple US sprint stakes winner Coronado Rose (by Coronado's Quest) and 2 minor US winners by Gulch and Thunder Gulch. The dam, unplaced in one start, is a sister to the US stakes winners and Grade 3 placed European Rose and a half-sister to a stakes winner in Australia by Danehill. The second dam, Lakab (by Manila), a fair 7.6f winner, is a half-sister to the Group winners Wixim, Run Softly and Berceau. (A G D Hogarth)

929. SENNOCKIAN STORM ★★★
*b.f. Storm Cat – Winning Season
(Lemon Drop Kid).*
April 18. First foal. $300,000Y. Keeneland September. M Johnston. The dam, a stakes winner and Grade 2 placed in the USA, is a half-sister to the US stakes winner and Grade 2 placed Laguna Seca. The second dam, Topicount (by Private Account), a US Grade 2 and Grade 3 winner, is a half-sister to 5 winners. (The Vine Accord)

930. SHAMA'ADAN ★★★
b.c. Shamardal – Trick (Shirley Heights).
March 16. Eighth foal. 50,000Y. Tattersalls October 2. M Johnston. Half-brother to the fairly useful 2-y-o 6f winner and 1m listed-placed White Rabbit (by Zilzal), to the quite useful 6f (at 2 yrs) to 11.8f winner Cap Ferrat (by Robellino), the fair 14f winner Onyergo (by Polish Precedent), the modest 2-y-o 6f winner Shinner (by Charnwood Forest) and a winner in Germany by Alhaarth. The dam, a fair 10f winner, is a half-sister to 6 winners. The second dam, Hocus (by High Top), a quite useful 3-y-o 7f winner, is a half-sister to 10 winners including the Group 1 5f Flying Childers and Group 1 6f Middle Park Stakes winner Hittite Glory. (Mr A Jaber)

931. STEP IN TIME (IRE) ★★★
*b.c. Giant's Causeway – Cash Run
(Seeking The Gold).*
April 25. Fifth foal. €50,000Y. Goffs Million. M Johnston. Closely related to the Irish 2-y-o listed 7f winner and dual Group 3 second Great War Eagle (by Storm Cat). The dam won the Grade 1 Breeders Cup Juvenile Fillies' and two Grade 2 events and is a half-sister to the US Grade 1 King's Bishop Stakes winner and sire Forestry. The second dam, Shared Interest (by Pleasant Colony), won the Grade 1 Ruffian Handicap and is a half-sister to the dual Grade 1 Vosburgh Stakes winner Sewickley. (S R Counsell)

932. UNNAMED ★★★
b.c. Bertolini – Aquaba (Damascus).
March 31. Closely related to the quite useful 2008 2-y-o 5f and 6f winner Palo Verde and to the fair 3-y-o 7f winner Auvergne (both by Green Desert) and half-brother to the useful listed 6f Blue Seal Stakes winner Polska (by Danzig), the useful winner of five races over 5f including the Ballyogan Stakes Millstream (by Dayjur), the quite useful 2-y-o 5f winner Waterstone (by Cape Cross), the Irish 1m and 10f winner Woodsia (by Woodman) and a 5f UAE winner by Lammtarra. The dam, a Grade 3 stakes winner in the USA, won from 7f to 9f and is a half-sister to five winners. The second dam, Elect (by Vaguely Noble), a very useful winner of 3 races from 10f to 12.3f, was third in the Sun Chariot Stakes and is a half-sister to the dams of the Group 1 winners Sadeem and Too Chic. (Hamdan al Maktoum).

933. UNNAMED ★★★
*ch.c. Shamardal – Australian Dreams
(Magic Ring).*

February 16. Third foal. 160,000Y. Tattersalls October 1. John Ferguson. The dam, a listed winner of 7 races at 3 and 4 yrs in Germany, is a half-sister to 6 winners including the smart Group 3 5f Palace House Stakes and subsequent US Grade 3 9f winner Needwood Blade and the US Grade 3 winner Islay Mist. The second dam, Finlaggan (by Be My Chief), a quite useful 11f to 2m winner, is a half-sister to 7 winners. (Hamdan al Maktoum).

934. UNNAMED ★★★

b.c. Cape Cross – Autumn Wealth
(Cadeaux Genereux).
January 24. First foal. 115,000Y. Tattersalls October 2. John Ferguson. The dam, a useful 5f (at 2 yrs) and 6f winner, was second in the Group 2 5f Temple Stakes and is a half-sister to 2 winners. The second dam, Cyclone Flyer (by College Chapel), a modest 5f winner at 3 yrs, is a half-sister to 8 winners including the high-class Group 2 Temple Stakes and Group 2 Kings Stand Stakes winner Bolshoi and the useful sprinters Mariinsky, Great Chaddington and Tod. (Hamdan al Maktoum).

935. UNNAMED ★★★

b.c. Shamardal – Balalaika (Sadler's Wells).
March 5. Seventh foal. 150,000Y. Tattersalls October 1. John Ferguson. Half-brother to the very smart UAE Group 2 and Group 3 10f Select Stakes winner Alkaadhem (by Green Desert), to the fairly useful 1m and 10f winner Lookalike (by Rainbow Quest) and a winner in Greece by Machiavellian. The dam, a useful 4-y-o listed 9f winner, is a sister to the high-class Group 2 10f Prince of Wales's Stakes and dual US Grade 2 winner Stagecraft and a half-sister to 5 winners including the Group 3 Strensall Stakes winner Mullins Bay and the very useful dual 1m listed winner Hyabella. The second dam, Bella Colora (by Bellypha), won the Group 2 Prix de l'Opera and the Group 3 7f Waterford Candelabra Stakes, was third in the 1,000 Guineas and is a half-sister to the Irish Oaks winner Colorspin (herself the dam of the Group 1 winners Zee Zee Top, Opera House and Kayf Tara) and to the Irish Champion Stakes winner Cezanne. (Hamdan al Maktoum).

936. UNNAMED ★★★

b.c. Cape Cross – Carry On Katie (Fasliyev).
February 3. Second foal. Brother to Charles Dickens, unplaced in one start at 2 yrs in 2008. The dam won 3 races at 2 yrs including the Group 1 6f Cheveley Park Stakes and the Group 2 6f Lowther Stakes. The second dam, Dinka Raja (by Woodman), a minor French 3-y-o 1m winner, is a half-sister to 3 winners. (Hamdan Al Maktoum).

937. UNNAMED ★★★

b.c. Cape Cross – Court Lane (Machiavellian).
February 24. Closely related to the moderate 2008 6f placed 2-y-o Chambers and to the smart 2-y-o dual 5f winner and Group 1 6f Middle Park Stakes third Holborn (both by Green Desert) and half-brother to the modest 2-y-o 7f winner Show Trial (by Jade Robbery). The dam, a quite useful 2-y-o 6f winner and subsequently a 1m winner in France, is a half-sister to the quite useful 2001 2-y-o 5f winner Morouj. The second dam, Chicarica (by The Minstrel), a smart 2-y-o filly, won the Group 3 6f Cherry Hinton Stakes, was placed in the Fred Darling Stakes and the Cork And Orrery Stakes and is a half-sister to the smart 2-y-o Romeo Romani. (Sheikh Mohammed).

938. UNNAMED ★★★

b.c. Danehill Dancer – Courtier (Saddlers' Hall).
January 12. Sixth foal. €40,000Y. Goffs Million. M Johnston. Brother to the useful 2-y-o Group 3 Solario Stakes winner and Group 1 Gran Criterium Stakes third Barbajuan and half-brother to the fair 7f winner of 4 races Trimlestown (by Orpen) and the quite useful 1m (at 2 yrs) and 10f winner Oligarch (by Monashee Mountain). The dam is an unraced sister to one minor winner and a half-sister to two more. The second dam, Queen's Visit (by Top Command), is a placed half-sister to 5 winners including the Royal Lodge Stakes second Khozaam. (The Originals).

939. UNNAMED ★★★

b.c. Dubai Destination – Desert Lynx
(Green Desert).

February 9. Seventh foal. 32,000Y. Tattersalls October 1. John Ferguson. Half-brother to the useful 5f, 6f (both at 2 yrs) and listed 7f winner Nufoos (by Zafonic), to the fairly useful 2-y-o sprint winner of 3 races Valiant Romeo (by Primo Dominie), the quite useful dual 10f winner Bee Sting (by Selkirk), the quite useful 2-y-o 5f and 6f winner Sand Cat (by Cadeaux Genereux) and the fair 6f and 7f 3-y-o winner Neon Blue (by Atraf). The dam, a fair dual 6f winner, is a sister one winner and a half-sister to the very smart dual listed 5f winner Watching. The second dam, Sweeping (by Indian King), a useful 2-y-o 6f winner, is a half-sister to 10 winners. (Hamdan Al Maktoum)

940. UNNAMED ★★★
b.c. Shamardal – Dubai Surprise (King's Best).
March 4. First foal. 150,000Y. Tattersalls October 1. John Ferguson. The dam, a winner of 4 races here and in Italy including the Group 1 Premio Lydia Tesio and the Group 3 Prestige Stakes, was second in the Group 1 Criterium de Saint-Cloud and is a half-sister to 2 winners. The second dam, Toujours Irish (by Irish River), is an unraced half-sister to 7 winners including the French multiple Group winner Athyka. (Hamdan Al Maktoum)

941. UNNAMED ★★★
ch.c. Barathea – Echo River (Irish River).
January 31. Third foal. Brother to the quite useful triple 7f winner (including at 2 yrs) Ravi River and to the unraced 2008 2-y-o Karta (by Diktat). The dam was a useful 2-y-o 6f and listed 7f winner. The second dam, Monaassabaat (by Zilzal), a very useful 6f (at 2 yrs) and listed 10f Virginia Stakes winner, is a half-sister to the US 1m stakes winner Air Dancer and to the Group 2 Criterium de Maisons-Laffitte winner Bitooh. (Hamdan Al Maktoum)

942. UNNAMED ★★★★
ch.c. Storm Cat – Lead Story (Editor's Note).
January 9. Second foal. $600,000Y. Keeneland September. M Johnston. The dam won 8 races including three Grade 2 events and is a half-sister to another stakes winner. The second dam, Gwenjinsky (by Seattle Dancer), is a placed half-sister to the US Grade 1 winners Unbridled Elaine and Glitterwoman. (Hamdan Al Maktoum)

943. UNNAMED ★★★★
ch.c. Exceed And Excel – Licence To Thrill (Wolfhound).
April 29. Fifth foal. 75,000Y. Tattersalls October 1. John Ferguson. Half-brother to the modest 2008 5f placed 2-y-o Cheap Thrills (by Bertolini), to the useful 2-y-o dual 5f winner Group Therapy (by Choisir), the dual 5f winner (including at 2 yrs) and Group 3 5f Norfolk Stakes third Classic Encounter (by Lujain) and the modest 6f all-weather winner Gimme Some Lovin (by Desert Style). The dam, a quite useful dual 5f all-weather winner, is a half-sister to 4 winners including the useful 2-y-o 5f winner Master Of Passion. The second dam, Crime Of Passion (by Dragonara Palace), winner of the Group 3 Cherry Hinton Stakes and third in the Group 1 Prix Robert Papin, is a half-sister to 4 winners including the Ayr Gold Cup winner Primula Boy. (Hamdan Al Maktoum)

944. UNNAMED ★★★
gr.c. El Prado – Lovely Later (Green Dancer).
April 9. Eighth foal. $400,000Y. Keeneland September. M Johnston. Half-brother to the US Grade 3 winner Lovely Afternoon (by Afternoon Deelites) and to the US stakes winner and Grade 3 placed With Patience (by With Approval). The dam is an unraced half-sister to 2 winners including the dam of the listed winner Fatefully. The second dam, Fate's Reward (by Key To The Mint), won 4 races in the USA at 2 to 4 yrs and is a sister to the US Grade 1 winner Devil's Orchid. (Hamdan Al Maktoum)

945. UNNAMED ★★★
ch.f. Medicean – Mare Nostrum (Caerleon).
January 24. Fourth foal. $340,000Y. Keeneland September. M Johnston. Half-sister to the quite useful 2008 2-y-o 7f winner Roman Republic (by Cape Cross) and to the minor French 2-y-o winner Hurricane Mist (by Spinning World). The dam won the Group 3 Prix Vanteaux and was placed in the Prix Vermeille and Prix Saint-Alary

and is a half-sister to 7 winners including the US Grade 1 winner Aube Indienne. The second dam, Salvora (by Spectacular Bid), won once at 3 yrs in France and is a half-sister to 7 winners and to the dam of the Australian triple Grade 1 winner Flying Spur. (Hamdan Al Maktoum)

946. UNNAMED ★★★★
ch.c. Shamardal – Mood Swings (Shirley Heights).
March 4. Ninth foal. 100,000Y. Tattersalls October 1. John Ferguson. Half-brother to the useful 2008 2-y-o 7f winner and Group 2 7f Futurity Stakes third Grand Ducal (by Danehill Dancer), to the useful 2-y-o 6f winner and listed placed Hurricane Floyd (by Pennekamp), the Irish 7f (at 2 yrs) and 1m winner and listed-placed Best Side (by King's Best), the fairly useful 6f (at 2 yrs) and 1m winner Al Khaleeej (by Sakhee), the fairly useful 1m and 10f winner Tears Of A Clown (by Galileo) and the fair 3-y-o 5f winner Psychic (by Alhaarth). The dam, a fair 2-y-o 6f winner, is a sister to the listed 2-y-o Sweet Solera Stakes winner Catwalk and a half-sister to 5 winners. The second dam, Moogie (by Young Generation), a useful 2-y-o 6f winner, was fourth in the Coronation Stakes and is a half-sister to 6 winners. (Hamdan Al Maktoum)

947. UNNAMED ★★★
b.c. Green Desert – Pioneer Bride (Gone West).
February 14. Brother to the useful 6f to 9f winner of 6 races Yamal. The dam is an unraced half-sister to the high-class Group 2 10f Prince of Wales's Stakes winner Faithful Son, to the very smart Coventry Stakes and Prix Quincey winner Always Fair and the dams of the Irish Oaks winner Lailani and the dual Group 3 winner Naheef. The second dam, Carduel (by Buckpasser), won over 8.5f in the USA at 2 yrs and is a half-sister to the very useful Irish 10f colt Punctilio. (Hamdan Al Maktoum)

948. UNNAMED ★★★★
b.c. Dubawi – Satin Flower (Shadeed).
March 4. Half-brother to the very smart 2-y-o Group 1 6f Middle Park Stakes winner Lujain, to the useful 2-y-o 6f winner and Group 3 6f Coventry Stakes second Botanical, the very useful 6f (at 2 yrs) to 9f winner of 4 races Satin Kiss (all by Seeking The Gold), the very useful listed 7f (at 2 yrs) and listed 12f winner Lilium (by Nashwan) and the fairly useful 2-y-o 5f winner Deceptor (by Machiavellian). The dam, a smart winner of the Group 3 7f Jersey Stakes and second in the Grade 1 9f Queen Elizabeth II Challenge Cup, is a half-sister to 7 winners including the US Grade 1 10f Santa Anita Handicap winner Martial Law. The second dam, Sateen (by Round Table), won two 6f stakes events in the USA. (Hamdan Al Maktoum)

949. UNNAMED ★★★★
b.c. Bahamian Bounty – See You Later (Emarati).
April 9. Fifth living foal. 210,000Y. Tattersalls October 1. John Ferguson. Half-brother to the very useful 5f (including at 2 yrs) and listed 6f winner of 6 races Aahayson (by Noverre), to the fairly useful 6f and 7f winner Thebes (by Cadeaux Genereux) and the quite useful 2-y-o 5f winner Annatalia (by Pivotal). The dam, a fairly useful dual 5f winner (including at 2 yrs), was listed-placed 3 times and is a half-sister to 6 winners including the very smart 2-y-o Group 3 Horris Hill Stakes winner Peak To Creek. The second dam, Rivers Rhapsody (by Dominion), a useful winner of the listed 5f Scarborough Stakes and third in the Group 2 5f Temple Stakes, is a half-sister to the Group 3 5f Prix d'Arenberg winner Regal Scintilla. (Hamdan Al Maktoum)

950. UNNAMED ★★
ch.f. Elusive Quality – Silent Eskimo (Eskimo).
April 16. Sixth foal. $375,000Y. Keeneland September. M Johnston. Half-sister to 2 winners including the minor US stakes-placed Silent Fusaichi (by Fusaichi Pegasus). The dam won 5 graded stakes events in the USA and was Grade 1 placed. The second dam, Slide Out Front (by Silent Review), a US stakes winner of 8 races, was Grad 1 placed. (Hamdan Al Maktoum)

951. UNNAMED ★★★
ch.c. Shamardal – Slap Shot (Lycius).
February 21. Second foal. 85,000Y. Tattersalls December. John Ferguson. Half-brother to the quite useful 2008 2-y-o 7f winner Samara Valley (by Dalakhani). The dam won 6 races in Italy including the Group 3 Gran Premio Citta di Napoli and was second in the Group 1 5f Prix de l'Abbaye and is a half-sister to 2 winners in Turkey. The second dam, Katanning (by Green Desert), is a placed half-sister to one winner. (Hamdan Al Maktoum)

952. UNNAMED ★★★
b.f. Cape Cross – Snow Polina (Trempolino).
February 19. Fourth foal. 70,000Y. Tattersalls October 2. M Johnston. The dam won the Grade 1 9f Beverly D Stakes and the Grade 2 Black Helen Handicap in the USA and a listed 10f event in France and is a half-sister to 2 winners. The second dam, Snow House (by Vacarme), won 8 races including 2 listed events in France, was Group 3 placed over 10f and is a half-sister to 10 winners. (Hamdan Al Maktoum)

953. UNNAMED ★★★★
ch.c. Shamardal – Wolf Cleugh (Last Tycoon).
March 29. Eighth foal. 190,000Y. Tattersalls October 1. John Ferguson. Half-brother to the 2008 Irish 6f fourth placed 2-y-o Alexander Youth (by Exceed And Excel), to the Group 2 5f Prix du Gros-Chene and dual Group 3 5f winner Moss Vale (by Shinko Forest), the fairly useful dual 1m winner Natural Force (by King's Best), the quite useful 2-y-o dual 6f winner Cape Vale (by Cape Cross) and the quite useful 10f winner of 3 races Street Life (by Dolphin Street). The dam is an unplaced half-sister to 8 winners including the Irish listed 6f winner King's College. The second dam, Santa Roseanna (by Caracol), won the listed 9f The Minstrel Stakes, was second in the Group 2 6f Moyglare Stud Stakes and is a half-sister to 9 winners. (Hamdan Al Maktoum)

SYLVESTER KIRK
954. ASTONISHMENT ★★★★
b.c. Desert Style – Lucky Norwegian (Almutawakel).
January 22. First foal. 4,800Y. Tattersalls December. Not sold. The dam won one race in Norway at 3 yrs and is a half-sister to 3 other minor winners. The second dam, Echoes (by Niniski), won the Group 3 Prix Corrida and is a half-sister to 5 winners.
"A cracking little horse, he was a January foal and he's just a bit 'up behind' at the moment but he goes well and has a great attitude. He'll be early enough and he's done few bits of work already. If he carries on the way he is doing he'll be out in early May".

955. CREEVY ★★★
b.f. Trans Island – Kilbride Lass (Lahib).
April 29. Sixth living foal. 8,000Y. Doncaster St Leger. S Kirk. Half-sister to the fairly useful 6f (including at 2 yrs) and 7f winner of 6 races and listed-placed Fathsta (by Fath), to the fairly useful 6f (at 2 yrs) and 5f winner Consensus (by Common Grounds), the quite useful 2m all-weather winner Boumahou (by Desert Story) and a minor winner in Italy by Cape Cross. The dam is an unraced half-sister to 4 winners including the Grade 1 Canadian International winner Phoenix Reach. The second dam, Carroll's Canyon (by Hatim), is an unraced full or half-sister to 10 winners including the Prix de l'Arc de Triomphe winner Carroll House.
"A tall, leggy, backward filly that moves really well. Doing everything nicely, she's a little bit light of bone but if she copes with training she'll be quite a nice filly. She's done a fair bit already so I think she'll be fine". TRAINER'S BARGAIN BUY

956. FREE FOR ALL (IRE) ★★★★
b.br.c. Statue Of Liberty – Allegorica (Alzao).
February 12. Fifth foal. €26,000foal. Goffs. Littleton Stud. Half-brother to the useful Irish 6f, 7f and 1m winner Miss Gorica (by Mull Of Kintyre) and to the fair 5f (at 2 yrs) to 1m winner Celtic Spa (by Celtic Swing). The dam won 4 races from 5f to 7f and from 2-5 yrs and is a

half-sister to one winner. The second dam, Anne de Beaujeu (by Ahonoora), a listed-placed winner of 5 races in Ireland from 5f (at 2 yrs) to 7f, is a half-sister to 5 winners including the dual Group 3 winner Ahohoney. (J C Smith).

"A smashing horse, he was an early foal, he's strong, mature and as big as most of my three-year-olds. I like him a lot and he'll definitely be a two-year-old. I've just eased off him because he had a bit of a cough but he'll be out early. Going off his physique and his attitude he could be as nice as any I've had".

957. GALLANT EAGLE (IRE) ★★★

ch.c. Hawk Wing – Generous Gesture (Fasliyev).
April 12. Second foal. €20,000foal. Goffs. Littleton Stud. The dam, a fair dual 6f winner, is a half-sister to the smart dual listed 1m winner Harvest Queen. The second dam, Royal Bounty (by Generous), a quite useful 2-y-o 7.5f winner, is a half-sister to 3 minor winners here and abroad. (J C Smith).

"A beautiful mover, he's a little bit unfurnished and he's pretty forward mentally – probably too much for his own good. If I manage him properly he'll be OK in the second half of the season".

958. SCOTTISH BOOGIE ★★★

b.c. Tobougg – Scottish Spice (Selkirk).
March 22. Fourth foal. The dam, a fairly useful dual 2-y-o 7f and 4-y-o 1m winner, is a half-sister to one winner out of the French 11f winner Dilwara (by Lashkari). (J C Smith).

"A real nice two-year-old. The dam was a good filly but she hasn't bred anything yet and that's my only concern. He's going along sharp enough, he's strong and bang there so you should see him out early. Hopefully we can start the mare off with a winner".

959. HULCOTE ROSE (IRE) ★★★

b.f. Rock Of Gibraltar – Siksikawa (Mark Of Esteem).
February 21. Fourth foal. Deauville August. €95,000Y. Jeremy Brummitt. The dam, unplaced in one start, is a half-sister to 7 winners including the Grade 1 Hollywood Derby winner Labeeb and the Grade 2 winners Fanmore and Alrassaam. The second dam, Lady Blackfoot (by Prince Tenderfoot), a listed winner in Ireland, was fourth in the Group 1 Phoenix Stakes.

"A nice filly that goes well, she's strong enough and getting stronger as we go along. She's got a middle-distance pedigree and is probably one for the late summer onwards, but she's sharp enough so don't be surprised if we have a try with her a little bit earlier".

960. STARBOARD BOW ★★

b.c. Observatory – Overboard (Rainbow Quest).
February 22. Fourth foal. 11,000Y. Tattersalls October 2. Not sold. Half-brother to the quite useful 10f winner Bin End (by King's Best), to the fair dual 12f winner Sea Admiral (by Sinndar) and the modest 12f and hurdles winner Summer Of Love (by Fasliyev). The dam, placed over 12f, is a half-sister to 4 winners including the Group 3 6f Coventry Stakes winner Red Sea and the useful 7f (at 2 yrs) and Italian Group 3 12f winner Sailing. The second dam, Up Anchor (by Slip Anchor), won four races including the Group 3 12f St Simon Stakes, was third in the Italian Oaks and is a half-sister to 5 winners including the triple US Grade 3 winner at around 8.5f Just Class.

"A nice horse but he's backward and he'll have a couple of runs at the back-end before making a nice three-year-old".

961. TEST PILOT ★★★

b.c. Haafhd – Chinchilla (Inchinor).
April 18. Second foal. 34,000Y. Tattersalls October 2. Not sold. Half-brother to the Italian winner of 3 races at 2 and 3 yrs Mendace (by Bering). The dam is an unraced half-sister to 4 winners including the 2-y-o Group 3 Solario Stakes winner Chicmond. The second dam, Chicobin (by J O Tobin), is an unraced half-sister to 2 minor winners in the USA.

"He's probably still got some growing to do but he's precocious mentally. A real nice horse, he's well-balanced and a good mover. He's just a little light of bone and just a little bit immature physically. One for the middle part of the season and he's doing well".

962. WING OF FAITH ★★★
ch.c. Kirkwall – Angel Wing (Barathea).
February 11. First foal. The dam is an unraced half-sister to one winner. The second dam, Lochangel (by Night Shift), a very smart winner of the Group 1 5f Nunthorpe Stakes, is a half-sister to the champion sprinter Lochsong. (J C Smith).

"*A strong, well-made colt. He's a nice horse that's coping well with everything I'm asking him to do. We'll carry on with him and he shouldn't be too long before we run him*".

963. UNNAMED ★★★
b.c. Azamour – Irina (Polar Falcon).
March 9. Fourth foal. 30,000Y. S Kirk. Tattersalls October 2. S Kirk. Half-brother to the fairly useful 7f to 9f winner of 4 races (including at 2 yrs) Icemancometh (by Marju) and to the modest 7f winner of 4 races (including at 2 yrs) Imperial Lucky (by Imperial Ballet). The dam, a fairly useful Irish 7f and 1m winner at 3 and 4 yrs, is a half-sister to one winner. The second dam, Bird Of Love (by Ela-Mana-Mou), is a placed half-sister to 6 winners including the Australian Grade 1 winner Water Boatman and the Group 3 winner Hill Hopper (herself dam of the Group 1 Fillies' Mile and Coronation Stakes winner Nannina). (L Breslin).

"*A lovely horse that's doing really well, he's a bit on the weak side so he has to furnish and grow up. A beautiful mover and a colt with a good attitude, he'll be one for the second half of the season*".

964. UNNAMED ★★
b.f. Rock Of Gibraltar – Love And Affection (Exclusive Era).
January 30. Thirteenth foal. 35,000Y. Tattersalls October 2. S Kirk. Sister to the Group 3 Gordon Stakes winner and Group 1 placed Yellowstone, closely related to the 2-y-o 8.6f all-weather winner Danamour (by Dansili) and half-sister to the useful 7f (including at 2 yrs) and hurdles winner Londoner (by Sky Classic), the quite useful 12f and hurdles winner Always (by Dynaformer), the quite useful 10f winner Groom's Affection (by Groom Dancer) and 3 minor winners in the USA by Flying Paster (2) Dixieland Band and Bolger. The dam, a winner from 5f to 1m including a minor stakes at 3 yrs, was second in the Grade 1 6f Spinaway Stakes at 2 yrs and is closely related to the Prix d'Ispahan and Budweiser International Stakes winner Zoman. The second dam, A Little Affection (by King Emperor), a US stakes winner of 7 races, is a half-sister to 6 winners.

"*She's small and light. That's why she didn't cost as much as her pedigree would suggest. The mare's getting on a bit but the pedigree is superb. Physically she wouldn't be your first choice but we sacrificed that in that hope that she can go and win a race because she'd be a nice filly to send to the paddocks. She has a wonderful attitude, she goes along well and we'll just give her time to mature*".

965. UNNAMED ★★
b.f. Cadeaux Genereux – Triple Green (Green Desert).
March 24. Seventh foal. Half-sister to the fairly useful 7f and 1m winner of 7 races Titan Triumph (by Zamindar), to the fairly useful 10f winner Burning Moon (by Bering) and the quite useful 1m (at 2 yrs) to 12f winner Fair Gale (by Storming Home). The dam, a fair 1m placed 3-y-o, is a half-sister to 8 winners including the Group 2 10f Sun Chariot Stakes winner Talented. The second dam, Triple Reef (by Mill Reef), is an unraced half-sister to 13 winners including the smart middle-distance winners Maysoon, Richard of York and Third Watch and the dams of the Group winners Lend A Hand, Sea Wave, Tamure and Three Cheers. (Mr N Ormiston).

"*A small filly, she's nice and similar to her half-brother Fair Gale except she's a bit smaller. Being by Cadeaux she could be anything. I haven't done an awful lot with her but she moves well*".

966. UNNAMED ★★★★
b.f. Invincible Spirit – Attymon Lill (Marju).
February 22. Second foal. 55,000Y. Tattersalls October 2. S Kirk. Half-sister to the unplaced 2008 2-y-o Baby Is Here (by Namid). The dam is an unplaced half-sister to one winner. The

second dam, Guest Room (by Be My Guest), is an unraced half-sister to the multiple Group 1 winner Sun Princess.
"An athletic filly with the scope to be more than just a nice two-year-old. She's sharp enough and you should keep an eye out for her".

967. UNNAMED ★★
b.c. Dansili – Michelle Ma Belle (Shareef Dancer).
March 19. Half-brother to the modest 2008 7f placed 2-y-o Cousin Charlie (by Choisir). The dam, a fairly useful 5f and 6f winner (including at 2 yrs), was listed-placed and is a half-sister to several winners. The second dam, April Magic (by Chief Singer), was unraced.
"He had a problem with a bad tooth and I had to leave him alone so I haven't done a lot with him but he'll be worth putting in the book".

968 UNNAMED ★★★
b.c. Fasliyev – Velvet Slipper (Muhtafal).
April 4. 9,000Y. Doncaster Autumn. Not sold. Half-brother to the fair 1m winner of 3 races Statute Book (by Statue Of Liberty). The dam, a modest 7f placed maiden, is a half-sister to 6 winners including the useful 2-y-o 6f and 7f winner Muhab. The second dam, Magic Slipper (by Habitat), a useful 10f and 11.5f winner, is a half-sister to 6 winners including the 1,000 Guineas winner Fairy Footsteps and the St Leger winner Light Cavalry.
"The half-brother surprised me because he's got physical problems but he's gone out and won 3 races. The fellow is nicer, he might take a bit of time but he does everything nicely. Again, he's probably mentally too precocious for his own good so I've backed off him a bit. He'll reward us later on and be a nice horse".

969. UNNAMED ★★★
b.c. Night Shift – Cookie Cutter (Fasliyev).
April 13. First foal. 16,000Y. Tattersalls October 2. S Kirk. The dam, a modest 4-y-o 6f winner, is a half-sister to 2 winners including the Irish listed 6f winner and Group 3 7f Ballycorus Stakes third Poco A Poco. The second dam, Cut The Red Tape (by Sure Blade), a fair 2-y-o 7f winner, is a half-sister to 4 winners including the smart Group 2 Beefeater Gin Celebration Mile and Group 3 7f Beeswing Stakes winner Bold Russian and the fairly useful 9f winner Axe.
"A sharp horse, he's precocious enough and ready to go but he may end up wanting a nursery later on because I think he'll grow and develop, so I'll keep my eye on him".

970. UNNAMED ★★
b.c. Val Royal – Blue Kestrel (Bluebird).
April 12. Eighth foal. €20,000Y. Tattersalls Ireland. S Kirk. Half-brother to the quite useful 13f to 2m and hurdles winner Fortune Island (by Val Royal), to the fair 1m, 9f and hurdles winner Blackhall Crew (by Grand Lodge) and a minor winner in France by Montjeu.
"A colt with a staying pedigree, but he's a real nice horse and there are two shares left to sell in him! He's one for the second half of the season over seven furlongs before training on to be a decent three-year-old".

971. UNNAMED ★★
b.f. Piccolo – Runs In The Family (Distant Relative).
Apil 3. Eighth foal. 11,500Y. Doncaster St Leger. J Brummitt. Sister to the quite useful 6f (including at 2 yrs) and 5f winner of 5 races Angel Sprints and half-sister to the Italian winner of 6 races, including at 2 yrs, Red Bamboo (by Daggers Drawn) and the Italian 2-y-o winner of 3 races Jolly God (by Compton Place). The dam, a fair 5f and 6f winner of 4 races, is a half-sister to 4 other minor winners. The second dam, Stoneydale (by Tickled Pink), won 5 races at 2 and 4 yrs and is a half-sister to 6 winners.
"She's a quite nice, sharp filly and she goes along well. I think she'll be good enough to win a little maiden auction".

WILLIAM KNIGHT

972. ALAIA (IRE) ★★★
b.f. Sinndar – Alasana (Darshaan).
March 30. Tenth living foal. €280,000Y. Goffs Million. BBA (Ire). 170,000Y. Tattersalls December. Norris/Huntingdon. Half-sister to

7 winners including the 7f (at 2 yrs) and listed 1m winner and Grade 1 E P Taylor Stakes second Alasha (by Barathea), the 10f winner Alamouna (by Indian Ridge), the 1m and 10f winner Almiyan (by King's Best), the 7f and 1m winner Alafzar (by Green Desert) – all 3 quite useful - and a minor winner in France by Daylami. The dam won twice in France over 1m and 9f and is a half-sister to the Prix Maurice de Nieuil winner Altayan and the Grand Prix de Vichy winner Altashar. The second dam, Aleema (by Red God), won over 9f in France and is a half-sister to the disqualified Oaks winner Aliysa. (M J Taylor & L Taylor).

"A very nice filly, despite her pedigree she's not going to be a late two-year-old and hopefully she'll be one for June or July. Quite forward, she's well-balanced and a lovely mover and I see her starting at seven furlongs".

973. BOSTON BLUE ★★
b.c. Halling – City Of Gold (Sadler's Wells).
April 17. Sixth foal. 52,000Y. Tattersalls October 2. A Skiffington. Brother to Mabuya, unplaced in 2 starts at 2 yrs in 2008 and to a minor winner in Japan by Sunday Silence. The dam, a fairly useful 7f (at 2 yrs) and 12f winner, is a sister to the Group 3 10f Gordon Richards Stakes winner Scribe and the German listed winner Northern Hal and a half-sister to 5 winners. The second dam, Northern Script (by Arts And Letters), a fairly useful 1m winner, is a half-sister to 10 winners including the Melbourne Cup and Grand Prix de Paris winner At Talaq and Annoconnor, a winner of four Grade 1 events in the USA. (Mr & Mrs I H Bendelow).

"A nice, scopey colt, he'll be a back-end two-year-old over seven furlongs and a mile. He just filling out his frame at the moment but he's a lovely mover. He has a Derby entry and will be trained with his three-year-old career in mind".

974. COOL KITTEN (IRE) ★★★
b.f. One Cool Cat – Zoom Lens (Caerleon).
April 11. Eleventh foal. 30,000Y. Tattersalls October 3. Elmhurst Bloodstock. Half-sister to the smart 2-y-o Group 2 1m Royal Lodge Stakes winner Atlantis Prince (by Tagula), to the fairly useful 2-y-o dual 1m winner Close Up, the Austrian winner Light Meter (both by Cadeaux Genereux), the fairly useful 2-y-o 1m winner Zeis (by Bahhare), the fair 1m winner Photo Flash (by Bahamian Bounty), the fair 2-y-o 5f winner Blue Movie (by Bluebird) and a minor winner in France by Desert Prince. The dam, placed once over 7f at 2 yrs, is a half-sister to 4 winners including the middle-distance winner Itqan (herself dam of the Group 1 Gran Criterium and US Grade 3 winner Hello) and to the placed dam of the Group 2 Prix Dollar winner Dano-Mast. The second dam, Photo (by Blakeney), a quite useful 1m and 9f winner, is a half-sister to 8 winners and to the unplaced dam of the Australian Grade 1 winner Nick's Joy. (Mr T G Roddick).

"She looks quite precocious and she's going nicely at the moment. She's small and racey and she'll be a six furlong two-year-old to start with".

975. FLYING DESTINATION ★★★
ch.c. Dubai Destination – Fly For Fame (Shaadi).
April 26. Half-brother to the fair Irish 12f and 13f winner Fire Finch (by Halling), to the fair dual 10f and hurdles winner Air Chief (by Dr Fong), the modest 10f winner Fittonia (by Ashkalani) and a minor 10f winner in France by Bering. The dam, a useful French 10f (at 2 yrs) and 12f winner, is a half-sister to 6 winners including the French listed winner Fixed Wing. The second dam, Fly Me (by Luthier), won the Group 3 10.5f Prix Corrida and the Group 3 10.5f Prix de Flore and is a half-sister to the Group 1 Grand Prix de Paris winner Galiani. (The Pheasnt Rew Partnership).

"A bonny little horse I bought outside the ring for only 3 grand. He'll definitely win his races, albeit at a level, and he'll make a June/July two-year-old". TRAINER'S BARGAIN BUY

976. LUCKY BREEZE (IRE) ★★★
b.f. Key Of Luck – Lasting Chance (American Chance).
March 31. Fifth foal. 25,000Y. Tattersalls October 2. Blandford Bloodstock. Half-sister to

the very smart 7f (at 2 yrs) and listed 10f winner and subsequent Hong Kong Derby winner Collection (by Peintre Celebre) and to the fair 7f and 1m winner Dapple Dawn (by Celtic Swing). The dam won 4 races in Canada including a Grade 3 event and is a half-sister to 8 winners. The second dam, Baildancer (by Bailjumper), a stakes-placed winner in the USA, is a half-sister to 4 winners. (Mrs S M Mitchell).

"A big, scopey filly, she's a bit 'on the leg' at the moment but she's a well-balanced, good mover. One for September time I should think".

977. MISSIONAIRE (USA) ★★★★
b.br.c. El Corredor – Fapindy (A P Indy).
January 27. Third foal. $320,000Y. Keeneland September. Westfield Place Corp. Half-brother to the US stakes-placed winner Point Me The Way (by Point Given). The dam, a minor winner at 3 yrs in the USA, is a half-sister to 4 winners including two stakes winners. The second dam, Aroz (by Fappiano), won at 4 yrs and is a half-sister to 10 winners including the US Grade 3 winner Rose Bouquet. (Bluehills Racing Ltd).

"A lovely colt, he oozes class and is a very well-balanced colt and a good mover. He'll be out in mid-summer and I think he could have the speed for six furlongs".

978. SHEER FORCE (IRE) ★★★
b.c. Invincible Spirit – Imperial Graf (Blushing John).
May 9. Seventh foal. 68,000Y. Tattersalls October 2. Bluehills Racing. Half-brother to the fairly useful 2008 2-y-o 5f winner Ginobili (by Fasliyev), to the useful Irish 7f winner of 4 races at 2 and 3 yrs Dynamo Dancer (by Danehill Dancer), the modest 6f to 1m all-weather winner Noble Locks (by Night Shift) and 3 winners in Italy by Bigstone, Rossini and Royal Abjar. The dam was placed at 3 yrs in Italy and is a half-sister to 4 winners. The second dam, Sharp Ascent (by Sharpen Up), won the Grade 3 Honeymoon Handicap in the USA and is a half-sister to 6 winners. (Bluehills Racing Ltd).

"A nice horse, he's a May foal with a rounded action that goes along nicely and he'll make a two-year-old in June or July".

979. PRINCE OF DREAMS ★★★
b.c. Sadler's Wells – Questina (Rainbow Quest).
May 2. Eighth foal. 140,000Y. Tattersalls October 1. Elmhurst Bloodstock. Closely related to the Group 3 10f Prix Corrida and Group 3 10.5f Prix de Flore winner Trumbaka (by In The Wings) and half-brother to the unplaced 2008 2-y-o Spirit Of Dubai (by Cape Cross) and the French listed 9f winner Arctic Hunt (by Bering). The dam won twice at 3 yrs in France and is a half-sister to 6 winners. The second dam, Soviet Squaw (by Nureyev), won once at 3 yrs in France and is a full or half-sister to 8 winners including the Italian Group 1 winner Antheus. (Mr T G Roddick).

"She has a lot of class about her, she's leggy and finds everything easy for one that's more of a three-year-old type. She'll be out over a mile later in the season and I think she's capable of winning as a two-year-old".

980. TECHNOPHOBE (IRE) ★★
ch.c. Noverre – Staylily (Grand Lodge).
February 27. Third foal. 50,000Y. Doncaster St Leger. Norris/Huntingdon. Brother to the fairly useful dual 7f winner Candle Sahara and half-brother to the quite useful 6f winner of 4 races Kyle (by Kyllachy). The dam is an unraced half-sister to 4 winners including the US stakes winner and Grade 1 placed She's Classy. The second dam, Stately Dance (by Stately Don), won twice in the USA and is a half-sister to the Coronation Cup winner Be My Native. (Mr & Mrs B Willis).

"He's growing at the moment and is 'up behind' but he's going to make up into a big, strapping colt. He's a nice type and should make a two-year-old by August time".

981. UNNAMED ★★★
gr.f. Verglas – Mango Groove (Unfuwain).
January 17. First foal. 18,000Y. Tattersalls October 2. Norris/Huntingdon. The dam is an unplaced half-sister to 3 winners including very useful 2-y-o 6f winner and Group 3 placed Feared In Flight. The second dam, Solar Crystal (Alzao), won the Group 3 1m May Hill Stakes, was third in the Group 1 1m Prix Marcel Boussac

and is a half-sister to the Group 3 12f Lancashire Oaks winner State Crystal and the Irish Derby third Tchaikovsky. (O J Williams).
"A good-sized filly, she looks relatively precocious. She's a bit hot, temperament-wise, but she has definite ability, she's a nice mover and I like her".

982. UNNAMED ★★
b.f. Exceed And Excel – Mo Stopher (Sharpo).
March 8. Half-sister to the fair dual 7f winner Robin Sharp, to the fair 6f winner Steppin Out (both by First Trump), the modest 5f and 6f winner Calabaza (by Zaha), the modest dual 1m winner Spirit's Awakening and the poor 2m winner Unleaded (both by Danzig Connection). The dam is an unplaced full sister to 3 winners. (Canisbay Bloodstock).
"A filly with a good action, she's gone a bit weak on me at the moment. One for July or August. She goes along OK and at a level I think she'll be alright".

DAVID LANIGAN
983. LIGHTING SPEED ★★★★
b.f. Xaar – Crown Of Light (Mtoto).
March 23. Sixth foal. Half-sister to the quite useful 1m and 10f winner Augustine, to the modest French 1m winner Royal Tiara (both by Machiavellian) and the smart 7f (at 2 yrs) to 14f winner and listed-placed Balkan Knight (by Selkirk). The dam, a smart 7f (at 2 yrs) and 11.5f winner, was third in the Oaks and is a half-sister to the very useful 2-y-o listed 1m Stardom Stakes winner and Group 1 Grand Criterium third Alboostan and the useful 7.5f and 8.5f winner Romanzof. The second dam, Russian Countess (by Nureyev), a useful French 2-y-o 1m winner and listed-placed, is a half-sister to 5 winners. (Dr Ali Ridha).
"A very nice filly for the back-end over seven furlongs".

984. LOGOS ASTRA (USA) ★★★★
b.c. Elusive Quality – Wild Planet (Nureyev).
February 7. Sixth foal. Half-brother to the US Grade 2 Dahlia Handicap winner Surya (by Unbridled), to the French 1m winner Mundus Novus (by Unbridled's Song) and the French 2-y-o 1m winner Wind Silence (by A P Indy). The dam won at 2 yrs and was third in the Group 3 Prestige Stakes and is a half-sister to 6 winners. The second dam, Ivory Wings (by Sir Ivor), a listed winner over 12f, is a half-sister to the multiple US Grade 1 winner Miss Oceana, the Prix Jean Prat winner Kitwood and the dam of the Coronation Stakes winner Magic Of Life.
"A smashing colt that goes very nicely. He'll need a bit of time but he should be out by the end of June or early July. A well-made horse, he's very easy to do anything with and he's my favourite at the moment. I wouldn't be surprised if he had the speed to go six furlongs but he'll probably be better over seven. A compact little horse with a bit of quality about him and he has the scope to go on as a three-year-old as well".

985. STAR TWILIGHT ★★★
b.f. King's Best – Star Express (Sadler's Wells).
March 8. Sister to the moderate 6f winner Haedi. The dam, a minor 12f winner in France, is a sister to the Group 3 7f Greenham Stakes winner and Irish 2,000 Guineas fourth Yalaietanee and a half-sister to the Group 3 5f Molecomb Stakes winner Sahara Star (herself dam of the Group 2 5f Flying Childers Stakes winner Land Of Dreams). The second dam, Vaigly Star (by Star Appeal), a smart sprint winner of 3 races, was second in the Group 1 July Cup and a half-sister to the high-class sprinter Vaigly Great.
"A nice filly, she's not the best looker in the world but her temperament's not too bad for a King's Best. She'll be alright over six furlongs".

986. UNNAMED ★★★
ch.c. Halling – Cheerleader (Singspiel).
February 12. First foal. The dam, quite useful 10f winner, is a half-sister to the smart US Grade 2 1m Colonel F W Koester Handicap and German Group 3 1m winner Ventiquattrofogli and to the German 6f to 11f listed winner Irish Fighter. The second dam, India Atlanta (by Ahonoora), is an unraced half-sister to 6 winners including the German Group 3 1m winner Sinyar.

"A big, tall, leggy horse, he's nice but he's one for the back-end of the season. He goes very well and he'll be alright this year".

987. UNNAMED ★★★
b.c. Whipper – Civic Duty (Definite Article).
April 8. Second foal. 40,000Y. Tattersalls October 2. Rabbah Bloodstock. The dam, a fair Irish 4-y-o 6f and 7f winner of 5 races, is a half-sister to 3 winners. The second dam, Just Society (by Devil's Bag), an Irish 5f and 6f winner, is a half-sister to 3 winners.
"A nice, compact horse with a bit of strength. He'll be a six furlong type two-year-old in July or August".

988. UNNAMED ★★★
ch.c. Dubawi – Extreme Beauty (Rahy).
January 25. First foal. 140,000Y. Tattersalls October 1. Troy Steve. The dam, a quite useful 6f (at 2 yrs) and 7f winner, is a half-sister to 5 winners including the US Grade 2 and dual Grade 3 winner Go Between (by Point Given). The second dam, Mediation (by Caerleon), won the listed Irish 1,000 Guineas Trial and was Group 3 placed here and in the USA.
"A nice, solid horse that won't be too big, he'll make a two-year-old over six furlongs".

989. UNNAMED ★★★
ch.c. Doyen – Fudge (Polar Falcon).
February 25. 25,000Y. Tattersalls October 3. Rabbah Bloodstock. Half-brother to the modest 2008 6f placed 2-y-o Gilbertian (by Sakhee), to the useful 5f (at 2 yrs) to 7f winner of 4 races and Group 2 third Gloved Hand (by Royal Applause), the fair 10f and all-weather 12f winner Jackie Kiely (by Vettori), and the moderate 7f and 1m winners Rigat (by Dansili) and Magroom (by Compton Place). The dam is an unraced half-sister to 7 winners including the quite useful 1m to 10f winner Summer Fashion (herself dam of the Group winners Definite Article, Salford City and Salford Express). The second dam, My Candy (by Lorenzaccio), is a placed half-sister to 7 winners including the Ballymoss Stakes and Royal Whip Stakes winner Candy Cane.

"A strong horse, not the best walker in the world but he has a good action when cantering. He'll want seven furlongs as a two-year-old and will be a better horse next year". TRAINER'S BARGAIN BUY

990. UNNAMED ★★★
b.f. Dubawi – Have Faith (Machiavellian).
March 8. Second foal. Half-sister to Congregation (by Cape Cross), unplaced in 2 starts at 2 yrs in 2008. The dam, a quite useful 2-y-o 7f winner, is a sister to the useful UAE winner of 7 races Opportunist and a half-sister to the Group 2 1m Matron Stakes winner Favourable Terms. The second dam, Fatefully (by Private Account), a smart winner of 4 races including a listed event over 1m, is a half-sister to 2 minor winners.
"A small filly that needs to strengthen a bit and just needs a bit of time. She'll be a July/August two-year-old and six furlongs should suit her".

991. UNNAMED ★★★★
b.f. Dansili – Makara (Lion Cavern).
March 31. Fourth foal. 70,000Y. Tattersalls October 1. Rabbah Bloodstock. Sister to the French winner of 3 races at 2 and 3 yrs Asque and half-sister to the fairly useful Irish 2-y-o 5f and 6f winner Fourpenny Lane (by Efisio). The dam is an unraced half-sister to 5 winners including the useful 5f (at 2 yrs) and listed 7f winner Kalindi. The second dam, Rohita (by Waajib), a fairly useful 2-y-o 5f and 6f winner, was third in the Group 3 6f Cherry Hinton Stakes and is a half-sister to 5 winners.
"A quality filly, she could be very nice. She's only trotting at the moment and whatever she does this year she'll be better as a three-year-old. I'll probably start her off at six furlongs but she'll be better over seven. A very nice filly".

992. UNNAMED ★★★
ch.f. Dubawi – Miss Honorine (Highest Honor).
April 21. Third foal. 55,000Y. Tattersalls October 2. Rabbah Bloodstock. Half-sister to Mirabile Dictu (by King's Best), unplaced in one start at 2 yrs in 2008 and to the fairly useful

2-y-o 6f winner Master Chef (by Oasis Dream). The dam won 4 races at 3 and 4 yrs in Ireland including three listed events from 1m to 10f and is a half-sister to 7 winners. The second dam, Nini Princesse (by Niniski), won 6 races from 2 to 4 yrs in France and is a sister to the US Grade 1 winner Louis Cyphre and a half-sister to the Group 2 winner Psychobabble.
"A small, compact filly, she's nice and she should win races".

993. UNNAMED ★★★
b.c. *Motivator – Park Romance (Dr Fong).*
February 12. First foal. 75,000Y. Tattersalls October 1. Rabbah Bloodstock. The dam, a fairly useful 2-y-o 6f winner, is a half-sister to 4 winners including the 6f (at 2 yrs) and Group 3 7f Ballycorus Stakes winner Rum Charger. The second dam, Park Charger (by Tirol), a useful winner over 1m and 10f at 3 yrs in Ireland, was listed-placed several times and is a half-sister to 9 winners.
"He'll be alright. At the moment he just looks like a two-year-old without much scope but they can do anything during the summer. He'll win races".

994. UNNAMED ★★★
b.f. *Selkirk – State Secret (Green Desert).*
March 1. Fourth foal. 67,000Y. Tattersalls October 1. David Lanigan. Half-sister to the fair dual 1m winner and listed Masaka Stakes second Song Of Silence (by Unbridled's Song). The dam, a winner over 6.5f at 2 yrs, was fourth in the Group 3 1m Prix d'Aumale and is a half-sister to 8 winners including the 2-y-o Group 2 Criterium de Maisons-Laffitte winner Bitooh and the dams of the Group/Grade 1 winners Storming Home, Music Note and Musical Chimes. The second dam, It's In The Air (by Mr Prospector), a joint-champion 2-y-o filly in the USA, won from 6f to 10f.
"She could be a nice two-year-old, she's a big, strong filly and whatever she does this year she'll be much better as a three-year-old. She's very nice and could be anything".

995. UNNAMED ★★★
b.f. *Dynaformer – String Quartet (Sadler's Wells).*
April 16. Sixth foal. $175,000Y. Keeneland September. Rabbah Bloodstock. Half-sister to the smart 1m winner (at 2 yrs) and Group 2 12f Princess Of Wales's Stakes second Shahin (by Kingmambo). The dam, a 12.5f listed winner in France and third in the Group 3 Lancashire Oaks, is a sister to the Irish listed 10f winner Casey Tibbs and a half-sister to 4 winners. The second dam, Fleur Royale (by Mill Reef), won the Group 2 Pretty Polly Stakes, was second in the Irish Oaks and is a half-sister to 4 winners.
"A sharp filly, especially for a Dynaformer. There's plenty of speed in the pedigree and she'll make a two-year-old later in the season".

996. UNNAMED ★★
b.f. *Bahri – Triple Zee (Zilzal).*
March 7. Seventh foal. 16,000Y. Tattersalls October 1. Rabbah Bloodstock. Half-sister to the useful 2-y-o 7f winner and Group 3 Diomed Stakes second Cauvery (by Exit To Nowhere), to the fair 8.7f winner Redarsene (by Sakhee) and the fair 2-y-o 7.5f winner Three Pennies (by Pennekamp). The dam is an unraced half-sister to one minor winner. The second dam, Zuaetreh (by Raise A Native), is a placed half-sister to 4 winners.
"She'll be alright and will need some time but will probably make a two-year-old at the back-end of the season".

997. UNNAMED ★★★★
b.c. *King's Best – Broadway Hit (Sadler's Wells).*
April 27. First foal. 20,000Y. Tattersalls October 1. D Lanigan. The dam is an unraced half-sister to 5 winners including the smart 2-y-o Group 1 1m Prix Marcel Boussac winner and Group 1 10f Nassau Stakes second Sulk, the Group1 Hong Kong Cup winner and Epsom Derby second Eagle Mountain and the smart 1m listed winner Wallace. The second dam, Masskana (by Darshaan), a minor 9f and 10f winner in France, is a half-sister to the US Grade 3 Arcadia Handicap winner Madjaristan and the Group 2 Gallinule Stakes winner Massyar.

"A nice, quality horse. He didn't come in till late but he's very nice and worth looking out for. He goes very well and he should be sharp enough for six furlongs".

GER LYONS
998. DAYS AHEAD (IRE) ★★
ch.g. Kheleyf – Hushaby (Eurobus).
March 31. Fourth foal. €31,000Y. Tattersalls Ireland. Ger Lyons. Half-brother to a winner over hurdles by Lend A Hand. The dam is an unraced half-sister to 7 winners including the Group 3 Ormonde Stakes winner Brunico. The second dam, Cartridge (by Jim French), won twice at 3 yrs and is a half-sister to 3 winners. (W Bellew).

"When I saw him at the sales I thought there was just something about him I liked. He doesn't have a particularly good pedigree but he's a big, strapping horse. I'm getting on with him, he has a good attitude and a good action, but he's one for the middle-to-back-end of the season". Last year Ger's wife gave the two-year-olds Native American Indian names. This year she's naming them after ipod tunes!"

999. LOVE LOCKDOWN ★★★
gr.c. Verglas – Out Of Thanks (Sadler's Wells).
May 10. Second foal. €35,000Y. Tattersalls Ireland. Ger Lyons. Half-brother to the 2008 6f placed 2-y-o Out Of Honour (by Highest Honor). The dam, a fairly useful dual 10f winner in Ireland, is a half-sister to 3 winners. The second dam, Trust In Luck (by Nashwan), an Irish 7f winner, is a half-sister to 9 winners including the Grade 1 winner Dress To Thrill.

"He'll make his debut at Naas in mid-April. He's sharp and being by Verglas he'll want some cut in the ground. He was a May foal but hopefully by the time of his second birthday he'll already be a winner. A lovely, big-striding horse, he'll be a grand horse as the year goes on".

1000. MISTER TEE ★★★★
b.c. Danehill Dancer – Clipper (Salse).
March 8. Sixth foal. 56,000Y. Doncaster St Leger. Emerald Bloodstock. Brother to the quite useful Irish 6f and 7f winner of 3 races Subtle Shimmer. The dam, a useful 2-y-o 1m winner and 10f placed 3-y-o, is a half-sister to 3 winners including the listed-placed Genoa. The second dam, Yawl (by Rainbow Quest), a very useful winner of 2 races over 7f at 2 yrs including the Group 3 Rockfel Stakes, is a half-sister to 7 winners. (W Bellew).

"He's a cracking horse and he'll start in mid-April. You can't have too many Danehill Dancer's – I've had a few nice ones and this colt is every bit as good as they were. He'll be a smart horse if he delivers on the track what he does at home. He's ready to run and you'll be seeing him soon over five furlongs".

1001. NEON TIGER ★★★
b.c. Bahamian Bounty – Sharplaw Star (Xaar).
January 13. First foal. 55,000Y. Doncaster St Leger. Emerald Bloodstock. The dam, a fairly useful 2-y-o dual 5f winner, was third in the Group 3 5f Queen Mary Stakes and is a half-sister to 2 winners. The second dam, Hamsah (by Green Desert), a quite useful 2-y-o dual 5f winner, was listed-placed and is a half-sister to the Irish 2,000 Guineas winner Wassl and to the dam of the Queen Mary Stakes winner On Tiptoes.

"I like him but he'll be a middle-to-back-end colt. I'm in no rush with him".

1002. REGGAE ROCK ★★
b.c. Red Ransom – Calonnog (Peintre Celebre).
March 28. Second foal. 26,000Y. Doncaster St Leger. Emerald Bloodstock. The dam, a modest 12f placed maiden, is a half-sister to 2 winners including the US Grade 1 winner Sunshine Street. The second dam, Meadow Spirit (by Chief's Crown), is an unplaced half-sister to the US Grade 1 winner Dawn's Curtsey.

"A nice horse but he's going to take time. I think he'll need seven furlongs from mid-summer onwards, he has a nice attitude and I like him but it's too early to say anymore than that".

1003. RUSTY HALO ★★★
gr.c. Verglas – Summer Crush (Summer Squall).
May 5. Third foal. €27,000Y. Goffs. Ger Lyons. Half-brother to the fairly useful Irish 2-y-o 7f

winner and listed 12f placed Blackberry Boy (by Desert Prince) and to the fair 10f and hurdles winner Havetoavit (by Theatrical). The dam is an unplaced half-sister to 7 winners including the Group 1 Racing Post Trophy winner Saratoga Springs. The second dam, Population (by General Assembly), is a placed half-sister to the Group/Grade 1 winners Play It Safe and Providential.

"A nice horse, I thought he was going to be early but he'll be another month. I like my two Verglas two-year-olds, they're the ones showing me the most early doors. Being by Verglas I'm expecting he'll prefer softish ground".

1004. WEALDMORE WAVE (IRE) ★★★★
b.c. Oratorio – Multicolour Wave
(Rainbow Quest).
April 28. Fifth foal. €120,000Y. Goffs Million. Bobby O'Ryan. Closely related to the French 9.5f winner Photophore (by Clodovil) and half-brother to the 2008 2-y-o Group 3 7f Prix du Calvados winner Elusive Wave (by Elusive City), to the Irish 2-y-o 7f winner Million Spirits (by Invincible Spirit) and the Irish 2-y-o 7f winner and listed-placed Million Waves (by Mull Of Kintyre). The dam is a placed half-sister to 4 winners. The second dam, Echoes (by Niniski), won the Group 3 Prix Corrida, was Group 2 placed and is a half-sister to 5 winners.

"If I had a Royal Ascot horse I think it could be him. I think he's a very smart horse, he has a lovely attitude and hopefully he'll win next time out, over six furlongs. I like him a lot".

1005. UNNAMED ★★
b.f. Alhaarth – Montana Lady (Be My Guest).
March 6. €10,000Y. Goffs. Ger Lyons. Half-sister to the modest 2008 2-y-o 5f winner Red Cell (by Kheleyf), to the quite useful Irish 2-y-o 6f winner Nebraska Lady (by Lujain) and the modest 10f winner Landikhaya (by Kris Kin). The dam won over 7f at 3 yrs in Ireland and is a half-sister to 3 winners in Italy. The second dam, Invisible Halo (by Halo), won over 6f at 2 yrs and is a half-sister to 5 minor winners.

"The fillies are taking time to come to themselves but she's actually grown into a nice,
big, scopey filly. She's doing everything I've asked but she's one for the second half of the season".

GEORGE MARGARSON
1006. EXCELLENT GUEST ★★★
b.c. Exceed And Excel – Princess Speedfit
(Desert Prince).
February 22. Third foal. Half-brother to the useful 2008 2-y-o listed 6f winner of 3 races Imperial Guest (by Imperial Dancer). The dam was a fair 8.3f winner at 3 yrs and is a half-sister to the French listed 12f Prix de la Porte de Madrid and Group 2 placed Sibling Rival. The second dam, Perfect Sister (by Perrault), a minor French winner, is a half-sister to the US Grade 1 winner Frankly Perfect and the French listed winner and US Grade 1 placed Franc Argument. (J D Guest).

"A well-grown, strong type and similar to Imperial Guest at this stage last year. Showing plenty of promise".

1007. OUR GEORGIE GIRL ★★★
ch.f. Zafeen – Rosina May
(Danehill Dancer).
January 18. Third foal. Half-sister to 2 unplaced horses by Josr Algarhoud. The dam won all her 3 starts, over 5f at 2 yrs. The second dam, Gay Paris (by Paris House, was unraced.

"She's a well-grown, strong filly and is showing plenty of promise. She should be seen out in mid-April given continued progress as her mother was unbeaten 3 from 3 as a two-year-old".

1008. THALIWARRU ★★★
b.c. Barathea – Autumn Pearl (Orpen).
April 15. Sixth foal. 30,000Y. Tattersalls October 2. Angie Sykes. The dam won 3 races at 2 and 3 yrs, was second in the Group 2 Temple Stakes and is a half-sister to 2 winners abroad. The second dam, Cyclone Flyer (by College Chapel), won once at 3 yrs and is a half-sister to 8 winners including the Group 2 King's Stand Stakes.

"He's a small, compact, sprinting type and is well-forward and showing plenty of speed".

1009. YOUNG SIMON ★★★
ch.c. Piccolo – Fragrant Cloud (Zilzal).
April 21. Brother to the fair 2-y-o dual 5f winner Hephaestus. The dam is a 12f placed half-sister to numerous winners including the smart and genuine Group 3 7f Hungerford Stakes and Group 3 7f Prix du Palais-Royal winner Young Ern. The second dam, Stardyn (by Star Appeal), a poor middle-distance placed handicapper, is a half-sister to 4 winners.
"A leggy sort that will not be seen out until June but he's a very athletic horse and a lovely, well-balanced mover".

1010. UNNAMED ★★
ch.c. Kyllachy – Dame Jude (Dilum).
May 11. Fifth foal. Half-brother to the fair 2-y-o 7f winner Bertocelli (by Vettori). The dam, a fair dual 5f winner at 2 yrs, is out of the poor sprint maiden Three Lucky (by Final Straw).
"He's a late foal but looks a sprinting type as his pedigree would suggest and he should be seen out in late May".

1011. UNNAMED ★★
b.f. Red Ransom – Fiveofive (Fairy King).
April 21. Half-sister to Medici Code (by Medicean), a quite useful 1m and 9f winner here and subsequently a dual Grade 2 winner in the USA, to the quite useful 2-y-o 5f and 6f winner and listed-placed Polly Alexander (by Foxhound), the fair and 1m and 10f winner Lilli Marlene (by Sri Pekan), the fair 2-y-o 7f winner My Only Sunshine (by First Trump) and to the fair 12f winner Sweet Angeline (by Deploy). The dam, a modest 5f (at 2 yrs) and 1m winner, is a half-sister to 4 winners including the Group 3 6f July Stakes third The Old Firm. The second dam, North Hut (by Northfields), ran twice unplaced and is a half-sister to 4 winners.
"She's a nice sort that will need a bit of time but should make a two-year-old later in the year".

ALAN McCABE

1012. FRATELLINO ★★★
ch.c. Auction House – Vida (Wolfhound).
April 14. 2,200Y. Doncaster Autumn Sales. Brother to the fair 6f (at 2 yrs) and 8.7f winner of 4 races Common Diva. The dam is an unplaced half-sister to the useful dual 6f winner and listed-placed Maghaarb. The second dam, Fida (by Persian Heights), is a half-sister to the top-class Coronation Stakes, Irish 1,000 Guineas and Eclipse Stakes winner Kooyonga and to the Irish listed winner and Group-placed Hatton Gardens – herself dam of the South African Grade 1 winner Kundalini. (Sale of the Century).
"A very pleasing individual, we were going to run him in the Brocklesbury but he got eliminated, so we took him to Beverley and he won a maiden auction. He's a very compact, sprinting type but the family get further so we hope he'll do the same in time".

1013. OPUS DEI ★★★★
b.c. Oasis Dream – Grail (Quest For Fame).
April 1. Sixth foal. 15,000Y. Tattersalls October 1. A McCabe. Half-brother to the fairly useful 2-y-o 6f winner Divine Right (by Observatory) and to the quite useful 4-y-o 7f winner Aliceinwonderland (by Danehill). The dam won once over 12f in France and is a half-sister to 5 winners including the Group 3 Coventry Stakes winner and subsequent US Grade 2 winner Three Valleys. The second dam, Skiable (by Niniski), won four times at up to 9f in France and the USA and is a half-sister to the outstanding broodmare Hasili (dam of the Group/Grade 1 winners Banks Hill, Intercontinental and Heat Haze and the Group 2 winners Cacique and Dansili). (B Morton).
"A beautiful horse, I'm very fond of him. He'll be one for the middle of the season over six and seven furlongs and he's a very, very nice horse. We're not going to rush him, he's not backward but he's not just going to be a horse for this year, he's a three-year-old in the making".
TRAINER'S BARGAIN BUY

1014. PETROCELLI ★★★
b.c. Piccolo – Sarcita (Primo Dominie).
March 24. Half-brother to the smart listed 6f winner and Group 3 placed Snow Kid (by Indian Ridge) and to the useful 2-y-o 5f winner and Group 2 6f Richmond Stakes second Sarson (by Efisio). The dam, a very useful sprint winner of

6 races including the Portland Handicap is a half-sister to 6 winners including the Group 2 5f Flying Childers Stakes winner Mrs P. The second dam, Zinzi (by Song), won over 5f at 4 yrs in Ireland and is a half-sister to 4 winners including the Irish listed winner Checker Express. (Mr Raymond Tooth).

"This is a very nice horse, he's working really well and he could up a nice five/six furlong horse. It's a nice family and I used to ride the dam at David Elsworth's where she was trained to win the Portland Handicap".

1015. SANDY TOES ★★★
b.c. Footstepsinthesand – Scrooby Baby (Mind Games).
April 23. First foal. The dam, a modest dual 6f placed 2-y-o, is a half-sister to the high-class 2-y-o Milk It Mick, winner of the Group 1 7f Dewhurst Stakes. The second dam, Lunar Music (by Komaite), a modest 5f winner of 3 races at 2 and 4 yrs, is a full or half-sister to 4 winners. (The Sexy Six).

"He's very precocious, I like him but he's on the small side and he'll start off at five furlongs in May".

1016. SLIKBACK JACK ★★★
ch.c. Dr Fong – Duelling (Diesis).
April 2. First foal. 8,000Y. Doncaster. Doncaster St Leger. A McCabe. The dam, a quite useful 2-y-o 6f winner, is a half-sister to the useful 2-y-o listed 1m placed Super Sleuth. The second dam, Enemy Action (by Forty Niner), a very useful 2-y-o dual 6f winner, is a half-sister to the smart Daggers Drawn (by Diesis), winner of the Group 2 6f Richmond Stakes and the Group 2 7f Laurent Perrier Rose Champagne Stakes. (B Morton).

"A very nice horse, I like him a lot. He's precocious enough and when the six furlong races start he'll be ready. He's what I'd call a 'handy' two-year-old and he'll probably end up staying a mile".

1017. TRUE LOVES KISS ★★★
ch.f. Tobougg – Bob's Princess (Bob's Return).
February 24. 6,500Y. Doncaster Festival Sales. A McCabe. Half-sister to the quite useful 7f and 12f winner The Oil Magnate (by Dr Fong), to the fair 5f to 7f 2-y-o winner Ingleby Princess (by Bold Edge), the modest 10f and 12f winner Bob's Your Uncle (by Zilzal) and the moderate 8.7f winner Bob Baileys (by Mister Baileys). The dam, a fair 2-y-o 7f winner, is a half-sister to several winners. (Mr K N Lane & Mr J Kennerley).

"A nice, sharp two-year-old, she's ready to run and she could make up into a nice three-year-old as well".

1018. TURF TIME ★★★
b.c. Zafeen – Next Time (Danetime).
February 1. First foal. The dam, a moderate 5f placed maiden, is a half-sister to the useful listed 5f Field Marshal Stakes winner No Time and to 2 minor winners abroad. The second dam, Muckross Park (by Nomination), a moderate sprint maiden, is a sister to the useful Nominator, a winner of 6 races including the listed 7f Somerville Tattersall Stakes and a half-sister to 4 winners. (The Sexy Six).

"He'll be out over five furlongs in May but he's likely to be better over six. A nice, compact little horse, he has 'two-year-old' written all over him".

1019. UNNAMED ★★★
ch.f. Tobougg – Park Ave Princess (Titus Livius).
March 12. First foal. The dam, a quite useful 2-y-o dual 7f winner, is a half-sister to numerous minor winners here and abroad. The second dam, Satinette (by Shirley Heights), won the Group 3 1m May Hill Stakes and is a half-sister to 9 winners. (The Sexy Six).

"She's going to need a bit of time but she'll start off at six furlongs and she's nice. She's a bit weak at the moment but she's growing and these Tobougg's often take that little bit of time to mature".

ED McMAHON
1020. AALSMEER ★★★
b.f. Invincible Spirit – Flower Market (Cadeaux Genereux).
February 15. First foal. Doncaster St Leger. 32,000Y. J Fretwell. The dam, a fair 2-y-o 6f

winner, is a half-sister to 7 winners including the fair 2-y-o dual 7f winner Relinquished, the fairly useful 2-y-o 6f winner Marching Song and the fairly useful 2-y-o 6f winner Medley. The second dam, Marl (by Lycius), a fairly useful 2-y-o 5.2f winner, is a half-sister to several winners including the very useful 2-y-o listed 5f National Stakes winner Rowaasi. (J C Fretwell).
"She's not over-big but she's sharp enough. A nice filly, she'll probably be one of our first two-year-olds to run. A five furlong type, she might stay an easy six later on".

1021. ASTROPHYSICAL JET ★★★
b.f. *Dubawi – Common Knowledge (Rainbow Quest).*
February 10. Fourth foal. 42,000Y. Tattersalls October 2. E McMahon. Half-sister to the unraced 2008 2-y-o Manoeuvre and to the quite useful 12f winner Coin Of The Realm (both by Galileo). The dam is an unraced half-sister to 6 winners including the Group 2 12f Jockey Club Stakes and dual US Grade 2 winner Blueprint and the listed 10f winner Fairy Godmother. The second dam, Highbrow (by Shirley Heights), a very useful 2-y-o 1m winner, was second in the Group 2 12f Ribblesdale Stakes, is closely related to the good middle-distance colt Milford and a half-sister to the Princess of Wales's Stakes winner Height of Fashion – herself the dam of Nashwan, Nayef and Unfuwain. (Ladas).
"She's a nice, big filly with a good pedigree and I think she was a good buy. She's just cantering at the moment and I see her as being a seven furlong type in June or July. A well-made filly with a very good temperament".

1022. BLADES HARMONY ★★★
b.c. *Needwood Blade – Yabint El Sham (Sizzling Melody).*
May 18. Third foal. 30,000Y. Doncaster Festival. R L Bedding. Half-brother to the fair 2-y-o 5f winner Nigella (by Band On The Run). The dam, a quite useful 2-y-o 5f winner, is a half-sister to 4 winners including the useful listed 9f winner Yabint El Sultan. The second dam, Dalby Dancer (by Bustiki), a fair winner of 7 races at up to 2m, is a half-sister to 2 winners over hurdles. (R L Bedding).
"I'm just stepping him up now. He's a May foal and very much like another Needwood Blade I had last year called Blades Princess. He's likely to want a little bit of cut in the ground and he will make a two-year-old".

1023. COURT GOWN (IRE) ★★
b.f. *Zafeen – Silk Law (Barathea).*
February 5. 20,000Y. Doncaster St Leger. J C Fretwell. Half-sister to the fair 1m (at 2 yrs) and 14f winner Lady Sorcerer (by Diktat) and to the modest 2-y-o 10f winner Ms Rainbow Runner (by Josr Algarhoud). The dam was a quite useful 6f and 6.8f 2-y-o winner. The second dam, Jural (by Kris), a useful winner of the Group 3 1m Curragh Futurity Stakes and the 7f Sweet Solera Stakes, was second in the Group 1 Fillies Mile and is a half-sister to the useful 6f to 9.5f winner Committal. (J C Fretwell).
"She's a nice, big filly by the first season sire Zafeen. She looks like a six/seven furlong filly to start with and she's one for the second half of the season".

1024. EVICTION (IRE) ★★★★
b.c. *Kheleyf – La Belle Katherine (Lyphard).*
March 10. Seventh foal. 27,000Y. Doncaster St Leger. John Fretwell. Half-brother to the quite useful 7f (at 2 yrs) and 1m winner of 7 races Stevedore (by Docksider), to the quite useful 5f (at 2 yrs) to 9f all-weather winner Aventura (by Sri Pekan), the fair 3-y-o 6f winner Criss Cross (by Lahib), the modest 2-y-o 1m winner Distant Diamond (by Distant Music) and the modest 2-y-o 5f winner Tom Tower (by Cape Cross). The dam was unplaced in France and is a half-sister to 3 minor winners. The second dam, Little Scioto (by Little Current), won 2 minor races in the USA and is a half-sister to 7 winners. (Premspace Ltd).
"A nice, big horse, he's just a bit backward mentally but I've entered him in one of the big two-year-old races because I think he'll make up into a nice horse. He should equip himself fairly well as a two-year-old". TRAINER'S BARGAIN BUY

1025. GWYNEDD (IRE) ★★★
br.f. Bertolini – Bethesda (Distant Relative).
March 21. Fifth foal. 28,000Y. Doncaster St Leger. J Fretwell. Half-sister to the fairly useful 2008 2-y-o dual 5f winner Masamah (by Exceed And Excel) and to the fair 2-y-o 5f all-weather winner Fluttering Rose (by Compton Place). The dam, a fairly useful 5.7f and 6f winner at 4 yrs, is a half-sister to 4 winners including the Group 1 6f Middle Park Stakes winner Fard. The second dam, Anneli Rose (by Superlative), a plating-class winner of one race over 6f on the all-weather at 3 yrs, is a half-sister to the Middle Park Stakes and Flying Childers Stakes winner Gallic League. (J C Fretwell).
"She's a nice enough filly and I don't doubt she'll win, but at a level. I think she'll probably be better over six furlongs than five and she's a bit temperamental as I believe Bertolini's can be".

1026. LOOK WHOS NEXT ★★★
ch.c. Compton Place – Look Here's Carol (Safawan).
February 15. First foal. The dam, a fairly useful 6f and 7f winner of 3 races, was listed-placed and is a half-sister to several winners including the smart listed 6f winner Now Look Here. The second dam, Where's Carol (by Anfield), was a fair 2-y-o 6f winner of 4 races on the all-weather. (S L Edwards).
"The dam was small but she had a big engine. He's small too but he has a good action and I don't think it'll be long before he's out. He's a bit hot headed but he's just a bit light and I'd like him to put a bit of weight on. I should think he'll be sharp but I expect him to improve by the time he gets into the nursery races later on".

1027. MILITARY CALL ★★★
b.c. Royal Applause – Trump Street (First Trump).
February 21. Fifth foal. 42,000Y. Doncaster St Leger. J Fretwell. Half-brother to the quite useful 2-y-o 5f winner Top Bid (by Auction House), to the fair 2-y-o 6f winner Street Cred (by Bold Edge) and the moderate 5f winner Trumpita (by Bertolini). The dam, a fair 6f winner at 4 yrs, is a half-sister to 4 winners. The second dam, Pepeke (by Mummy's Pet), a fair 3-y-o 7f winner, is a half-sister to 6 winners. (J C Fretwell).
"He looks an absolute picture and he's had a glossy coat all winter but he needs a run to make him grow up. I've no doubt he'll win but what grade I'm not sure. I've done plenty of work with him but the penny hasn't quite dropped yet".

1028. REVOLTINTHEDESERT ★★★
b.f. Dubai Destination – Cloud Hill (Danehill).
March 5. Third foal. 18,000Y. Doncaster St Leger. J C Fretwell. Half-sister to the modest 2009 5f and 6f placed 3-y-o Beaux Yeux (by Cadeaux Genereux) and to the fair 10f winner Mista Rossa (by Red Ransom). The dam is an unraced half-sister to 3 winners including the Cheshire Oaks winner and Yorkshire Oaks and St Leger second High And Low and the very useful 12f to 14.6f winner Corradini and to the unraced dam of the triple Group 1 winner American Post. The second dam, Cruising Height (by Shirley Heights), a very useful 10.6f and 12.2f winner, was second in the Group 3 Lancashire Oaks and is a half-sister to the Park Hill Stakes winner Trampship. (J C Fretwell).
"She's a nice, big filly and has a very good action, so we'll be looking at setting her off at six furlongs and she'll probably end up over a mile at the end of the season".

1029. STARLIGHT MUSE (IRE) ★★★
gr.f. Desert Style – Downland (El Prado).
January 24. First foal. 10,000Y. Tattersalls October 2. Not sold. The dam, a moderate 7f placed 3-y-o, is a half-sister to 3 winners including the useful 2-y-o 5f winner and Group 2 6f Gimcrack Stakes and Group 2 6f Mill Reef Stakes placed Ma Yoram. The second dam, Quelle Affaire (by Riverman), is a French placed sister to the Group 3 7f Concorde Stakes winner and Queen Anne Stakes second Rami and a half-sister to the Group 3 6.5f Prix Eclipse winner Crack Regiment and the listed Prix Yacowlef winner La Grand Epoque. (Mr N J Hughes).
"I've got her entered for the Supersprint and although she had a little setback earlier in the year she looks a nice, big filly with a bit of scope.

I don't doubt she'll make a nice two-year-old, it's just a case of when we get her there".

1030. STERNLIGHT (IRE) ★★
b.c. *Kheleyf – Sail By Night (Nureyev).*
April 29. Fifth foal. 30,000Y. Doncaster St Leger. J Fretwell. Half-brother to 2 winners in Italy by Alhaarth. The dam is an unraced half-sister to 4 winners including the US stakes winning dam of the US Graded stakes winners Forest Music and Shooter. The second dam, Defer (by Damascus), is an unraced half-sister to 3 winners including the US Grade 1 winner Mining. (J C Fretwell).
"He's a got a bit of growing to do and he's just doing strong canters up to half-speeds. The owner always buys nice sorts and this colt has a nice action. Whether he's as good as our other Kheleyf I don't know yet".

1031. TOTALLY INVINCIBLE (IRE) ★★★
b.f. *Invincible Spirit – Sebastene (Machiavellian).*
February 5. First foal. 32,000Y. Doncaster St Leger. J Fretwell. The dam, placed once at 2 yrs, is a half-sister to 4 minor winners. The second dam, Spring Easy (by Alzao), ran once unplaced and is a half-sister to 8 winners including the Group 3 winner Legend Maker (herself dam of the 1,000 Guineas winner Virginia Waters). (Premspace Ltd).
"She's a bit on the small side but she's sharp enough and she'll probably be helped by a bit of cut in the ground. We'll have to pick her starting point carefully and that may be on the all-weather".

1032. UNNAMED ★★
b.br.f. *Shamardal – Noushkey (Polish Precedent).*
January 23. Seventh foal. 31,000Y. Tattersalls October 3. Ed McMahon. Half-sister to the quite useful 11f winner Anaamil (by Darshaan) and to a winner in Greece by Fantastic Light. The dam, a winner over 7f (at 2 yrs) and the Group 3 12f Lancashire Oaks, is a half-sister to 9 winners including the Group 1 2m 2f Prix du Cadran winner San Sebastian and the German listed winner and Group 1 placed Chesa Plana (herself dam of the Japan Cup and Grand Prix de Saint-Cloud winner Alkaased). The second dam, Top Of The League (by High Top), a quite useful 2-y-o 7f winner, is a half-sister to 3 winners. (Mr M W Crane).
"A lovely filly, she's a little bit temperamental but she has a good action and is very athletic. She'll be running at the back-end of the season on good ground and is primarily bred for her three-year-old career".

1033. UNNAMED ★★★
b.c. *Kyllachy – Valandraud (College Chapel).*
March 10. Fourth foal. 32,000Y. Doncaster St Leger. J Fretwell. Half-brother to Rio Ther (by Bertolini), a winner of 7 races in Italy from 2 to 5 yrs. The dam is an unraced half-sister to 2 winners. The second dam, Guana Bay (by Cadeaux Genereux), is an unraced sister to one winner and a half-sister to 5 winners including the Group 2 winners Prince Sabo and Millyant. (J C Fretwell).
"A nice, big sort, he's very professional and knows his game. The Kyllachy's can get a bit temperamental, so we're just easing him into the job. How good he is I don't know but he's definitely going to make a two-year-old".

BRIAN MEEHAN

1034. ARCANO (IRE) ★★★
b.c. *Oasis Dream – Tariysha (Daylami).*
February 14. First foal. 90,000Y. Tattersalls October 1. McKeever St Lawrence. The dam is an unraced half-sister to 2 winners. The second dam, The second dam, Tarwiya (by Dominion), won the Group 3 7f C L Weld Park Stakes, was third in the Irish 1,000 Guineas and is a half-sister to 5 winners including the Group 3 Norfolk Stakes winner Blue Dakota. (Brimacombe, McNally, Vinciguerra, Sangster).
"He's a six/seven furlong type two-year-old and he should be racing by the end of May. A nice type".

1035. AULTCHARN (FR) ★★★★♠
b.c. *Kyllachy – Nuit Sans Fn (Lead On Time).*
March 1. Sixth foal. 120,000Y. Tattersalls

October 1. Hugo Merry. Half-brother to the French listed 1m winner Matin De Tempete (by Cardoun), to the fairly useful 2-y-o 6f winner Amour Sans Fin (by Kendor) and a winner over jumps in France by Ocean Of Wisdom. The dam is an unplaced half-sister to 9 winners. The second dam, Feerie Boreale (by Irish River), a French 2-y-o winner and third in the Prix Marcel Boussac, is a half-sister to 6 winners including the Group 1 Grand Prix de Paris winner Jeune Noir. (Brimacombe, McNally, Vinciguerra, Sangster).
"He's a very nice horse, we'll probably be running him in May and he looks very good".

1036. CHRISTMAS CARNIVAL ★★★
ch.c. Cadeaux Genereux – Ellebanna (Tina's Pet).
March 10. Eleventh foal. 70,000Y. Tattersalls October 2. McKeever St Lawrence. Brother to the fair 1m winner (on his only start) City Bonus and half-brother to the smart 1m Royal Hunt Cup winner Mine (by Primo Dominie), to the useful 3-y-o 7f winner King Midas (by Bluebird), the fairly useful 7f winner of 5 races Gift Of Gold (by Statoblest), the modest 7f all-weather winner Ours (by Mark Of Esteem) and a winner in Belgium by Distant Relative. The dam, a fair winner of 3 races over 5f, is a half-sister to 8 winners including the high-class sprinter Bolshoi, winner of the Group 2 Kings Stand Stakes and the Group 2 Temple Stakes. The second dam, Mainly Dry (by The Brianstan), is an unraced half-sister to 4 winners. (Jaber Abdullah).
"One for the late summer onwards, he's a typical Cadeaux Genereux in that he needs that bit of time. I'd expect him to stay seven furlongs later on and he's a nice, big horse".

1037. COJO (IRE) ★★★★
b.f. Rock Of Gibraltar – Love Excelling (Polish Precedent).
March 15. Third foal. 115,000Y. Tattersalls October 1. McKeever St Lawrence. Half-sister to the fairly useful Irish dual 10f winner Angels Story (by Galileo). The dam ran once unplaced and is a half-sister to 5 winners including the high-class Group 1 12f Oaks and listed Lupe Stakes winner Love Divine (herself dam of the St Leger winner Sixties Icon) and the listed 12f winner Floreeda. The second dam, La Sky (by Law Society), a useful 10f winner and second in the Group 3 Lancashire Oaks, is closely related to the Champion Stakes winner Legal Case and a half-sister to 4 winners. (Exors of the late F C T Wilson).
"A nice filly and she should be racing in mid-May over six furlongs. She goes really well".

1038. CONNIPTION (IRE) ★★★
b.f. Danehill Dancer – Showbiz (Sadler's Wells).
February 26. First foal. 225,000Y. Tattersalls October 1. Margaret O'Toole. The dam, a quite useful Irish 2-y-o 7f winner, is a half-sister to 2 listed-placed winners. The second dam, Movie Legend (by Affirmed), was placed over 1m in Ireland and is a sister to the Irish 1,000 Guineas winner Trusted Partner (dam of the high-class filly Dress To Thrill), to the Italian Group 2 winner Easy To Copy (dam of the Irish triple Group 3 winner Two-Twenty-Two), the US Grade 3 winner Low Key Affair and the Irish listed winner Epicure's Garden (dam of the Irish Group 2 Blandford Stakes winner Lisieux Rose). (Exors of the late F C T Wilson).
"A lovely filly, we've done quite a lot with her and we're going to back off her now because I wouldn't expect her to be out before August time".

1039. CONTREDANSE (IRE) ★★★★ ♠
br.f. Danehill Dancer – Ahdaab (Rahy).
April 16. Fifth foal. 200,000Y. Tattersalls October 1. McKeever St Lawrence. Sister to the fairly useful 2008 Irish 2-y-o 7f winner and Group 1 Racing Post Trophy fourth Set Sail and to the Canadian Grade 2 Nassau Stakes winner Callwood Dancer and closely related to the fair 2-y-o 5f and subsequent US 3-y-o winner Walklikeanegyptian (by Danehill). The dam, placed once over 10f, is a half-sister to 8 winners including the Group 1 1m Queen Elizabeth II Stakes winner Maroof and to the placed dam of the Irish Derby winner Desert King. The second

dam, Dish Dash (by Bustino), won the Group 2 12f Ribblesdale Stakes and is a half-sister to 6 winners. (Exors of the late F C T Wilson).
"A similar type, if a bit more forward than the previous filly by Danehill Dancer, Conniption. There's plenty of size to her, she's a lovely filly that should be out in June and I like her a lot".

1040. DANCING DAVID (IRE) ★★★★
b.c. Danehill Dancer – Seek Easy
(Seeking The Gold).
May 3. Fourth foal. $475,000Y. Keeneland September. Not sold. Half-brother to the quite useful 12f winner (from two starts) Ordination (by Fantastic Light) and to a 3-y-o winner in Japan by Boundary. The dam is an unraced half-sister to 3 winners including the US Grade 2 winner Conserve. The second dam, Slew And Easy (by Slew O'Gold), won once at 4 yrs in the USA and is a half-sister to 13 winners including the champion Canadian horses La Voyageuse, L'Enjoleur and Medaille d'Or. (Mr Catesby W Clay).
"Very much one for later one – possibly August or September. Quite small but a good-looking horse, I like him a lot and I'd say he'd be one to follow".

1041. DOLPHIN'S DREAM ★★★
b.f. Medicean – Arriving
(Most Welcome).
February 28. Eighth foal. 30,000Y. Doncaster St Leger. McKeever St Lawrence. Half-sister to the useful listed 7f winner of 4 races Attune, to the quite useful 10f winner Adventuress (both by Singspiel), the fair 7f and 10f winner Asharon (by Efisio) and the modest 7f winner Artistry (by Night Shift). The dam was a useful 10f to 11.4f winner of 3 races including the listed Middleton Stakes and was second in the Group 2 Sun Chariot Stakes. The second dam, Affirmation (by Tina's Pet), won over 5f (at 2 yrs) and 10f and is a half-sister to 5 winners including the Royal Hunt Cup winner Teamwork. (Jaber Abdullah).
"She'd be the type to start around June time, she's a nice type with a nice temperament. A straightforward filly".

1042. DUTY AND DESTINY (IRE) ★★★★
b.f. Montjeu – Swilly (Irish River).
April 18. Fifth foal. €180,000Y. Goffs Million. Demi O'Byrne. Sister to the quite useful Irish 10f winner Mississippian. The dam is an unplaced half-sister to 7 winners including the Group 2 Premio Lydia Tesio winner Grey Way (herself dam of the Italian dual Group 1 winner Distant Way). The second dam, Northern Naiad (by Nureyev), is a placed half-sister to 7 winners. (Sangster Family).
"She shows a lot of speed for a Montjeu, we've done a lot of work with her and we'll probably run her when we get to the six furlong races. She's very forward for a Montjeu and she looks very nice".

1043. EDGEWATER (IRE) ★★
b.g. Bahamian Bounty – Esteemed Lady
(Mark Of Esteem).
February 28. Second foal. 60,000Y. Tattersalls October 2. McKeever St Lawrence. Half-brother to the unraced 2008 2-y-o Sleepy Blue Ocean (by Oasis Dream). The dam, placed once over 6f at 2 yrs, is a half-sister to 4 winners including the 2-y-o Group 2 6f Richmond Stakes winner Revenue. The second dam, Bareilly (by Lyphard), is an unraced three-parts sister to the Group 3 1m Prix de la Grotte winner Baya and the Italian Group 2 winner Narrative. (B V Sangster).
"He wants a bit of time and I was a bit disappointed with how he did over the winter. He's improving now but we're going to give him a little break. I think he's one for the mid-to-late season, but he's a nice sort of horse".

1044. FIELD DAY (IRE) ★★
b.f. Cape Cross – Naval Affair (Last Tycoon).
March 15. Half-sister to the quite useful 1m and 12f winner War At Sea (by Bering). The dam, a useful 2-y-o 7f winner, is a half-sister to 3 listed winners. The second dam, Sailor's Mate (by Shirley Heights), won the Group 3 Meld Stakes and is a half-sister to 8 winners. (Ballymacoll Stud).
"She hasn't been in that long and we'll give her plenty of time. One for the back-end, but a nice filly".

220 TWO YEAR OLDS OF 2009

1045. HE'S INVINCIBLE ★★★★
b.c. *Invincible Spirit – Adamas (Fairy King).*
March 22. Third foal. €120,000Y. Goffs Million. McKeever St Lawrence. Half-brother to the modest 2008 1m placed 2-y-o Crystallize (by Bertolini) and to the modest 7f and 1m winner Private Peachey (by Shinko Forest). The dam, a modest 1m winner of 2 races at 3 and 5 yrs, is a half-sister to 2 other minor winners. The second dam, Corynida (by Alleged), is an unraced half-sister to 5 winners here and abroad. (Brimacombe, McNally, Vinciguerra, Sangster).
"He'll be racing in early May and he's a good horse I'd say. Goes very well".

1046. HIGH HOLBORN (IRE) ★★★★
b.c. *Danehill Dancer – Wedding Morn (Sadler's Wells).*
March 18. Second foal. 42,000Y. Doncaster St Leger. McKeever St Lawrence. Brother to the unplaced 2008 2-y-o Suakin Dancer. The dam is an unplaced half-sister to 2 winners. The second dam, Wedding Bouquet (by Kings Lake), a useful 5f to 7f winner (including the Group 3 C L Park Stakes), was Group 1 placed in Ireland at 2 yrs and subsequently won the Grade 3 6.5f Monrovia Handicap in the USA and is closely related to the outstanding Derby, Irish Derby and King George winner Generous and a half-sister to the Oaks winner and good broodmare Imagine. (R C Tooth).
"Quite sharp, he'll be racing in early May and I think he's a good colt".

1047. HOLD YOUR COLOUR (IRE) ★★★
gr.c. *Verglas – Azia (Desert Story).*
March 25. Second foal. 30,000Y. Doncaster St Leger. McKeever St Lawrence. Brother to the unplaced 2008 2-y-o Taste The Wine. The dam, a 2-y-o 7f winner in Ireland, is out of the unraced Safdara (by Shahrastani), is an unraced half-sister to 10 winners including the Group 2 Lockinge Stakes winner Safawan.
"He should be ready soon and he'll be one of our earliest ones. He goes very well and he's straightforward like all the Verglas's. A nice colt". TRAINER'S BARGAIN BUY

1048. INSIDE TRACK (IRE) ★★
b.g. *Bertolini – True Crystal (Sadler's Wells).*
February 27. Fourth foal. 9,000Y. Tattersalls October 2. McKeever St Lawrence. The dam, a fairly useful 10f winner, is a half-sister to 2 winners. The second dam, State Crystal (by High Estate), was a very useful winner of the Group 3 12f Lancashire Oaks and was placed in the Yorkshire Oaks and the Prix Vermeille. She is a half-sister to 6 winners including the Group 1 Fillies Mile winner Crystal Music and the Group 3 winners Dubai Success and Solar Crystal. (N B Attenborough).
"With Bertolini as the sire you might think he'd be sharp but the dam's side suggests he'll take a bit of time. A nice, strong horse, he'll be ready by the end of May I should think".

1049. LADY OF THE DESERT (USA) ★★★
ch.f. *Rahy – Queen's Logic (Grand Lodge).*
March 12. Half-sister to the fair 2008 7f placed 2-y-o and 2009 9f winner Dunes Queen (by Elusive Quality) and to the quite useful 2-y-o 1m winner Go On Be A Tiger (by Machiavellian). The dam, a champion 2-y-o filly and winner of the Group 1 6f Cheveley Park Stakes and the Group 2 6f Lowther Stakes, is a half-sister to the top-class multiple Group 1 winner Dylan Thomas. The second dam, Lagrion (by Diesis), was placed 5 times in Ireland and stayed 12f and is a full or half-sister to 3 winners. (Jaber Abdullah).
"A nice, sharp filly, we gave her a bit of time off and she's back now. I like her".

1050. L FRANK BAUM (IRE) ★★
b.c. *Sinndar – Rainbow City (Rainbow Quest).*
April 22. Half-brother to the quite useful 14f winner City Stable (by Machiavellian). The dam, a quite useful 10f winner, is a sister to the Group 2 13.3f Geoffrey Freer Stakes winner Multicolored, closely related to the Group 1 Grand Prix de Saint-Cloud winner Gamut and a half-sister to the useful 7f (at 2 yrs) and listed 10f winner Athens Belle. The second dam, the French 10f and 12f winner Greektown (by Ela-Mana-Mou) is a half-sister to the high-class stayer Sought Out (dam of the Derby winner

North Light) and to Scots Lass (dam of the Group 2 Great Voltigeur Stakes winner Bonny Scot). (Ballymacoll Stud Farm).
"Very much one for the back-end, but he goes very well and he's a nice colt".

1051. MAATH GOOL ★★★
b.c. Dubawi – My First Romance (Danehill).
March 27. Tenth foal. 62,000Y. Tattersalls October 2. Rabbah Bloodstock. Half-brother to the promising 2008 2-y-o 6f winner Alkhafif (by Royal Applause), to Group 3 5f Queen Mary Stakes winners Romantic Myth (by Mind Games) and Romantic Liason (by Primo Dominie), the useful 2-y-o 5f winner Power Packed (by Puissance), the fairly useful dual 5f winner Zargus (by Zamindar), the quite useful 2-y-o 7f winner Wedaad (by Fantastic Light), the fair 7f winner Romantic Destiny (by Dubai Destination) and the fair 2-y-o 5.5f winner Chance For Romance (by Entrepreneur). The dam ran twice unplaced and is a half-sister to 6 minor winners here and abroad. The second dam, Front Line Romance (by Caerleon), won once and was Group 3 placed over 1m at 2 yrs in Ireland and is a full or half-sister to 10 winners including the muliple Italian Group 3 winner Knight Line Dancer. (Jaber Abdullah).
"He's taking a bit of time and we've decided to give him a break, so we won't get him out until mid to late summer. He goes very well, he's straightforward and he'll be better being given a bit of time".

1052. MANDARIN EXPRESS ★★★
ch.f. Dubai Destination – Hsi Wang Mu (by Dr Fong).
March 11. Half-sister to the fair 7f and 1m placed 2-y-o Ysing Yi (by Singspiel). The dam, a moderate 7f (at 2 yrs) and 9f placed 2-y-o, is a half-sister to the useful 6f and 7f winner and listedplaced Against The Grain and the smart 2-y-o 5f and 6f and subsequent US Grade 2 Oak Tree Derby winner Devious Boy. The second dam, Oh Hebe (Night Shift), a fair 3-y-o 7f winner, is a half-sister to 6 winners including the listed winners Calypso Grant and Poppy Carew. (Mr Catesby W Clay).

"A nice horse, he'll want six or seven but he's quite sharp and forward and I'll run him sometime in late May over six furlongs and he's a nice, positive, straightforward colt".

1053. MANHATTAN FOX (USA) ★★★★
ch.c. Elusive Quality – Safeen (Storm Cat).
March 23. Fourth foal. Half-brother to the quite useful 2008 7f and 1m placed 2-y-o Alhaque (by Galileo). The dam is an unraced half-sister to the listed winner and Italian Group 3 winner Revere. The second dam, Bint Pasha (by Affirmed), won the Prix Vermeille, the Yorkshire Oaks and the Group 2 Pretty Polly Stakes. (Mr Catesby W Clay).
"He's very nice and I like him a lot. He may be ready in late May or early June and he looks a very smart colt".

1054. MASSACHUSETTS ★★
ch.c. Singspiel – Royal Passion (Ahonoora).
April 7. Brother to the fairly useful 2-y-o 7f winner Manchurian and half-brother to the fair 2008 2-y-o dual 7f winner Silent Hero (by Oasis Dream), the useful 7f (at 2 yrs) and 10.3f winner Attache (by Wolfhound), to the useful sprint winner of numerous races (including at 2 yrs) Tadeo (by Primo Dominie), the modest dual 7f and 9f winner Midnight Lace (by Tomba) and the modest 2-y-o 6f winner Chaska (by Reprimand). The dam, a fair triple 10f winner, is a half-sister to 4 winners. The second dam, Courtesy Call (by Northfields), is a placed half-sister to 5 winners. (Mrs P Good).
"He hasn't arrived yet and I haven't seen him but I believe he's very nice. Being by Singspiel I expect he'll need time though".

1055. MONTPARNASSE (IRE) ★★★★★
b.c. Montjeu – Capades Dancer (Gate Dancer).
April 19. Half-brother to the Group 2 10f Prix d'Harcourt winner Vangelis, to the multiple French listed winner Marechal (both by Highest Honor) and the French 9f winner Great Gorge (by Gulch). The dam won in the USA and is a half-sister to the US Grade 1 2-y-o 8.5f winner Capades. (Lady Rothschild).

"He hasn't been in that long but he takes his work very easily. His pedigree says he's going to need time but he does look very nice".

1056. MOONLIGHT MISCHIEF (IRE) ★★
b.f. Galileo – Muwali (Kingmambo).
January 22. First foal. 90,000Y. Tattersalls October 1. Not sold. The dam is an unplaced half-sister to 3 winners. The second dam, Housa Dancer (by Fabulous Dancer), won 2 listed events in France and the USA and was Grade 1 placed and is a half-sister to the Group 2 Prix Niel winner Housamix. (Sangster Family).
"A nice filly, she goes well but being by Galileo we won't be in any hurry with her".

1057. NEW CHRISTMAS (USA) ★★★★
gr.c. Smoke Glacken – Occhi Verdi (Mujtahid).
February 8. Fifth foal. 48,000Y. Tattersalls October 2. McKeever St Lawrence. Half-brother to 2 minor winners in the USA by Menifee and Royal Academy and to the listed-placed Skadrak (by Forest Camp). The dam won at 2 yrs and subsequently in the USA, was Grade 1 placed and is a half-sister to 3 winners. The second dam, Mali (by Storm Bird), won once at 3 yrs in France and is a half-sister to 4 winners. (Jaber Abdullah).
"A sharp sort and I like him a lot. He'll probably be ready by mid May and he goes very well".

1058. PIN CUSHION ★★★★
ch.f. Pivotal – Frizzante (Efisio).
March 20. The dam won 7 races including the Group 1 July Cup and is a half-sister to 4 winners including the Stewards Cup winner Zidane and the dual 6f listed winner Firenze. The second dam, Juliet Bravo (by Glow), a modest 2-y-o 5f winner, is a half-sister to the very smart filly Donna Viola, a winner of 11 races here and abroad including the Grade 1 Yellow Ribbon Handicap, the Grade 1 Gamely Handicap and the Group 2 Prix de l'Opera. (Lady Rothschild).
"A very smart filly, she's very forward in her work but not in her coat. So we're just waiting with her for a bit, but she looks a good filly".

1059. PLEASANT DAY (IRE) ★★★
b.c. Noverre – Sunblush (Timber Country).
March 7. First foal. €40,000Y. Goffs Million. McKeever St Lawrence. The dam ran unplaced twice and is a half-sister to 4 winners including the Group 2 Rockfel Stakes winner Cairns. The second dam, Tanami (by Green Desert), a very useful 5f and 6f winner and second in the Group 1 Cheveley Park Stakes, is a half-sister to 3 winners including the dam of the Cheveley Park Stakes winner Wannabe Grand. (Jaber Abdullah).
"A very tough, hardy sort of horse and like all the Noverre's he's very straightforward and good-looking. I guess he's going to want seven furlongs or a mile but he's quite forward".

1060. PUBLIC SERVICE (IRE) ★★★★
ch.c. Danehill Dancer – Sintra (Kris).
January 10. First foal. €80,000Y. Goffs Million. Citywest Inc. Ltd. The dam, a minor French 1m winner, is a half-sister to 7 winners including US stakes winner Aliena and the US Grade 2 placed Brianda and Bedmar. The second dam, Gracious Line (by Fabulous Dancer), a minor French 3-y-o winner, is a half-sister to the Group 3 winners Gay Minstrel and Greenway. (The Hon. Earle I Mack).
"A very sharp colt, he's got plenty of speed and he'll be running in May. I think he's got a fair amount of ability and I like him a lot".

1061. RAKAAN (IRE) ★★★
ch.c. Bahamian Bounty – Petite Spectre (Spectrum).
January 23. First foal. 140,000Y. Tattersalls October 1. Tony Nerses. The dam, a fair 2-y-o 6f all-weather winner, is a half-sister to 7 winners including the useful 2-y-o Group 3 7f C L Weld Park Stakes winner Rag Top and the fair 2-y-o 7f winner Seamstress (herself dam of the 2-y-o listed winner Elhamri). The second dam, Petite Epaulette (by Night Shift), a fair 5f winner at 2 yrs, is a sister to the Sweet Solera Stakes second The Jotter and a half-sister to the Group 1 1m Gran Criterium second Line Dancer. (Saleh Al Homaizi & Imad Al Sagar).
"A very nice colt, he's really come to himself in the last few weeks and I'm happy with him".

1062. SECRET QUEEN ★★★★
b.f. Zafeen – Gold Queen
(Grand Lodge).
January 18. The dam, a quite useful 2-y-o 7.5f winner, is a half-sister to the fairly useful listed 1m winner Silver Pivotal. The second dam, Silver Colours (by Silver Hawk), a useful 2-y-o listed 1m winner, is a half-sister to 3 winners including the Japanese Grade 2 winner God Of Chance and the Royal Lodge Stakes third Desaru. (Jaber Abdullah).
"She's quite forward and will be running in early May. A nice, sharp filly, I like her a lot".

1063. SMOG (IRE) ★★★
gr.c. Verglas – Dollysister (Alydar).
February 26. Eighth foal. 30,000Y. Tattersalls October 1. Stephen Dartnell. Half-brother to the US stakes-placed winner Skamper (by Skip Away) and to 2 minor winners in France and Japan by Sillery and Red Ransom. The dam won once at 3 yrs in France and is a half-sister to 8 winners including the French Group 3 winners Beau Sultan and Dalna. The second dam, Devalois (by Nureyev), won the Grade 2 E P Taylor Stakes and the Group 3 Prix Cleopatre and is a half-sister to 9 winners including the French Group 3 winner Dunphy. (S Dartnell).
"He goes well and is just coming back after a little break. I'm very happy with him and he'll be ready to run in mid-May".

1064. SPARKLE PARK ★★
b.f. Kyllachy – Petonellajill (Petong).
April 13. Seventh living foal. Closely related to the useful 7f and 7.6f winner and listed-placed Violet Park (by Pivotal) and half-sister to the modest 7f and 1m winner Golden Prospect (by Lujain) and the moderate 6f to 10f winner Piquet (by Mind Games). The dam, a fair 7f winner, is a half-sister to 2 minor winners. The second dam, Crackerjill (by Sparkler), won over hurdles and is a half-sister to 2 minor winners. (Mrs J & D E Cash).
"She's just come in so I can't anything about her, but she looks well".

1065. TULLE (IRE) ★★
b.f. Sinndar – Dragnet (Rainbow Quest).
March 18. Third foal. Half-sister to the useful dual 1m winner and listed-placed Lang Shining (by Dr Fong). The dam, a fair 10f winner, is a sister to the Irish 2,000 Guineas and Champion Stakes winner Spectrum and to the useful 7f and 1m winner Stream Of Gold and a half-sister to the useful 1m winner Nash House. The second dam, River Dancer (by Irish River), a smart French winner over 5f (at 2 yrs) and the 1m Prix de la Calonne, was third in the French 1,000 Guineas. (Ballymacoll Stud Farm).
"A nice filly that wants plenty of time. One for August or September over seven furlongs and a mile".

1066. TWILIGHT MEMORY ★★★
ch.f. Smart Strike – Southern Swing
(Dixieland Band).
February 2. Sixth foal. $300,000Y. Keeneland September. Blandford Bloodstock. Half-sister to the US winner and Grade 1 placed Erinsouthernman, to the minor US stakes winner Mr Pee Vee (both by Eltish) and 2 minor US winners by Dynaformer and Lemon Drop Kid. The dam, a minor winner at 3 yrs in the USA, is a half-sister to 5 winners including the US Grade 3 winner Jaded Dancer. The second dam, Lien (by Never Bend), was a stakes winner of 7 races in the USA and Grade 3 placed. (Sangster Family).
"She's had a break but she's back in now and she looks great. So we're just starting to get on with her now".

1067. WATER BISCUIT ★★★
b.f. Bertolini – Waterfall One (Nashwan).
January 26. Half-sister to the unplaced 2008 2-y-o Water Hen (by Diktat). The dam is an unplaced half-sister to 3 winners. The second dam, Spout (by Salse), was a very smart winner of the Group 3 12f John Porter Stakes and the Group 3 Lancashire Oaks and is a half-sister to numerous winners including the French listed winner Mon Domino. (Lady Rothschild).
"She's had a break and we're just getting on with her, she's working nicely and she'll be out sometime in May".

1068. YOUM JAMIL (USA) ★★★★★
gr.c. Mizzen Mast – Millie's Choice (Taufan).
February 2. Tenth foal. 140,000Y. Tattersalls December. Gill Richardson. Half-brother to the US Grade 3 winner and Grade 1 placed Millie's Quest (by Quest For Fame), to the fairly useful 2-y-o 6f winner Eat Pie (by Thunder Gulch), the US stakes-placed winners Honeypenny (by Royal Academy) and Millie's Trick (by Phone Trick) and 2 minor winners in the USA by Hennessy and Stravinsky. The dam, an Irish listed 7f winner of 7 races, is a half-sister to 2 winners including the dam of the dual Grade 1 winner Doctor Dino. The second dam, Salagangai (by Sallust), is an unraced half-sister to 6 winners. (Jaber Abdullah).
"A lovely colt, he wants a fair bit of time because he's tall so he's one for the second half of the season, but I think he could be a five star job".

1069. ZAFEEN SPEED ★★
ch.c. Zafeen – Dakhla Oasis (Night Shift).
January 23. Third foal. Half-brother to the fair 2008 2-y-o 6f winner Dubai's Gazal (by Fraam). The dam, winner of the Group 2 German 1,000 Guineas, is a sister to 2 winners including the Group 3 6f Prix de Seine-et-Oise and German Group 3 6f Benazet-Rennen winner Dyhim Diamond and a half-sister to the US 2-y-o Grade 1 8.5f Starlet Stakes winner Creaking Board (herself dam of the US Grade 3 winner Crowd Pleaser). The second dam, Happy Landing (by Homing), was placed twice in France at 3 yrs and is a half-sister to 4 minor winners. (Jaber Abdullah).
"A big horse but he's in work and he shows a lot of speed. Because he's a big two-year-old we'll play it by ear and let him tell us when he's ready".

1070. UNNAMED ★★★
ch.c. Avonbridge – Amazed (Clantime).
February 8. Fifth foal. 40,000Y. Doncaster St Leger. McKeever St Lawrence. Closely related to the useful 2-y-o 5f and 6f and 3-y-o listed 5f winner Dazed And Amazed (by Averti) and half-brother to the quite useful 2-y-o 5f winner Nawaaff (by Compton Place). The dam, a modest 5f placed 3-y-o, is a sister to the Group 3 Prix du Petit Couvert winner Bishops Court and a half-sister to 5 winners including the listed winning sprinter Astonished. The second dam, Indigo (by Primo Dominie), a quite useful 2-y-o 5f winner, is a half-sister to 5 winners. (Clipper Logistics).
"A nice, sharp colt that goes really well. He should be ready in May".

1071. UNNAMED ★★★
ch.c. Danehill Dancer – Autumnal (Indian Ridge).
April 3. Second foal. The dam was a useful winner of the 2-y-o 5f Windsor Castle Stakes and over 6f at 2 yrs and is a sister to the useful sprint winners Mazepa and Lord Pacal and a half-sister to the quite useful sprint winner of 12 races Storyteller. The second dam, Please Believe Me (by Try My Best), a fairly useful 2-y-o 5f winner, is out of the Group 3 12f Princess Royal Stakes winner Believer. (Paul & Jenny Green).
"A very nice, typical Danehill Dancer and he shows a lot of ability, but he's quite forward for one of them".

1072. UNNAMED ★★★
b.c. Captain Rio – Be My Wish (Be My Chief).
February 25. Fifth foal. 20,000Y. Doncaster St Leger. McKeever St Lawrence. Half-brother to the moderate 2m winner Himba (by Vettori). The dam, a fair 6f and 7f winner, is a half-sister to 7 winners. The second dam, Spinner (by Blue Cashmere), was a modest sprint winner and a half-sister to the smart sprinter Clantime. (Abbott Racing Ltd).
"He was off for part of the spring with sore shins but he's back in training and I like him a lot. He won't take long before he's ready".

1073. UNNAMED ★★
b.c. Green Tune – Calling Card (Bering).
February 16. Fifth foal. 36,000Y. Doncaster St Leger. McKeever St Lawrence. Half-brother to the minor Italian 3-y-o 1m winner Daily Call (by Daylami). The dam, a useful French 10.5f winner, was listed-placed and is a half-sister to

5 winners. The second dam, Cheeky Charm (by Nureyev), ran unplaced twice and is closely related to the listed winners Theatrical Charmer and Mohaajir and a half-sister to 7 winners. (Mrs S Tucker).

"A lovely mid-season type horse, he goes really well but we need to hang on to him for a bit".

1074. UNNAMED ★★★★
b.f. *Fasliyev – Danseuse du Bois (Woodman).*
April 14. Fifth foal. 40,000Y. Doncaster St Leger. McKeever St Lawrence. Sister to the fairly useful 2008 2-y-o 5f winner and listed placed Saucy Brown and half-sister to a 3-y-o winner in Italy by Danehill Dancer and a minor winner abroad by Montjeu. The dam is an unplaced half-sister to the minor winner Zappeuse, herself dam of the French Group 3 winner and US Grade 1 third Danzon. The second dam, Danseuse du Nord (by Kahyasi), won over 1m at 2 yrs in France and was third in both the Group 2 Prix de Malleret and the Group 3 Prix de Royaumont and is a half-sister to 11 winners including the French 1,000 Guineas and Prix de la Foret winner Danseuse du Soir (herself dam of the Group 1 Gran Criterium winner Scintillo).

"She looks very sharp and I like her a lot. I think she'll be winning early".

1075. UNNAMED ★★★
b.c. *Fasliyev – Miss Megs (Croco Rouge).*
March 24. Second foal. 30,000Y. Tattersalls October 2. McKeever St Lawrence. Half-brother to Golden Pool (by Fasliyev), a moderate fourth over 6f at 2 yrs in 2008. The dam, a fair 9f and 11f winner in Ireland, is a half-sister to 3 winners including the listed winner Santa Isobel. The second dam, Atlantic Record (by Slip Anchor), is an unraced half-sister to 4 winners. (Abbott Racing Ltd).

"A very forward colt, he's sharp and shows a lot of speed. A typical Fasliyev that should be out in a month".

1076. UNNAMED ★★★★
b.f. *Tiznow – Moss (Woodman).*
March 19. Tenth foal. €170,000Y. Goffs Million. BBA (Ire). Half-sister to the US listed stakes winner and Grade 2 placed Dover Dere (by Cherokee Run), to the fairly useful 2-y-o 7f winners and listed-placed Wahsheeq (by Green Desert) and Elrehaan (by Sadler's Wells), the quite useful 10f winner Rousing Thunder (by Theatrical) and the fair 2-y-o 6f winner Maggies Farm (by Forest Wildcat). The dam ran once unplaced in the USA and is a half-sister to 6 winners including the William Hill Sprint Championship and Prix de l'Abbaye winner Committed (herself dam of the US Grade 1 winner Pharma). The second dam, Minstinguette (by Boldnesian), ran once unplaced and is a half-sister to the US Grade 1 winner and good broodmare Miss Toshiba. (Mr D R Fleming).

"She's doing really well, she's a very nice filly and quite forward for a Tiznow. We'll still give her plenty of time and she'll probably be ready by July".

1077. UNNAMED ★★★
gr.f. *Verglas – Native Force (Indian Ridge).*
January 31. Third foal. €220,000Y. Goffs Million. Hugo Merry. Half-sister to the Group 1 Golden Jubilee Stakes and Group 1 Nunthorpe Stakes winner Kingsgate Native (by Mujadil) and the 7f seller winner Assumption (by Beckett). The dam, a quite useful 1m winner, is a half-sister to 2 winners. The second dam, La Pellegrina (by Be My Guest), is a placed half-sister to 5 winners including the 1,000 Guineas winner Las Meninas. (Mr A Rosen).

"She looks a sharp filly, she probably needs six furlongs and she'll be ready pretty soon.

1078. UNNAMED ★★★★
br.c. *Danehill Dancer – Pina Colada (Sabrehill).*
March 18. Third foal. €50,000Y. Goffs Million. McKeever St Lawrence. The dam, a winner of 3 races here and in the USA including a minor stakes, was Grade 2 placed and is a half-sister 4 winners. The second dam, Drei (by Lyphard), is a placed half-sister to 3 winners. (Bayardo).

"A lovely colt, not as forward as a couple of my other Danehill Dancer's but he's a very, very attractive colt for the middle of the season. Look out for him".

1079. UNNAMED ★★★
b.c. Noverre – Ricadonna (Kris).
March 8. 58,000Y. Tattersalls October 2. McKeever St Lawrence. Half-brother to the unplaced 2008 2-y-o Valid Point (by Val Royal), to the French 2-y-o listed 7.5f winner Iron Fist (by Desert Style) and to the Italian 1m winner of 4 races from 2 to 4 yrs Pavoncella (by Bachir). The dam is an unraced half-sister to 4 winners including the Group 2 Prix Robert Papin winner Greenlander. The second dam, Pripet (by Alleged), a quite useful 2m winner, is a sister to the 1,000 Guineas and Oaks winner Midway Lady. (J L Allbritton).
"He's very forward physically and is a six/seven furlong type two-year-old. I like him a lot".

1080. UNNAMED ★★★
ch.c. Johannesburg – Security Interest (Belong To Me).
April 26. Third foal. 78,000Y. Tattersalls October 1. Hugo Merry. Half-brother to the minor US 2-y-o winner Atash (by Smoke Glacken). The dam is an unraced half-sister to 3 minor winners in the USA. The second dam, Shes Got The Facts (by Known Fact), a stakes winner of 4 races at 3 yrs in the USA, is a sister to the US Grade 3 winner Fancy Freda and a half-sister to 5 winners. (Bayardo).
"He'll be one of our first runners, certainly over six furlongs, he's very good-looking and we like him a lot".

1081. UNNAMED ★★★★
b.br.f. Indian Charlie – Shahalo (Halo).
April 15. Ninth foal. $460,000Y. Keeneland September. Hugo Merry. Sister to the US Grade 2 and Grade 3 winner Bwana Charlie and to the US winner and Grade 2 placed My Pal Charlie and half-sister to the US Grade 3 winner Bwana Bull (by Holy Bull) and the US stakes-placed winner Ten Halos (by Marquetry). The dam was unplaced in 2 starts and is out of the US Grade 3 winner and Grade 1 third White Mischief (by Dance In Time). (Mr A Rosen).
"She's one for the middle of the season but she's had a break and it won't be long before she's in full work. I'll give her plenty of time, but she's a nice filly you should take note of."

1082. UNNAMED ★★★
ch.c. Indian Ridge – Silvia Diletta (Mark Of Esteem).
May 3. Fourth foal. €55,000Y. Goffs Million. McKeever St Lawrence. Brother to the minor Italian 3-y-o winner Sparkling Ridge and half-brother to another by Fasliyev. The dam, a listed-paced winner at 2 and 3 yrs in Italy, is a half-sister to 8 winners including the dual Italian listed winner King Park. The second dam, Grande Gioia (by Dara Monarch), won at 3 yrs in Italy and is a half-sister to 5 winners. (Bayardo).
"He goes really well. He's typical of the sire, he's likely to want six or seven furlongs, very forward and very professional. A good-looking horse that should be ready in late May".

1083. UNNAMED ★★★★
b.f. Cape Cross – Speech Room (Gulch).
February 17. 72,000foal. Tattersalls December. Charlie Gordon-Watson. The dam, placed once over 5f in Ireland at 3 yrs, is a half-sister to 6 winners including the Group 3 winners Woodland Melody and Saintly Speech. The second dam, Eloquent Minister (by Deputy Minister), a very useful sprint winner of 2 listed events at Doncaster and in Ireland, also won in the USA and is a half-sister to 8 winners. (Sangster Family).
"One for the middle of the season onwards. She's a beautifully made filly, has a lovely pedigree and she goes well. We'll be expecting a lot from her".

1084. UNNAMED ★★★★♠
b.c. Kyllachy – Talighta (Barathea).
February 7. Sixth foal. 58,000Y. Doncaster St Leger. McKeever St Lawrence. Half-brother to the fairly useful 5f (at 2 yrs) and 6f winner of 6 races Forces Sweetheart (by Allied Forces) to the quite useful dual 5f (at 2 yrs) and 1m winner Espartano, the fair 5f and 6f winner of 4 races (including at 2 yrs) Geoffdaw (both by Vettori) and the fair 2-y-o 5f winners Melandre (by Lujain) and Kuringai (by Royal Applause). The dam was placed fourth once over 5f in Ireland and is a half-sister to 3 winners. The second dam, Morcote (by Magical Wonder), won the

Group 3 7f Park Stakes in Ireland and is a half-sister to 5 winners.
"A very similar type to another Kyllachy two-year-old colt we have called Aultcharn. He's going to start off at six furlongs in May and he looks a proper horse".

ROD MILLMAN

1085. APACHE KID (IRE) ★★★
b.c. Antonius Pius – She's The Tops (Shernazar).
March 29. Eleventh foal. 30,000Y. Doncaster St Leger. Will Edmeades. Half-brother to the smart Group 2 10f Pretty Polly Stakes winner and Group 1 second Lady Upstage (by Alzao), to the useful 6f (at 2 yrs) winner and 1m listed second Lycility (by Lycius), the fairly useful 17.2f winner The Blues Academy (by Royal Academy) and the fair 2-y-o 7f winner Orpen Prince (by Orpen). The dam, a quite useful 12f winner and a half-sister to one winner, is out of the modest 10f winner Troytops (by Troy), herself a half-sister to the Lockinge Stakes winner and Derby second Most Welcome. (Karmaa Racing Ltd).
"A nice individual and very well-mannered, he's come to hand early but he'll be better over six furlongs. Not over-big, but definitely big enough".

1086. JO BOY ★★★
b.c. Royal Applause – Bad Kitty (Mt Livermore).
March 6. Second foal. 32,000Y. Doncaster St Leger. Will Edmeades. The dam won 3 races at 2 yrs in the USA including a stakes event and is a half-sister to 2 winners. The second dam, Purr Pleasure (by El Gran Senor), won 4 minor races at 2 to 4 yrs in the USA and is a half-sister to 7 winners. (Karmaa Racing Ltd).
"Quite a big colt, he'll need a bit of time and he'll be out in July. He has a touch of quality and he's just not mature enough yet".

1087. LENKIEWICZ ★★★
gr.f. Oratorio – Philadelphie (Anabaa).
April 13. First foal. 10,000Y. Doncaster St Leger. The dam won once over 10f at 3 yrs in France. The second dam, Printanniere (by Thatching), won once at 2 yrs in France and is a half-sister to 4 winners including the Group 1 Prix de la Foret winner Poplar Bluff. (B R Millman).
"She's got quite a nice pedigree, but she's had a bit of a cough so she's had some time off and she'll be running in mid-May. She's very fast".

1088. MACROY ★★★
b.c. Makbul – Royal Orchid (Shalford).
April 28. Brother to the fair 5f and 7f winner Castano and half-brother to the quite useful 5f and 6f winner of 4 races Maddie's A Jem (by College Chapel) and the modest 5f all-weather winner Imtalkinggibberish (by Pursuit Of Love). The dam, a fair maiden, was placed over 5f and 7f at 2 yrs and is a half-sister to 5 winners including the listed placed Ho Leng. The second dam, Indigo Blue (Bluebird), is a placed half-sister to 5 winners including the smart sprinter Mistertopogigo.
"He's had a setback and won't be ready until June. He's well put together, he's small and looks very much like a nice horse I had called Maktavish, who was also by Makbul. He's quite quick and will make a sprinting type two-year-old".

1089. MRS BOSS ★★★
b.f. Makbul – Chorus (Bandmaster).
January 30. The dam was a modest winner of 5 races from 5f to 7f. The second dam, Name That Tune (by Fayruz), was unplaced. (Mrs L S Millman).
"She's by Makbul, one of my favourite sires, who has unfortunately retired now. She looks very much like a nice horse I had called Ocean Blaze. She's a big two-year-old and out of one of our own mares. She's working nicely and she'll be out in mid-May. The dam was never really sound but she still won 6 races and my children learned to ride on her!"

1090. PRINCESS SEREN ★★
b.f. King's Best – Gold Field (Unfuwain).
March 31. Fourth foal. 16,000Y. Tattersalls October 2. Not sold. The dam won 5 races in France over middle-distances at 3 and 4 yrs including a listed event and is a half-sister to 3 winners. The second dam, Gemmologie (by Crystal Glitters), won once at 2 yrs in France and

is a half-sister to 9 winners.
"Strong and well put together, I see her being out over six furlongs and she'll move up from there".

1091. TRUE RED ★★★
ch.f. Redback – Red Trance (Soviet Star).
April 14. 1,000Y. Tattersalls October. Not sold. The dam, a fair 2-y-o 5f winner, is a half-sister to 2 winners including the fairly useful 3-y-o 1m winner and Group 3 Prix Miesque third Arabian Spell. The second dam, Truly Bewitched (by Affirmed), a quite useful 2-y-o 6f winner, is a half-sister to 5 winners including the US Grade 2 winner Chinese Dragon.
"One of the smallest fillies I've ever had with ability. An easy-moving filly, she was just touched off on her debut but she needs a fast five furlongs and firm ground".

1092. TUCKER'S LAW ★★★
b.c. Country Reel – Silvereine (Bering).
April 7. Sixth foal. 10,000Y. Tattersalls October 3. Rod Millman. Half-brother to 3 minor winners abroad by Emperor Jones, Green Tune and Groom Dancer. The dam, a minor French 3-y-o winner, is a half-sister to 5 winners. The second dam, Silverqueen (by Alydar), won once at 3 yrs in France and is a half-sister to 10 winners including the Group 1 Prix Jean Prat winner and sire Sillery.
"He's quite sharp and he'll be out in mid-May over five furlongs. I had a half-brother by Elnadim who showed a lot of promise but he got injured and was never the same again. This horse has a lot of natural speed but he'll get further later on".

TERRY MILLS

Once again Assistant Trainer Richard Ryan was kind enough to discuss the Loretta Lodge two-year-olds with me.

1093. OLD DEVIL MOON (IRE) ★★★
br.c. Johannesburg – Tencarola (Night Shift).
January 21. Fourth foal. 36,000Y. Tattersalls October 2. T Mills. Half-brother to a minor winner in the USA by Gulch. The dam, a listed-placed 3-y-o winner in France, is a half-sister to 4 winners. The second dam, Vanya (by Busted), won the listed Prix d'Automne and is a full or half-sister to 7 winners including the French Group 3 winner Muroto.
"A very forward horse, he's showing plenty of speed, has done a couple of bits of work and we're pleased with him. He should be out in May and he's a five/six furlong type".

1094. UNNAMED ★★★
ch.f. Kyllachy – Comeraincomeshine (Night Shift).
March 6. Second foal. 26,000Y. Tattersalls October 1. Not sold. Half-sister to the useful 2008 2-y-o dual 5f winner and Group 3 6f Firth Of Clyde Stakes third Danehill Destiny (by Danehill Dancer). The dam, a modest 5.5f winner, is a half-sister to 5 winners including the high-class Group 1 1m Queen Elizabeth II Stakes winner Where Or When and the smart 10f and 12f winner and Group 1 St Leger fourth All The Way. The second dam, Future Past (by Super Concorde), a winner of 4 races at up to 9f in the USA, is a half-sister to 8 winners.
"She's going to take a little time to come to hand. She's slower-maturing than her half-sister but she'll be OK in time. I think it's one feature of the Pivotal gene that Kyllachy's aren't usually early types anyway. She's not over-big but she's neatly made".

1095. UNNAMED ★★★★
ch.c. Giant's Causeway – Eliza (Mt Livermore).
February 4. Eleventh foal. 50,000 2-y-o. Tattersalls Craven Breeze Up Sales. Closely related to the US 2-y-o winner and Grade 2 placed Miss Doolittle (herself the dam of a stakes winner) and to the minor US winner of 3 races Dominique's Cat (both by Storm Cat) and half-brother to the fairly useful 5f and 7f 2-y-o winner and listed Chesham Stakes second Country Song (by Fusaichi Pegasus) and a minor US 3-y-o winner by Theatrical. The dam, winner of the Grade 1 Breeders Cup Juvenile Fillies and the Grade 1 Santa Anita Oaks, is a half-sister to 9 winners including the Grade 1 Santa Anita Derby winner Dinard. The second dam, Daring

Bidder (by Bold Bidder), was unraced.
"He's literally just arrived as he bought at the Newmarket Breeze Up Sales this week. Obviously it's too soon to judge but he moves well and I don't think he was too expensive considering the pedigree".

1096. UNNAMED ★★★★
gr.c. Verglas – Gwyneth (Zafonic).
March 9. First foal. 60,000Y. Tattersalls October 2. T Mills. The dam is an unplaced half-sister to 6 winners including the Italian Group 3 winner Guest Connections. The second dam, Llyn Gwynant (by Persian Bold), won the Group 3 1m Desmond Stakes and the Group 3 1m Matron Stakes and is a half-sister to 2 winners. (T G Mills).
"He's a nice, quality horse, he's doing work at the moment and he may well run over six furlongs. We might get him out prior to Ascot to see if we should take him there, but I think he'll get better as the season goes on. He's one to look forward to and he's a very good-actioned horse".

1097. UNNAMED ★★★★
b.c. Montjeu – Magnificient Style (Silver Hawk).
April 21. 230,000foal. Tattersalls December. New Cross Bloodstock. Closely related to the Group 1 Fillies' Mile winner Playful Act, to the Group 3 11.5f Lingfield Derby Trial winner Percussionist and the 10f winner and Group 3 10f Prix de Psyche second Changing Skies (all by Sadler's Wells) and half-brother to the Group 2 1m Sun Chariot Stakes and Group 2 14.6f Park Hill Stakes winner Echoes In Eternity (by Spinning World), the US stakes winner and Grade 3 placed Stylelistick (by Storm Cat) and the 1m (at 2 yrs) and listed 9f winner and Group 2 placed Petara Bay (by Peintre Celebre). The dam won the Group 3 10.5f Musidora Stakes and is a half-sister to the Grade 1 10f Charles H Strub Stakes winner Siberian Summer. The second dam, Mia Karina (by Icecapade), a minor 3-y-o winner in France, is a half-sister to the dam of the US Grade 1 Pegasus Handicap winner Silver Ending. (T G Mills).
"A very nice horse, he's obviously a horse for next year's Derby – all being well! A very agile mover, he's very light on his feet, neatly-made and very correct. He's a very pleasing horse and we look forward to seeing him later in the season".

1098. UNNAMED ★★★★
ch.f. Pivotal – Sweet Firebird (Sadler's Wells).
March 16. First foal. 320,000Y. Tattersalls October 1. T Mills. The dam, a useful Irish 10f winner and third in the Group 3 10f Blue Wind Stakes, is a sister to the 2-y-o 7.5f winner and Group 2 1m Royal Lodge Stakes second Moscow Ballet and a half-sister to 6 winners including the top-class Group 1 July Cup and Group 1 Nunthorpe Stakes winner Stravinsky. The second dam, Fire The Groom (by Blushing Groom), a smart winner of 5 races trained at around 1m, subsequently won the Grade 1 9.5f Beverly D Stakes and the Grade 2 Wilshire Handicap and is a half-sister to the Group 1 6f Vernons Sprint Cup winner Dowsing.
"She's got a lot of quality and she's a strong, well-made filly. She won't be rushed, so we'll see her in the second half of the season with some cut in the ground, probably at around six or seven furlongs".

STAN MOORE

1099. ANT MUSIC (IRE) ★★★
b.c. Antonius Pius – Day Is Dawning (Green Forest).
March 6. Seventh foal. 35,000Y. Doncaster St Leger. Bobby O'Ryan. Half-brother to the quite useful Irish 7f winner Sa'ed, to the fair 6f and 7f winner of 7 races Flying Edge (both by Flying Spur) and a 2-y-o winner in Italy by Turtle Island. The dam is an unraced half-sister to 3 winners. The second dam, Grand Morning (by King Of Clubs), won the listed Marble Hill Stakes and is a half-sister to 6 winners. (P M Cunningham).
"This is a good-looking two-year-old, he's a good walker and he's already had his first race. He'll be a six-to-seven furlong two-year-old and there's plenty of size about him. He'll probably appreciate a bit of cut in the ground and he'll win his races".

1100. CHAT DE SOIE (IRE) ★★★
b.f. Barathea – Margay (Irish River).
March 15. Fourth foal. €12,000Y. Goffs October. Stan Moore. Half-sister to the unlaced 2008 2-y-o Lock N' Load (by Johannesburg) and to a minor 3-y-o winner in the USA by Hennessy. The dam, an Irish 2-y-o 7f winner, was second in the Group 2 German 1,000 Guineas and is a half-sister to 3 winners. The second dam, Almarai (by Vaguely Noble), is a placed half-sister to 5 winners including the US Grade 1 winner Buckhar. (Mrs S Briddon).
"A really nice filly, she has a lovely pedigree and she could be anything. I see her being one of our better two-year-olds and seven furlongs should suit her this year".

1101. EMMA JEAN LASS (IRE) ★★★
b.f. Choisir – Enlisted (Sadler's Wells).
January 17. Fifth foal. 12,000Y. Doncaster St Leger. Stan Moore. Half-sister to the 10f to 12f winner of 6 races Mull Of Dubai (by Mull Of Kintyre), to the modest 2-y-o 7f winner Regimental Dance (by Groom Dancer), the moderate 1m winner Lady Predominant (by Primo Dominie) and a 9f winner in Spain by Peintre Celebre. The dam, a quite useful 10f winner, is a half-sister to 6 winners including the May Hill Stakes second Self Assured. The second dam, Impudent Miss (by Persian Bold), a useful winner of 3 races from 5f to 1m at 2 yrs in Ireland including the Group 3 Silken Glider Stakes, is a half-sister to the smart sprinter Sayyaf. (R Ambrose, W Reilly, S Moore).
"She was beaten a short head first time out but she was backward in her coat and she'll improve. I have one eye on the Albany Stakes with her, she's genuine, has plenty of pace and will definitely win races".

1102. FRAMEIT (IRE) ★★★
b.c. Antonius Pius – Delisha (Salse).
March 10. €22,000Y. Goffs Million. Not sold. Half-brother to the very smart Group 3 6f Phoenix Sprint Stakes winner Al Qasi (by Elnadim), to the moderate 1m and 9f winner Margot Mine (by Choisir) and two multiple winners in Italy by Be My Guest and Victory Note. The dam won once at 3 yrs in Germany and is a half-sister to 5 winners including the Group 1 Hong Kong Mile winner Ecclesiastical. The second dam, Rachael Tennessee (by Matsadoon), was placed once in the USA and is a half-sister to 7 winners including the top-class miler Lear Fan.
"A really nice horse, he's quite big and won't be over-raced this year. I'll start him around June time and towards the back-end I think he'll be one of our nicer ones. He's a proper horse, with quality". TRAINER'S BARGAIN BUY

1103. KINKY AFRO (IRE) ★★★
b.f. Modigliani – Feet Of Flame (Theatrical).
April 24. €17,000Y. Goffs Sportsman's. Stan Moore. Half-sister to the fairly useful 2008 2-y-o 8.7f winner Fullback (by Redback) and to the fair 2-y-o winner 7f Orpen Fire (by Orpen). The dam is a placed half-sister to one winner in the USA. The second dam, Red Hot Dancer (by Seattle Dancer), is a US placed half-sister to 5 winners including the minor US stakes winner at around 1m Madame Secretary (herself dam of the French One Thousand Guineas winner Ta Rib), the useful stayer Zero Watt and the Stewards Cup winner Green Ruby.
"A half-sister to a nice two-year-old of ours last year, Fullback, this is a big, strong filly that'll be best at up to seven furlongs. She has quality and if you saw her coming you'd think she was a colt".

1104. SOMNIUM ★★★★
b.c. Oasis Dream – Finity (Diesis).
March 15. Third foal. €25,000Y. Tattersalls Ireland. Stan Moore. Brother to the fair 2008 2-y-o 6f winner Flintlock. The dam, a useful 2-y-o 7f winner, was third in the Group 3 7f C L Weld Park Stakes and is a half-sister to 2 winners. The second dam, Silversword (by Highest Honor), a winner at 3 yrs in France and Group 3 placed, is a full or half-sister to 6 winners. (Mr P & Mr T Wilkinson).
"A real nice horse, when we bought him his dam hadn't bred a winner but since then both her first foals have won. He's one of our better horses, I'll kick start his season in May over six

furlongs and aim him for the Tattersalls Sales race in Ireland. One to look out for".

1105. WELIKETOBOUGGIE ★★★
b.c. Tobougg – Country Spirit (Sayf El Arab).
March 29. Tenth foal. €17,000Y. Tattersalls Ireland. Stan Moore. Half-brother to the unplaced 2008 2-y-o Spiritual Bond (by Monsieur Bond), to the quite useful 5f (at 2 yrs) and 1m winner Millennium Magic (by Magic Ring), the fair 5f and 6f winner Semenovskii (by Fraam) and 2 minor winners abroad by Magic Ring and Bertolini). The dam is an unraced half-sister to 4 minor winners. The second dam, Queen And Country (by Town And Country), is an unplaced half-sister to 7 winners. (Wall to Wall Partnership).
"One of the best looking two-year-olds we have, his sire Tobougg breeds tough horses and this colt is definitely up to winning races. I have the Sales race in Ireland in mind for a few of my horses and this is one of them".

1106. UNNAMED ★★★
b.f. High Chaparral – Diary (Green Desert).
February 10. Third foal. 28,000 2-y-o. Doncaster Breeze Up. Stan Moore. Half-sister to the smart 2008 2-y-o listed 6f Redcar Two-Year-Old Trophy winner Total Gallery (by Namid). The dam won 3 races over 7f at 3 yrs and is a half-sister to 3 winners including the Triumph Hurd;e winner Made In Japan. The second dam, Darrerry (by Darshaan), won 3 races at 3 and 4 yrs.
"I have her half-brother Total Gallery who we think will make up into a high-class horse. This filly breezed well at the sale and she'll be a nice six furlong two-year-old. She isn't as big as her half-brother and looks a two-year-old type".

1107. UNNAMED ★★
b.c. Elusive City – Lizanne (Theatrical).
April 4. Seventh foal. €27,000Y. Goffs. Rathbarry Stud. Half-brother to the unplaced 2008 2-y-o Allexes (by Exceed And Excel). The dam is an unraced half-sister to 12 winners including Hawkster (a winner of three Grade 1 events in the USA), the French listed 5f winner and Group 1 placed Silver Kite and the Group 3 1m Prix de la Grotte winner and Irish Oaks third Silver Lane (herself the dam of 3 listed winners). The second dam, Strait Lane (by Chieftain), is an unraced half-sister to 2 stakes winners in the USA.
"He's quite a big two-year-old and he'll make up into a nice colt. Showing nice paces at home, I haven't done much with him but whatever he's been asked to do he's done well. Six furlongs should be his distance".

1108. UNNAMED ★★★
b.c. Soviet Star – Walnut Lady (Forzando).
April 21. Fifth foal. €3,500Y. Goffs October. Stan Moore. Brother to the quite useful 7f (at 2 yrs) to 10f winner of 6 races Alfie Tupper and half-brother to the quite useful 6f winner of 5 races at 3 and 4 yrs Expensive Art (by Cape Cross). The dam won a 5f seller at Southwell at 2 yrs prior to winning 3 races in France where she was listed-placed twice at up to 6f. The second dam, Princess Tateum (by Tate Gallery), won over 1m, 10f and over hurdles and is a half-sister to 5 winners.
"He'll be a tough horse and one that will take plenty of racing. He's working well, he has a good, solid pedigree and will start off at six furlongs in May".

PATRICK MORRIS
1109. BILLIONAIRE BOY ★★★
b.c. Acclamation – Shalwell (Shalford).
April 16. Sixth foal. 100,000Y. Doncaster St Leger. Bobby O'Ryan. Half-brother to the modest 2-y-o 6f winner Megell (by Entrepreneur). The dam is an unraced half-sister to 7 winners including the French and Irish 2,000 Guineas winner Bachir. The second dam, Morning Welcome (by Be My Guest), is a placed half-sister to 9 winners including the US Grade 3 winner Down Again. (Rob Lloyd Racing Ltd).
"A big colt, he's good-brained and six/seven furlongs will be his sort of trip this year".

1110. SECRET MILLIONAIRE ★★★
b.c. Kyllachy – Mithl Al Hawa (Salse).
April 18. Tenth foal. 56,000 2-y-o. Goffs

Kempton Breeze Up. O'Ryan/Cloverdale. Half-brother to 5 winners including the fairly useful 7f and 1m winner Cornflower Fields (by Cadeaux Genereux) and the quite useful 1m and 9f winner Eastern Spice (by Polish Precedent). The dam, a useful 2-y-o 6f winner, is a half-sister to 9 winners including the Group placed Abraham Lincoln, Moon King, South Dakota and Devil Moon and the dam of the Group 2 Cherry Hinton Stakes winner Jewel In The Sand. The second dam, Moon Drop (by Dominion), a useful listed winner of 3 races over 5f and 6f, is a half-sister to 7 winners including the very useful 7f and 12f winner Beldale Star.
"He breezed well at the sale and he's a sharp-looking, two-year-old type. An out and out five furlong horse".

1111. WAR ANGEL ★★
b.g. Verglas – Ibtihal (Hamas).
March 26. Third foal. 35,000Y. Doncaster St Leger. Bobby O'Ryan. Half-brother to the fair Irish 2-y-o 8.5f winner Lily Whitford (by Intikhab). The dam is a placed half-sister to 6 winners. The second dam, Taqreem (by Nashwan), is a placed half-sister to 7 winners including Rosia Bay (Group 1 Yorkshire Oaks) and Ibn Bey (triple Group 1 winner).
"His first run will be dependent on the ground because he'll appreciate a bit of cut, but we expect him out in May. He's a nice, hardy sort and he'll be a six/seven furlong type two-year-old".

1112. UNNAMED ★★★
b.f. Exceed And Excel – Royal Lady
(Royal Academy).
March 4. Fourth foal. 31,000Y. Doncaster St Leger. Bobby O'Ryan. The dam is an unplaced half-sister to 6 winners including the US Grade 1 placed Bouccaneer. The second dam, Shahoune (by Blushing Groom), is a placed half-sister to the US dual Grade 3 winner Amal Hayati. (Rob Lloyd Racing Ltd).
"This filly is a brilliant mover – you wouldn't see a better one. We haven't pushed her yet and she'll be one for the middle of the season over six and seven furlongs. She's an athletic, scopey filly".

1113. UNNAMED ★★★
b.f. Xaar – Sadalsud (Shaadi).
February 10. Seventh foal. 50,000Y. Doncaster Festival. Bobby O'Ryan. Half-brother to the smart 6f (at 2 yrs) and Group 3 Sandown Sprint winner Acien Regime (by King's Best) and to 2 minor winners in Italy by Lycius and Lion Cavern. The dam, a winner of 7 races at 2 to 5 yrs in Italy and is a half-sister to 3 winners. The second dam, Ring The Changes (by Auction Ring), won once at 3 yrs and is a half-sister to 10 winners including 4 stakes winners and the dam of the Group 1 winners Royal Applause, Lyric Fantasy and In Command. (Rob Lloyd Racing Ltd).
"A lovely, big filly, she'll want seven furlongs this year and I see her being out in mid-season. She's entered for the Watership Down Stud Sales race".

HUGHIE MORRISON
1114. BETHLEHEM (IRE) ★★
b.c. Oratorio – Bumble (Rainbow Quest).
February 27. Fifth foal. 80,000Y. Tattersalls October 2. Kern/Lillingston. Half-brother to the useful 5f winner of 4 races and 2-y-o Group 2 6f July Stakes second Northern Empire (by Namid), to the quite useful Minus Fifteen 9by Trans Island) and the fair 1m all-weather winner Scutch Mill (by Alhaarth). The dam is an unraced half-sister to 6 winners including the Group 1 Racing Post Trophy winner Be My Chief. The second dam, Lady Be Mine (by Sir Ivor), a minor 3-y-o 1m winner, is a half-sister to 6 winners including Mixed Applause (dam of both the high-class miler Shavian and the Ascot Gold Cup winner Paean). (Findlay & Bloom).
"He's a very nice horse but he's 'up behind' and is one for the autumn. He's a charming character and a proper horse hopefully, everything's in the right place and he finds everything easy".

1115. CELESTIAL GIRL ★★
b.f. Dubai Destination – Brightest Star
(Unfuwain).
April 14. Fourth foal. 38,000Y. Tattersalls October 2. Not sold. Half-sister to King's Starlet (by King's Best), unplaced in 2 starts at 2 yrs in

2008, to the Italian 1m to 10f winner of 14 races from 3 to 6 yrs Strepadent (by Diesis) and a hurdles winner by Giant's Causeway. The dam was placed over 10f and 11f is a half-sister to the Oaks winner Lady Carla. The second dam, Shirley Superstar (by Shirley Heights), a fairly useful 2-y-o 7f winner, is a half-sister to 2 winners. (Helena Springfield Ltd).

"She hasn't come in yet, I've seen her and she's a typical Dubai Destination in that she's quite 'buzzy'. She needs gelding but she's a filly! Whether she's any good or not I couldn't say at the moment".

1116. COSIMO DE MEDICI ★★★
b.c. *Medicean – Wish (Danehill)*.
March 5. Fifth foal. 55,000Y. Tattersalls October 2. Kern/Lillingston. Half-brother to the 2008 French 7f and 1m placed 2-y-o Antinea (by Royal Applause), to the fair Irish 5f and 7f winner Wildwish (by Alhaarth) and the minor dual Italian 3-y-o winner Queen Cheap (by Daylami). The dam, a quite useful 2-y-o 6f winner Wish, is a half-sister to 3 winners. The second dam, Dazzle (by Gone West), a smart winner of the Group 3 6f Cherry Hinton Stakes and placed in both the Cheveley Park Stakes and the 1,000 Guineas. (Findlay & Bloom).

"He's quite 'up behind' and needs to level out, but funnily enough Robert Winston rode him out the other day and said I should kick-on with him. But I won't do that until he's level".

1117. DANCE TEMPO ★★
b.c. *Dansili – Musical Twist (Woodman)*.
February 6. 41,000foal. Tattersalls December. Lakin Bloodstock. Half-brother to a minor French 11f winner by Singspiel and to a 3-y-o winner in Greece by Atticus. The dam was placed from 6f to 1m and is a half-sister to 3 winners including the Group 2 6f Mill Reef Stakes third and subsequent US winner Belasco. The second dam, Musicale (by The Minstrel), winner of the Group 3 6f Cherry Hinton Stakes and the 7f Rockfel Stakes at 2 yrs and the Group 3 7.3f Gainsborough Stud Fred Darling Stakes at 3 yrs, is a half-sister to 6 winners. (Mr A N Solomons).

"A lovely big horse but one for the autumn".

1118. FORMULATION (IRE) ★★
b.c. *Danehill Dancer – Formal Approval (Kingmambo)*.
February 24. First foal. 90,000Y. Tattersalls October 1. Amanda Skiffington. The dam is a placed half-sister to 6 winners including the Group 3 6f Princess Margaret Stakes winner Sainly Speech, the Group 3 7f Prix du Calvados winner Woodland Melody and the good Japanese 10f winner Maruka Diesis. The second dam, Eloquent Minister (by Deputy Minister), a very useful sprint winner of 2 listed events at Doncaster and in Ireland, also won in the USA and is a half-sister to 8 winners. (Bob Tullett & Michael Kerr-Dineen).

"A lovely, big, rangy horse, he's definitely one for the autumn".

1119. HOT PURSUITS ★★★
b.f. *Pastoral Pursuits – Perfect Partner (Be My Chief)*.
January 29. 7,000foal. Tattersalls December. I Eavis. Half-sister to the modest 2-y-o 6f winner Molly Dancer (by Emarati). The dam is an unraced half-sister to 6 winners including the 6f Ayr Gold Cup and Washington Singer Stakes winner Funfair Wane and to the Italian listed 7.5f winner Cabcharge Striker. The second dam, the fairly useful listed 2-y-o 6f winner Ivory Bride (by Domynsky), is a half-sister to the useful listed 8.5f and listed 10f winner Putuna and the useful sprinter Lochonica.

"She's quite forward and she has a superb temperament. Very straightforward, she's cantering upsides and all being well she'll start over at six furlongs in May. She wants to do it and I think the sire will do well".

1120. IMPERIAL WARRIOR ★★★
ch.c. *Imperial Dancer – Tribal Lady (Absalom)*.
February 19. 17,000Y. Italy. Sbara Nuova. Half-brother to the quite useful 6f and 7f winner of 8 races Wyatt Earp, to the quite useful winner of 3 races at around 1m Triccolo (both by Piccolo), the Italian listed 9f winner Ira Funesta (by Definite Article), the Italian winner of 12 races Tito Claudio (by Aragon) and the quite useful 7.5f to 9f winner of 4 races Parting Shot (by

Young Ern). The dam, a fair 2-y-o 5f and 6f winner, is a half-sister to 6 minor winners. The second dam, Placid Pet (by Mummy's Pet), a modest 1m winner, is a sister to the Vernons Sprint Cup winner Runnett.

"You definitely need to put this one in the book. He's quite forward and has done a few bits of work on the grass. He wants to do it and I think all being well he'll run in May over six furlongs. He seems to pick things up pretty quick. He's a half-brother to plenty of winners and he'll make a two-year-old".

1121. ISLAND RHAPSODY ★★

ch.f. Bahamian Bounty – Lovely Lyca
(Night Shift).
March 16. 20,000Y. Tattersalls October 3. Norris/Huntingdon. Half-sister to the fair 2008 2-y-o 1m winner Brooksby (by Diktat), to the quite useful 2-y-o 6f winner and listed-placed Jeanmaire (by Dansili), the quite useful 3-y-o 1m winner Polish Off (by Polish Precedent), the fair 3-y-o 7.5f winner Lyca Ballerina (by Marju) and the modest 7f and 1m winner Sophia Gardens (by Barathea). The dam, a fair 1m and 11.8f winner, is a sister to the listed 1m winner Barboukh (herself dam of the Group 3 10f Prix Exbury winner Barbola) and a half-sister to 5 winners. The second dam, Turban (by Glint Of Gold), a fair 10f and 11.7f winner, is a half-sister to the top-class middle-distance colt Old Vic and the dual Group 3 12f winner Splash Of Colour.

"She's had a few irritating little problems so we haven't been able to do much with her. She's very laid-back like her half-sister Jeanmaire, so we'll push on with her and she should be a June/July two-year-old".

1122. PASTORAL PLAYER ★★★★

b.c. Pastoral Pursuits – Copy-Cat
(Lion Cavern).
March 21. Fifth foal. 35,000Y. Tattersalls October 2. Hugh Morrison. Half-brother to the fairly useful 2-y-o 7f and subsequent Hong Kong winner Copywriter (by Efisio), to the fairly useful 2-y-o 6f winner Chataway (by Mujahid) and the quite useful 2-y-o 5f winner Gilt Linked (by Compton Place). The dam is an unplaced half-sister to 7 winners including the very useful Group 3 5f King George Stakes winner Averti. The second dam, Imperial Jade (by Lochnager), a useful sprint winner of 4 races and second in the Group 2 Lowther Stakes, is a sister to the Greenlands Stakes, Palace House Stakes and Temple Stakes winner Reesh and a half-sister to 3 winners. (The Pursuits Partnership).

"Yes, he's a racehorse all right. He's quite sharp but he's not small and he's on his toes – probably because he finds everything easy. I did a bit of work with him a couple of weeks ago and that was enough to show me he's got speed, so I'd be disappointed if he didn't win at two".

1123. PRAYER HALL ★★

b.c. Oratorio – Timber Tops
(Timber Country).
March 3. First foal. 57,000Y. Tattersalls October 2. Charlie Gordon-Watson. The dam is an unplaced half-sister to 5 winners including the Group 3 Prix Vanteaux winner Campsie Fells. The second dam, Queen's View (by Lomond), a very useful 6f (at 2 yrs) and 7f winner, was second in the Group 3 Rockfel Stakes and is a half-sister to 6 winners including the Irish listed winner Millstreet. (Mr & Mrs Hugh Scott-Barrett).

"He canters away quite easily but he needs to grow a bit and I'd be surprised if he ran before the autumn. You'd think he'd get a trip".

1124. QUEEN'S GRACE ★★★

ch.f. Bahamian Bounty – Palace Affair
(Pursuit Of Love).
February 23. Half-sister to the modest 7f and 1m winner April Fool (by Pivotal). The dam, a smart listed winner of 6 races from 5f to 7f, is a half-sister to the high-class Group 1 6f July Cup winner Sakhee's Secret and to the very useful 6f to 8.3f winner Duke Of Modena. The second dam, Palace Street (by Secreto), a useful winner over 6f and 7f including the listed Cammidge Trophy, is a half-sister to the Extel Handicap winner Indian Trail and the Italian Group 3 winner Sfriss. (Miss B Swire).

"She's quite sharp-looking and she's got plenty of speed. We're focusing her talent and you'd hope she'd make a two-year-old. She moves well and has grown a bit lately but she could be a runner in May".

1125. SIX DIAMONDS ★★★
b.f. Exceed And Excel – Daltak (Night Shift).
February 17. Sixth foal. 4,000Y. Tattersalls October 3. Not sold. Half-sister to the fair 2-y-o 6f all-weather winner Scarlet Empress (by Second Empire). The dam is an unraced half-sister to 7 winners including the listed winner and Group 2 5f Temple Stakes second Dominio (herself dam of the Group 2 Kings Stand Stakes winner Dominica) and the very smart Group 1 5f Nunthorpe Stakes winner Ya Malak. The second dam, La Tuerta (by Hot Spark), a fairly useful sprint winner of 3 races, is a half-sister to 8 winners including Cadeaux Genereux.
"She's quite sharp, quite forward and a straightforward type. She wants to do it and hopefully she'll be out before the end of May. The fact that the dam hasn't produced much wouldn't put me off – I'd have bought her myself". TRAINER'S BARGAIN BUY

1126. STADIUM OF LIGHT (IRE) ★★★
b.c. Fantastic Light – Treble Seven (Fusaichi Pegasus).
January 26. First foal. 20,000Y. Tattersalls October 3. Norris/Huntingdon. The dam, placed once over 1m, is a half-sister to the very smart filly Lovers Knot, winner of the Group 2 1m Falmouth Stakes and the US Grade 3 De La Rose Handicap and to the very useful 1m (at 2 yrs) and 9f winner and listed-placed Foodbroker Founder. The second dam, Nemea (by The Minstrel), a fairly useful 10f winner, stayed 2m and is a half-sister to 8 winners including the useful 12f winners Topsider Man and Bryan Station and the useful stayer Muir Station. (Dr J Wilson).
"A typical Fantastic Light in that he's a bit of a prat, but we quite like him! He's quite 'together', he's not over-big or backward and I would think he'll make a two-year-old by August. He was cheap".

1127. TIGER CAT ★★
b.f. Tiger Hill – Great Verdict (Christmas Tree).
April 1. Half-sister to Repealed (by Reset), unplaced in one start at 2 yrs in 2008, to the very smart South African Grade 1 13f and UAE Grade 3 12f winner Greys Inn (by Zabeel) and the quite useful 10f winner Masterofthecourt (by Horse Chestnut). The dam is an unraced half-sister to the top-class Australian winner Zedative. (Mrs B Oppenheimer).
"A nice, big, rangy filly, you'd be wrong to think of racing her this summer. She's one for the back-end of the year and particularly as a three-year-old"

1128. UNNAMED ★★
b.f. Montjeu – Discreet Brief (Darshaan).
April 25. Third foal. €140,000Y. Goffs Million. Kern/Lillingston. Closely related to the fairly useful 1m 2f winner Secret Dancer (by Sadler's Wells) and half-sister to the unraced 2008 2-y-o Doggerbank (by Oasis Dream). The dam won the Group 3 Park Hill Stakes, was Group 3 placed in Italy and is a half-sister to 2 winners. The second dam, Quiet Counsel (by Law Society), won once at 3 yrs and is a half-sister to 7 winners including the Group 1 Yorkshire Oaks winner Key Change. (Anthony Rogers & Mr J Dodd).
"Very much one for the back-end of the season, she's a very attractive filly. She was returned from the sales as a box walker but she's never done that in her life – not even a sign of it. She's a leggy, backward looking filly but the best Montjeu fillies are big, so I'd be quite hopeful for her".

1129. UNNAMED ★★
b.br.f. Efisio – Dwingeloo (Dancing Dissident).
May 15. Seventh foal. Sister to Miss Vegas, a winner of 7 races including the US Grade 3 Senorita Stakes and a listed event in Italy and half-sister to the Italian winner at 2 and 3 yrs and listed-placed Vegas Queen (by Celtic Swing) and the fair 6f winner of 4 races Realt Na Mara (by Tagula). The dam, a 2-y-o 5f winner, is a half-sister to 7 winners. The second dam, Thank One's Stars (by Alzao), is an unraced half-sister

to 5 winners. (Mrs G C Maxwell & Partners).
"Yet to come in to the yard, there's nothing stunning about her but she'll be a mid-to-late summer two-year-old".

1130. UNNAMED ★★
b.c. Zafeen – Roofer (Barathea).
May 12. Half-brother to the modest 2008 1m placed 2-y-o Assail and to the fair 2-y-o 5f winner Relkida (both by Bertolini). The dam was placed 5 times from 7f to 10f and is a half-sister to the Group 2 German 2,000 Guineas winner Brunel. The second dam, Castlerahan (by Thatching), was unraced. (Mr M Watson & Ms Deborah Collett).
"A big, strong horse with a nice character, he was a late foal and he's only just being broken at the moment, but he's a nice horse – better looking than his half-brother Assail. They really like him at the pre-training yard but he'll be one for the all-weather in November/December time".

1131. UNNAMED ★★★
ch.c. Bahamian Bounty – Sefemm (Alhaarth).
January 23. First foal. 36,000Y. Tattersalls October 2. Hugh Morrison. The dam is an unraced half-sister to 4 minor winners. The second dam, Pennsylvania (by Northjet), is an unplaced half-sister to 6 winners including the dam of the US Grade 1 winner Unaccounted For. (Mr & Mrs G Paulus & Mr R Behan).
"He's laid-back, big and strong but I'm not sure whether he'll go backward on us or not yet. I've x-rayed his knees and they are mature enough, so hopefully he'll be a late summer two-year-old".

WILLIE MUIR
1132. BE A DEVIL ★★★
ch.c. Dubai Destination – Devil's Imp (Cadeaux Genereux).
March 28. Seventh foal. 35,000Y. Doncaster St Leger. W Muir. Half-brother to the 2008 Irish 2-y-o 6f winner Droumeragh (by Royal Applause), to the Group 2 7f Challenge Stakes winner Miss Lucifer (by Noverre) and the fairly useful (at 2 yrs) and 7f winner Desert Imp (by Cadeaux Genereux). The dam, a fair 6f and 7f winner, is a half-sister to the Group 2 12f King Edward VII Stakes winner Amfortas and the Group 3 10.5f Prix de Royaumont winner Legend Maker (dam of the 1,000 Guineas winner Virginia Waters). The second dam, High Spirited (by Shirley Heights), was quite useful and won two of her seven races over 14f and 2m at 3 yrs. She is a sister to the Group 1 Premio Roma winner High Hawk (herself dam of the Breeders Cup Turf winner In the Wings) and a half-sister to the dams of the Derby winner High Rise and the Rothmans International winner Infamy. (Foursome Thoroughbreds).
"He's a real strong, 'butty' type of two-year-old. He grew a fair bit so I've taken my time with him but he has a stallion's pedigree. I think if he'd been by a more fashionable stallion he'd have made 200 Grand. He will make a two-year-old, he's strong and has big quarters and he's very laid-back".

1133. BLUE ZEPHYR ★★★
br.c. Pastoral Pursuits – Pippa's Dancer (by Desert Style).
February 21. First foal. 12,000Y. Doncaster St Leger. Not sold. The dam, a fair 5f and 6f winner of 4 races, is a half-sister to several winners including the smart dual 6f winner (including at 2 yrs) Strahan. The second dam, Soreze (Gallic League), a useful Irish 2-y-o listed 5f Marble Hill Stakes winner, is a half-sister to 5 winners. (Mr M P Graham).
"I trained the mother and she won four sprints despite having a problem with her foot. This lad has no problems, he's shown me he's got ability and he'll definitely win this year. Pastoral Pursuits looks like he'll be a sharp stallion and I think this colt is nice and he'll improve for his first run".

1134. FAWLEY GREEN ★★★★
b.c. Shamardal – Wars (Green Desert).
March 11. Fourth foal. 30,000Y. Doncaster St Leger. W Muir. Half-brother to the quite useful 2-y-o 6f winner Heroes, to the Irish 2-y-o 7f winner Redrightreturning (both by Diktat) and the fair 7f winner Usk Poppy (by Mark Of

Esteem). The dam is a placed sister to the very smart 7f and 1m performer Gabr and a half-sister to 4 winners including the smart middle-distance horse Kutta. The second dam, Ardassine (by Ahonoora), a 12f winner in Ireland, was fourth in the Group 3 Irish 1,000 Guineas Trial and is a half-sister to 7 winners. (W R Muir).

"A strong colt, I think he's lovely. He through a splint so I took my time with him and it's settled down nicely now. I think the sire will be a great stallion and I love this colt to look at. He'll be out in mid-season and he looks like he could be a quality two-year-old. He looks like his Dad in that he's got scope and is a big, strong, hardy colt".

1135. HIGH APPROACH ★★★★
b.c. *Dalakhani – Jawaher (Dancing Brave)*.
March 3. Ninth foal. 26,000Y. Tattersalls October 1. Mr D Joseph. Half-brother to Zomaradah (by Deploy), a winner of 6 races including the Group 1 Italian Oaks and herself dam of the high-class miler Dubawi, to the quite useful 12f, 14f and hurdles winner Nichol Fifty (by Old Vic) and 2 minor winners abroad by Dihistan and Water Cay. The dam was placed over 1m and 9f and is a half-sister to the Derby winner High Rise out of the winning stayer High Tern (by High Line), herself a half-sister to Group 1 winner High Hawk (the dam of In The Wings). (David & Gwyn Joseph).

"This could be a nice animal and if he continues to mature and improve he could be better than average. He's related to Dubawi and he could be anything. He wasn't expensive, he's quite strong which is unlike most Dalakhani's because they're normally 'on the leg' and take forever. This colt shows he's got something but I need to take my time with him. I'm happy with everything he's done so far".

1136. KILDANGAN GIRL ★★
b.f. *Refuse To Bend – Paola Maria (Daylami)*.
March 19. Second foal. 5,000Y. Tattersalls October 2. Not sold. Half-sister to Peace In Paradise (by Dubai Destination), unplaced in two starts at 2 yrs in 2008. The dam is an unraced half-sister to 4 winners including the useful 9.5f winner and Group 2 placed Queen Of Naples. The second dam, Napoleon's Sister (by Alzao), a useful 10f listed winner, is a half-sister to the top-class colts Oath (winner of the Derby) and Pelder (winner of the Group 1 1m Gran Criterium, the Group 1 1m Premio Parioli and the Group 1 10.5f Prix Ganay). (Mr P C Bourke).

"She's got some speed but I backed off her a bit because she hadn't come to hand properly. She'll be a two-year-old if anything, because she's on the small side".

1137. LILY RIO ★★★
b.br.f. *Marju – Jinsiyah (Housebuster)*.
April 19. Seventh foal. €80,000Y. Goffs Million. Not sold. Half-sister to the modest 2008 5f placed 2-y-o Raimond Ridge (by Namid), to the smart listed 5f and 6f winner of 13 races Indian Maiden (by Indian Ridge), the quite useful Irish dual 7f winner Kingsdale Orion (by Intikhab) and the fair 7f and 10.5f winner Neqaawi (by Alhaarth). The dam, a useful 2-y-o 7f winner, is a half-sister to 5 winners including the fairly useful dual 1m winner Bintalshaati. The second dam, the fair staying maiden Minifah (by Nureyev), is a placed half-sister to 8 winners including the Kentucky Derby winner Winning Colors. (Mrs J Doyle).

"She's a big, tall filly that's never stopped growing and 'doing'. She looks fantastic and she moves well. I think at the back-end of the season we'll have a really nice filly on our hands and I do like the stallion. She'd be high up on my list of nice fillies with a future".

1138. MERCHANT OF MEDICI ★★★★
b.c. *Medicean – Regal Rose (Danehill)*.
March 1. Third foal. 13,000Y. Tattersalls October 2. W Muir. Brother to the fairly useful 2-y-o 6f winner Regal Royale and half-brother to the fair 2-y-o 7f winner Regal Riband (by Fantastic Light). The dam won both her starts including the Group 1 6f Cheveley Park Stakes. She is a sister to the Japanese 10f stakes winner Generalist and a half-sister to 7 winners. The second dam, Ruthless Rose (by Conquistador

Cielo), ran twice unplaced and is a half-sister to 9 winners including the high-class miler Shaadi. (Jones, Haim, Kennedy).

"He was cheap, he's out of a really good mare and I would say he's a very nice horse. He's bigger than a sharp two-year-old but he has the speed now. I'll hopefully be running him at the end of May and he's a lovely individual that could be classy". TRAINER'S BARGAIN BUY

1139. NEFYN ★★★
b.f. *Tiger Hill – Bread Of Heaven (Machiavellian).*
March 16. Second foal. 60,000Y. Tattersalls October 1. Not sold. Half-sister to the unplaced 2008 2-y-o Scarlets (by Red Ransom). The dam, a quite useful 2-y-o 6f winner, is a half-sister to 4 winners including the Group 2 1m Prix du Rond-Point and Group 3 8.5f Diomed Stakes winner Trans Island and the Italian Group 3 winner Welsh Diva. The second dam, Khubza (by Green Desert), a quite useful 3-y-o 7f winner, is a half-sister to 7 winners including the Group 2 winners Barrow Creek and Last Resort and the listed winners Arctic Char and Heard A Whisper. (Usk Valley Stud).

"A big, tall Tiger Hill filly that moves well and looks well. But she is big so I'll wait until she tells she's ready. She has the size and scope to be good and she's done everything nicely so far".

1140. OPTIMISTIC DUKE ★★★
ch.c. *Bachelor Duke – Gronchi Rosa (Nashwan).*
March 17. Second foal. 26,000Y. Doncaster St Leger. Not sold. Brother to the fair 2008 2-y-o 7f winner Cavendish Road. The dam won 2 races at 2 and 3 yrs in Italy and is a half-sister to 2 winners including the Group 3 placed Euribor. The second dam, Anna Grassi (by Bound For Honour), won a listed event in Italy and is a half-sister to 6 winners. (Linkslade Optimists).

"He'll take a bit of time, I train his full-brother Cavendish Road and this colt is bigger, nicer and stronger".

1141. STORMGLASS ★★★★
ch.c. *Galileo – Aberdovey (Mister Baileys).*
February 7. First foal. 110,000Y. Tattersalls October 1. W Muir. The dam, a fair 6f (at 2 yrs) and 1m winner, is a half-sister to the dual 10f and subsequent minor US stakes winner and Grade 2 placed Solva. The second dam, Annapurna (by Brief Truce), a useful 7f winner (at 2 yrs) and 9f listed placed, is a half-sister to 4 winners including the very useful 2-y-o Group 3 7f Rockfel Stakes and listed 7f winner Name Of Love. (C Edginton, M Graham & K Mercer).

"I've always wanted a Galileo and I hope I've bought one as good as New Approach! I wouldn't rush him and he's probably the apple of my eye. One for the second half of the season and I'll bring him along like a proper horse".

1142. TOTALLY OURS ★★
b.br.f. *Singspiel – Totally Yours (by Desert Sun).*
April 20. First foal. 5,000Y. Tattersalls October 1. Not sold. The dam, a quite useful 2-y-o 6f winner, is a half-sister to the 2-y-o Group 1 7f Dewhurst Stakes winner Tout Seul (by Ali-Royal). The second dam, Total Aloof (Groom Dancer), a fair dual 5f winner at 3 yrs, is a half-sister to 2 winners in Japan. (Foursome Thoroughbreds).

"I trained the mother and bred this filly. She's really growing and is now starting to develop into a big, tall filly so I won't rush her. The dam won at two and was beaten a short head in the Sales race in Ireland where she was beaten a short head. This filly won't be early but I really like her and she could be a really classy individual".

1143. TUDOR PRINCESS ★★
b.f. *King's Best – Santorini (Spinning World).*
February 15. Fourth foal. 30,000Y. Doncaster St Leger. Not sold. Half-sister to the modest 1m and 10f winner South Wales (by Sakhee), to the quite useful 5f to 7f winner of 8 races Methally (by Red Ransom) and the modest 7f winner Park Valley Prince (by Noverre). The dam is an unraced half-sister to the dual US Grade 1 Flower Bowl Invitational winner Dimitrova and to the multiple Group 1 winner (including the St Leger and Coronation Cup) Mutafaweq. The second dam, The Caretaker (by Caerleon), won 4 races in Ireland over 7f and 1m including 4 listed events, was Grade 3 placed in the USA

and is a half-sister to 8 winners. (Usk Valley Stud).
"She's a good mover and is unlike any King's Best I've ever had in that she's so chilled and laid-back. She's got length and she looks like she wants time but she moves well. I haven't done a lot with her yet and she's a filly I've got to look after at this time of the year".

1144. WELSH ANGEL ★★★
b.f. *Dubai Destination – Bright Halo (Bigstone).*
April 28. Third foal. 240,000Y. Tattersalls October 1. Not sold. Half-sister to the useful 6f (at 2 yrs) and listed 1m winner and Group 2 6f Mill Reef Stakes third Nantyglo (by Mark Of Esteem), to the fairly useful 1m (at 2 yrs) and 12f winner Resplendent Light (by Fantastic Light) and the moderate 2m 1f winner Arabian Sun (by Singspiel). The dam, a minor French 3-y-o 9f winner, is a half-sister to 7 winners including the Group 1 Irish Oaks winner Moonstone, the Group 1 10f Prix Saint-Alary winner Cerulean Sky and the Breeders Cup second L'Ancresse. The second dam, Solo de Lune (by Law Society), a French 11f winner, is a half-sister to 6 winners including the Grade 2 E P Taylor Stakes winner Truly A Dream and the French Group 2 winner Wareed. (Usk Valley Stud).
"I love this filly and I think she's got a serious amount of class. She's big, but a lot stronger than her half-brother Resplendent Light was at this stage. A nice filly, the owner was never going to sell her unless he got serious money and I'm lucky to be able to train her. She'll make a two-year-old in the second half of the season".

1145. UNNAMED ★★★
gr.g. *Oasis Dream – Barathiki (Barathea).*
March 10. Half-brother to the quite useful 2008 2-y-o 6f winner and listed 6f Bosra Sham Stakes third Albertine Rose (by Namid). The dam, a quite useful 2-y-o dual 6f winner, is a half-sister to 3 winners including the useful Peacock Alley, a winner of 3 races at around 7f and listed-placed. The second dam, Tagiki (by Doyoun), won once over 7f at 2 yrs in Italy and is a half-sister to 6 winners including the listed Ulster Harp Derby winner Tijara. (Mr & Mrs G Middlebrook).
"He's only just come in but he's a really lovely-looking individual from a nice family and he'll make a two-year-old. Once he strengthens up he'll hopefully emulate Albertine Rose who was listed-placed for us last season".

1146. UNNAMED ★★★
b.c. *Le Vie Dei Colori – Camassina (Taufan).*
April 9. €20,000Y. Goffs Million. Emerald Bloodstock. Half-brother to the fair 2008 2-y-o 6f winner On Offer (by Clodovil), to the fairly useful Irish 7f (at 2 yrs) and 1m winner Bricks And Porter (by College Chapel), the fair 2-y-o 5f winner Mujassina and the moderate Irish 7f winner Idle Journey (both by Mujadil). The dam was placed once over 7f at 3 yrs and is a half-sister to one winner. The second dam, Kaskazi (by Dancing Brave), won twice at 3 yrs and is a half-sister to 6 winners.
"I like this colt and he reminds me of Enforcer (Le Vie dei Colori and Enforcer are both by Efisio). I still need to sell a bit of him but I really like the colt. I've got after him, he shows he's got ability and I'm now just laying off him a bit because he's a big, tall horse and I wouldn't want to be too early with him. He's got the character that Enforcer had and I think he's a horse that will win two-year-old races".

1147. UNNAMED ★★
ch.c. *Medicean – Castaway Queen (Selkirk).*
March 23. Second living foal. 28,000Y. Tattersalls October 1. Not sold. The dam was placed 13 times from 6f (at 2 yrs) to 10f and is a half-sister to 8 winners including the useful 6f to 9.4f all-weather winner and subsequent US Grade 3 All American Handicap winner Mister Fire Eyes and the Hong Kong stakes winner Bumper Storm. The second dam, Surfing (by Grundy), a fair 7f placed maiden, is a sister to the Group 3 Prix d'Arenburg winner Glancing and a half-sister to the Group 1 Middle Park Stakes winner Bassenthwaite.
"He's quite a nice colt. I trained the dam who was placed loads of times but I just couldn't get her to put head in front. It's a strong family and this colt has got everything in place and has a bit of character about him. He just might be a

1148. UNNAMED ★★★
ch.c. Compton Place – Centre Court (Second Set).
February 25. Seventh foal. 32,000Y. Tattersalls October 1. Not sold. Brother to the fairly useful 2-y-o 7f winner and listed placed The Old Fella and half-brother to the modest 2-y-o 5.2f winner Service (by College Chapel). The dam, a fair 2-y-o 5f winner, is a half-sister to 3 winners including the useful winner of 4 races at around 7f Rasan. The second dam, Raffle (by Balidar), a quite useful 3-y-o 5.8f winner, is a half-sister to the good sprinters Mummy's Pet, Parsimony and Arch Sculptor.
"He's not over-big – the family are that way – but he's built like a tank. His full-brother was pretty useful and I think this is a lovely horse. I'll leave him until May and then start pushing on and doing a bit more with him".

1149. UNNAMED ★★★
b.f. Sakhee – Classical Dancer (Dr Fong).
February 24. Second foal. 95,000foal. Tattersalls December. Horizon Bloodstock. Half-sister to the fair 2008 7f and 1m 2-y-o winner Zaaqya (by Nayef). The dam, a fairly useful 8.3f winner, was listed-placed twice and is a half-sister to 3 winners including the Group 1 Premio Roma winner Imperial Dancer. The second dam, Gorgeous Dancer (by Nordico), an Irish 3-y-o 1m winner and third in the listed Irish Oaks Trial, is a half-sister to 3 winners. (M J Caddy).
"She has a great pedigree and I bought her as a foal for the owner. I'll try and turn her into a black-type filly if I can, she's developing at the moment so I've eased off her at the moment and she has a bit of scope".

1150. UNNAMED ★★★★
b.c. Avonbridge – Final Shot (Dalsaan).
March 20. Thirteenth foal. Doncaster St Leger. 30,000Y. W Muir. Half-brother to 10 winners including the very useful dual 6f winner and Group 3 Coventry Stakes second Sir Nicholas (by Cadeaux Genereux), subsequently very successful in Hong Kong, the smart 5f (at 2 yrs) and 6f winner and Ayr Gold Cup second Double Action (by Reprimand), the very useful 2-y-o listed 6f Sirenia Stakes winner Lipstick (by Zamindar), the useful 7f (at 2 yrs) and 10f winner High Command (by Galileo), the fairly useful 2-y-o 5.7f winner Final Pursuit (by Pursuit Of Love), the quite useful 6f winner of 6 races (including at 2 yrs) We Have A Dream (by Oasis Dream), the fair 8.5f all-weather winner Magical Shot (by Magic Ring) and the fair 2-y-o 6f winner Miss Waterline (by Rock City). The dam, a quite useful filly, won 3 races including the Ayr Gold Cup. The second dam, Isadora Duncan (by Primera), is a placed half-sister to the dam of the Yorkshire Oaks and Nassau Stakes winner Connaught Bridge. (W Muir).
"I really like him, he's got a fantastic attitude and the mare's bred loads of winners. He's correct, strong and doing his work well. He has a fantastic temperament, he'll be a treat to train and he'll be a two-year-old".

1151. UNNAMED ★★★
b.c. Fasliyev – Petite Epaulette (Night Shift).
March 20. Twelfth foal. 15,000Y. Doncaster St Leger. Not sold. Brother to the fairly useful 7.6f and subsequent US 1m winner Red Top and half-brother to the useful 2-y-o Group 3 7f C L Weld Park Stakes winner Rag Top, to the fair 2-y-o 7f winner Seamstress (herself dam of the 2-y-o listed winner Elhamri), the quite useful 2-y-o 5f winner Dress Code (all by Barathea), the fairly useful 2-y-o dual 5f winner Lady Sarka (by Lake Coniston), the quite useful 2-y-o 5f winner Shalford's Honour (by Shalford), the fair 2-y-o 6f all-weather winner Petite Spectre (by Spectrum) and the modest 7f winner One Giant Leap (by Pivotal). The dam, a fair 5f winner at 2 yrs, is a sister to the Sweet Solera Stakes second The Jotter and a half-sister to the Group 1 1m Gran Criterium second Line Dancer. The second dam, Note Book (by Mummy's Pet), a fairly useful 6f winner, is a sister to the Norfolk Stakes winner Colmore Row and a half-sister to the Horris Hill Stakes winner Long Row.
"It's a good family, the mare's getting old but

she's bred a lot of winners. This colt is solid and strong and he moves well. I'll start to do a bit more with him now and I'm thinking that by the end of May or early June he'll come out and do us some good. Fasliyev's like fast ground and he's starting to come to hand right now. He's done everything right and he's built to be fast".

1152. UNNAMED ★★★
b.c. Dr Fong – Saint Ann (Geiger Counter).
March 31. Seventh foal. 25,000Y. Tattersalls October 2. Tim Easterby. Half-brother to the fairly useful 2-y-o 1m winner and listed Predominate Stakes second Sienna Storm (by Peintre Celebre) and to the quite useful 1m all-weather winner Heversham (by Octagonal). The dam, placed fourth once at 2 yrs, is a half-sister to 4 winners. The second dam, Swan Princess (by So Blessed), won the Group 1 Phoenix Stakes and is a half-sister to 6 winners including Primo Dominie.

"He looks fantastic and is probably one of the most mature bodied horses you'd see as a two-year-old. He's got a bit of class and ability and despite it being a family that can get a distance he shows he's got speed. A Dr Fong won the Chesham Stakes at Royal Ascot last year and if this colt is good enough that's where I'll try and aim him".

1153. UNNAMED ★★★
b.f. Fantastic Light – Seven Of Nine (Alzao).
April 19. Fourth foal. Half-sister to the fair 2008 2-y-o 7f winner Lyra's Daemon (by Singspiel) and to a winner in Greece by Hernando. The dam is an unplaced sister to the 2-y-o dual 7f winner and Group 3 Scottish Classic third Rabi and a half-sister to 3 winners. The dam is an unplaced half-sister to the fairly useful 3-y-o 9.6f winner Sharadiya (by Akarad). (M J Caddy).

"Her half-sister won her second start for us last year and this filly is a bit stronger than she was at this time. I like her a lot, I won't rush her and I think she's nice".

1154. UNNAMED ★★
ch.c. Cadeaux Genereux – Umniya (by Bluebird).
March 3. First foal. The dam, a quite useful 2-y-o 6f winner, was fourth in the Group 1 Moyglare Stud Stakes and is a half-sister to several winners including the dual listed 6f winner (including at 2 yrs) Lady Links. The second dam, Sparky's Song (Electric), a moderate 10.2f and 12f winner, is a half-sister to the very smart Group 1 6.5f winner Bold Edge and to the listed winner and Group 3 5f Temple Stakes second Brave Edge.

"I haven't sold him yet but he's got a great pedigree. He has typical Cadeaux Genereux front legs (a bit off-set) and during his early training he through a splint so he's had a month back at the stud. He's due to come back in any time, I like him and although he cost 30 Grand as a foal the owner would be happy with half that because he can't keep all his horses. He'd be a cheap horse if anyone wants him because he's not over-big, he's 'butty' and strong".

JEREMY NOSEDA
1155. ADVERTISEMENT (USA) ★★★★
b.br.c. Mr Greeley – Banner (A P Indy).
February 8. Second foal. $300,000Y. Keeneland September. Not sold. The dam is an unraced sister to the winner and US Grade 2 placed A P Five Hundred and a half-sister to the US stakes winner Gold Streamer. The second dam, Banner Dancer (by Danzig), is a placed half-sister to the triple US Grade 1 winner Sacahuista.

"Bought at the Calder Breeze Up Sales in Florida, he spent a short time at Vinery Stud in Florida and I'm pleased to say he's with me now. He's a July type two-year-old, he's a good goer and I like the way he goes about things. He should be a six/seven furlong two-year-old".

1156. AWESOME ACT (USA) ★★★★
ch.c. Awesome Again – Houdini's Honey (Mr Prospector).
April 17. Fourth foal. $240,000Y. Keeneland September. Jane Allison. The dam, a quite useful 10f winner, was later successful in the USA and is a sister to Machiavellian and to the high-class French 2-y-o Coup de Genie. The second dam, Coup de Folie (by Halo), won four races from 6f to 10f including the Group 3 1m Prix

d'Aumale and was stakes-placed in the USA.
"After the Calder Sales he was in pre-training in Florida before arriving in Newmarket. He's a nice, straightforward colt and he's done everything right. He looks like making a two-year-old from mid-July onwards and he has a little resemblance to a very good two-year-old I had called Wilko. I don't know if it's right or wrong to try and relive the dream!"

1157. BIT OF BLING ★★★
b.f. Dansili – Bling Bling (Indian Ridge).
March 9. First foal. The dam is an unplaced sister to the very smart dual listed 5f winner Watching and a half-sister to numerous winners. The second dam, Sweeping (by Indian King), was a useful 2-y-o 6f winner, was placed over 8.5f at 3 yrs and is a half-sister to 9 winners.
"She'll take bit of time and is one for the last three months of the season. I haven't done much with her, but she moves well. I like my two-year-olds but they have to be the most backward group I've ever had and most of them have been bought very much with their three-year-old careers in mind".

1158. BRANNAGH (USA) ★★★★
ch.c. Hennessy – Green Room (Theatrical).
April 19. Second foal. 105,000Y. Tattersalls October 1. J Noseda. Half-brother to the very smart 2008 Group 2 7f Mill Reef Stakes winner and Group 1 7f Dewhurst Stakes second Lord Shanakill (by Speightstown). The dam is an unraced half-sister to 5 winners including the Group 1 Yellow Ribbon Handicap winner Spanish Fern. The second dam, Chain Fern (by Blushing Groom), is an unraced sister to the Irish 1,000 Guineas and Coronation Stakes winner Al Bahathri (dam of the 2,000 Guineas and Champion Stakes winner Haafhd).
"A good moving horse and very athletic, he's grown a bit recently but I see him as a summer 2-y-o and he'll win his races at two".

1159. CALL TO REASON (IRE) ★★★
ch.f. Pivotal – Venturi (Danehill Dancer).
March 22. Second foal. 65,000Y. Tattersalls October 1. Not sold. The dam, winner of the Group 3 7f C L Weld Park Stakes, was subsequently second in two US Grade 3 events and is a half-sister to one winner. The second dam, Zagreb Flyer (by Old Vic), is an unraced half-sister to 8 winners including the listed winner and Group 1 Italian Oaks second Flying Girl.
"A big, scopey filly, she's done well and I feel she's a July type two-year-old. She's done everything right and I'd hope to see her racing from the middle of July onwards. I think she'll do a job at two and be a six/seven furlong two-year-old".

1160. CALM STORM ★★★
b.c. Whipper – Dark Hyacinth (Darshaan).
February 9. €170,000Y. Deauville August. Charlie Gordon-Watson. Half-brother to the Italian winner and listed-placed Dark Indian (by Indian Ridge) and to the moderate 2-y-o 6f winner Korolieva (by Xaar) and the moderate 7f and 11f winner Melledgan (by Catrail). The dam, placed at up to 1m 5f in Ireland at 3 yrs, is a half-sister to 6 minor winners. The second dam, Priddy Blue (by Blue Cashmere), is an unplaced half-sister to the dams of Tony Bin (Prix de l'Arc de Triomphe), Dibidale (Irish Oaks and Yorkshire Oaks) and Cracaval (Chester Vase).
"He goes alright, he's a good mover and is one for the mid-summer. I haven't done an awful lot with him at present but he's a good-moving, good balanced horse and I think he'll win as a two-year-old".

1161. CANDOTOO (IRE) ★★★
b.f. Cape Cross - Leopard Hunt (Diesis).
March 19. Second foal. 25,000Y. Tattersalls October 1. Not sold. Half-sister to the unplaced 2008 2-y-o 6f Safari Song (by War Chant). The dam, a fairly useful 2-y-o 7f winner, was listed-placed and is a sister to the very useful 7f listed winner and 1,000 Guineas fourth Capistrano Day and a half-sister to 4 winners including the useful 2-y-o 6f winner and listed-placed Bring Plenty. The second dam, Alcando (by Alzao), a smart winner of the listed 6f Firth of Clyde Stakes at 2 yrs and the 10f Group 3 Prix de Psyche at 3 yrs, subsequently won the Grade 1

Beverly Hills Handicap and is a half-sister to 5 winners.

"A good-moving filly, I see her as being a seven furlong two-year-old from late July onwards. She has a good attitude and she'll do a job at two but I haven't done enough with her to say any more than that at present".

1162. CARNACKI (USA) ★★★
b.c. Ghostzapper – Guana (Sillery).
February 18. The dam won over 1m in France, was listed-placed and is a half-sister to the French 1m (at 2 yrs) and listed 7f winner Great News.

"A good moving horse and he's one that I like. He's a two-year-old for July time and is an interesting horse to have around".

1163. CHEYNE WALK (USA) ★★★
b.f. Royal Academy – Lady Liberty (Noble Bijou).
February 2. $170,000foal. Keeneland November. Thoroughbred Advisory. Brother to the very useful 2-y-o 1m Curragh Futurity Stakes winner Equal Rights and half-brother to 4 winners including the listed 15f and hurdles winner Adopted Hero, the quite useful 12f winner Majority Rule (both by Sadler's Wells) and the Australian Grade 2 winner Freedom Fields (by Bluebird). The dam won the Grade 1 12f Australian Oaks and is a half-sister to 4 winners including the New Zealand Grade 3 winner Marquess. The second dam, Yvette (by Sovereign Edition), won once in New Zealand.

"She's a nice filly, she'll take time and is physically developing at the moment. She should be one for the last third of the season over seven furlongs and a mile".

1164. DANCE EAST ★★★★
b.f. Shamardal – Russian Dance (Nureyev).
January 30. Second foal. Half-sister to the modest 2008 5f placed 2-y-o Cecilia's Lass (by Dr Fong). The dam, a fairly useful 2-y-o 6f winner, is a half-sister to 7 winners including the Group 1 Racing Post Trophy winner Saratoga Springs. The second dam, Population (by General Assembly), is a placed half-sister to the Group/Grade 1 winners Play It Safe and Providential.

"A good type and an athletic filly, she does everything the right way. I would hope she'd make a two-year-old in mid-summer and she has the scope to train on. She should definitely go and do something this year".

1165. DESERT LIAISON ★★★
b.f. Dansili – Toffee Nosed (Selkirk).
February 20. Fifth foal. Deauville August. €160,000Y. Charlie Gordon-Watson. Half-sister to a minor French 2-y-o winner by Desert Prince. The dam, a listed winner and third in the Group 3 Nell Gwyn Stakes, is a half-sister to 5 winners. The second dam, Ever Welcome (by Be My Guest), a minor winner, is a half-sister to the Group 3 Matron Stakes winner Chanzi.

"She's a good mover and she's quite forward. Initially I'd thought she'd be one for later on but she's done well and could actually be ready for the end of June or early July. Probably a seven furlong type, she's a good-moving filly that does everything right".

1166. EMPEROR'S STRIDE ★★★
b.c. Kyllachy – Red Flame (Selkirk).
January 26. Third foal. 52,000Y. Tattersalls October 2. Charlie Gordon-Watson. The dam, placed fourth twice at 3 yrs, is a half-sister to the useful dual listed 6f winner of 5 races Falcon Hill. The second dam, Branston Jewel (by Prince Sabo), a fairly useful 2-y-o dual 5f winner, was second in the Group 3 5.5f Prix d'Arenburg and is a half-sister to 11 winners including the Group Sandown Mile winner Desert Deer and the very useful and tough mare Branston Abby.

"Quite a heavy horse, he'll take a bit of time as he's quite loaded through his shoulders and we'll have to be patient with him. Definitely one for the second half of the season".

1167. FRIVOLITY ★★★
ch.f. Pivotal – Gay Gallanta (Woodman).
May 15. Eighth foal. Half-sister to the smart 2-y-o Group 2 6f Mill Reef Stakes winner Byron, to the fairly useful 7f and 1m winner Gallantry, the quite useful 6f winner Light Hearted (all by

Green Desert), the useful 1m and 10.3f winner Gallant Hero, the fairly useful 9f winner Gallant (both by Rainbow Quest), the useful 10.4f listed-placed maiden Gay Heroine (by Caerleon) and the quite useful 2-y-o 6f winner Gallivant (by Danehill). The dam, a very smart winner of the Group 1 6f Cheveley Park Stakes and the Group 3 5f Queen Mary Stakes, was second in the 1m Falmouth Stakes and is a half-sister to the smart Group 2 10f Gallinule Stakes winner Sportsworld. The second dam, Gallanta (by Nureyev), a useful winner of 3 races from 5.5f to 1m including the Prix de Coburg, was second in the Group 1 Prix Morny and is a half-sister to the top-class French middle-distance colt Gay Mecene and to the dam of Wolfhound. (Cheveley Park Stud).

"I can't quite make my mind up about this filly because although she's a late foal she looks an early type and is quite 'together'. She's cantering away now and I'll know a lot more in about a month's time".

1168. HIGH IMPORTANCE (USA) ★★★
b.c. Arch – Music Lane (Miswaki).
March 6. Tenth foal. $260,000Y. Keeneland September. Charlie Gordon-Watson. Brother to 2 minor winners in Japan and Canada, closely related to the minor US stakes-placed winner Music Way (by Kris S) and half-brother to a stakes-placed winner in Japan by Silver Hawk. The dam, a minor US 4-y-o winner, is a half-sister to 11 winners including the multiple US Grade 1 winner Hawkster.

"A good-looking horse with plenty of scope. He moves well but he's very much one for seven furlongs and a mile in the autumn".

1169. ILLUSTRIOUS PRINCE (IRE) ★★★
b.c. Acclamation – Sacred Love (Barathea).
March 26. Third foal. 72,000Y. Tattersalls October 2. Charlie Gordon-Watson. Brother to the unraced 2008 2-y-o Mastoora. The dam, placed fourth once over 1m, is a half-sister to 5 winners. The second dam, Abstraction (by Rainbow Quest), is an unraced sister to 2 listed winners and a half-sister to 7 winners including the US triple Grade 1 winner Wandesta.

"He's going to take a bit of time as he's not wintered as well as I'd have liked. He's a good-moving horse but I'm only just upping the tempo with him. He should be in action in mid-summer".

1170. JUNKET ★★
b.f. Medicean – Gallivant (Danehill).
January 22. Third foal. Half-sister to Pumpkin (by Pivotal), unplaced in one start at 2 yrs in 2008. The dam, a quite useful 2-y-o 6f winner, is a closely related to the smart 2-y-o Group 2 6f Mill Reef Stakes winner Byron and a half-sister to 3 winners including the useful 1m and 10.3f winner Gallant Hero. The second dam, Gay Gallanta (by Woodman), a very smart winner of the Group 1 6f Cheveley Park Stakes and the Group 3 5f Queen Mary Stakes, was second in the 1m Falmouth Stakes and is a half-sister to 10 winners including the Group 2 10f Gallinule Stakes winner Sportsworld. (Cheveley Park Stud).

"She's only just some in so I don't know enough about her to pass judgement yet".

1171. KEY ART (IRE) ★★★★
b.c. Kheleyf – Gift Of Spring (Gilded Time).
March 20. Second foal. €100,000Y. Goffs Million. A Stroud. Half-brother to the quite useful 2-y-o 5f winner Vegas Baby (by Kheleyf). The dam, placed at 3 yrs in France, is a half-sister to 6 winners including the listed-placed and smart broodmare Witch Of Fife. The second dam, Fife (by Lomond), a winner at 3 yrs and third in the listed Lupe Stakes, is a half-sister to 5 winners including the dam of the Prix Vermeille winner Pearly Shells.

"He's just started working and he's a nice, sprinting two-year-old type with a good attitude. I think he goes pretty well and he'll definitely be winning. I'd be looking to get him on the racecourse in May".

1172. MEXICAN ROSE ★★
b.f. Galileo – Mexican Hawk (Silver Hawk).
May 7. Fourth foal. 120,000Y. Tattersalls October 1. Not sold. Half-sister to Eyes Like A Hawk (by Diktat), unplaced in one start at 2 yrs

in 2008 and to the quite useful 9f and 12f winner Elegant Hawk (by Generous). The dam, a fairly useful 1.2f winner, is a half-sister to 7 winners. The second dam, Viva Zapata (by Affirmed), won the Group 2 Prix du Gros Chene and is a half-sister to 7 winners.
"A good-moving filly and a good type but she's a May foal and scopey. Definitely one for the autumn".

1173. NEBULA STORM (IRE) ★★★★★
b.c. Galileo – Epping
(Charnwood Forest).
January 22. Fourth foal. 460,000Y. Tattersalls October 1. Sir Robert Ogden. Brother to the smart 10f winner and Group 1 St Leger second The Last Drop. The dam, a quite useful 3-y-o 7f winner, is a half-sister to 4 winners including the French listed winner and multiple Group-placed Self Defense. The second dam, Dansara (by Dancing Brave), is an unraced half-sister to 10 winners including the Irish Oaks winner Princess Pati and the Great Voltigeur Stakes winner Seymour Hicks.
"A lovely moving colt, he should develop into a two-year-old from July onwards and he's already shown me speed. I do like him and he has the potential to be a quality horse. A lovely individual, he'll do a job this year and he could be one of the nicest I have".

1174. PARADISE DREAM ★★★★ ♠
b.c. Kyllachy – Wunders Dream (Averti).
March 14. Second foal. 110,000Y. Tattersalls October 1. Charlie Gordon-Watson. The dam, winner of 4 races at 2 yrs including the Group 2 5f Flying Childers Stakes and the Group 3 5f Molecomb Stakes, is a half-sister to 3 winners including the Irish Group 3 winner Grecian Dancer. The second dam, Pizzicato (by Statoblest), a modest 5f and 5.3f winner at 3 yrs, is a half-sister to 5 winners including the high-class Hong Kong horses Mensa and Firebolt.
"He's just coming into fast work now and he looks a speedy type. He has a great attitude and he's a lovely, laid-back colt that has the make and shape of a two-year-old sprinting type. I like the way he goes about things".

1175. PARK TWILIGHT (IRE) ★★★★
b.f. Bertolini – Sunset Café (Red Sunset).
April 24. Eleventh foal. Half-sister to the fair 2008 Irish 2-y-o 7f winner Oasis Sunset (by Oasis Dream), to the 2-y-o Group 1 6f Cheveley Park Stakes winner Seazun (by Zieten), the dual 1m winner and listed-placed Albertinelli, the useful Group 3 placed Albert Einstein (both by Danehill), the 2-y-o 7f winner and listed-placed Mahogany (by Orpen) and the fair all-weather 1m and 2m winner Pipe Music (by Mujadil). The dam, a minor Irish 12f winner, is a sister to the Group 3 Prix Foy winner Beeshi and a half-sister to 8 winners including the John Smiths Magnet Cup winner Chaumiere and the dam of the high-class 10f colt Insatiable. The second dam, Cafe Au Lait (by Espresso), was a fairly useful winner of 3 races and stayed middle-distances.
"She's one of four of my two-year-olds that have been in fast work. She goes well, looks a two-year-old type, has a great attitude and a good action. She'll definitely be doing a job over six furlongs from May onwards. She's a filly that I like and she's nice, straightforward two-year-old that'll earn her corn".

1176. PERENNIAL ★★
b.c. Kingsalsa – Red Peony (Montjeu).
March 13. First foal. The dam, a useful 7f (at 2 yrs) and 12f winner and Group 3 7f Prestige Stakes third, is a half-sister to 3 winners. The second dam, Red Azalea (by Shirley Heights), a fairly useful 7f (at 2 yrs) and 10f winner, is a half-sister to 4 winners including the Group 3 Prestige Stakes winner and French 1,000 Guineas third Red Camellia (herself dam of the Fillies Mile winner Red Bloom). (Cheveley Park Stud).
"He won't run until the autumn, he's a great-moving horse with a lovely attitude but he'll take plenty of time".

1177. PICNIC PARTY ★★★
ch.f. Indian Ridge – Antediluvian (Air Express).
January 27. First foal. The dam, a very useful 7f (at 2 yrs) and 1m listed winner of 3 races, is a half-sister to the fairly useful dual 7f winner Ekhtiaar and the fairly useful 2-y-o 6f winner

Mine Host. The second dam, Divina Mia (by Dowsing), a modest 2-y-o 6f winner, stayed 11f and is a half-sister to the dam of the Australian Grade 1 winner Markham.

"A filly I hoped would to come to hand early, she is picking up now and I'm in the middle of deciding what to do with her. She has progressed a lot in the last month, she'll definitely make a two-year-old and she'll be a six furlong type".

1178. PLAY WITH CAUTION (USA) ★★★

b.br.c. Johannesburg – I'm A Caution
(A P Indy).
April 14. First foal. $140,000 2-y-o. Calder Breeze Up. John McCormack. The dam, a minor US 3-y-o winner, is a sister to the winner and Grade 3 placed A P Magic. The second dam, Magicalmysterycat (by Storm Cat), won the Grade 2 Landaluce Stakes and the Grade 2 Schuylerville Stakes and is a half-sister to the Grade 2 winner Burmilla.

"He came out of the Calder sale, he's just arrived here and he's more of a second half of the season two-year-old but he breezed well over there so we'll keep our fingers crossed".

1179. POINT NORTH (IRE) ★★★★

b.c. Danehill Dancer – Briolette
(Sadler's Wells).
February 21. First foal. 500,000Y. Tattersalls October 1. Sir R Ogden. The dam won the listed 10f Trigo Stakes, was second in the Group 3 12f Princess Royal Stakes and is a sister to the Irish listed winner Peach Out Of Reach and a half-sister to 6 winners including the Grade 1 12f Breeders Cup Turf, Grade 1 12f Japan Cup, Group 1 10f Grosser Preis von Baden and Group 1 10f Coral-Eclipse Stakes winner Pilsudski. The second dam, Cocotte (by Troy), a very useful 10.2f winner, was second in the Group 3 Prix de Psyche, fourth in the Group 2 10f Nassau Stakes and is a half-sister to the listed winner Gay Captain.

"I think he'll make a two-year-old by July time and he's a good type that moves well, Strong and scopey, he's a horse that I like. A spot-on seven furlong two-year-old from July onwards".

1180. PROGRESS (IRE) ★★★

br.f. Green Desert – Mille (Dubai Millennium).
February 4. First foal. €50,000Y. Goffs Million. Citywest Inc Ltd. The dam is an unraced half-sister to 7 winners including the US Grade 1 San Juan Capistrano Handicap winner Passinetti. The second dam, Cloeilia (by Lyphard), is a placed half-sister to 11 winners including the Group winners Keos, Proskona and Korveya (herself the dam of the Group 1 winners Hector Protector, Bosra Sham and Shanghai).

"A straightforward filly, I'm just beginning to pick up the tempo with her and she looks the type to make a two-year-old from the back-end of May/June onwards over six furlongs. A solid individual".

1181. QUEEN OF MEAN ★★

b.f. Pivotal – Tyranny (Machiavellian).
March 12. Third foal. Half-sister to the modest 7f placed 2-y-o Good For Her (by Rock Of Gibraltar). The dam, a fairly useful dual 7f winner, is a half-sister to the listed 1m and subsequent US Grade 2 winner Spotlight. The second dam, Dust Dancer (by Suave Dancer), won 4 races including the Group 3 10f Prix de la Nonette and is a half-sister to 6 winners including the Group 3 7.3f Fred Darling Stakes winner Bulaxie (herself dam of the Group 2 winner Claxon) and the dual French listed winner Zimzalabim. (Normandie Stud).

"She's just having a little break now. She's a good-moving filly but she'll take a little time".

1182. REGAL PARK (IRE) ★★★

b.c. Montjeu – Classic Park (Robellino).
January 13. Seventh foal. 180,000Y. Tattersalls October 1. D Metcalfe. Half-brother to the French 2-y-o 1m winner, Group 1 1m Criterium International third and Epsom Derby second Walk In The Park (by Montjeu), to the smart 1m winner Secret World (by Spinning World) and the quite useful Irish 6f and 7f winner Mufradat (by Desert Prince). The dam won 3 races including the Irish 1,000 Guineas and is a half-sister to 9 winners including the US Grade 2 winner Rumpipumpy. The second dam, Wanton (by Kris), a useful 2-y-o 5f winner and third in

the Group 2 Flying Childers Stakes, is a half-sister to 8 winners including the listed 5f St Hugh's Stakes winner and Group 2 5f Prix du Gros-Chene second Easy Option.

"A good type and a good-moving horse with the right attitude. He's just cantering at present and I haven't done a lot with him, but he has the make and shape of a horse to be a back-end two-year-old and to go on as a three-year-old".

1183. RICH AND RECKLESS ★★★
b.f. Starcraft - Krynica (Danzig).
January 18. First foal. The dam was a quite useful 2-y-o 6f winner. The second dam, Bionic (by Zafonic), a very useful 2-y-o 7f winner, is a half-sister to Day Flight, a winner of 6 races at up to 13.5f including three Group 3 12f events.
"She's a little bit more forward than my other Starcraft two-year-old and I'd hope that mid-summer onwards over seven furlongs would be her time. She's straightforward and I like the way she goes about her business".

1184. RITUAL (IRE) ★★★
b.c. Cape Cross – Silver Queen (Arazi).
May 5. Fifth foal. 115,000Y. Tattersalls October 1. John Warren. Half-brother to the Italian Group 3 6f winner Kuaicoss (by Lujain) and to a minor winner in Italy by Indian Danehill. The dam was placed over 10f and is a half-sister to 4 winners. The second dam, Love Of Silver (by Arctic Tern), won the 2-y-o Group 3 7f Prestige Stakes.
"A good type and a good-looking horse, physically he's developing all the time and I think he's a two-year-old for seven furlongs from August onwards. I quite like him but he just needs a bit of time".

1185. ROCKEMAR (USA) ★★★
b.f. Rock Hard Ten – Madame Cerito (Diesis).
The dam, an Irish 3-y-o 1m winner, was listed-placed at 2 yrs and is a half-sister to the 1m all-weather 2-y-o and subsequent German Group 1 10f winner Ransom O'War. The second dam, Sombreffe (Polish Precedent), a fair 7f all-weather winner, is closely related to the Group 2 Mill Reef Stakes winner Russian Bond and the Group 2 Temple Stakes winner Snaadee and a half-sister to the Group 3 Prix de Conde winner Cristofori.

"The stallion, a son of Kris S, was very good on the dirt and the dam's side of the pedigree is turf. This is a lovely scopey filly that should take a bit of time and is one for the back-end, but she's a good moving filly with scope and given time she'll do a job".

1186. SAHARIA (IRE) ★★★
b.c. Oratorio – Inchiri (Sadler's Wells).
May 1. Fifth foal. 37,000Y. Tattersalls October 1. Timeform Betfair Racing Club. Half-brother to Hawk's Eye (by Hawk Wing), placed fourth twice over 6f at 2 yrs in 2008, to the fairly useful dual 12f winner Inchwood (by Dubai Destination) and the quite useful 2-y-o dual 7f winner Celtic Step (by Selkirk). The dam, a very useful 12f listed winner, is a half-sister to 2 winners. The second dam, Inchyre (by Shirley Heights), a useful 1m winner, is a half-sister to 7 winners including the very smart and tough triple Group 3 7f winner and sire Inchinor.
"A nice two-year-old colt that should be running in mid-season".

1187. SEA CHANGE (IRE) ★★★
b.c. Danehill Dancer – Ibtikar (Private Account).
April 2. Thirteenth foal. 290,000Y. Tattersalls October 1. John Warren. Half-sister to the unraced 2008 2-y-o Pallas Athena (by Sadler's Wells) and to 6 winners including the US stakes-placed Vegas Venture (by Gold Fever) and the South African stakes-placed Brown Linnet (by King Of Kings). The dam, a poor 6f (at 2 yrs) and 2m placed maiden, is closely related to the Grade 1 Hollywood Gold Cup, Charles H. Strub Stakes and Californian Stakes winner Desert Wine and a half-sister to 6 winners including the dual Grade 1 winner Menifee and to the unraced dam of the dual Group 1 winner Fasliyev. The second dam, Anne Campbell (by Never Bend), won three races in the USA including a minor stakes event.
"He's a nice, scopey horse that has grown and changed a lot since the sale. I do like him and he's a good mover and has done everything

right. I view him as a horse for the seven furlong maidens from August onwards. He'll do a job as a two-year-old".

1188. SECRET SPELL ★★
ch.f. Pivotal – It's A Secret (Polish Precedent).
March 26. Fifth foal. Sister to the unraced 2008 2-y-o Secret Witness. The dam, a fairly useful 1m and 9f winner, is a half-sister to 7 winners including the useful 2-y-o 6f winner and Group 3 10.4f Musidora Stakes third Obsessive. The second dam, Secret Obsession (by Secretariat), a fairly useful 10f winner, is a half-sister to 6 winners including the Group 2 12f King Edward VII Stakes winner Beyton. (Cheveley Park Stud).
"A backward filly, she's coming along and she moves well but I don't know enough about her yet and she's going to take a little time".

1189. SPACECRAFT (IRE) ★★★
b.c. Starcraft – Brazilian Samba (Sadler's Wells).
January 18. First foal. 200,000Y. Tattersalls October 1. Badgers Bloodstock. The dam is an unraced half-sister to 3 winners including the 2-y-o Group 3 6f Swordlestown Stud Sprint Stakes winner Brazilian Bride and the 2-y-o 7.5f winner and Group 3 7f second Brazilian Star. The second dam, Braziliz (by Kingmambo), placed fourth once over 5f at 2 yrs, is a half-sister to 8 winners including Or Vision (dam of the Irish 2,000 Guineas winner Saffron Walden, the Grade 1 E P Taylor Stakes winner Insight and the Group 1 7f Prix de la Foret winner Dolphin Street).
"A good, solid type and more of a September two-year-old over seven furlongs. He looks like a horse that will come in the autumn but do his job then".

1190. SQUALL ★★★
b.c. Dubawi – Exciting Times (Jeune Homme).
May 23. Fifth foal. 400,000Y. Tattersalls October 1. M H Goodbody. Half-brother to the US Grade 1 Beverly D Stakes, Group 2 Prix de Sandringham and dual US Grade 2 winner Gorella (by Grape Tree Road), to the US stakes and French listed winner Porto Santo (by Kingsalsa) and the French listed-placed winner Thanks Again (by Anabaa Blue). The dam is a placed half-sister to 7 winners. The second dam, Eloura (by Top Ville), won twice in France and is a half-sister to 4 other minor winners.
"A nice, athletic horse that moves well. I like him and although he's a late foal I'd still hope to see him coming to hand over six and seven furlongs from the end of July onwards. He's done everything right and despite his late foaling date if you looked at him you'd think he'd be up and running at two".

1191. STATE CAPITAL ★★
b.f. Pivotal – Dublino (Lear Fan).
March 31. The dam, a French 2-y-o 1m winner, subsequently won the Grade 1 Del Mar Oaks, was Grade 1 placed several times and is a half-sister to several winners. The second dam, Tuscoga (by Theatrical), was unplaced in 2 starts and is a sister to the Grade 1 Matriarch Stakes winner Duda and a half-sister to 5 winners.
"A solid filly, she moves well but she'll be a back-end two-year-old".

1192. THEOLOGY ★★
b.c. Galileo – Biographie (Mtoto).
April 24. Second foal. 70,000Y. Tattersalls October 1. John Warren. The dam, a dual winner in Italy at 3 and 4 yrs, was listed-placed and is a half-sister to 4 winners including the dual French Group 3 winner Di Moi Oui. The second dam, Biosphere (by Pharly), won 3 races in Italy and was listed-placed and is a half-sister to 4 winners.
"A good mover and a good type, he's a horse that I like and he moves well but he won't be on the track until the autumn".

1193. WARLING (IRE) ★★★★
br.f. Montjeu – Walkamia (Linamix).
February 7. Second foal. Half-sister to the fairly useful 2008 2-y-o 6f and 7f winner War Native (by Cape Cross). The dam won the Group 3 10.5f Prix Fille de l'Air and is a sister to the Group 2 11f Prix Noailles winner Walk On Mix. The second dam, Walk On Air (by Cure The Blues), is a placed half-sister to 7 winners including the Group 1 Prix Vermeille winner Walensee.

"A really good-looking filly and a great mover, she's going to take time. She's got plenty of quality but is very much one for the back-end of the year".

1194. UNNAMED ★★★★
b.c. Invincible Spirit – Bridelina (Linamix).
March 24. Seventh foal. 70,000Y. Tattersalls October 2. Charlie Gordon-Watson. Half-brother to the 2008 2-y-o 6f winner Brierty (by Statue Of Liberty), to the Irish 2-y-o 6.5f winner De Roberto (by Barathea), the 5.6f winner Lunces Lad (by Xaar), the 1m winner Blue Spartan (by Spartacus) – all quite useful - and the Swiss 2-y-o winner White Tiger (by Tiger Hill). The dam won over 1m and 10f at Longchamp at 3 yrs and is a half-sister to 3 winners including the US stakes winner and Grade 3 placed Society Dream. The second dam, Society Bride (by Blushing Groom), is a placed half-sister to 5 winners.
"A straightforward, rather aggressive horse. I think he'll do a job at two and he reminds me in a way of a nice horse I had last year, Kingship Spirit. He'll be a six/seven furlong horse".

1195. UNNAMED ★★★
b.c. Oratorio – Chalice Wells (Sadler's Wells).
March 3. Third foal. 110,000Y. Tattersalls October 1. Demi O'Byrne. The dam is an unraced sister to the Group 1 Coronation Cup and triple Group 1 Ascot Gold Cup winner Yeats and a half-sister to the Group 2 Royal Whip Stakes winner Solskjaer and the Japanese stakes winner and Grade 1 fourth Tsukuba Symphony. The second dam, Lyndonville (by Top Ville), a minor Irish 3-y-o 14f winner, is a half-sister to 4 winners including the Group 1 Fillies Mile winner Ivanka.
"A good type, he goes well and I'd like to think he'd make a two-year-old by July. He's does everything right and he's quite a nice horse. I like him".

1196. UNNAMED ★★
b.c. Galileo – Cradle Of Love (Roberto).
May 31. Tenth foal. €70,000Y. Goffs Million. Demi O'Byrne. Half-brother to the fairly useful 1m to 12f winner of 11 races Captain's Log, to the fair dual 1m winner School Days (both by Slip Anchor), the quite useful 6f winner of 6 races Ivory Dawn (by Batshoof), the Italian winner of 9 races Stracch (by Polish Precedent) and a minor winner in Italy by Salse. The dam, a quite useful 3-y-o 9f winner, is a sister to the Nassau Stakes winner Mamaluna and the US stakes winners Saucy Bobbie and Point Cedar and a half-sister to 11 winners. The second dam, Kadesh (by Lucky Mel), won a 5f stakes event in the USA at 2 yrs and was second in the Grade 2 Hollywood Lassie Stakes.
"A lovely, quality horse and great mover. He's well-balanced but as a late foal he's going to take time and is one for the back-end of the year".

1197. UNNAMED ★★
b.c. Galileo – Dalawara (Top Ville).
May 22. Half-brother to the smart 1m (at 2 yrs) to 14f winner and Ascot Gold Cup fourth Heron Island (by Shirley Heights). The dam is an unplaced sister to the Prix Vermeille winner Darara and a half-sister to the French Derby winner and high-class sire Darshaan and the Prix de Royallieu winner Dalara. The second dam, Delsy (by Abdos), won over 12f and was third in the Prix de Pomone. (Mr M Tabor).
"A lovely, good-moving, well-balanced horse, he's cantering along but although he's a quality horse and he's one I like, he is a late foal. So he's going to be a back-end of the season type two-year-old".

1198. UNNAMED ★★★★
ch.f. Danehill Dancer – En Garde (Irish River).
February 14. Seventh foal. 210,000Y. Tattersalls October 1. Blandford Bloodstock. Half-sister to the fairly useful 7f (at 2 yrs) and 1m winner Rifleman (by Starborough), to the quite useful 10f winner Fabia and the minor French 3-y-o winner Marie de Bansha (both by Sadler's Wells). The dam, a quite useful 2-y-o 5.7f winner, is a half-sister to 7 winners including the top-class Group 1 1m Queen Elizabeth II Stakes and Group 1 9.3f Prix d'Ispahan winner Observatory and the Group 2 Prix de Malleret winner High

Praise. The second dam, Stellaria (by Roberto), won from 5f to 8.5f including the listed 6f Rose Bowl Stakes and is a half-sister to 8 winners.
"A lovely, big scopey colt, he does everything right and I would think he'll be a horse for July onwards. He'll definitely do a job at two and he's a big, imposing individual that I like".

1199. UNNAMED ★★★★
ch.c. Indian Ridge – Miss Assertive (Zafonic).
April 17. Second foal. €80,000Y. Goffs Million. Jane Allison. Half-brother to the useful 6f (at 2 yrs) and listed 7f winner Meydan Princess (by Choisir). The dam, a quite useful 2-y-o 6f winner, was listed-placed twice and is a half-sister to the useful all-weather 1m (including at 2 yrs) to 10f winner and subsequent US Grade 3 winner Ascertain. The second dam, Self Assured (by Ahonoora), a fairly useful 7f winner at 2 yrs, was second in the Group 3 1m May Hill Stakes and is a half-sister to 6 winners.
"Another one of the two-year-olds that's just gone into fast work. He's very much a five/six furlong two-year-old type, he's straightforward and 'together' and he'll probably be out by the end of April. He'll win his races".

1200. UNNAMED ★★★
b.f. Galileo – Sharakawa (Darshaan).
April 26. €240,000foal. Goffs. M V Magnier. Sister to the quite useful 11f and 12f winner Watchful and half-sister to the 2-y-o dual 7f winner and Group 3 Scottish Classic third Rabi (by Alzao), to the 1m (at 2 yrs) and hurdles winner Ebinzayd (by Rahy), the Group 3 Coventry Stakes third and hurdles winner Kawagino (by Perugino), the quite useful 1m winner Tanto Faz (by Rock Of Gibraltar) and the minor 4-y-o Irish 7f winner Appleblossom Girl (by Peintre Celebre). The dam is an unraced half-sister to 4 winners including the Group 3 placed Mempari. The second dam, Sharaya (by Youth), won the Group 1 Prix Vermeille and is a half-sister to the Group 2 Grand Prix d'Evry winner Sharaniya.
"A good type with plenty of scope, she moves well and is a filly for the autumn. I haven't done a lot with her because she's a scopey filly and very much a three-year-old in the making".

1201. UNNAMED ★★★
ch.c. Forest Wildcat – Spinner (Conquistador Cielo).
March 23. Eighth foal. $240,000 2-y-o. Calder Breeze Up. John McCormack. Half-brother to 5 winners including the US stakes winners Brittsker (by Bounding Basque) and Ferragamo (by Vindication). The dam is an unraced half-sister to 8 winners including the US triple Grade 1 winner Left Bank. The second dam, Marchesseaux (by Dr Blum), was a stakes-placed winner of 13 races.
"A good type that breezed well at the Sales. He arrived in Newmarket in early April and looks like a horse I'd hope to have on the track by the end of May".

1202. UNNAMED ★★★
b.c. Danehill Dancer – Streetcar (In The Wings).
April 29. Seventh foal. €380,000Y. Goffs Million. Jane Allison. Closely related to the US Grade 1 winner and Irish 1,000 Guineas third Luas Line (by Danehill) and the fair Irish 9.5f winner Street Style (by Rock Of Gibraltar). The dam was placed fourth once over 8.5f at 2 yrs and is a half-sister to 9 winners including the Group 3 May Hill Stakes winner Intimate Guest and the dam of the US Grade 1 winner Prince Arch. The second dam, As You Desire Me (by Kalamoun), won 2 listed events in France over 7.5f and 1m and is a half-sister to 7 winners including the Group 2 King Edward VII Stakes winner Classic Example.
"A good-looking type that moves well, he has a very laid-back attitude and he's done well over the last few weeks. I do like him and he's one for the end of July or August".

1203. UNNAMED ★★★
b.c. Trans Island – Where's Charlotte (Sure Blade).
March 10. Sixth foal. 55,000Y. Tattersalls October 2. Jane Allison. Brother to the 5f winner of 5 races (including at 2 yrs) and dual Group 3 placed Bond City and half-brother to the quite useful 7f (at 2 yrs) to 12f winner of 5 races Quince (by Fruits Of Love), the modest 5f

winner Admiral Bond (by Titus Livius) and the moderate 8.6f winner Eight Ellington (by Ali-Royal). The dam, a modest sprint maiden, is a half-sister to the listed winner Pea Green. The second dam, One Degree (by Crooner), won at 2 and 4 yrs and is a full or half-sister to 3 winners. *"A good mover and a straightforward type for the middle of the summer onwards".*

1204. UNNAMED ★★★
gr.f. Mr Greeley – Winning Colors (Caro).
March 3. Half-sister to the Japanese Group 3 placed Golden Colors (by Mr Prospector). The dam, a champion 3-y-o filly in the USA, won the Kentucky Derby, the Santa Anita Derby and the Santa Anita Oaks and is a half-sister to the 10f winner and multiple Group placed Shareek. The second dam, All Rainbows (by Bold Hour), won three 8.5f stakes races in the USA and is a half-sister to the champion filly Chris Evert (herself grandam of the champion colt Chief's Crown) and to the dams of Beyton (King Edward VII Stakes winner), Missed the Storm (US Grade 1 winner) and Two Timing (Group 2 10f Prince of Wales's Stakes winner).
"A nice filly, the mare was pretty old when she was conceived but she bares no resemblance to an old mare's foal. She's a good type, she's done everything well and I like her but she's very much one for the last third of the season".

AIDAN O'BRIEN
1205. AIR CHIEF MARSHAL (IRE) ★★★★
b.c. Danehill Dancer – Hawala (Warning).
March 25. Sixth foal. €320,000Y. Goffs Million. Demi O'Byrne. Brother to the listed 6f (at 2 yrs) and listed 7f winner and Group 3 placed Misu Bond and half-brother to the quite useful 2008 6f placed 2-y-o Winged Harriet (by Hawk Wing), to the dual sprint listed winner and Group 3 placed Slip Dance (by Celtic Swing), the fairly useful 2-y-o 7f and 1m winner Numen (by Fath) and the minor French 3-y-o winner Hawazi (by Ashkalani). The dam, a useful 8.3f winner, is a half-sister to the French Group 3 winner Afaf. The second dam, the minor French 3-y-o winner Halawa (by Dancing Brave), is a half-sister to 7 winners.

1206. ALFRED NOBEL ★★★★
b.c. Danehill Dancer – Glinting Desert (Desert Prince).
January 23. First foal. 220,000Y. Tattersalls October 1. J Magnier. The dam, a fair 2-y-o 7f winner, is a half-sister to 2 winners. The second dam, Dazzling Park (by Warning), a very smart winner of the Group 3 1m Matron Stakes and a listed 9f event, was placed in the Group 1 Irish Champion Stakes and the Irish 1,000 Guineas. She is a half-sister to 7 winners including the Derby, Champion Stakes, Dewhurst Stakes and National Stakes winner New Approach.

1207. BEETHOVEN (IRE) ★★★★
b.c. Oratorio – Queen Titi (Sadler's Wells).
April 2. First foal. €260,000Y. Goffs Million. Hugo Merry. The dam won 2 races in Ireland at 3 yrs including the listed 1m Garnet Stakes and is a sister to the Irish Group 3 winner Psalm and a half-sister to the very useful 1m winner and subsequent US stakes-placed winner The Editor. The second dam, Litani River (by Irish River), was listed placed and is a sister to the listed winner and top-class broodmare Or Vision (dam of the Group 1 winners Dolphin Street, Insight and Saffron Walden) and a half-sister to 7 winners including the dam of the Group 1 winners Sequoyah and Listen. (Mrs Sue Magnier).

1208. CABARET (IRE) ★★★
b.f. Galileo – Witch Of Fife (Lear Fan).
May 4. Seventh living foal. €300,000Y. Goffs Million. J Magnier. Half-sister to the Group 3 Solario Stakes winner Drumfire (by Danehill Dancer), to the useful 2-y-o 6f winner, Group 2 6f Gimcrack Stakes second and subsequent Hong Kong stakes winner Ho Choi (by Pivotal) and the moderate 1m winner Witchcraft (by Zilzal). The dam, a fairly useful 2-y-o 6f and 7f winner and third in the listed 7f Sweet Solera Stakes, is a half-sister to 5 winners out of the fairly useful 1m winner Fife (by Lomond), herself a half-sister to 5 winners including the dam of the US Grade 1 winner Frenchpark and the Prix Vermeille winner Pearly Shells.

1209. DON CARLOS (GER) ★★★
b.c. Galileo – Dapprima
(Shareef Dancer).
March 17. Ninth foal. 300,000Y. Tattersalls October 1. Demi O'Byrne. Closely related to the German Group 3 winner Davidoff (by Montjeu) and half-brother to the German Group 2 winner Denaro, to the German listed winner Duellant (both by Dashing Blade) and 3 minor winners abroad by Danehill, Fasliyev and Platini. The dam, a listed winner in Germany and second in the Group 2 German 1,000 Guineas, is a half-sister to 8 winners. The second dam, Diaspora (by Sparkler), won twice and was second in the German 1,000 Guineas and is a half-sister to 7 winners.

1210. DREAMALITTLEDREAM (IRE) ★★★★
b.f. Danehill Dancer – Belsay (Belmez).
April 20. Ninth foal. €340,000Y. Goffs Million. Demi O'Byrne. Closely related to the fair 2008 6f and 1m placed 2-y-o Furious Belle and to the fairly useful Irish 1m (at 2 yrs) and 7.5f winner Pyrenees and half-sister to the 6f, 7f (at 2 yrs) and Group 3 Craven Stakes winner and Group 2 second Killybegs (by Orpen), the fair 6f (at 2 yrs) and 1m winner Tsaroxy, the minor German 3-y-o winner Beaumont (both by Xaar) and the Irish 2-y-o 6f winner Lady's Mantle (by Sri Pekan). The dam ran unplaced twice and is a half-sister to 4 winners including the Group 3 7f Nell Gwyn Stakes winner and 1,000 Guineas third Crystal Gazing. The second dam, Crystal Bright (by Bold Lad, Ire), won once in the USA and is a half-sister to 4 minor winners.

1211. DYNASTY ★★★★
b.c. Danehill Dancer – Dash To The Top
(Montjeu).
March 30. First foal. 300,000Y. Tattersalls October 1. Demi O'Byrne. The dam, a very useful 2-y-o 1m winner and Group 1 Fillies' Mile third, is a half-sister to the listed 10.8f winner Dash To The Front. The second dam, Millennium Dash (by Nashwan), a fairly useful 10.2f winner, is a half-sister to 4 winners and to the unplaced dam of the Sun Chariot Stakes winner Kissogram.

1212. FAMOUS (IRE) ★★★★
ch.f. Danehill Dancer – Starlight Dreams
(Black Tie Affair).
February 13. Seventh foal. €1,000,000Y. Goffs Million. Demi O'Byrne. Sister to the 2008 2-y-o Group 1 Phoenix Stakes winner Mastercraftsman, closely related to the US Grade 3 winner Locust Grove (by Rock Of Gibraltar) and half-sister to the 2-y-o 6f seller winner Nordhock (by Luhuk). The dam, a 2-y-o winner in the USA, is a half-sister to 5 winners including the listed Zetland Stakes winner Matahif. The second dam, Reves Celeste (by Lyphard), a quite useful 1m winner, is a three-parts sister to the Ribblesdale Stakes winner Thawakib (dam of the 'Arc' winner Sakhee) and a half-sister to the high-class Celestial Storm.

1213. LILLIE LANGRY (IRE) ★★★
b.br.f. Danehill Dancer – Hoity Toity (Darshaan).
February 27. Third foal. 230,000Y. Tattersalls October 1. McKeever St Lawrence. The dam is an unraced half-sister to 4 winners. The second dam, Hiwaayati (by Shadeed), is an unraced half-sister to Great Commotion (winner of the Group 3 6f Cork and Orrery Stakes and the Group 3 7f Beeswing Stakes and second in both the July Cup and the Irish 2,000 Guineas) and to Lead on Time (winner of the Group 2 7f Criterium de Maisons-Laffitte and the Group 2 6.5f Prix Maurice de Gheest).

1214. MARK TWAIN (IRE) ★★★
b.c. Rock Of Gibraltar – Lady Windermere
(Lake Coniston).
April 24. Sixth foal. 150,000Y. Tattersalls October 1. J Magnier. Half-brother to the unraced 2008 2-y-o Russian Jar (by Xaar) and to the useful Irish listed 6f winner and Group 3 placed Absolutelyfabulous (by Mozart). The dam is an unraced half-sister to 4 winners including the Group 1 Fillies' Mile winner Listen and the Group 1 7f Moyglare Stud Stakes winner and high-class broodmare Sequoyah. The second dam, Brigid (by Irish River), a minor French 3-y-o 1m winner, is a sister to the listed 7f Prix de l'Obelisque winner Or Vision (herself dam of the Group/Grade 1 winners Dolphin

Street, Insight and Saffron Walden) and a half-sister to 6 winners.

1215. MINOAN (FR) ★★★
b.c. Danehill Dancer – Mirina (Pursuit Of Love).
May 7. Fifth live foal. Deauville August. €200,000Y. Demi O'Byrne. Half-brother to the German Group 3 winner Marine Bleue (by Desert Prince) and to the French listed winner Mystic Spirit (by Invincible Spirit). The dam, a minor French 3-y-o winner, is a half-sister to 6 winners including the dam of the Group 1 Grand Prix de Paris winner Mirio. The second dam, Mirea (by The Minstrel), won once at 2 yrs.

1216. PLANATORY ★★★
b.f. Galileo – Zietory (Zieten).
March 14. Second foal. 320,000Y. Tattersalls October 1. J Magnier. Sister to Parabola, unplaced in one start at 2 yrs in 2008. The dam, a 2-y-o 6f and 3-y-o dual 1m listed winner, is a half-sister to 3 winners. The second dam, Fairy Story (by Persian Bold), won 5 races over 7f (including at 2 yrs) and is a half-sister to 4 winners.

1217. POSTELLION ★★★
b.c. Galileo – Peace Time (Surumu).
April 22. Sixth foal. 230,000Y. Tattersalls October 1. Demi O'Byrne. Half-brother to the German dual Group 3 1m winner Peace Royale (by Sholokov), to the German Group 3 1m winner Peaceful Love, the fair triple 1m winner Prince Evelith and a minor winner abroad (all by Dashing Blade). The dam, a German listed-placed winner, is a half-sister to 7 winners in Germany. The second dam, Princess Of Spain (by King Of Spain), was a listed-placed winner in Germany.

1218. SEVEN SUMMITS (IRE) ★★★
b.c. Danehill Dancer – Mandavilla
(Sadler's Wells).
January 22. First foal. Closely related to the Irish 10f and 12f winner Excalibur (by Danehill) and half-brother to the useful 12f winner and listed-placed Mazaya (by Sadler's Wells), the useful Irish 12f to 2m winner Sharazan (by Akarad), the French 1m winner and listed placed Shamsiya (by The Minstrel) and 2 minor winners in France by Shahrastani. The dam was a smart winner of the Group 2 12f Grand Prix d'Evry, the Group 3 12f Prix Minerve and the Group 3 12.5f Prix de Royallieu and is a half-sister to the Prix Vermeille winner Sharaya and the US Grade 3 winner Shannkara. The second dam, Shanizadeh (by Baldric II), was a useful French 6f and 1m winner. (Mrs S Magnier).

1219. STRING OF PEARLS (IRE) ★★★
b.f. Danehill Dancer – Evangeline
(Sadler's Wells).
May 11. Fourth foal. 400,000Y. Tattersalls October 2. Demi O'Byrne. Half-sister to the 2008 2-y-o Group 2 6f Lowther Stakes winner Infamous Angel (by Exceed And Excel). The dam is an unraced half-sister to 4 winners including the listed winner Sgt Pepper. The second dam, Amandine (by Darshaan), won once at 3 yrs in France and is a half-sister to 3 winners.

1220. UNNAMED ★★★★
b.c. Galileo – Approach (Darshaan).
February 22. The dam, a 7.5f (at 2 yrs) and listed 10f winner, was second in a US Grade 2 9.5f event and is a sister to the very useful 2-y-o 8.5f winner and Group 1 Prix Marcel Boussac fourth Intrigued and a half-sister to the French 2,000 Guineas and US Grade 1 winner Aussie Rules. The second dam, Last Second (by Alzao), winner of the 10f Nassau Stakes and the 10f Sun Chariot Stakes, is a half-sister to 7 winners including the Moyglare Stud Stakes third Alouette (herself dam of the Group 1 winners Albanova and Alborada) and to the placed dam of the Group 1 winners Yesterday and Quarter Moon. (Derek Smith).

1221. UNNAMED ★★★★
b.c. Sadler's Wells – Asnieres
(Spend A Buck).
January 27. Brother to the 1m (at 2 yrs) and Group 3 10.5f winner Prix de Flore winner Australie and half-brother to the Irish listed-placed 2-y-o and 5f 3-y-o winner Keepers Hill (by Danehill) and the quite useful 2-y-o 7f

winner Forgotten Voice (by Danehill Dancer). The dam, a minor winner in France at 4 yrs, is a half-sister to the Breeders Cup Classic and 9.3f Prix d'Ispahan winner Arcangues, to the Prix de Psyche winner and French 1,000 Guineas second Agathe (dam of the triple Group 1 winner Alexandrie) and the dam of the 1,000 Guineas winner Cape Verdi. The second dam, Albertine (by Irish River), a winner of 2 races and third in the Group 2 Prix de l'Opera, was smart at up to 10f and is a half-sister to the French Group winners Acoma, Ashmore and Art Bleu. (Mr M Tabor).

1222. UNNAMED ★★★★
b.c. Sadler's Wells – Brigid
(Irish River).
April 4. Ninth foal. Brother to the 2008 2-y-o Liffey Dancer, to the Group 1 7f Moyglare Stud Stakes winner Sequoyah (the dam of Henrythenavigator), the 2-y-o Group 1 Fillies' Mile winner Listen and the fair 7f winner Clara Bow and half-brother to the Irish listed 5.6f winner and Group 3 7f placed Oyster Catcher (by Bluebird). The dam, a minor French 3-y-o 1m winner, is a sister to the French listed 7f winner Or Vision (herself dam of the Group/ Grade 1 winners Dolphin Street, Insight and Saffron Walden) and a half-sister to 6 winners. The second dam, Luv Luvin' (by Raise a Native), won 2 races in the USA and was stakes-placed. (Mrs Sue Magnier).

1223. UNNAMED ★★★
b.c. Sadler's Wells – By Charter
(Shirley Heights).
April 3. Twelfth foal. 500,000Y. Tattersalls October 1. J Magnier. Closely related to the Group 2 Prix Hocquart winner Anton Chekhov (by Montjeu) and half-brother to the Group 2 2m Lonsdale Stakes winner First Charter, to the fair 14f winner High Charter (both by Polish Precedent), the smart 10f winner and Group 1 Italian Derby second Private Charter (by Singspiel), the fairly useful 2-y-o 6f winner Ridge Runner (by Indian Ridge), the fairly useful 12f winner and listed placed Careful Timing (by Caerleon), the quite useful 2-y-o 7f all-weather winner Magna Carta (by Royal Academy) and the fair 2-y-o 7f winner Green Charter (by Green Desert). The dam, a useful 2-y-o 7f winner and second in two listed events over middle-distances, is a sister to the Group 2 winner Zinaad and a half-sister to 5 winners including the Group 2 winner Time Allowed. The second dam, Time Charter (by Saritamer), was an exceptional filly and winner of the Oaks, the King George VI and Queen Elizabeth Diamond Stakes, the Champion Stakes, Coronation Cup, Prix Foy and Sun Chariot Stakes.

1224. UNNAMED ★★★
b.c. Montjeu – Bywayofthestars (Danehill).
February 11. The dam is a placed half-sister to numerous winners including the Group 1 Irish Oaks winner Moonstone, the Group 1 10f Prix Saint-Alary winner Cerulean Sky and the Breeders Cup second L'Ancresse. The second dam, Solo de Lune (by Law Society), a French 11f winner, is a half-sister to 6 winners including the Grade 2 E P Taylor Stakes winner Truly A Dream and the French Group 2 winner Wareed. (Mr M Tabor).

1225. UNNAMED ★★★★
b.c. Sadler's Wells – Danilova (Lyphard).
May 1. Brother to the 2-y-o Group 2 7f Debutante Stakes winner Silk And Scarlet and half-brother to the smart Group 3 6f Prix de Seine-et-Oise winner Danger Over, the fair 8.3f and 9.4f winner Danakil (both by Warning), the quite useful 11.7f placed Cartesian (by Shirley Heights) and the modest Irish 1m winner Potsdam (by Rainbow Quest). The dam is an unraced half-sister to the high-class middle-distance colt Sanglamore – winner of the French Derby and the 9.3f Prix d'Ispahan – and the very useful listed 10f winner Opera Score. The second dam, Ballinderry (by Irish River), won the Group 2 12f Ribblesdale Stakes and is a half-sister to numerous good winners including Sharpman (placed in the French 2,000 Guineas and the French Derby), Mot d'Or (Prix Hocquart) and Lydian (Grosser Preis von Berlin and Gran Premio de Milano). (Mrs Sue Magnier).

1226. UNNAMED ★★★
b.c. *Galileo – Dime Bag (High Line).*
February 16. Closely related to the quite useful 8.3f winner Nouveau Riche (by Entrepreneur) and half-brother to the smart Group 3 Prix La Rochette winner Guys And Dolls (by Efisio), the smart 1m (including at 2 yrs) to 11f listed winner Pawn Broker (by Selkirk), the useful dual 7f 2-y-o winner and Group 3 placed Blushing Bride (by Distant Relative) and the fairly useful Irish 7f winner Blushing Melody (by Never So Bold). The dam, a quite useful winner of 4 races at up to 2m (including on the all-weather), is a half-sister to 7 minor winners. The second dam, Blue Guitar (by Cure The Blues), a fairly useful winner of 2 races over 1m and 8.3f, is a half-sister to the listed winners Polished Silver and Melody. (Mr M Tabor).

1227. UNNAMED ★★★★
b.br.f. *Storm Cat – Farda Amiga (Broad Brush).*
April 7. Fourth foal. $650,000Y. **Keeneland September. Demi O'Byrne.** The dam, a champion 3-y-o filly in the USA, won the Grade 1 Kentucky Oaks and the Grade 1 Alabama Stakes. The second dam, Fly North (by Pleasant Colony), was a stakes winner in Canada.

1228. UNNAMED ★★★★
b.br.c. *Storm Cat – Get Lucky (Mr Prospector).*
February 23. Twelfth foal. $2,000,000Y. **Saratoga August. M V Magnier.** Half-brother to 6 winners including the US Graded stakes winners Accelerator and Daydreaming and to the unraced dam of the US Grade 1 winner Bluegrass Cat (by Storm Cat). The dam, winner of 5 races including the Grade 3 Affectionately Handicap in the USA, is a sister to the US Grade 1 Travers Stakes winner Rhythm and a half-sister to the US Grade 1 placed Offbeat. The second dam, Dance Number (by Northern Dancer), won 8 races including the Grade 1 Beldame Stakes and the Grade 2 Shuvee Handicap and is a half-sister to the high-class racehorse and sire Private Account.

1229. UNNAMED ★★★
b.c. *Sadler's Wells – Gryada (Shirley Heights).*
April 14. Eighth foal. 200,000Y. **Tattersalls October 1. Demi O'Byrne.** Closely related to the 2008 2-y-o Group 1 10f Criterium de Saint-Cloud winner Fame And Glory, to the fair Irish 10f winner Yummy Mummy (both by Montjeu) and to a minor winner in Germany by Galileo and half-brother to the smart 10.2f and 12f winner Grampian, to the fair 2-y-o 1m all-weather winner Gryskirk (both by Selkirk), the useful 10f and 12.3f winner Guaranda and the quite useful 11f winner Graham Island (both by Acatenango). The dam, a fairly useful 2-y-o 7f and 8.3f winner and third in the Group 3 1m Premio Dormello, is a full or half-sister to 4 middle-distance winners. The second dam, Grimpola (by Windwurf), won over 6f and 1m in Germany including the Group 2 German 1,000 Guineas and stayed 12f.

1230. UNNAMED ★★★
ch.c. *Galileo – Healing Music (Bering).*
April 10. The dam, a French listed-placed 2-y-o winner, is a half-sister to the French listed winner and subsequent Grade 1 Hollywood Derby second Fast And Furious. The second dam, Helvellyn (by Gone West), a quite useful 8.3f winner, is a half-sister to 6 winners. (Mrs Sue Magnier).

1231. UNNAMED ★★★★
b.br.c. *Giant's Causeway – Imagine (Sadler's Wells).*
February 6. Half-brother to the 2-y-o Group 1 7f Prix Jean Luc Lagardere winner Horatio Nelson (by Danehill) and to the 2-y-o Group 2 7f Rockfel Stakes winner Kitty Matcham (by Rock Of Gibraltar). The dam, winner of the Irish 1,000 Guineas and Epsom Oaks, is a half-sister to Generous, winner of the Derby, the Irish Derby, the King George VI and Queen Elizabeth Diamond Stakes and the Dewhurst Stakes. The second dam, Doff The Derby (by Master Derby), is an unraced half-sister to the Prix Ganay winner Trillion (herself dam of the outstanding racemare Triptych). (Mrs Sue Magnier).

1232. UNNAMED ★★★
b.c. Galileo – Kissogram (Caerleon).
March 20. Fourth foal. 150,000Y. Tattersalls October 1. Demi O'Byrne. The dam won 3 races including the Group 2 10f Sun Chariot Stakes and the listed Atalanta Stakes and is a half-sister to 3 winners. The second dam, Alligram (by Alysheba), is an unplaced half-sister to 5 winners out of Queen Elizabeth II Stakes and Coronation Stakes winner Milligram.

1233. UNNAMED ★★★
b.c. Danehill Dancer – Kitty O'Shea (Sadler's Wells).
February 24. First foal. The dam ran twice and won both races over 1m (including at 2 yrs and a listed event at 3 yrs). She is a sister to the Group 1 Racing Post Trophy and Group 1 St Leger winner Brian Boru and a half-sister to the Group 3 12.5f Prix de Royallieu winner Moon Search. The second dam, Eva Luna (by Alleged), won the Group 3 14.6f Park Hill Stakes and is a half-sister to several winners. (Mrs S Magnier).

1234. UNNAMED ★★★
b.c. Montjeu – Krissante (Kris).
February 14. Half-brother to the 2-y-o Group 1 7f Grand Criterium winner Okawango (by Kingmambo) and to the moderate French 9.5f winner Class King (by Royal Academy). The dam is a placed half-sister to several winners including the Group 3 10.5f Prix Cleopatre winner Brooklyn's Dance (herself dam of 2 French listed winners). The second dam, Vallee Dansante (by Lyphard), won once in France and is a full or half-sister to 12 winners including the French 2,000 Guineas winner and good sire Green Dancer and the US Grade 2 winner Val Danseur and to the unplaced dam of the Dewhurst Stakes winner Alhaarth. (Derek Smith).

1235. UNNAMED ★★★
b.c. Galileo – Lady Karr (Mark Of Esteem).
February 18. First foal. 250,000foal. Tattersalls December. T Hyde. The dam, a fair 12f winner, is a sister to 2 winners including the Dewhurst Stakes and Derby winner Sir Percy and a half-sister to the very useful 1m to 10f winner and Group 3 Scottish Classic third Blue Lion. The second dam, Percy's Lass (by Blakeney), a very useful winner from 6f (at 2 yrs) to 11.5f including the Group 3 September Stakes, is a half-sister to 6 winners including the Grade 1 10f E P Taylor Stakes winner Braiswick.

1236. UNNAMED ★★★★
b.c. Sadler's Wells – L'Ancresse (Darshaan).
January 26. The dam, a 7f (at 2 yrs) and listed 12f winner, was second in the Group 1 Breeders Cup Filly Mare & Turf and is a half-sister to 7 winners including the Group 1 Irish Oaks winner Moonstone and the Group 1 10f Prix Saint-Alary winner Cerulean Sky. The second dam, Solo de Lune (by Law Society), a French 11f winner, is a half-sister to 6 winners including the Grade 2 E P Taylor Stakes winner Truly A Dream and the French Group 2 winner Wareed. (Mrs Sue Magnier).

1237. UNNAMED ★★★
ch.c. Galileo – Laurel Delight (Presidium).
April 20. Eighth foal. €330,000Y. Goffs Million. Demi O'Byrne. Half-brother to the US Grade 2 Argent Dixie Stakes and Grade 2 Kelso Breeders Cup Handicap winner and Grade 1 second Mr O'Brien (by Mukaddamah), to the fair 2-y-o 5f winner Laurel Pleasure (by Selkirk) and a winner in Italy by Emperor Jones. The dam, a useful winner of 4 races over 5f, is a half-sister to 5 winners including the high-class sprinter Paris House. The second dam, Foudroyer (by Artaius), ran unplaced twice.

1238. UNNAMED ★★★
b.c. Montjeu – Leaping Water (Sure Blade).
April 13. Tenth living foal. 200,000Y. Tattersalls October 1. Demi O'Byrne. Brother to the fair 2008 2-y-o 1m debut winner Cascata and half-brother to 2 winners including the US dual Grade 2 winner and Grade 1 placed Grammarian (by Definite Article). The dam is an unraced half-sister to the high-class St James's Palace Stakes and Prix Jean Prat winner Starborough, the Criterium de Saint-Cloud and Criterium International winner Ballingarry, the

Racing Post Trophy winner Aristotle and the Prix de Royaumont winner Spanish Falls. The second dam, Flamenco Wave (by Desert Wine), won the Group 1 Moyglare Stud Stakes.

1239. UNNAMED ★★★
b.c. Montjeu – Madeira Mist (Grand Lodge).
March 8. Second foal. 360,000Y. Tattersalls October 1. Demi O'Byrne. Half-brother to the unplaced 2008 2-y-o Storm Mist (by Giant's Causeway). The dam won 8 races in the USA and Canada including the Grade 3 Dance Smartly Handicap and is a half-sister to 5 winners including the Irish listed winner Misty Heights. The second dam, Mountains Of Mist (by Shirley Heights), a quite useful 10f winner, is a half-sister to 7 winners including the Group 2 Lowther Stakes winner Enthused.

1240. UNNAMED ★★★★
ch.c. Kingmambo – Maryinsky (Sadler's Wells).
March 7. Brother to the very smart 2-y-o Group 1 Criterium International winner Thewayyouare and half-brother to the high-class Pretty Polly Stakes, Irish Oaks, Nassau Stakes and Yorkshire Oaks winner (all Group 1 events) Peeping Fawn (by Danehill). The dam, a 2-y-o 7f winner, was second in the Group 1 Fillies Mile and is a half-sister to the Grade 2 9f Demoiselle Stakes winner Better Than Honour, to the smart Group 2 1m Beresford Stakes winner Turnberry Isle and the Group 2 1m Prix d'Astarte winner Smolensk. The second dam, Blush With Pride (by Blushing Groom), won the Grade 1 9f Kentucky Oaks and the Grade 1 8.5f Santa Susana Stakes and is a half-sister to the smart winners Gielgud, Malinowski and Monroe (herself dam of the Dewhurst Stakes winner Xaar) and to the dam of El Gran Senor and Try My Best.

1241. UNNAMED ★★★
b.c. Montjeu – Masskana (Darshaan).
March 29. Closely related to the quite useful 10f winner Anna Pallida (by Sadler's Wells) and half-brother to the very smart Group 1 10f Hong Kong Cup, Group 2 1m Beresford Stakes and Group 2 10f Royal Whip Stakes winner Eagle Mountain (by Rock Of Gibraltar), the smart 2-y-o Group 1 1m Prix Marcel Boussac winner and Group 1 10f Nassau Stakes second Sulk (by Selkirk), the smart 1m listed winner Wallace (by Royal Academy) and the modest 9f winner Twilight World (by Night Shift). The dam, a minor 9f and 10f winner in France, is a half-sister to the US Grade 3 Arcadia Handicap winner Madjaristan and the Group 2 Gallinule Stakes winner Massyar. The second dam, Masarika (by Thatch), won the French 1,000 Guineas and the Prix Robert Papin and is a half-sister to 4 winners. (Derek Smith).

1242. UNNAMED ★★★
b.c. Oratorio – Moonlight Dance (Alysheba).
April 25. Tenth foal. Deauville August. €400,000Y. Demi O'Byrne. Closely related to the minor French winner Maitre du Jeu (by Rock Of Gibraltar) and half-brother to the French listed winner Memory Maker (by Lure), the listed winner and Group 1 French Oaks second Millionaia (by Peintre Celebre) and the 10f winner Memoire (by Sadler's Wells). The dam, winner of the Group 1 10f Prix Saint-Alary, is a half-sister to the Dante Stakes winner Claude Monet and the smart winners Magdalena and Marignan. The second dam, Madelia (by Caro), won the French 1,000 Guineas, the Prix Saint-Alary and the Prix de Diane and is a half-sister to the Prix du Moulin winner Mount Hagen and two other good French horses in Monsanto and Malecite.

1243. UNNAMED ★★★
b.c. Montjeu – My Emma (Marju).
February 15. Half-brother to the smart 12f and listed 14f winner Moments Of Joy (by Darshaan) and to the useful 11.5f winner Light Of Morn (by Daylami). The dam, a smart winner of the Group 1 12f Prix Vermeille, is a half-sister to 5 winners including the Group 1 St Leger and Group 1 Ascot Gold Cup winner Classic Cliché. The second dam, Pato (by High Top), a fairly useful 2-y-o 7f and triple 4-y-o 10f winner, is a sister to the very smart sprinter Crews Hill. (Mr M Tabor).

1244. UNNAMED ★★★★
b.c. Sadler's Wells – Necklace (Darshaan).
February 20. Brother to the fair 2008 Irish 1m placed 2-y-o Sapphire Bracelet. The dam won the 2-y-o Group 1 7f Moyglare Stud Stakes and was Grade 1 placed in the USA. The second dam, Spinning The Yarn (by Barathea), ran once unplaced and is closely related to the top-class King George VI and Queen Elizabeth Diamond Stakes winner Opera House and the Ascot Gold Cup and Irish St Leger winner Kayf Tara and a half-sister to the Group 1 Prix de l'Opera winner Zee Zee Top. (Mr M Tabor).

1245. UNNAMED ★★★
b.c. Galileo – Numidie (Baillamont).
May 8. Eleventh foal. Deauville August. €260,000Y. Demi O'Byrne. Half-brother to 7 winners including the Group 1 Prix Saint-Alary winner Reve d'Oscar, the Group 2 Prix Hocquart winner Numide and the listed 3-y-o winner Sir Eric (all by Highest Honor). The dam won twice in France including a listed event at Evry and is a half-sister to 3 minor winners in France. The second dam, Yamuna (by Green Dancer), won twice in France and is a half-sister to 7 winners including the dam of the Group 2 Prix de Royallieu winner Fabulous Hostess.

1246. UNNAMED ★★★
b.c. Montjeu – Onereuse (Sanglamore).
February 10. Sixth living foal. €240,000Y. Goffs Million. Demi O'Byrne. Closely related to Francisco Goya (by Galileo), placed fourth over 1m on his only start at 2 yrs in 2008 and to the Group 1 10f Prix Saint-Alary winner and Group 1 Prix Vermeille third Fidelite (by In The Wings) and half-brother the French 10f and jumps winner Amour Multiple (by Poliglote) and a winner in Greece by Rock Of Gibraltar. The dam was placed over 1m and 10f in France and is a half-sister to 8 winners including the Irish Derby winner Winged Love. The second dam, J'ai Deux Amours (by Top Ville), winner of the listed 1m Prix de Lieurey at 3 yrs, dead-heated for third in the Group 2 9.2f Prix de l'Opera and is a half-sister to 8 winners.

1247. UNNAMED ★★★
b.c. Montjeu – Pink Cristal (Dilum).
February 14. Fifth foal. 250,000Y. Tattersalls October 1. J Magnier. Closely related to the 2-y-o 7f and subsequent US Grade 2 Sunset Handicap winner Always First (by Barathea) and half-brother to the fairly useful 1m winner Motaqareb (by Grand Lodge) and the fairly useful 7f winner Orientalist Art (by Green Desert). The dam was a smart winner of 2 races at 3 yrs including a listed event over 1m at Ascot. She is a half-sister to 8 winners including the German Group 2 and Group 3 Scottish Classic winner Crystal Hearted and the dam of the Group winners Crystal Music, State Crystal, Dubai Success and Solar Crystal. The second dam, Crystal Fountain (by Great Nephew), was unplaced on her only start and is a half-sister to Royal Palace and Glass Slipper (dam of the classic winners Fairy Footsteps and Light Cavalry).

1248. UNNAMED ★★★
b.f. Arch – Samut (Danehill).
January 28. Fourth foal. $500,000Y. Keeneland September. Demi O'Byrne. Half-sister to the Italian stakes winner Iuturna (by Intidab). The dam, a fairly useful 2-y-o 7.5f winner, is a sister to the useful 3-y-o dual 7f winner and Group 3 5f Queen Mary Stakes second Al Ihsas, closely related to the Irish listed 8.5f winner Anna Karenina and the listed placed winner Makam and a half-sister to 3 winners. The second dam, Simaat (by Mr Prospector), a fair 1m winner, is a half-sister to 2 winners.

1249. UNNAMED ★★★★
ch.c. Kingmambo – Sequoyah (Sadler's Wells).
February 24. Brother to the 2,000 Guineas, Irish 2,000 Guineas, St James's Palace Stakes and Sussex Stakes winner Henrythenavigator and to the Group 3 Irish 1,000 Guineas Trial winner Queen Cleopatra and half-brother to the fairly useful Irish 2-y-o 7.5f winner Abide With Me (by Danehill). The dam, winner of the Group 1 7f Moyglare Stud Stakes, is a sister to the 2-y-o Group 1 Fillies' Mile winner Listen and a half-sister to the Irish listed 5.6f winner and Group 3

7f placed Oyster Catcher. The second dam, Brigid (by Irish River), a minor French 3-y-o 1m winner, is a sister to the French listed 7f winner Or Vision (herself dam of the Group/Grade 1 winners Dolphin Street, Insight and Saffron Walden) and a half-sister to 6 winners. (Mrs Sue Magnier).

1250. UNNAMED ★★★
ch.c. Giant's Causeway – Sheepscot (Easy Goer).
April 11. Seventh foal. $725,000Y. Keeneland September. Demi O'Byrne. Half-brother to 4 winners including the Group 1 St James's Palace Stakes winner Astronomer Royal (by Danzig) and the US Grade 2 Pan American Handicap winner Navesink River (by Unbridled). The dam, a minor stakes winner of 5 races in the USA, is a half-sister to 7 winners including the dual US Grade 1 winner Vicar. The second dam, Escrow Agent (by El Gran Senor), won at 2 yrs in Ireland and was stakes-placed in the USA.

1251. UNNAMED ★★★★
b.c. Sadler's Wells – Shouk (Shirley Heights).
April 23. Brother to the smart 2008 listed 2-y-o 1m winner and Group 2 1m Beresford Stakes third Masterofthehorse and to the high-class 1m (at 2 yrs), Oaks, Irish Oaks and Yorkshire Oaks winner Alexandrova, closely related to the 2-y-o Group 1 6f Cheveley Park Stakes winner Magical Romance, the fairly useful 2-y-o 7f winner and subsequent Canadian Grade 3 placed Saree (both by Barathea) and the smart 10f winner and Group 2 placed Washington Irving (by Montjeu) and half-brother to the modest 10f all-weather winner Grand Wizard (by Grand Lodge). The dam, a quite useful 10.5f winner, is closely related to the listed winner and Group 3 Park Hill Stakes third Puce and a half-sister to 6 winners. The second dam, Souk (by Ahonoora), a fairly useful 7f winner, was listed placed over 1m and is a half-sister to 3 winners. (Mrs Sue Magnier).

1252. UNNAMED ★★★★
b.c. Montjeu – Sophisticat (Storm Cat).
February 22. Half-brother to the 2008 Irish 2-y-o 6f winner and Group 1 6f Cheveley Park Stakes third Pursuit Of Glory (by Fusaichi Pegasus) and to the French listed winner Sefroua (by Kingmambo). The dam, a very smart Group 1 1m Coronation Stakes winner, is a sister to the US Grade 2 9f winner Grand Reward and a half-sister to the US Grade 2 winner Harlington (by Unbridled) and the US listed winner Serena's Tune. The second dam, Serena's Song (by Rahy), was an outstanding US winner of eleven Grade 1 events and is a half-sisterto the US Grade 3 Golden Rod Stakes winner Vivid Imagination. (Mr M Tabor).

1253. UNNAMED ★★★
b.c. Galileo – Special Oasis (Green Desert).
March 27. Half-brother to the fairly useful 7f, 1m and hurdles winner Golden Chalice (by Selkirk). The dam is an unraced half-sister to 7 winners including the Group 1 Juddmonte International winner One So Wonderful, the Group 3 7f Rockfel Stakes winner and Irish 1,000 Guineas third Relatively Special (herself the dam of 2 stakes winners) and the Group 2 Dante Stakes winner Alnasr Alwasheek. The second dam, Someone Special (by Habitat), a useful 3-y-o 7f winner, was third in the Coronation Stakes and is a half-sister to the top-class miler Milligram. (Mr Michael Tabor).

1254. UNNAMED ★★★
b.c. Galileo – Splendid (Mujtahid).
May 17. Eighth foal. €500,000Y. Goffs Million. Demi O'Byrne. Half-brother to the quite useful 2008 2-y-o 7f winner Fanditha (by Danehill Dancer), to the quite useful 2-y-o 6f winner Packing Hero (by Black Minnaloushe), the US stakes-placed winner of 5 races Bohunk (by Polish Numbers) and a minor US 4-y-o winner by Rahy. The dam is a placed half-sister to 4 winners including the very useful 1m (at 2 yrs) and 12f winner Peking Opera. The second dam, Braneakins (by Sallust), won 3 races over 12f in Ireland and is a half-sister to 7 winners including the Cheveley Park Stakes winners Park Appeal (the dam of Cape Cross) and Desirable (dam of the 1,000 Guineas winner Shadayid), the Irish Oaks winner Alydaress and the unraced dam of the 1,000 Guineas winner Russian Rhythm.

1255. UNNAMED ★★★
b.c. Montjeu – Sweeten Up
(Shirley Heights).
April 7. Closely related to the 2-y-o Group 1 10f Criterium de Saint-Cloud winner Alberto Giacometti (by Sadler's Wells) and half-brother to the German 10f winner Marco Andre (by Zilzal). The dam ran just twice, being placed at 2 yrs and is a sister to the smart German 1m (at 2 yrs) and 9f winner Sharan. The second dam, Honeybeta (by Habitat), was a useful winner at up to 12f. (Derek Smith).

1256. UNNAMED ★★★
b.c. Galileo – Tammany Hall (Petorius).
April 20. Half-brother to the the fairly useful Irish 2-y-o 6f winner I Key (by Fasliyev). The dam is an unraced half-sister to 4 winners including the 2-y-o Group 3 6f Coventry Stakes winner CD Europe. The second dam, Woodland Orchid (by Woodman), is an unplaced half-sister to the Group 3 winners D'Anjou and Truth Or Dare. (Mrs Sue Magnier).

1257. UNNAMED ★★★
b.f. Giant's Causeway – Tee Kay
(Gold Meridian).
March 19. Eighth foal. $400,000Y. Keeneland September. Demi O'Byrne. Half-sister to 5 winners including the Japanese champion and Horse of the Year Symboli Kris S (by Kris S), 2 minor US winners by Grand Slam and Kingmambo and a minor winner in Japan by Fusaichi Pegasus. The dam won 6 races in the USA including the Grade 3 Martha Washington Stakes and is a half-sister to several winners. The second dam, Tri Argo (by Tri Jet), was a US stakes winner of 6 races.

1258. UNNAMED ★★★
b.c. Giant's Causeway – Valentine Band
(Dixieland Band).
March 23. The dam, a very useful 10f winner, is a half-sister to the French 7f (at 2 yrs) and listed 1m winner Multiplex, to the very useful 10f and Irish Group 3 14f winner Memorise, the useful 7.5f winner and listed 1m placed Sparkling Water and the useful 2-y-o 7f winner Fully Invested. The second dam, Shirley Valentine (by Shirley Heights), a useful 12f winner, was fourth in the Park Hill Stakes and the Lancashire Oaks and is a sister to the high class Irish Derby second Deploy and a half-sister to the Derby and Irish Derby winner Commander in Chief, the champion 2-y-o and miler Warning and the Grade 1 10f Flower Bowl Invitational Handicap winner Yashmak. (Mrs Sue Magnier).

1259. UNNAMED ★★★
b.c. Montjeu – Vanishing Prairie
(Alysheba).
February 6. Tenth foal. 650,000Y. Tattersalls October 1. Demi O'Byrne. Closely related to the listed Glorious Stakes winner and Melbourne Cup second Purple Moon (by Galileo) and to the Group 3 Prix Penelope winner La Sylphide (by Barathea) and half-brother to 6 winners including the Group 1 Grand Prix de Paris and Group 1 Prix Jean Prat winner Vespone and the French listed-placed Verdi (both by Llandaff). The dam won over 10f and 12f in Ireland and is a half-sister to the Group 2 winners Vetheuil and Verveine (herself dam of the Group/Grade 1 winners Vallee Enchantee and Volga). The second dam, Venise (by Nureyev), is an unraced three-parts sister to the Mill Reef Stakes and Richmond Stakes winner Vacarme and a half-sister to the Prix Jacques le Marois winner Vin de France.

1260. UNNAMED ★★★
ch.c. Giant's Causeway – Words Of War
(Lord At War).
April 16. Ninth foal. $590,000Y. Keeneland September. Demi O'Byrne. Closely related to a minor US 3-y-o winner by Storm Cat and half-brother to the Grade 2 Suburban Handicap and Grade 2 Dwyer Stakes winner E Dubai (by Mr Prospector), the Grade 1 Del Mar Oaks winner No Matter What (by Nureyev) and 2 winners in Japan and the USA by Coronado's Quest and Danzig. The dam, US stakes winner of 9 races, is a sister to the Grade 3 Miesque Stakes winner Ascutney and a half-sister to 8 winners. The second dam, Right Word (by Verbatim), is a placed sister to the stakes winner Spruce Song.

JEDD O'KEEFFE

1261. ARCH WALKER ★★★
ch.c. Choisir – Clunie (Inchinor).
March 13. 26,000Y. Doncaster Festival. Jedd O'Keeffe. Half-brother to the quite useful triple 6f winner Filligree (by Kyllachy), to the quite useful 2-y-o 6f winner Propellor (by Pivotal), the fair 2-y-o 7.5f winner Porcelain (by Peintre Celebre) and the moderate 1m winner Poker (by Hector Protector). The dam, a quite useful triple 6f winner, is a half-sister to the quite useful 2-y-o 6f winner Indeedyedo. The second dam, Bonita (by Primo Dominie), a modest 6f and 7f winner, is a half-sister to one winner. (A Walker).
"I love him to bits. He's a real two-year-old – very powerful with a good backside on him. Quite a flashy chestnut, he's going really well and he might be racing in late April. I'm very happy with him and he should win a race or two".

1262. FANTASTIC FAVOUR ★★
b.c. Fantastic Light – Dixie Favor (Dixieland Band).
March 20. Eleventh foal. 26,000Y. Doncaster St Leger. J O'Keeffe. Half-brother to the Italian listed winner and Group 2 Italian 1,000 Guineas third Kiralik, to the fair middle-distance winner of 5 races Favorisio, the hurdles winner Currahee (all by Efisio), the 2-y-o Group 3 6f Princess Margaret Stakes and subsequent US 3-y-o Grade 2 8.5f winner and Grade 1 9f third River Belle (by Lahib), the useful 3-y-o 7.5f and 1m winner Rio Riva (by Pivotal) and the poor 5f all-weather winner Stately Favour (by Statoblest). The dam was a quite useful Irish 6f (at 2 yrs) to 1m winner. The second dam, Femme Favor (by Forli), is an unraced half-sister to 4 winners. (Ken & Delia Shaw – KGS Consulting LLP).
"He's quite big and backward, but he is the most gorgeous looking horse. Not one to be rushed but he's my favourite in terms of looks. One for a mile at the back-end and much more of a three-year-old type".

1263. FIFTY MOORE ★★★★
b.c. Selkirk – Franglais (Lion Cavern).
March 24. Fourth foal. 10,000Y. Tattersalls October. J O'Keeffe. Half-brother to the 2008 2-y-o listed 5f Windsor Castle Stakes winner Flashman's Papers (by Exceed And Excel) and to the quite useful dual 6f winner Temple Of Thebes (by Bahri). The dam won 3 races from 6f to 1m at 3 and 4 yrs in Germany and is a half-sister to 3 winners including the Grade 1 E P Taylor Stakes winner Fraulein. The second dam, Francfurter (by Legend Of France), was a quite useful 3-y-o dual 10f winner. (Colin & Melanie Moore).
"When I saw him at the Sales I didn't think for a moment I'd be able to afford him, particularly as his half-brother Flashmans Papers won at Royal Ascot last year. He's a lovely horse and quite big but just like another of my two-year-olds, Magic Footsteps, he's surprising me how well he's going now. One for the second half of the season, he's a dream to train and I'll start him off at six furlongs in May. He'll probably want a bit of give in the ground". TRAINER'S BARGAIN BUY

1264. IRISH EYES ★★
b.c. Mark Of Esteem – Diabaig (Precocious).
February 5. Second foal. 10,000Y. Tattersalls October 3. Jedd O'Keeffe. Half-brother to the fairly useful 1m winner of 5 races Ailincala (by Pursuit Of Love), the fair 10f winners Highland Love and Wester Ross (both by Fruits Of Love) and 2 hurdles winners by Bin Ajwaad and Victory Note. The dam, a fair 1m winner, is a half-sister to 4 minor winners. The second dam, Silka (by Lypheor), won once at 2 yrs in Italy and is a half-sister to 4 other minor winners. (Ken & Delia Shaw – KGS Consulting LLP).
"I trained the half-brother Highland Love who won two races for us last year. It's a good, solid, hardy family and they all try hard. He had a little setback earlier on but he's fine again now and he'll make a back-end two-year-old over seven furlongs or a mile".

1265. POWERFUL PIERRE ★★★
ch.c. Compton Place – Alzianah (Alzao).
February 8. Tenth foal. 32,000Y. Doncaster St Leger. Jedd O'Keeffe. Brother to the fairly useful 2-y-o 5f winner Crosby Hall and half-brother to the fairly useful 2-y-o 6f winner Desperate Dan (by Danzero), the fairly useful 2-y-o 6f winner Sirjoshua Reynolds (by Kyllachy), the quite useful triple 5f winner (including at 2 yrs) Leozian, the fair 5f and all-weather 6f winner Patientes Virtis (both by Lion Cavern), the fair 7f all-weather winner Voluptuous (by Polish Precedent) and the fair 2-y-o 5f all-weather winner Waffles Of Amin (by Owington). The dam, a fairly useful 5f and 6f winner, was second in the Ayr Gold Cup and third in the Group 3 6f Prix de Meautry and is a half-sister to 5 winners. The second dam, Ghassanah (by Pas de Seul), a fair 7f winner, is a half-sister to 10 winners including the Italian Derby winner Don Orazio. (Ken & Delia Shaw – KGS Consulting LLP).

"A lovely looking two-year-old from a good family. The dam was trained by James Bethell and he tells me this colt is the nicest one from the mare. I thought this colt would be very early, but he's still coming along nicely and he'll be out in May".

1266. MAGIC FOOTSTEPS ★★★
b.c. Footstepsinthesand – Dayville (Dayjur).
February 9. Ninth foal. 25,000Y. Doncaster St Leger. J O'Keeffe. Half-brother to the quite useful 5f and 6f winner and listed-placed Day By Day (by Kyllachy), to the quite useful 2-y-o 1m all-weather winner Musical Day (by Singspiel), the quite useful 10f and 12f winner My Daisychain (by Hector Protector) and the Irish 3-y-o 5f winner Alexander Ballet (by Mind Games). The dam, a quite useful triple 6f winner, is a half-sister to 4 winners including the Grade 1 Yellow Ribbon Handicap winner Spanish Fern. The second dam, Chain Fern (by Blushing Groom), is an unraced sister to the Irish 1,000 Guineas and Coronation Stakes winner Al Bahathri (herself dam of the 2,000 Guineas and Champion Stakes winner Haafhd). (Ken & Delia Shaw – KGS Consulting LLP).

"He could be racing in early May. He's really surprising me because he's quite big and yet he shows good speed. A real nice horse with a good temperament, I've got to the stage where I can't hold him back any longer! He'll start off at six furlongs".

JAMIE OSBORNE

1267. CARRIES LASS ★★★
br.f. Auction House – Carranita (Anita's Prince).
The dam won 16 races from 5f to 7f and from 2 to 8 yrs including 4 listed events and is a full or half-sister to 7 winners. The second dam, Take More (by Frontal), was a listed-placed winner in Germany. (Mr Michael Turner).

"A sharp-looking filly that should be racing in May".

1268. JASMINE SCENT ★★★
ch.f. Namid – Sky Galaxy (Sky Classic).
February 7. €8,000Y. Tattersalls Ireland. Not sold. The dam, a quite useful 2-y-o 6f winner, is a half-sister to the useful 2-y-o 5f winner and Group 3 5f Queen Mary Stakes third Moonshine Girl. The second dam, Fly To The Moon (by Blushing Groom), a fairly useful 3-y-o 1m winner, is a sister to the Group 1 Heinz "57" Phoenix Stakes winner Digamist and a half-sister to several winners.

"She's very solid and a straightforward filly that shows a bit of speed and she could be one of the first runners".

1269. POLISH STEPS ★★★★
b.f. Footstepsinthesand – Polish Spring (Polish Precedent).
March 26. The dam, a useful winner here and in the USA from 6f (at 2 yrs) to 8.5f including a stakes event, is a half-sister to numerous winners including the French listed 11f winner Go Boldly. The second dam, Diavolina (by Lear Fan), a French 10f winner at 3 yrs, is a half-sister to 7 winners. (Mr Michael Turner).

"She shows speed and could be one of my first runners. I like her and she looks to be a nice two-year-old".

1270. UNNAMED ★★★
b.c. Alhaarth – Aguilas Perla (Indian Ridge).
April 8. Fourth foal. €40,000Y. Goffs Million. David Redvers. Half-brother to the fair 2-y-o 6f winner Annes Rocket (by Fasliyev), to the fairly useful Irish 2-y-o 5f and 7f winner and listed-placed Spirit Of Pearl (by Invincible Spirit) and the modest Irish 6f winner Hazelwood Ridge (by Mozart). The dam is an unraced sister to the Irish listed 7f winner Cool Clarity and a half-sister to the listed winners Artistic Blue and Queen Of Palms. The second dam, Tapolite (by Tap On Wood), won the listed 7f Tyros Stakes, is a sister to the 2-y-o Group 3 1m Killavullen Stakes winner Sedulous and a half-sister to 3 winners.
"A nice little colt, he should be one for the first half of the season and he's done a couple of bits of work. I don't think he's a five furlong horse but he should be out sometime in May. A lovely moving horse, I think he's forward enough for the first six furlong races".

1271. UNNAMED ★★★★
b.c. Exceed And Excel – Almost Amber (Mt Livermore).
January 25. Fifth foal. €58,000Y. Goffs Million. David Redvers. Half-brother to the quite useful 2-y-o 6f and subsequent South African winner Little Dalham, to the fair 2-y-o 6f winner Our Ruby (both by Diktat) and the modest 7f and 1m winner Ten To The Dozen (by Royal Applause). The dam, a fairly useful 2-y-o 5f winner, is a half-sister to 5 winners in the USA and Japan including the multiple Japanese stakes winner Grab Your Heart. The second dam, Kelly Amber (by Highland Park), was a minor stakes-winning sprinter in the USA.
"Probably the sharpest of my two-year-olds, he has bags of speed and he's an early foal from a fast family. He's very mature and will probably be my first runner. I own him and he's for sale but I'm happy to keep him because he should be an early season winner at least".

1272. UNNAMED ★★★
ch.c. Tagula – Alserna (Alhaarth).
April 23. Fourth foal. 1,000Y. Goffs Sportsmans. David Redvers. The dam, a fairly useful Irish 9f and 10f winner, is a half-sister to 2 winners. The second dam, Shahaamh (by Reference Point), won at 3 yrs and is a half-sister to 6 winners.
"A very good-moving horse and he could be ready for the first half of the season. He was virtually given to me at Goffs and I'm pleased I've got him. We've had some luck with Tagula's before and he looks like he's got a bit of speed".
TRAINER'S BARGAIN BUY

1273. UNNAMED ★★
b.c. Danehill Dancer – Arpege (Sadler's Wells).
March 24. Fourth foal. Closely related to Alystar (by Rock Of Gibraltar), unplaced in one start at 2 yrs in 2008 and to the fairly useful French 10f and 11f winner and listed-placed Beau Vengerov (by Danehill). The dam is an unraced sister to the smart German Group 2 8.5f and Italian Group 2 1m winner Crimson Tide, closely related to the US Grade 2 and Group 3 Prix de Sandringham winner Pharatta and a half-sister to the US stakes winner and Group 1 Prix Marcel Boussac fourth La Vida Loca. The second dam, Sharata (by Darshaan), is an unraced half-sister to the Derby and Irish Derby winner Shahrastani.
"A very tall colt and most definitely one for later on. A lovely horse with a nice pedigree, he's a good mover and very athletic. He just wants a bit of time".

1274. UNNAMED ★★
b.c. Singspiel – Bayleaf (Efisio).
April 6. Sixth living foal. 30,000Y. Tattersalls October 2. David Redvers. Half-brother to the useful 5f, 6f (at 2 yrs) and 10f winner of 6 races and Group 3 5f Molecomb Stakes third Folio (by Perugino). The dam, a useful 2-y-o 5f winner, was listed-placed and is a sister to the 2-y-o 5f winner, Group 3 Molecomb Stakes third and subsequent US winner of 3 races at up to 6f Baize (herself dam of the US Grade 1 Del Mar Oaks winner Singhalese). The second dam, Bayonne (by Bay Express), a dual 5f winner at 3 yrs, is a half-sister to 7 winners.
"He has a sort of 'forward' physique for a Singspiel and although he's probably unlikely to

be one for the first half of the season we'll give him the chance to be. I'm happy enough with him and he's a nice horse".

1275. UNNAMED ★★★
b.c. *Kheleyf – Bron Hilda (Namaqualand).*
April 10. Fifth foal. €17,000Y. Goffs Sportsmans. David Redvers. The dam is a placed half-sister to 6 winners including the Irish Group 3 winner Rainbows For All. The second dam, Maura's Guest (by Be My Guest), is an unraced half-sister to 3 stakes winners.
"He's done well over the winter and strengthened up. He looks like he could be quite sharp, he's got a bit of boot and I'll kick on with him".

1276. UNNAMED ★★
b.f. *Whipper – Cheyenne Spirit (Indian Ridge).*
May 5. €30,000Y. Goffs October. David Redvers. Half-sister to the useful 2-y-o dual 6f winner and subsequent US stakes winner Alinga (by King's Theatre) and to the modest 9f winner Shoooz (by Soviet Star). The dam, a useful winner of 7 races including a listed event over 6f, is a half-sister to 5 winners including the dam of the Group 3 winner Ashdown Express. The second dam, Bazaar Promise (by Native Bazaar), is an unplaced sister to the very useful sprinter Crofthall.
"I'm just not as far forward with her as I'd like to be and I wouldn't have a view of her ability yet. She's probably going to come in the second half of the season".

1277. UNNAMED ★★★
b.c. *Chineur – Church Mice (Petardia).*
April 28. Fourth foal. €8,000Y. Goffs Sportsman's. David Redvers. Half-brother to the fairly useful 6f (at 2 yrs) to 1m winner Red Rumour (by Redback) and to the fair 2-y-o 6f winner Dustry (by Chevalier). The dam, a quite useful 5f (at 2 yrs) and 6f winner, is a half-sister to 2 winners. The second dam, Negria (by Al Hareb), a German 2-y-o 6f winner, is a half-sister to 7 winners.
"He has a sharp look to him, the mare has bred two juvenile winners and this lad looks like he could do the same. So I'd be happy enough with him".

1278. UNNAMED ★★★
b.c. *Lujain – Discoed (Distinctly North).*
February 28. Second foal. The dam is an unplaced half-sister to the Group 1 Dewhurst Stakes and subsequent US Grade 1 winner Milk It Mick. The second dam, Lucky Candy (by Lucky Wednesday), is an unplaced half-sister to 5 winners.
"I had the mare's two-year-old last year and he was OK but sadly he broke a leg and had to be put down. This is a good-moving horse and we'll kick on with him shortly. He won't be useless".

1279. UNNAMED ★★★
gr.c. *Clodovil – Genetta (Green Desert).*
March 23. Tenth foal. €35,000Y. Tattersalls Ireland. Jamie Osborne. Half-brother to the quite useful 6f (at 2 yrs) to 1m winner of 8 races Tiber Tiger (by Titus Livius), to the fair 1m and 11f winner Raybaan (by Flying Spur), the modest Irish 12f, 13f and hurdles winner Harcas (by Priolo) and a 2-y-o winner in the Czech Republic by No Excuse Needed. The dam is a placed half-sister to 10 minor winners. The second dam, Gatchina (by Habitat), won twice at 3 yrs and is a half-sister to Kalaglow.
"Quite a sharp, forward colt, there's quite a mixture in the pedigree because the family have won over all sorts of distances, but he should be running in May".

1280. UNNAMED ★★
b.c. *Johannesburg – Hit It Here Cafe (Grand Slam).*
March 6. First foal. 37,000Y. Tattersalls October 2. David Redvers. The dam was placed once in the USA and is a half-sister to 7 winners including the multiple Canadian stakes winner Strawberry Moon. The second dam, Strawberry's Charm (by Strawberry Road), a minor winner in the USA, is a half-sister to 5 winners.
"One for the second half of the season, he's a good mover and a nice, solid colt".

1281. UNNAMED ★★
b.c. *Arakan – Isticanna (Far North)*.
February 8. 28,000Y. Tattersalls October 2. Not sold. Half-brother to the Group 3 10f Sandown Classic Trial winner Chancellor (by Halling), so the useful 6f and 7f winner Purple Haze (by Spectrum), the fairly useful Italian listed 7.5f winner Whatcombe (by Alleged), the fair 5f winner Ragged Jack (by Cape Cross), the modest 1m (at 2 yrs) and 10f winner Seama (by Affirmed) and the 7f all-weather seller winner High Flown (by Lear Fan). The dam, a useful 2-y-o 5f and Italian 6f listed winner, is a half-sister to 6 winners including the dam of the US dual Grade 2 winner Uncharted Haven. The second dam, Guest Night (by Sir Ivor), a very useful 7f and 9f winner, is a half-sister to 4 winners.
"There's a mixture in the pedigree but he looks quite forward and strong. Probably not one for the first half of the season".

1282. UNNAMED ★★★
b.c. *Footstepsinthesand – Lady Wells (Sadler's Wells)*.
March 23. Third foal. €40,000Y. Goffs Million. David Redvers. Half-brother to the 10.5f winner Manshoor (by Linamix), the dam, a minor French 12f winner, is a half-sister to 8 winners including the Group 3 7f Prix du Calvados winner Shigeru Summit. The second dam, Riveryev (by Irish River), is a placed half-sister to 6 winners.
"He's more of a second half of the season two-year-old really, but he's a nice, solid type of horse and very good-looking".

1283. UNNAMED ★★★
b.br.f. *Gone West – Maugusta (Saint Ballado)*.
April 22. First foal. €39,000Y. Goffs Million. Not sold. The dam is an unraced half-sister to 4 winners including the Japanese stakes winner Fifty Oner. The second dam, Heraklia (by Irish River), is an unraced half-sister to 5 winners, including 2 listed winners abroad.
"She's quite sharp. I wouldn't have a lot of experience with Gone West fillies but she moves very well and she's got a bit of speed. I'll be trying to get her out by the end of May".

1284. UNNAMED ★★★★
b.c. *Azamour – Naazeq (Nashwan)*.
February 10. Ninth foal. €50,000Y. Goffs Million. David Redvers. Half-brother to the 7f, 1m and subsequent US Grade 1 placed stakes winner Tamweel, to the fair 9.5f all-weather winner Thunder Canyon (both by Gulch), the fairly useful 12f winner Mostarsil (by Kingmambo) and to the quite useful 7f winner Sharapova (by Elusive Quality). The dam, a quite useful 10.5f winner, is a full or half-sister to 9 winners including the very useful 10f winner Shaya. The second dam, Gharam (by Green Dancer), a very useful 2-y-o 6f winner, was third in the French 1,000 Guineas and is a half-sister to the US Grade 1 9f winner Talinum.
"A gorgeous horse. Of the ones with a lomger term future he'd probably be my pick. A very good-looking, good-moving horse but I wouldn't be in a rush with him. A high quality horse from a family that improves with age".

1285. UNNAMED ★★★
b.c. *Elusive City – Night Spirit (Night Shift)*.
April 21. Eighth foal. 25,000Y. Tattersalls October 2. David Redvers. Half-brother to the minor French 2-y-o winner Dukeside (by Bachelor Duke), to the quite useful 2-y-o 6f winner Kalhan Sands (by Okavango), the modest dual 6f winner Victoria Peek (by Cape Cross) and a 2-y-o winner in Italy by Spectrum. The dam won once over 6f at 3 yrs and is a half-sister to 5 winners. The second dam, Brentsville (by Arctic Tern), won once at 2 yrs and is a half-sister to 7 winners.
"He's grown a lot and I'm not as far forward with him as I'd like to be. I'll be kicking on with him as soon as I can. He's just getting stronger now and he's a very nice, good-moving horse. I'll give him a chance to start before Ascot because he looks as if he might be that type, but I may have to wait a bit longer".

1286. UNNAMED ★★★
b.f. *Acclamation – Rye (Charnwood Forest)*.
February 20. Second foal. €60,000Y. Goffs Million. Not sold. Sister to the fair 2008 2-y-o 5f winner River Rye (by Acclamation). The dam,

a fair 3-y-o 1m all-weather winner, is a sister to the useful 2-y-o 6f and 7f winner Forwood and a half-sister to 3 winners. The second dam, Silver Hut (by Silver Hawk), a quite useful 2-y-o 1m winner at York, is a half-sister to 6 minor winners. *"She looks quite sharp and typical of Acclamation's two-year-old fillies, so she's definitely one for the first half of the season and she looks quite quick. I trained the mother and sold her to Amanda Skiffington who bred this filly".*

1287. UNNAMED ★★
b.f. Montjeu – Shaanara (by Darshaan).
January 17. €30,000Y. Goffs. Oaks Farm Stables. Half-sister to the modest 10f winner Fantastic Lass (by Fantastic Light). The dam, a quite useful 2-y-o 7f winner, is a half-sister to the smart Group 3 7f Gladness Stakes winner Cool Edge and to a listed-placed winner in Italy by Classic Secret. The second dam, Mochara (by Last Fandango), placed once over 5f at 2 yrs in Ireland, is a half-sister to 4 winners.
"She's not enormous and she's a good mover that looks to have a good brain on her for a Montjeu filly, but she won't be ready until later in the season".

1288. UNNAMED ★★★
ch.c. Eurosilver – Short Shadow (Out Of Place).
February 17. Second foal. 25,000Y. Tattersalls October 2. D Redvers. Half-brother to the quite useful 2008 2-y-o 6f winner Blown It (by More Than Ready). The dam, a stakes-placed winner of one race in the USA, is a half-sister to 4 winners. The second dam, Last Reflection (by Nostrum), a stakes-placed winner of 8 races in the USA, is a half-sister to 10 winners.
"The sire was a very good dirt and turf horse in America and we had the dam's two-year-old last year, Blown It. This lad is bigger and probably not as forward as Blown It but he's a lovely mover and he's one for the second half of the season. Probably a nice one".

JOHN OXX

1289. ALIWIYYA (IRE) ★★★
br.f. Anabaa – Aliya (Darshaan).
April 29. Half-sister to the quite useful 2008 Irish 2-y-o 1m winner Aliyfa (by Spinning World), to the Irish 9f winner Alisar (by Entrepreneur) and the Irish 12f winners Alandi (by Galileo) and Ayla (by Daylami). The dam, a dual 12f winner in Ireland, is a sister to the high-class Group 3 12f Lingfield Oaks Trial winner and disqualified Epsom Oaks winner Aliysa and a half-sister to several winners including the useful 2-y-o 7f winner and Group 2 Park Hill Stakes third Altiyna. The second dam, Alannya (by Relko), a smart 1m winner in France, is a half-sister to the dam of the French 2,000 Guineas winner Nishapour and the Rothmans International winner Nassipour. (H H Aga Khan).
"She's a nice filly and it's a good staying family but hopefully Anabaa will put a bit of speed and precocity in it. She's well-made and hopefully she'll run by mid-summer, she's not a backward type".

1290. BASS ROCK ★★★★★
b.c. Pivotal – Massarra (Danehill).
March 21. Third foal. 400,000Y. Tattersalls October 1. M H Goodbody. Half-brother to the unraced 2008 2-y-o Middle Persia (by Dalakhani) and to the quite useful 10f winner Tebee (by Selkirk). The dam, a useful listed 6f winner and second in the Group 2 Prix Robert Papin at 2 yrs, is a sister to one winner, closely related to the Group 1 6f Haydock Park Sprint Cup winner Invincible Spirit and a half-sister to 7 winners including the Group 3 winners Acts Of Grace and Sadian. The second dam, Rafha (by Kris), a very smart winner over 6f (at 2 yrs) and the Group 1 10.5f Prix de Diane, the Group 3 Lingfield Oaks Trial and the Group 3 May Hill Stakes, is a half-sister to 9 winners. (Mr T Barr).
"A nice horse that's had a good winter and he's ready to do some fast work. He looks the part and obviously with a pedigree like his you'd hope he had ability but he hasn't been tested yet. He's a lovely horse and we're likely to start him off at six furlongs in mid-summer".

1291. EBANOUR (IRE) ★★★★
ch.c. Indian Ridge – Ebadiyla (Sadler's Wells).
April 21. Half-brother to the quite useful 2008 7f and 1m placed 2-y-o Ebashan (by King's Best), to the useful 1m winner and Group 1 National Stakes third Eyshal (by Green Desert), the useful Irish 10f winner Ehsan (by Sinndar), the dual 12f and very smart hurdles winner Ebaziyan (by Daylami) and the quite useful 12f winner Ebalista (by Selkirk). The dam won the Group 1 Irish Oaks and the Group 1 Prix Royal-Oak and is a half-sister to the smart Group 1 7f Moyglare Stud Stakes winner Edabiya and the high-class Ascot Gold Cup winner Enzeli. The second dam, Ebaziya (by Darshaan), won from 7f (at 2 yrs) to 12f including three listed races and was third in the Group 2 12f Blandford Stakes. (H H Aga Khan).
"A lovely colt, he won't be precocious and is one for later in the year, but he's got a great temperament, he's a nice mover and I'd say he'd be a seven furlong horse. A lot of Indian Ridge horses like a bit of ease in the ground and so did the dam, so you'd expect this colt will be the same. He's a beautiful looking horse".

1292. HANAKIYYA (IRE) ★★★
b.f. Danehill Dancer – Handaza (Be My Guest).
January 24. Half-sister to the Irish Group 3 7.5f Concorde Stakes winner Hamairi (by Spectrum), to the Irish 5f (at 2 yrs) and 3-y-o listed 6f winner Hanabad (by Cadeaux Genereux), the quite useful Irish 12f winner Hadarama (by Sinndar) and the modest Irish 10f winner Hannda (by Dr Devious). The dam, a 1m winner at 3 yrs in Ireland, is out of Hazaradjat (by Darshaan), herself a half-sister to the Middle Park Stakes winner Hittite Glory. (H H Aga Khan).
"She's not as forward as she should be because of a few setbacks over the winter. Hopefully we'll be able to make up for lost time now and I see her being out in the second half of the year. It's a good family and it's very active at the moment".

1293. JULIE'S JET (IRE) ★★★★
b.f. Cape Cross – Julie Jalouse (Kris S).
April 4. Third foal. Half-sister to the 2008 7f placed 2-y-o Jesse James (by King's Best). The dam won a listed race in Ireland prior to winning four races in the USA including the Grade 2 Orchid Handicap and is a half-sister to 4 winners including the US Grade 2 winner Mariensky. The second dam, Julie La Rousse (by Lomond), won the Grade 3 Suwannee River Handicap and is half-sister to 3 winners. (Lady O'Reilly).
"She a lovely filly out of a good mare I trained for Lady O'Reilly, hopefully she'll be out in late June or July. She'll probably want seven furlongs".

1294. KALADENA (IRE) ★★★★
br.f. Daylami – Kalamba (Green Dancer).
April 29. Half-sister to the top-class Champion Stakes and Breeders Cup Turf winner Kalanisi (by Doyoun), to the high-class 1m listed winner and Group 1 St James's Palace Stakes second Kalaman (by Desert Prince), the useful 9f (at 2 yrs) and listed 10f and 12f winner Kaloura (by Sinndar), the fairly useful 12f winner Kalambari (by Kahyasi) and the minor French 9f winner Kalambara (by Bluebird). The dam was placed over 9f and 10f. The second dam, Kareena (by Riverman), a very useful winner of 4 races including the listed 1m Fern Hill Stakes, is a half-sister to the Group 3 Supreme Stakes winner Kerita. (H H Aga Khan).
"She's a very good-looking filly, a good goer and about to go into fast work. She's not really bred to be a two-year-old but she's very mature and goes ell, so I can see her being out from July onwards. She's particularly good-looking, well-proportioned and well-grown without being backward looking".

1295. KERALOUN (IRE) ★★★★★
b.c. Dalakhani – Kermiyana (Green Desert).
January 27. Half-brother to the useful Irish 12f winner Kerdem (by Rainbow Quest). The dam won the listed 1m Brownstown Stakes at 3 yrs in Ireland. The second dam, Keraka (by Storm Bird), won the Group 3 6f Anglesey Stakes at 2 yrs. (H H Aga Khan).
"This is a particularly nice horse, one of the nicest we have. He's good-looking, a great

mover and quite precocious even though he's by Dalakhani. I could see him being out by July or so and the dam was quite speedy. He quite mature and looks like a three-year-old now. A very nice horse".

1296. KEREDARI (IRE) ★★★
b.c. Oasis Dream – Kerataka (Doyoun).
February 21. Half-brother to the fairly useful 9f to 12f winner Kerashan (by Sinndar). The dam, an Irish 3-y-o 1m winner, is a half-sister to the 2-y-o Group 3 6f Anglesey Stakes winner Keraka. The second dam, Kerita (by Formidable), won the Group 3 7f Supreme Stakes at Goodwood. (H H Aga Khan).
"He was a little backward in the beginning but he's matured quickly and he's a good-looking horse about to enter some fast work. He looks nice".

1297. LINGAPOUR (USA) ★★★★
ch.c. Gulch – Lidakiya (Kahyasi).
March 6. Half-brother to the dual 7f (at 2 yrs) and Group 2 German 6f and Group 2 UAE 1m winner Linngari (by Indian Ridge), to the quite useful Irish 2-y-o 7f winner Lidana (by King's Best) and the modest 12f all-weather winner Lilakiva (by Dr Fong). The dam, a useful 10f and 12f winner, is a half-sister to the fairly useful 10f winner Lishtar and to the Irish 9f winner of 3 races and listed placed Livadiya. The second dam, Lilissa (by Doyoun), a French 9f and 10.5f winner, is a half-sister to 5 winners including the Group 3 12f Prix Minerve winner Linnga. (H H Aga Khan).
"A very nice, very good-looking horse about to start doing some fast work. He'll want fast ground and he's promising".

1298. SACRED ARIA ★★★
ch.f. Motivator – Portrait Of A Lady (Peintre Celebre)
February 3. First foal. Half-sister to the 2008 2-y-o 7f winner and Group 3 7f Killavullan Stakes second Vitruvian Man (by Montjeu). The dam was a fairly useful listed-placed 12f winner of 3 races. The second dam, Starlight Smile (Green Dancer), is an unraced half-sister to 4 winners including the dam of the Irish Derby winner Grey Swallow. (Plantation Stud).
"She's not a big filly and she's bit light, but she's very racey and I'm hoping she'll be out in July or so. Her half-brother Vitruvian Man is a nice colt that began his career in August as a two-year-old so she should be out by that time too".

1299. SHAREEN (IRE) ★★★★
b.f. Bahri – Sharesha (Ashkalani).
February 28. Half-sister to the useful 6f (at 2 yrs) and 7f winner and listed-placed Sharleez (by Marju). The dam was a fairly useful Irish 10f winner out of Sharemata (by Doyoun). (H H Aga Khan).
"This is a particularly nice filly with a very fluent stride. She's quite strong and mature-looking and I'm hoping she'll be out in June. She's promising".

1300. TROAS (IRE) ★★★
ch.c. Dalakhani – Amathusia (Selkirk).
March 15. Second foal. €100,000Y. Goffs Million. BBA (Ire). The dam is an unraced half-sister to 9 winners including the Group 1 Gran Premio d'Italia winner Posidonas. The second dam, Tamassos (by Dance In Time), won at 3 yrs and is a half-sister to the Group 1 Juddmonte International winner Ile de Chypre. (Mr A Christodoulou).
"He might need a little bit of time but he's well put together, a nice colt and a good mover. One for later in the year but hopefully we'll see what he's made of at two".

1301. UNNAMED ★★★★
b.f. Sadler's Wells – Asmara (Lear Fan).
March 2. Closely related to the Group 1 St James's Palace Stakes and Group 1 Irish Champion Stakes winner Azamour (by Night Shift) and to the 3-y-o 7f winner Arawan (by Entrepreneur), and half-sister to the 2008 2-y-o Group 2 7f Futurity Stakes winner and Greoup 1 National Stakes third Arazan (by Anabaa), to the fairly useful Irish 7f winner Ardistan (by Selkirk), the Irish 2-y-o 7f winners Ahsanabad and Surveyor (both by Muhtarram), the Irish 2-y-o dual 7f winner Arameen (by Halling) and the fair

Irish 14f and hurdles winner Ardalan (by Sinndar). The dam, a useful winner in Ireland at up to 10f, is a half-sister to the high-class Prix Ganay and Prix d'Harcourt winner Astarabad. The second dam, Anaza (by Darshaan), only ran at 2 yrs when she was a useful 1m winner in France. (H H Aga Khan).
"She's really good-looking, very racey and doesn't look backward, so she should be out in the second half of the season. She's more close-coupled and sharper-looking than her half-brother Azamour".

1302. UNNAMED ★★★★
b.br.f. Key Of Luck – Atalina (Linamix).
May 4. Fifth foal. €110,000Y. Goffs Million. Kevin Ross. Sister to the fairly useful 1m and 10f winner Australia Day and half-sister to the Group 3 Park Express Stakes winner Marjalina (by Marju). The dam won once over 12.5f in France and is a half-sister to 4 winners including the French listed winners Atabaa and Paix Blanche. The second dam, Alma Ata (by Rheffic), won a listed race in France and is a half-sister to 5 winners. (Mr C Jones).
"A nice, big, rangy filly, she's a very fluent mover and particularly nice looking. We like her and she'll be a second half of the year two-year-old".

1303. UNNAMED ★★★
b.f. Azamour – Balanka (Alzao).
March 2. Ninth foal. Half-sister to the fairly useful 2008 Irish 2-y-o 7f winner Baliyana (by Dalakhani), to the very smart Group 2 10f King Edward VII Stakes winner Balakheri (by Theatrical), the French 11f winner Balankiya (by Darshaan) and the fair 12f winners Belanak (by Sinndar) and Balakan (by Selkirk). The dam, a French listed winner and second in the Group 2 9.2f Prix de l'Opera, is a half-sister to several winners. The second dam, Banana Peel (by Green Dancer), won 2 races in the USA at 4 yrs and is a half-sister to 10 winners including the Group 3 Grand Prix de Vichy winner Bulington and the French listed winners Catman and Beaune (herself the dam of Bering). (H H Aga Khan).
"A sharp looking filly that goes well, she's about to start some fast work and I like the look of her. I wouldn't rule out her starting out over six furlongs despite her dam staying beyond a mile".

1304. UNNAMED ★★★
b.f. Alhaarth – Ebatana (Rainbow Quest).
March 6. Third foal. Half-sister to the fairly useful Irish 12f and hurdles winner Ebadiyan (by Darshaan). The dam, placed over 10f and 12f in Ireland, is a half-sister to 3 winners including the Hong Kong Grade 3 winner Eyshal. The second dam, Ebadilya (by Sadler's Wells), won the Group 1 Irish Oaks and the Group 1 Prix Royal-Oak and is a half-sister to the smart Group 1 7f Moyglare Stud Stakes winner Edabiya and the Ascot Gold Cup winner Enzeli. (H H Aga Khan).
"This is a nice filly and hopefully she'll be out in June, she's a fluent mover but she'll want a bit of a trip because there's plenty of stamina there".

1305. UNNAMED ★★★
b.f. Azamour – Elasouna (Rainbow Quest).
April 18. The dam, a 2-y-o 7f winner and listed placed over 12f, is a sister to the Group 1 7f Moyglare Stud Stakes winner Edabiya and a half-sister to the Irish Oaks and Prix Royal-Oak winner Ebadiyla and the Ascot Gold Cup winner Enzeli (by Kahyasi). The second dam, Wbaziya (by Darshaan), won from 7f (at 2 yrs) to 12f including three listed races and was third in the Group 2 12f Blandford Stakes.
"The dam was small and this filly is on the small side too. But she's a nice filly, very fluent and one for later in the year".

1306. UNNAMED ★★★★
gr.f. Daylami – Hazariya (Xaar).
March 4. The dam, winner of the Group 3 7f Athasi Stakes and a listed event over 7f, is a half-sister to the Group 3 Blue Wind Stakes winner Hazarista and a half-sister to numerous minor winners. The second dam, Hazaradjat (by Darshaan), won twice at 2 and 3 yrs and is a half-sister to 10 winners including the Group 1 Flying Childers Stakes winner Hittite Glory. (H H Aga Khan).

"Another very good-looking, quite mature filly. She's a nice filly and she'll be out in the second half of the year".

1307. UNNAMED ★★★★
ch.f. Medicean – Masakala
(Cadeaux Genereux).
March 19. Half-sister to the fairly useful 2008 Irish 2-y-o 7f winner Mariyca (by Daylami) and to the fair 11f to 13f winner Maysa (by Marju). The dam, a minor Irish 7f winner, is a half-sister to the 1m Irish Cambridgeshire winner and subsequent Grade 1 Hong King Derby fourth Beverly Green (named Masani in Ireland). The second dam, Masawa (by Alzao), an Irish 3-y-o 1m winner, is a half-sister to the very useful Group 2 10f Gallinule Stakes winner Massyar and to the French 1m to 10f and subsequent Grade 3 1m Arcadia Stakes winner Madjaristan. (H H Aga Khan).
"She's a very good-looking filly and she moves well. She won't start fast work until sometime in May but she has a very good temperament and the dam breeds horses with ability. So when you see what a nice type she is you'd be disappointed if she had little ability".

1308. UNNAMED ★★★
b.f. Azamour – Sinnariya (Persian Bold).
April 28. The dam, placed once over 13f from 3 starts, is a half-sister to 5 winners including the top-class middle-distance colt Sinndar, winner of the Derby, the Irish Derby and the Prix de l'Arc de Triomphe. The second dam, Sinntara (by Lashkari), won 4 races in Ireland at up to 2m. (H H Aga Khan).
"She's racey, a smart sort of filly, a very good mover and very switched on and alert. The dam was a bit hot, so we'll have to see if she passes that trait on".

1309. UNNAMED ★★★
b.f. Kalanisi – Sinntara (Lashkari).
February 25. Half-sister to the top-class middle-distance colt Sinndar (by Grand Lodge), winner of the Derby, the Irish Derby and the Prix de l'Arc de Triomphe, to the fairly useful 1m winner (at 2 yrs) and listed-placed Simawa (by Anabaa), the modest 2m winner Sirinndi (by Shahrastani), the fair 20f Ascot Stakes and hurdles winner Sindapour (by Priolo) and the minor Irish 12f winner Sinndiya (by Pharly). The dam won 4 races in Ireland at up to 2m. The second dam, Sidama (by Top Ville), won over 12f in France and is a half-sister to the high-class middle-distance colt Sadjiyd. (H H Aga Khan).
"A very good-looking filly, she's a nice mover and a really good sort. One for the autumn".

1310. UNNAMED ★★★★
b.f. Azamour – Takarouna (Green Dancer).
April 2. Half-sister to the 2008 Irish 2-y-o 7f winner and listed 1m third Tanoura (by Dalakhani), to the Group 3 12f Meld Stakes winner Takarian (by Doyoun), subsequently winner of the Bay Meadows Derby in the USA, the smart Irish 10f and 12f winner Takali (by Kris), the Irish 2-y-o 6f winner Takariya (by Arazi) and the fair French 10.5f winner Takaniya (by Rainbow Quest). The dam, a very useful winner of the Group 2 12f Pretty Polly Stakes at the Curragh, is a sister to the smart Group 2 Dante Stakes winner Torjoun and a half-sister to the quite useful 2m Northumberland Plate winner Tamarpour (by Sir Ivor). The second dam, Tarsila (by High Top), won over 1m and 9f and is a sister to Top Ville. (H H Aga Khan).
"A particularly nice filly, well-grown and mature looking. I'd hope to get her out in June or July and she shows promise".

AMANDA PERRETT
1311. ATAKORA (IRE) ★★★
b.f. King's Best – Orinoco (Darshaan).
April 7. Half-sister to the fairly useful 10f and 12f winner Bandama (by Green Desert), to the quite useful dual 12f winner Intiquilla (by Galileo) and the fair 10f winner Riverscape (by Peintre Celebre). The dam was unplaced in one start and is a full or half-sister to 6 winners including the very smart 7f (at 2 yrs) and Group 1 12f Irish Oaks winner Winona. The second dam, My Potters (by Irish River), an Irish 3-y-o 1m handicap winner, is a half-sister to numerous winners including the champion US sprinter My Juliet (herself the dam of two Grade 1 winners)

and the good middle-distance colt Lyphard's Special. (Lady Clague).
"An athletic filly, sharper than the other members of the family we've had and she'll make a two-year-old. She does have the 'King's Best' temperament but we're getting the better of her!"

1312. BLUE SPARKLE (IRE) ★★★
b.f. *Acclamation – Westlife (Mind Games).*
April 12. Fourth foal. €85,000Y. Goffs Million. Gill Richardson. Half-sister to the 2-y-o 6f seller winner Pearo (by Captain Rio). The dam is an unplaced half-sister to the listed Roses Stakes winner Pepperoni. The second dam, Enchantica (by Timeless Times), is a placed half-sister to 7 winners. (Green Dot Partnership).
"A five/six furlong type two-year-old he'll be ready to roll in May".

1313. BRAMSHAW (USA) ★★★
b.br.c. *Langfuhr – Milagra (Maria's Mon).*
January 21. Third foal. $130,000Y. Keeneland September. James Delahooke. Half-brother to the Canadian stakes winner Bear Holiday (by Harlan's Holiday). The dam, a minor winner of 4 races at 4 yrs in the USA, is a half-sister to 3 winners including the Grade 1 placed Rhlana (herself dam of the US Grade 2 winner Behindatthebar). The second dam, Tatiani (by Fappiano), is an unplaced half-sister to 2 stakes-placed winners. (G Harwood).
"He's over 16.1 hands already but he has everything going for him and he looks a classy prospect. The dam's only had one runner and that was a listed winner and this a big, rangy horse that should hopefully do well later on this season and next year".

1314. GREEN EARTH (IRE) ★★★
b.c. *Cape Cross – Inchyre (Shirley Heights).*
April 15. Seventh foal. 45,000Y. Tattersalls October 1. Amanda Perrett. Closely related to Miss Tango Hotel (by Green Desert), placed second over 6f from 2 starts at 2 yrs in 2008 and half-brother to the very useful 12f listed winner Inchiri (by Sadler's Wells), the very useful 2-y-o 8.3f winner and Oaks fourth Inchberry (by Barathea), the useful 9.5f to 11f winner Whirly Bird (by Nashwan) and the fair 7f winner of 3 races Benedetto (by Fasliyev). The dam, a useful 1m winner and listed-placed over 12f, is a half-sister to 7 winners including the very smart and tough triple Group 3 7f winner Inchinor. The second dam, Inchmurrin (by Lomond), a winner of 6 races including the Group 2 Child Stakes and second in the Group 1 Coronation Stakes, is a half-sister to 7 winners including the Mill Reef Stakes winner Welney. (Green Dot Partnership).
"A six furlong type two-year-old. It's a family we've had plenty of winners from and they're all tough, hardy, sound horses".

1315. GREEN ENERGY ★★
b.c. *Rainbow Quest – Carambola (Danehill).*
March 27. Sixth foal. 50,000Y. Tattersalls October 2. Amanda Perrett. Half-brother to the fairly useful 1m winner and listed-placed Lady Stardust (by Spinning World). The dam, a useful listed Leopardstown 1,000 Guineas Trial winner and second in the Group 3 1m Matron Stakes, is a sister to the useful 2-y-o 6f winner and South African Grade 1 second Toreador and a half-sister to 7 winners including the Irish 1,000 Guineas winner Matiya. The second dam, Purchasepaperchase (by Young Generation), a useful winner of three races including the listed 1m Atalanta Stakes, was second in the Group 1 Prix Saint-Alary. (Green Dot Partnership).
"He wants a bit of time and although the dam hasn't done too well so far with her foals, this colt looks a nice horse. Seven furlongs later in the year".

1316. HUFF AND PUFF ★★★
b.c. *Azamour – Coyote (Indian Ridge).*
March 2. Fifth foal. 70,000Y. Tattersalls October 1. Amanda Perrett. Half-brother to the useful 2008 2-y-o 1m and subsequent Group 3 1m Park Express Stakes winner Oh Goodness Me (by Galileo) and to the useful 10f and listed 12f winner Eradicate (by Montjeu). The dam, a fairly useful 1m winner, was listed-placed and is a half-sister to one winner. The second dam, Caramba (by Belmez), a smart winner of the Group 2 1m Falmouth Stakes and the Group 2

10f Nassau Stakes, is a half-sister to 7 winners including the Moyglare Stud Stakes and Falmouth Stakes winner Lemon Souffle. (A D Spence).

"His sister won the Guineas trial last month at the Curragh. A nice horse and a big, scopey individual. The ones from this family aren't necessarily precocious but they all win and this is a nice horse for the future".

1317. LAGO INDIANO (IRE) ★★★★
b.c. Namid – My Potters (Irish River).
March. Half-brother to the very smart 7f (at 2 yrs) and Group 1 12f Irish Oaks winner Winona (by Alzao), to the Irish 6f (at 2 yrs) and Group 3 7f Killavullen Stakes third Carlisle Bay (by Darshaan), the fairly useful 11.5f winner Gold Quest (by Rainbow Quest), the Irish 1m winner Azarouak (by Danehill) and the minor Irish 1m (at 2 yrs) and 14f winner Western Seas (by Caerleon). The dam, an Irish 3-y-o 1m handicap winner, is a half-sister to numerous winners including the champion US sprinter My Juliet (herself the dam of two Grade 1 winners), the good middle-distance colt Lyphard's Special and the 2-y-o 6f Blue Seal Stakes winner New Trends. The second dam, My Bupers (by Bupers), was placed at 3 yrs. (Lady Clague).

"I think he's a lovely, good-bodied colt and we should see a fair bit of him this year. Hopefully he'll have a bit of class".

1318. LIFE AND SOUL (IRE) ★★★★
b.c. Azamour – Way For Life (Platini).
February 21. Fourth foal. 115,000Y. Tattersalls October 1. A Perrett. Half-brother to the useful Irish 1m (at 2 yrs) and 7f winner Mr Medici (by Medicean), to the Italian listed winner Viapervita (Spectrum) and the German listed-placed 2-y-o winner Winning Time (by Night Shift). The dam, a listed-placed winner at 2 and 3 in Germany, is a half-sister to 6 winners including the champion German 2-y-o filly Waitowin. The second dam, Waitotara (by Habitat), won at 4 yrs. (A D Spence).

"There is a pedigree update because Mr Medici was recently placed in the Hong Kong Derby. This is a really nice, forward-going colt that should be a seven furlong type this year. I just have an idea that he may be a Chesham Stakes horse".

1319. RED INTRIGUE (IRE) ★★
b.f. Selkirk – Red Affair (Generous).
March 12. Sister to the useful dual 6f (at 2 yrs) and 7f winner Red Liason and half-sister to the very useful Group 3 7f Brownstown Stakes winner Redstone Dancer (by Namid) and the quite useful Irish 1m winner So Well Red (by Sadler's Wells). The dam, an Irish listed 10f winner, is a half-sister to the smart 7.6f to 10f winner Brilliant Red and to the useful 12f to 14f winner and Group 3 2m Queens Vase third Kassab (by Caerleon). The second dam, Red Comes Up (by Blushing Groom), was placed 6 times in France and is a sister to Rainbow Quest. (Lady Clague).

"She's going to want a bit of time I think. She's nice but given the pedigree she'll want a trip".

1320. ROXY FLOWER (IRE) ★★
b.f. Rock Of Gibraltar – Dyna Flyer (Marquetry).
March 16. Second foal. 35,000Y. Tattersalls October 1. Gill Richardson. Half-sister to Bad Baron (by Lomitas), placed fourth twice over 7f at 2 yrs in 2008. The dam, a stakes-placed winner of 4 races at 2 and 3 yrs in the USA, is a half-sister to 5 winners including the Japanese £2 million earner Biko Pegasus. The second dam, Condessa (by Condorcet), won the Group 1 Yorkshire Oaks and the Group 3 Musidora Stakes and is a half-sister to 3 winners. (F Cotton & Mrs S Conway).

"A filly with a bit of size and scope, she's a little bit immature at the moment and she'll be a middle-distance type next year. But I hope we'll see her in seven furlongs races later this season.

1321. STREET ENTERTAINER (IRE) ★★
br.c. Danehill Dancer – Opera Ridge (Indian Ridge).
February 20. First foal. 65,000Y. Tattersalls October 2. Not sold. The dam was placed over 10f in France and is a half-sister to 7 winners including the French Group winners Stretarez

and Street Shaana. The second dam, Street Opera (by Sadler's Wells), a minor Irish 14f winner, is a half-sister to 10 winners including the very smart Group 1 Grand Prix de Paris winner Grape Tree Road, the smart Group 2 Geoffrey Freer Stakes winner Red Route and the smart Group 3 Queens Vase winner Windsor Castle. (G D P Materna).

"A first foal but he's a big, strapping, typical Danehill Dancer with good bone. He's nice but I haven't done much with him yet as he just needs a bit of time, although he is a February foal".

1322. TIGRESS HILL ★★★★
b.f. Tiger Hill – Inchberry (Barathea).
April 2. Third foal. Half-sister to the modest 14f winner Berry Baby (by Rainbow Quest). The dam, placed 7 times including when second in a listed event over 1m at 2 yrs and fourth in the Oaks, is a half-sister to the very useful 12f listed winner Inchiri. The second dam, Inchyre (by Shirley Heights), a useful 1m winner, is a half-sister to 7 winners including the very smart and tough triple Group 3 7f winner and sire Inchinor. (Woodcote Stud).

"A lovely filly – but a middle-distance filly for next year. She's leggy but shows plenty of ability considering her size".

1323. TROVARE (USA) ★★★★
b.c. Smart Strike – Abita
(Dynaformer).
May 18. $195,000Y. Keeneland September. Not sold. Half-brother to the fairly useful 2-y-o 6f winner Gone Fast and to the minor US 4-y-o winner Vixana (both by Gone West). The dam, a US 6f to 9f winner at 3 and 4 yrs, is a half-sister to the Group/Grade 3 winners Majuscule and Royal Cielo and the smart 10f to 12f winner Luhuk. The second dam, Royal Stance (by Dr Fager), is an unraced half-sister to the Yorkshire Oaks winner Awaasif. (J P Connolly).

"The dam's bred two from two and although this is a late May foal he's a very nice individual and it'll be worth keeping a eye out for him later in the year".

1324. VIVIANI (IRE) ★★★★
ch.c. Galileo – Bintalreef (Diesis).
April 24. Fifth foal. 300,000Y. Tattersalls October 1. Gill Richardson. The dam, a useful French 2-y-o 7f winner, is a half-sister to 5 winners including the US stakes winner and Grade 3 1m placed Solar Bound. The second dam, Solar Star (by Lear Fan), a fairly useful 2-y-o 6f winner, is a half-sister to 6 winners including the US triple Grade 3 winner Gold Land.

"A nice, neat colt, I would think we'll see him in six furlong races sometime in June. He's a well-bred horse and we have a lot to look forward to with him. I haven't done much with him yet, I don't think he's going to grow much more, he looks well and is just about to start some faster work".

1325. VOYSEY (IRE) ★★
b.c. Dalakhani – Gothic Dream (Nashwan).
April 22. Closely related to the listed 10f and listed 14f winner Pugin (by Darshaan) and half-brother to the quite useful 2008 2-y-o 1m winner Hurakan (by Daylami), the listed 12f winner Chartres (by Danehill), the quite useful 10f and 12f winner Nosferatu (by In The Wings), the fair Irish 9f winner Sogno Verde (by Green Desert), the modest 12f winner Pointed Arch (by Rock Of Gibraltar) and the Irish 2m winner Gothic Theme (by Zafonic). The dam won over 7f in Ireland at 2 yrs and was third in the Irish Oaks. The second dam, Dark Lomond (by Lomond), won the Irish St Leger and is a half-sister to numerous winners including the Blandford Stakes winner South Atlantic. (Lady Clague).

"It's a good, hardy, staying family and he looks like being the same, just having a couple of runs at the back-end of this year. We've had plenty of winners from this family and he is as good an individual as we've had from the mare".

1326. WARNING SONG (USA) ★★★
b.br.c. Successful Appeal – Tia Lea
(Songandaprayer).
February 14. First foal. $75,000Y. Keeneland September. J Delahooke. The dam is a placed

half-sister to 4 minor winners. The second dam, Valid Expression (by Valid Appeal), is an unplaced sister to a stakes winner and a half-sister to 8 winners. (Guy Harwood).

"He's one that Dad bought in the States and he's been catching our eye in recent weeks. There's plenty of speed in the family, I like him and he's tough and hardy. I can see him possibly being our first two-year-old runner".

1327. UNNAMED ★★★
b.c. Oasis Dream – Balmy (Zafonic).
April 28. Second living foal. Half-brother to the quite useful 2008 1m placed 2-y-o Coiled Spring (by Observatory). The dam, a fairly useful 1m winner, is a sister to winner in Greece and a half-sister to the very useful French 6f (at 2 yrs) and 1m listed winner Barricade and the useful 14f winner War Cabinet. The second dam, Balleta (by Lyphard), a quite useful 3-y-o 10f winner, also won 3 races in the USA, is a sister to the great 'Arc', 'King George' and 2,000 Guineas winner Dancing Brave and to Jolypha (winner of the Group 1 12f Prix Vermeille and Group 1 10.5f Prix de Diane). (Khalid Abdulla).

"A lovely horse that will just want a bit of time. He's had a few niggles such as sore shins and he's already 16 hands, but he'll be worth waiting for. He's a proper horse and Oasis Dream should add a touch of speed".

1328. UNNAMED ★★★
b.f. Aptitude – Private Line (Private Account).
April 19. Half-sister to the Group 3 10.5f Prix Fille de'Air winner Dance Dress (by Nureyev), to the useful 10f winner Conclude (by Distant View), the fairly useful 1m winner and listed-placed Discuss (by Danzig) and the fair 11f and hurdles winner Colophany (by Distant View). The dam, a useful 7f (at 2 yrs) and listed 1m winner, is a half-sister to French 2-y-o listed 1m Prix de Lieurey winner and Group 1 placed Most Precious and the very useful dual 7f winner High Summer. The second dam, Miss Summer (by Luthier), won the listed 1m Prix de Saint-Cyr and is a half-sister to the Group 2 Prix Hocquart winner Mot d'Or, the Group 1 Gran Premio de Milano winner Lydian, the Group 2 Ribblesdale Stakes winner Ballinderry (herself the dam of Sanglamore) and the French Two Thousand Guineas second Sharpman. (Khalid Abdulla).

"A scopey filly, she's a nice individual for later in the year. She's well-bred and although there haven't been many Aptitude's over here they are doing well on the turf in America. She has plenty of size and scope and is pleasing to the eye".

1329. UNNAMED ★★★
b.f. Aptitude – Proflare (Mr Prospector).
April 6. Half-sister to numerous winners including the US Grade 2 winners True Flare and Apple Of Kent (by Kris S) and the Group 3 Prix de la Porte Maillot winner War Zone (by Danzig), the French 2-y-o Group 3 7f Prix Thomas Bryon winner Set Alight (by Hennessy). The dam won twice and was listed-placed in France. (Khalid Abdulla).

"A sharper, smaller type than my other Aptitude filly, she'll be out in May over six furlongs".

1330. UNNAMED ★★★
b.c. Dansili – Sound Asleep (Woodman).
April 19. Third foal. Half-brother to the modest 12f winner Warming Up (by Kalanisi). The dam is an unraced half-sister to one winner in the USA. The second dam, Sleep Easy (by Seattle Slew), won the Grade 1 Hollywood Oaks and the Grade 2 Railbird Stakes and is a half-sister to 5 winners including the US dual Grade 1 winner Aptitude. (Khalid Abdulla).

"A bonny little colt, he's not over-big and you can't go far wrong with a Dansili. I should think he'll be running over six/seven furlongs from July time onwards".

1331. UNNAMED ★★★
b.f. Red Ransom – Tamalain (Royal Academy).
February 20. First foal. The dam, a modest 1m and 10f placed maiden, is a sister to the Group 3 6f Coventry Stakes winner CD Europe and a half-sister to 3 winners including the French 1m winner and listed Prix Yacowlef second Cedar Sea. The second dam, Woodland Orchid (by Woodman), is an unplaced half-sister to the Group 3 Derrinstown Stud Derby Trial winner

Truth Or Dare, the UAE Group3 winner D'Anjou and the listed winner Sandstone. (Mr and Mrs R Scott).
"This is the first foal of a mare we trained. A February foal, she's 15 hands and we'll be driving her towards the early season six furlong races. She's one of the first home-breds for her owners and as the mare has a colt foal by the sire it's important that we get a win out of this filly".

1332. UNNAMED ★★★★
b.f. Zamindar – Tentative (Distant View).
February 26. The dam, a fairly useful 2-y-o triple 5f winner, was listed-placed and is a half-sister to numerous winners including the Grade 1 Eddie Read handicap winner Monzante and the useful French 2-y-o 7f winner Alpha Plus. The second dam, Danzante (by Danzig)a sprint winner in France and in the USA, is a half-sister to the Breeders Cup Classic winner Skywalker and to the French Group 3 7f winner Nidd. (Khalid Abdulla).
"A sharp filly, she's working well now and we'll have her out in May. She's a good-size but there's plenty of speed in the family – the dam was a five furlong performer herself".

JON PORTMAN
1333. BATHWICK ZARA ★★
b.f. Xaar – Anapola (Polish Precedent).
March 18. 800Y. Tattersalls October 4. J Portman. Half-sister to the fair 2008 2-y-o 7f winner Blazing Buck (by Fraam). The dam won twice at 3 yrs in Germany and is a half-sister to 8 winners. The second dam, Angelica (by Gay Mecene), a German listed winner, is half-sister to the German Group 1 winner Ataxerxes. (J Portman).
"Quite small but compact and a very good mover, she'll probably come into her own over seven furlongs with a bit of give in the ground. For just 800 Guineas she looks very good value".
TRAINER'S BARGAIN BUY

1334. CUCKOO ROCK (IRE) ★★★
b.c. Refuse To Bend – Ringmoor Down (Pivotal).
April 1. First foal. The dam won 6 races including over 6f at 2 yrs, the Group 3 5f King George Stakes and the Group 3 Flying Five and is a half-sister to 6 winners. The second dam, Floppie (by Law Society), a minor 3-y-o winner in France, is a sister to a listed-placed winner there and a half-sister to 4 winners including the French listed winner Love Shack. (Prof C D Green).
"He needs a bit of time but he might be quite nice. We're not moving along with him at the moment, he's quite small, stocky and strong. I would have thought he'd be out by the end of July over seven furlongs".

1335. EXISTENTIALIST ★★★
b.f. Exceed And Excel – Owdbetts (High Estate).
April 27. Seventh foal. 19,000Y. Doncaster St Leger. Paul Moulton. Half-sister to the smart Group 3 5.2f and 6f Wokingham Handicap winner Ratio (by Pivotal), to the fairly useful 7f (at 2 yrs) and 6f winner Heywood (by Tobougg), the fair 2-y-o 6f winner Rochdale (by Bertolini) and the fair 2-y-o 6f winner Alice Blackthorn (by Forzando). The dam, a fair 7f to 10.2f winner of 4 races, is a half-sister to 3 minor winners. The second dam, Nora Yo Ya (by Ahonoora), ran once unplaced at 2 yrs and is a half-sister to 3 winners. (P Moulton).
"She might be running by the end of April, there's not much of her but she's a beautiful mover and is well put together. I like her, she's a nice filly and she looks like a two-year-old".

1336. HOUDA ★★★
ch.f. Trans Island – Islandagore (Indian Ridge).
February 28. Fourth foal. 15,000Y. Doncaster St Leger. J Portman. Half-sister to the quite useful 2008 2-y-o 7f winner (on only start) Island Sunset (by Trans Island), to the quite useful Irish 2-y-o 7f winner Tintean (by Clodovil), the fair 7f (at 2 yrs) and 1m winner Right Ted and to the fair 2-y-o 6f winner Toby's Dream (both by Mujadil). The dam, a 3-y-o 7f winner in Ireland, was second in a listed event over 9f on her only other start and is a half-sister to the 2-y-o listed 6f winner Lady Of Kildare. The second dam, Dancing Sunset (by Red Sunset), a smart winner of the Group 3 10f Royal Whip Stakes, is a full or half-sister to 5 winners

including the US stakes winner Truly. (Berkeley Racing).

"She's a very nice, very strong, solid filly. She had a little setback in February which means she won't run now until July but actually that may have done her a favour because until then I was getting quite excited about her. The family aren't very early two-year-olds anyway. I think a lot of her but when she comes back I just hope she doesn't have further problems".

1337. OAK LEAVES ★★★
b.f. Mark Of Esteem – Exotic Forest (Dominion).
March 21. Eleventh foal. Half-sister to the fairly useful 2-y-o 5f and 6f winner Mesmerize Me (by Mind Games), to the fairly useful 5f (at 2 yrs) to 1m winner of 5 races Threezedzz, the modest all-weather 5f and 6f winner Zoena (both by Emarati), the fair 2-y-o 6f all-weather winner Blue Charm (by Averti), the fair 1m winner Smoothly Does It (by Efisio) and a winner over hurdles by Tragic Role. The dam, a modest 3-y-o 1m winner, is a half-sister to 5 winners including the listed October Stakes winner Toffee Nosed. The second dam, Ever Welcome (by Be My Guest), won over 10f at 4 yrs and is a half-sister to 5 winners including the Group 3 1m Matron Stakes winner Chanzi. (The Hon. Mrs R Pease).

"She hasn't been with us long and she's a big filly, very strong and not an early type at all. It wouldn't surprise me if she showed something over six furlongs at the back-end".

1338. SPANISH ACCLAIM ★★★
b.c. Acclamation – Spanish Gold (Vettori).
April 7. Second foal. 90,000Y. Doncaster St Leger. J Portman. Half-brother to the fairly useful triple 6f winner (including at 2 yrs) Spanish Bounty (by Bahamian Bounty). The dam, an 8.5f winner, is a half-sister to 4 winners including the useful 1m Victoria Cup winner Bold King and the Group 2 Railway Stakes second Spanish Ace. The second dam, Spanish Heart (by King Of Spain), a quite useful winner of 4 races over 7f and 1m, is a half-sister to 7 winners. (The Farleigh Court Racing Partnership).

"He'll start his career in April and he has plenty of ability but also plenty of attitude. He's a very tricky ride at home and if he behaves badly on his debut he'll probably be gelded".

1339. UNNAMED ★★★
ch.f. Intikhab – Dawn Chorus (Mukaddamah).
April 6. Seventh foal. 6,000Y. Tattersalls October 2. J Portman. Half-sister to the useful Irish 7f winner and listed-placed Dangle (by Desert Style), to the Irish 7f (at 2 yrs) to 10f and subsequent Hong Kong stakes winner Solid Approach (by Definite Article), the quite useful Irish 5f winner Divert (by Averti), the quite useful Irish 7f winner Devious Diva (by Dr Devious) and the quite useful 2-y-o dual 6f winner La Campanella (by Tagula). The dam is an unraced half-sister to 5 winners including Barrier Reef, a winner of 8 races and second in the Group 3 Beresford Stakes. The second dam, Singing Millie (by Millfontaine), won twice in Ireland at 3 yrs and is a half-sister to 7 winners. (J Portman).

"She's quite narrow and there's not a lot of her but she's growing all the time, I like her and I think she could be out in late June. We'll start her at six but I can see her getting a mile in time".

KEVIN PRENDERGAST
1340. ALSALWA (IRE) ★★★★
b.f. Nayef – Ros The Boss (Danehill).
January 27. Third foal. Deauville August. €400,000Y. Shadwell France. Half-sister to the 2008 2-y-o winner Kate The Great (by Xaar). The dam, a quite useful 7f and 1m winner, is a half-sister to 3 winners including the Irish 2-y-o 1m and listed 9f winner Yehudi. The second dam, Bella Vitessa (by Thatching), is an unplaced half-sister to 6 winners including the German Group 1 12f Aral-Pokal winner Wind In Her Hair and the Grade 3 Vineland Handicap and Pretty Polly Stakes winner Capo di Monte. (Hamdan Al Maktoum).

"She's a filly we like a lot and she'll be racing before the end of May. She's compact, has plenty of quality and will probably start off at six fiurlongs but she might well stay a mile by the end of the year".

1341. ALSHAHBAA (IRE) ★★★
b.f. Alhaarth – Adaala (Sahm).
February 11. The dam, an Irish 7f (at 2 yrs) and listed 9f winner, is a half-sister to a winner in Denmark. The second dam, Alshoowg (by Riverman), is an unraced half-sister to 4 winners. (Hamdan Al-Maktoum).
"She's a bit backward but we like her. She's one for later in the year over seven furlongs".

1342. BRAZILIAN BEAUTY ★★★
b.f. Galileo – Braziliz (Kingmambo).
April 14. Sister to the very useful 2-y-o 7.5f winner and Group 3 7f second Brazilian Star, closely related to the Irish 3-y-o 6f winner Brazilian Sun (by Barathea) and half-sister to the quite useful 2008 2-y-o 5f and 7f winner Brazilian Spirit (by Invincible Spirit) and the 2-y-o Group 3 6f Swordlestown Stud Sprint Stakes winner Brazilian Bride (by Pivotal). The dam is an unplaced half-sister to the 2-y-o winner Or Vision (dam of the Irish 2,000 Guineas winner Saffron Walden, the Grade 1 E P Taylor Stakes winner Insight and the Group 1 7f Prix de la Foret winner Dolphin Street). The second dam, Luv Luvin' (by Raise a Native), won 2 races in the USA. (Lady O'Reilly).
"She's at home having a break but she'll be back in soon. One for September or October, so she won't be as early as her dam was as a two-year-old. She's not over big, but she's a nice, quality filly".

1343. CAPTAINOFTHEFLEET (IRE) ★★★★
ch.c. Refuse To Bend – Darabaka (Doyoun).
April 19. Tenth foal. €50,000Y. Goffs Million. Frank Barry. Half-brother to the Group 3 2m 2f Doncaster Cup winner Far Cry (by Pharly), to the minor Irish 1m 5f winner Sassenach (by Night Shift and herself the dam of 2 listed winners), the minor Irish 12f winner Misskinta (by Desert Sun) and the minor French 3-y-o winner Dariyba (by Kahyasi). The dam is an unraced half-sister to 6 winners including the Group 3 Prix Minerve winner Daralinsha (herself the dam of numerous winners) and the listed winner Darata (dam of the French Oaks winner Daryaba). The second dam, Darazina (by Labus), won once in France. (J Foley).
"A very, very nice horse. He goes really well and he has great presence. A big colt, seven furlongs will suit him to start with and you'd like him a lot".

1344. COASTAL WELLS (IRE) ★★★★
b.c. Sadler's Wells – Darling (Darshaan).
March 17. Fourth foal. €130,000Y. Goffs Million. Frank Barry. Half-brother to Tony's Treasure (by Sakhee), unplaced in one start at 2 yrs in Ireland in 2008. The dam is an unraced half-sister to 3 winners including the Group 3 winner Shemozzle. The second dam, Reactress (by Sharpen Up), a US 2-y-o stakes winner, is a half-sister to 6 winners. (Iona Equine Syndicate).
"He's not a big horse, but he's a quality individual that goes well. He looks a real Sadler's Wells and he'll come to hand over seven furlongs around Galway time".

1345. CRYSTAL GAL (IRE) ★★★★
b.f. Galileo – Park Crystal (Danehill).
April 25. Fourth foal. €70,000Y. Goffs Million. Frank Barry. Closely related to the unraced 2008 2-y-o Crimson Sky (by Montjeu). The dam is an unraced half-sister to 3 winners including the French 2-y-o 1m winner and Epsom Derby second Walk In The Park. The second dam, Classic Park (by Robellino), won 3 races including the Irish 1,000 Guineas and is a half-sister to 10 winners including the US Grade 2 winner Rumpipumpy. (P O'Grady).
"One for six furlongs to start with before we step her up to seven, she needs a bit of time but we like her a lot".

1346. DANCE HALL GIRL (IRE) ★★
b.f. Dansili – Dawn Raid (Docksider).
January 23. The dam, a quite useful Irish 3-y-o 7f winner, is a half-sister to the French and Irish 2,000 Guineas and Richmond Stakes winner Bachir, to the smart 7f (at 2 yrs) to 10f and hurdles winner Albuhera and the useful 2-y-o listed 7f winner Elliots World. The second dam, Morning Welcome (by Be My Guest), placed once over 12f at 3 yrs in Ireland, is a half-sister to 9 winners including the Irish listed Debutante

Stakes and subsequent US Grade 3 winner Down Again and to the dam of the Irish and French 2,000 Guineas winner Bachir. (Lady O'Reilly).
"She's was a January foal but she's much more of a three-year old type and won't be seen out until the back-end this season"

1347. EJTEYAAZ ★★
b.c. Red Ransom – Camaret (Danehill).
February 16. 42,000foal. Tattersalls December. Shadwell Estate Co. Half-brother to the useful dual 1m winner (including at 2 yrs) and listed placed La Conquistadora (by Pivotal). The dam, a fairly useful 7f winner, is a sister to the useful Irish 6f (at 2 yrs) and 7f winner Darwin and a half-sister to the modest 2-y-o 7f all-weather winner Tiger Dawn (by Anabaa) and the modest 10.2f winner Crozon (by Peintre Celebre). The second dam, Armorique (by Top Ville), a minor winner and listed placed at 3 yrs in France, is a half-sister to 8 winners including the French Group winners Modhish, Russian Snows and Truly Special. (Hamdan Al Maktoum).
"A big horse, he'll want seven furlongs, he's nice and we know the family well".

1348. FAMOUS WARRIOR (IRE) ★★★
b.c. Alhaarth – Oriental Fashion (Marju).
April 15. Brother to the very useful 2-y-o 6f and 7f winner Oriental Warrior and half-brother to the useful 7f and UAE 1m winner Green Coast, to the fairly useful 7f and 1m winner Desert Chief (both by Green Desert) and the Irish 2-y-o 7f winner Oriental Melody (by Sakhee). The dam won 3 races including the Group 2 1m Premio Ribot and is a half-sister to 3 winners including the US Grade 2 winner Makderah. The second dam, Wijdan (by Riverman), a useful 1m and 10.4f winner, is a sister to the 7f (at 2 yrs) and listed 1m winner Sarayir and a half-sister to Nashwan, Nayef and Unfuwain. (Hadi Al Tajir).
"I like him a lot, we haven't had him long but he's a good goer and a good galloper. I expect he'll want seven furlongs from mid-summer onwards".

1349. FARANDOONEY (IRE) ★★
b.g. Sahm – Sarina's Princess (Captain Bodgit).
January 28. First foal. €80,000Y. Tattersalls Ireland. Frank Barry. The dam, placed once at 3 yrs in the USA, is a half-sister to one minor winner. The second dam, Thistle Rose (by Artichoke), is an unraced half-sister to 10 winners. (Mr N Ormiston).
"A nice, big, seven furlong type horse and we've had a bit of luck with the sire".

1350. GIPSY ROSE (IRE) ★★★
b.f. Noverre – Lumber Jill (Woodman).
March 4. Fourth foal. €25,000Y. Tattersalls Ireland. Frank Barry. The dam won 2 races over 11f and 12f and is a half-sister to one winner. The second dam, Bineyah (by Sadler's Wells), won once at 3 yrs, was second in the Group 1 Yorkshire Oaks and is a sister to the Group 2 Royal Lodge Stakes winner Desert Secret.
"A nice filly, she'll make a two-year-old over seven furlongs and she goes well". TRAINER'S BARGAIN BUY

1351. GREEN ART ★★★
b.c. Dubai Destination – Seamstress (Barathea).
January 15. Fourth foal. Half-brother to the very useful 2-y-o listed 5f Windsor Castle Stakes and 5.2f Weatherbys Super Sprint winner Elhamri (by Noverre). The dam, a fair 2-y-o 7f winner, subsequently won over 1m in the USA and is a sister to 2 winners including the useful 2-y-o Group 3 7f C L Weld Park Stakes winner Rag Top and a half-sister to 4 winners including the fairly useful 7.6f and subsequent US 1m winner Red Top and the fairly useful 2-y-o dual 5f winner Lady Sarka. The second dam, Petite Epaulette (by Night Shift), a fair 5f winner at 2 yrs, is a full or half-sister to 3 winners. (Mr N Ormiston).
"A very nice horse and we like him. He'll want six furlongs to start with".

1352. HEDAAYA (IRE) ★★
ch.f. Indian Ridge – Nausicaa (Diesis).
March 9. Fourth foal. €210,000Y. Goffs Million. Shadwell Estate Co. Half-sister to the 2008 8.5f placed 2-y-o Heading East (by Dubai

Destination), to the fair 6f (at 2 yrs) and 1m winner Naughty Frida (by Royal Applause) and the quite useful 6f (at 2 yrs) and 7f winner Kafuu (by Danehill Dancer). The dam won 3 races at 2 and 3 yrs in France and the USA over 7f and 1m, was third in the Grade 3 Miesque Stakes and is a half-sister to 3 winners. The second dam, Blushing All Over (by Blushing Groom), won 6 races in France and the USA including a listed event and is a half-sister to 8 winners including the good broodmare Come On Rosi. (Hamdan Al Maktoum).
"She's going to take some time and we'll have to wait until the back-end with her".

1353. JADE JEWEL (IRE) ★★★
b.f. *Invincible Spirit – Jakarta Jade*
(Royal Abjar).
February 25. First foal. Half-sister to the quite useful 2009 Irish 3-y-o 1m winner Jakarta Jazz (by Marju). The dam, a useful 1m to 12f winner at 2 and 3 yrs, was listed-placed and is a half-sister to one winner. The second dam, Desert Frolic (Persian Bold), a fairly useful 11f to 13f winner, is a half-sister to 3 winners including the Group 2 12f King Edward VII Stakes winner Storming Home. (Lady O'Reilly).
"A nice filly, we'll start her off at six furlongs and move up from there. I trained the dam and she stayed twelve furlongs but Invincible Spirit will inject some speed into the pedigree. This is a grand, big filly so she won't early".

1354. JAMAAYEL (IRE) ★★★
b.f. *Shamardal – Walayef (Danzig).*
April 6. Third foal. Half-sister to the quite useful Irish 2-y-o 7f winner Reyaada (by Daylami). The dam, a listed 6f (at 2 yrs) and Group 3 7f Athasi Stakes winner, is a sister to the smart 2006 2-y-o 6f winner Haatef and to the Irish dual listed 6f winner Ulfah. The second dam, Sayedat Alhadh (by Mr Prospector), a US 7f winner, is a sister to the US Grade 2 7f winner Kayrawan and a half-sister to the useful winners Amaniy, Elsaamri and Mathkurh. (Hamdan Al Maktoum).
"She's very muscular and looks more of a sprinter than a stayer and she'll make a nice two-year-old later on".

1355. KILLEETER (IRE) ★★
ch.f. *Kheleyf – Moet (Mac's Imp).*
March 27. €25,000Y. Tattersalls Ireland. Frank Barry. Half-sister to the quite useful Irish 2-y-o 1m winner and listed-placed Dick Morris (by Kalanisi) and to the modest 12f to 2m winner of 10 races Champagne Shadow (by Kahyasi). The dam, a modest dual 3-y-o 6f winner, is a half-sister to 4 minor winners here and abroad. The second dam, Comfrey Glen (by Glenstal), is a placed half-sister to the Group 2 Premio Ribot winner Patriach. (Mr N Ormiston).
"She had a bit of a setback but when we get her racing she'll be one for five or six furlongs and she's a nice type".

1356. KING LEDLEY (USA) ★★★★
b.br.c. *Stormin Fever – Mt Kobla*
(Mt Livermore).
January 29. Second foal. €45,000Y. Goffs Million. Frank Barry. The dam won 2 minor races at 3 yrs in the USA. The second dam, Kobla (by Strawberry Road), is an unplaced sister to the US triple Grade 1 winner Ajina. (P O'Grady).
"A debut winner over 5f at the Curragh in March, he'll probably go for the five furlongs Marble Hill Stakes but he'll be better over six furlongs and hopefully he'll get to Royal Ascot".

1357. KINGSFORT ★★
b.br.c. *War Chant – Princess Kris (Kris).*
March 20. Eighth foal. €36,000Y. Goffs Sportsman's. Frank Barry. Half-brother to the US Grade 1 11f winner Prince Arch (by Arch) and half-sister to a minor winner in the USA. The dam, a quite useful 3-y-o 1m winner, is half-sister to 8 winners including the Group 3 May Hill Stakes winner Intimate Guest. The second dam, As You Desire Me (by Kalamoun), won 2 listed events in France over 7.5f and 1m and is a half-sister to 7 winners including the Group 2 King Edward VII Stakes winner Classic Example. (Mr N Ormiston).
"A big horse that'll want seven furlongs to a mile and we like him a lot".

1358. MIDNIGHT MOVER (IRE) ★★★
ch.f. *Bahamian Bounty – Promenade (Primo Dominie).*
March 24. The dam, a quite useful 2-y-o triple 5f winner, is a half-sister to the fairly useful 2-y-o dual 5f winner and Group 3 5f Queen Mary Stakes third Sharplaw Star and to the fairly useful Irish 2-y-o 5f winner and listed placed Sparkling Outlook. The second dam, Hamsah (by Green Desert), a quite useful 2-y-o dual 5f winner, was listed-placed and is a half-sister to the Irish 2,000 Guineas winner Wassl and to the dam of the Queen Mary Stakes winner On Tiptoes. (J McGrath).
"A nice filly, she's sharp. She did have a bit of of muscular trouble but she's coming on now and it's a quick family".

1359. MONTECCHIO (IRE) ★★★
gr.c. *Acclamation – Fritta Mista (Linamix).*
April 12. Fourth foal. 56,000Y. Doncaster St Leger. K Prendergast. Half-brother to the fairly useful 2-yo 6f and 7f winner and Group 2 May Hill Stakes third Sans Reward (by Barathea). The dam is a placed half-sister to one minor winner. The second dam, Sea Quest (by Rainbow Quest), is an unplaced half-sister to 9 winners including the Group 1 Yorkshire Oaks winner Hellenic (herself the dam of the Group 1 winners Islington, Greek Dance and Mountain High). (Mr J McGrath).
"Not a big horse but he's a nice two-year-old type and he'll probably run at Leopardstown in mid-April. He'd want seven furlongs now".

1360. MUJAAZEF ★★★
b.c. *Dubawi – Khubza (Green Desert).*
March 4. Tenth foal. 180,000Y. Tattersalls October 1. Shadwell Estate Co. Half-brother to Welsh Anthem (by Singspiel), placed fourth over 1m on her only start at 2 yrs in 2008, to the Group 2 1m Prix du Rond-Point and Group 3 8.5f Diomed Stakes winner Trans Island, the Italian Group 3 winner Welsh Diva, the useful 2-y-o 7f winner Nothing Daunted (all by Selkirk), the quite useful 2-y-o 6f winner Bread Of Heaven (by Machiavellian) and the fair 7f winner Welsh Cake (by Fantastic Light). The dam, a quite useful 3-y-o 7f winner, is a half-sister to 7 winners including the Group 2 winners Barrow Creek and Last Resort and the listed winners Arctic Char and Heard A Whisper. The second dam, Breadcrumb (by Final Straw), a very useful winner of 3 races at 3 yrs over 6f and 7f, is a half-sister to 4 winners including the high-class sprinter College Chapel. (Hamdan Al Maktoum).
"A nice horse, but he was late coming in. He rides well and does everything nicely and I'd say he'd want seven furlongs. He's a good type of horse".

1361. MUNAWEER (IRE) ★★
ch.c. *Mr Greeley – Tap Dance (Pleasant Tap).*
February 3. Fourth foal. $300,000Y. Keeneland September. Shadwell Estate Co. The dam won 5 races in the USA including the Grade 2 Bonnie Miss Stakes and is a full or half-sister to 5 winners. The second dam, Lyrical Prayer (by The Minstrel), is an unraced half-sister to 8 winners. (Hamdan Al Maktoum).
"He hasn't arrived from Dubai yet, but I believe he's a very nice horse".

1362. MUQALAD (IRE) ★★
b.c. *Indian Ridge – Tutu Much (Sadler's Wells).*
March 31. First foal. €300,000Y. Goffs Million. Shadwell Estate Co. The dam, a minor 12f winner on her only start, is a sister to French Ballerina (a winner of four listed events in Ireland from 1m to 2m) and a half-sister to 4 winners including the Group 1 Fillies Mile winner and Irish Oaks second Sunspangled. The second dam, Filia Ardross (by Ardross), a very smart filly, won three Group 2 events in Germany and the Group 3 10f Select Stakes at Goodwood. (Hamdan Al Maktoum).
"A nice horse, we like him a lot but it's a middle-distance family and he'll want seven furlongs to start off with".

1363. QUBOOL ★★★★
ch.f. *Trade Fair – Hidden Meaning (Cadeaux Genereux).*
April 18. Fifth foal. 80,000Y. Doncaster St Leger. F Barry. Half-sister to the very useful

2008 2-y-o listed 5f winner of 3 races and Group 2 placed Senor Mirasol (by Deportivo), to the French dual 10f winner Becher (by Vettori) and the modest 7f (at 2 yrs) to 1m seller winner Secret Meaning (by Mujahid). The dam is a placed half-sister to 5 winners including the dual Group 2 winner Niche and the dam of the Group 2 July Stakes winner Captain Hurricane. The second dam, Cubby Hole (by Town And Country), is a placed half-sister to 9 winners including Ascot Gold Cup winner Little Wolf. (Hamdan Al Maktoum).
"She goes well and she's a nice, big filly. I'd say she'd be suited by six furlongs and I like her a lot".

1364. SAAFIDAH (USA) ★★
b.br.f. Dynaformer – Jode (Danzig).
April 21. Thirteenth foal. $375,000Y. Keeneland September. Shadwell Estate Co. Half-sister to 6 winners including the Irish 1,000 Guineas winner Hula Angel (by Woodman), to the minor US stakes winner Schedule (by Brian's Time) and 2 winners in Japan by Seeking The Gold and Sunday Silence. The dam, a fair 2-y-o 6f winner here and in America at 3 yrs, is a sister to 2 winners and a half-sister to 9 winners including the Kentucky Derby winner Spend A Buck. The second dam, Belle de Jour (by Speak John), won over 6f in the USA. (Hamdan Al Maktoum).
"Yet to arrive from Dubai but I'm told she's a very nice filly".

1365. SAHAAYEB (IRE) ★★★
b.f. Indian Haven – Date Mate (Thorn Dance).
February 11. Fifth foal. 110,000Y. Tattersalls October 2. Shadwell Estate Co. Half-sister to the listed 2-y-o Woodcote Stakes winner and Group 1 Prix Jean-Luc Lagardere second Declaration Of War (by Okawango), to the quite useful 6f to 10f winner of 4 races Freak Occurrence (by Stravinsky) and a winner over hurdles by Idris. The dam, placed in the USA, is a half-sister to 4 winners including the dams of the Italian Group 1 winner Le Vie Dei Colori and the Queen Mary Stakes winner Shining Hour. The second dam, Doubling Time (by Timeless Moment), a smart winner at 3 yrs in France and second in the Group 3 10.5f Prix de Flore, is a full or half-sister to 8 winners including the Prix Ganay and Prix d'Ispahan winner Baillamont. (Hamdan Al Maktoum).
"She goes well and we like her. A nice filly, she'll be a six furlong type but probably needs some ease in the ground".

1366. SULOOK (IRE) ★★
b.c. Shinko Forest – Golden Dew (Montjeu).
February 24. First foal. 100,000Y. Tattersalls October 2. Shadwell Estate Co. The dam, placed fourth over 1m and 12f in Ireland, is a half-sister to 3 winners. The second dam, Golden Cat (by Storm Cat), won over 1m at 3 yrs in Ireland and was listed-placed and is a half-sister to 9 winners including the dual Irish listed winner Eurostorm. (Hamdan Al Maktoum).
"A big horse, he'll take some time. You would think he'd be early, being by Shinko Forest, but I don't get that impression".

1367. TERMAGANT (IRE) ★★★
b.f. Powerscourt – Rock Salt (Selkirk).
January 28. Second foal. €34,000Y. Goffs Sportsman's. Frank Barry. Half-sister to the fairly useful 2008 2-y-o 1m winner Splinter Cell (by Johannesburg). The dam, placed twice at 3 yrs in France, is a sister to the very smart Group 2 10f Prix Eugene Adam and Group 3 9f Prix de Guiche winner Kirkwall and a half-sister to 3 winners. The second dam, Kamkova (by Northern Dancer), a placed middle-distance stayer, is a half-sister to 10 winners including the top-class US middle-distance colt Vanlandingham.
"A very nice filly and I own her myself. This is a quality filly and she's from a good family. I'm looking for an owner if anyone is interested".

1368. VELVET FLICKER (IRE) ★★★
b.f. Fasliyev – Velvet Appeal (Petorius).
February 16. Eighth foal. €40,000Y. Goffs Million. Frank Barry. Sister to the fairly useful 1m winner of 5 races at 2 and 3 yrs The Illies and half-sister to the fairly useful 2-y-o 5f and 6f winner Macvel (by Mull Of Kintyre), the fairly

useful 6f (at 2 yrs) and 7f winner Nephetriti Way (by Docksider) and the useful triple 7f winner Craiova (by Turtle Island). The dam, a useful 1m winner at 3 yrs in Ireland, was fourth in the Group 1 Moyglare Stud Stakes, is a sister to the 2-y-o Group 3 Horris Hill Stakes and subsequent South African Group 1 winner Sapieha and a half-sister to 4 winners including the Group 2 15f Prix Hubert de Chaudenay winner Dajraan. The second dam, Sugarbird (by Star Appeal), won once at 2 yrs and is a half-sister to 6 winners.

"A very nice, quality filly and a two-year-old type with a good temperament. I'd be waiting for six furlongs with her".

1369. WRONG ANSWER (IRE) ★★★
gr.f. Verglas – Wrong Key
(Key Of Luck).
March 11. Half-sister to the quite useful Irish 2-y-o 1m winner Wrong Number (by King's Best). The dam, an Irish 7f (at 2 yrs) and listed 1m winner, was placed in the Group 2 1m Goffs International Stakes and the Group 2 10f Pretty Polly Stakes and is a sister to the 7f (at 2 yrs) and Group 3 10f and 12f winner Right Key. The second dam, Sarifa (by Kahyasi), is an unraced half-sister to one winner. (Lady O'Reilly).

"She's had a run and was only just touched off. She's not very big, but she's full of quality and she'll win all right".

SIR MARK PRESCOTT

This book is evidence of the fact that many owners, for whatever reason, don't name their horses until the summer is almost upon us. I enquired of Sir Mark how he managed to get a group of owners so disciplined that, almost without exception, every horse in the yard has it's name in print for all to see in the early March publication Horses In Training. He replied: "To have a horse in training with me, the owner has to agree to have his yearling named by Christmas Day". As someone who searches for hours trying to find out if horses have been named or not, I think that's an admirable arrangement!

1370. AGE OF REFINEMENT (IRE) ★★★★
ch.f. Pivotal – Dowager (Groom Dancer).
February 3. First foal. The dam, a useful 2-y-o 6f (listed) and 7f winner, is a half-sister to the useful 1m (at 2 yrs) and 10f winner Dower House and the fairly useful 6f (at 2 yrs) and 7f winner Zither. The second dam, Rose Noble (by Vaguely Noble), a modest 3-y-o 11.5f winner, is a half-sister to 6 winners including the champion two-year-old and high-class sire Grand Lodge, winner of the St James's Palace Stakes and the Dewhurst Stakes. (Plantation Stud).

"She'll make her debut in July and I would say she looks much more like a sprinter than a stayer. A smallish filly, she should make a two-year-old, probably over six furlongs".

1371. ALBACOCCA ★★
gr.f. With Approval – Ballymac Girl (Niniski).
January 26. Half-sister to the quite useful 2-y-o 5f winner Alizadora (by Zilzal) and the winning hurdler/chaser Coat Of Honour (by Mark Of Esteem). The dam, a modest winner of 5 races in Ireland at up to 15f, is a half-sister to 7 winners including the Nassau Stakes winner Last Second, the Irish Oaks third Arrikala and the Moyglare Stud Stakes third Alouette (herself dam of the Champion Stakes winner Alborada). The second dam, Alruccaba (by Crystal Palace), was a quite useful 2-y-o 6f winner. (Miss K Rausing).

"She's need plenty of time as she's a very tall and backward filly. Very much more a three-year-old type".

1372. ALLANNAH ABU ★★★★
b.f. Dubawi – Alexandrine (Nashwan).
April 23. Fifth foal. 180,000Y. Tattersalls October 1. BBA (Ire). Half-sister to the promising 2008 2-y-o 1m and 10f winner Alcalde (by Hernando), to the fairly useful 12f to 14f winner of 6 races and listed-placed Alambic (by Cozzene), the fair 2-y-o 1m all-weather winner Algarade (by Green Desert) and the modest 11f and 12f winner Astrodome (by Domedriver). The dam, a fair 10f to 13f winner of 4 races, is a half-sister to 7 winners including

the Nassau Stakes and Sun Chariot Stakes winner Last Second (dam of the French 2,000 Guineas winner Aussie Rules), the Doncaster Cup winner Alleluia (dam of the Prix Royal-Oak winner Allegretto) and the Moyglare Stud Stakes third Alouette (herself dam of the dual Champion Stakes winner Alborada and the triple German Group 1 winner Albanova) and to the placed dam of the Group 1 winners Yesterday and Quarter Moon. The second dam, Alruccaba (by Crystal Palace), a quite useful 2-y-o 6f winner, is out of a half-sister to the dams of Aliysa and Nishapour. (Ennistown Stud).
"A July type two-year-old, she's a very good-looking filly and isn't as big as the others from this dam. It's a family that stays, but on size she'd be the least likely to stay – and I've trained them all".

1373. ALMIRANTA ★★★★
gr.f. Galileo – Alvarita (Selkirk).
February 27. The dam was a French listed 10.5f winner. The second dam, Alborada (by Alzao), was a high-class winner of the Champion Stakes (twice), Nassau Stakes and Pretty Polly Stakes and is a sister to the smart listed 10.2f winner Albanova and a half-sister to the fairly useful dual middle-distance winner Alakananda. (Miss K Rausing).
"I should think she'll be the type for seven furlongs or a mile in August. She's a good-looking, medium-sized filly".

1374. ALTRUISTE ★★★★★
b.f. Montjeu – Alborada (Alzao).
January 24. Fourth foal. Half-sister to the French listed 10.5f winner Alvarita (by Selkirk). The dam was a high-class winner of the Champion Stakes (twice), Nassau Stakes and Pretty Polly Stakes and is a sister to the smart listed 10.2f winner Albanova and a half-sister to the fairly useful dual middle-distance winner Alakananda. The second dam, Alouette (by Darshaan), a useful 1m (at 2 yrs) and listed 12f winner, is a sister to the listed winner and Irish Oaks third Arrikala and to the placed Jude (dam of the Group 1 winners Yesterday and Quarter Moon) and a half-sister to the Nassau Stakes and Sun Chariot Stakes winner Last Second (dam of the French 2,000 Guineas winner Aussie Rules). (Miss K Rausing).
"We've trained them all and she looks like a July/August two-year-old. She's like her dam in that she's not over-big. The family tend to be better at three, but if they're good enough they win at two as well". This filly has a wonderful pedigree but as usual Sir Mark likes to keep us all guessing as to her ability! I'm going to stick my neck out and say she's a five star job! ST.

1375. ARCHITRAVE ★★★
ch.c. Hernando – White Palace (Shirley Heights).
May 10. Brother to the useful 7f (at 2 yrs) and listed 10f winner Portal and half-brother to the useful 1m and listed 10f winner Ice Palace (by Polar Falcon), the useful 7f winner of 4 races (including at 2 yrs) Palatial (by Green Desert) and the quite useful 11f winner Pediment (by Desert Prince). The dam was a quite useful 3-y-o 8.2f winner. The second dam, Blonde Prospect (by Mr Prospector), is an unplaced half-sister to the US listed winner Spectacular Bev and the dams of the US Grade 1 winner Link River and the Group 2 Queen's Vase winner Stelvio. (Cheveley Park Stud).
"An athletic, staying, mile-type two-year-old from August onwards. He looks like he'll want fast ground".

1376. ART MACHINE (USA) ★★★
ch.f. Sky Mesa – Grazia (Sharpo).
March 15. Fifth foal. Half-sister to the useful 7f and 1m winner of 6 races on the flat and one over hurdles Master Of Arts (by Swain) and to the dual Irish 7f winner (including at 2 yrs) Caprarola (by Rahy). The dam, a smart winner of the 6f Redcar Two-Year-Old Trophy and the listed 6f Hackwood Stakes, is closely related to the top-class middle-distance colt Halling. The second dam, Dance Machine (by Green Dancer), was a very useful winner of the listed 7f Sweet Solera Stakes at 2 yrs and a minor event over 10f at 3 yrs. (C Humphris).
"She grew a lot and was turned out but she's back in now. I trained the dam and she was fast

but this filly has much more size and scope. She's a half-sister to Master Of Arts who won six out of six for us last year and most of the family need soft ground".

1377. BARALAKA ★★★
ch.c. Barathea – Shakalaka Baby (Nashwan).
February 16. Third foal. 28,000Y. Tattersalls October 2. Sir M Prescott. The dam is an unraced half-sister to 9 winners including the dual Group 2 winner and sire Titus Livius. The second dam, Party Doll (by Be My Guest), a very useful winner of 4 races in France including 3 listed events from 5f to 1m, was Group 3 placed twice and is a half-sister to 10 winners.
"He was backward and turned out but he's back in training now. An August type two-year-old and likely to stay well".

1378. CAPTAIN'S PARADISE (IRE) ★★★★
b.f. Rock Of Gibraltar – Minnie Habit (Habitat).
April 13. Fourth foal. 115,000Y. Tattersalls October 1. Denford Stud. Half-sister to the Irish 2-y-o listed 9f winner On The Nile, the Irish listed 1m winner In The Limelight and the fair 10f winner Maganda (all by Sadler's Wells), to the Singapore Gold Cup and Gran Premio del Jockey Club winner Kutub (by In The Wings), the 2-y-o 6f winner Child Prodigy (by Ballad Rock) and the Irish 14f winner Blue Bit (by Bluebird) - both quite useful. The dam, an Irish 4-y-o 9f winner, is closely related to the 5f Curragh Stakes and 6f Railway Stakes winner Bermuda Classic (herself dam of the Coronation Stakes winner Shake The Yoke and the Phoenix Sprint Stakes winner Tropical) and a half-sister to 6 winners. The second dam, Minnie Tudor (by Tudor Melody), won over 6f (at 2 yrs) and 1m in Ireland. (Denford Stud).
"She looks as if she'll be out around July time, probably over six furlongs and she's a very pretty, well-made filly".

1379. FORK LIGHTNING (USA) ★★★★
gr.f. Storm Cat – Last Second (Alzao).
March 11. Half-sister to the French 2,000 Guineas and US Grade 1 winner Aussie Rules (by Danehill), to the useful 7.5f (at 2 yrs) and listed 10f winner and US Grade 2 second Approach, the very useful 2-y-o 8.5f winner and Group 1 Prix Marcel Boussac fourth Intrigued (both by Darshaan) and the quite useful 10f winner Bold Glance (by Kingmambo). The dam, winner of the 10f Nassau Stakes and the 10f Sun Chariot Stakes, is a half-sister to 7 winners including the Moyglare Stud Stakes third Alouette (herself dam of the Group 1 winners Albanova and Alborada) and to the placed dam of the Group 1 winners Yesterday and Quarter Moon. The second dam, Alruccaba (by Crystal Palace), a quite useful 2-y-o 6f winner, is out of a half-sister to the dams of Aliysa and Nishapour. (Denford Stud).
"Beautifully-bred, she's growing quite a lot. Her mother didn't run until early autumn and this filly looks to be the same sort. Very much her mother's daughter, she's a tall, elegant filly. I trained the dam for the same owner, Prince Faisal Salman".

1380. HONOURED (IRE) ★★★
ch.c. Mark Of Esteem – Traou Mad (Barathea).
February 11. Third foal. 55000Y. Tattersalls October 1. Sir M Prescott. Half-brother to the French 7.5f winner and listed-placed Roscoff (by Daylami). The dam, a French listed 2-y-o 5.5f winner, was Group 3 placed four times and is a half-sister to 6 winners including the Group 2 6f Gimcrack Stakes and dual Group 3 winner Josr Algharoud and to the Group 2 5f Prix du Gros-Chene winner Saint Marine. The second dam, Pont-Aven (by Try My Best), a very useful winner of 3 races including the Group 3 Prix de Saint-Georges, was second in the French 1,000 Guineas and is a half-sister to 6 winners. (Charles C Walker – Osborne House).
"A big, strong, heavy horse, he's just come back in the yard after being turned out. The dam was quite quick but this colt would be more Mark Of Esteem I would think".

1381. ILDIKO (USA) ★★
b.f. Yes It's True – Eternity (Suave Dancer).
February 20. Half-sister to the useful 1m (at 2 yrs) and 10f winner and listed-placed Sagredo (by Diesis), to the quite useful 13f and 14f

winner Artless (by Aptitude) and the modest 12f to 2m winner Etching (by Groom Dancer). The dam, a fair 11f and 12f winner, is a half-sister to numerous winners including the 2-y-o Group 2 Hoover Fillies Mile and Group 3 May Hill Stakes winner Tessla. The second dam, Chellita (by Habitat), ran once unplaced. (Dr Catherine Wills).

"She's in a field and won't come out of it until May 15th! She looks a nice three-year-old type – the dam breeds them that way".

1382. INTERLACE ★★★★
ch.f. Pivotal – Splice (Sharpo).
February 7. Sister to the very smart 6f and 7f winner of 7 races Feet So Fast and to the moderate 7f winner Cornerstone, closely related to the quite useful 7f all-weather (at 2 yrs) and 6f winner Rise (by Polar Falcon) and half-sister to the smart Group 2 6f Lowther Stakes and Group 3 Princess Margaret Stakes winner Soar (by Danzero) and the quite useful 2-y-o dual 5f winner Entwine (by Primo Dominie). The dam, a smart winner of the listed 6f Abernant Stakes, is a full or half-sister to several winners including the fairly useful 1m winner and subsequent Italian winner Alfujairah. The second dam, Soluce (by Junius), won the Group 3 Irish 1,000 Guineas Trial and is a half-sister to several winners. (Cheveley Park Stud).

"She's a possible two-year-old for June or July and she's a strong filly that will probably be a six furlong type".

1383. KING'S REALM (IRE) ★★
ch.c. King's Best – Sweet Home Alabama (Desert Prince).
March 30. Second foal. 47,000Y. Tattersalls October 1. Sir Mark Prescott. The dam, placed fourth over 7f and 1m, is a half-sister to the Group 2 1m Sussex Stakes winner Proclamation and to the German dual listed winner No Refuge. The second dam, Shamarra (by Zayyani), is an unraced half-sister to the smart middle-distance performer Shantaroun and to the dams of the Group 3 Meld Stakes and subsequent US Grade 2 winner Sardaniya and the Group 3 Prix du Lutece winner Shaiybara. (P J McSwiney – Osborne House).

"He'd be a three-year-old type, but he's a good-looking horse".

1384. LUCK OF THE DRAW (IRE) ★★★
b.g. Key Of Luck – Sarifa (Kahyasi).
March 28. Seventh foal. €60,000Y. Goffs Million. Sir M Prescott. Brother to the Irish 7f (at 2 yrs) and listed 1m winner and dual Group 2 placed Wrong Key, to the 7f (at 2 yrs) and Group 3 10f and 12f winner Right Key, the quite useful Irish 2-y-o 1m winner Right Or Wrong and the 10.5f and hurdles winner Starluck. The dam is an unraced half-sister to the Group 3 Prix du Palais Royale winner Saratan. The second dam, Sarafia (by Dalsaan), won at 3 yrs and is a half-sister to 3 winners including the listed winner and French 1,000 Guineas second Safita (herself dam of the Lockinge Stakes winner Safawan). (L A Larratt – Osborne House).

"He looks like he'll be a September two-year-old and more than likely a seven furlong type".

1385. LUTINE BELL ★★★
ch.g. Starcraft – Satin Bell (Midyan).
April 14. Seventh foal. Half-sister to the very useful 6f (at 2 yrs) and 9f winner Zabaglione (by Zilzal), to the quite useful 1m and 9f winner Strawberry Leaf (by Unfuwain) and the fair 12f winner Snake's Head (by Golden Snake). The dam, a useful 7f winner, is a half-sister to several winners including the useful listed 6f winner Star Tulip. The second dam, Silk Petal (by Petorius), a useful German listed 1m winner and third in the Group 3 10.5f Prix de Flore, is a half-sister to numerous winners including the dam of the Group 2 12f Ribblesdale Stakes winner Fairy Queen. (Mr Tom Wilson & Mr Nicholas Jones).

"Very big, but he's not as backward as he looks and I should think he'll run in July".

1386. MAIWAND ★★★
b.f. Reset – Iris May (Brief Truce).
April 1. Seventh foal. Half-sister to the useful dual 5f (at 2 yrs) and 1m winner and listed placed Joseph Henry (by Mujadil), to the quite useful 2-y-o 5f winner Royal Engineer (by Royal

Applause), the fair 2-y-o 6f winner Special Cuvee (by Reset) and the fair 2-y-o 7f all-weather winner Leonard Charles (by Best Of The Bests). The dam, a dual 5f winner, including at 2 yrs, is a half-sister to 4 winners including the very useful listed sprint winner Cathedral. The second dam, Choire Mhor (by Dominion), a useful winner of three races over 6f at 2 yrs, is a half-sister to 6 winners including the Group 3 Prix de la Jonchere winner Soft Currency and the listed winner Fawzi – both useful. (John Brown and Megan Dennis).

"She's small and strong and looks the sort of filly that will try hard. She'll be running in July".

1387. MME DE STAEL ★★
ch.f. Selkirk – Scandalette (Niniski).
April 3. Half-sister to the very smart Group 3 7f and 9f winner and Group 1 placed Gateman (by Owington), to the useful 7f (at 2 yrs) and 10f winner Lady Jane Rigby (by Oasis Dream), the fair 2-y-o dual 6f winner Diablerette, the fair 8.6f winner Devil's Island (both by Green Desert), the smart 1m Royal Hunt Cup winner Surprise Encounter (by Cadeaux Genereux) and the fairly useful 7f (at 2 yrs) and dual 12f winner Night Flyer (by Midyan). The dam is an unraced half-sister to 9 winners including the Group 1 July Cup winner Polish Patriot and the Italian listed winner Grand Cayman. The second dam, Maria Waleska (by Filiberto), won 6 races including the Group 1 Gran Premio d'Italia and the Group 1 Oaks d'Italia. (Miss K Rausing).

"Big and backward, he's still in a field and is unlikely to do much this year. That is unless he's good – and you never know!"

1388. MOTRICE ★★
gr.f. Motivator – Entente Cordiale (Affirmed).
March 20. Eleventh foal. Half-sister to the quite useful 2008 2-y-o 1m winner (from 2 starts) Quai d'Orsay (by Sulamani), to the smart 7f (at 2 yrs) to 12f winner of 12 races (including 7 listed events) Foreign Affairs, the very useful 10f winner Bien Entendu, the useful 2m winner of 4 races Affaire d'Amour and the quite useful 14f and 18f winner Esprit de Corps (all by Hernando) and the Italian 2-y-o winner of 4 races Last Result (by Northern Park). The dam ran once unplaced in France and is a half-sister to 5 winners including the Peruvian Grade 1 winner Natalie Too. The second dam, Likely Split (by Little Current), is a placed half-sister to 6 winners including the very smart French sprinters Ancient Regime (dam of 3 good sprinters herself) and Cricket Ball. (Miss K Rausing).

"Not very big, she's from a family that's done well for me and most of them stay well. She'll be a late two-year-old and she'll stay, but she is small".

1389. NEZHENKA ★★
b.f. With Approval – Ninotchka (Nijinsky).
May 12. Half-sister to the useful 2-y-o 6f winner and 7f Group 3 placed Nataliya (by Green Desert) and to the quite useful triple 12f winner Nadeszhda (by Nashwan). The dam, a listed winner in Italy and third in the Group 3 12f Lancashire Oaks and the Group 3 12f Princess Royal Stakes, is a half-sister to 5 winners. The second dam, Puget Sound (by High Top), was a fairly useful 7f and 1m winner and a half-sister to the Group 3 Oaks Trial Stakes winner Kiliniski. (Miss K Rausing).

"A very big, very scopey filly. She's in a field at present but she canters nicely".

1390. SUMERIAN ★★
ch.f. Medicean – Pitcroy (Unfuwain).
February 9. Sixth living foal. Half-brother to the useful 3-y-o listed 10f winner Succinct (by Hector Protector) and to the fairly useful 7f and 1m (including at 2 yrs) and German listed 1m winner Succession (by Groom Dancer). The dam, a useful 10f winner, is a half-sister to 8 winners including the very useful Group 3 7f Jersey Stakes winner Ardkinglass. The second dam, Reuval (by Sharpen Up), a useful winner of 2 races over 1m at 3 yrs, is closely related to the dams of the Group 2 winners Ozone Friendly, Reprimand and Wiorno. (Dr Catherine Wills).

"I had a good one called Succession out of the mare. This one wouldn't be nearly as precocious as she was however".

1391. TUSCAN GOLD ★★
ch.c. Medicean – Louella (El Gran Senor).
April 2. Seventh foal. 16,000Y. Tattersalls October 2. Sir M Prescott. Half-brother to the Group 1 Gran Premio di Milano winner Leadership (by Selkirk) and to 2 minor winners abroad by Groom Dancer and Hector Protector. The dam is a placed half-sister to 7 minor winners in Europe and the USA. The second dam, Celtic Loot (by Irish River), a minor US 4-y-o winner, is a half-sister to 2 winners. (The Green Door Partnership).
"He looks a nice, scopey horse but he'll make a two-year-old at some point. One for the back-end of the season".

1392. VIRGINIA HALL ★★★★
b.f. Medicean – Odette (Pursuit Of Love).
March 6. Seventh foal. Half-sister to the quite useful 2008 2-y-o 5f winner Cecily (by Oasis Dream), to the Group 3 6f Firth Of Clyde Stakes winner and Group 2 Rockfel Stakes second Violette (by Observatory), the listed 6f (at 2 yrs) and Group 3 7f Nell Gwyn Stakes winner Silca's Gift (by Cadeaux Genereux) and the fair 3-y-o 5f all-weather winner On Point (by Kris). The dam, a fair 3-y-o 5f and 5.7f winner, is a half-sister to 4 winners including the useful 6f (at 2 yrs) and 7f winner and Group 2 5f Flying Childers Stakes fourth Caballero. The second dam, On Tiptoes (by Shareef Dancer), a useful winner of 5 races at around 5f including the Group 3 Queen Mary Stakes, is a half-sister to 2 winners. (C G Rowles Nicholson).
"I see her being out around July time. It's a fast family and they all make two-year-olds – if they're any good that is!"

MICHAEL QUINLAN
1393. AUDRINNA (IRE) ★★
b.f. Oratorio – Zvezda (Nureyev).
May 3. Fourth foal. Half-sister to the fairly useful Irish 2-y-o Group 3 7f C L Weld Park Stakes third Silk Dress (by Gulch). The dam is an unplaced full or half-sister to 5 winners including the 7f (at 2 yrs) and subsequent US stakes winner and Group 1 Dewhurst Stakes and US Grade 1 third Zentsov Street. The second dam, Storm Fear (by Coastal), is a US placed half-sister to 9 winners including the dam of Bakharoff and Emperor Jones.
"She's had one piece of fast work that went alright. A May foal, she tries and she's one that'll be OK in a few weeks time".

1394. DIAMOND AFFAIR ★★★★
b.f. Namid – Subtle Affair (Barathea).
February 11. First foal. The dam, a quite useful dual 11f winner, is a half-sister to 8 winners including the useful 12.3f and 14f winner and Group 2 Henry II Stakes second Lochbuie, the Irish 7f (at 2 yrs) and 9f winner and Group 2 placed Prize Time and the useful 12f and 14f winner Direct Bearing. The second dam, Uncertain Affair (by Darshaan), a quite useful Irish 14f winner, is a half-sister to 3 winners.
"We trained the dam and we've also had a number of horses by Namid that haven't been any good, but this filly goes like the wind. You wouldn't necessarily expect it from the pedigree but she does have plenty of speed and she's a very straightforward filly that should be winning early on".

1395. ISHTAR ★★
gr.f. Verglas – Villa Deste (Bertolini).
February 11. First foal. The dam is an unraced half-sister to one winner. The second dam, Lady Two K (Grand Lodge), was a fairly useful winner of 4 races from 12f to 15f and was listed placed. (Plantation Stud).
"She'll win a little race and we should be starting her off at the end of April over five furlongs but she may prove to want six. She's small but has a good attitude".

1396. KEYTA BONITA ★★★ ♠
b.f. Denon – Miss Corinne (Mark Of Esteem).
February 16. First foal. 3,500Y. Tattersalls October 3. David McGreavy. The dam won 6 races in Italy from 3 to 5 yrs and is a half-sister to 4 minor winners here and abroad. The second dam, Percy's Girl (by Blakeney), a useful 10f and 10.3f winner, is a sister to the Group 3 September Stakes winner Percy's Lass (herself dam of the Derby winner Sir Percy) and a half-

sister to the very smart Grade 1 E. P.Taylor Stakes and Group 2 Sun Chariot Stakes winner Braiswick. (Mrs N McGreavy).

"A filly with a good pedigree, she's rangy and if she happens to win a race she'd be worth a lot more than she cost. Six and seven furlongs should suit her best but if she's up for it she might just start at five".

1397. STARBURST EXCEL ★★★
b.f. Exceed And Excel – Homeward (Kris).
February 26. Second foal. 12,000Y. Doncaster St Leger. Not sold. The dam is an unplaced half-sister to the Group 2 7f Challenge Stakes winner Susu and the fairly useful 6f winner of 7 races Cadeaux Cher. The second dam, Home Truth (by Known Fact), a useful winner of 3 races over 7f and 1m, was listed-placed. (J Haydon).

"I'm very fond of her, I think she's a lovely filly. We're about to start fast work with her and I'd be very disappointed if she wasn't smart. Very light when she came in, she's done really well and has a great attitude".

1398. YORKSTERS PRINCE ★★★ ♠
b.g. Beat Hollow – Odalisque (Machiavellian).
April 1. Sixth reported foal. 9,000Y. Tattersalls October 3. D McGreavy. Half-sister to the French 2-y-o 7.5f winner Fast Enough, to the modest 1m winner Turkish Sultan (both by Anabaa) and the French 3-y-o winner Onda Blu (by Desert King). The dam won once over 11f in France and is a half-sister to 3 winners including the dual listed winner Otaiti. The second dam, Ode (by Lord Avie), won the Group 2 Grand Prix d'Evry and is a half-sister to 6 winners. (B P York).

"A nice horse, we gelded him so he'll need a bit of time but he'll be OK".

1399. UNNAMED ★★
b.f. Elusive City – Accell (Magical Wonder).
March 9. Half-sister to the useful French 2-y-o 1m winner Guillaume Tell (by Rossini), subsequently Group 3 placed in France and the USA. The dam won over 1m and 12f in Ireland and is a half-sister to numerous winners. The second dam, Lough Graney (by Sallust), an Irish 12f winner, is a sister to the 2,000 Guineas winner Tap On Wood and the Irish listed winner Americus and a half-sister to 3 winners.

"A lovely looking filly, she isn't quite ready yet but she's nice enough and her temperament and constitution are good enough for her to come good at some stage. I think our horses this year are a nice, neat bunch that we can get on with – more so than in previous years. They seem to be quite forward this year and in general we're pleased with them".

1400. UNNAMED ★★★
b.c. Celtic Swing – Cape Finisterre (Cape Cross).
March 31. First foal. 15,000Y. Doncaster St Leger. David McGreavy. The dam is an unraced half-sister to one winner. The second dam, Trim Star (by Terimon), is a placed half-sister to 6 winners including the listed Galtres Stakes winner Startino.

"A sweet little fellow, this is a colt I really love. I need to hold on to him until the six furlong races start and he might even make up into a Chesham Stakes horse. You couldn't ask for a more genuine, straightforward horse and sometime this year I think he'll make up into a really nice two-year-old".

1401. UNNAMED ★★★
ch.f. More Than Ready – Red Piano (Red Ransom).
April 30. $125,000Y. Keeneland September. Ben McElroy. The dam was placed over 1m in France and won 2 minor races in the USA at 4 yrs. She is a half-sister to the US Grade 3 placed winner Stanislavsky. The second dam, Spinet (by Nureyev), is an unraced half-sister to the Irish 2,000Guineas winner Prince Of Birds. (EHR Partners).

"She's not here yet and I haven't seen her but she's supposed to be very nice. She's been prepped in Florida and we're looking forward to having her here".

1402. UNNAMED ★★
b.c. Elnadim – Roseau (Nashwan).
April 25. €9,500Y. Tattersalls Ireland. Not sold. Half-brother to two placed horses by Montjeu

and Danehill Dancer. The dam, a winner over 13f and over hurdles in Ireland, is a half-sister to 2 winners. The second dam, Fair Rosamunda (by Try My Best), won the listed Prix Massine and is a half-sister to 4 winners.

"A lovely looking horse but he's a bit backward at this stage so we'll have to wait and see how he progresses".

DAVID SIMCOCK
1403. AL EMARATI (USA) ★★
b.c. Eddington – Serene Nobility (His Majesty).
April 7. Twelfth foal. $70,000Y. Keeneland September. Blandford Bloodstock. Half-brother to 7 winners including the Group 2 Royal Lodge Stakes winner Mutaahab (by Dixieland Band), the fairly useful 7f winner of 3 races (including at 2 yrs) Noble Citizen (by Proud Citizen) and the US stakes winners Courtly Jazz and Covering Ground. The dam, a US stakes winner of 9 races at 3 to 5 yrs, is a half-sister to the US stakes winner Corax. The second dam, Peaceful Snow (by Hold Your Peace), a minor US 3-y-o winner, is a sister to the US Grade 2 winner Hold Your Tricks.

"A weak horse, he's very similar to his half-brother Noble Citizen who won a nursery at the end of his two-year-old career and has since run well in Dubai. He'll need time".

1404. ARABIAN PRIDE ★★★★
b.c. Cadeaux Genereux – Noble Peregrine (Lomond).
February 16. Tenth foal. 110,000Y. Tattersalls October 1. Rabbah Bloodstock. Half-brother to the 6f (at 2 yrs) and triple listed winner Dubai's Touch (by Dr Fong), to the smart 8.5f and 9f winner and Group 3 Diomed Stakes third Wannabe Around (by Primo Dominie), the useful triple 6f winner (including at 2 yrs) Grantley Adams (by Dansili), the useful 7.5f to 10f winner and French Group 3 1m third Nobelist (by Bering) and the fairly useful 7f (at 2 yrs) and 1m winner Noble Pursuit (by Pursuit Of Love). The dam, an Italian 10f winner, is closely related to the French 2-y-o listed 10f winner Noble Ballerina and a half-sister to 6 winners. The second dam, Noble Dust (by Dust Commander), is an unraced half-sister to 6 winners.

"He's likely to be our first two-year-old colt to run, probably in May. He goes very well, he's very natural and he looks a two-year-old. We've got some very well-related horses this year, with a lot of quality amongst them".

1405. CRAIGHALL ★★
b.f. Dubawi – Craigmill (Slip Anchor).
April 8. Eleventh foal. 55,000Y. Tattersalls October 2. Charles Wyatt. Half-sister to the quite useful 2008 2-y-o 1m winner Stirling Castle (by Dubai Destination), to the smart 1m winner and listed-placed Castleton, the fairly useful dual 10f winner Craigstown (both by Cape Cross), the German listed winner and Group 3 placed Fleurie Domaine (by Unfuwain), the fairly useful 12f and 2m winner Astyanax (by Hector Protector), the quite useful 10.5f winner Heather Mix (by Linamix), the quite useful 9.5f all-weather winner Oscillator (by Pivotal) and the German 2-y-o winner Global Champion (by Elnadim). The dam, a fair 2-y-o 7f winner, is a half-sister to the Group 3 Park Hill Stakes winner Coigach, to the listed Cheshire Oaks winner Kyle Rhea and the Park Hill Stakes second Applecross. The second dam, Rynechra (by Blakeney), was a useful 12f winner and a half-sister to 6 winners.

"Not the biggest, but she has a good attitude to life. She won't be particularly early but she does everything right"

1406. DUBAI ATLANTIS (USA) ★★
b.br.f. Street Cry – Tasha Yar (Cryptoclearance).
February 25. Fourth foal. $60,000Y. Keeneland September. Rabbah Bloodstock. Half-sister to the minor US stakes winner Lady Bell Dawn (by Clever Trick) and a minor US winner by Miswaki. The dam is an unraced half-sister to 3 winners. The second dam, Extra Touch (by Fit To Fight), a minor US 3-y-o winner, is a half-sister to 2 stakes winners.

"A big, leggy filly, she's had a few issues but she's not a bad type at all".

1407. DUBAI MEDIA (CAN) ★★★
b.f. Songandaprayer – Forty Gran
(El Gran Senor).
March 30. Fifth foal. $250,000Y. Keeneland September. Blandford Bloodstock. Half-sister to several winners including the 2008 US 2-y-o Grade 1 8.5f Breeders Futurity winner Square Eddie (by Smart Strike) and a stakes-placed winner in Canada by Pulpit. The dam won twice at 2 yrs and was stakes placed in the USA is a half-sister to 2 winners. The second dam, Forty Weight (by Quadratic), a US stakes winner of 7 races, was Grade 3 placed.

"A nice, big, rangy filly with a lot of scope. She's a horse I like".

1408. DUBAI PHANTOM ★★★★
ch.c. Dubawi – Anna Amalia (In The Wings).
March 2. Second foal. 42,000Y. Tattersalls October 1. Rabbah Bloodstock. Half-brother to the fairly useful 2008 2-y-o 7f winner Ave (by Danehill Dancer). The dam won once at 3 yrs in France and is a half-sister to 4 winners including the smart French 2-y-o Group 3 1m Prix d'Aumale winner and smart broodmare Anna Palariva. The second dam, Anna Of Saxony (by Ela-Mana-Mou), a very useful winner of the Group 2 14.6f Park Hill Stakes, is a half-sister to 9 winners including the Group 2 winners Annaba and Pozarica.

"A horse I like, he looks well worth the money he cost now and I'm very pleased with him. He's well put together, he does it all very well and there's nothing backward or weak about him. One for the six and seven furlong races".

1409. EXCEED POWER ★★★
ch.f. Exceed And Excel – Israar (Machiavellian).
March 17. First foal. 23,000Y. Tattersalls October 3. David Simcock. The dam is an unraced half-sister to 3 minor winners. The second dam, El Opera (by Sadler's Wells), a useful dual 7f winner, is a half-sister to 8 winners including the very useful Group 1 6f Heinz "57" Phoenix Stakes winner Pharaoh's Delight.

"She goes well and she's not bad at all. She was in the forward group of my two-year-olds and does everything right but she's had a slight setback. She'll still be early enough".

1410. JUMEIRAH PALM (USA) ★★★★
gr.f. Distorted Humor – Zoftig (Cozzene).
April 19. Fifth foal. $270,000Y. Keeneland September. Rabbah Bloodstock. Half-sister to the US Grade 1 Acorn Stakes winner Zaftig (by Gone West) and to a minor US 2-y-o winner by Danzig. The dam won the Grade 1 Selene Stakes. The second dam, Mrs Marcos (by Private Account), won 2 minor races at 4 yrs and is a half-sister to 4 winners.

"She goes well and she'll be a six/seven furlong two-year-old in July. Her half-sister Zaftig was placed in the Breeders Cup Distaff, so she was expensive. A filly with a lot of quality, she goes very well".

1411. LOVELY EYES ★★★
b.f. Red Ransom – Polygueza (Be My Guest).
March 29. Ninth foal. 55,000Y. Tattersalls October 1. Rabbah Bloodstock. Half-sister to the fair 2008 Irish 2-y-o 7f debut winner Maziona (by Dansili), to the very smart Group 3 Gordon Stakes winner and Group 1 St Leger, Group 2 Great Voltigeur and Group 2 Dante Stakes second The Geezer (by Halling), the Italian winner of 5 races from 2 to 5 years and listed-placed Big Sinisa (by Barathea), the quite useful 1m to 10f winner of 5 races Doctored (by Dr Devious) and the quite useful 2-y-o 7f and subsequent US winner Flight Captain (by In The Wings). The dam, a minor 3-y-o 7f winner in Ireland, is a half-sister to 4 winners including the Irish listed winner Lepoushka. The second dam, Polifontaine (by Bold Lad, Ire), won twice at 2 yrs in France and is a half-sister to the Irish 1,000 Guineas and Coronation Stakes winner Katies.

"A nice, very natural filly and more forward than you'd expect considering the pedigree".

1412. MAKING THE EVENT (USA) ★★
b.br.f. Pulpit – Glenarcy (Forestry).
April 12. Second foal. $55,000Y. Keeneland September. Rabbah Bloodstock. The dam is an unraced half-sister to two Group 1 winners in Brazil. The second dam, Joy Valley (by Ghadeer), was a Brazilian stakes winner.

"A big filly, she's very natural and does everything asked of her but she will take a lot of time".

1413. QUALITY MOVER (USA) ★★★★
b.br.f. Elusive Quality – Katherine Seymour
(Green Desert).
February 2. Third foal. 140,000Y. Keeneland September. Rabbah Bloodstock. Closely related to the quite useful 7f winner Liberation Spirit (by Gone West). The dam, a very useful 2-y-o 7f winner and third in the Group 2 7f Rockfel Stakes, is a half-sister to 3 winners. The second dam, Sudeley (by Dancing Brave), a modest 11.5f winner, is a half-sister to the high-class middle-distance colts Peacetime and Quiet Fling, to the Cambridgeshire winner Intermission (herself dam of the good sprinter Interval) and to the dams of the Group/Graded stakes winners Wandesta, De Quest and Flaming Torch.
"A lovely filly, I like her a lot. She's big and mature but I imagine she'll be running over six or seven furlongs in mid-summer".

1414. SHABAK HOM (USA) ★★★
b.c. Exceed And Excel – Shbakni
(Mr Prospector).
January 26. Sixth foal. Brother to the 2008 6f placed 2-y-o Secret Society and half-brother to the fairly useful 6f to 9f winner Membership (by Best Of The Bests). The dam was placed in France and the UAE at up to 9f and is a daughter of the Kentucky Derby winner Winning Colors (by Caro).
"A home-bred, he does everything right and is a fluent mover. He'll be a seven furlong two-year-old in the high summer".

1415. SHAMARDAL PHANTOM (IRE) ★★★
b.f. Shamardal – Ripalong (Revoque).
March 3. Second foal. 55,000Y. Tattersalls October 1. Rabbah Bloodstock. Half-sister to the quite useful 2008 2-y-o 6f winner Shamwari Lodge (by Hawk Wing). The dam is an unplaced half-sister to 7 winners including the Group 1 6f Haydock Park Sprint Cup and Group 3 5f Palace House Stakes winner Pipalong. The second dam, Limpopo (by Green Desert), a poor 5f placed 2-y-o, is a half-sister to 7 winners here and abroad.
"She came in very late and had a very bad mouth when we got her, so it took us a long time to break her. She's not the biggest but she's all there and she shows a good attitude to life. I'm very happy with her".

1416. TAYMOOR ★★★
b.c. Shamardal – Presto Vento (Air Express).
April 17. Third foal. 60,000Y. Tattersalls October 1. Rabbah Bloodstock. Half-brother to the fair 5f (at 2 yrs) and 6f winner Presto Levanter (by Rock Of Gibraltar). The dam was a useful 2-y-o 5f listed and 3-y-o 7f listed winner. The second dam, Placement (by Kris), is an unraced half-sister to 4 winners including the Group 2 Sun Chariot Stakes winner Danceabout and the French dual Group 3 winner Pole Position.
"He won't be that early – I'm looking at him being out in July over six or seven furlongs. He's very well put together, moves very well and does everything right, but he's quite a big horse so I've just eased off him for now".

1417. UNNAMED ★★★★
b.br.c. Mr Greeley – Anita Madden (Arch).
March 13. Second foal. $210,000Y. Keeneland September. Rabbah Bloodstock. The dam is an unraced half-sister to the US Grade 2 winner and Grade 1 placed Santa Caterina. The second dam, Purrfectly (by Storm Cat), won twice at 3 yrs and is a half-sister to the Fillies' Mile, Prix Marcel Boussac and French 1,00 Guineas winner Culture Vulture.
"A really attractive colt, he's well put together and one I like a lot. A very forward two-year-old, he'll probably start in May over six furlongs. He has a lot of attitude – he plays quite a lot – and he does everything very, very easily".

1418. UNNAMED ★★
b.f. Exceed And Excel – City Maiden
(Carson City).
January 29. Fourth living foal. 20,000Y. Tattersalls October 3. David Simcock. Half-sister to the fair 2008 2-y-o 6f winner First City

(by Diktat). The dam is an unraced half-sister to the French listed winner and Group 3 placed Vernoy. The second dam, Marble Maiden (by Lead On Time), won the Grade 2 All Along Stakes and the Group 3 Prix de Sandringham and is a half-sister to 5 winners.

"A big, leggy, gangly filly but a good actioned horse. We have the half-sister City Maiden who is quite useful but a totally different sort – you couldn't have two more contrasting fillies. This filly is narrow but she's good actioned and I don't dislike her. Seven furlongs will probably be her trip".

1419. UNNAMED ★★★
ch.c. *Distorted Humor – Escrow Agent*
(El Gran Senor).
May 10. Seventeenth foal. $310,000Y. Keeneland September. Rabbah Bloodstock. Half-brother to 6 winners including the Grade 1 Florida Derby and Grade 1 Fountain of Youth Stakes winner Vicar (by Wild Again), the fairly useful 10f winner Signatory (by Kris S), the minor US stakes winner Sheepscot (by Easy Goer and herself dam of the French 2,000 Guineas winner Astronomer Royal) and the US stakes-placed winners Weston Field (by Gulch), Mama Dean (by Woodman) and Magic Caver (by Spend A Buck). The dam won at 2 yrs in Ireland, was stakes-placed in the USA and is a half-sister to 6 winners. The second dam, Viva Sec (by Secretariat), was a stakes winner of 10 races in the USA.

"He's just having a growth spurt and has gone slightly weak, so he won't be seen out until July or August. An attractive horse and very well-related, he's doing OK".

1420. UNNAMED ★★★★
b.c. *Selkirk – Fatefully (Private Account).*
April 15. Fifth living foal. 55,000Y. Tattersalls October 3. Rabbah Bloodstock. Brother to the Group 1 Nassau Stakes and Group 2 1m Matron Stakes winner Favourable Terms and half-brother to the quite useful 2-y-o 7f winner Have Faith and the US 2-y-o 6.5f and subsequent UAE winner Opportunist (both by Machiavellian). The dam, a smart winner of 4 races including a listed event over 1m, is a half-sister to 4 minor winners. The second dam, Fateful (by Topsider), a fairly useful 6f (at 2 yrs) and 7f winner, is a half-sister to 2 winners.

"A big, strong horse, I'm delighted with him. In terms of physical improvement he's done as well as anything we've got from the Sales. He's got a lot of quality about him and he'll be a July/August two-year-old. He's a horse I like a lot and he's done very, very well since we got him".

1421. UNNAMED ★★
br.c. *Green Desert – Generous Option*
(Cadeaux Genereux).
February 28. First foal. The dam, a quite useful 6f (at 2 yrs) and 7f winner, is a half-sister to numerous winners including the dual Group 1 winner Court Masterpiece and the Group 3 5f winner Maybe Forever. The second dam, Easy Option (by Prince Sabo), a smart winner of the listed 5f St Hugh's Stakes and second in the Group 2 5f Prix du Gros-Chene, is a half-sister to 8 winners including the useful 2-y-o 5f winner and Group 2 Flying Childers Stakes third Wanton (herself dam of the Irish 1,000 Guineas winner Classic Park).

"A horse that carries a lot of condition, he had a bit of a setback a few weeks ago and he will need a bit of time but I don't dislike him".

1422. UNNAMED ★★★★
b.br.f. *Seeking The Gold – Kahlua Bay (Catrail).*
February 9. First foal. $300,000Y. Keeneland September. Rabbah Bloodstock. The dam is an unraced half-sister to 4 winners including the US triple Grade 1 winner Medaglia d'Oro. The second dam, Cappucino Bay (by Bailjumper), a minor US stakes winner of 5 races, is a half-sister to 2 winners.

"She's just lovely – a real, quality filly. She's big, mature, covers a lot of ground and does everything right. She'll be a seven furlong type but will get a mile easily".

1423. UNNAMED ★★★
b.f. *Kheleyf – Lady Liesel (Bin Ajwaad).*
February 17. First foal. 36,000Y. Tattersalls

October 3. Rabbah Bloodstock. The dam, a modest 6f to 1m placed maiden, is a half-sister to 3 winners. The second dam, Griddle Cake (by Be My Guest), is a placed full or half-sister to 5 winners including the Group 2 Great Voltigeur Stakes winner Bonny Scot and the dam of the 2,000 Guineas winner Golan.

"She'll probably be our first two-year-old filly to run. She's shows a a great attitude, is very willing and will probably start off in a six furlong maiden in early May. She goes well and she looks good value".

1424. UNNAMED ★★★
b.c. King's Best – Sheer Reason (Danzig).
April 14. 16,000Y. Doncaster St Leger. Not sold. Half-brother to the quite useful 2-y-o 7f and 1m winner Faith And Reason (by Sunday Silence) and to the fair 7f winner I'm Right (by Rahy). The dam won the listed 6f Criterium d'Evry at 2 yrs and is a closely related to the useful Group 3 12f Lingfield Oaks Trial winner Munnaya and a half-sister to the French 2-y-o listed 6f winner Mall Queen and the useful 2-y-o 6f winner Balla Jidaal. The second dam, Hiaam (by Alydar), won the Group 3 6f Princess Margaret Stakes at 2 yrs and listed events over 7.6f and 1m at 3 yrs. She is a half-sister to the champion Canadian 3-y-o Key to the Moon, the dual US Grade 1 winner Gorgeous and the Grade 1 Kentucky Oaks winner Seaside Attraction – herself dam of the US Grade 1 winner Golden Attraction. (Saeed Manana).

"He's got his traits in that he's quite a free sweater, but his mind is very good and as a ride he's excellent. He was good value I think and I do like him". TRAINER'S BARGAIN BUY

1425. UNNAMED ★★★★
b.f. Noverre – Summer Dreams (Sadler's Wells).
February 18. Fourth foal. 40,000Y. Tattersalls October 2. Blandford Bloodstock. Half-sister to the fairly useful 2-y-o 7f winner and Group 3 1m Autumn Stakes third Moudez (by Xaar). The dam was placed at up to 14f and is a half-sister to 5 winners including the German Derby winner All My Dreams. The second dam, Marie de Beaujeu (by Kenmare), won twice and was listed placed in France and is a half-sister to 4 winners.

"A filly I really like, she's a half-sister to a good horse I trained called Moudez. A very mature, very big two-year-old and I'd like to think we'll see her running over six or seven furlongs in June or July. I can see a lot of Moudez in her and she's very likeable".

1426. UNNAMED ★★
b.c. Zafeen – Talah (Danehill).
April 13. Sixth foal. Half-brother to the useful winner of 8 races including a listed 7f event Ceremonial Jade and to the modest 6f winner Sea Rover (both by Jade Robbery). The dam, a fairly useful second over 6f at 2 yrs on her only start, is a sister to the listed winner and French 1,000 Guineas second Firth Of Lorne and a half-sister to 5 winners including the smart 2-y-o 6f winner and Group 3 placed Shmoose. The second dam, Kerrera (by Diesis), a smart winner of the Group 3 Cherry Hinton Stakes and second in the 1,000 Guineas, is a half-sister to the high-class 2-y-o Rock City.

"A big horse, he's one for later on but he does everything right and for a big horse he's very natural".

BRIAN SMART
1427. ASKAN (IRE) ★★★
b.c. Arakan – Ask Carol (Foxhound).
March 16. First foal. 30,000Y. Doncaster St Leger. Prime Equestrian. The dam, a fairly useful 5-y-o 7f winner in Ireland, is a half-sister to 6 winners including the very useful Group 3 7f Jersey Stakes winner Sergeyev. The second dam, Escape Path (by Wolver Hollow), placed once over hurdles, is a half-sister to the Group 1 William Hill Futurity Stakes winner Sandy Creek. (Prime Equestrian)

1428. BENRISH (IRE) ★★★
b.c. Refuse To Bend – Miss Trish (Danetime).
January 31. First foal. 82,000Y. Doncaster St Leger. B Smart. The dam, an Irish 7f and 1m winner, was second in the Group 3 Ridgewood

Stakes and is a half-sister to 3 winners. The second dam, Fey Rouge (by Fayruz), is an unplaced full or half-sister to 9 winners. (Prime Equestrian)

1429. CEEDAL ★★★
ch.c. Shamardal – Tee Cee (Lion Cavern).
March 11. Sixth foal. 88,000Y. Doncaster St Leger. Blandford Bloodstock. Half-brother to the fair 2008 5.8f and 7f placed 2-y-o Flyit (by King's Best), to the useful 2-y-o triple 6f winner and listed placed Yajbill (by Royal Applause), the quite useful 2-y-o 7f winner Bold Crusader (by Cape Cross) and the fair 7f all-weather winner Fantastic Cee (by Noverre). The dam, a fair 3-y-o 7f winner, is a half-sister to 5 winners including the useful 7f and 1m winner Bishr. The second dam, Hawayah (by Shareef Dancer), a modest 2-y-o 7f winner, is a half-sister to 6 winners. (Prime Equestrian)

1430. CEEDWELL ★★★
ch.f. Exceed And Excel – Muja Farewell (Mujtahid).
March 17. Fourth foal. 65,000Y. Doncaster St Leger. Prime Equestrian. The dam, a fairly useful 5f winner of 4 races (including at 2 yrs), is a half-sister to 2 winners including the quite useful 2-y-o 5f winner and listed-placed Dolce Piccata (by Piccolo). The second dam, Highland Rhapsody (by Kris), a fair 6f winner at 3 yrs, is a half-sister to 4 winners including the German Group 3 winner Miss Gazon. (Prime Equestrian)

1431. CHUSHKA ★★★
ch.f. Pivotal – Ravine (Indian Ridge).
March 10. Sixth foal. 75,000Y. Doncaster St Leger. Crossfields Racing. Half-sister to the 2-y-o Group 2 6f July Stakes winner Captain Hurricane (by Desert Style), to the minor US 3-y-o winner Cassablanca (by Royal Applause) and the modest 3-y-o 7f winner Nelly's Glen (by Efisio). The dam, a quite useful 6f and 7f winner at 3 yrs, is a half-sister to 4 winners including the smart Lowther Stakes, Nell Gwyn Stakes and Falmouth Stakes winner Niche. The second dam, Cubby Hole (by Town And Country), placed over 12f and 2m, is a half-sister to 9 winners including the Ascot Gold Cup winner Little Wolf and to the unraced dam of the high-class sprinter Sheikh Albadou. (Crossfields Racing)

1432. COMHEART ★★★
b.f. Compton Place – Change Of Heart (Revoque).
April 4. Third foal. 25,000Y. Doncaster St Leger. Prime Equestrian. Half-sister to the modest 2-y-o 6f winner Lady Salama (by Fasliyev) and to the fair 2-y-o 6f winner Geestring (by Diktat). The dam, placed over 7f at 2 yrs, is a half-sister to 3 winners including the Group 3 Cornwallis Stakes third Fast Heart. The second dam, Heart Of India (by Try My Best), is an unraced half-sister to 9 winners including King's Stand Stakes and Temple Stakes winner Bolshoi. (Prime Equestrian)

1433. CULADIE ★★★
br.c. Kheleyf – Acicula (Night Shift).
April 17. Sixth foal. 38,000Y. Doncaster St Leger. Prime Equestrian. Half-brother to the smart 2008 Group 3 6f Sirenia Stakes winner Elnawin, to the quite useful 2-y-o 6f and 7f winner Elna Bright (both by Emarati), the 5f and 6f seller winner Raphoola (by Raphane) and the moderate 7f and 1m winner Alucica (by Celtic Swing). The dam, a useful 2-y-o 5f and 6f winner, is a half-sister to 5 winners. The second dam, Crystal City (by Kris), a minor 10f winner at 3 yrs in France, is out of the Yorkshire Oaks winner Untold. (Prime Equestrian)

1434. ELUSIST (IRE) ★★★
b.f. Elusive City – Imperialist (Imperial Frontier).
April 20. Fifth foal. 38,000Y. Doncaster St Leger. Prime Equestrian. Half-sister to the fair 2008 2-y-o 7f winner Captain Imperial (by Captain Rio) and to the moderate dual 6f winner (including at 2 yrs) Slipasearcher (by Danehill Dancer). The dam, a fairly useful 2-y-o dual 5f winner, was third in the listed 6f Sirenia Stakes and is a half-sister to 4 minor winners. The second dam, Petrine (by Petorius), was an unplaced half-sister to 8 winners. (Prime Equestrian)

1435. EXGRAY (IRE) ★★★
gr.f. Exceed And Excel – Mrs Gray
(Red Sunset).
March 31. Thirteenth foal. 42,000Y. Doncaster St Leger. Prime Equestrian. Half-sister to the very useful 6f and 7f (at 2 yrs) and subsequent US stakes winner Steelaninch, to the quite useful 2-y-o 1m winner Snowey Mountain (both by Inchinor), the quite useful 7f (at 2 yrs) to 10f winner Anuvasteel (by Vettori), the fair 4-y-o 6f winner Lucayan Beach (by Cyrano de Bergerac), the fair 7f (at 2 yrs) and 10f winner Flying Applause (by Royal Applause), a winner of 8 races in Sweden by Rambo Dancer and a bumpers winner by Rock Hopper. The dam, a modest 2-y-o 5f winner, is a full or half-sister to 11 winners here and abroad including the German 2-y-o Group 2 6f winner Amigo Sucio and the dam of the Group 2 Prix Robert Papin winner Rolly Polly. The second dam, Haunting (by Lord Gayle), is a placed half-sister to 7 minor winners. (Prime Equestrian)

1436. MONALINI (IRE) ★★★
b.c. Bertolini – Mona Em (Catrail).
March 4. Fourth foal. 40,000Y. Doncaster St Leger. McKeever St Lawrence. Half-brother to the French listed 10f winner Nice Applause (by Royal Applause) and to the minor French 2-y-o winner Monatora (by Hector Protector). The dam, a French listed sprint winner, is a half-sister to 3 winners including the Irish 2,000 Guineas fourth Maumee. The second dam, Moy Water (by Tirol), an Irish 1m (at 2 yrs) and 9f winner, is a half-sister to 8 winners including the very useful listed sprint winners Bufalino and Maledetto. (Pinnacle Bertolini Partnership

1437. RENESSE ★★★
ch.c. Hennessy – Read Federica
(Fusaichi Pegasus).
March 14. First foal. 65,000Y. Doncaster St Leger. Prime Equestrian. The dam, a fairly useful 2-y-o 7f winner, is a half-sister to one winner. The second dam, Reading Habit (by Half A Year), won a listed stakes in the USA and is a full or half-sister to 5 winners. (Prime Equestrian)

1438. WAREEN ★★★
b.f. War Chant – Carinae (Nureyev).
April 10. Fourth foal. 52,000Y. Doncaster St Leger. Prime Equestrian. Half-sister to the fair 2008 2-y-o 5f winner Carina Nebula (by Grand Slam) and to the minor US 2-y-o winner Sweet And Sassy (by Lear Fan). The dam, a useful 2-y-o 6f winner, was listed placed here and in the USA and is a half-sister to the smart 2-y-o 7f and 1m winner and Group 3 1m UAE 2,000 Guineas third Rallying Cry (by War Chant). The second dam, Turning Wheel (by Seeking The Wheel), winner of the Group 3 10f La Coupe de Maisons-Laffitte, is a half-sister to 7 winners including the 1,000 Guineas third Ajfan and the listed winners Space Cruiser and Minds Music. (Prime Equestrian)

1439. WAUSE ★★★
b.c. Whipper – Apple Sauce (Prince Sabo).
April 28. Sixth foal. 34,000Y. Doncaster St Leger. Prime Equestrian. Half-brother to the fair dual 5f winner Steelcut (by Iron Mask), to the modest 3-y-o all-weather dual 5f winner Cut And Dried (by Daggers Drawn) and a winner in Belgium by Shinko Forest. The dam, a fair 3-y-o 5f winner, is a half-sister to 4 winners including the Group 2 5f Flying Childers Stakes winner Sizzling Melody. The second dam, Mrs Bacon (by Balliol), a quite useful 2-y-o 5f winner, is a half-sister to 2 winners. (Prime Equestrian)

1440. UNNAMED ★★★
ch.c. Bahamian Bounty – Hill Welcome
(Most Welcome).
March 31. Sixth foal. 50,000Y. Tattersalls October 2. McKeever St Lawrence. Brother to the useful 2-y-o dual 5f winner and Group 3 Molecomb Stakes second Mary Read and half-brother to the quite useful 2008 2-y-o 6f winner Dubai Hills (by Dubai Destination), the useful 2-y-o 6f winner and listed-placed Tiana (by Diktat) and the quite useful dual 5f winner Jack Rackham (by Kyllachy). The dam was placed twice at 2 yrs and stayed 7f and is a half-sister to 5 winners including the Group 1 6f Middle Park Stakes winner Stalker and the 2-y-o listed 5f winner and Group 3 third Regal Peace. The

second dam, Tarvie (by Swing Easy), won 3 races and was a useful sprinter. (Mrs F Denniff)

1441. UNNAMED ★★★
b.c. Bahamian Bounty – Molly Moon (Primo Dominie).
January 18. Second foal. 30,000Y. Tattersalls October 3. McKeever St Lawrence. Half-brother to the fair 2008 6f placed 2-y-o Battle (by Compton Place). The dam, a useful 2-y-o dual 5f winner, is a half-sister to the smart dual Group 3 sprint winner The Trader. The second dam, Snowing (by Tate Gallery), a quite useful dual 5f winner at 3 yrs, is a half-sister to 2 minor winners. (EKOS Pinnacle Partnership)

TOMMY STACK

1442. AISY (IRE) ★★★
b.f. Oasis Dream – Granny Kelly (Irish River).
February 25. Seventh foal. 55,000Y. Tattersalls October 1. Not sold. Half-brother to the quite useful 2-y-o 6f and Italian 7.5f listed winner Six Hitter (by Boundary), to the quite useful dual 7f winner (including at 2 yrs) Hustle (by Choisir) and a minor 10f winner in France by Montjeu. The dam, placed once over 7f at 2 yrs in Ireland, is a half-sister to 4 minor winners. The second dam, Devilante (by Devil's Bag), a minor US 3-y-o winner, is a half-sister to 5 winners including the US stakes winner and Grade 2 placed Arrowtown.
"She finished fourth on her debut and was a bit green but hopefully she'll improve for that and won't be long in winning. She's not over big but she's a sharp, precocious filly and five/six furlongs is her trip".

1443. BANGATHELATCH (IRE) ★★★
b.c. Choisir – Vinicky (Kingmambo).
March 3. Sixth foal. €32,000Y. Tattersalls Ireland. Half-brother to the useful 2008 Irish 2-y-o dual 6f winner Pady The Pro (by Exceed And Excel) and to a winner in Greece by Fasliyev. The dam is an unplaced half-sister to 7 winners. The second dam, L'Incestueuse (by Lypheor), won 3 races in France and is a half-sister to 4 winners.
"He'll set off over six furlongs in late May or early June. He seems to nicely but he'll want fast ground".

1444. BROCANTEUR (IRE) ★★★
b.c. Chineur – Shining Desert (Green Desert).
March 13. Seventh foal. 38,000Y. Tattersalls October 1. Five Star Bloodstock. Half-brother to the unplaced 2008 2-y-o Shining Times (by Danetime), to the Italian winner of 13 races from 2 to 6 yrs Bryan Gold (by Bahhare), the modest triple 6f winner Maison Dieu (by King Charlemagne) and the Italian winner (including at 2 yrs), Compton Flowers (by Compton Place). The dam, a quite useful 2-y-o 5f winner, is a half-sister to 2 winners. The second dam, Riyoom (by Vaguely Noble), won over 1m in Ireland at 2 yrs, is a half-sister to 5 winners including the dual US Grade 3 winner Lt Lao.
"A big, fine imposing colt, he seems to move well and he should be running in May. He'll probably want the ground on the fast side and he's likely to start off at six furlongs".

1445. CAPULET MONTEQUE (IRE) ★★★
b.f. Camacho – Family At War (Explodent).
April 25. Thirteenth foal. €37,000Y. Goffs Million. James Stack. Half-sister to the very useful listed Scarborough Stakes winner and Group 2 Kings Stand Stakes second Flanders (herself dam of the US Grade 3 winner Louvain), to the quite useful 6f winner Disputed and a 5f winner in Macau (all by Common Grounds), the listed winner Ascot Family (by Desert Style), the fair 2-y-o 5f and 6f winner Magic Myth, the modest 2-y-o 5f winner Elsie Hart, the modest 10.2f winner Diddymu (all by Revoque) and a winner in Belgium by Distant Music. The dam, a fair 2-y-o 5f winner, is a half-sister to 4 minor winners in the USA. The second dam, Sometimes Perfect (by Bold Bidder), a minor 2-y-o 6f winner in the USA, is a half-sister to 6 winners including the French listed winner and Group 1 Grand Prix de Saint-Cloud third Gain and the German Group 3 winner Krotz.
"A good-looking filly and she looks like she's going to be precocious. On pedigree you wouldn't expect her to get far and we'll set her off

at five furlongs and see where we go from there. She seems like a nice filly".

1446. CARAZAM (IRE) ★★
b.c. Azamour – Carallia
(Common Grounds).
April 23. Second foal. €60,000Y. Goffs Million. Not sold. The dam won over 6f at 2 yrs in Ireland and was listed-placed and is a half-sister to 3 winners including the Group 1 Prix de la Foret winner Caradak. The second dam, Caraiyma (by Shahrastani), won over 9f in Ireland and is a sister to the Irish dual Group 3 winner Cajarian.
"A well-balanced colt, looking at him I'd say he'd want seven furlongs and I don't think he'll take long to come to hand. I see him being out around June time".

1447. CLASHNACREE ★★★★
b.c. Footstepsinthesand – Miss Moore (Tagula).
March 13. Third foal. €70,000Y. Goffs Million. C McCormack. The dam, a moderate Irish 8.5f winner, is a half-sister to 5 winners. The second dam, Thatcherite (by Final Straw), is an unraced half-sister to 7 winners including the Group 3 winners Kampala, Millionaire and State Occasion.
"He goes nicely and he's a very good mover. We'll set him off in May over six furlongs and he'll have no problem getting seven but he will want fast ground".

1448. LOLLY FOR DOLLY (IRE) ★★★
b.f. Oratorio – Heart Stopping (Chester House).
March 17. First foal. 57,000Y. Tattersalls October 2. C McCormack. The dam, a modest 1m placed 3-y-o, is a half-sister to the listed winner and Group 3 Fred Darling Stakes third Short Dance. The second dam, Clog Dance (by Pursuit Of Love), a useful maiden, was second in the Group 3 7f Rockfel Stakes and the listed 10f Pretty Polly Stakes and is a half-sister to 5 winners including the smart 14f Ebor Handicap winner Tuning.
"A grand, scopey filly, she's coming along quite nicely. A good mover, she'll probably appreciate seven furlongs".

1449. MARCUS GALERIUS (IRE) ★★★
b.c. Antonius Pius – Surprise Me
(Imperial Frontier).
May 1. Second foal. €10,000Y. Tattersalls Ireland. James Carney. The dam, a modest Irish 5f winner at 5 yrs, is a half-sister to a winner abroad and to a Bumper winner. The second dam, Ushimado (by Ela-Mana-Mou), an Irish 10f and hurdles winner, is a half-sister to 7 other minor winners.
"He goes nicely and he'll be out in May over six furlongs. His pedigree is very light but he's a good-looking colt". TRAINER'S BARGAIN BUY

1450. NUBAR BOY ★★★
ch.c. Compton Place – Out Like Magic
(Magic Ring).
March 14. Fifth foal. 35,000Y. Doncaster St Leger. Irish Racing Shares. Half-brother to the quite useful 2-y-o 6f winner Bahamian Magic (by Royal Applause) and to a minor winner in Greece by Vettori. The dam, a quite useful 2-y-o 5f winner, is a half-sister to 4 winners including the listed Heron Stakes second In Like Flynn. The second dam, Thevetia (by Mummy's Pet), is a placed half-sister to 7 winners.
"He goes nicely, he probably wants six furlongs and fast ground. A big, strapping horse, he should be quite early".

1451. PLUM SUGAR (IRE) ★★★
b.f. Footstepsinthesand – Bush Baby (Zamindar).
February 7. Third foal. Half-sister to the quite useful 2008 2-y-o 6f winner Aakef (by Exceed And Excel). The dam is an unplaced half-sister to 9 winners including the very smart Group 2 12f Ribblesdale Stakes winner Gull Nook (herself dam of the top-class colt Pentire), the equally smart Group 3 12f Princess Royal Stakes winner Banket and the useful Group 3 Ormonde Stakes winner Mr Pintips. The second dam, Bempton (by Blakeney), was placed three times at up to 11f and is a half-sister to Shirley Heights.
"She's a fine, big filly and a good-mover. I imagine she'll be racing from mid-summer onwards but we haven't done an awful lot with her yet. She's a good-looking filly, so hopefully she'll have an engine".

1452. RAHYA CLASS (IRE) ★★★
b.f. Rahy – It's On The Air (King's Theatre).
January 25. First foal. €125,000Y. Goffs Million. De Burgh/Farrington. The dam is an unraced half-sister to 6 winners including the Champion Stakes and dual US Grade 1 winner Storming Home. The second dam, Try To Catch Me (by Shareef Dancer), a winner at 3 yrs in France, is a half-sister to 8 winners including the French Group 2 winner Bitooh.

"She shouldn't take too long and I should imagine she'd be out in late May or early June. Having said that I think she'll want seven furlongs, she moves nicely and we're happy with her".

1453. SHABASSH ★★★
b.c. Antonius Pius – Basin Street Blues (Dolphin Street).
February 8. Fourth foal. €130,000Y. Goffs Million. C McCormack. Half-brother to the fairly useful 2-y-o dual 6f and subsequent US winner Varsity Blues (by Fasliyev). The dam won over 7f and 1m at 3 yrs and is a half-sister to 7 minor winners. The second dam, Music Of The Night (by Blushing Groom), is an unraced half-sister to 9 winners including the dual Group 1 winner Prima Voce.

"He'll start off at Leopardstown over six furlongs in mid-April. He probably wouldn't want the ground too soft and he looks to be progressive".

1454. WALK ON BYE (IRE) ★★★★
b.f. Danehill Dancer – Pipalong (Pips Pride).
April 22. Fifth foal. €68,000Y. Goffs Million. James Stack. Sister to Alliance, a minor winner of 2 races at 2 yrs abroad. The dam won 10 races including the Group 1 6f Haydock Park Sprint Cup, the Group 3 Duke Of York Stakes and the Group 3 Palace House Stakes and is a half-sister to 6 winners including the fairly useful 2-y-o 6f listed winner Out Of Africa. The second dam, Limpopo (by Green Desert), a poor 5f placed 2-y-o, is a half-sister to 7 winners here and abroad.

"A nice filly, she seems to have a bit of toe and probably won't get much further than six or seven furlongs I should imagine. She goes nicely and she's a good-looking filly. We're getting quite excited about her and it won't be long before she's out".

1455. WOODROW CALL (IRE) ★★★
b.c. Desert Style – Majudel (Revoque).
March 3. Second foal. 50,000Y. Doncaster St Leger. Fozzy Stack. Brother to the modest 4-y-o 1m winner Navene. The dam is an unraced full or half-sister to 6 winners including the Group 3 Futurity Stakes winner and Group 1 Dewhurst Stakes third Impressionist. The second dam, Yashville (by Top Ville), is an unraced half-sister to 8 winners.

"He's a fine, big, good-looking colt that should be suited by six/seven furlongs and be racing from late May onwards".

1456. UNNAMED ★★★
b.f. Galileo – Christel Flame (Darshaan).
January 29. Second foal. €52,000Y. Goffs Million. Angie Sykes. Half-sister to the 2-y-o 7f seller winner Coffee Cup (by Royal Academy). The dam won 3 races in France at around 12f including a listed event and is a half-sister to 5 winners. The second dam, Kirkby Belle (by Bay Express), is a placed half-sister to 5 winners.

"A big filly, she'll take a bit of time but she's a good mover. One for the back-end of the season".

1457. UNNAMED ★★★
b.f. Galileo – Fear And Greed (Brief Truce).
March 5. Half-sister to the fair 2-y-o 6f winner Falcolnry (by Hawk Wing) and to the minor Irish 5f winner Live In Fear (by Fasliyev). The dam, an Irish 2-y-o 6f winner and second in the Group 1 7f Moyglare Stud Stakes, is a half-sister to the 2-y-o 6.5f Goffs Challenge winner Serious Play. The second dam, Zing Ping (by Thatching), a quite useful 2-y-o 7f placed maiden, is a half-sister to 4 winners here and abroad.

"Not really a typical Galileo, she shouldn't take too long to come to hand and she's going along quite nicely".

1458. UNNAMED ★★★★
b.c. *Antonius Pius – Kotdiji (Mtoto).*
April 6. Fourth foal. €110,000Y. Goffs Million. Irish Racing Shares. Half-brother to the fair 2008 7f and 1m placed 2-y-o Polly's Mark (by Mark Of Esteem). The dam is an unraced half-sister to 4 winners including the 1,000 Guineas winner Ameerat and to the smart UAE 7.5f/1m winner Walmooh. The second dam, Walimu (by Top Ville), a quite useful winner of 3 races from 1m to 12f, is a half-sister to 6 winners.

"A big, fine, good-looking horse and he appears to be a good-mover. He'll take a bit of time and is probably one for the middle of the summer. We're very happy with him and he seems to have all the right credentials".

1459. UNNAMED ★★★
b.f. *Galileo – Most Precious (Nureyev).*
May 2. Twelfth foal. 220,000Y. Tattersalls October 1. Charlie Gordon-Watson. Half-sister to the French 1,000 Guineas and US Grade 1 winner Matiara, to the French listed winner and US Grade 2 placed Precious Ring (both by Bering), the 2-y-o Group 2 6f Richmond Stakes winner Pyrus and the Group 2 Prix du Muguet winner Marathon (by Diesis). The dam won the listed Prix de Lieurey, was placed in the Group 1 Prix de la Salamandre and Group 1 Grand Criterium and is a half-sister to 8 winners including the listed Atalanta Stakes winner Private Line. The second dam, Miss Summer (by Luthier), won the listed 1m Prix de Saint-Cyr and is a half-sister to the Group 2 Prix Hocquart winner Mot d'Or, the Group 1 Gran Premio de Milano winner Lydian and the Group 2 Ribblesdale Stakes winner and high-class broodmare Ballinderry.

"She's a very nice filly and a good mover with a great pedigree. She hasn't done much yet but hopefully she'll be up to running at the back-end of the season. She'll probably want good ground".

1460. UNNAMED ★★★
b.f. *Montjeu – Saganeca (Sagace).*
February 8. Twelfth foal. Closely related to the 2-y-o 1m winner and Group 3 Chester Vase second Almighty (by Sadler's Wells) and half-sister to 6 winners including the Prix de l'Arc de Triomphe winner Sagamix, to the Group 2 Prix de Malleret winner Sage Et Jolie, the minor French 2-y-o winner Saga d'Ouilly (all by Linamix), the Group 1 Criterium de Saint-Cloud winner Sagacity (by Highest Honor) and the useful 12f and 13f winner and listed-placed Shastye (by Danehill). The dam was a very smart winner of the Group 3 12.5f Prix de Royallieu. The second dam, Haglette (by Hagley), won 3 races in the USA and is a half-sister to the smart French 7f and 1m winner Round Top.

"She seems quite a nice filly and despite her pedigree she isn't that backward, so she should be up for a couple of runs at the back-end".

1461. UNNAMED ★★★
b.c. *Oratorio – Swiss Roll (Entrepreneur).*
March 23. Second foal. €70,000Y. Goffs Million. Irish Racing Shares. The dam, an Irish 12f and 14f winner, was listed placed and is a sister to the smart Irish 2-y-o 7f winner and Group 1 7f National Stakes second Berenson and a half-sister to one winner. The second dam, On Air (by Chief Singer), a fairly useful dual 10f and hurdles winner, is a half-sister to 6 winners including the Prix de Malleret winner Another Dancer.

"A grand, hard-knocking colt, he'll be out as soon as the seven furlong maidens start".

SIR MICHAEL STOUTE

1462. ARAKANA (IRE) ★★★
b.c. *Danehill Dancer – Castle Quest (Grand Lodge).*
February 28. Fourth foal. 420,000Y. Tattersalls October 2. Maxine Cowdrey. Half-brother to the quite useful UAE 7f and 1m winner City Of Poets (by Alhaarth). The dam, an Irish 3-y-o listed 1m winner, is a half-sister to 4 winners including the Group 2 Nassau Stakes winner Siringas. The second dam, In Unison (by Bellypha), won over 1m at 3 yrs and is a half-sister to the Group 1 6f Haydock Park Sprint Cup winner Cherokee Rose. (Mrs E Moran)

1463. CHIEFDOM PRINCE ★★★
br.c. *Dansili – Jouet (Reprimand).*
April 15. Sixth foal. 220,000Y. Tattersalls October 1. Charlie Gordon-Watson. Half-brother to the very useful listed 6f winner Rising Shadow (by Efisio), to the fair 1m and 8.3f winner Night Cru (by Night Shift) and the modest 6f winner Bonne (by Namid). The dam, a fair 7f placed 3-y-o, is a sister to the dual Group 3 winning sprinter Deep Finesse and a half-sister to 5 winners including the dam of the Cornwallis Stakes winner Halmahera. The second dam, Babycham Sparkle (by So Blessed), a quite useful 5f and 6f winner, is a half-sister to 6 winners and to the dams of the Group winners Premiere Cuvee, Monsieur Bond and River Falls. (Saeed Suhail)

1464. CONDUCT (IRE) ★★★
gr.c. *Selkirk – Coventina (Daylami).*
February 28. First foal. 56,000Y. Tattersalls October 2. John Warren. The dam, a useful 1m (at 2 yrs) and 2m winner, is a half-sister to 2 winners including the useful 2-y-o dual 1m winner Ladies Best. The second dam, Lady Of The Lake (by Caerleon), a useful 2m listed winner of 4 races, is a half-sister to 5 winners including the Italian Group 3 winner Guest Connections. (Highclere Thoroughbred Racing)

1465. EFFERVESCE (IRE) ★★★★
ch.f. *Galileo – Royal Fizz (Royal Academy).*
April 7. Eighth foal. 280,000Y. Tattersalls October 1. Cheveley Park Stud. Half-sister to the useful 2-y-o dual 7f winner and listed-placed Grand Marque (by Grand Lodge), to the useful dual 6f winner (including at 2 yrs) Hitchens (by Acclamation) and to a winner of 4 races 3 and 4 yrs in Belgium by Brief Truce. The dam won once over 6.5f at 2 yrs in France and is a half-sister to 6 winners here and abroad including the £1m Hong Kong earner Floral Pegasus. The second dam, Crown Crest (by Mill Reef), won once at 3 yrs and is a sister to the high-class middle-distance horses Glint Of Gold and Diamond Shoal. (Cheveley Park Stud)

1466. ELEANORA DUSE (IRE) ★★
b.f. *Azamour – Drama Class (Caerleon).*
March 19. Half-sister to the listed 10f winner and Group 1 12f Irish Oaks second Scottish Stage (by Selkirk) and to the fairly useful 10f winner Voice Coach (by Alhaarth). The dam, a useful 10.2f winner, is a half-sister to the Group 2 10.3f winner Stage Gift. The second dam, Stage Struck (by Sadler's Wells), a quite useful 12f winner, is a sister to the high-class Group 1 7f Dewhurst Stakes winner (in a dead-heat) Prince of Dance and to the useful middle-distance winners Ballet Prince and Golden Ball. (Ballymacoll Stud)

1467. FANCY VIVID (IRE) ★★★
b.f. *Galileo – Starchy (Cadeaux Genereux).*
March 28. First foal. €400,000Y. Goffs Million. Simon Christian. The dam, a fair 2-y-o 6f winner, is a sister to the smart Group 2 5f Flying Childers Stakes and Group 3 5f King George V Stakes winner Land Of Dreams (herself dam of the dual listed winner Into The Dark) and a half-sister to 5 winners. The second dam, Sahara Star (by Green Desert), winner of the Group 3 5f Molecomb Stakes, was third in the Lowther Stakes and is a half-sister to the Group 3 7f Greenham Stakes winner and Irish 2,000 Guineas fourth Yalaietanee. (Patrick Fahey)

1468. GIANT'S PLAY (USA) ★★★★
b.f. *Giant's Causeway – Playful Act (Sadler's Wells).*
January 17. First foal. $850,000Y. Keeneland September. John Warren. The dam, a Group 1 Fillies' Mile, Group 2 Lancashire Oaks and Group 2 May Hill Stakes winner, is a sister to the Group 2 Yorkshire Cup winner Percussionist and a half-sister to the Group 2 Sun Chariot Stakes and Group 2 Park Hill Stakes winner Echoes In Eternity. The second dam, Magnificent Style (by Silver Hawk), won the Group 3 10.5f Musidora Stakes and is a half-sister to the Grade 1 10f Charles H Strub Stakes winner Siberian Summer. (Mrs R Jacobs)

1469. INQAATH ★★★
ch.c. Mr Greeley – Sparkle Of Stones (Sadler's Wells).
January 23. First foal. 320,000Y. Tattersalls October 1. Shadwell Estate Co. The dam is an unraced sister to the useful French 1m and 11f winner Synergetic and a half-sister to 5 winners including the very smart Group 3 7f Greenham Stakes winner and 2,000 Guineas second Enrique and the smart sprinter/miler Piperi. The second dam, Gwydion (by Raise A Cup), won the Group 3 5f Queen Mary Stakes, the listed 6f Hackwood Stakes and the listed 5f Bentinck Stakes and is a half-sister to 5 winners. (Hamdan Al Maktoum).

1470. ISLAND DREAMS ★★★
b.f. Giant's Causeway – Camanoe (Gone West).
May 5. Half-sister to 3 winners including July Jasmine (by Empire Maker), a 7f winner at 2 yrs in 2008 and the Group 2 Sandown Mile and Group 3 1m Joel Stakes winner Rob Roy (by Lear Fan). The dam was unplaced in 2 starts and is a half-sister to the US Grade 1 Yellow Ribbon Invitational winner Super Staff, to the French and US Grade 2 Public Purse and the minor US stakes winner Mr Adorable. The second dam, Prodigeous (by Pharly), won 4 races at 3 and 4 yrs in France and is a half-sister to the minor US stakes winner Sheila Shine. (Khalid Abdulla).

1471. ISTIMLAAK (IRE) ★★★★ ♠
b.c. Marju – Zither (Zafonic).
March 8. Third foal. 150,000Y. Tattersalls October 1. Shadwell Estate Co. Half-brother to the fair 8.5f winner Themwerethedays (by Olden Times). The dam, a fairly useful 6f (at 2 yrs) and 7f winner, is a half-sister to the useful 2-y-o listed 6f winner Dowager and the useful 1m (at 2 yrs) and 10f winner Dower House. The second dam, Rose Noble (by Vaguely Noble), a modest 3-y-o 11.5f winner, is a half-sister to 6 winners including the champion two-year-old and high-class sire Grand Lodge, winner of the Dewhurst Stakes and the St James's Palace Stakes. (Hamdan Al Maktoum).

1472. KING'S PARADE ★★★
b.c. Dynaformer – Bay Tree (Daylami).
February 12. First foal. 220,000Y. Tattersalls October 1. Charlie Gordon-Watson. The dam, useful 2-y-o listed 7f winner, is a half-sister to 4 winners including the Group 1 6f Haydock Sprint Cup winner Tante Rose. The second dam, My Branch (by Distant Relative), a very useful winner of the listed 6f Firth Of Clyde Stakes (at 2 yrs) and the listed 7f Sceptre Stakes, was second in the Group 1 Cheveley Park Stakes and third in the Irish 1,000 Guineas and is a half-sister to 5 winners. (Saeed Suhail).

1473. LOYALTY ★★★
b.c. Medicean – Ecoutila (Rahy).
February 19. Third foal. 88,000Y. Tattersalls October 1. John Warren. Half-brother to the 2008 2-y-o listed 1m winner Enticement (by Montjeu) and to the minor French 2-y-o winner Betilla (by Bering). The dam is an unraced half-sister to the US winner and Grade 2 placed Listen Indy. The second dam, Ecoute (by Manila), a winner of 2 listed events in France and the USA and third in the Group 1 Prix Saint-Alary, is a half-sister to 5 winners including the Group 1 winners Pas de Reponse and Green Tune. (Highclere Thoroughbred Racing).

1474. MAGNETIC FORCE (IRE) ★★★★ ♠
gr.c. Verglas – Upperville (Selkirk).
February 19. Second foal. €160,000Y. Goffs Million. Charlie Gordon-Watson. Half-brother to Blue Ridge Lane (by Indian Ridge), unplaced in one start at 2 yrs in 2008. The dam, a fair Irish 12f winner, is a half-sister to 6 winners including the useful Irish listed 12f winner Mutakarrim and the very useful Irish listed 10f winner Nafisah. The second dam, Alyakkh (by Sadler's Wells), a fair 3-y-o 1m winner, is a half-sister to the Champion Stakes and 2,000 Guineas winner Haafhd and to the 1m listed stakes winner and Group 1 Coronation Stakes second Hasbah.

1475. MAIN SPRING ★★★
b.f. Pivotal – Fairy Godmother (Fairy King).
March 16. Half-sister to the useful 2008 2-y-o 1m winner and Group 3 1m Autumn Stakes

third Four Winds (by Red Ransom) and to the quite useful dual 10f winner Kingdom Of Fife (by Kingmambo). The dam, a listed 10f winner, is a half-sister to the Group 2 12f Jockey Club Stakes winner Blueprint. The second dam, Highbrow (by Shirley Heights), a very useful 2-y-o 1m winner, was second in the Group 2 12f Ribblesdale Stakes, is closely related to the good middle-distance colt Milford and a half-sister to the Princess of Wales's Stakes winner Height of Fashion — herself the dam of Nashwan, Nayef and Unfuwain. (The Queen).

1476. MARKAZZI ★★★
b.c. Dansili – Bandanna (Bandmaster).
April 5. Fourth foal. 300,000Y. Tattersalls October 1. Shadwell Estate Co. Half-brother to the fairly useful 2-y-o 5.5f winner Art Sale (by Compton Place) and to the quite useful 2-y-o 5f winner Rowayton (by Lujain). The dam, a fairly useful 5f and 6f winner of 6 races (including at 2 yrs), is a half-sister to 5 winners including the Group 3 July Stakes winner Rich Ground. The second dam, Gratclo (by Belfort), a modest winner of 5 races from 2 to 4 yrs, is a half-sister to 4 winners. (Hamdan Al Maktoum)

1477. RAHAALA ★★★
b.f. Indian Ridge – Mythie (Octagonal).
April 5. Second foal. 170,000foal. Tattersalls December. Shadwell Estate Co. Half-sister to the fairly useful 2008 2-y-o 6f winner Versaki (by Verglas). The dam, a minor French 3-y-o winner, is a half-sister to 4 winners including the French listed winner Mytographie. The second dam, Mythologie (by Bering), won twice and is a half-sister to 7 winners.(Hamdan Al Maktoum)

1478. READYMADE ★★
b.c. Dubai Destination – Onda Nova (Keos).
February 23. Second foal. €140,000Y. Goffs Million. Not sold. The dam, a winner of 3 races in France at 2 and 3 yrs including the listed Prix Imprudence, is a half-sister to 6 winners and to the placed dams of the Group 1 winners Shiva and Light Shift and the Brazilian Grade 1 winners Nonno Luigi and Jeune-Turc. The second dam, Northern Trick (by Northern Dancer), won the Prix de Diane and the Prix Vermeille, was second in the Prix de l'Arc de Triomphe and is a half-sister to the US Grade 1 Jockey Club Gold Cup winner On The Sly. (Niarchos Family)

1479. SIR WALTER RALEIGH ★★
b.c. Galileo – Elizabethan Age (King's Best).
March 1. First foal. 120,000Y. Tattersalls October 1. John Warren. The dam, a fair 7f winner, is a half-sister to the useful dual 10f winner Drill Sergeant. The second dam, Dolydille (by Dolphin Street), won 7 races including 2 listed events, from 9f to 12f and is a half-sister to 9 winners including the Irish listed 1m winner and high-class broodmare La Meilleure. (Highclere Thoroughbred Racing)

1480. SPECIFIC DREAM ★★★★
b.f. Danehill Dancer – Specifically (Sky Classic).
April 15. Ninth foal. Sister to the 1,000 Guineas and Group 2 Rockfel Stakes winner Speciosa and half-sister to the US Grade 3 stakes winner of 11 races and Grade 1 placed Major Rhythm (by Rhythm), the minor US winner of 6 races Bold Classic (by Pembroke), the fair 1m and 10f winner Liberally (by Statue Of Liberty), the fair 9.7f and 10f winner Thundermill (by Thunder Gulch) and the modest all-weather 5f and 6f winner Shadow Jumper (by Dayjur). The dam won once at 2 yrs in the USA and is a half-sister to 7 winners including the Group 1 Champion Stakes, Grand Prix de Saint-Cloud and Hong Kong Cup winner Pride. The second dam, Specificity (by Alleged), a useful winner of the listed 12.2f George Stubbs Stakes, is a half-sister to the 10 winners including the St Leger and Irish St Leger winner Touching Wood. (Mrs R C Jacobs)

1481. STARSHINE ★★★★
b.f. Danehill Dancer – In The Limelight (Sadler's Wells).
January 16. Third foal. 100,000Y. Tattersalls October 1. John Warren. The dam, an Irish listed 1m winner, is a sister to the Irish listed winner On The Nile, closely related to the Singapore Gold Cup, Group 1 Gran Premio del

Jockey Club and dual German Group 1 winner Kutub and a half-sister to 3 winners. The second dam, Minnie Habit (by Habitat), an Irish 4-y-o 9f winner, is closely related to the dual sprint Group 3 winner Bermuda Classic (herself dam of the Coronation Stakes winner Shake The Yoke) and a half-sister to 6 winners. (The Queen).

1482. SUGHERA (IRE) ★★★
b.f. *Alhaarth – Gold Bar (Barathea).*
March 7. The dam, a 10f placed maiden, is closely related to the high-class Group 1 7f Dewhurst Stakes dead-heater Prince of Dance and to the Group 2 Scottish Derby winner Princely Venture. The second dam, Sun Princess (by English Prince), a top-class winner of the Oaks, the St Leger and the Yorkshire Oaks, is a half-sister to the high-class middle-distance colt Saddlers Hall. (Ballymacoll Stud).

1483. TIMELESS STRIDE (IRE) ★★★
b.c. *Kyllachy – Trois Heures Apres (Soviet Star).*
March 28. Eighth foal. 100,000Y. Tattersalls October 2. Charlie Gordon-Watson. Half-brother to the quite useful 2-y-o 6f and 7f winner and 1m listed placed Laurentina (by Cadeaux Genereux), to the French 9m to 10f winner of 9 races and listed placed Rising Talent (by Bering), the fairly useful 10f winner Feaat (by Unfuwain), the fair 1m winner Groomsman (by Groom Dancer) and a minor winner in Italy by King's Theatre. The dam is an unraced half-sister to 4 winners including the very useful 7f (at 2 yrs) and 10f listed winner and Oaks third Mezzogiorno (herself dam of the Group 2 Blandford Stakes winner Monturani). The second dam, Aigue (by High Top), a fairly useful 4-y-o dual 1m winner, is a sister to the listed middle-distance winner Torchon. (Saeed Suhail)

1484. UNNAMED ★★★★
b.c. *Montjeu – Altruiste (Diesis).*
March 30. Second foal. €420,000Y. Goffs Million. Demi O'Byrne. The dam is an unraced half-sister to the 2,000 Guineas winner King's Best and to the Arc winner Urban Sea (herself dam of the Derby, Irish Derby and King George VI winner Galileo, the dual Group 1 winner Black Sam Bellamy and the US Grade 1 My Typhoon) and the Group 3 winner Allez Les Trois (dam of the French Derby winner Anabaa Blue). The second dam, Allegretta (by Lombard), a useful 2-y-o 1m and 9f winner and second in the Lingfield Oaks Trial, is a sister to the German St Leger winner Anno. (Mr J Magnier,/Mr M Tabor/D Smith)

1485. UNNAMED ★★★
b.br.c. *Dynaformer – Arabian Spell (Desert Prince).*
March 14. Second foal. $380,000Y. Keeneland September. Charlie Gordon-Watson. The dam, a 1m winner and third in the Group 3 Prix Miesque, is a half-sister to 2 winners including the useful 7f and 1m winner Truly Enchanting. The second dam, Truly Bewitched (by Affirmed), a quite useful 2-y-o 6f winner, is a half-sister to 4 winners including the US Grade 2 winner Chinese Dragon. (Saeed Suhail)

1486. UNNAMED ★★★★
b.f. *Oasis Dream – Arrive (Kahyasi).*
March 29. Sister to the Group 6f Princess Margaret Stakes and Group 7f Oak Tree Stakes winner Visit and half-sister to the Group 1 10f Pretty Polly Stakes and Group 3 10f Middleton Stakes winner Promising Lead (by Danehill), The dam, a very useful 10f (at 2 yrs) and listed 13.8f winner, is a half-sister to the 2-y-o 5f winner (stayed 1m) Hasili (herself dam of the top-class performers Banks Hill, Heat Haze and Dansili). The second dam, Kerali (by High Line), a quite useful 3-y-o 7f winner, is a half-sister to numerous winners including the Group 3 6f July Stakes winner Bold Fact and the Group 1 Nunthorpe Stakes winner So Factual. (Khalid Abdulla)

1487. UNNAMED ★★★
b.c. *Smart Strike – Colonella (Pleasant Colony).*
February 19. Third foal. $500,000Y. Keeneland September. Charlie Gordon-Watson. Brother to the US Grade 3 winner Pleasant Strike and half-brother to a minor US winner by Lemon Drop Kid. The dam, a winner at 3 yrs, is a sister to the

US Grade 2 winner Colonial Minstrel and a half-sister to the US Grade 3 winner Minidar. The second dam, Minstrella (by The Minstrel), won the Group 1 Cheveley Park Stakes. (Saeed Suhail)

1488. UNNAMED ★★★★
ch.c. Selkirk – Ithaca (Distant View).
March 31. Second foal. Half-brother to the 2008 2-y-o 7f winner and Group 2 7f Champagne Stakes second Zacinto (by Dansili). The dam, a useful 2-y-o 7f winner and second in the Group 3 7f Prestige Stakes, is a half-sister to several winners including the useful dual 10f winner Many Volumes. The second dam, Reams Of Verse (by Nureyev), won the Oaks, the Fillies Mile, the Musidora Stakes and the May Hill Stakes and is a half-sister to numerous winners including the high-class Group 1 10f Coral Eclipse Stakes and Group 1 10f Phoenix Champion Stakes winner Elmaamul. (Khalid Abdulla).

1489. UNNAMED ★★★
b.c. Gone West – Light Jig (Danehill).
March 17. The dam, a US Grade 1 10f Yellow Ribbon Stakes winner, is a half-sister to numerous winners including the very useful French 2-y-o listed 1m winner Battle Dore. The second dam, Nashmeel (by Blushing Groom), was a very smart winner of three races over 1m including the Group 2 Prix d'Astarte and was second in the Prix Jacques le Marois (to Miesque), the Yellow Ribbon Invitational and the Matriarch Stakes. (Khalid Abdulla).

1490. UNNAMED ★★
b.f. Dalakhani – Not Before Time (Polish Precedent).
May 4. Closely related to the Group 3 10.4f Musidora Stakes winner and Group 1 Prix de Diane third Time Away (by Darshaan) and half-sister to the 10f winner and Group 1 French Oaks second Time Ahead (by Spectrum), the useful dual 1m winner Duntulm (by Sakhee), the fairly useful 10f and 12.4f winner Original Spin (by Machiavellian), the quite useful 10f winners Ringing Hill (by Charnwood Forest) and Time Loss (by Kenmare) and the fair 1m winner Time Over (by Mark Of Esteem). The dam is an unraced half-sister to the very useful Group 3 12f Jockey Club Stakes winner Zinaad and to the very useful Group 3 12f Princess Royal Stakes winner Time Allowed. The second dam, Time Charter (by Saritamer), was an exceptionally talented filly and winner of the Oaks, the King George VI and Queen Elizabeth Diamond Stakes, the Champion Stakes, the Coronation Cup, the Prix Foy and the Sun Chariot Stakes. (R Barnett).

1491. UNNAMED ★★★
b.c. Singspiel – Orford Ness (Selkirk).
March 24. Closely related to the Group 2 10f Prix Dollar winner Weightless (by In The Wings) and half-brother to the smart 7f (at 2 yrs) and listed 8.3f winner Home Affairs (by Dansili), the useful 6f and 7f winner Main Aim (by Oasis Dream) and the French 10.5f winner Castle Rising (by Indian Ridge). The dam won twice including the Group 3 1m Prix de Sandringham and is a half-sister to the French 10f winner and Group 2 10f Prix Eugene Adam second Aware. The second dam, the fairly useful 10f and 10.5f winner Nesaah (by Topsider) is a half-sister to the very useful Group 2 12f Prix de Malleret winner Privity and the Group 3 9f Prix Saint Roman winner Zindari. (Khalid Abdulla).

1492. UNNAMED ★★★
b.f. King's Best – Quiff (Sadler's Wells).
January 22. First foal. The dam won the Group 1 Yorkshire Oaks and is a sister to the useful 10f winner and Group 3 Chester Vase second Arabian Gulf. The second dam, Wince (by Selkirk), won the 1,000 Guineas and the Group 3 Fred Darling Stakes and is a half-sister to 3 winners including the very smart middle-distance winner Ulundi.

1493. UNNAMED ★★★ ♠
b.c. Arch – Remediate (Miswaki).
March 23. Fourth foal. €115,000Y. Goffs Million. Charlie Gordon-Watson. Half-brother to a minor winner in the USA by Belong To Me. The dam won 4 minor races in the USA and is a

half-sister to 4 winners. The second dam, Interlope (by Lemhi Gold), a listed-placed 2-y-o winner in the USA, is a half-sister to 3 winners. (Saeed Suhail)

1494. UNNAMED ★★★★
b.c. Dansili – Summer Breeze (Rainbow Quest).
March 4. Half-brother to the very smart 1m (at 2 yrs) and Group 3 12.3f Chester Vase winner Doctor Fremantle and to the dual 12f winner and listed-placed Summer Shower (by Sadler's Wells). The dam won over 1m at 2 yrs, was third in the Group 3 1m Prix des Reservoirs and is sister to the high-class Rothmans International and Prix Royal-Oak winner Raintrap and to the very smart Criterium de Saint-Cloud and Prix du Conseil de Paris winner Sunshack. The second dam, Suntrap (by Roberto), a useful dual 7f winner at 2 yrs, was third in the Group 3 Prix d'Aumale and is a half-sister to the Group 2 German winner Non Partisan and the Grade 3 Canadian stakes winner Jalaajel. (Khalid Abdulla).

1495. UNNAMED ★★★★
b.c. Sadler's Wells – Wince (Selkirk).
April 11. Brother to the Group 1 Yorkshire Oaks winner Quiff and to the useful 10f winner and Group 3 Chester Vase second Arabian Gulf. The dam won the 1,000 Guineas and the Group 3 Fred Darling Stakes and is a half-sister to 3 winners including the very smart middle-distance winner Ulundi. The second dam, Flit (by Lyphard), is a half-sister to the Grade 1 Washington Lassie Stakes winner Contredance, the listed Roses Stakes winner Old Alliance and the Graded stakes winners Shotiche and Skimble (herself dam of the US Grade 1 winner Skimming). (Khalid Abdulla).

SAEED BIN SUROOR (GODOLPHIN)

I must say "Thank You" to Diana Cooper for once again discussing the Godolphin horses with me.

1496. AMEER (IRE) ★★★
b.c. Monsun – Ailette (Second Set).
April 5. Fourth foal. 240,000Y. Tattersalls October 1. John Gosden. Half-brother to the German 2-y-o 7.5f winner Asinara (by Big Shuffle). The dam won once at 2 yrs in Germany and is a half-sister to 7 winners including the Group 1 German 2,000 Guineas winner Aviso and the dam of the Group 1 German Oaks winner Amarette. The second dam, Akasma (by Windwurf), won 3 races at 3 yrs in Germany, is a half-sister to 5 winners including the German Group 2 winner Ajano.
"More of a three-year-old prospect but the dam won at two and this colt is a three-parts brother to a German 2,000 Guineas winner, so we'd expect him to be out mid-season".

1497. ARABIAN FALCON (IRE) ★★★
b.c. Lomitas – Flying Squaw (Be My Chief).
February 20. Seventh foal. 100,000Y. Tattersalls October 1. John Ferguson. Brother to the very smart Group 3 10.3f Huxley Stakes and 2-y-o listed 7f winner Championship Point and half-brother to the fair 7f winner Straight Sets (by Pivotal) and the fair 8.5f winner Flying Carpet (by Barathea). The dam, winner of the Group 2 6f Moet and Chandon Rennen at 2 yrs, is a half-sister to 7 winners including the quite useful 5f and 6f winner Cauda Equina. The second dam, Sea Fret (by Habat), a fairly useful 2-y-o 6f winner, was listed-placed and is a half-sister to the winners and Lancashire Oaks placed fillies Main Sail and Sextant.
"This colt is straightforward, thriving on his work and if he continues to progress could be racing in June or July."

1498. ARABIAN HISTORY (USA) ★★★★
b.c. Kingmambo – Weekend In Seattle (Seattle Slew).
May 9. Ninth foal. $1,000,000Y. Keeneland September. John Ferguson. Brother to the US winner of 3 races and Grade 1 Travers Stakes second Mambo In Seattle, closely related to a minor US winner by Seeking The Gold and half-brother to 2 more by Danzig and War Chant. The dam, a winner of 3 races in the USA, was third in the Grade 1 CCA Oaks and is a sister to the multiple Grade 1 winner and sire A P Indy

and a half-sister to numerous winners including the dual US Grade 1 winner Summer Squall. The second dam, Weekend Surprise (by Secretariat), won two Grade 3 events in the USA and is a sister to the Group 1 Haydock Park Sprint Cup winner Wolfhound.

"This colt is a May-foal and still has plenty of daylight under him, but he is a very fluent mover and an exciting prospect for the back-end of the season."

1499. ASRAAB (IRE) ★★★★
b.c. Oasis Dream – Alexander Queen (King's Best).
February 22. First foal. €220,000Y. Goffs Million. John Ferguson. The dam, a fairly useful 2-y-o 5f winner, is a half-sister to the Group 3 Palace House Stakes winner and Group 1 placed Dandy Man. The second dam, Lady Alexander (by Night Shift), won the Group 3 6.3f Anglesey Stakes and Group 3 5f Molecomb Stakes.

"This is a flashy bay colt that thrives in his work. He should be relatively early and have the speed for five furlongs".

1500. ATLANTIS STAR ★★★
b.c. Cape Cross – Ladeena (Dubai Millennium).
February 8. First foal. 200,000Y. Tattersalls October 1. John Ferguson. The dam, a fair 7f winner at 3 yrs, is a half-sister to the quite useful 2-y-o 1m winner Elmonjed. The second dam, Aqaarid (by Nashwan), a smart winner of the Group 1 Fillies Mile and the Group 3 7.3f Fred Darling Stakes, was second in the 1,000 Guineas and is a half-sister to 2 winners.

"He is still a bit weak and growing but is a nice type for the second half of the season."

1501. BAB AL SHAMS (IRE) ★★★
b.c. Cape Cross – Shimna (Mr Prospector).
February 13. Sixth foal. 200,000Y. Tattersalls October 1. John Ferguson. Brother to the unraced 2008 2-y-o Black Eagle, closely related to the useful 2-y-o 7f winner Santa Fe (by Green Desert) and half-brother to the useful 1m (at 2 yrs) and 10f winner and Group 3 Derby Trial second Hazeymm (by Marju) and the fairly useful 1m (at 2 yrs) and dual 10f winner Sahrati

(by In The Wings). The dam, placed fourth over 10f in Ireland on her only outing, is a half-sister to the St Leger and Gran Premio del Jockey Club winner Shantou. The second dam, Shaima (by Shareef Dancer), a very useful 7.3f (at 2 yrs) and 9f listed winner here, later won the Grade 2 12f Long Island Handicap and is a half-sister to 6 winners including the Prix Saint Alary winner Rosefinch.

"He is still quite tall and weak but moves well and is an interesting prospect for the second half of the season."

1502. BINT ALMATAR (USA) ★★★★
b.f. Kingmambo – Firth of Lorne (Danehill).
January 17. First foal. The dam, a French 2-y-o listed 1m winner and second in the French 1,000 Guineas, was Grade 2 placed in the USA is a half-sister to 5 winners including the smart 2-y-o 6f winner and Group 3 placed Shmoose. The second dam, Kerrera (by Diesis), a smart winner of the Group 3 Cherry Hinton Stakes and second in the 1,000 Guineas, is a half-sister to the high-class 2-y-o Rock City.

"An attractive, well-made filly who is beginning to strengthen up. We would like to see her racing in mid-summer."

1503. BRONZE PRINCE ★★★★
b.c. Oasis Dream – Sweet Pea (Persian Bold).
February 26. Sixth foal. 220,000Y. Tattersalls October 1. John Ferguson. Half-brother to the modest 2008 6f placed 2-y-o Sicilian Pink (by Beat Hollow), to the Group 3 Princess Margaret Stakes and Group 3 Nell Gwyn Stakes winner Scarlet Runner (by Night Shift) and the minor Irish 12f winner Scent (by Groom Dancer). The dam, a fairly useful winner of 4 races at around 1m, is a half-sister to 4 winners including the useful listed 6f winner Star Tulip. The second dam, Silk Petal (by Petorius), a useful German listed 1m winner and third in the Group 3 10.5f Prix de Flore, is a half-sister to 5 winners including the good broodmare Dedicated Lady (dam of the Group 2 winners Fairy Queen and Tashawak).

"A very neat colt, he'll make a two-year-old before mid-summer and we like him".

1504. BURJ NAHAR ★★★
b.c. Shamardal – Melikah (Lammtarra).
March 18. Fifth foal. Half-brother to the French 2008 2-y-o 7f debut winner Valedictory (by Dubai Destination) and to the fair 10f and 11f winner Villarrica (by Selkirk). The dam was a smart winner of the listed 10f Pretty Polly Stakes and was third in the Oaks. She is a half-sister to the Derby, Irish Derby and King George VI and Queen Elizabeth Diamond Stakes winner Galileo, to the Group 1 12f Gran Premio del Jockey Club and Group 1 10.5f Tattersalls Gold Cup winner Black Sam Bellamy and the smart 1m (at 2 yrs) and Group 2 10f Gallinule Stakes winner Urban Ocean. The second dam, Urban Sea (by Miswaki), a top-class winner of 8 races from 1m (at 2 yrs) to 12f including the Group 1 Prix de l'Arc de Triomphe and the Group 2 Prix d'Harcourt, is closely related to the 2,000 Guineas winner King's Best and a half-sister to numerous winners including the smart Allez Les Trois, winner of the Group 3 10.5f Prix de Flore and herself dam of the French Derby winner Anabaa Blue.
"A nice 10-12f colt for next year, he will probably start over 7f later in the season."

1505. CARIBOU ISLAND ★★★
b.c. Dansili – Lake Nipigon (Selkirk).
March 1. First foal. Deauville August. €160,000Y. John Ferguson. The dam is an unraced half-sister to 6 winners including the Group 3 placed Equity Princess. The second dam, Hawait Al Barr (by Green Desert), a useful 12f to 2m winner, is out of a half-sister to the dam of the Kentucky Derby and Preakness Stakes winner Real Quiet.
"A well-grown but lazy colt who keeps producing more each time he is asked but it remains to be seen if he has the speed for 6f."

1506. EMIRATES DREAM (USA) ★★★★★
b.c. Kingmambo – My Boston Gal (Boston Harbor).
February 18. Second foal. $850,000Y. Keeneland September. John Ferguson. The dam won 5 races including two Grade 2 events in the USA and is a half-sister to one winner. The second dam, Western League (by Forty Niner), is an unraced half-sister to the Group 2 Cherry Hinton Stakes winner Storm Star.
"He is a lovely, classy mover but is not expected to be early. One for mid-summer onwards and he should be a miler next year".

1507. FROZEN POWER (IRE) ★★★★
b.c. Oasis Dream – Musical Treat (Royal Academy).
February 17. Fourth living foal. 500,000Y. Tattersalls October 1. John Ferguson. Half-sister to the Prix Marcel Boussac, 1,000 Guineas and Irish 1,000 Guineas winner Finsceal Beo (by Mr Greeley), to the quite useful 7f winner and listed placed Musical Bar (by Barathea) and a 3-y-o winner abroad by Red Ransom. The dam, a useful 3-y-o 7f winner and listed-placed twice, subsequently won 4 races at 4 yrs in Canada and the USA and is a half-sister to 6 winners. The second dam, Mountain Ash (by Dominion), won 10 races here and in Italy including the Group 3 Premio Royal Mares and is a half-sister to 7 winners.
"It will be difficult to match up to his half-sister's ability, but he is an athletic, forward type who could race in June."

1508. IBN SINA (IRE) ★★★
gr.c. Dalakhani – Sara Moon (Barathea).
January 19. Fourth foal. Deauville August. €500,000Y. John Ferguson. The dam, placed 4 times at 2 and 3 yrs in France, is a half-sister to 1 winner. The second dam, Diner de Lune (by Be My Guest), a French 2-y-o listed winner, is a half-sister to 2 winners including the Group 1 placed L'Ancresse and Cerulean Sky.
"A nice, tough, strong colt who is still very much an unknown quantity. He is a middle-distance type for next season and does everything asked of him with ease."

1509. IZAAJ (USA) ★★★★
ch.c. Giant's Causeway – Miss Coronado (Coronado's Quest).
January 15. The dam, a US Grade 2 8.5f Davona Dale Stakes winner, is a half-sister to the Group 3 7f Nell Gwyn Stakes and subsequent US dual

Grade 3 winner Karen's Caper and to the minor US stakes-placed winner Stone Cat. The second dam, Miss Caerleona (Caerleon), was a useful French 10f performer and subsequently won the Grade 3 Cardinal Handicap in the USA.

"This colt is doing well, is very professional and at the moment looks likely to be one of our first runners."

1510. LAMH ALBASSER (USA) ★★★★
ch.c. Mr Greeley – Madame Boulangere (Royal Applause).
March 10. Third foal. $450,000Y. Saratoga August. John Ferguson. The dam, a useful dual 6f winner (including at 2 yrs), was listed-placed and is a half-sister to one winner. The second dam, Jazz (by Sharrood), a fair 7f (at 2 yrs) and 10f placed maiden, is a half-sister to 12 winners including the fairly useful 2-y-o 5f winner Chasing Moonbeams, the Italian Group 2 placed Finian's Rainbow and the French Group 2 placed Carmot. (Mrs Carmen Burrell & Mr Jonathan Harvey).

"He is well-balanced and coming together quite quickly. There is plenty of speed in his family and he should start over 6f."

1511. NAFURA ★★★
b.f. Dubawi – Mysterial (Alleged).
March 28. Half-sister to the high-class Group 1 1m Prix Jacques le Marois and Group 1 1m Prix du Moulin winner Librettist, to the useful 7f and 1m winner Amarna (both by Danzig), the Group 1 1m Queen Anne Stakes and Group 2 7f Champagne Stakes winner Dubai Destination and the useful 10f and 10.5f winner Destination Dubai (both by Kingmambo). The dam ran unplaced twice and is a half-sister to the top-class Prix de l'Abbaye and July Cup winner Agnes World and to the champion Japanese sprinter/miler Hishi Akebono. The second dam, Mysteries (by Seattle Slew), was third in the Group 3 Musidora Stakes and is out of the Group 3 Prix Quincey winner Phydilla. (Sheikh Mohammed).

"This filly has a lot of size, like many of her dam's progeny. She is still a bit weak and won't be early."

1512. NASHAMA (IRE) ★★★★
b.f. Pivotal – Lurina (Lure).
March 23. Fifth foal. 480,000Y. Tattersalls October 1. John Ferguson. Half-sister to the dual 1m (at 2 yrs), Group 2 Great Voltigeur Stakes and Group 3 Classic Trial winner Centennial (by Dalakhani). The dam, a smart 1m winner, was third in the Group 2 1m Prix de Sandringham and is a half-sister to 6 winners including the dual Group 1 winner Croco Rouge and the listed winner Alidiva (herself dam of the Group 1 winners Sleepytime, Ali Royal and Taipan). The second dam, Alligatrix (by Alleged), a very useful 2-y-o 7f winner, was third in the Group 3 Hoover Fillies Mile and is a half-sister to 6 winners.

"This filly is athletic and has a lot of quality. A lovely prospect for this season and the next."

1513. NEXT MOVE (IRE) ★★★
b.c. Tiger Hill – Cinnamon Rose (Trempolino).
April 25. Seventh foal. 140,000Y. Tattersalls October 1. John Ferguson. Half-brother to the Group 1 7f Moyglare Stud Stakes winner Chelsea Rose (by Desert King), to the Irish 6f (at 2 yrs) and listed 1m and subsequent US winner and Grade 2 placed European (by Great Commotion), the quite useful 7f (at 2 yrs) and 12f winner Woodcutter (by Daylami), the Japanese 3-y-o winner Admire Golgo (by Fasliyev) and the minor French and Spanish winner of 4 races Ruente (by Persian Bold). The dam, an Irish 10f winner, is a half-sister to 6 winners including the Group 2 Prix Eugene Adam winner River Warden and the US Grade 3 winner Sweettuc. The second dam, Sweet Simone (by Green Dancer), is a placed half-sister to 7 winners.

"He is probably a mile and a half type for next year but he is a well-balanced nice colt who we look forward to seeing out later in the season."

1514. PERFECT NOTE ★★★
b.f. Shamardal – Mezzo Soprano (by Darshaan).
April 19. Third foal. Half-sister to the French 11f winner Claremont (by Sadler's Wells). The dam won 4 races including the Group 1 12f Prix

Vermeille and the listed 12f Galtres Stakes. The second dam, Morn Of Song (by Blushing Groom), a quite useful 3-y-o 7.6f winner, is a sister to the Grade 2 Bel Air Handicap winner and sire Rahy and a half-sister to the top-class middle-distance colt and sire Singspiel, winner of the Japan Cup, the Dubai World Cup, the Juddmonte International etc., and the useful 9f and 10.2f winner Rakeen – subsequently a Grade 2 winner in South Africa.

"Another middle-distance type for next season who will need some time to strengthen and will have her first start over 7f at the end of the summer."

1515. POET'S VOICE ★★★
b.c. Dubawi – Bright Tiara (Chief's Crown).
March 7. Half-brother to the Japanese $3.5 million earner Gold Tiara, to the fairly useful 2-y-o 6f and 6.5f winner Swan Nebula (both by Seeking The Gold), the minor US stakes winner Queen's Park (by Relaunch) and the minor US 3-y-o winner Best Boot (by Storm Boot). The dam, a minor 2-y-o winner in the USA, is a sister to the Grade 1 Brooklyn Handicap winner Chief Honcho and a half-sister to 10 winners including the dam of the US dual Grade 2 winner American Chance. The second dam, Expressive Dance (by Riva Ridge), won 12 races including three Grade 3 events in the USA and is a half-sister to the Grade 1 winner and sire General Assembly.

"This colt is a lovely mover who will probably need 10f next year, but he is doing all that is asked of him at the moment. He has a big frame but is strengthening nicely and should be out late-summer."

1516. POWERFUL MELODY (USA) ★★★
b.br.c. Dynaformer – Song Track (Dixieland Band).
February 15. Second foal. $550,000Y. Keeneland September. John Ferguson. The dam, a minor winner of 2 races at 3 yrs in the USA, is a half-sister to the US Grade 3 winners High Cotton and Symphony Sid. The second dam, Happy Tune (by A P Indy), is an unraced half-sister to the US dual Grade 1 winner Storm Song and a half-sister to the US Grade 2 winner Diamond Omi.

"He will not be early but is strengthening all the time and looks like a seven furlong type for the second half of the season."

1517. QAMAR ★★★
gr.c. Pivotal – Karliyna (Rainbow Quest).
March 12. First foal. 280,000Y. Tattersalls October 1. John Ferguson. The dam, a fairly useful 10f winner, is a half-sister to 6 winners including the 2-y-o Group 3 1m May Hill Stakes winner and Group 1 Prix Marcel Boussac second Karasta and the Group 2 2m 2f Doncaster Cup dead-heat winner Kasthari. The second dam, Karliyka (by Last Tycoon), a French winner of 4 races, was listed placed over 1m and 10f and is a half-sister to 4 winners.

"There is plenty of two-year-old form in this colt's family and we would expect him to race mid-summer."

1518. SIYAADAH ★★★★
b.f. Shamardal – River Belle (Lahib).
January 29. First foal. 110,000Y. Tattersalls October 1. John Ferguson. The dam, winner of the Group 3 6f Princess Margaret Stakes and subsequently the US Grade 2 8.5f Mrs Revere Stakes, was Grade 1 placed and is a half-sister to the Italian listed winner and Group 2 Italian 1,000 Guineas third Kiralik and the useful 7.5f and 1m winner of 5 races Rio Riva. The second dam, Dixie Favor (by Dixieland Band), was a quite useful Irish 6f (at 2 yrs) to 1m winner of 3 races.

"A big filly, she is coming together nicely. Her dam won the Princess Margaret and this filly should have her first start in June or July."

1519. SWEET SONNET (USA) ★★★★
ch.f. Seeking The Gold – Minister's Melody (Deputy Minister).
March 23. Sister to the US Grade 1 9f Wood Memorial Stakes and dual Grade 3 winner Bob and John. The dam was a Grade 3 winner and Grade 1 placed in the USA. The second dam, My Song For You (by Seattle Song), a stakes-placed winner in the USA, is a half-sister to the Grade

1 winners Capote and Exceller.
"A beautifully bred filly who is doing very well and pleasing. We would hope to see her race in June."

1520. UNNAMED ★★★
b.br.c. Dynaformer – Thunder Kitten
(Storm Cat).
April 9. Brother to the Group 2 12f Ribblesdale Stakes and listed 10f Height Of Fashion Stakes winner and dual Group 1 placed Michita and half-brother to the US 6f to 1m winner and Grade 3 placed Thunder Mission (by Pulpit). The dam, a US 6.5f to 8.5f winner (including a Grade 3), is a half-sister to the Japanese Group 1 1m winner Nobo True. The second dam, Nastique (by Naskra), was a US Grade 1 winner at up to 10f.
"A tough, athletic type, he should start over seven furlongs and be ready in late summer."

ALAN SWINBANK
1521. BOSS'S DESTINATION ★★★
b.c. Dubai Destination – Blushing Sunrise
(Cox's Ridge).
March 28. Sixth reported foal. €28,000Y. Goffs Million. J J O'Leary. Half-brother to the fair 1m and 9.2f winner Sharp Needle (by Mark Of Esteem), to the modest dual 10f winner Rosy Dawn (by Bertolini) and a bumpers winner by Green Dancer. The dam, a 6.5f winner in the USA, is a half-sister to 5 minor winners. The second dam, She Won't Blush (by Blushing Groom), is an unplaced half-sister to the US Grade 1 winner Senor Pete. (Mr G Bell).
"He's done very well and he'll probably be our first runner. More of a back-end type to look at, but he's sharp enough for six and he's showing enough to win a race or two".

1522. YESNABAY (USA) ★★★★
b.br.c. Grand Slam – Speedy Sonata
(Stravinsky).
January 31. First foal. 36,000Y. Tattersalls October 2. J J O'Leary. The dam won 6 races from 2 to 4 yrs in the USA and was stakes-placed and is a half-sister to 2 winners. The second dam, Sandshell (by Silver Hawk), is a placed sister to the Prix de Diane winner Lady In Silver and a half-sister to 8 winners. (Mrs I Gibson).
"He could be the best of our two-year-olds. He's been working very well, he wouldn't be far off a run and he has plenty of scope. I can see him starting at six furlongs, winning a race and maybe being sold to race in Hong Kong – at least that's the plan! He's a nice horse".

1523. UNNAMED ★★★
ch.c. Smarty Jones – Ascot Starre
(Ascot Knight).
April 21. Fifth foal. 21,000Y. Tattersalls December. J Glover. Half-brother to the US Grade 2 winner Greeley's Galaxy (by Mr Greeley). The dam won 3 races at 2 and 3 yrs and is a half-sister to the multiple Grade 3 winner License Fee. The second dam, Star Deputy (by Deputy Minister), a minor US 4-y-o winner, is a half-sister to 4 winners. (Mr S Anderson).
"This is a nice horse and he'll probably have a run before the end of May over six furlongs although he'll be better a bit later on over seven. A big, scopey horse, he's been working well".

1524. UNNAMED ★★
b.c. Fasliyev – Congress (Dancing Brave).
April 6. Tenth foal. Half-brother to the Irish 7f (at 2 yrs) and listed 10f winner Royal Intrigue (by Royal Applause), the fairly useful 1m winner United Nations (by Halling), the quite useful 2-y-o 7f winner Hawaana (by Bahri), to the quite useful 7.7f winner Serra Negra (by Kris) and the fair 6f all-weather winner Promessa (by Reprimand). The dam, a quite useful 2-y-o 1m winner, is a sister to the high-class Cherokee Rose, a winner of 5 races from 6f to 7f including the Group 1 6f Haydock Park Sprint Cup and the Group 1 Prix Maurice de Gheest and a half-sister to 3 winners. The second dam, Celtic Assembly (by Secretariat), a fairly useful 10.6f winner, was second in the Lupe Stakes and is a full or half-sister to 13 winners including the Group 1 Prix du Cadran winner Molesnes. (Mr N Funnel).
"He's doing OK but he's going to be a seven furlong or mile two-year-old. He'll be a nice horse given time".

TOM TATE

1525. ACROSS THE SEA (USA) ★★
gr.c. Giant's Causeway – Trust Your Heart (Relaunch).
May 23. Sixth foal. $200,000Y. Keeneland September. Tom Tate. Half-brother to 3 winners including the US Grade 3 placed Special Grayce (by Smart Strike) and the stakes placed Trust Your Luck (by Mr Greeley). The dam, a US 2-y-o winner, was stakes-placed and is a half-sister to numerous winners including the US Grade 3 placed Aunt Henny and the dam of the US Grade 1 winner Ever A Friend. The second dam, Ms.Patty B (by Grey Dawn II), won 3 minor races in the USA and is a half-sister to 10 winners. (JMH Lifestyle Ltd).
"He was a late foal and is backward but he's a fine-looking horse and one for the autumn".

1526. CALDERCRUIX (USA) ★★
ch.c. Rahy – Al Theraab (Roberto).
May 25. Twelfth foal. $140,000Y. Keeneland September. Tom Tate. Half-brother to the Group 2 Beresford Stakes winner Albert Hall, to the listed French Prix Yacowlef winner Barsine, the useful French 6f and 7f winner Algallarens (all by Danehill), the useful 7f (at 2 yrs) to 8.5f winner of 8 races Flighty Fellow (by Flying Spur), the quite useful 7f winner Sabhaan (by Green Desert) and the French 1m winner Ebdaa (by Nashwan). The dam, a quite useful 1m winner, is a half-sister to the US stakes winner Meadowlamb. The second dam, Golden Lamb (by Graustark), won at 3 yrs and is a sister to several good US horses including the Grade 3 winner Java Moon and the dam of the champion US turf horse Sunshine Forever. (JMH Lifestyle).
"A quality horse, he really is a nice specimen but he was a late foal and he won't see action until much later in the year. Like a lot of Rahy's he's not the easiest to have to deal with".

1527. COUNT BERTONI (IRE) ★★★★
b.c. Bertolini – Queen Sceptre (Fairy King).
March 3. Eighth foal. Deauville August. €52,000Y. Tom Tate. Half-brother to the useful 7f and 1m winner of 4 races Minority Report (by Rainbow Quest) and to the quite useful 12f winner North Parade (by Nayef). The dam, a useful 2-y-o winner of 2 races including the listed 6f Firth of Clyde Stakes, subsequently won a small stakes event in the USA. The second dam, Happy Smile (by Royal Match), a fairly useful Irish middle-distance winner of 4 races, is a sister to the Group 2 10f Pretty Polly Stakes and US Grade 2 winner Happy Bride and a half-sister to the Group 2 12f Blandford Stakes winner Topanoora. (Mr P J Martin).
"He's always been very forward and he's a fine, big horse. If we don't do something with him everyday he'll buck his rider off. A big, powerful beast with plenty of toe, he'll hopefully be racing over six furlongs in May".

1528. KARAMOJO BELL ★★
b.c. Selkirk – Shabby Chic (Red Ransom).
April 13. Seventh foal. 90,000Y. Tattersalls October 1. Tom Tate. Half-brother to Ruler Of All (by Sadler's Wells), unplaced in one start at 2 yrs in 2008, to the 1m (at 2 yrs) and Group 2 Italian Oaks winner Fashion Statement (by Rainbow Quest) and the fairly useful dual 12f winner Kerriemuir Lass (by Celtic Swing). The dam won the listed 10f Prix de Liancourt and was third in both the Grade 1 Yellow Ribbon Stakes and the Group 3 Prix Chloe. She is a sister to the Oaks winner Casual Look and a half-sister to 5 winners. The second dam, Style Setter (by Manila), a stakes-placed winner of 3 races in the USA, is a half-sister to 2 winners. (JMH Lifestyle Ltd).
"He's a very nice, big, scopey animal and again he'd be an autumn horse. It's a good family and he's a fair specimen alright".

1529. KYLLADDY ★★★
ch.c. Kyllachy – Chance For Romance (by Entrepreneur).
March 14. Second foal. 10,000Y. Doncaster St Leger. Tom Tate. The dam, a fair 2-y-o 5.5f winner, is a half-sister to 6 winners including the Group 3 5f Queen Mary Stakes winners Romantic Myth and Romantic Liason and the useful 2-y-o 5f winner Power Packed. The second dam, My First Romance (Danehill), ran

twice unplaced and is a half-sister to 6 minor winners here and abroad. (P J Martin).
"He's one of our forward ones and he'll run soon so he's worth a mention".

1530. LEVIATHAN ★★★
b.c. *Dubawi – Gipsy Moth (Efisio).*
February 19. 22,000Y. Doncaster St Leger. Mr T Tate. Half-sister to the smart 7f to 10f (listed) winner Illustrious Blue (by Dansili), to the fairly useful triple 6f winner Mullein (by Oasis Dream), the quite useful 7f winner Fly Free (by Halling) and the quite useful 5f (including at 2 yrs) and 6f winner of 8 races Romany Nights (by Night Shift). The dam, a quite useful dual 5f winner at 2 yrs, subsequently won a listed event in Germany and is a half-sister to 3 winners including the useful listed 1m winner and Group 2 Falmouth Stakes second Heavenly Whisper. The second dam, Rock The Boat (by Slip Anchor), a modest 6f (at 2 yrs) and 1m placed maiden, is a half-sister to 9 winners including the 1,000 Guineas second Kerrera and the high-class multiple Group winner Rock City. (Mr P Moulton).
"He's quite forward and he's very, very strong. One of our heaviest two-year-olds, he's a very powerful horse and I would hope he'd run before mid-summer, probably over six furlongs".

1531. SADLER'S MARK ★★★★
b.c. *Sadler's Wells – Waldmark (Mark Of Esteem).*
March 1. Third foal. 160,000Y. Tattersalls October 1. Tom Tate. The dam, a smart 2-y-o 7f winner, was second in the Group 2 1m Falmouth Stakes and is a half-sister to 3 winners including the German listed winner and Group 3 placed Waldvogel. The second dam, Wurftaube (by Acatenango), won two Group 2 events over 12f and 14f in Germany and is a half-sister to 7 winners. (JMH Lifestyle Ltd).
"He's a big, powerful, potential three-year-old type and I should think he's taken a lot after his dam's side in that he's a tall, elegant horse. Having said that he's just started to pick up now and looks like an autumn two-year-old. He isn't slow!"

1532. THE CAPED CRUSADER ★★★
b.c. *Cape Cross – Phariseek (Rainbow Quest).*
March 31. Fourth foal. €100,000Y. Goffs Million. Tom Tate. Half-sister to the fair Irish 1m winner Young Lochinvar (by Pivotal) and to the fair Irish 6f winner Toberanthawn (by Danehill Dancer). The dam, an Irish 2-y-o 7f winner, was listed-placed twice and is a half-sister to 5 winners including the Irish 2-y-o listed 6f winner Pharmacist (herself dam of the Breeders Cup Turf winner Red Rocks). The second dam, Pharaoh's Delight (by Fairy King), a half-sister to 8 winners, was a very useful 2-y-o winner of the Group 1 5f Phoenix Stakes. (Mrs Sylvia Clegg & Louise Worthington).
"He'll be a six furlong horse, he's quite forward, has plenty of scope and a good bit of class and speed".

1533. THINKS ITS ALL OVER ★★★
b.c. *Tiznow – A P Petal (A P Indy).*
February 22. Third foal. Deauville August. €55,000Y. Tom Tate. Half-brother to the 2008 2-y-o Causeway King (by Giant's Causeway). The dam is an unraced half-sister to 10 winners including the dual US Grade 3 winner Lotus Pool and the dams of the Group 2 winners Lear Spear and Montgomery's Arch. (JMH Lifesytle Ltd).
"He's a grand horse. I bought him in Deauville in August, he was broken in September and he's never missed a day since. He'd be over 16 hands now and he's a lovely, big, honest horse. A tall, powerful type, he should be racing by August and I wouldn't be betting against him when he runs!

1534. TING TING (USA) ★★
b.f. *Empire Maker – My Sweet Heart (You And I).*
March 13. Second foal. $180,000Y. Keeneland September. Tom Tate. The dam, a minor US 3-y-o winner of 2 races, is a half-sister to the Kentucky Derby and Preakness Stakes winner War Emblem. The second dam, Sweetest Lady (by Lord At War), a minor US winner of 5 races at 3 and 4 yrs, is a half-sister to 6 winners. (JMH Lifestyle Ltd).
"She's a classy, potential three-year-old stayer".

1535. TRULY PINK ★★★
ch.f. Mr Greeley – Tincture (Dr Fong).
April 16. First foal. 130,000Y. Tattersalls October 1. Jane Chapple-Hyam. The dam was third in the listed Cheshire Oaks and is a half-sister to 6 winners including the US Grade 3 Cardinal Handicap winner Miss Caerleona (herself dam of the Group winners Karen's Caper and Miss Coronado) and the French listed-placed Mr Academy and Mister Shoot. The second dam, Miss d'Ouilly (by Bikala), won a listed event over 9f in France and is a half-sister to 6 winners including the Prix Jacques le Marois winner Miss Satamixa and the dam of the Group/Graded stakes winners Mister Riv, Mister Sicy and Manninamix.
"A nice, quality filly, she'll be an autumn type and is big and strong".

1536. WALVIS BAY ★★★★
b.c. Footstepsinthesand – Limpopo (Green Desert).
April 8. Fourteenth foal. €45,000Y. Goffs Million. Tom Tate. Half-brother to the fairly useful 2008 Group 3 6f placed 2-y-o Silver Shoon (by Fasliyev), to the Group 1 6f Haydock Park Sprint Cup and Group 3 5f Palace House Stakes winner Pipalong (by Pips Pride), the useful 2-y-o 5f winner and Group 2 5f Flying Childers Stakes second China Eyes (by Fasliyev), the fairly useful 2-y-o 6f listed winner Out Of Africa (by Common Grounds), the quite useful 2-y-o 7f winner Corton, the quite useful 7f to 12f winner Smoothie (both by Definite Article), the French 5f and 6f winner of 5 races at 2 and 3 yrs Raja (by Pivotal) and the minor US winner of 2 races Henry Kitchener (both by Common Grounds). The dam, a poor 5f placed 2-y-o, is a half-sister to 7 winners here and abroad. The second dam, Grey Goddess (by Godswalk), was a smart winner of 5 races in Ireland from 7f to 8.5f including the Group 3 Gladness Stakes and the Group 3 Matron Stakes. (Mrs Sylvia Clegg & Louise Worthington).
"A very early-maturing colt that's showing early speed. I'll run him as soon as I can and I'd say he's quick in all departments!"

1537. UNNAMED ★★★
b.c. More Than Ready – Amour Mio (Private Terms).
January 24. Third foal. 125,000Y. Tattersalls October 1. Jane Chapple-Hyam. The dam is an unraced half-sister to 11 winners including the German Group 2 winner Nicholas and the dam of the dual Group 1 winner Strategic Choice. The second dam, Lulu Mon Amour (by Tom Rolfe), won twice at around 1m in the USA and is a half-sister to 6 winners.
"A big, strong individual that should be racing in July or August. He's a good sort."

1538. UNNAMED ★★★★
ch.f. Redback – Flames (Blushing Flame).
April 27. Fifth foal. Doncaster St Leger. 25,000Y. Hugo Merry. 210,000 2-y-o. Craven Breeze-Up Sales. Tom Tate. Sister to the fairly useful 2008 2-y-o dual 7f winner and 2009 3-y-o Group 3 7f Fred Darling Stakes winner Lahaleeb and half-sister to the fairly useful dual 6f (at 2 yrs) and listed 1m Masaka Stakes winner Precocious Star (by Bold Fact). The dam is an unraced half-sister to 4 winners including the listed winner Dance Partner. The second dam, Dancing Debut (by Polar Falcon), is a placed full or half-sister to 4 winners.
"We bought her this week at the Breeze Ups and she's a really cracking filly. She's hopefully one we can train to come out in the summer. I'm very lucky to have her".

1539. UNNAMED ★★
ch.c. Nayef – Reveuse de Jour (Sadler's Wells).
April 2. Tenth foal. 48,000Y. Tattersalls October 1. Tom Tate. Half-brother to the quite useful all-weather 7f and 8.6f winner Grand Jour (by Grand Lodge), to the minor French 2-y-o winner Dream Of Day (by Machiavellian), the fair Irish 1m winner Day Ticket (by Mtoto) and a jumps winner in France by Exit To Nowhere. The dam, a fair 7f placed 3-y-o, is a half-sister to 8 winners including the Group 2 6f Lowther Stakes winner Enthused. The second dam, Magic Of Life (by Seattle Slew), a smart winner of the Group 1 1m Coronation Stakes, is a half-sister to 4 winners. (Mr T P Tate).

"Quite strong and a good mover, he's a nice, quality horse but he's backward and won't be out until much later on".

MARK TOMPKINS

1540. AKULA (IRE) ★★★
ch.c. Soviet Star – Danielli (Danehill).
February 12. First foal. €30,000Y. Goffs Million. M Tompkins. The dam, placed second 4 times at up to 13f in Ireland, is a sister to the Group 3 C L Weld Park Stakes winner Eva's Request and a half-sister to 7 winners including the Group 1 7f Moyglare Stud Stakes winner Priory Belle and the Group 3 7f Concorde Stakes winner Wild Bluebell. The second dam, Ingabelle (by Taufan), won the Group 3 Phoenix Sprint Stakes and is a half-sister to 4 winners. (Jay Three Racing).
"A strong, attractive, good-natured horse. He's going to be much better next year but he's out of a Danehill mare and I've always liked Soviet Star. He'll certainly be OK and will be out in mid-summer. He's in the Goffs Million so we'll see how he goes".

1541. AMNO DANCER ★★★
b.c. Namid – Special Dancer (Shareef Dancer).
March 2. Fourth foal. €12,000Y. Goffs Million. M Tompkins. Half-brother to the unplaced 2008 2-y-o Ja One (by Acclamation) and to the French 11f to 15f winner Special Reggae (by Xaar). The dam won 3 races at 3 yrs in Italy and is a half-sister to 7 winners including the Group 3 Meld Stakes winner Cajarian and the dam of the Group 1 Prix de la Foret winner Caradak. The second dam, Caraniya (by Darshaan), a quite useful 1m (at 2 yrs) and 12f winner, is a half-sister to 7 winners. (Mr D P Noblett).
"Another one I bought at Goffs, he's showing me plenty and he's a big, strong, rangy horse and very similar to his sire in looks. My two-year-olds are a much stronger and more forward bunch than I normally have. He'll be out in May and the boys couldn't believe I bought him for only 12 Grand". TRAINER'S BARGAIN BUY

1542. ASTROMOON ★★★
b.f. Beat Hollow – Astromancer (Silver Hawk).
March 16. Second foal. Half-sister to Astrodiva (by Where Or When), unplaced in one start at 2 yrs in 2008. The dam, a moderate 4-y-o 14f winner, is a half-sister to one winner. The second dam, Colour Dance (by Rainbow Quest), is an unplaced full or half-sister to 4 winners including the very useful French 1m listed winner and Group 1 Prix Morny third Barricade. (Mystic Meg Ltd).
"She's a lovely, big, strong filly by a sire I've always liked. She got a bit of a cold in the early spring but she's fine now and from mid-season onwards I think she could develop into a very nice filly".

1543. BLINKA ME ★★★★
b.c. Tiger Hill – Easy To Love (Diesis).
January 7. Sixth foal. 10,000Y. Tattersalls October 2. Not sold. Half-brother to the very promising 2008 2-y-o 7f winner Pezula Bay (by Oasis Dream) and to the fairly useful 2-y-o 7f and 1m winner and listed-placed Easy Lover (by Pivotal). The dam, a quite useful 4-y-o 11.5f winner, is a sister to the Oaks winner Love Divine (herself dam of the St Leger winner Sixties Icon) and a half-sister to 3 winners including the listed 12f winner Floreeda. The second dam, La Sky (by Law Society), a useful 10f winner and second in the Lancashire Oaks, is closely related to the Champion Stakes winner Legal Case and a half-sister to 4 winners.
"A lovely colt from a very good family, he's big and strong and he'll definitely be alright from mid-season onwards. I should think he'll be one to follow later on this year and next season. A January foal, I think he might surprise a few people if he doesn't grow on me and he could be quite an exciting horse".

1544. CAPTAIN CLINT ★★
b.c. Captain Rio – Lake Poopo (Persian Heights).
May 8. Eighth foal. €9,000Y. Tattersalls Ireland. M Tompkins. Half-brother to the fair 2-y-o 5f winner Mr Klick (by Tendulkar) and to 2 winners in Germany and Spain by Be My Guest and Up And At 'em. The dam, a quite useful 3-y-o 13f and 15f winner, is a half-sister to 9 winners including 2 listed winners in Germany and Italy.

The second dam, Bolivia (by Windwurf), was a useful German 2-y-o listed winner and a full or half-sister to 9 winners.

"He's a May foal but he's a strong, well-grown horse and is just the right size. If he doesn't grow on me he'll be quite early, probably starting in May. We quite like him and I think he'll be alright".

1545. CORNISH BEAU ★★
ch.c. Pearl Of Love – Marimar
(Grand Lodge).
February 23. Fifth foal. €10,500Y. Tattersalls Ireland. M Tompkins. Half-brother to the modest 7f to 9f winner Freda's Choice (by Shinko Forest) and to a winner in Greece by Revoque. The dam won twice in Italy at 3 and 4 yrs and is a half-sister to 6 other minor winners. The second dam, Marionetta (by Nijinsky), is a placed half-sister to 6 winners. (Mr M Winter).

"He's a lovely natured horse. A big colt, he'll be a colt for the middle of the season onwards and he'll be better next year. The sire's dead now which usually means his stock do well so I bought two of them! I like them both and this colt goes well enough but he's big and will need time".

1546. EDWARD WHYMPER ★★
ch.c. Bahamian Bounty – Sosumi
(Be My Chief).
January 15. Fourth foal. 8,000Y. Tattersalls December. Not sold. Half-brother to the unplaced 2008 2-y-o Missou Maiden (by Medicean), to the fair 1m winner Tevez (by Sakhee) and the 2-y-o 1m seller winner Benayoun (by Inchinor). The dam, a useful 2-y-o dual 5f winner, was fourth in the Group 3 Prix du Calvados. The second dam, Princess Deya (by Be My Guest), ran twice unplaced and is a half-sister to the Eclipse Stakes winner Compton Admiral and the Group 1 1m Queen Elizabeth II Stakes winner Summoner. (Sakal Family).

"A great, big, rangy horse. All he's done is grow and he's one of our home-breds. We've always liked him and he'll be running from mid-season onwards".

1547. FASETTE ★★
b.f. Fasliyev – Londonnet (Catrail).
February 23. 1,000Y. Tatersalls October 3. M Tompkins. Half-sister to a minor French 10f winner by Beat Hollow. The dam ran once unplaced and is a half-sister to 4 winners including the dual listed winner Keld. The second dam, Society Ball (by Law Society), a fair 12f all-weather and hurdles winner, is a half-sister to 3 winners including the listed winner and useful broodmare Well Beyond. (Raceworld).

"A big, well-grown filly, she's as strong as an ox and has a great stride on her. We'll get on with her and she'll give us a lot of fun".

1548. KATHLEEN FRANCES ★★
b.f. Sakhee – Trew Class (by Inchinor).
February 16. First foal. The dam, a fairly useful 10f winner of 5 races, was listed-placed and is a sister to the useful dual 1m winner Inverness. The second dam, Inimitable (by Polish Precedent), a modest 10f winner, is a half-sister to 3 winners including the smart hurdler Puntal. (Russell Trew Ltd).

"The first foal of a mare we trained, this filly is by Sakhee who I've always liked as a sire. She's a bit like her mother in that she's a rangy, very scopey filly who will be one for the second half of the season. She has a good outlook and attitude to the whole job".

1549. LABRETELLA (IRE) ★★★
b.f. Bahamian Bounty – Known Class
(Known Fact).
March 21. Eighth foal. 8,000Y. Tattersalls October 2. M Tompkins. Half-sister to the fair dual 7f winner Royal Applord (by Royal Applause), to 3 winners in the USA including the 2-y-o winner and stakes-placed Tocha (by Indian Charlie) and a winner over hurdles by Groom Dancer. The dam is a placed half-sister to 2 minor winners. The second dam, Club Class (by Roberto), was third in the Group 3 Cheshire Oaks and subsequently won 4 races in the USA and is a full or half-sister to 9 winners. (Mr J Ellis).

"She's quite forward and I should think she'll be running in May. I've had quite a few nice

Bahamian Bounty's, this is a filly with a bit of an attitude and she's been going nicely this spring. She's not a tiny thing, she's well-grown and all she wants to do is please".

1550. NUMBER ONE GUY ★★★★
br.c. Rock Of Gibraltar – Dubious (Darshaan).
April 5. Fourth foal. 70,000Y. Tattersalls October 2. M Tompkins. Half-brother to the moderate 1m 4f winner Linby (by Dr Fong). The dam ran once unplaced in the USA and is a half-sister to 7 winners including Shady Heights, winner of the Group 1 International Stakes (on disqualification) and second in both the Eclipse Stakes and the Phoenix Champion Stakes. The second dam, Vaguely (by Bold Lad, Ire), was a fairly useful 1m (at 2 yrs) and 10f winner. (GPD Ltd).

"We like him a lot and he's the most expensive one we've got. He was a bit nervous when I first got him but he's matured now, he's grown and developed and I really like him. He shows plenty of ability and he looks to have gears".

1551. POWER OF DREAMS ★★
b.c. Pearl Of Love – Pussie Willow (Catrail).
April 2. Fifth foal. €12,000Y. Tattersalls Ireland. M Tompkins. The dam, placed over 5f at 2 yrs, is a full or half-sister to 5 winners including the German listed winner Symboli Kildare. The second dam, Quiche (by Formidable), a fair dual 6f winner, is a half-sister to 3 winners.

"A lovely horse of a good hard colour, all he wants to do is eat, sleep and go out and canter. He's thriving at the moment and he'll be running in May or June. A run sometimes just takes the edge of them and makes them see sense!"

1552. RED BARCELONA ★★★
ch.c. Indian Haven – Purepleasureseeker (Grand Lodge).
February 19. Second foal. 12,000Y. Tattersalls October 3. M Tompkins. The dam is a half-sister to the useful 2-y-o Group 3 6.5f Prix Eclipse winner Potaro. The second dam, Bianca Cappello (by Glenstal), is an unplaced half-sister to Idris, a winner of four Group 3 events in Ireland at up to 12f and to the winner and US Grade 3 placed Sweet Mazarine.

"He's a very nice horse with a lovely temperament. He's just grown a bit so I need to back off him a bit but he'll be racing in May or June and he has plenty of ability. All these horses will be lovely as three-year-olds but they're nice horses now".

1553. RED SMOKEY (IRE) ★★
ch.c. Tagula – Red Slipper (Alzao).
April 16. Second foal. €15,500Y. Tattersalls Ireland. M Tompkins. The dam, placed once at 3 yrs in France, is a half-sister to 3 winners including the smart dual listed 10f winner and good broodmare Foodbroker Fancy. The second dam, Red Rita (by Kefaah), a fairly useful 4-y-o 6f winner, was second in the Group 3 6f Cherry Hinton Stakes and the Group 3 6f Princess Margaret Stakes at 2 yrs and is a half-sister to 3 minor winners. (Judi Dench, Bryan Agar & Partners).

"This is a filly from a fast family and we got on with her early on but she went a bit weak. We like her a lot, she was a mid-April foal so there's no rush with her although I think she's a five or six furlong filly".

1554. SPIRIT LAND ★★★
ch.c. Indian Haven – Reborn (Idris).
April 8. Third foal. €5,000Y. Tattersalls Ireland. M Tompkins. The dam, placed once over 1m from 8 starts, is a is a half-sister to 2 winners. The second dam, Tantum Ergo (by Tanfirion), won the Group 3 C L Weld Park Stakes and is a half-sister to 7 winners including the dam of the Melbourne Cup winner Might And Power.

"He's not very big but he's strong. An April foal, we were getting on with him but he started to go 'up behind' so we backed off him. He has the right attitude, he's tough, a great mover and he'll definitely be a two-year-old".

1555. TED SPREAD ★★
b.c. Beat Hollow – Highbrook (Alphabatim).
March 6. Half-brother to the quite useful 6f (at 2 yrs) to 10f and hurdles winner Niagara

(by Rainbows For Life) and to the fair 2-yo 6f winner Pink Sapphire (by Bluebird). The dam, a quite useful 10f to 13f and hurdles winner, is a half-sister to 5 minor winners in the USA. The second dam, Tellspot (by Tell), is a placed half-sister to 10 winners.

"He's a big, strong horse out of a mare that did well for me. He's going to be one for the mid-season onwards and he goes well enough now. He'll make up into a good three-year-old, he has the right attitude and looks the part".

1556. WATCH CHAIN ★★
b.c. Traditionally – Dangle
(Desert Style).
March 12. Second foal. €3,800Y. Tattersalls Ireland. Not sold. The dam, a useful Irish 7f winner, was listed-placed and is a half-sister to 4 winners including the Irish 7f (at 2 yrs) to 10f and subsequent Hong Kong stakes winner Solid Approach. The second dam, Dawn Chorus (by Mukaddamah), is an unraced half-sister to 5 winners including Barrier Reef, a winner of 8 races and second in the Group 3 Beresford Stakes.

"The sire isn't very popular but this colt goes well enough, I quite like him and he's a big, strong horse. A bit of a 'Jack the Lad' but he has the right attitude and he should be alright in mid-summer".

1557. ZENARINDA ★★
b.f. Zamindar – Tenpence
(Bob Back).
March 31. Third foal. The dam, unplaced in two starts, is a sister to the 2-y-o 1m winner and Group 3 Prix Saint-Roman second Ten Bob I and a half-sister to one winner. The second dam, Tiempo (by King Of Spain), was unplaced.

"A filly we bred ourselves, she has her own outlook to life – all she wants to do is get on with it. She's grown a lot and she'll be big and strong in the end. Being out of a Bob Back mare she should stay well, she'll be one for the mid-season onwards and will make a lovely three-year-old. She'll definitely be alright".

MARCUS TREGONING

1558. AETOS ★★
b.c. Royal Applause – Hagwah (Dancing Brave).
April 22. Eighth foal. 72,000Y. Tattersalls October 2. M Tregoning. Half-brother to the fair 2008 2-y-o 7f winner Nizhoni Dancer (by Bahamian Bounty), to the very useful 10f and 12f winner Trust Rule (by Selkirk), the fair 8.6f all-weather winner Sydney Symphony (by Daylami) and the minor German and Dutch winner of 7 races King's Regards (by Machiavellian). The dam, a very useful multiple listed winner from 1m to 12f, is a half-sister to the US Grade 1 winner Sarafan (previously a very useful 2-y-o listed 1m winner here). The second dam, Saraa Ree (by Caro), a useful 7f winner, is a half-sister to 5 winners. (Sir Alex Ferguson & Sotiros Hassiakos).

"I think he's more of a back-end two-year-old because he had a few niggling problems early on and he's grown an awful lot. A nice mover, he's a big, scopey horse and hopefully he'll be fine later on".

1559. BALATOMA (IRE) ★★★
b.f. Mr Greeley – Honfleur (Sadler's Wells).
May 14. Ninth foal. 85,000Y. Tattersalls October 1. M Tregoning. Closely related to the Irish 2-y-o and subsequent Hong Kong winner and Group 3 Tetrarch Stakes second Creekview (by Gone West), to the smart Irish 1m winner Book Of Kings (by Kingmambo), the fairly useful 3-y-o 1m winner Argentan (by Gulch) and a minor winner at 3 yrs in the USA. The dam, a useful winner of 2 races including a listed event in France over 13.5f, is a sister to the Prix de l'Arc de Triomphe winner Carnegie, closely related to the Group 2 Prix Guillaume d'Ornano winner Antisaar and a half-sister to the Group 3 St Simon Stakes winner Lake Erie. The second dam, Detroit (by Riverman), won the Prix de l'Arc de Triomphe and is a half-sister to the Cheveley Park Stakes winner Durtal (herself dam of the Ascot Gold Cup winner Gildoran). (N Bizakov).

"She's a very nice filly and we thought she would cost far too much money – we expected her to reach 100,000. It's a very good family although I think it's fair to say that recently it

hasn't struck a chord. If this one does come right she's an exciting broodmare prospect for the owner. She's quite tall but she's sharp cantering now and moves very well".

1560. BOOM AND BUST (IRE) ★★★
b.c. Footstepsinthesand – Forest Call (Wolfhound).
April 28. Sixth foal. 25,000Y. Tattersalls December. M Tregoning. Half-brother to a 2-y-o winner in Japan by Hawk Wing. The dam, a modest 5f and 1m placed maiden, is a half-sister to 3 winners including the Group 1 Coronation Stakes winner Balisada. The second dam, Balnaha (by Lomond), a modest 3-y-o 1m winner, is a sister to Inchmurrin (winner of the Child Stakes and herself dam of the very smart and tough colt Inchinor) and a half-sister to 6 winners including the Mill Reef Stakes winner Welney. (Mr J Singh).
"A nice type, he's robust enough and he's changed out of all recognition since the sales. He won't be early but he's a particularly nicely balanced horse.

1561. DARSHONIN ★★★★
ch.c. Pivotal – Incheni (Nashwan).
March 21. Second foal. 200,000Y. Tattersalls October 1. M Tregoning. The dam, a useful 7f (at 2 yrs) and listed 10f winner, is a sister to the very useful 2-y-o 7f winner Inchlonaig and a half-sister to 6 winners including the triple Group 3 7f winner and sire Inchinor, the useful 1m winner and 12f listed-placed Inchyre, the useful 6f winner Inchcape and the fairly useful 1m listed winner Ingozi. The second dam, Inchmurrin (by Lomond), a very useful winner of three races at 2 yrs over 5f and three races at 3 yrs including the Child Stakes, was second in the Group 1 1m Coronation Stakes and is a half-sister to 7 winners including the Mill Reef Stakes winner Welney. (N Bizakov).
"I know the Coolmore team liked this horse and I suspect the purchase wasn't made because at the sale he was a rig. I knew that, but he's now got two fully formed testicles. So that was a coup, really, because it's difficult to buy a Pivotal and especially one that's not too big. He's an ideal size for a two-year-old, a very nice horse and one that goes along nicely with the Indian Ridge colt. He's full of quality".

1562. DOON KALAL (IRE) ★★
b c. Dubai Destination – Muwajaha (Night Shift).
April 25. Half-brother to Kassa Ed (by Marju), unplaced in one start at 2 yrs in 2008. The dam, a fairly useful 6f winner, is a half-sister to the very useful 2-y-o listed 5f winner and subsequent French 3-y-o 5f listed winner Khasayl, the quite useful 10f and hurdles winner of 10 races Mazeed (both by Lycius), the useful listed 2-y-o 7f winner Muklah (by Singspiel), the useful 3-y-o dual 7f winner Al Aali (by Lahib), the quite useful 1m (at 2 yrs) and 10f winner Nebl (by Persian Bold) and the fair 6f winner Hewaraat (by Fasliyev). The second dam, Maraatib (by Green Desert), a quite useful 5f and 6f winner, is a half-sister to 6 winners. (Sheikh Ahmed Al Maktoum).
"He's OK and has done a few sharp canters, he's going alright and is one for the mid-season and beyond".

1563. ESHTYAAQ ★★★
b.c. Mark Of Esteem – Fleet Hill (Warrshan).
February 9. Sixth foal. 270,000Y. Tattersalls October 2. Shadwell Estate Co. Brother to the Group 3 Lingfield Classic Trial and Group 3 Dee Stakes winner African Dream and half-brother to the useful 11f and 12f winner and listed-placed Cresta Gold (by Halling), the Irish 9f winner and listed-placed Fenella's Link (by Linamix), the fairly useful 6f and 7f winner and listed-placed Lone Wolfe (by Foxhound) and a winner in the USA by Miner's Mark. The dam, winner of the listed Superlative Stakes and third in the Group 3 Rockfel Stakes, is a half-sister to 6 winners including the useful listed 6f Sandy Lane Stakes winner Lee Artiste. The second dam, Mirkan Honey (by Ballymore), a quite useful Irish 4-y-o 16f winner, is a half-sister to 12 winners. (Hamdan Al Maktoum).
"This colt colt such a lot of money because apparently he's a much nicer horse than his

brother African Dream ever was. African Dream was the horse that put Peter Chapple-Hyam back on the map when he returned from Hong Kong. This colt is a back-end performer because he's in Dubai and he won't be arriving until late April. He's quite a big horse but a lovely looking colt".

1564. GAKALINA (IRE) ★★
ch.f. *Galileo – Ramona (Desert King)*.
March 2. Fifth foal. 200,000Y. Tattersalls October 1. M Tregoning. Sister to the useful Group 3 7f Athasi Stakes winner Prima Luce and half-sister to the 2008 Irish 7f placed 2-y-o Toraidhe (by High Chaparral), the fair Irish 10f winner Home You Stroll (by Selkirk) and the modest Irish 6f winner Sheer Silk (by Fasliyev). The dam is an unraced half-sister to 8 winners including the Group 2 5f Kings Stand Stakes winner Cassandra Go (herself dam of the Irish 1,000 Guineas winner Halfway To Heaven) and the smart Group 3 6f Coventry Stakes winner and Irish 2,000 Guineas second Verglas. The second dam, Rahaam (by Secreto), a fairly useful 3-y-o 7f winner, is a half-sister to 8 winners including the French 2,000 Guineas third Glory Forever. (N Bizakov).
"A backward filly, she was bought because the owner would like to start a stud. She's very immature at present and is one for the mile maidens at the back-end".

1565. HAADEETH ★★★
b.g. *Oasis Dream – Musical Key (Key Of Luck)*.
February 25. Third foal. 80,000Y. Doncaster St Leger. Shadwell Estate Co. Half-brother to the quite useful 2008 2-y-o 7f winner Key Signature (by Dansili). The dam, a fair maiden, was fourth twice over 5f at 2 yrs and is a half-sister to 6 winners including the high-class Hong Kong horses Mensa and Firebolt and the dam of the Group 2 Flying Childers winner Wunders Dream. The second dam, Musianica (by Music Boy), was a fairly useful 2-y-o 6f winner. (Hamdan Al Maktoum).
"He's been gelded and that's improved his temperament a lot. He'll be a two-year-old and he's a good mover that's done well lately. Quite big and powerful, he won't be out early but I expect he'll be out from July onwards over seven furlongs".

1566. HUWAAYA (USA) ★★
b.f. *Rahy – Sarayir (Mr Prospector)*.
April 13. Sister to the fair 12f winner Atayeb and half-sister to the fairly useful and promising 2008 2-y-o 7f winner Ghanaati (by Giant's Causeway), the very useful dual 1m winner Mawatheeq (by Danzig), the quite useful 1m winner Itqaan (by Danzig) and the quite useful 10f winner Sundus (by Fairy King). The dam, winner of a 1m listed event, is closely related to the Champion Stakes winner Nayef and a half-sister to Nashwan and Unfuwain. The second dam, Height Of Fashion (by Bustino), a high-class winner of 5 races from 7f to 12f including the Group 2 Princess of Wales's Stakes, is a half-sister to the good middle-distance colt Milford. (Hamdan Al Maktoum).
"She's quite nice and looks the part. Tall (like most of the family) she'll make a back-end two-year-old as long as her temperament remains alright (considering she's by Rahy)".

1567. ILSTON LORD (IRE) ★★★★
b.c. *One Cool Cat – Canouan (Sadler's Wells)*.
March 5. Third foal. 7,000Y. Tattersalls December. M Tregoning. The dam was placed 5 times in Ireland including in a listed event and is a half-sister to 5 winners including the Group 1 Irish Oaks winner Winona. The second dam, My Potters (by Irish River), an Irish 3-y-o 1m handicap winner, is a half-sister to numerous winners including the champion US sprinter My Juliet (herself the dam of two Grade 1 winners) and the good middle-distance colt Lyphard's Special. (David & Gwyn Joseph).
"I think he was a steal. He has a good page and I think he was cheap because a lot of the One Cool Cat's get gelded because they're quite flighty. This one isn't like that at all, he's very nice and he has a 'seven furlong page'. I'm very pleased with him and he'd be in the bunch of my nicer horses". **TRAINER'S BARGAIN BUY**

1568. ISHRAAQAT ★★
ch.f. *Singspiel – Elshamms (Zafonic)*.
May 1. Sixth foal. Closely related to the fairly useful Irish 7f and 10f winner Aqraan (by In The Wings) and half-sister to the useful triple 6f (including at 2 yrs) and subsequent UAE listed 5f winner Taqseem (by Fantastic Light) and the moderate 6f winner Minwir (by Green Desert). The dam, a fairly useful 2-y-o 7f winner and third in the Group 3 Prestige Stakes, is a half-sister to numerous winners including the very useful 10f winner Shaya. The second dam, Gharam (by Green Dancer), a very useful 2-y-o 6f winner, was third in the French 1,000 Guineas and is a half-sister to the US Grade 1 9f winner Talinum. (Hamdan Al Maktoum).
"She's OK, but currently in Dubai so she'll be one for later on this season".

1569. JAYAASH (USA) ★★★
ch.c. *Seeking The Gold – Misterah (Alhaarth)*.
February 19. Brother to the useful listed 1m winner and Group 3 7f Oak Tree Stakes third Shabiba. The dam, a very useful listed 6f (at 2 yrs) and Group 3 7f Nell Gwyn Stakes winner, is sister to the quite useful 5f (at 2 yrs) to 12f winner Mustajed and a half-sister to the useful 2-y-o 6f winner Muqtarb. The second dam, Jasarah (by Green Desert), was a fair 7f placed maiden. (Hamdan Al Maktoum).
"He's a nice horse. I trained the filly and she was good. One of the nicer ones due to arrive from Dubai, he's a solid colt and they do like him".

1570. JUWIREYA ★★★★
b.f. *Nayef – Katayeb (Machiavellian)*.
March 26. Second foal. Half-sister to Tahkeem (by Green Desert), unplaced in one start at 2 yrs in 2008. The dam, unplaced on her only start, is a half-sister to the Group 1 12f Italian Derby winner and 'King George' second White Muzzle, to the Group 2 German St Leger winner Fair Question and the listed 10f winner Elfaslah. The second dam, Fair of the Furze (by Ela-Mana-Mou), won the Group 2 10f Tattersalls Rogers Gold Cup and is a half-sister to the listed winners Majestic Role, Norman Style and Proconsular. (Hamdan Al Maktoum).

"She's a nice filly – I have the three-year-old which is a different type altogether. One thing you have to say about Nayef is that his stock look incredibly sound – just as he was. I like this filly a lot, she's very active and she'll be one for seven furlongs this season".

1571. LATANSAA ★★★★★
b.c. *Indian Ridge – Sahool (Unfuwain)*.
April 21. Second foal. Half-brother to the unraced 2008 2-y-o Arwaah (by Dalakhani). The dam, a 1m (at 2 yrs) and listed 12f winner, was second in the Group 2 Lancashire Oaks and is a half-sister to 2 winners. The second dam, Mathaayl (by Shadeed), a quite useful 6f and 10f winner, is a half-sister to 3 winners including the dams of the Group/Graded stakes winners Kayrawan, Asfurah and Istintaj. (Hamdan Al Maktoum).
"I have the unraced three-year-old filly by Dalakhani and she's very nice. This Indian Ridge colt is too. He's a straightforward, good-tempered horse that knows his stuff and we just have to wait a bit with him because he could be a nice horse a bit later on. I like him and I trained the dam who was also a decent filly. He's the star of all my two-year-olds at the moment".

1572. MAKFI ★★★★
b.c. *Dubawi – Dhelaal (Green Desert)*.
March 4. First foal. The dam is an unraced half-sister to 7 winners including the champion 2-y-o Alhaarth, winner of the Dewhurst Stakes, the Laurent Perrier Champagne Stakes, the Prix Dollar, the Budweiser American Bowl International Stakes and the Prix du Rond-Point and a half-sister to the very useful 2-y-o Group 3 7f Prix du Calvados winner Green Pola. The second dam, Irish Valley (by Irish River), is an unplaced half-sister to 10 winners, notably the Observer Gold Cup, French 2,000 Guineas and 10.5f Prix Lupin winner and good sire Green Dancer, the US Grade 3 winner Ercolano and the US Graded stakes winner Val Danseur. (Hamdan Al Maktoum).
"Dubawi seems to be stamping nice looking horses. This is a straightforward, perfectly racey colt and he does go OK. We'd be happy with

him so far and he'll probably make a two-year-old over six furlongs by mid-season".

1573. MOOBEYN ★★
ch.c. Selkirk – Key Academy (Royal Academy).
March 23. Sixth foal. 155,000Y. Tattersalls October 1. M Tregoning. Half-brother to the quite useful 2-y-o 8.5f winner Keenes Day (by Daylami), to the quite useful 2-y-o dual 6f winner Adaptation (by Spectrum) and the fair 2-y-o 1m winner Razed (by King's Best). The dam, a quite useful 12f winner, subsequently won at 5 yrs in the USA and was stakes placed. She is a half-sister to 7 winners including the Grade 1 Beverly Hills Handicap and Grade 1 Matriarch Stakes winner Squeak. The second dam, Santa Linda (by Sir Ivor), is an unraced half-sister to 5 winners including the Group 1 Premio Roma winner Noble Saint. (Sheikh Ahmed Al Maktoum).
"Quite a big horse, he's one for the second half of the season and I haven't done enough with him to make an assessment really".

1574. PRIORS GOLD ★★★★
ch.c. Sakhee – Complimentary Pass (Danehlll).
January 21. Sixth foal. 135,000Y. Tattersalls October 1. Peter Doyle. Half-brother to the fairly useful 2008 2-y-o 7f winner Mafaaz (by Medicean), to the useful 2-y-o 7f winner and Group 3 7f Acomb Stakes second Gweebarra (by Lomitas) and to the modest 1m and 10f winner Spunger (by Fraam). The dam, a quite useful 1m placed maiden, is a half-sister to 5 minor winners. The second dam, Capo Di Monte (by Final Straw), a smart 6f (at 2 yrs), dual 10f listed and subsequent Grade 3 11f winner in the USA, is a half-sister to 5 winners including the Group 1 12f Aral-Pokal winner Wind In Her Hair (herself dam of the Japan Cup winner Deep Impact). (Lady Tennant).
"One thing I'd say about Sakhee's stock is that they are good-brained horses. We love this colt and we paid quite a bit of money for him. He's a nice, straightforward colt but you wouldn't expect a Sakhee to be particularly early. He'll come along in his own time, probably in mid-summer".

1575. RASMY ★★★
b.c. Red Ransom – Shadow Dancing (Unfuwain).
May 31. Third foal. 68,000Y. Tattersalls October 2. Shadwell Estate Co. Half-brother to the fair 2008 2-y-o 1m winner Hazy Dancer (by Oasis Dream). The dam, winner of the listed Cheshire Oaks, was third in the Oaks and second in the Group 2 Ribblesdale Stakes and in the Group 2 Prix de Pomone and is a half-sister to 6 winners. The second dam, Salchow (by Niniski), won the Cheshire Oaks, was second in the Park Hill Stakes and is a half-sister to 7 winners. (Hamdan Al Maktoum).
"He's still in Dubai but I'm particularly interested in him because I trained the dam and I have the three-year-old half-sister. There's stamina in abundance in the pedigree and this colt is a late foal but at the back end of the season I think he'll be nice".

1576. SHAAYEQ (IRE) ★★★
b.c. Dubawi – Shohrah (Giant's Causeway).
February 10. First foal. The dam, a useful 2-y-o 6f winner, is a half-sister to the useful 7f winner and 1m listed second Ma-Arif. The second dam, Taqreem (by Nashwan), was second four times over middle-distances and is a half-sister to the high class middle distance colt Ibn Bey, winner of 4 Group 1 events including the Irish St Leger and second in the Breeders Cup Classic and to the very smart Group 1 Yorkshire Oaks winner Roseate Tern. (Hamdan Al Maktoum).
"I trained the dam who won her first start but didn't train on. This is a perfectly nice horse and I know they like him in Dubai. Let's hope that when he comes here he does well, but bear in mind that those coming from Dubai are never early".

1577. STARSTREAMER (IRE) ★★★★
ch.f. Captain Rio – Petra Nova (First Trump).
January 22. Fifth foal. 32,000Y. Doncaster St Leger. M Tregoning. Sister to the quite useful dual 5f winner Mey Blossom and half-sister to the 1m seller winner Tafilah (by Foxhound) and the moderate 7.5f winner Paris Heights (by Paris House). The dam was placed over 5f at 2 yrs and

is a half-sister to 8 winners. The second dam, Spinner (by Blue Cashmere), won once at 3 yrs and is a half-sister to the smart sprinter Clantime. (R C C Villers).

"I'm very happy with her and she's done as much any two-year-old I've got in the yard. One day I'm hoping to be able to go to Goodwood with her. It's a speedy family and she's sound, so in May we'll start charging her up a bit. Captain Rio horses excel on the all-weather but hopefully this filly will act on any surface. She'll be quick enough".

1578. TATAWOR (IRE) ★★★
b.c. Kheleyf – Romea (Muhtarram).
March 26. First foal. 65,000Y. Tattersalls October 2. Shadwell Estate Co. The dam won 2 races at 3 and 4 yrs in Italy and is a half-sister to 3 winners including the US Grade 3 winner Where We Left Off. The second dam, Rekindled Affair (by Rainbow Quest), is an unraced half-sister to 4 winners and to the unraced smart broodmare Summer Trysting (the dam of two Group winners). (Hamdan Al Maktoum).

"A nice-moving, straightforward colt and a sharp enough, well-balanced type".

1579. UDABAA (IRE) ★★★★
b.br.c. Alhaarth – Addaya (Persian Bold).
February 21. Ninth foal. 190,000Y. Tattersalls October 1. Shadwell Estate Co. Half-brother to Endeavoured (by Peintre Celebre), unplaced in 2 starts at 2 yrs in 2008, to the Group 2 Celebration Mile and listed 7f winner Priors Lodge (by Grand Lodge), the useful 7f to 8.5f winner and listed-placed Penny Cross, the fair 10f all-weather winner Kentmere (both by Efisio), the fair 9f to 14f winner Alonso de Guzman, the fair 12f and 2m winner Night Cruise (both by Docksider) and the modest 7f all-weather winner Mystical Star (by Nicolotte). The dam ran once unplaced and is a half-sister to 8 winners abroad. The second dam, Night Of Stars (by Sadler's Wells), won a listed event in Germany over 1m and is a half-sister to the Beeswing Stakes, Hungerford Stakes and Kiveton Park Stakes winner Hadeer. (Hamdan Al Maktoum).

"He's quite a tallish colt but he's been here all winter, rather than in Dubai, so I've been able to do what I want with him. He will be a two-year-old and he's a sensible type just like his half-brother Priors Lodge. He cost a lot of money because he was a very good looking colt and several people wanted him. We do like him, he's very straightforward and a great mover. We'll see him in mid-summer".

1580. UNNAMED ★★★
b.f. Observatory – Annex (Anabaa).
February 27. Half-sister to the French 7f (at 2 yrs) and 1m winner and listed-placed Alsace (by King's Best). The dam, a 7f winner at 3 yrs in Deauville, is a half-sister to the US Grade 2 1m and Group 3 1m Prix Quincey winner Bon Point. The second dam, Twixt (by Kings Lake), won over 7f in France and is a half-sister to the Group 2 Maurice de Gheest winner Interval, to the Grade 2 La Prevoyante Handicap winner Interim and to the dam of the Hoover Fillies Mile winner Invited Guest. (Mr N A Penston & Mr Jas Singh).

"She's a perfectly nice filly. A little bit immature and backward, she'll be arriving at the yard very shortly but I've seen her recently and I thought she'd done very well. She'll be a two-year-old a bit later on".

ED VAUGHAN
1581. BUSINESS BAY (USA) ★★★★
b.br.c. Salt Lake – Jeweled Lady (General Meeting).
March 29. Fifth foal. 40,000Y. Tattersalls October 2. John Ferguson. Half-brother to the US stakes winner and Grade 1 placed Saucey Evening (by More Than Ready) and to a minor US 3-y-o winner by Petionville. The dam is an unraced sister to the US triple Grade 1 winner General Challenge and a half-sister to the US Grade 1 winner Notable Career. The second dam, Excellent Lady (by Smarten), won 4 races in the USA and is a half-sister to 4 winners.

"He's the apple of my eye at the moment. A lovely horse and a week after we bought him the half-sister Saucey Evening was fourth in the Breeders Cup Juvenile Turf. This fellow will need a mile but he's a smashing physical specimen – there wouldn't be a better looking two-year-old in Newmarket".

1582. ELEGANTLY (IRE) ★★
b.f. Rock Of Gibraltar – Solar Crystal (Alzao).
April 19. Ninth foal. 35,000Y. Tattersalls October 2. Blandford Bloodstock. Sister to the unplaced 2008 2-y-o Solar Graphite and half-sister to the smart 2-y-o 6f winner and Group 1 Racing Post Trophy third Feared In Flight (by Hawk Wing), the useful 2-y-o 7f winner, listed-placed and hurdles winner Lunar Crystal (by Shirley Heights) and the quite useful 10f winner Crystal (by Danehill). The dam, a smart 2-y-o, won the Group 3 1m May Hill Stakes, was third in the Group 1 1m Prix Marcel Boussac and is a half-sister to 6 winners including the Group 1 Fillies' Mile winner Crystal Music and the Group 3 winners Dubai Success and State Crystal. The second dam, Crystal Spray (by Beldale Flutter), a minor Irish 4-y-o 14f winner, is a half-sister to 8 winners including the Group 2 winner Crystal Hearted. (The Eloquently Partnership).
"A very nice filly but I can see her being a ten furlong three-year-old. She's done very well of late after going through a growing stage and she should be alright for a mile this year".

1583. EMIRATES HILLS ★★
b.f. Dubawi – Starstone (Diktat).
April 4. First foal. 55,000Y. Tattersalls October 1. Darley Stud. The dam is an unraced half-sister to the Group 1 July Cup winner Pastoral Pursuits and the Group 1 Haydock Park Sprint Cup winner Goodricke. The second dam, Star (by Bahamian Bounty), a quite useful 5f winner, is a half-sister to 7 winners including the useful 2-y-o listed 5f winner Four-Legged-Friend and the US Grade 3 7f winner Superstrike. (A Saeed).
"A first foal, she's a sharp two-year-old type but she's just not doing it for me at the moment, so although she's a straightforward filly she just hasn't come to herself at the moment".

1584. FALCON CITY (CAN) ★★
ch.f. Street Cry – Ascot Tobie (Ascot Knight).
May 21. Sixth foal. $200,000Y. Keeneland September. Darley Stud. Sister to a minor 2-y-o winner in Japan and half-sister to a minor winner in Canada by Mizzen Mast. The dam, a stakes-placed winner at 3 yrs in Canada, is a half-sister to 6 winners. The second dam, Jackjon (by Caucasus), was a stakes-placed winner in Canada. (A Saeed).
"A late foal, she's a lovely specimen and when we bought her she looked a two-year-old type but she's done nothing but grow. Street Cry's tend to do better with age and I think she could be a very nice filly one day".

1585. ROMANCEA (USA) ★★★★
ch.f. Mr Greeley – Two Halos (Saint Ballado).
February 17. First foal. $400,000Y. Keeneland September. Darley Stud. The dam is an unraced half-sister to one winner. The second dam, Top Secret (by Afleet), won 11 races including for Graded stakes events in the USA, was Grade 1 placed and is a full or half-sister to 2 stakes winners. (A Saeed).
"I love this filly, she got pneumonia in January so we were held up for a bit but she's a big, good-looking filly with a lovely action. As a physical type she's very similar to the Guineas winner Finsceal Beo. Seven furlongs should suit her this year and she'll probably go a mile next season".

1586. SEEKING DUBAI ★★★
b.f. Dubawi – Placement (Kris).
February 5. Seventh foal. 55,000Y. Tattersalls October 1. Rabbah Bloodstock. Half-sister to the useful 5f listed (at 2 yrs) and 7f listed winner Presto Vento (by Air Express) and to the quite useful 10f winner Amanjena (by Green Desert). The dam is an unraced half-sister to 4 winners including the Group 2 Sun Chariot Stakes winner Danceabout and the Group 3 6f Prix de Meautry winner Pole Position. The second dam, Putupon (by Mummy's Pet), a fairly useful 2-y-o 5f winner, is a sister to the Gimcrack Stakes

winner Precocious and a half-sister to 9 winners including Jupiter Island (Japan Cup) and Pushy (Queen Mary Stakes). (A Saeed).
"She goes well, looks sharp and might be quick enough for five furlongs. She's done one piece of work and did OK. I'm sure she'll win a five furlong fillies' race. Fully grown and quite small, she's an all-out early two-year-old".

1587. SHAMS ALBAWADI (USA) ★★★★
b.br.f. Gone West – Lucky (Sadler's Wells).
January 17. Second foal. 130,000Y. Tattersalls October 1. Not sold. The dam, winner of the Group 3 7f Athasi Stakes, is a sister to the Irish 1,000 Guineas Trial winner and Irish 1,000 Guineas second Amethyst and to the 2,000 Guineas and Group 1 National Stakes winner King Of Kings and a half-sister to the Group 2 5.5f Prix Robert Papin winner General Monash. The second dam, Zummerudd (by Habitat), is an unplaced sister to the Irish Group 3 and US Grade 3 winner Ancestral. (A Saeed).
"This filly is the bees knees but she's had a problem with a stifle cyst which we've attended to and we'll just have to see how she progresses. A filly with a very natural way of going, she's a lovely model with a lovely pedigree but if we see her this year it'll be late in the season. A filly with a lot of ability".

1588. UNNAMED ★★★
b.br.c. Key Of Luck – Ascot Cyclone (Rahy).
April 21. Half-brother to the useful 2-y-o 5f and 7f winner Asia Winds (by Machiavellian), the useful 2-y-o dual 6f winner Fancy Lady (by Cadeaux Genereux), the quite useful 10f winner Daylami Star (by Daylami) and the modest 12f winner Kochanski (by King's Best). The dam, a fairly useful 5.7f (at 2 yrs) and 7f winner, is a half-sister to the 2-y-o 6f winner and Group 1 7f Prix de la Salamandre second Bin Nashwan, the US Grade 2 winner Magellan and the 6f winner and Group 3 7f Supreme Stakes second Alanees (by Cadeaux Genereux) – all 3 very useful. The second dam, Dabaweyaa (by Shareef Dancer), was a smart winner of the 1m Atalanta Stakes and was placed in the 1,000 Guineas and the Kiveton Park Stakes. She is a half-sister to the Group 3 winning sprinter Bruckner, the 12f Galtres Stakes winner Ma Femme and the smart Hoover Fillies Mile and Nassau Stakes winner Acclimatise. (Mohammed Obaida).
"A nice horse that's doing everything right, he's just a little bit soft in his pasterns and he needs to strengthen up a bit up front. He looks the type that should be out in July and he's a very good looking horse that goes well".

1589. UNNAMED ★★★★
b.br.f. Malibu Moon – Baldellia (Grape Tree Road).
February 25. Third foal. $150,000Y. Keeneland September. Rabbah Bloodstock. The dam won the listed Prix des Lilas. The second dam, Benevole (by Groom Dancer), is a placed half-sister to 3 listed winners including the smart broodmare Frenetique. (N Mourad).
"By a sire that did well with cheap mares and managed to upgrade them, he's got a very high percentage of winners to runners. His progeny are not really turf horses but I took a punt and if she goes on grass she'll be out in mid-season. I like her very much and she looks like a colt. Not overly big, she's very well boned, has a great hind end and six or seven furlongs should be right for her".

1590. UNNAMED ★★
ch.f. Compton Place – Barboukh (Night Shift).
March 18. 26,000Y. Tattersalls October. Rabbah Bloodstock. Half-sister to the Group 3 10f Prix Exbury winner and Group 1 Premio Presidente della Repubblica third Barbola (by Diesis) and the fairly useful 10f winner Tarboush (by Polish Precedent). The dam, a fairly useful winner of the 1m listed Fern Hill Stakes, is a half-sister to 6 winners. The second dam, Turban (by Glint Of Gold), a fair 10f and 11.7f winner at 3 yrs, is a half-sister to 6 winners including the top-class French and Irish Derby winner Old Vic.
"Although she looks precocious her pedigree suggests she might want a trip".

1591. UNNAMED ★★
ch.f. Barathea – Coeur de la Mer (Caerleon).
January 30. Third foal. 26,000Y. Tattersalls

October 3. McKeever St Lawrence. Half-sister to the useful 5f (at 2 yrs) and 6f winner and listed-placed Evens And Odds (by Johannesburg). The dam, a quite useful 2-y-o 1m winner, is a half-sister to the 3 winners including the listed-placed Ski Academy. The second dam, Cochineal (by Vaguely Noble), is an unplaced half-sister to 7 winners in the USA.

"A huge filly but mature, she has a lovely action but looks like a mile and a half filly next year. We'll give her a run at the back-end".

1592. UNNAMED ★★★★
b.c. Noverre – Polish Affair
(Polish Patriot).
March 16. Sixth living foal. 42,000Y. Tattersalls October 2. McKeever St Lawrence. Half-brother to the modest 2008 fourth placed 2-y-o Tarruji (by Verglas) and to 3 winners in Germany including the Group 2 German 1,000 Guineas winner Portella and the listed-placed Predator (all by Protektor). The dam, placed twice at 2 and 3 yrs in Germany, is a half-sister to 6 winners. The second dam, Have A Flutter (by Auction Ring), is a placed full or half-sister to 5 winners. (S Rashid).

"A lovely, really good-moving horse. A real athlete, I'd love to start him at six furlongs but I imagine he'll need seven furlongs. I could get him ready to run in April but the six furlong races aren't there. An out-an-out two-year-old type".

1593. UNNAMED ★★★
ch.c. Shamardal – Polly Perkins (Pivotal).
February 13. First foal. 50,000Y. Tattersalls October 1. Rabbah Bloodstock. The dam, a useful 2-y-o dual listed 5f winner, is a half-sister to one winner. The second dam, Prospering (by Prince Sabo), a moderate 7f winner at 3 yrs, is a half-sister to 6 winners. (Mr M Al Shafar).

"An out-and-out two-year-old type, earlier on I thought he'd be my first runner but unfortunately he had a niggling problem. He's back cantering now and he's one I wanted to have ready early because he was such a sharp looking two-year-old. Fully grown, he's small and really sharp".

1594. UNNAMED ★★
b.c. Cape Cross – Silver Bracelet
(Machiavellian).
March 20. Fourth foal. Closely related to Stoic (by Green Desert), unplaced in one start at 2 yrs in 2008 and half-brother to the minor French 1m winner Dark Beauty (by Singspiel). The dam, a fairly useful 8.3f winner, was third in the listed Masaka Stakes and is a half-sister to one winner out of the very useful 2-y-o Group 3 7f Prestige Stakes winner and Group 1 Prix Marcel Boussac third Love Of Silver (by Arctic Tern) – herself a half-sister to 6 winners. (Ali Saeed).

"He had an accident at stud so he lost time as a result and went backward but he's a lovely horse with a nice way of going. A little bit slack of his pasterns, we'll take our time with him but he has a great attitude and he should be a seven furlong horse".

1595. UNNAMED ★★
b.c. Dubai Destination – Tidie France
(Cape Town).
February 14. First foal. 32,000Y. Tattersalls October 2. McKeever St Lawrence. The dam, placed once at 3 yrs in France, is a half-sister to 6 winners. The second dam, Talon d'Aiguille (by Big Spruce), won at 3 yrs in France and was third in the Group 3 10.5f Prix de Flore. She is a half-sister to the high-class French filly Proskona and to the smart Prix Chloe winner Korveya – herself dam of the classic winners Bosra Sham, Hector Protector and Shanghai. (Salem Rashid).

"A nice horse, he looks a two-year-old but we haven't done a lot with him and he'll need fast ground or polytrack. He could be OK".

1596. UNNAMED ★★★★
b.br.f. Tale Of The Cat – Gaily Lady
(Silver Hawk).
January 29. Sixth foal. 26,000Y. Tattersalls October 2. Half-sister to 3 minor winners in the USA and Japan by Carnegie, Dancing Partner and French Deputy. The dam won 2 races in Japan and is out of the US Grade 1 winner Gaily Gaily (by Cure The Blues), herself a half-sister to the Italian 2,00 Guineas winner Gay Burslem. (The Grange House Partnership).

"A very nice filly that should make a two-year-old, she's certainly worth adding to your list".
TRAINER'S BARGAIN BUY

1597. UNNAMED ★★
b.c. Azamour – Bonheur (Royal Academy).
April 5. Fifth foal. Half-brother to the Group 3 Irish 1,000 Guineas Trial winner Carribean Sunset (by Danehill Dancer), to the minor French 2-y-o winner Happy Lodge (by Grand Lodge) and the fair 12f winner Ommadawn (by Montjeu). The dam won over 6f at 3 yrs in Ireland and is a half-sister to 7 winners including the German 1,000 Guineas winner Quebrada. The second dam, Queen To Conquer (by King's Bishop), won the Grade 1 Yellow Ribbon Handicap and is a half-sister to 5 winners.
"He has a lovely action and he'll be a nice horse on fast ground towards the back-end of the season".

DERMOT WELD
1598. AIDED AND ABETTED (IRE) ★★★
ch.c. Danehill Dancer – Lady Luck (Kris).
May 1. Half-brother to the very smart 7f (at 2 yrs) and Group 2 10f Leopardstown Derby Trial winner and dual Derby placed Casual Conquest (by Hernando), to the Irish 2-y-o listed 7f winner Elusive Double (by Grand Lodge) and the quite useful Irish 9f winner Media Asset (by Polish Precedent). The dam won over 1m in Ireland and is a half-sister to several winners including the Irish Group 3 Boland Stakes winner Social Harmony. The second dam, Latest Chapter (by Ahonoora), is an unraced half-sister to the Grade 1 Belmont Stakes winner Go And Go. (Moyglare Stud Farm).

1599. ALBURJ (USA) ★★★
b.c. Dynaformer – Rumansy (Theatrical).
March 25. Half-brother to the quite useful Irish 2-y-o 7f winner Labaqa (by Rahy). The dam is a placed sister to the US Grade 3 Generous Stakes winner Startac. The second dam, Uenga (Mr Prospector), won a minor event at 2 yrs in France and is a half-sister to 5 winners including the US Grade 2 winner Jade Flush. (Hamdan Al-Maktoum).

1600. ANAVERNA (IRE) ★★★
b.f. Galileo – Agnetha (Big Shuffle).
April 16. Fourth foal. Closely related to the quite useful Irish 7f winner Scarlet O'Hara (by Sadler's Wells) and half-sister to the fair UAE 7f winner Pure Bluff (by Indian Ridge). The dam was a smart winner of the listed Silver Flash Stakes (at 2 yrs) and the Group 3 5f King George 200th Anniversary Stakes at 3 yrs. She is a sister to the smart German Group 2 sprint winner Areion and to the Irish listed winner Anna Frid and a half-sister to 4 winners. The second dam, Aerleona (by Caerleon), a German 2-y-o 6f winner, is a half-sister to 5 winners including the Fillies' Mile winner Nepula. (Mrs C L Weld).

1601. ATYAAB ★★★
b.f. Green Desert – Aspen Leaves (Woodman).
March 21. Fifth foal. Sister to the fair 3-y-o 7f winner Deira Dubai and half-sister to the fair 2008 2-y-o 7f winner Awfeyaa (by Haafhd) and the useful Irish 10f winner Agenda (by Sadler's Wells). The dam, a minor Irish 7f winner, is a sister to the champion American 2-y-o colt Timber Country and a half-sister to the very smart Group 2 13.5f Prix de Pomone winner Colorado Dancer (herself the dam of Dubai Millennium), the Grade 1 Gamely Handicap winner Northern Aspen, the Group 1 July Cup winner Hamas, the Group 1 Grand Prix de Paris winner Fort Wood and the Prix d'Astarte winner Elle Seule (herself dam of the Group 1 winners Elnadim and Mehthaaf). The second dam, Fall Aspen (by Pretense) – clearly one of the finest broodmares of recent times – won 8 races notably the Grade 1 7f Matron Stakes. (Hamdan Al Maktoum).

1602. BETHRAH (IRE) ★★★
br.f. Marju – Reve d'Iman (Highest Honor).
March 21. Second foal. €160,000Y. Goffs Million. Shadwell Estate Co. The dam, a minor 3-y-o winner in France, is a sister to the Group 1 Prix Saint-Alary winner Reve d'Oscar, the Group 2 Prix Hocquart winner Numide and the listed 3-y-o winner Sir Eric. The second dam, Numidie (by Baillamont), won a listed race in France and is a half-sister to 3 minor winners. (Hamdan Al Maktoum).

1603. BYGONE AGE (IRE) ★★★
b.c. Whipper – Twiggy's Sister (Flying Spur).
March 11. Third foal. €125,000Y. Goffs Million. Blandford Bloodstock. Half-brother to the quite useful 2008 2-y-o triple 5f winner Visterre (by Noverre). The dam, a useful triple 7f winner in Ireland at 4 and 5 yrs, was listed-placed and is a half-sister to 3 winners. The second dam, Winsome Girl (by Music Boy), won once over 1m in Ireland at 4 yrs and is a half-sister to 6 winners. (Dr R Lambe).

1604. CLEAR ALTERNATIVE (IRE) ★★★
ch.c. Indian Ridge – Token Gesture (Alzao).
April 30. Ninth foal. Brother to the useful 10f winner and Group 3 10f Gallinule Stakes third Central Station and to the Irish 2-y-o 7f winner and Group 2 1m Beresford Stakes second Relaxed Gesture and half-brother to the fair 2008 2-y-o 7f winner Braveheart Move (by Cape Cross), the Irish 1m and subsequent US Grade 2 9.5f American Derby winner Evolving Tactics (by Machiavellian) and the Irish 1m, 12f and hurdles winner Turn Of Phrase (by Cadeaux Genereux). The dam, a smart winner of the Group 3 7f C L Weld Park Stakes, is a half-sister to the US Grade 2 9f winner Wait Till Monday, to the useful Irish 10f to 12.3f winner Blazing Spectacle and the useful Irish middle-distance stayer and Triumph Hurdle winner Rare Holiday. The second dam, Temporary Lull (by Super Concorde), is an unraced sister to the Nell Gwyn Stakes winner Martha Stevens. (Moyglare Stud Farm).

1605. COOL MARBLE (IRE) ★★★
b.c. Oasis Dream – Nini Princesse (Niniski).
March 27. Tenth foal. €70,000Y. Goffs Million. Blandford Bloodstock. Half-brother to the dual listed winner and Group 3 placed Miss Honorine, to the French winner of 3 races Princesse Baie (both by Highest Honor), the French trained winner and smart hurdler Blue Canyon (by Bering), the fair 1m winner Mekong Melody (by Cape Cross) and 3 minor French 3-y-o winners by Darshaan, Grand Lodge and Night Shift. The dam, a winner of 6 races from 2 to 4 yrs and from 1m to 10f in France, is a sister to the US Grade 1 winner and Group 1 Criterium de Saint-Cloud second Louis Cyphre and a half-sister to 7 winners including the Group 2 Prix Robert Papin winner Psychobabble. The second dam, Princesse Timide (by Blushing Groom), won twice in France and was listed placed 5 times. (Dr R Lambe).

1606. DEFINITE SEASON (IRE) ★★★
ch.c. Refuse To Bend – Sun Seasons (Salse).
April 29. The dam, a fairly useful Irish 7f winner, is a half-sister to numerous winners including the Group 2 11f Blandford Stakes winner Lisieux Rose. The second dam, Epicure's Garden (by Affirmed), a useful Irish 7f (at 2 yrs) to 9f winner, is a sister to the Irish 1,000 Guineas winner Trusted Partner (dam of the high-class filly Dress To Thrill). (Moyglare Stud Farm).

1607. DHABIA (USA) ★★★
b.f. Gulch – Fatwa (Lahib).
May 4. Half-sister to the quite useful 2008 2-y-o 5f winner Raedah (by Elusive Quality) and to the modest dual 10f winner Chant de Guerre (by War Chant). The dam, a fairly useful 3-y-o 6f winner, was second in the Group 3 7f Fred Darling Stakes and is a full or half-sister to numerous winners including the useful 6f (at 2 yrs) and 1m winner Hirasah. The second dam, Mayaasa (by Lyphard), a fair 1/2f winner, is closely related to the Group 1 Queen Elizabeth II Stakes winner Maroof. (Hamdan Al Maktoum).

1608. DRIVE HOME (USA) ★★★
b.br.c. Mr Greeley – Unique Pose (Sadler's Wells).
April 3. First foal. The dam, an Irish 6f (at 2 yrs) and 10f winner, was listed-placed and is a sister to the Irish 3-y-o 7f winner and 2-y-o Group 3 7f C L Weld Park Stakes third Easy Sunshine. The second dam, Desert Ease (by Green Desert), an Irish 2-y-o listed 6f winner, is a half-sister to several winners including the Group 3 Tetrarch Stakes and Group 3 7f Concorde Stakes winner Two-Twenty-Two. (Moyglare Stud Farm).

1609. EWAAN (IRE) ★★★
b.c. Intikhab – Blue Crystal (Lure).
February 17. Fifth foal. €90,000Y. Goffs

Million. Shadwell Estate Co. Half-brother to the Italian 2-y-o winner and listed placed Golden Liberty (by Statue Of Liberty) and to a minor winner in Italy by Grand Lodge. The dam, a fair 10.5f winner in Ireland, is a half-sister to 3 minor winners. The second dam, Crystal Cross (by Roberto), a quite useful winner of 4 races at up to 14f, is a half-sister to the Group 1 Haydock Park Sprint Cup winner Iktamal, the French Group 2 winner First Magnitude and the Grade 2 Arkansas Derby winner Rockamundo. (Hamdan Al Maktoum).

1610. FLAME KEEPER (IRE) ★★★★
ch.f. *Pivotal – Cool Clarity (Indian Ridge)*.
February 14. The dam, an Irish listed 7f winner, is a half-sister to the 2-y-o listed 7f Tyros Stakes winner and Group 3 7f Boland Stakes second Artistic Blue and to the Irish listed 7.5f winner Queen Of Palms. The second dam, Tapolite (by Tap On Wood), won the listed 7f Tyros Stakes, is a sister to the 2-y-o Group 3 1m Killavullen Stakes winner Sedulous and a half-sister to 4 winners. (Moyglare Stud Farm).

1611. HISTORIC OCCASION (IRE) ★★★
b.c. *Royal Applause – Intriguing (Fasliyev)*.
February 17. First foal. €165,000Y. Goffs Million. Bobby O'Ryan. The dam, a quite useful 2-y-o 6f winner, is a half-sister to 7 winners including the Group 3 6f Greenlands Stakes winner Nautical Pet, the poor 11f all-weather winner Laa Jadeed (both by Petorius), the quite useful 10f winner Green In Blue (by Kahyasi), the fair dual 1m winner Roi de la Mer (by Fairy King), the fair 10f all-weather winner Brazilian Mood (by Doyoun), the Irish 9f and 14f winner Touching Moment (by Pennine Walk) and the modest 7-y-o 6f winner Waders Dream (by Doulab). The second dam, Sea Mistress (by Habitat), is an unraced half-sister to 2 minor winners. (Dr R Lambe).

1612. JARAYAAN ★★★
b.c. *Needwood Blade – Bold Bunny (Piccolo)*.
February 27. First foal. 56,000Y. Doncaster St Leger. Shadwell Estate Co. The dam, a moderate 6f placed 3-y-o, is a half-sister to 6 winners including the listed winners Warbler and Silly Bold. The second dam, Bold And Beautiful (by Bold Lad, Ire), a useful 1m winner, was Group 3 placed twice in Germany is a half-sister to 4 winners. (Hamdan Al Maktoum).

1613. JOAN D'ARC (IRE) ★★★
b.f. *Invincible Spirit – Prakara (Indian Ridge)*.
March 21. First foal. €90,000Y. Goffs Million. Bobby O'Ryan. The dam was placed fourth once over 1m and is a half-sister to 3 winners including the 2-y-o Group 2 6f Mill Reef Stakes and listed 7f winner Bouncing Bowdler. The second dam, Prima Volta (by Primo Dominie), a quite useful 6f (at 2 yrs) and 9f winner, is a half-sister to 5 minor winners. (Newtown Amner Stud).

1614. KEY SECURE (IRE) ★★★
b.f. *Sadler's Wells – Market Slide (Gulch)*.
February 22. Sister to Refuse To Bend, a top-class winner of four Group 1 races from 7f (at 2 yrs) to 10f, to the very useful 2-y-o 7f winner and Group 2 Beresford Stakes second Domestic Fund and the fairly useful Irish 12f winner Ripple Of Pride and half-sister to the Melbourne Cup winner Media Puzzle (by Theatrical). The dam, an Irish 6f (at 2 yrs) and 6.5f winner, is closely related to the minor Irish 7f winner First Breeze and a half-sister to the Breeders Cup Classic second Twilight Agenda and the minor Irish 7f winner Early Memory. (Moyglare Stud Farm).

1615. LEGENDARY LAD (IRE) ★★★
b.c. *Dubawi – Lishaway (Polish Precedent)*.
February 3. Eighth foal. €120,000Y. Goffs Million. D K Weld. Half-brother to the Group 3 Solario Stakes winner Foss Way (by Desert Prince) and to a listed winner abroad by Medicean. The dam is a placed half-sister to 9 winners including the French Group winners Blushing Gleam, Danzigaway and Gold Away. The second dam, Blushing Away (by Blushing Groom), won in France at 3 yrs and was listed-placed and is a half-sister to 5 winners. (Dr R Lambe).

1616. LISSELAN PRINCESS ★★★
b.f. Verglas – Erreur (Desert King).
January 24. First foal. 34,000Y. Doncaster St Leger. Bobby O'Ryan. The dam, a quite useful 3-y-o 6f winner, is a half-sister to 5 winners including the French dual listed winner and Group 3 placed Felicita. The second dam, Abergwle (by Absalom), ran twice unplaced and is a half-sister to 4 winners. (Lisselan Farms).

1617. MARKET PUZZLE (IRE) ★★★
ch.c. Bahamian Bounty – Trempjane (Lujain).
February 15. First foal. 62,000Y. Doncaster St Leger. Bobby O'Ryan. The dam, a fair 2-y-o 6f winner, is a half-sister to the 5.8f (at 2 yrs here) and subsequent four-time US Graded stakes winner Katdogawn. The second dam, Trempkate (by Trempolino), a French 2-y-o 9f winner, is a half-sister to 6 winners including the Group 3 Brownstown Stakes winner Perfect Touch. (Mr D R Keough).

1618. MINSKY MINE (IRE) ★★★
b.c. Montjeu – Summer Trysting (Alleged).
March 27. Ninth foal. Half-brother to the Irish 2-y-o 7f listed and subsequent US Grade 2 9.5f Arlington Derby winner Simple Exchange (by Danehill), to the Irish 7f (at 2 yrs), Group 3 Brigadier Gerard Stakes and Group 3 Newbury Dubai Duty Free 'Arc' Trial winner Sights On Gold, the fairly useful Irish 8.5f winner Romantic Venture (both by Indian Ridge), the fairly useful Irish 9f winner Beat The Heat (by Salse) and the fair Irish 12f winner Tempting Paradise (by Grand Lodge). The dam was placed at up to 12f in Ireland and is a half-sister to the smart performer at up to 10f Smooth Performance. The second dam, Seasonal Pickup (by The Minstrel), won four listed races in Ireland and is a half-sister to the dam of Grey Swallow. (Moyglare Stud Farm).

1619. MUTAMALEQ (IRE) ★★★
b.c. Refuse To Bend – Chaturanga (Night Shift).
March 30. Eighth foal. 150,000Y. Tattersalls October 1. Shadwell Estate Co. Half-brother to the fairly useful Irish 8.5f winner and Group 3 placed Mooretown Lady (by Montjeu), to the fair 11.7f winner Battledress, the Irish 7f (at 2 yrs) and 6f winner Cocorica (by Croco Rouge) and the fair 9.4f all-weather winner Folaann (by Pennekamp). The dam is an unraced half-sister to 6 winners including the Irish listed 10f winner and Group 2 9.8f Prix Dollar second Strategic and the Group 2 Prix Eugene Adam winner Sobieski. The second dam, Game Plan (by Darshaan), won the Group 2 10f Pretty Polly Stakes, was second in the Oaks and is a half-sister to 10 winners including the Oaks winner Shahtoush. (Hamdan Al Maktoum).

1620. NUNAVIK (IRE) ★★
b.f. Indian Ridge – In Anticipation (Sadler's Wells).
February 2. Sister to the useful Irish 1m winner Legal Jousting and half-sister to the Group 2 12f Ribblesdale Stakes winner Irresistible Jewel (by Danehill), the listed 12f winner Diamond Trim (by Highest Honor), the quite useful Irish 1m winner Silent Confession (by Selkirk), the quite useful 7f to 10f winner of 14 races Intricate Web (by Warning) and the quite useful Irish 12f winner Instant Sparkle (by Danehill). The dam won over 12f and 14f in Ireland. The second dam, Aptostar (by Fappiano), won 6 races in the USA including the Grade 1 Acorn Stakes and the Grade 2 Bed O'Roses Handicap and is a half-sister to the US Grade 2 winner Man Alright. (Moyglare Stud Farm).

1621. PALM RIDGE (IRE) ★★
ch.c. Indian Ridge – Queen Of Palms (Desert Prince).
March 22. Second foal. Brother to the unplaced 2008 2-y-o Little Calla. The dam, an Irish listed 7.5f 3-y-o winner, is a half-sister to the Irish listed winners Artistic Blue and Cool Clarity. The second dam, Tapolite (by Tap On Wood), won the listed 7f Tyros Stakes, is a sister to the 2-y-o Group 3 1m Killavullen Stakes winner Sedulous and a half-sister to 4 winners. (Mrs A Coughlan).

1622. SAISON (IRE) ★★★
b.f. Indian Ridge – Summer Spice (Key Of Luck).
May 10. Third foal. €75,000Y. Goffs Sportsman's. D K Weld. Half-sister to the 2008

2-y-o 7f winner (on her only start) Anice Stellato (by Dalakhani). The dam, a quite useful 2-y-o 6f winner, is a half-sister to the very smart Group 1 7f National Stakes and Group 2 10f Tattersalls Rogers Gold Cup winner Definite Article, to the Group 2 Dante Stakes winner Salford Express and the Group 3 7f Greenham Stakes winner Salford City. The second dam, Summer Fashion (by Moorestyle), a quite useful winner of 6 races from 1m to 10f, is a half-sister to 6 winners. (Irish National Stud).

1623. SENSE OF PURPOSE (IRE) ★★★
ch.f. Galileo – Super Gift (Darshaan).
February 25. Closely related to Dance Pass (by Sadler's Wells), placed fourth over 1m at 2 yrs on her only start at 2 yrs in 2008 and half-sister to the Irish 7f winner Rare Delight (by Indian Ridge), to the quite useful Irish 7f and 1m winner Polite Reply (by Be My Guest) and the fair Irish 10f winner All In A Mix (by Definite Article). The dam, a dual 2-y-o 1m winner and second in the Group 3 C L Weld Park Stakes, is a half-sister to 2 winners out of the Group 3 1m Italian winner Bubinka (by Nashua). (Moyglare Stud Farm).

1624. STROKE OF LOVE (USA) ★★★
b.f. Smart Strike – Hymn Of Love (Baratea).
January 22. The dam, an Irish listed 1m winner, is a half-sister to several winners including the Irish 6f and subsequent US winner Still As Sweet. The second dam, Perils Of Joy (by Rainbow Quest), a 3-y-o 1m winner in Ireland, is a half-sister to 5 winners including the Italian Group 3 winner Sweetened Offer. (Moyglare Stud Farm).

1625. STUNNING VIEW (IRE) ★★★
ch.c. Shamardal – Sabaah (Nureyev).
February 4. Eleventh foal. €160,000Y. Goffs Million. D K Weld. Half-brother to the top-class National Stakes, Irish 2,000 Guineas and Irish Derby winner Desert King, to the useful 2-y-o 6f and 7f winner and Group 2 7f Champagne Stakes third Chianti, the fairly useful 6f and 1m winner Desertion (all by Danehill), the Irish 10f listed winner Cairdeas (by Darshaan), the useful 7f winner of 4 races Wahj (by Indian Ridge) and the French 2-y-o 6.6f all-weather winner Bright Morning (by Dubai Millennium). The dam, a modest 8.2f placed maiden, is a full or half-sister to 8 winners including the Group 1 1m Queen Elizabeth II Stakes winner Maroof and to the placed dam of the Canadian Grade 2 winner Callwood Dancer. The second dam, Dish Dash (by Nureyev), won the Group 2 12f Ribblesdale Stakes and is a half-sister to 6 winners. (Dr R Lambe).

1626. TRUTH SEEKING (IRE) ★★★
ch.f. Seeking The Gold – Touch Of Truth (Storm Cat).
March 15. Fifth foal. Sister to the useful Irish 7f and German listed 1m winner Society Hostess. The dam is a lightly raced unplaced half-sister to several winners including the Breeders Cup Classic second Twilight Agenda. (Moyglare Stud Farm).

1627. UNACCOMPANIED (IRE) ★★★
b.f. Danehill Dancer – Legend Has It (Sadler's Wells).
April 14. Second foal. The dam, a quite useful 9f and 12f winner, is a half-sister to one winner. The second dam, Magical Cliché (by Affirmed), was placed 4 times at up to 1m and is a sister to several good winners including the Group 2 Premio Legnano winner Easy To Copy and the Irish 1,000 Guineas winner Trusted Partner (dam of the high-class filly Dress To Thrill). (Moyglare Stud Farm).

1628. WAAHEB (USA) ★★★
b.c. Elusive Quality – Nafisah (Lahib).
April 9. Half-brother to the useful UAE Group 3 1m winner of 5 races Snaafy (by Kingmambo). The dam, a very useful 7f (at 2 yrs), 9f and listed 10f winner, is a half-sister to 6 winners including the Irish 12f listed and hurdles winner Mutakarrim. The second dam, Alyakkh (by Sadler's Wells), a fair 3-y-o 1m winner, is a full or half-sister to 6 winners including the Champion Stakes and 2,000 Guineas winner Haafhd. (Hamdan Al Maktoum).

1629. WAAJIDA ★★★
b.f. *Dubawi – Ruby Affair (Night Shift)*.
March 2. Seventh foal. 50,000Y. Tattersalls October 2. Shadwell Estate Co. Half-sister to the quite useful 2008 2-y-o 5f winner Red Kyte (by Hawk Wing), to the very useful 6f (including at 2 yrs) and 6.5f winner Khabfair (by Intikhab), the useful 2-y-o 6f winner Hammadi (by Red Ransom) and the quite useful 2-y-o 6f all-weather winner Frances Cadell (by Cadeaux Genereux). The dam, a modest 7f placed 3-y-o, is a half-sister to the 2,000 Guineas winner Island Sands. The second dam, Tiavanita (by J O Tobin), is a half-sister to 8 winners including the Group 2 Great Voltigeur Stakes winner Corrupt. (Hamdan Al Maktoum).

1630. WHISKEY BAY (IRE) ★★★
b.c. *Acclamation – Samriah (Wassl)*.
April 10. Ninth foal. €87,000Y. Goffs Million. Blandford Bloodstock. Half-brother to the useful 2-y-o 6f winner and Group 3 Princess Margaret Stakes third Voile (by Barathea), to the fairly useful 2-y-o 5f winner of 5 races Baby Grand, the Hong Kong winner of 4 races One Step Ahead (both by Mukaddamah), the quite useful 6f (at 2 yrs) and 2m winner Cedar Master (by Soviet Lad) and the fair 2-y-o 7f winner Bishop's Wood (by Charnwood Forest). The dam is an unraced half-sister to 5 minor winners. The second dam, Top Treat (by Topsider), a winner of 3 races, was fourth in the Group 3 Beeswing Stakes and is a half-sister to 5 winners. (Dr R Lambe).

1631. ZULU PRINCIPLE ★★★★
b.c. *Tiger Hill – Tu Eres Mi Amore (Sadler's Wells)*.
March 19. Second foal. The dam is an unplaced sister to the 2-y-o Group 1 Fillies' Mile winner Listen and to the Group 1 7f Moyglare Stud Stakes winner and smart broodmare Sequoyah (the dam of Henrythenavigator). The second dam, Brigid (by Irish River), a minor French 3-y-o 1m winner, is a sister to the listed 7f Prix de l'Obelisque winner Or Vision (herself dam of the Group/Grade 1 winners Dolphin Street, Insight and Saffron Walden) and a half-sister to 6 winners. (Plantation Stud).

1632. UNNAMED ★★★
b.f. *Dansili – Aspiring Diva (Distant View)*.
April 28. Sister to the listed 5f winner Daring Diva and half-sister to the fairly useful 2-y-o 6f winner Striking Spirit (by Oasis Dream). The dam, placed at up to 1m in France, is a half-sister to numerous winners including the useful 10.2f winner Private Song. The second dam, Queen Of Song (by His Majesty), won 14 races in the USA including the Grade 2 8.5f Shuvee Handicap and the Grade 3 8.5f Sixty Sails Handicap (twice), was Grade 1 placed and is a sister to the Grade 1 Jersey Derby winner Cormorant. (Khalid Abdulla).

1633. UNNAMED ★★★
b.f. *Oasis Dream – Avoidance (Cryptoclearance)*.
May 12. Third foal. Sister to the quite useful 2008 Irish 2-y-o 7f winner Broad Meaning. The dam, a fairly useful 7f and 1m winner at 2 yrs, is a half-sister to several winners including the useful 1m and 10f winner Averted View. The second dam, Averti (by Known Fact), a fairly useful 7f (at 2 yrs) and 6f winner, is a half-sister to the US Grade 1 winner Defensive Play. (Khalid Abdulla).

1634. UNNAMED ★★★
b.f. *Dansili – Biloxi (Caerleon)*.
March 18. Fourth foal. The dam is an unraced sister to the useful 10f winner Yaralino and a half-sister to the 1m (at 2 yrs) and Group 1 10f Grand Prix de Paris winner Beat Hollow. The second dam, Wemyss Bight (by Dancing Brave), won 5 races including the Group 1 12f Irish Oaks, the Group 2 12f Prix de Malleret, the Group 3 10.5f Prix Cleopatre and the Group 3 10.5f Prix Penelope. (Khalid Abdulla).

1635. UNNAMED ★★★
b.f. *Royal Anthem – Shining Bright (Rainbow Quest)*.
February 16. Half-sister to the 7f (at 2 yrs) and Group 2 12f Ribblesdale Stakes winner Spanish Sun, to the smart 7f (at 2 yrs) and triple listed 10f winner Spanish Moon, the quite useful dual 1m winner Certain Promise (all by El Prado), the

fairly useful middle-distance winners Eagle's Cross (by Trempolino) and Galvanise (by Run Softly) and the French 1m winner Cut Glass (by Diesis). The dam, a French 10f winner, is a half-sister to the Group 2 12f Grand Prix de Chantilly winner Daring Miss and the Group 3 12f Prix de Royaumont winner Apogee. The second dam, Bourbon Girl (by Ile de Bourbon), a 2-y-o 7f winner, was second in the Oaks and the Irish Oaks. (Khalid Abdulla).

PETER WINKWORTH

I need to say thank you to assistant trainer Anton Pearson for discussing these horses with me.

1636. IT'S A DEAL (IRE) ★★★
b.f. Indian Haven – Gold And Blue (Bluebird).
March 19. 8,000Y. Doncaster St Leger. David Redvers. Half-sister to the useful 6f winner (including at 2 yrs) Blue Star, to the fairly useful 2-y-o 5f and 6f winner Blue Reigns, the modest 7f winner Blue Mystique (all by Whittingham), the fairly useful all-weather 5f (at 2 yrs) and 6f winner Blue Kite (by Silver Kite), the quite useful triple 5f winner (including at 2 yrs) Westbrook Blue (by Kingsinger), the quite useful 5f winner of 8 races Jodeeka (by Fraam) and the fair 6f winner of 4 races Bid For Gold (by Auction Ring). The dam was a lightly-raced Irish maiden. (Badger's Set).
"A lovely filly but she's growing and I won't be rushing her. She's a nice individual and I like her a lot but we'll have to see how she progresses".

1637. MARCUS CICERO (IRE) ★★
b.g. Le Vie Dei Colori – Stroke Of Six (Woodborough).
April 22. Third living foal. 18,000Y. Tattersalls October 2. David Redvers. Half-brother to the fairly useful 2008 2-y-o 6f and 7f winner Sohcahtoa (by Val Royal) and to the fair 2-y-o 7f winner Miss Phoebe (by Catcher In The Rye). The dam, a quite useful 6f (at 2 yrs) and 1m winner, is a full or half-sister to 6 winners including the Group 2 10f Prix Eugene Adam winner Revelation. The second dam, Angelus Chimes (by Northfields), a quite useful Irish 4-y-o 12f winner, is a half-sister to 4 winners.
"Certainly not the same as his half-brother Sohcahtoa, but he's alright and he's beginning to show me something now. Certainly no forlorn hope".

1638. OIL STRIKE ★★★ ♠
b.c. Lucky Story – Willisa (Polar Falcon).
April 19. Eighth foal. 20,000Y. Doncaster Festival. David Redvers. Half-brother to the fair 7f (at 2 yrs) and 6f winner Polar Annie (by Fraam) and to the modest 5f (at 2 yrs) to 1m winner of 5 races Waterpark (by Namaqualand). The dam, a modest 3-y-o 7f winner, is a half-sister to 5 winners including the Group 3 placed Alzianah. The second dam, Ghassanah (by Pas de Seul), a fair 7f winner, is a half-sister to 10 winners including the Italian Derby winner Don Orazio. (Mr D C Holden).
"He looks a nice horse. I love the sire because his stock all seem to be big, good-looking horses. How early he'll be I don't know, but I like him and he'll definitely win this year".

1639. RAINE'S CROSS ★★★★
b.c. Cape Cross – Branston Jewel (Prince Sabo).
February 22. Seventh reported foal. 12,500Y. Doncaster Festival. David Redvers. Half-brother to the useful dual listed 6f winner of 5 races Falcon Hill (by Polar Falcon) and to the unplaced 2005 2-y-o Willows World (by Agnes World). The dam, a fairly useful 2-y-o dual 5f winner, was second in the Group 3 5.5f Prix d'Arenburg and is a half-sister to 9 winners including the Group Sandown Mile winner Desert Deer and the very useful and tough mare Branston Abby, a winner of 24 races at up to 7f including numerous listed events. The second dam, Tuxford Hideaway (by Cawston's Clown), a useful sprint winner of two races at 2 yrs, is a half-sister to 4 winners. (Mr D C Holden).
"He's done really well lately and I think he's a very nice horse. He's come to hand quickly for a Cape Cross and yet he's not just a two-year-old type because he does have scope".
TRAINER'S BARGAIN BUY

1640. SAFARI SPECIAL ★★★
ch.c. Pastoral Pursuits – Quiz Time (Efisio).
February 16. 8,000foal. Tattersalls December.
Closely related to the useful 2-y-o 5f and listed 6f winner Cool Question (by Polar Falcon), to the fairly useful 5f (at 2 yrs) and 7f winner Quaroma, the quite useful 5f to 7f winner Countdown (both by Pivotal) and half-brother to a winner in Spain at up to 9f by Pursuit Of Love. The dam, a fairly useful 2-y-o 5f winner, was second in the listed St Hugh's Stakes and is a half-sister to 6 winners including the Group 3 Premio Dormello winner Brockette. The second dam, Explosiva (by Explodent), won once at 2 yrs and is a half-sister to 8 winners. (Team Safari).
"He'll be worth putting in the book for sure. He'll be alright and he's a five furlong type two-year-old".

1641. UNNAMED ★★★
b.f. Danehill Dancer – Sun On The Sea (Bering).
April 10. Second foal. 54,000Y. Tattersalls October 1. David Redvers. The dam, a listed 10f winner, is a half-sister to 4 winners including the US stakes winner and Grade 3 placed Beau Temps. The second dam, Shimmer (by Green Dancer), won 3 races at 3 and 4 yrs in France and was second in the Group 3 Prix de Psyche. (Mr T Butterfield & Mr J Strong).
"A beautiful filly, I've done no fast work with her because she's quite big and you won't see her until the back-end of the year".

STALLION REFERENCE

This section deals with those sires represented by four or more two-year-olds in the book. Amongst the stallions listed in this section are most of the best sires of America and Europe, horses like the US-based sires Distorted Humor, Dynaformer, Giant's Causeway, Gone West, Kingmambo, Seeking The Gold and Storm Cat. The top European sires include Cape Cross, Danehill Dancer, Dansili, Galileo, Green Desert, Indian Ridge, Invincible Spirit, Montjeu, Pivotal, Sadler's Wells and Selkirk.

ACCLAMATION 2000 *Royal Applause – Princess Athena (Ahonoora)*. Racing record: Won 6 times, including Diadem Stakes. Also placed in King's Stand and Nunthorpe. Stud record: First crop now four-year-olds, he was an instant hit with his first crop in 2007, notably with his Group 1 winner Dark Angel. Not quite so good in 2008, but he still had the King's Stand winner Equiano. Standing at Rathbarry Stud, Ireland. 2009 fee: €25,000.

ALHAARTH 1993 *Unfuwain – Irish Valley (Irish River)*. Racing record: Champion 2-y-o of 1995 when winner of 4 group races, notably Dewhurst Stakes. Showed very smart form up to 10f at 3/4 yrs, winning three Group 2 events. Stud record: First runners in 2001. Sire of high-class Haafhd (2000 Guineas and Champion Stakes), very smart performers Bandari and Phoenix Reach (Canadian International, Hong Kong Vase and Dubai Sheema Classic), and smart performers Bouguereau, Dominica, Hoh Buzzard, Maharib and Mutajarred. Standing at Derrinstown Stud, Ireland. 2009 fee: €8,000.

ANABAA 1992 *Danzig – Balbonella (Gay Mecene)*. Racing record: Won 8 races including the July Cup and the Prix Maurice de Gheest. Stud record: First runners in 2000. Sire of Anabaa Blue (Prix du Jockey Club), Martillo, and Precision (Hong Kong Cup), all 3 very smart, and of smart performers Amonita, Ana Marie, Celtic Slipper, Blue Ksar, Loup Breton, Marshall, Miss Anabaa, Passager, Rouvres, Shaard, Tarzan City and Victorieux. Standing at Haras du Quesnay in France. 2009 fee: €30,000.

ANTONIUS PIUS 2001 *Danzig – Catchascatchcan (Pursuit of Love)*. Racing record: Won the Group 2 Railway Stakes at 2 yrs. Placed in the French 2,000 Guineas, St James's Palace Stakes and Breeders Cup Mile. Stud record: First European runners in 2009 (shuttles to Australia where his first winner came in November 2008). Standing at Coolmore Stud, Ireland. 2009 fee: €5,000.

ARAKAN *Nureyev – Far Across (Common Grounds)*. Racing record: Won 6 races including the Group 3 Criterion Stakes, the Group 3 Supreme Stakes (both 7f), the listed Abernant Stakes and the City Of York Stakes (both 6f). Stud record: First runners in 2009. Standing at Ballyhane Stud. 2009 fee: €2,500.

AVONBRIDGE 2000 *Averti – Alessia (Caerleon)*. Racing record: Won the Prix de l'Abbaye and the Palace House Stakes, second in the July Cup. Stud record: First runners in 2009. Standing at Whitsbury Manor Stud. 2009 fee: £4,500.

AZAMOUR 2001 *Night Shift – Azmara (Lear Fan)*. Race record: Won St James's Palace Stakes, Irish Champion Stakes, Prince of Wales's Stakes and King George VI and Queen Elizabeth Diamond Stakes. Stud record: First crop runners in 2009. Standing at Gilltown Stud, Ireland. 2009 fee: €15,000.

BACHELOR DUKE 2001 *Miswaki – Gossamer (Seattle Slew)*. Racing record: Won Irish 2,000 Guineas. Stud record: His first crop of runners in 2008 yielded four winners here and 3 in Ireland. Standing at Ballylynch Stud, Ireland. 2009 fee: €7,500.

BAHAMIAN BOUNTY 1994 *Cadeaux Genereux – Clarentia (Ballad Rock)*. Racing Record: Winner of 3 races at 2 yrs, notably Prix Morny and Middle Park. Also fourth in July Cup at 3 yrs. Stud record: First runners in 2001. Sire of high-class performer Pastoral Pursuits (July Cup), very smart Goodricke (Sprint Cup) and smart performers Gallagher, Babadona, Dubaian Gift, Naahy, Paradise Isle and Topatoo. Had 22 individual two-year-old winners in 2008. Standing at the National Stud, Newmarket. 2009 fee: £10,000.

BARATHEA 1990 *Sadler's Wells – Brocade (Habitat)*. Racing record: 5 wins, notably

Breeders Cup Mile and Irish 2000 Guineas. Stud record: First runners in 1998. Sire of high-class Tobougg (Prix de la Salamandre and Dewhurst) and Tante Rose (Sprint Cup), and numerous smart performers including Alasha, Cornelius, Hazarista, Jumbajukiba, Lost Soldier Three, One Off, Opera Cape, Pongee, Port Vila, Raincoat, Sanaya, Shield, Sina Cova and Stotsfold. Standing at Rathbarry Stud, Ireland. 2009 fee: €15,000.

BERTOLINI 1996 *Danzig – Aquilega (Alydar)*. Racing record: Won 2 races, including July Stakes at 2 yrs, and placed in July Cup, Sprint Cup and Nunthorpe Stakes. Stud record: First runners in 2005. Sire of the smart winners Moorhouse Lad and Prime Defender and the useful performers Blades Girl, Bobs Surprise, Come Out Fighting, Donna Blini (Cheveley Park), Mac Gille Eoin, Signor Peltro and Tabaret. Standing at Overbury Stud, Gloucestershire. 2009 fee: £4,000.

CADEAUX GENEREUX 1985 *Young Generation – Smarten Up (Sharpen Up)*. Racing record: 7 wins notably July Cup and William Hill Sprint Championship. Stud record: Best winners include high-class Bijou d'Inde (St James's Palace Stakes), Donativum (Grade 1 Breeders Cup Juvenile) and Touch of The Blues (Atto Mile in Canada), very smart Gift Horse and numerous smart performers including Bahamian Bounty (Middle Park Stakes), Embassy (Cheveley Park Stakes), Hoh Magic (Prix Morny), Major Cadeaux (Group 2 Sandown Mile) and Toylsome (Group 1). Standing at Whitsbury Manor Stud, Hampshire. 2009 fee: £10,000.

CAMACHO 2002 *Danehill – Arabesque (Zafonic)*. Racing record: Won a listed race over 6f and was second in the Group 3 7f Jersey Stakes. Stud record: First runners in 2009. Standing at Morristown Lattin Stud, Ireland. 2009 fee: €4,000.

CAPE CROSS 1994 *Green Desert – Park Appeal (Ahonoora)*. Racing record: Won 4 races, including Lockinge Stakes, Queen Anne Stakes and Celebration Mile. Stud record: First runners in 2003. Sire of top-class Ouija Board (7 Group 1 wins including the Oaks & the Breeders' Cup Filly and Mare Turf), very smart Hazyview, and numerous smart performers including Borthwick Girl, Cape Fear, Castleton, Charlie Farnsbarns, Crossing The Line, Crosspeace, Crystal Capella, Halicarnassus, Hatta Fort, Mac Love, Madid, Mazuna, Musicanna, Privy Seal and Russian Cross. Standing at Kildangan Stud, Ireland. 2009 fee: €35,000.

CAPTAIN RIO 2000 *Pivotal – Beloved Visitor (Miswaki)*. Racing record: Won 4 times, including Criterium de Maisons-Laffitte at 2 yrs. Stud record: From 2 crops racing sire of the New Zealand Grade 1 winner Il Quello Veloce, the smart Capt Chaos and Captain Dunne and the Group 3 Sirenia Stakes winner Philario. 20 individual two-year-old winners in England and Ireland last year. Standing at Ballyhane Stud, Ireland. 2009 fee: €5,000.

CHINEUR 2001 *Fasliyev – Wardara (Sharpo)*. Race record: Won Kings Stand Stakes and Prix de Saint-Georges. Stud record: First runners in 2009. Standing at Tally Ho Stud, Ireland. €5,000.

CHOISIR 2000 *Danehill Dancer – Great Selection (Lunchtime)*. Racing record: Group 1 winner in both Australia and Britain, including King's Stand Stakes and Golden Jubilee Stakes. Stud record: From 2 crops racing sire of the Group 2 Challenge Stakes winner Stimulation and the listed winners Fat Boy, Luna Nel Pozzo & Porto Marmay. Standing at Coolmore Stud, Ireland. 2009 fee: €8,000.

CLODOVIL 2001 *Danehill – Clodora (Linamix)*. Racing record: Won 5 races, including Poule d'Essai des Poulains. Stud record: First crop were two-year-olds in 2007. Best winners to date are the Falmouth Stakes winner Nahoodh and the very useful Beacon Lodge and Secret Asset. Standing at Rathasker Stud, Ireland. 2009 fee: €12,000.

COMPTON PLACE 1994 *Indian Ridge – Nosey (Nebbiolo)*. Racing record: Won 3 races, notably July Cup. Stud record: First runners in 2002. Sire of the high-class Borderlescott, smart Boogie Street and Intrepid Jack, US Grade 2 winner Passified, the Group 2 winner Godfrey Street and numerous useful performers, including Compton's Eleven, If Paradise, Judd Street, Hunter Street, Pacific Pride and Prolific. Standing at Whitsbury Manor Stud, Hampshire.

2009 fee: £7,500.

DALAKHANI 2001 *Darshaan – Daltawa (Miswaki)*. Racing record: Won 8 of 9 starts, including Prix du Jockey Club and Arc. Stud record: First crop were two-year-olds in 2007. Standing at Gilltown Stud, Ireland. 2009 fee: €50,000. Sire of 2 classic winners from his first crop in Conduit (St Leger) and Moonstone (Irish Oaks) and also worthy of note are the dual Group winner Centennial and the smart Chinese White.

DANEHILL DANCER 1993 *Danehill – Mira Adonde (Sharpen Up)*. Racing Record: Winner of 4 races, including Heinz 57 Phoenix Stakes and National Stakes at 2 yrs and Greenham at 3. Stud record: First runners in 2001. Sire of high-class performer Choisir (Golden Jubilee Stakes), leading 2008 two-year-olds Mastercraftsman and Again, very smart Alexander Tango (US Grade 1 Garden City Stakes winner), Indesatchel and Where Or When (Queen Elizabeth II Stakes) & numerous smart performers including Alexander Tango, Anna Pavlova, Blue Sky Thinking, Express Wish, Fast Company, Ice Queen, Jeremy, Lady Dominatrix, Lizard Island, Medicine Path, Miss Beatrix (Moyglare Stud Stakes), Monsieur Bond, Pride Of nation, Snaefell and Speciosa (1,000 Guineas). Standing at Coolmore Stud, Ireland. 2009 fee: Private (was €115,000).

DANROAD 1999 *Danehill – Strawberry Girl (Strawberry Road)*. Racing record: Won 6 races over 6f in New Zealand, including a Group 2 and was Group 1 placed. Stud record: Had a two-year-old Group 1 winner in Australia in his first crop (Rockdale) and his first European crop are runners in 2009. Standing at Rathmuck Stud, Ireland. 2009 fee: €3,500.

DANSILI 1996 *Danehill – Hasili (Kahyasi)*. Racing record: Won 5 races in France, and placed in six Group/Grade 1 events including Sussex Stakes and Breeders' Cup Mile. Stud record: First runners in 2004. Sire of top-class Rail Link (Arc, Grand Prix de Paris, Prix Niel), Zambezi Sun (Group 1 Grand Prix de Paris) and numerous very smart performers including Dansant, Delegator, Grecian Dancer, Home Affairs, Illustrious Blue, Passage Of Time, Price Tag (US Grade 1 winner and first past post in Poule d'Essai des Pouliches), Proviso, Sense Of Joy, Shaweel (Gimcrack Stakes), Silver Touch and Strategic Prince. Standing at Banstead Manor Stud, Newmarket. 2009 fee: £65,000.

DISTORTED HUMOR 1993 *Forty Niner – Danzig's Beauty (Danzig)*. Racing record: Won 11 races in the USA including the Champagne Stakes, Futurity Stakes, Haskell Invitational and Travers Stakes (all Grade 1). Champion 2-y-o. Stud record: Sire of nine Grade 1 winners (Commentator, Coronado's Quest, Ecton Park, Editor's Note, Flower Alley, Funny Cide, Gold Fever, Marley Vale & Nine Keys). Standing at Win Star Farm, Kentucky. 2009 fee $150,000.

DIXIE UNION 1997 *Dixieland Band – She's Tops (Capote)*. Racing record: Won 7 races including the Haskell Invitational and the Malibu Stakes (both Grade 1 events in the USA). Stud record: Sire of the US Grade 1 winner Dixie Chatter, the Group 2 Cherry Hinton Stakes winner Sander Camillo and the US Grade 2 winners Justwhistledixie, Most Distinguished and Nothing But Fun. Standing at Standing at Lane's End Farm, Kentucky. 2009 fee: $35,000.

DOMEDRIVER *Indian Ridge – Napoli (Baillamont)*. Racing record: Won 6 races, including Breeders' Cup Mile. Stud record: First crop now two-year-olds. Standing at Fresnay-le-Buffard.

DOYEN 2000 *Sadler's Wells – Moon Cactus (Kris)*. Racing record: Won the King George VI and Queen Elizabeth Diamond Stakes, Hardwicke Stakes. Stud record: First runners in 2009. Standing at Gestut Auenquelle in Germany. 2009 fee: €5,000.

DR FONG 1995 *Kris S – Spring Flight (Miswaki)*. Racing record: Won 5 races, including St James's Palace Stakes. Stud record: First runners in 2003. Sire of the US Grade 1 winner Shamdinan, the smart performers Andronikos, Ask For The Moon, Doctor Brown, Dubai's Touch, Fong's Thong, Forward Move, Group Captain, Metropolitan Man and Spotlight, and of numerous very useful performers. Standing at Highclere Stud, Berkshire. 2009 fee: £6,000.

DUBAI DESTINATION *Kingmambo – Mysterial (Alleged)*. Racing record: Won 4 times, including

Champagne Stakes and Queen Anne Stakes. Stud record: First crop were two-year-olds in 2007 and included the Group 1 winner Ibn Khaldun and the smart gelding Charm School. Standing at Dalham Hall Stud, Newmarket. 2009 fee: £7,000.

DUBAWI 2002 *Dubai Millennium – Zomaradah (Deploy)*. Race record: Won the National Stakes at 2 and the Irish 2,000 Guineas and Prix Jacques le Marois at 3. Third in the Derby. Stud record: First runners in 2009. Standing at Dalham Hall Stud, Newmarket. 2009 fee: £15,000.

DYNAFORMER 1985 *Roberto – Andover Way (His Majesty)*. Racing record: 7 wins in USA including Grade 2 Florida Derby and Grade 2 Discovery Handicap. Stud record: Best winners include the Group 1 winner Lucarno, the 2008 Group 1 Fillies' Mile winner Rainbow View, Group 2 Ribblesdale winner Michita, the very smart Beat All and (in USA) Grade 1 winners Barbaro, Dynaforce, Film Maker and Perfect Drift, and numerous smart performers including Dynever, Ocean Silk, Sharp Susan and Spanish John. Standing at Three Chimneys Farm, Kentucky. 2009 fee: $150,000.

ELUSIVE CITY 2000 *Elusive Quality – Star of Paris (Dayjur)*. Racing record: Won Group 1 Prix Morny and Group 2 Richmond Stakes. Also placed in Middle Park. Stud record: First crop were two-year-olds in 2008 and included the smart winners Elusive Wave and Soul City. Standing at Irish National Stud. 2009 fee: €12,500.

ELUSIVE QUALITY 1993 *Gone West – Touch of Greatness (Hero's Honor)*. Racing record: Won 9 races in USA, including Grade 3 events at 7f/1m. Stud record: Sire of top-class Kentucky Derby/Preakness Stakes winner Smarty Jones, Breeders Cup Classic and Queen Elizabeth II Stakes winner Raven's Pass, Prix Morny winner Elusive City and numerous US graded stakes winners, including Chimichurri, Elusive Diva, Girl Warrior, Maryfield, Omega Code, Quality Road Royal Michele and True Quality, and the 2008 Group 3 Horris Hill Stakes winner Evasive. Standing at Darley, Kentucky. 2009 fee: $75,000.

EXCEED AND EXCEL 2000 *Danehill – Patrona (Lomond)*. Racing record: Champion sprinter in Australia, won 7 races including the Grade 1 Newmarket H'cap, the Grade 1 Dubai Racing Club Cup and the Grade 2 Todman Stakes. Stud record: First northern hemisphere runners in 2008 and he got off to a very good start with smart winners like Infamous Angel (Lowther Stakes) and the Royal Ascot winner Flashmans Papers. His 2007 Australasian two-year-old winners include the Group 3 winners Exceedingly Good, Believe 'n' Succeed & Wilander. Standing at Dalham Hall Stud, Newmarket. 2009 fee: £12,000.

FANTASTIC LIGHT 1996 *Rahy – Jood (Nijinsky)*. Racing record: Won 12 races, including Prince of Wales's Stakes, Irish Champion Stakes and Breeders' Cup Turf. Stud record: First runners in 2005. Sire of Group 1 winner Scintillo, smart performers Detonator, Imperial Star, Luberon, New Guinea and Prince of Light, and of very useful performers Roshani, Scintillo and Som Tala. Standing at Dalham Hall Stud, Newmarket. Now standing in Australia/Japan.

FASLIYEV 1997 *Nureyev – Mr P'S Princess (Mr Prospector)*. Racing record: Unbeaten in 5 starts at 2 yrs (only season to race), including Coventry Stakes, Heinz 57 Phoenix Stakes and Prix Morny. Stud record: First runners in 2003. Sire of Carry On Katie (Cheveley Park Stakes), very smart performer Chineur, smart performers Fyodor, City Leader, Kings Point, Lady Deauville, Much Faster, Russian Valour, Russki and Steppe Dancer and numerous useful performers. Now standing in Japan.

FIREBREAK 1999 *Charnwood Forest – Breakaway (Song)*. Racing record: Won the Godolphin Mile in Dubai (twice), Challenge Stakes and Hong Kong Mile. Stud record: First runners in 2009. Standing at Bearstone Stud. 2009 fee: £3000.

FOOTSTEPSINTHESAND 2002 *Giant's Causeway – Glatisant (Rainbow Quest)*. Racing record: Won all 3 of his starts, notably the 2,000 Guineas. Stud record: First European runners in 2009. Standing at Coolmore Stud, Ireland. 2009 fee: €12,500.

GALILEO 1998 *Sadler's Wells – Urban Sea (Miswaki)*. Racing record: Won 6 races, including

Derby, Irish Derby and King George And Queen Elizabeth Diamond Stakes. Stud record: First runners in 2005. Sire of champion 2-y-o's Teofilo and New Approach (subsequent Derby, Champion Stakes and Irish Champion Stakes winner) and of Sixties Icon (St Leger), Red Rocks (Breeders' Cup Turf), Allegretto (Prix Royal-Oak), Lush Lashes (Coronation Stakes and Sun Chariot Stakes), Soldier Of Fortune (Irish Derby) and Nightime (Irish 1000 Guineas). Standing at Coolmore Stud, Ireland. 2009 fee: Private (€150,000).

GIANT'S CAUSEWAY 1997 *Storm Cat – Mariah's Storm (Rahy)*. Racing record: Won 9 races, 6 of them Group 1 events, including Prix de la Salamandre, Juddmonte International and Sussex Stakes. Stud record: First runners in 2004. Sire of high-class Shamardal (Dewhurst Stakes, St James's Palace Stakes and Prix du Jockey Club), very smart Footstepsinthesand (2000 Guineas) and a number of very smart performers including Aragorn (dual US Grade winner), Heatseeker (Santa Anita Handicap), Maids Causeway (Coronation Stakes), My Typhoon (US Grade 1 winner), Oonagh Maccool and First Samurai (US 2-y-o Grade 1 winner). Standing at Ashford Stud, Kentucky. 2009 fee: $125,000.

GONE WEST 1984 *Mr Prospector – Secrettame (Secretariat)*. Racing record: 6 wins including Grade 1 Dwyer Stakes. Stud record: Best winners include North American performers Came Home (Pacific Classic), Commendable (Belmont Stakes), Da Hoss (Breeders' Cup Mile), Johar (Breeders' Cup Turf), Link River (John A. Morris Handicap), March Side (Canadian International), Speightstown (Breeders Cup Sprint), West By West (Nassau County Handicap) and Zaftig (Acorn Stakes), the smart Japanese horse Zafolia and in Europe the top-class colt Zafonic (4 Group 1 wins including Dewhurst Stakes and 2000 Guineas). He's also the sire of the good sires Mr Greeley and Zamindar. Standing at Mill Ridge Farm, Kentucky. 2009 fee: $65,000.

GREEN DESERT 1983 *Danzig – Foreign Courier (Sir Ivor)*. Racing record: 5 wins including July Cup, Vernons Sprint Cup and Flying Childers Stakes. Stud record: Best winners (all very smart or better) include Alkaadhem, Cape Cross (Lockinge Stakes), Desert Lord (Prix de l'Abbaye), Desert Prince (Irish 2000 Guineas, Prix du Moulin, Queen Elizabeth Stakes), Desert Style, Desert Sun, Gabr, Invincible Spirit (Haydock Sprint Cup), Oasis Dream (Middle Park, July Cup, Nunthorpe Stakes), Owington (July Cup), Sheikh Albadou (Nunthorpe Stakes/Haydock Sprint Cup), Tamarisk (Haydock Sprint Cup) and Tropical. Standing at Nunnery Stud, Norfolk. 2009 fee: £25,000.

HAAFHD 2001 *Alhaarth – Al Bahathri (Blushing Groom)*. Racing record: Won 5 races, notably 2,000 Guineas and Champion Stakes. Stud record: First crop were two-year-olds in 2008. The sire of 13 winners in England and Ireland. Standing at Shadwell Stud, Norfolk. 2009 fee: £8,000.

HALLING 1991 *Diesis – Dance Machine (Green Dancer)*. Racing record: Won 12 races including Coral-Eclipse Stakes (twice), Juddmonte International (twice) and Prix d'Ispahan. Stud record: First runners in 2000. Sire of high-class Norse Dancer, very smart Hala Bek and The Geezer, and of numerous smart performers including Bauer, Chancellor, Coastal Path, Dandoun, Foodbroker Fancy, Franklins Gardens, Hattan, Hero's Journey, Mkuzi, Parasol, Pinson and Vanderlin. Standing at Dalham Hall Stud, Newmarket. 2009 fee: £8000.

HAWK WING 2000 *Woodman – La Lorgnette (Val de l'Orne)*. Racing record: Won 5 times, including National Stakes, Eclipse and Lockinge. Stud record: First crop were two-year-olds in 2007. Best winners to date include the smart Feared In Flight and The Bogberry. Standing at Coolmore Stud, Ireland.

HERNANDO 1990 *Niniski – Whakilyric (Miswaki)*. Racing record: Won 7 races including Prix Lupin and Prix du Jockey Club. Stud record: First runners in 1999. Sire of high-class Look Here (Oaks), Holding Court (Prix du Jockey Club) and Sulamani (Prix du Jockey Club, Arlington Million, Turf Classic Invitational, Juddmonte International), very smart performers Asian Heights Casual Conquest, Foreign Affairs, Mr Combustible, Songerie and Tau Ceti and numerous smart performers.

Standing at Lanwades Stud, Newmarket. 2009 fee: £12,000.

HIGH CHAPARRAL 2000 *Sadler's Wells – Kasora (Darshaan)*. Racing record: Won 10 races, including Derby, Irish Champion Stakes and Breeders' Cup Turf (last event twice). Stud record: First crop were two-year-olds in 2007. Disappointing start with St Leger runner-up Unsung Heroine by far his best performer to date. Standing at Coolmore Stud, Ireland. 2009 fee: €10,000.

INDIAN HAVEN 2000 *Indian Ridge – Madame Dubois (Legend Of France)*. Racing record: Won 3 races including the Group 1 Irish 2,000 Guineas. Stud record: First crop were 2-y-o's of 2008 and included the smart winners Ashram and Aspen Darlin. Standing at the Irish National Stud. 2009 fee: €7,500.

INDIAN RIDGE 1985 *Ahonoora – Hillbrow (Swing Easy)*. Racing record: Won 5 races including Kings Stand Stakes, Duke of York Stakes and Jersey Stakes. Stud record: Best winners include Compton Place (July Cup), Domedriver (Breeders' Cup Mile), Indian Haven (Irish 2000 Guineas), Indian Ink (Coronation Stakes), Linngari (Premio Vittorio di Capua), Relaxed Gesture (Canadian International), Ridgewood Pearl (Irish 1,000 Guineas, Coronation Stakes, Prix du Moulin, Breeders Cup Mile) and Namid (Prix de l'Abbaye), high-class Imperial Stride and Nayyir, and very smart Definite Article & Handsome Ridge and Sleeping Indian. Died in 2006.

INTIKHAB 1994 *Red Ransom – Crafty Example (Crafty Prospector)*. Racing record: 8 wins including Diomed and Queen Anne Stakes. Stud record: First runners in 2003. Sire of Red Evie (Lockinge Stakes & Matron Stakes), smart Bonnie Charlie (2008 two-year-old), Hoh Mike, Khabfair and Motashaar, and numerous very useful performers including Fine Silver, Leg Spinner, Les Fazzani and Tropical Strait. Standing at Derrinstown Stud, Ireland. 2009 fee: €7,000.

INVINCIBLE SPIRIT 1997 *Green Desert – Rafha (Kris)*. Racing record: 7 wins, notably Sprint Cup at 5 yrs. Stud record: First runners in 2006. Sire of dual Group 1 winner Lawman (French Derby & Prix Jean Prat), Fleeting Spirit (Temple Stakes, Flying Childers Stakes and Molecomb Stakes), Gimcrack Stakes and Stewards Cup winner Conquest, smart performers Allied Powers, Captain Marvellous and Staying On, and of useful performers Bahama Mama, Hurricane Spirit, Invincible Force and Kingship Spirit. Standing at Irish National Stud. 2009 fee: €60,000.

JOHANNESBURG 1999 *Hennessy – Myth (Ogygian)*. Racing record: Unbeaten at 2 yrs, when 7 wins included Phoenix Stakes, Prix Morny, Middle Park and Breeders' Cup Juvenile. Below form at 3 yrs. Stud record: First runners in 2006. Sire of the Prix d'Ispahan winner Sageburg and the smart performers Diamond Tycoon, Hammody, Jupiter Pluvius, Rabatash and Tombi, the US Grade 1 winner Scat Daddy and US Grade 2 winner Eaton's Gift. Standing at Ashford Stud, Kentucky. 2009 fee: $35,000.

KEY OF LUCK 1991 *Chief's Crown – Balbonella (Gay Mecene)*. Racing record: Winner of Prix d'Arenberg at 2 yrs and Dubai Duty Free at 5 yrs, when also runner-up in US Grade 1 9.5f event. Stud record: First runners in 2001. Sire of top-class Alamshar (Irish Derby, King George VI and Queen Elizabeth Diamond Stakes), smart performers Miss Emma, Profit's Reality and Right Key, and of numerous useful performers. Standing at Tara Stud, Ireland. 2009 fee: €9,000.

KHELEYF 2001 *Green Desert – Society Lady (Mr Prospector)*. Racing record: Won 3 races including the Group 3 Jersey Stakes. Stud record: First crop were two-year-olds in 2008 and his British and Irish winners numbered an exceptional 29, plus the Middle Park Stakes runner-up Sayif. Standing at Dalham Hall Stud, Newmarket. 2009 fee: £12,000.

KINGMAMBO 1990 *Mr Prospector – Miesque (Nureyev)*. Racing record: Won the French 2,000 Guineas, the Prix du Moulin and the St James's Palace Stakes. Stud record: His European Group 1 winners include Henrythenavigator, King's Best (both 2,000 Guineas), Russian Rhythm, Virginia Waters (both 1,000 Guineas), Rule Of Law (St Leger), Divine Proportions, Bluemamba (both French 1,000 Guineas), Light Shift (Oaks), Dubai Destination (Queen Anne Stakes) and Okawango (Grand Criterium). Also the Japan

Cup and French Group 1 winner Alkaased, Belmont Stakes winner Lemon Drop Kid and the Japanese champions El Condor Pasa and Kingkamehameha. Standing at Lane's End Farm, Kentucky. 2009 fee: $250,000.

KING'S BEST 1997 *Kingmambo – Allegretta (Lombard)*. Racing record: Won 3 races, including 2000 Guineas. Stud record: First runners in 2004. Sire of high-class Proclamation (Sussex Stakes) and Creachadoir, the very smart Ancien Regime, Army Of Angels, Best Alibi, King's Apostle, Notability and Spice Route and the smart performers Dubai Surprise, Elliots World and Oiseau Rare. Standing at Kildangan Stud, Ireland. 2009 fee: €15,000.

KYLLACHY 1998 *Pivotal – Pretty Poppy (Song)*. Racing record: Winner of 6 races, including Nunthorpe Stakes at 4 yrs. Stud record: First runners in 2006. Sire of Group 2 winners Arabian Gleam and Tariq, the very smart sprinter Corrybrough, smart 2008 two-year-old Awinnersgame and numerous other smart performers. Standing at Cheveley Park Stud, Newmarket. 2009 fee: £12,000.

LE VIE DEI COLORI 2000 *Efisio – Mystic Tempo (El Gran Senor)*. Racing record: Won 12 races in Italy (notably the Premio Parioli and the Premio Vittorio di Capua) and 2 races here including the Challenge Stakes. Stud record: First runners in 2009. Dead.

LION HEART 2001 *Tale Of The Cat – Satin Sunrise (Mr Leader)*. Racing record: Won the Hollywood Futurity and the Haskell Invitational (both Grade 1 events). Stud record: Had a good start with his first crop of 2-y-o's in 2008. His best performers included the US Grade 2 winner Azul Leon and the Grade 3 winners Heart Ashley and Silent Valor. Standing at Ashford Stud, Kentucky. 2009 fee: $20,000.

LOMITAS 1988 *Niniski – La Colorada (Surumu)*. Racing record: Won 10 races, including 3 Group 1 events in Germany at 3 yrs. Stud record: Sire of Arlington Million winner Silvano, German Derby winner Belenus, Italian Oaks winner Meridiana, German St Leger winner Liquido, US graded stakes winners Blue Moon and Sumitas, the very smart winners Championship Point, Veracity and the Group 3 winner Trick Or Treat.

LUCKY STORY 2001 *Kris S – Spring Flight (Miswaki)*. Racing record: Won 4 races including the Group 2 Champagne Stakes and Group 2 Vintage Stakes. Stud record: First crop (bred in Japan) were two-year-olds in 2007. His first European crop did well considering there were only 21 runners. They included the high-class Coventry Stakes winner Art Connoisseur. Standing at Tweenhills Stud. 2009 fee: £3,000.

MARJU 1988 *Last Tycoon – Flame of Tara (Artaius)*. Racing record: 3 wins including St James's Palace Stakes and runner-up in Derby. Stud record: First runners in 1993. Sire of the high-class Soviet Song (5 Group 1 events, including Sussex Stakes), very smart performer in Hong Kong Indigenous and of numerous smart performers including Asset, Brunel, My Emma (Prix Vermeille) and Sil Sila (Prix de Diane). Standing at Derrinstown Stud, Ireland. 2009 fee: €20,000.

MEDICEAN 1997 *Machiavellian – Mystic Goddess (Storm Bird)*. Racing record: 6 wins included Lockinge Stakes and Eclipse. Stud record: First runners in 2005. Sire of very smart Dutch Art (Prix Morny, Middle Park), smart performer Nannina (Fillies' Mile, Coronation Stakes), the very smart miler Bankable, German Group 3 winner Love Academy and the very smart Al Shemali, Cartimandua, and Medici Code. Standing at Cheveley Park Stud. 2009 fee: £15,000.

MONTJEU 1996 *Sadler's Wells – Floripedes (Top Ville)*. Racing record: Won 11 races, including Prix de l'Arc de Triomphe and King George VI and Queen Elizabeth Diamond Stakes. Stud record: First runners in 2004. An outstanding stallion son of Sadler's Wells. Sire of top-class Hurricane Run (Irish Derby, Prix de l'Arc de Triomphe, Tattersalls Gold Cup and King George), Authorized (Racing Post Trophy, Derby & Juddmonte International) and Motivator (Racing Post Trophy and Derby), the high-class Scorpion (Grand Prix de Paris and St Leger), Alessandro Volta, Frozen Fire, Honolulu, Corre Caminos (Prix Ganay), Macarthur and Papal Bull, and the very smart Dash To The Top, Falstaff, Walk In The Park. Standing at Coolmore Stud, Ireland. 2009 fee: Private (was €125,000).

MOTIVATOR 2002 *Montjeu – Out West (Gone West)*. Racing record: Won the Derby, the Racing Post Trophy and the Dante Stakes. Stud record: First runners in 2009. Standing at The Royal Studs. 2009 fee: £10,000.

MR GREELEY 1992 *Gone West – Long Legend (Reviewer)*. Racing record: Triple Grade 3 winner in USA and runner-up in Breeders' Cup Sprint. Stud record: First runners in 1999. Sire of Finsceal Beo (English & Irish 1,000 Guineas), Saoirse Abu (Phoenix Stakes, Moyglare Stud Stakes), very smart El Corredor (Cigar Mile Handicap) and several smart performers including Reel Buddy (Sussex Stakes). Standing at Gainesway Farm, Kentucky. 2009 fee: €100,000.

MUJADIL 1988 *Storm Bird – Vallee Secrete (Secretariat)*. Racing record: 3 wins (at 2 yrs) including Group 3 Cornwallis Stakes. Stud record: Best winners include Kingsgate Native (Nunthorpe Stakes), Bouncing Bowdler (Group 2 Mill Reef Stakes), Galeota (Group 2 Mill Reef Stakes), the Group 3 winners Daunting Lady, Leggy Lou, Master Plasta, Satri and Show Me The Money and numerous useful performers. Standing at Rathasker Stud, Ireland. 2009 fee: €10,000.

NAMID 1996 *Indian Ridge – Dawnsio (Tate Gallery)*. Racing record: Won 5 races, including Prix de l'Abbaye. Stud record: First runners in 2004. Sire of smart performers Hogmaneigh, Redstone Dancer and Resplendent Glory and several useful performers including Blue Dakota, Buachaill Dona, Burning Incense, Pike Bishop and That's Hot. Standing at Rathbarry Stud, Ireland. 2009 fee: €5,000.

NAYEF 1999 *Gulch – Height of Fashion (Bustino)*. Racing record: Won 9 races, including Champion Stakes and Juddmonte International Stakes. Stud record: First crop were two-year-olds in 2007. His best winners are Tamayiz (dual Group 1 winner in France), Lady Marian (Prix de l'Opera), Spacious (Group 2 May Hill Stakes winner and 1,000 Guineas second) and the smart Confront and Top Lock. Standing at Nunnery Stud, Norfolk. 2009 fee: £15,000.

NEEDWOOD BLADE 1998 *Pivotal – Finlaggan (Be My Chief)*. Racing record: Won 9 races here and in the USA including the Group 3 5f Palace House Stakes and the Grade 3 9f Bay Meadows Breeders Cup Handicap. Stud record: His first crop are 2-y-o's in 2008 yielded 5 individual winners. Standing at Mickley Stud. 2009 fee: £3,000.

NOVERRE 1998 *Rahy – Danseur Fabuleux (Northern Dancer)*. Racing record: Won 4 races at 2 yrs, including Champagne Stakes, and Sussex Stakes at 3 yrs. Placed in 7 Group 1 events afterwards. Stud record: First runners in 2006. Sire of the Group 2 Challenge Stakes winner Miss Lucifer, the Group 3 Albany Stakes winner Nijoom Dubai, the very smart Summit Surge, the smart sprinter Aahayson and the useful performer Elhamri. Exported to India.

OASIS DREAM 2001 *Green Desert – Hop (Dancing Brave)*. Racing record: Won 4 races, including Middle Park Stakes, July Cup and Nunthorpe Stakes. Stud record: First crop were two-year-olds in 2007. His best performers to date are the high-class Jersey Stakes winner Aqlaam and the smart winners Captain Gerrard, On Our Way, Perfect Stride, Prohibit, Starlit Sands, Visit, Tiscan Evening and Young Pretender. Sired an outstanding total of 37 two-year-old winners in 2008 – a new world record. Standing at Banstead Manor Stud, Newmarket. 2009 fee: £30,000.

OBSERVATORY 1997 *Distant View – Stellaria (Roberto)*. Racing record: 6 wins included Queen Elizabeth II Stakes and Prix d'Ispahan. Stud record: First runners in 2005. Sire of the very smart African Rose and Twice Over and the useful performers Nidhaal, Star Cluster, The Grey Berry and Violette, but only one two-year-old winner to his name in 2008. Standing at Banstead Manor Stud, Newmarket. 2009 fee: £10,000.

ONE COOL CAT 2001 *Storm Cat – Tacha (Mr Prospector)*. Racing record: At two in Ireland won Group 1 6f Phoenix Stakes and Group 1 7f National Stakes. Stud record: First crop were two-year-olds in 2008 and numbered 15 individual winners in England and Ireland. Standing at Coolmore Stud, Ireland. 2009 fee: €9,000.

ORATORIO 2002 *Danehill – Mahrah (Vaguely*

Noble). Racing record: Won the Prix Jean-Luc Lagardere (at 2) and the Eclipse Stakes and Irish Champion Stakes. Standing at Coolmore Stud, Ireland. 2009 fee: €12,500.

PASTORAL PURSUITS 2001 *Bahamian Bounty – Star (Most Welcome)*. Racing record: Won 6 races including the July Cup, Sirenia Stakes and Park Stakes. Stud record: First crop runners in 2009. Standing at the National Stud. 2009 fee: £4,500.

PICCOLO 1991 *Warning – Woodwind (Whistling Wind)*. Racing record: 4 wins including Nunthorpe Stakes and Kings Stand Stakes. Stud record: First runners in 1999. Sire of smart performers Aegean Dancer, Bond Boy (Steward's Cup winner), Hoh Hoh Hoh, Hunting Lion, La Cucaracha (Nunthorpe Stakes), Lipocco, Pan Jammer and Winker Watson. Standing at Lavington Stud, West Sussex. 2009 fee: £5,000.

PIVOTAL 1993 *Polar Falcon – Fearless Revival (Cozzene)*. Racing record: 4 wins including the Nunthorpe Stakes and King's Stand Stakes. Stud record: First runners in 2000. An outstanding sire whose best winners include the high-class Excellent Art (St James's Palace Stakes), Falco (French 2,000 Guineas), Halfway To Heaven (Irish 1,00 Guineas, Nassau Stakes and Sun Chariot Stakes, Kyllachy (Nunthorpe Stakes) and Somnus (Sprint Cup, Prix de la Foret, Prix Maurice de Gheest), and very smart Beauty Is Truth (Group 2 Prix du Gros-Chene), Captain Rio (Group 2 Criterium des Maisons-Laffitte), Chorist (Pretty Polly Stakes), Golden Apples (triple US Grade 1 winner), Leo (Group 2 Royal Lodge Stakes), Peeress (Lockinge Stakes, Sun Chariot Stakes) and Pivotal Point (Group 2 Diadem Stakes) and numerous smart performers including Megahertz (2 US Grade 1 events), Silvester Lady (German Oaks) and Saoire (Irish 1000 Guineas). Standing at Cheveley Park Stud, Newmarket. 2009 fee: £65,000.

PROUD CITIZEN 1999 *Gone West –Drums Of Freedom (Green Forest)*. Racing record: Won 3 races including the Grade 3 Lexington Stakes and second the Kentucky Derby. Stud record: Retired to stud in 2004. First crop were 2-y-o's in 2007. Sire of the US Grade 1 Alabama Stakes winner Proud Spell and the Group 3 Somerville Tattersall Stakes winner River Proud. Standing at Airdrie Stud, Kentucky. 2009 fee: $30,000.

RAHY 1985 *Blushing Groom – Glorious Song (Halo)*. Racing record: Won 3 races in Britain, 2 at 2 yrs when second in Middle Park Stakes. Later Grade 2 1m winner in US. Half-brother to Singspiel. Stud record: Best winners include top-class Fantastic Light (7 Group/Grade 1 successes, including Irish Champion Stakes and Breeders' Cup Turf), and high-class Hawksley Hill, Noverre (Sussex Stakes, also first past post in French 2000 Guineas), Rio de la Plata (Prix Jean-Luc Lagardere) and Serena's Song (won 11 US Grade 1 events). Standing at Three Chimneys Farm, Kentucky. 2009 fee: $50,000.

RAKTI 1999 *Polish Precedent – Ragera (Rainbow Quest)*. Racing record: Won the Italian Derby, Champion Stakes, Prince of Wales's Stakes, Queen Elizabeth II Stakes and Lockinge Stakes. Stud record: First runners in 2009. Standing at the Irish National Stud. 2009 fee: €6,000.

REDBACK 1999 *Mark of Esteem – Patsy Western (Precocious)*. Racing record: Won Solario Stakes and Greenham Stakes. Stud record: Winners include the Group 2 Queen Mary Stakes winner Gilded, Lahaleeb (Group 2 Rockfel Stakes), listed winner Sonny Red & Group 1 placed Redolent. Standing at Tally-Ho Stud, Ireland. 2009 fee: €5,000.

RED RANSOM 1987 *Roberto – Arabia (Damascus)*. Racing record: 2 wins in US, at 5f and 6f, from three outings. Stud record: Best performers include outstanding miler Intikhab, high-class Ekraar and Electrocutionist (Dubai World Cup, Juddmonte International), very smart performers Casual Look (Oaks), China Visit (Group 2 Prix du Rond-Point), Bail Out Becky (Del Mar Oaks), Perfect Sting (Queen Elizabeth II Challenge Cup and BC Filly and Mare Turf), Red Clubs (Haydock Park Sprint Cup), Australian Grade 1 winners Red Dazzler & Charge Forward, the German Group 1 winner Ransom O'War and the smart 2008 two-year-old Four Winds. Now standing at Vinery Stud, Australia. 2009 fee: AUS$66,000.

REFUSE TO BEND 2000 *Sadler's Wells – Market Slide (Gulch)*. Racing record: Won 7 races including National Stakes, 2,000 Guineas, Eclipse Stakes & Queen Anne Stakes. Stud record: His first crop were two-year-olds in 2008 and included 12 individual two-year-old winners, notably the smart Liberation. Standing at Kildangan Stud, Ireland. 2009 fee: €12,000.

ROCK OF GIBRALTAR 1999 *Danehill – Offshore Boom (Be My Guest)*. Racing record: Won 7 Group 1 races, including Dewhurst Stakes, 2000 Guineas and Sussex Stakes. Stud record: First runners in 2006. Sire of the high-class performers Eagle Mountain and Mount Nelson (Group 1 Eclipse Stakes and Criterium International), South African Grade 1 winner Seventh Rock, Group 2 Rockfel Stakes winner Kitty Matcham and very smart General Eliott and Yellowstone. Standing at Coolmore Stud, Ireland. 2009 fee: €27,500.

ROYAL APPLAUSE 1993 *Waajib – Flying Melody (Auction Ring)*. Racing record: Winner of 9 races, including Middle Park at 2 yrs and Haydock Park Sprint Cup at 4. Stud record: First runners in 2001. Sire of the US dual Grade 1 winner Ticker Tape, Group/Grade 2 winners Acclamation, Lovelace, Mister Cosmi & Nevisian Lad, and numerous smart performers including Auditorium, Majestic Missile and Peak To Creek. Had 14 two-year-old winners in England in 2008, notably the very smart Finjaan. Standing at The Royal Studs, Norfolk. 2009 fee: £9,000.

SADLER'S WELLS 1981 *Northern Dancer – Fairy Bridge (Bold Reason)*. Racing record: Winner of Irish 2,000 Guineas, Phoenix Champion Stakes and Coral-Eclipse Stakes. Stud record: A great sire of numerous Group/Grade 1 winners including top-class performers Doyen, Galileo, High Chaparral, Kayf Tara, Montjeu, Northern Spur, Old Vic, Salsabil and Yeats. Retired from stud.

SAKHEE 1997 *Bahri – Thawakib (Sadler's Wells)*. Racing record: Won 8 races, including Juddmonte International and Prix de l'Arc de Triomphe, and runner-up in Derby. Stud record: First runners in 2006. Sire of the Group 1 July Cup winner Sakhee's Secret and the very smart Presvis, Regal Flush and Samuel. Standing at Nunnery Stud, Norfolk. 2009 fee: £8,000.

SEEKING THE GOLD 1985 *Mr Prospector –*
Con Game (Buckpasser). Racing record: 8 wins in USA, notably Grade 1 events Dwyer Stakes and Super Derby. Stud record: First runners in 1993. Best winners include outstanding Dubai Millennium (Dubai World Cup, Prix Jacques le Marois, Queen Elizabeth II Stakes), high-class Cape Town, Heavenly Prize, Jazil (Belmont Stakes) and Pleasant Home (Breeders' Cup Distaff), Japanese Grade 1 winner Gold Tiara and very smart Bob and John, Dream Supreme, Flanders, Fort Dignity, Meiner Love and Seeking The Pearl (Prix Maurice de Gheest and Japanese Group 1 event). Retired from stud.

SELKIRK 1988 *Sharpen Up – Annie Edge (Nebbiolo)*. Racing record: 6 wins including Queen Elizabeth II Stakes, Lockinge Stakes, Beefeater Gin Celebration Mile and Challenge Stakes. Stud record: A leading British-based sire. Sire of the high-class Leadership, very smart Altieri (Premio Presidente Repubblica twice), Border Arrow, Etlaala, Highest, Kastoria, Pipedreamer, Prince Kirk (Prix d'Ispahan), Kastoria (Irish St Leger), Scott's View, Squeak, Tam Lin, The Trader, Tranquil Tiger and numerous smart performers including Field of Hope (Prix de la Foret), Red Bloom (Fillies' Mile), Sulk (Prix Marcel Boussac), Wince (1000 Guineas) and Wordly (Grade 2 La Jolla Handicap). Standing at Lanwades Stud in Newmarket. 2009 fee: £25,000.

SHAMARDAL 2002 *Giant's Causeway – Helsinki (Machiavellian)*. Racing record: Won Dewhurst Stakes, French 2,000 Guineas, French Derby and St James's Palace Stakes. Stud record: First European runners in 2009. Standing at Kildangan Stud, Ireland. 2009 fee: €20,000.

SINGSPIEL 1992 *In The Wings – Glorious Song (Halo)*. Racing record: Winner of 9 races, notably Canadian International and Japan Cup at 4 yrs and Dubai World Cup, Coronation Cup and Juddmonte International at 5. Stud record: First runners in 2001. Sire of top-class performer Moon Ballad, US dual Grade 1 winner Lahudood, high-class Lohengrin (in Japan), very smart Asakusa Den'en (Japanese Group 1 winner), Confidential Lady (Prix de Diane), Da Re Mi, Folk Opera (E P Taylor Stakes), Lateral (Gran Criterium), Papineau (Gold Cup),

Silkwood (Ribblesdale Stakes), Singhalese (Grade 1 Del Mar Oaks) and of numerous smart performers. Standing at Dalham Hall Stud, Newmarket. 2009 fee: £15,000.

SINNDAR 1997 *Grand Lodge – Sinntara (Lashkari)*. Racing record: Won 7 races, including Derby and Prix de l'Arc de Triomphe. Stud record: First runners in 2004. Sire of the top-class colt Youmzain, the very smart performer Shawanda (Irish Oaks and Prix Vermeille) and Four Sins (Blandford Stakes), the smart Albahja, Aqaleem, Pictavia and Visindar (Prix Greffulhe) and very useful Kerashan and Red Gala. Standing at Haras du Bonneval, France. 2009 fee: On application (was €20,000).

SMART STRIKE 1992 *Mr Prospector – Classy 'n Smart (Smarten)*. Racing record: Won 8 races in the USA including the Grade 2 8.5f Philip H Iselin Handicap and the Grade 3 Salvator Mile. Stud record: Best winners include the top-class colt Curlin (Preakness Stakes, Dubai World Cup, Breeders Cup Classic), the Grade 1 winners Soaring Free, English Channel, Square Eddie, Shadow Cast and Fleetstreet Dancer. Standing at Lane's End Farm. 2009 fee: €125,000.

STARCRAFT 2000 *Soviet Star – Flying Floozie (Pompeii Court)*. Racing record: Won 9 races in Australia/New Zealand including three Group 1 events. Subsequently won the Prix du Moulin and the Queen Elizabeth II Stakes. Stud record: First runners appear this year. Now in Australia.

STORM CAT 1983 *Storm Bird – Terlingua (Secretariat)*. Racing record: 4 wins from 6f to 8.5f notably Grade 1 Young America Stakes. Stud record: Best winners include Group/Grade 1 winners After Market, Aljabr, Black Minnaloushe, Cat Thief, Catinca, Desert Stormer, Forestry, Giant's Causeway, Good Reward, Hennessy, High Yield, Nebraska, One Cool Cat, Sharp Cat, Storm Flag Flying, Sweet Catomine, Tabasco Cat, Tornado and Vision And Verse, all at least very smart.

STREET CRY 1998 *Machiavellian – Helen Street (Troy)*. Racing record: 5 wins including Dubai World Cup. Stud record: First runners in 2006. Sire of the Group/Grade 1 winners Street Sense (Breeders' Cup Juvenile, Kentucky Derby, Travers Stakes), Cry And Catch Me (Oak Leaf Stakes), Majestic Roi (Sun Chariot Stakes), Street Boss (Triple Bend Invitational, Bing Crosby H'cap), Street Hero (Norfolk Stakes) and Zenyatta (Breeders Cup Ladies' Classic). Standing at Jonabell Stud Farm, Kentucky (also shuttling to Australia). 2009 fee: $150,000.

TAGULA 1993 *Taufan – Twin Island (Standaan)*. Racing record: Won 4 races including the Group 1 6f Prix Morny (at 2 yrs) and the Group 3 7f Supreme Stakes. Stud record: Sires plenty of winners, amongst the best being the Group 3 winner Tax Free, the smart Beaver Patrol and the listed winners Drawnfromthepast and King Orchisios. Standing at the Rathbarry Stud. 2009 fee: €5,000.

TIGER HILL 1995 *Danehill – The Filly (Appiani II)*. Racing record: Won 17 races including three Group 1 events in Germany. Stud record: Compiled an excellent record in Germany (including the Group 1 winners Iota and Konigstiger and a multitude of other stakes winners) prior to coming to England. This is his first British crop of two-year-olds. Standing at Dalham Hall Stud. 2009 fee: £12,000.

TOBOUGG 1998 *Barathea – Lacovia (Majestic Light)*. Racing record: Won 3 times at 2 yrs including Dewhurst Stakes and subsequently placed in 4 other Group 1 events including Derby and Eclipse. Stud record: First runners in 2006 when he was the leading British-based first season sire. Sire of the Grade 1 New Zealand 1,000 Guineas winner The Pooka, listed winners Biz Bar, Market Day and Sweet Lilly, the smart Sanbuch, The Betchworth Kid and Tobosa and the 2008 filly Penny's Gift. Standing at Dalham Hall Stud, Newmarket. 2009 fee: £2,500.

TRADE FAIR 2000 *Zafonic – Danefair (Danehill)*. Racing record: Won the Group 3 Criterion Stakes, the Group 3 Minstrel Stakes and two listed events. Stud record: His first runners appear in 2009. Standing at Tweenhills Stud. 2009 fee: £3,000.

TRANS ISLAND 1995 *Selkirk – Khubza (Green Desert)*. Racing record: Won 6 races including the Group 2 Prix du Rond-Point and the Group 3 Diomed Stakes. Stud record: His best winners include the smart sprinter Bond City and the smart listed 7f winner Kalahari Gold. Standing at Rathasker Stud, Ireland. 2009 fee: €3,000.

VERGLAS 1994 *Highest Honor – Rahaam (Secreto)*. Racing record: Won 3 races including the Group 3 6f Coventry Stakes. Stud record: Sire of the Group 1 Prix Jean Prat winner Stormy River, the US dual Grade 2 winner Blackdoun, Group 3 winner Silver Frost and the smart 2008 2-y-o Alhaban. Standing at the Irish National Stud. 2009 fee: €12,500.

WAR CHANT 1997 *Danzig – Hollywood Wildcat (Kris S)*. Racing record: Won 5 races including the Grade 1 Breeders Cup Mile. Stud record: Sire of the US dual Grade 2 winner Brilliant, the US Grade 3 winners Chattahoochee War, Karen's Caper and En Roblar & Sea Chanter, Irish Group 3 winner Norman Invader and the French Group 3 winner Asperity. Standing at Three Chimneys Farm, Kentucky. 2009 fee: $15,000.

WHIPPER 2001 *Miesque's Son – Myth To Reality (Sadler's Wells)*. Racing record: Won the Prix Morny and the Prix Maurice de Gheest. Stud record: First runners in 2009. Standing at Ballylinch Stud, Ireland. 2009 fee: €12,400.

WITH APPROVAL *Caro – Passing Mood (Buckpasser)*. Racing record: Raced in Canada where he won the Triple Crown (Queen's Plate, Breeders Stakes and Prince Of Wales's Stakes). Stud record: His best winners include the Group/Grade 2 winners T H Approval, Talkin Man, Lasting Approval, Allende and Just Approval, and the smart English winners Lonesome Dude and Frosty Welcome. Standing at Lanwades Stud. 2009 fee: £4,500.

XAAR 1995 *Zafonic – Monroe (Sir Ivor)*. Racing record: Champion 2-y-o of 1997, when his 4 wins included Prix de la Salamandre and Dewhurst Stakes. Won only once after but placed in Group 1 events at 10f. Stud record: First runners in 2004. Sire of smart Balthazaar's Gift (Group 2 Criterium de Maisons-Laffitte), Royal Power (Group 2 German 2,000 Guineas) and Tony James (Group 2 Gimcrack Stakes), the Australian Grade 2 winner No Questions, Group 3 winners Hazariya, Overclock and Wake Up Maggie, the useful winners Coeur Courageux, Dickensian, Mystical Land, Qadar and Sir Xaar and the smart 2008 2-y-o The Cheka. Now standing in Japan.

ZAFEEN 2000 *Zafonic – Shy Lady (Kaldoun)*. Racing record: Won St James's Palace Stakes and second in 2,000 Guineas. Stud record: First runners appear in 2009. Standing at Overbury Stud. 2009 fee: £3000.

ZAMINDAR 1994 *Gone West – Zaizafon (The Minstrel)*. Racing record: Won the Group 3 Prix de Cabourg at 2 yrs and was placed in the Prix Morny and the Prix de la Salamandre. Stud record: Has sired a number of very good fillies, notably the outstanding Zarkava, the high-class miler Darjina and the Prix Saint-Alary winner Coquerelle. Not so good with his British runners and was recalled from a stint in the USA when his brother Zafonic died. 2009 fee: £15,000.

RACING TRENDS

The tables in this section focus on particular two-year-old races that seem to have the knack of producing winners that improve the following year as three-year-olds. Some of these races have long been important races on the two-year-old calendar (the Dewhurst Stakes for example), but some others will come as a surprise. This type of analysis can enable us to select some of the best of this year's classic generation.

In last year's book the selected races highlighted five Group race winners and another three listed winners. Most notably they included the top-class Derby, Irish Champion Stakes and Champion Stakes winner New Approach, the 1,000 Guineas winner Natagora, the Falmouth Stakes winner Nahoodh and the dual Group winners Centennial and Twice Over.

Previous selections have included the classic winners George Washington, Haafhd, King Of Kings, Pennekamp, Mister Baileys, Refuse To Bend, Rock Of Gibraltar, Rodrigo de Triano and Zafonic (all 2,000 Guineas), Finsceal Beo (English & Irish 1,000 Guineas), Bosra Sham, Cape Verdi, Harayir, Russian Rhythm, Sayyedati (1,000 Guineas), Gossamer and Marling (Irish 1,000 Guineas), Dubawi (Irish 2,000 Guineas), Culture Vulture (French 1,000 Guineas), American Post (French 2,000 Guineas), Shamardal (French 2,000 Guineas and French Derby), Authorized, Sir Percy, High Chaparral, Motivator and Dr Devious (Derby), Lammtarra, Sinndar (Derby and 'Arc'), Alamshar (Irish Derby and the 'Arc'), Desert King, (Irish 2,000 Guineas and Irish Derby), Reams Of Verse (Oaks), Celtic Swing (French Derby), Rule Of Law, Brian Boru, Silver Patriarch and Bob's Return (St Leger), Aussie Rules (French 2,000 Guineas) along with the Prix de l'Arc de Triomphe winner Sakhee and a multitude of other top-class winners.

In the tables, the figure in the third column indicates the number of wins recorded as a three-year-old, with GW signifying a Group race winner at that age.

The horses listed below are the winners of the featured races in 2008. Anyone looking for horses to follow in the Group and Classic events of this season might well want to bear them in mind. I feel that those in bold text are particularly worthy of close scrutiny.

ASHRAM	HELIODOR	**LAHALEEB**
MASTERCRAFTSMAN	**RAINBOW VIEW**	TAAMEER
CROWDED HOUSE	INFAMOUS ANGEL	**LASSARINA**
NAAQOOS	RAYENI	**WESTPHALIA**
CRY OF FREEDOM	INTENSE FOCUS	
ORIZABA	SERIOUS ATTITUDE	

LOWTHER STAKES York, 6 furlongs, August

1991	Culture Vulture	2 GW
1992	Niche	2 GW
1993	Velvet Moon	1
1994	Harayir	4 GW
1995	Dance Sequence	0
1996	Bianca Nera	0
1997	Cape Verdi	1 GW
1998	Bint Allayl	NR
1999	Jemima	0
2000	Enthused	0
2001	Queen's Logic	1 GW
2002	Russian Rhythm	3 GW
2003	Carry On Katie	0
2004	Soar	0
2005	Flashy Wings	0
2006	Silk Blossom	0
2007	Nahoodh	1 GW
2008	Infamous Angel	

Despite a few disappointing years, this race usually has a big say in the following season's 1,000 Guineas. For example Harayir, Cape Verdi and Russian Rhythm won the English 1,000 and Culture Vulture and Al Bahathri took the respective French and Irish versions. Add on the top-class sprinters Habibti and Polonia (both winners prior to 1991) and clearly this race is an important pointer, as emphasized last year when Nahoodh won the Falmouth Stakes. A speedy filly by Exceed and Excel, Infamous Angel wasn't asked to go beyond six furlongs last year although being out of a Sadler's Wells mare one could argue she should stay further. Her paddock value is already established and she may not enhance that further this year.

DEWHURST STAKES
Newmarket, 7 furlongs, October

1991	Dr Devious	2 GW
1992	Zafonic	1 GW
1993	Grand Lodge	1 GW
1994	Pennekamp	2 GW
1995	Alhaarth	1 GW
1996	In Command	0
1997	Xaar	1 GW
1998	Mujahid	0
1999	Distant Music	1 GW
2000	Tobougg	0
2001	Rock Of Gibraltar	5 GW
2002	Tout Seul	0
2003	Milk It Mick	0
2004	Shamardal	3 GW
2005	Sir Percy	1 GW
2006	Teofilo	NR
2007	New Approach	3 GW
2008	Intense Focus	

The Dewhurst Stakes remains our premier race for two-year-old colts. Rock of Gibraltar was a real star of course, but other outstanding colts in this line up include Shamardal, Zafonic, Dr Devious, Grand Lodge and Sir Percy. New Approach can now be added to that illustrious list, with 3 Group 1 wins to his name in 2008 (the Derby, Champion Stakes and Irish Champion). Intense Focus provided a big surprise to most of us and gave his trainer Jim Bolger a hat trick of wins in this race. Further Group One success in Europe may prove beyond him.

ZETLAND STAKES
Newmarket, 10 furlongs, October/November

1991	Bonny Scot	2 GW
1992	Bob's Return	3 GW
1993	Double Trigger	1 GW
1994	Double Eclipse	1
1995	Gentilhomme	0
1996	Silver Patriarch	2 GW
1997	Trigger Happy	0
1998	Adnaan	1
1999	Monte Carlo	0
2000	Worthily	0
2001	Alexandra Three D	2 GW
2002	Forest Magic	NR
2003	Fun And Games	NR
2004	Ayam Zaman	0
2005	Under The Rainbow	0
2006	Empire Day	NR
2007	Twice Over	2 GW
2008	Heliodor	

Previous winners of this race include the St Leger and Coronation Cup winner Silver Patriarch, the good four-year-olds Double Eclipse and Rock Hopper, Bob's Return (St Leger) and the Ascot Gold Cup winner Double Trigger – surely the most notable of them all. In 2008, Twice Over won both the Group 2 Prix Eugene Adam and the Group 3 Craven Stakes for Henry Cecil. Heliodor was campaigned throughout the season, starting in five furlong events, but only found winning form over once he was asked to tackle nine and ten furlongs. He's a fairly useful colt and can win again.

CHAMPAGNE STAKES
(formerly the Laurent Perrier Champagne Stakes) Doncaster, 7 furlongs, September

1991	Rodrigo de Triano	4 GW
1992	Petardia	1
1993	Unblest	1 GW
1994	Sri Pekan	NR
1995	Alhaarth	1 GW
1996	Bahhare	0
1997	Daggers Drawn	0
1998	Auction House	0
1999	Distant Music	1 GW
2000	Noverre	1 GW
2001	Dubai Destination	0
2002	Almushahar	0
2003	Lucky Story	0
2004	Etlaala	0
2005	Close To You	1
	Silent Times (dead-heat)	0
2006	Vital Equine	0
2007	McCartney	0
2008	Westphalia	

The bare figures don't look good, but Dubai Destination came good as a 4-y-o and both Lucky Story and Etlaala were high-class colts, so this race continues to be worth checking out as the following season's big 3-y-o races are concerned. Rodrigo de Triano and Don't Forget Me both won the English 2,000 Guineas and the Irish 2,000 Guineas and Noverre was unlucky not to end the season with two Group 1 victories to his name. After winning this race Westphalia only just failed the land the Breeders Cup Juvenile, so further Group race success this year would hardly come as a surprise.

CHEVELEY PARK STAKES
Newmarket, 6 furlongs, October

1991	Marling	3 GW
1992	Sayyedati	2 GW
1993	Prophecy	0
1994	Gay Gallanta	0
1995	Blue Duster	1
1996	Pas de Reponse	2 GW
1997	Embassy	NR
1998	Wannabe Grand	1
1999	Seazun	0
2000	Regal Rose	NR
2001	Queen's Logic	1 GW
2002	Airwave	1 GW
2003	Carry On Katie	0
2004	Magical Romance	0
2005	Donna Blini	1
2006	Indian Ink	1 GW
2007	Natagora	2 GW
2008	Serious Attitude	

A number of these fillies have gone on to further Group race success, although it is some years now since a classic winner emerged. Indian Ink, saved her best day for Royal Ascot having previously been fifth in the 1,000 Guineas. Natagora raised the profile of this race even further last year when winning the 1,000 Guineas. Serious Attitude was an absolute bargain at only 7,500 Guineas and although one can't imagine her winning a classic she may well improve further. A mile may prove the limit to her stamina and let's hope she can win another Group race for Rae Guest

WASHINGTON SINGER STAKES
Newbury, 7 furlongs, August

1991	Rodrigo de Triano	4 GW
1992	Tenby	2 GW
1993	Colonel Collins	0
1994	Lammtarra	3 GW
1995	Mons	0
1996	State Fair	0
1997	Bahr	2 GW
1998	Valentine Girl	0
1999	Mana-Mou-Bay	0
2000	Prizeman	0
2001	Funfair Wane	1
2002	Muqbil	1 GW
2003	Haafhd	3 GW
2004	Kings Quay	0
2005	Innocent Air	1
2006	Dubai's Touch	2
2007	Sharp Nephew	1
2008	Cry of Freedom	

As can be seen from the table, this race can provide us with Group or Classic pointers and in that regard Lammtarra, Rodrigo de Triano and Haafhd were outstanding. After winning this race Cry of Freedom seemed to find pattern races beyond him, but who is to say Mark Johnston won't find further improvement in him this season?

VEUVE CLICQUOT VINTAGE STAKES
Goodwood, 7 furlongs, July

1991	Dr Devious	2 GW
1992	Maroof	1
1993	Mister Baileys	1 GW
1994	Eltish	0
1995	Alhaarth	1 GW
1996	Putra	0
1997	Central Park	2 GW
1998	Aljabr	1 GW
1999	Ekraar	3 GW
2000	No Excuse Needed	1 GW
2001	Naheef	1 GW
2002	Dublin	1
2003	Lucky Story	0
2004	Shamardal	3 GW
2005	Sir Percy	1 GW
2006	Strategic Prince	0
2007	Rio De La Plata	0
2008	Orizaba	

All in all, this race is very informative in terms of sorting out future stars, with the classic winners Sir Percy, Shamardal, Don't Forget Me, Dr Devious and Mister Baileys and the King George winner Petoski standing out. Aljabr, Central Park, Ekraar and No Excuse Needed were all high-class colts too. A smart colt, Orizaba is now with Godolphin and he should win another race at up to a mile.

NATIONAL STAKES Curragh, 7f, September

1991	El Prado	0
1992	Fatherland	0
1993	Manntari	1
1994	Definite Article	1
1995	Danehill Dancer	1 GW
1996	Desert King	3 GW
1997	King Of Kings	1 GW
1998	Mus-If	0
1999	Sinndar	5 GW
2000	Beckett	1
2001	Hawk Wing	1 GW
2002	Refuse To Bend	3 GW
2003	One Cool Cat	1 GW
2004	Dubawi	2 GW
2005	George Washington	2 GW
2006	Teofilo	NR
2007	New Approach	3 GW
2008	Mastercraftsman	

As one can see by the list of recent winners, this race is as important as any for figuring out the following year's top performers. New Approach was outstanding last year, when winning the Derby, the Champion Stakes and the Irish Champion. After winning this race Mastercraftsman disappointed in the Prix Jean-Luc Lagardere, but that should not detract from his excellent prospects of winning more races at the highest level in 2009.

RACING POST TROPHY
Doncaster, 8 furlongs, October

1991	Seattle Rhyme	0
1992	Armiger	1 GW
1993	King's Theatre	2 GW
1994	Celtic Swing	2 GW
1995	Beauchamp King	1 GW
1996	Medaaly	0
1997	Saratoga Springs	1 GW
1998	Commander Collins	0
1999	Aristotle	0
2000	Dilshaan	1 GW
2001	High Chapparal	5 GW
2002	Brian Boru	1 GW
2003	American Post	3 GW
2004	Motivator	2 GW
2005	Palace Episode	0
2006	Authorized	3 GW
2007	Ibn Khaldun	0
2008	Crowded House	

Some notable performers have won this race, including one of my own favourites the French Derby winner Celtic Swing, the outstanding colt High Chaparral and the Derby heroes Motivator and Authorized. A son of Rainbow Quest, Crowded House was very impressive winning this race. He can win more Group One events from anywhere between a mile and twelve furlongs and at the moment Epsom Derby glory is beckoning.

FILLIES CONDITIONS RACE
Newbury, 7 furlongs, September

1991	Freewheel	1
1992	Sueboog	1 GW
1993	Balanchine	2 GW
1994	Musetta	1
1995	Wild Rumour	0
1996	Etoile	0
1997	Amabel	NR
1998	Fragrant Oasis	1
1999	Veil Of Avalon	1
2000	Palatial	1
2001	Fraulein	2 GW
2002	L'Ancresse	1
2003	Silk Fan	1
2004	Shanghai Lily	0
2005	Mostaqeleh	0
2006	Darrfonah	1
2007	Rosa Grace	1
2008	Lassarina	

The brilliant fillies Balanchine and Milligram stand out in this group and although the race has thrown up a few disappointments of late, both Fraulein and L'Ancresse came up with excellent performances over the Atlantic, with the former taking Canada's Grade 1 E P Taylor Stakes and Ballydoyle's L'Ancresse only just getting touched off in the Breeders Cup Filly & Mare Turf. Rae Guest's filly, Rosa Grace, kept up the good record by winning a listed event last year. Lassarina attempted the Rockfel Stakes after winning this race and although she wasn't good enough that day one can see her winning again at up to a mile.

HAYNES, HANSON AND CLARK STAKES
Newbury, 8 furlongs, September

1991	Zinaad	1
1992	Pembroke	1
1993	King's Theatre	2 GW
1994	Munwar	2 GW
1995	Mick's Love	1
1996	King Sound	1
1997	Duck Row	0
1998	Boatman	0
1999	Ethmaar	0
2000	Nayef	4 GW
2001	Fight Your Corner	1 GW
2002	Saturn	0
2003	Elshadi	0
2004	Merchant	NR
2005	Winged Cupid	NR
2006	Teslin	2
2007	Centennial	2 GW
2008	Taameer	

The high-class horses Rainbow Quest, Unfuwain, King's Theatre and Nayef have all won this race and indeed Shergar won it in 1980, but it's been a while since those glory days. Centennial, a son of Dalakhani, managed two Group race wins in 2008. Taameer finished second in the Autumn Stakes on his only subsequent start. He's a very smart colt and should win a good race in 2009

MEON VALLEY STUD FILLIES' MILE
Ascot, 8 furlongs, September

1991	Midnight Air	0
1992	Ivanka	0
1993	Fairy Heights	0
1994	Aqaarid	1 GW
1995	Bosra Sham	3 GW
1996	Reams of Verse	2 GW
1997	Glorosia	0
1998	Sunspangled	0
1999	Teggiano	0
2000	Crystal Music	0
2001	Gossamer	1 GW
2002	Soviet Song	0
2003	Red Bloom	1 GW
2004	Playful Act	1 GW
2005	Nannina	1 GW
2006	Simply Perfect	1 GW
2007	Listen	0
2008	Rainbow View	

Diminuendo (in 1987), Bosra Sham, Reams of Verse, Gossamer and Soviet Song stand out amongst recent winners of this race, although the latter had to wait until after her 3-y-o career before reaching her full potential. Rainbow View looks to be a very special filly and further Group One victories are clearly on the card.

RACING TRENDS

SOMERVILLE TATTERSALL STAKES
Newmarket, 7 furlongs, September/October

1991	Tertian	0
1992	Nominator	0
1993	Grand Lodge	1 GW
1994	Annus Mirabilis	1
1995	Even Top	1 GW
1996	Grapeshot	1
1997	Haami	1
1998	Enrique	1 GW
1999	Scarteen Fox	0
2000	King Charlemagne	3 GW
2001	Where Or When	2 GW
2002	Governor Brown	NR
2003	Milk It Mick	0
2004	Diktatorial	0
2005	Aussie Rules	2 GW
2006	Thousand Words	0
2007	River Proud	1
2008	Ashram	

The bare figures in this table don't really tell the whole story, for there are some very good horses here. The Group winners speak for themselves but Milk It Mick, Opening Verse and Annus Mirabilis all went on to win good races abroad and Haami was certainly a smart colt too. Aussie Rules won the French 2,000 Guineas and a Grade 1 event in the USA. River Proud won a listed race in 2008 to continue the good record of winners of this race. A smart colt, Ashram is now with Godolphin. He ran well in defeat in the Dewhurst Stakes and he can win again at up to a mile.

KILLAVULLAN STAKES
Leopardstown, 7 furlongs October

1991	Misako-Togo	3
1992	Asema	3 GW
1993	Broadmara	0
1994	Kill The Crab	2 GW
1995	Aylesbury	0
1996	Shell Ginger	0
1997	Kincara Palace	1
1998	Athlumney Lady	0
1999	Monashee Mountain	2 GW
2000	Perigee Moon	0
2001	Stonemason	0
2002	New South Wales	1
2003	Grey Swallow	2 GW
2004	Footstepsinthesand	1 GW
2005	Frost Giant	1 GW
2006	Confuchias	1 GW
2007	Jupiter Pluvius	0
2008	Rayeni	

During the period researched, seven of the winners subsequently went on to Group success as three-year-olds, most notably the Irish Derby winner Grey Swallow and the English 2,000 Guineas winner Footstepsinthesand. Unbeaten in both his two-year-old starts, Rayeni (a son of Indian Ridge) should win another Group race this year, but trainer John Oxx tells me he's had a slight setback so whether he'll be ready for any of the Guineas races is questionable.

ROCKFEL STAKES
Newmarket, 7 furlongs, October

1991	Musicale	1 GW
1992	Yawl	0
1993	Relatively Special	0
1994	Germane	0
1995	Bint Salsabil	1
1996	Moonlight Paradise	0
1997	Name Of Love	NR
1998	Hula Angel	1 GW
1999	Lahan	1 GW
2000	Sayedah	0
2001	Distant Valley	0
2002	Luvah Girl	1 in USA
2003	Cairns	0
2004	Maids Causeway	1 GW
2005	Speciosa	1 GW
2006	Finsceal Beo	2 GW
2007	Kitty Matcham	0
2008	Lahaleeb	

Three Newmarket 1,000 Guineas winners have hailed from the winners of this race in the last 10 years – Lahan, Speciosa and Finsceal Beo. For good measure Maids Causeway won the Coronation Stakes and Hula Angel won the Irish 1,000 Guineas (a race Finsceal Beo also added to her tally). Lahaleeb won three races last year and she improved as the season went on. She stays a mile and will add another pattern race or two to her tally – maybe at an even higher level than at Group 3.

PRIC JEAN-LUC LAGARDERE – formerly the Grand Criterium, Longchamp, 7 furlongs (1 mile before 2001)

2001	Rock Of Gibraltar	5 GW
2002	Hold That Tiger	0
2003	American Post	3 GW
2004	Oratorio	2 GW
2005	Horatio Nelson	0
2006	Holy Roman Emperor	NR
2007	Rio de la Plata	0
2008	Naaqoos	

The last 3 winners have all failed to win as three-year-olds but Horatio Nelson sadly had to be put down after an injury in the Derby. A son of Oasis Dream, Naaqoos disappointed in his prep race for the Guineas in April, but his trainer Freddie Head still has a good colt on his hands. He was impressive when winning this race and can surely find further Group race glory this year.

LATE NAMES

Names that were confirmed after the indexing had been completed.

96. BAKONGO (IRE)
99. PASTEL BLUE (IRE)
166. MISHEER
172. AMTAAR
176. IPTKAAR (USA)
178. NIDEEB
179. SLASL
182. JAWAL
184. SARMAD (USA)
186. ZINJBAR (USA)
187. RUMOOL
188. SAIF ALARAB (IRE)
190. NIRAN (IRE)
206. ART EXCELLENCE
207. ART JEWEL (IRE)
254. FASHION FLOW
506. AQUARIUS STAR (IRE)
520. I'MNEVERWRONG (IRE)
521. CHRISTMAS COMING
522. REGENCY ART (IRE)
524. I'MALWAYSRIGHT (IRE)
562. BAILEYS GLEAM
651. ZELOS DREAM (IRE)
826. BIN SHAMARDAL (IRE)
829. HASTY (IRE)
883. SAJJHAA
884. SARRSAR
885. SHOBOBB
889. DAHAKAA
890. GAY MIRAGE (GER)
892. NADDWAH
917. FRONTLEY
933. WADNAAN
935. DOCTOR ZHIGAGO
937. FIRST INSTANCE
938. ORIGINAL DANCER (IRE)
939. CARACAL
940. SAND SKIER
948. DUELLIST
949. TAKE TEN
953. JARROW (IRE)
966. IF I WERE A BOY (IRE)
1033. FINAL ANSWER
1129. BE GRATEFUL (IRE)
1150. STRIKE SHOT
1195. JOLLY ROGER (IRE)
1196. ROMAN GLADIATOR (IRE)
1197. ALFONSO THE GREAT (IRE)
1227. LOVINGONYOURMIND (USA)
1248. CRAZYFORLOVINGYOU
1400. ABRIACHAN
1441. BAJAN FLASH
1537. EDWARD LONGSHANKS

HORSE INDEX

Aalsmeer 1020
Aalya (IRE) 473
Aattash (IRE) 257
Above Limits 401
Abrasive (IRE) 656
Abu Wathab 305
Across The Sea (USA) 1525
Activate 64
Admin 42
Admiral Cochrane (IRE) 894
Admission 65
Advertisement (USA) 1155
Aetos 1558
Affirmable 835
Afsare 373
Age Of Refinement (IRE) 1370
Agony And Ecstacy 43
Aided And Abetted (IRE) 1598
Air Chief Marshal (IRE) 1205
Aisy (IRE) 1442
Akamon 432
Akula (IRE) 1540
Al Emarati (USA) 1403
Al Khimiya (IRE) 198
Al Muthanaa 657
Alaia (IRE) 972
Albacocca 1371
Albeed 474
Alburj (USA) 1599
Alfred Nobel 1206
Alice Sara (USA) 163
Aliwiyya (IRE) 1289
All My Heart 510
All We Know 225
Allannah Abu 1372
Almadaar 433
Almiranta 1373
Almutham (USA) 475
Alnaseem (USA) 476
Alrasm (IRE) 855
Alsalwa (IRE) 1340
Alshahbaa (IRE) 1341
Altruiste 1374
Alwarqaa 784
Always In Fashion (IRE) 705
Amber Nectar (IRE) 636
Ambrogina 144
Ameer (IRE) 1496
American Spirit (IRE) 564
Amno Dancer 1541
Amtaar 172
Anaverna (IRE) 1600
Angel Of Fashion 785
Angie's Nap (USA) 434
Anna's Boy 101

Ant Music (IRE) 1099
Apache Kid (IRE) 1085
Appley Bridge 211
Arabian Falcon (IRE) 1497
Arabian History (USA) 1498
Arabian Pride 1404
Arakana (IRE) 1382
Arcano (IRE) 1034
Arch Walker 1261
Architrave 1375
Ardent 565
Art Machine (USA) 1376
Askan (IRE) 1427
Asraab (IRE) 1499
Astonishment 954
Astromoon 1542
Astrophysical Jet 1021
Atacama Crossing (IRE) 786
Atakora (IRE) 1311
Atasari (IRE) 121
Athwaab 375
Atlantis Star 1500
Attestation 658
Atyaab 1601
Audrinna (IRE) 1393
Autcharn (FR) 1035
Averroes (IRE) 463
Avonrose 918
Awesome Act (USA) 1156
Awzaan 919
Ayam Zainah 258
Azita 374
Azizi 659

Bab Al Shams (IRE) 1501
Babycakes (IRE) 66
Bahamian Music (IRE) 532
Bahamian Sun 402
Bakongo (IRE) 96
Balatoma (IRE) 1559
Balducci 1
Ballachulish 214
Balsha (USA) 436
Banana Republic (IRE) 357
Bangathelatch (IRE) 1443
Banks And Braes 706
Baoli 707
Baralaka 1377
Barzan 403
Bashir Bil Zain 259
Bass Rock 1290
Bateau Bleu 777
Bathwick Zara 1333
Bazaruto 566
Be A Devil 1132
Be Invincible (IRE) 788
Beachfire (IRE) 567

Beat The Rush 212
Beauchamp Yorker 215
Bebopalula (IRE) 787
Beethoven (IRE) 1207
Beggar's Opera (IRE) 568
Benrish (IRE) 1428
Berling 477
Best Intent 856
Bethlehem (IRE) 1114
Bethrah (IRE) 1602
Beyond Desire 857
Beyond The City (USA) 708
Big Audio (IRE) 709
Billionaire Boy 1109
Bint Almatar (USA) 1502
Bit Of Bling 1157
Bitter Man (IRE) 260
Blades Harmony 1022
Blancmange 660
Blinka Me 1543
Blitzing 661
Blue Angel (IRE) 710
Blue Lyric 375
Blue Sparkle (IRE) 1312
Blue Zealot 67
Blue Zephyr 1133
Bob Goes Electric (IRE) 106
Boga 261
Bombardino 836
Boom And Bust (IRE) 1560
Boss's Destination 1
Boston Blue 973
Bougainvilia (IRE) 711
Bouncy Bouncy (IRE) 68
Boycott (IRE) 569
Bramshaw (USA) 1313
Brannagh (USA) 1158
Bravo Bravo 909
Brazilian Beauty 1342
Breakheart 2
Brisbane (IRE) 570
Brocanteur (IRE) 1444
Bronze Prince 1503
Brunette (IRE) 712
Burj Nahar 1504
Business Bay (USA) 1581
Bygone Age (IRE) 1603

Cabaret (IRE) 1208
Cailocht (IRE) 122
Caldercruix (USA) 1526
Call To Reason (IRE) 1159
Calm Storm 1160
Calypso Star (IRE) 713
Candleshoe (IRE) 714
Candotoo (IRE) 1161
Canford Cliffs 715

Cansili Star 858
Caol Ila 551
Captain Clint 1544
Captain's Paradise (IRE) 1378
Captainofthefleet (IRE) 1343
Capulet Monteque (IRE) 1445
Carazam (IRE) 1446
Caribou Island 1505
Carnaby Street (IRE) 716
Carnacki (USA) 1162
Carraiglawn (IRE) 123
Carries Lass 1267
Cash Queen Anna (IRE) 789
Caucus 478
Caviar 717
Ceedal 1429
Ceedwell 1430
Ceilidh House 44
Celestial Girl 1115
Celtic Ransom 837
Centurio 330
Chabal (IRE) 124
Chachamaidee (IRE) 226
Chain Of Events 790
Champagnelifestyle 791
Channel Squadron (IRE) 227
Chat De Soie (IRE) 1100
Cheetah 376
Chelsea Morning (USA) 792
Cherry Bee 920
Cheyne Walk (USA) 1163
Chiefdom Prince 1463
Chink Of Light 3
Choir Solo 571
Christmas Carnival 1036
Church Melody 662
Church Of England 69
Chushka 1431
Cian Rooney 417
City Of Rome (IRE) 718
City View (IRE) 125
Clan Piper 572
Clarietta 479
Clashnacree 1447
Classic Colori (IRE) 404
Clayton Flick (IRE) 331
Clear Alternative (IRE) 1604
Clear Hills (IRE) 70
Clifton Encore (USA) 405
Cloud's End 663
Cloudy City (USA) 921
Coastal Wells (IRE) 1344
Cojo (IRE) 1037
Collect Art (IRE) 71
Colourbearer (IRE) 573

TWO YEAR OLDS OF 2009

Comheart 1432
Commissionaire 574
Compton Street 4
Compton Way 793
Conciliatory 640
Conduct (IRE) 1464
Conniption (IRE) 1038
Contract Caterer (IRE) 503
Contredanse (IRE) 1039
Cool Kitten (IRE) 974
Cool Marble (IRE) 1605
Cool Valentine 5
Coolminx (IRE) 418
Coordinated Cut (IRE) 306
Cornish Beau 1545
Coronaria 664
Cosimo De Medici 1116
Cotton King 575
Count Bertoni (IRE) 1527
Count Of Anjou (USA) 719
Country Princess (FR) 45
Court Gown (IRE) 1023
Craighall 1405
Cre Na Coille (IRE) 126
Creevy 955
Crown (IRE) 720
Crystal Gal (IRE) 1345
Cuckoo Rock (IRE) 1334
Culadie 1433
Cultured Pride (IRE) 721
Cunning Plan (IRE) 307
Cuthbert (IRE) 895

Dalalaat (GER) 665
Dance East 1164
Dance For Julie (IRE) 778
Dance Hall Girl (IRE) 1346
Dance Tempo 1117
Dancing David (IRE) 1040
Dancing Dude (IRE) 922
Dancing Freddy (IRE) 552
Danger Mulally 6
Danny's Choice 46
Danube (IRE) 228
Daredevil Dancer (USA) 533
Darshonin 1561
Dashing Doc (IRE) 511
Days Ahead (IRE) 998
Dea Mhein (IRE) 127
Deal 722
Decorative 859
Deely Plaza 723
Definite Season (IRE) 1606
Deirdre 576
Desert Liaison 1165
Destiny's Dancer 779
Dhaafer 666
Dhaamer (IRE) 577
Dhabia (USA) 1607
Dhan Dhana (IRE) 667

Dherghaam (IRE) 437
Di Stefano 262
Diam Queen (GER) 377
Diamond Affair 1394
Dispol Keasha 37
Divine Call 668
Divine Choice (IRE) 38
Divorcefromreality 419
Dixie Bright (USA) 553
Dizziness 332
Dolphin's Dream 1041
Dolphina (USA) 229
Don Carlos (GER) 1209
Don't Tell Mary (IRE) 406
Doon Kalal (IRE) 1562
Dorback 216
Dorooje (IRE) 860
Doyenne Dream 526
Dream Of Gerontius (IRE) 724
Dream Speed (IRE) 7
Dream Spinner 480
Dream Venture 725
Dreamalittledream (IRE) 1210
Drive Home (USA) 1608
Dromore 8
Dubai Atlantis (USA) 1406
Dubai Media (CAN) 1407
Dubai Phantom 1408
Dubawi Heights 199
Dutiful 263
Duty And Destiny (IRE) 1042
Duty Driven 512
Dylanesque 861
Dynasty 1211

Ebanour (IRE) 1291
Eclipsed (USA) 107
Edgewater (IRE) 1043
Edward Whymper 1546
Effervesce (IRE) 1465
Ejaab 669
Ejteyaaz 1347
Elation 923
Eleanora Duse (IRE) 1466
Elegantly (IRE) 1582
Elenore 333
Ellbeedee (IRE) 862
Eltheeb 481
Elusist (IRE) 1434
Emirates Dream (USA) 1506
Emirates Hills 1583
Emma Jean Lass (IRE) 1101
Emperor's Stride 1166
Engulf (IRE) 670
Erfaan 794
Ertikaan 863
Esaar (USA) 795

Eshtyaaq 1563
Essexbridge 726
Eviction (IRE) 1024
Ewaan (IRE) 1609
Exceed Power 1409
Excellent Day (IRE) 264
Excellent Guest 1006
Exgray (IRE) 1435
Existentialist 1335
Extreme Green 9

Fabulosity 671
Fair Trade 513
Faited To Pretend (IRE) 200
Faithful Duchess (IRE) 438
Falakee 308
Falcon City (CAN) 1584
Falcun 378
Fallen Idol 578
Famous (IRE) 1212
Famous Warrior (IRE) 1348
Fancy Star 796
Fancy Vivid (IRE) 1467
Fantastic Favour 1262
Fantastic Prince 358
Farandooney (IRE) 1349
Farmer Giles (IRE) 72
Fasette 1547
Fashion Flow 254
Fawley Green 1134
Fearless Falcon 73
Felsham 217
Ferdoos 864
Ferris Wheel (IRE) 359
Field Day (IRE) 1044
Fifty Moore 1263
Final Turn 218
Finalment 145
Fine Sight 727
Fireback 10
Fireflash 420
Firinne (IRE) 128
First Cat 728
Flambeau 219
Flame Keeper (IRE) 1610
Flapjack 729
Florentine Ruler (USA) 230
Floridita 924
Flouncing (IRE) 672
Fly Silca Fly (IRE) 265
Flying Destination 975
Fonterutoli (IRE) 146
Footsie (IRE) 554
Footsie Footsie (IRE) 797
Footstepsofspring (FR) 730
Forest Crown 47
Fork Lightning (USA) 1379
Formulation (IRE) 1118
Frameit (IRE) 1102
Fratellino 1012

Free For All (IRE) 956
Free Judgement (USA) 129
Fremont (IRE) 731
Frequency 439
Frivolity 1167
Frozen Power (IRE) 1507
Full Mandate (IRE) 732

Gakalina (IRE) 1564
Gallant Eagle (IRE) 957
Gallic Star (IRE) 266
Ghost (IRE) 798
Ghostwing 421
Giant's Play (USA) 1468
Gift Of Love (IRE) 514
Gile Na Greine (IRE) 130
Ginger Grey 201
Gipsy Countess (IRE) 131
Gipsy Rose (IRE) 1350
Glamour Profession (IRE) 733
Glass Of Red (IRE) 48
Gojeri (IRE) 865
Gold Rules 379
Golden Waters 910
Gomrath (IRE) 267
Goodwood Diva 482
Goolagong (IRE) 49
Gracious Melange 147
Grammercy (IRE) 74
Grand Mary (IRE) 360
Grand Zafeen 268
Greek Key 75
Greeley Bright (USA) 555
Green Art 1351
Green Earth (IRE) 1314
Green Energy 1315
Green Lightning 925
Green Moon (IRE) 464
Grey Bunting 799
Gritstone 534
Guesswork 896
Guidecca Ten 11
Gulf Punch 734
Gundaroo 483
Gwynedd (IRE) 1025

Haadeeth 1565
Haatheq (USA) 484
Habaayib 440
Habbah 579
Hairspray 269
Hajjan (USA) 485
Half Sister (IRE) 735
Hamloola 673
Hanakiyya (IRE) 1292
Hayek 897
Hayzoom 309
He's Invincible 1045
Hearts Of Fire 504

INDEX OF HORSES 357

Heavenly Quest (IRE) 580
Hedaaya (IRE) 1352
Helaku (IRE) 736
Heliocentric 737
Herculean 674
Heslington 192
Hidden Fire 515
Higgy's Ragazzo (FR) 738
High Approach 1135
High Holborn (IRE) 1046
High Importance (USA) 1168
High Ransom 866
Highland Quaich 516
Hill Of Miller 641
Hill Tribe 108
Historic Occasion (IRE) 1611
Hold You Colour (IRE) 1047
Honoured (IRE) 1380
Hooligan Sean 220
Hot Prospect 867
Hot Pursuits 1119
Houda 1336
Hounds Ditch 911
House Of Frills 39
House Red (IRE) 800
Hovering Hawk (IRE) 801
Huff And Puff 1316
Hulcote Rose (IRE) 959
Humidor (IRE) 334
Huwaaya 441
Huwaaya (USA) 1566

Ibn Sina (IRE) 1508
Ijaaza (USA) 442
Il Portico 270
Ildiko (USA) 1381
Illustrious Prince (IRE) 1169
Ilston Lord (IRE) 1567
Imperial Delight 221
Imperial Warrior 1120
In Vigo 898
Inqaath 1469
Inside Track (IRE) 1048
Interlace 1382
Internet Express (USA) 109
Invincible Prince (IRE) 50
Invincible Soul (IRE) 739
Invitee 443
Ipswich Lad 12
Iqtinaa 675
Irish Eyes 1264
Iron Condor 527
Isdaar (IRE) 581
Ishraaqat 1568
Ishtar 1395
Ishtar Gate (USA) 361
Island Dreams 1470
Island Rhapsody 1121
Isotia 148

Istimlaak (IRE) 1471
It's A Deal (IRE) 1636
Itsthursday Already 556
Itwasonlyakiss 838
Izaaj (USA) 1509

Jacqueline Quest (IRE) 231
Jade Jewel (IRE) 1353
Jamaayel (IRE) 1354
Jarayaan 1612
Jasmine Scent 1268
Jawal 182
Jayaash (USA) 1569
Jazz Age (IRE) 582
Jean Jeannie 676
Jehu 271
Jemima Nicholas 677
Jibrrya 272
Jo Boy 1086
Joan d'Arc (IRE) 1613
Juicy Pear (IRE) 76
Julie's Jet (IRE) 1293
Jumeirah Palm (USA) 1410
Junket 1170
Juwireya 1570

Kaizan (IRE) 77
Kajima 740
Kaladena (IRE) 1294
Kalam Daleel (IRE) 273
Kalk Bay 678
Kanaf (IRE) 444
Karamojo Bell 1528
Kate Skate 362
Katehari (IRE) 13
Kathleen Frances 1548
Kavak 149
Kayaan 679
Keenes Royale 780
Kensei 51
Kenswick 505
Keraloun (IRE) 1295
Kerchak (USA) 899
Keredari (IRE) 1296
Key Art (IRE) 1171
Key Light (IRE) 839
Key Secure (IRE) 1614
Keyta Bonita 1396
Khajally (IRE) 445
Kildangan Girl 1136
Killeeter (IRE) 1355
King Ledley (USA) 1356
King's Approach (IRE) 741
King's Parade 1472
King's Realm (IRE) 1383
Kingsfort 1357
Kingsgate Choice (IRE) 110
Kinky Afro (IRE) 1103
Kithonia 232

Kitty Kiernan 132
Kitty Wells 380
Kleio 233
Knockdolian (IRE) 335
Kona Coast 583
Kuilsriver (IRE) 111
Kydatee Kilt 363
Kylladdy 1529

L Frank Baum (IRE) 1050
L'Enchanteresse (IRE) 79
Laazem (IRE) 584
Labretella (IRE) 1549
Lady Mcbeth (IRE) 680
Lady McGonagall (USA) 78
Lady Navara (IRE) 193
Lady Of Akita (USA) 585
Lady Of The Desert (USA) 1049
Lady Slippers (IRE) 465
Lago Indiano (IRE) 1317
Lamh Albasser (USA) 1510
Lanizza 446
Latansaa 1571
Lathaat 486
Lauberhorn 912
Le Volcan D'Or 926
Legendary Lad (IRE) 1615
Leitzu (IRE) 274
Leleyf (IRE) 275
Lenkiewicz 1087
Letsplayball 840
Leviathan 1530
Licence To Kill 927
Liebelei (USA) 466
Life And Soul (IRE) 1318
Lighting Speed 983
Lillie Langry (IRE) 1213
Lilly Valentine (IRE) 742
Lily Rio 1137
Lingapour (USA) 1297
Liquid Asset (FR) 14
Lisselan Princess 1616
Listello (USA) 467
Little Oz (IRE) 447
Loden 381
Lofthouse 276
Logos Astra (USA) 984
Lolly For Dolly (IRE) 1448
Look Whos Next 1026
Lord Aratan (GER) 448
Lord Zenith 15
Lost Horizon (IRE) 743
Love Action (IRE) 744
Love Lockdown 999
Love Match 336
Lovely Eyes 1411
Loyaliste (FR) 745
Loyalty 1473
Luan Cincise (IRE) 133

Luck Of The Draw (IRE) 1384
Lucky Breeze (IRE) 976
Lucky Diva 642
Lucky Flyer 643
Lucky General (IRE) 746
Lulawin 557
Lutine Bell 1385

Maarek 586
Maath Gool 1051
Macroy 1088
Madame Roulin (IRE) 80
Madlool (IRE) 681
Magic Footsteps 1266
Magic Lantern 747
Magnetic Force (IRE) 1474
Magnus Thrax (USA) 748
Maid To Dream 587
Main Spring 1475
Maiwand 1386
Make It Big 682
Makfi 1572
Making The Event (USA) 1412
Mandarin Express 1052
Manhattan Fox (USA) 1053
Marchin Star 194
Marcus Cicero (IRE) 1637
Marcus Galerius (IRE) 1449
Marfach (USA) 134
Marigold Miss (IRE) 802
Mark Twain (IRE) 1214
Markazzi 1476
Market Puzzle (IRE) 1617
Marksbury 528
Maroon 803
Marrayah 868
Mascagni (IRE) 150
Mass Rally 588
Massachusetts 1054
Master OF Dance (IRE) 749
Mawzoon (IRE) 869
Mazammorra (USA) 151
Mecox Bay (IRE) 16
Medalia 529
Media Hype 382
Meezaan (IRE) 589
Melinoise 644
Merchant Of Medici 1138
Mexican Rose 1172
Midfielder (USA) 590
Midnight Mover (IRE) 1358
Mighty Aphrodite 645
Mighty Clarets (IRE) 535
Military Call 1027
Miniyamba (IRE) 487
Minoan (FR) 1215
Minsky Mine (IRE) 1618
Miracle Wish (IRE) 52

358 TWO YEAR OLDS OF 2009

Misheer 166
Miss Chaumiere 81
Miss Dreamy 781
Miss Whippy 82
Missionaire (USA) 977
Mister Tee 1000
Mistic Magic (IRE) 364
Mizayin (IRE) 277
Mme de Stael 1387
Mon Cadeaux 17
Monalini (IRE) 1436
Monograph 841
Monsieur Chevalier (IRE) 750
Mont Agel 83
Montecchio (IRE) 1359
Montelissima (IRE) 449
Montparnasse (IRE) 1055
Moobeyn 1573
Moonlight Mischief (IRE) 1056
Moonline Dancer (FR) 751
Moonraker's Choice (IRE) 752
Moose Moran (USA) 234
Mororless 53
Motirani 84
Motrice 1388
Mount Juliet (IRE) 202
Mountain Quest 85
Mrs Boss 1089
Mubareraat 683
Mudaaraah 488
Mufarrh (IRE) 489
Mujaazef 1360
Munaweer (IRE) 1361
Munsarim 490
Muqalad (IRE) 1362
Musaafer (IRE) 870
Musiara 278
Mutamaleq (IRE) 1619
My Manikato 383

Naasef 491
Nadeen (IRE) 279
Nadinska 280
Nafura 1511
Najoom Zaman (IRE) 384
Nashama (IRE) 1512
Nave (USA) 928
Nebula Storm (IRE) 1173
Nefyn 1139
Neon Tiger 1001
Nerves Of Steel (IRE) 365
New Christmas (USA) 1057
Next Move (IRE) 1513
Nezhenka 1389
Nideeb 178
Niran (IRE) 190
Nizaa (USA) 804

Noafal (IRE) 871
Notorize 54
Nubar Boy 1450
Number One Guy 1550
Nunavik (IRE) 1620
Nutela 152

Oak Leaves 1337
Oasis Dancer 55
Oil Strike 1638
Old Devil Moon (IRE) 1093
Old Money 468
Olympic Ceremony 536
Olympic Medal 337
On Her Way 235
On The Cusp (IRE) 872
One Good Emperor (IRE) 112
Opera Gal (IRE) 18
Optimistic Duke 1140
Opus Dei 1013
Oriental Cat 591
Orion The Hunter 366
Our Boy Barrington (IRE) 753
Our Dream Queen 805
Our Georgie Girl 1007
Outshine 592

Painswick (USA) 492
Paleo (IRE) 754
Palisades Park 755
Palm Ridge (IRE) 1621
Paradise Dream 1174
Parbold Hill 40
Park Twilight (IRE) 1175
Parvaaz (IRE) 873
Pastel Blue (IRE) 99
Pastoral Player 1122
Patachou 646
Pebble Beach (IRE) 684
Pedantic 385
Peeblesonthebeach 842
Pepper Lane 41
Perennial 1176
Perfect Ending (IRE) 537
Perfect Note 1514
Perse 900
Persian Heroine (IRE) 493
Persona Non Grata (IRE) 338
Petrocelli 1014
Picnic Party 1177
Pin Cushion 1058
Pink Coat 281
Pink Symphony 367
Pintura 282
Pipette 19
Pittodrie Star (IRE) 20
Planatory 1216

Planet Red 756
Play With Caution (USA) 1178
Pleasant Day (IRE) 1059
Plum Sugar (IRE) 1451
Plume 757
Plus ULtra (IRE) 236
Poet's Voice 1515
Point North (IRE) 1179
Polish Steps 1269
Poltergeist 758
Polyphemus (USA) 339
Port of Tyne 340
Portman Boy 21
Pose (IRE) 759
Postellion 1217
Pounced 593
Power Of Dreams 1551
Powerful Melody (USA) 1516
Powerful Pierre 1265
Praesepe 685
Prayer Hall 1123
Primo De Vida (IRE) 56
Prince Of Dreams 979
Princess Aurora (USA) 407
Princess Seren 1090
Priors Gold 1574
Prisoner 686
Professor Bollini 469
Progress (IRE) 1180
Prompter 86
Protaras (USA) 237
Public Service (IRE) 1060

Qamar 1517
Qanoon 687
Quadrille 760
Quaestor (IRE) 408
Quality Mover (USA) 1413
Qubool 1363
Qudwah (IRE) 874
Queen of Mean 1181
Queen Of Wands 494
Queen's Envoy 386
Queen's Grace 1124
Quick Reaction 761

Radio City 57
Ragsta (IRE) 762
Rahaala 1477
Rahya Class (IRE) 1452
Rainbow Six 153
Raine's Cross 1639
Rainsoorough 283
Rakaan (IRE) 1061
Rakitam (IRE) 409
Rashaad (IRE) 806
Rasmy 1575
Rasselas (IRE) 807

Readymade 1478
Red Amy 87
Red Avalanche (IRE) 368
Red Badge (IRE) 763
Red Barcelona 1552
Red Intrigue (IRE) 1319
Red Jazz (USA) 808
Red Roar (IRE) 102
Red Smokey (IRE) 1553
Redden 688
Regal Park (IRE) 1182
Reggae Rock 1002
Reiteration (USA) 135
Renesse 1437
Resolute Road 809
Revoltinthedesert 1028
Rezwaan 450
Rich And Reckless 1183
Ride A Rainbow 875
Rigidity 238
Ritual (IRE) 1184
River Landing 58
Robinson Cruso 876
Rock A Doodle Doo (IRE) 901
Rock Medley (IRE) 136
Rockabilly Rebel 810
Rockemar (USA) 1185
Roise (IRE) 137
Romancea (USA) 1585
Roodle 913
Rose Alba (IRE) 495
Roxy Flower (IRE) 1320
Royal Assent 22
Royal Box 764
Royal Cheer 422
Royal Desert 284
Royal Etiquette 470
Rumool 187
Rusty Halo 1003
Ruthie Babe 689

Saafidah (USA) 1364
Saary 451
Sabii Sands (IRE) 765
Sacred Aria 1298
Saderaat (USA) 496
Sadler's Mark 1531
Safari Special 1640
Safwaan 690
Saggiatore 452
Sahaayeb (IRE) 1365
Saharia (IRE) 1186
Saif Alarab (IRE) 188
Saison (IRE) 1622
Sakile 310
Salvation 88
San Cassiano (IRE) 59
San Jeminiano (IRE) 311
Sandy Toes 1015

INDEX OF HORSES 359

Sarbola 877
Satwa Excel 453
Satwa Royal 454
Satwa Son 455
Scarcity (IRE) 456
Scilly Breeze 647
Scottish Boogie 958
Sea Change (IRE) 1187
Sea Dubai 766
Seaside Sizzler 60
Secret Millionaire 1110
Secret Queen 1062
Secret Spell 1188
Seeking Dubai 1586
Senate 594
Sennockian Storm 929
Sensationally 387
Sense Of Purpose (IRE) 1623
Sent From Heaven (IRE) 811
Serious Spirit 648
Seven Summits (IRE) 1218
Seyaaq (USA) 812
Shaayeq (IRE) 1576
Shabak Hom (USA) 1414
Shabassh 1453
Shama'adan 930
Shamardal Phantom (IRE) 1415
Shams Albawadi (USA) 1587
Sharaayeen 813
Shareen (IRE) 1299
Sharp Shoes 423
She's A Character 538
Sheer Force (IRE) 978
Sheiling (IRE) 424
Shimanishiki 341
Shipwrecked 649
Side Glance 23
Silk Runner (IRE) 843
Silkenveil (IRE) 425
Simenon 24
Sir Pitt 595
Sir Walter Raleigh 1479
Six Diamonds 1125
Six Wives 691
Siyaadah 1518
Slasl 179
Slice (IRE) 914
Slikback Jack 1016
Smog (IRE) 1063
Snoqualmie Star 517
Soccer (USA) 410
Somnium 1104
Song Of The Desert 518
Song To The Moon (IRE) 25
Sooraah 692
Sory 388
Sounds Of Thunder 471

Space War 596
Spacecraft (IRE) 1189
Spanish Acclaim 1338
Sparkle Park 1064
Specialising 285
Specific Dream 1480
Spirit Land 1554
Spoken 342
Spring Heather (IRE) 497
Spying 426
Squall 1190
St Ignatius 61
Stadium Of Light (IRE) 1126
Stags Leap (IRE) 767
Star Power (IRE) 138
Star Twilight 985
Star Zafeen 286
Starboard Bow 960
Starburst Excel 1397
Starcraft Revival 389
Stargaze (IRE) 26
Starlight Muse (IRE) 1029
Starshine 1481
Starstreamer (IRE) 1577
Start Right 390
State Capital 1191
State Fair 369
Statuesque 472
Step In Time (IRE) 931
Sternlight (IRE) 1030
Stormglass 1141
Street Entertainer (IRE) 1321
Strictly Dncing 27
String Of Pearls (IRE) 1219
Stroke Of Love (USA) 1624
Stunning View (IRE) 1625
Style Queen (IRE) 139
Subtefuge 239
Suffolk Punch (IRE) 28
Sughera (IRE) 1482
Suited And Booted 768
Sulook (IRE) 1366
Sumerian 1390
Summa Cum Laude 427
Sun Raider (IRE) 814
Sunarise (IRE) 769
Super Collider 878
Super Hoofer (IRE) 140
Superstitious (USA) 164
Surooh (USA) 498
Swan Wings 29
Sweet Caroline (IRE) 815
Sweet Sonnet (USA) 1519
Swiftly Done (IRE) 391
Swilly Ferry (USA) 816
Syrian 89

Taajub (IRE) 693
Tadhkeer 694
Taher 312

Tamaathul 817
Tappanappa (IRE) 30
Tarita (IRE) 770
Tartan Trip 31
Tartufo Dolce 558
Tasmeem (IRE) 818
Tatawor (IRE) 1578
Tawaabb 287
Taymoor 1416
Technophobe (IRE) 980
Ted Spread 1555
Telescopic 902
Tell Halaf 90
Termagant (IRE) 1367
Tesslam 879
Test Pilot 961
Texas Queen 288
Thaliwarru 1008
That's My Style 597
The Caped Crusader 1532
The Confessor 222
The Kidnapper 344
The Only Boss (IRE) 695
Theladyinquestion 32
Theladyisatramp 91
Theology 1192
Thereafter (USA) 343
Thinks Its All Over 1533
Thistlestar 428
Thomas Baines (USA) 92
Three's A Crowd 519
Thrill 598
Tiger Bright 345
Tiger Cat 1127
Tiger Court 457
Tiger Hawk 203
Tiger Star 530
Tigers Charm 903
Tigranes The Great (IRE) 154
Tigress Hill 1322
Timeless Stride (IRE) 1483
Ting Ting (USA) 1534
Tioman Two 370
Tipperary Boutique (IRE) 819
Tiradito (USA) 155
Tislaam (IRE) 289
Titivation 93
Tiz The Whiz (USA) 141
Tobermory Boy 559
Toga Tiger (IRE) 290
Tomintoul Singer (USA) 240
Tomodachi (IRE) 156
Too Putra (IRE) 346
Torran Sound 531
Totally Invincible (IRE) 1031
Totally Ours 1142
Tower 599
Toy Razor 223

Trade Secret 195
Tranquil Waters (IRE) 820
Trelawny Wells 291
Trewarthenick 33
Troas (IRE) 1300
Tropical Treat 62
Trovare (USA) 1323
True Loves Kiss 1017
True Red 1091
Truly Pink 1535
Trust Deed 600
Truth Seeking (IRE) 1626
Tucker's Law 1092
Tudor Princess 1143
Tulle (IRE) 1065
Turf Time 1018
Tuscan Gold 1391
Twice As Nice 771
Twilight Memory 1066
Twinkling Ice (USA) 637
Tymora (USA) 241

Udabaa (IRE) 1579
Unaccompanied (IRE) 1627
Up At Last 696

Valenzani 601
Valiant Knight (FR) 772
Vanilla Loan (IRE) 157
Varachi 458
Velvet Band 371
Velvet Flicker (IRE) 1368
Ventura Cove (IRE) 539
Viking Dancer 34
Virginia Hall 1392
Visual Element (USA) 347
Vita Nova (IRE) 242
Vita Venturi (IRE) 142
Viviani (IRE) 1324
Volatilis 844
Voysey (IRE) 1325

Waabel 880
Waaheb (USA) 1628
Waajida 1629
Walcot Square (IRE) 348
Walk On Bye (IRE) 1454
Walkingonthemoon 411
Wallgate 213
Walvis Bay 1536
War Angel 1111
Wareen 1438
Warling (IRE) 1193
Warlu Way 499
Warning Song (USA) 1326
Waseet 500
Watch Chain 1556
Water Biscuit 1067
Wause 1439
Weathervane 602

Weeping Willow (IRE) 603
Wealdmore Wave (IRE) 1004
Weliketobouggie 1105
Welsh Angel 1144
West Leake Star (IRE) 821
Westernize 94
What An Issue 697
Whirly Dancer 243
Whiskey Bay (IRE) 1630
Whistle Blower 604
White Finch (USA) 35
Wigan Lane 540
Wigmore Hall 95
William Morgan (IRE) 541
Wing Of Faith 962
Winged 822
Wisecraic 412
Woodrow Call (IRE) 1455
Wriggle (IRE) 698
Wrong Answer (IRE) 1369

Xaara Star (IRE) 915
Yaa Wayl (IRE) 881
Yabtree (IRE) 349
Yankee Bright 560
Yarra River 36
Yes Oh Yes (USA) 143
Yesnabay (USA) 1522
Yorksters Prince 1398
Youm Al Mizayin 292
Youm Jamil (USA) 1068
Youm Mutamiez (USA) 392
Young Simon 1009

Zafeen Spead 1069
Zahoo (IRE) 501
Zelos Spirit 650
Zenarinda 1557
Zero Seven 165
Zigato 605
Zulu Principle 1631

Unnamed 63, 97-98, 100, 103-105, 113-118, 120, 158-162, 167-171, 173-177, 180-181, 183-186, 189, 191, 196-197, 204-210, 224, 244-253, 255-256, 293-304, 313-329, 350-356, 372, 393-400, 413-416, 429-431, 459-462, 502, 506-509, 520-525, 542-550, 561-563, 606-635, 638-639, 651-655, 699-704, 773-776, 782-783, 823-834, 845-854, 882-893, 904-908, 916-917, 932-953, 963-971, 981-982, 986-997, 1005, 1010-1011, 1019, 1032-1033, 1070-1084, 1094-1098, 1106-1108, 1112-1113, 1128-1131, 1145-1154, 1194-1204, 1220-1260, 1270-1288, 1301-1310, 1327-1332, 1339, 1399-1402, 1417-1426, 1440-1441, 1456-1461, 1484-1495, 1520, 1523-1524, 1537-1539, 1580, 1588-1597, 1632-1635, 1641

INDEX OF DAMS

DAM INDEX

Dams appear under the reference number of their offspring.

A P Petal 1533
Aberdovey 1141
Abita 1323
Accell 1399
Acicula 1433
Adaala 1341
Adamas 1045
Addaya 1579
Aeraiocht 125
Affair Of State 91
Affianced 123
After All 234
Agnetha 1600
Agony Aunt 43
Aguilas Perla 1270
Ahdaab 1039
Ahdaaf 435
Ailette 1496
Akanta 432
Akrimina 882
Al Desima 795
Al Persian 692
Al Sifaat 784
Al Theraab 1526
Alabaq 498
Alakananda 238
Alasana 972
Alborada 1374
Alegria 529
Alexander Anapolis 157
Alexander Ballet 504
Alexander Icequeen 870
Alexander Phantom 798
Alexander Queen 1499
Alexandrine 1372
Aliya 1289
Aljafliyah 695
All Embracing 670
All For Laura 166
All Is Fair 510
All My Yesterdays 109
Allegorica 956
Allencat 606
Allied Cause 386
Almond Flower 874
Almost Amber 1271
Almurooj 666
Alnasreya 437
Alpine Gold 470
Alserna 1272
Alshadiyah 484
Alstemeria 132
Alter Ego 429
Altruiste 1484
Alvarita 1373
Alvernia 343

Always Mine 705
Alzianah 1265
Amaryllis 19
Amathusia 1300
Amazed 1070
Amazing Dream 903
Amber Mill 430
Amistad 167
Amour Mio 1537
Amybdancing 533
Anaamil 883
Anapola 1333
Anchorage 723
Angel Wing 962
Angelic Song 925
Anita Madden 1417
Ann's Annie 274
Anna Amalia 1408
Anneliina 823
Annex 1580
Anniversary 225
Anqood 21
Antediluvian 1177
Anthos 664
Anthyllis 520
Antonia's Folly 103
Aonach Mor 726
Apache Star 306
Applaud 371
Apple Sauce 1439
Appointed One 574
Approach 1220
April Evening 133
Aqaarid 339
Aquaba 932
Aquila Oculus 154
Arabesque 607
Arabian Spell 1485
Arboreta 38
Aries 756
Arjuzah 577
Armorique 293
Arpege 1273
Arrive 1486
Arriving 1041
Artifice 239
Arutua 761
Ascot Cyclone 1588
Ascot Starre 1523
Ascot Tobie 1584
Ask Carol 1427
Asmara 1301
Asnieres 1221
Aspen Leaves 1601
Aspiring Diva 1632
Astorg 878
Astromancer 1542
Atalina 1302
Atlantide 487
Attraction 923

Attymon Lill 966
Aunt Flo 158
Aunt Pearl 313
Aunty Mary 863
Aunty Rose 521
Aura Of Glory 203
Aurelia 801, 822
Australian Dreams 933
Australie 447
Autumn Melody 393
Autumn Pearl 1008
Autumn Wealth 934
Autumnal 1071
Averami 23
Avila 168
Avoidance 1633
Ayun 474
Azia 1047
Azra 121

Baby Bunting 539
Bad Kitty 1086
Badawi 96
Bahr 884
Balalaika 935
Balanka 1303
Baldellia 1589
Ballet 513
Ballet Ballon 87
Ballymac Girl 1371
Balmy 1327
Balnaha 4
Bandanna 1476
Banner 1155
Baralinka 369
Barathiki 1145
Baroukh 1590
Basin Street Blues 1453
Bay Tree 1472
Bayalika 758
Bayleaf 1274
Be Glad 244
Be My Wish 1072
Beacon Silver 286
Beading 841
Bee One 516
Beechnut 58
Bella Bellisimo 835
Bella Tusa 78
Belle Argentine 885
Belle Genius 412
Belle Of Honour 820
Belsay 1210
Belterra 608
Bendis 411
Bentley's Bush 52
Beraysim 886
Beryl 404
Bethesda 1025
Bezant 603

Bibi Karam 561
Bienandanza 609
Billet 138
Biloxi 1634
Bint Al Hammour 169
Bint Kaldoun 915
Bintalreef 1324
Binya 792
Biographie 1192
Birdie 88
Birdsong 16
Birthday Suit 153
Blaze Of Colour 864
Blinding 661
Bling Bling 1157
Blue Cloud 710
Blue Crystal 1609
Blue Dream 660
Blue Holly 750
Blue Icon 472
Blue Indigo 204
Blue Kestrel 970
Blue Lullaby 518
Blue Siren 34
Blue Symphony 367
Blushing Barada 314
Blushing Sunrise 1521
Bob's Princess 1017
Bold Bunny 1612
Bolivia 720
Bombazine 394
Bonash 610
Bond Shakira 315
Bonheur 1597
Bonita Gail 410
Bonne Mere 294
Bonnie Doon 706
Border Minstral 217
Bourbonella 681
Brand 22
Branston Berry 61
Branston Gem 316
Branston Jewel 1639
Brazilian Samba 1189
Braziliz 1342
Bread Of Heaven 1139
Break Of Day 112
Bridelina 1194
Brigadiers Bird 196
Bright Halo 1144
Bright Tiara 1515
Brightest Star 1115
Brigid 1222
Brigids Cross 684
Briolette 1179
Broadway Hit 997
Bron Hilda 1275
Brooklyn's Sky 755
Buckle 544
Bumble 1114

TWO YEAR OLDS OF 2009

Bush Baby 1451
Bush Cat 611
By Charter 1223
Bywayofthestars 1224

Caladira 227
Calligraphy 113
Calling Card 1073
Calonnog 1002
Camanoe 1470
Camaret 1347
Camassina 1146
Canis Star 858
Canouan 1567
Canterbury Lace 226
Capades Dancer 1055
Cape Finisterre 1400
Cape Trafalgar 534
Cappadoce 76
Carallia 1446
Carambola 1315
Carefree Cheetah 436
Caressing 612
Carinae 1438
Carollan 644
Carpet Lady 768
Carranita 1267
Carry On Katie 936
Carson Dancer 139
Cash Run 931
Cashel Queen 789
Castaway Queen 1147
Castle Quest 1462
Catcher Applause 444
Catnipped 613
Catsuit 114
Cavernista 538
Cayman Sound 614
Ceirseach 137
Celtic Heroine 875
Celtic Silhouette 59
Centifolia 573
Centre Court 1148
Cephalonie 580
Cerulean Sky 446
Chaffinch 350
Chalice Wells 1195
Chalosse 271
Chance For Romance 1529
Chancey Squaw 585
Changari 193
Change Of Heart 1432
Change Partners 797
Chanterelle 675
Chaturanga 1619
Cheerleader 986
Cheyenne Spirit 1276
Child Prodigy 223
China Beauty 699
Chinchilla 961
Choirgirl 571
Chorist 662
Chorus 1089

Christel Flame 1456
Church Mice 1277
Cidaris 159
Cin Isa Luv 401
Cindy's Star 800
Cinnamon Rose 1513
City Maiden 1418
City Of Gold 973
Civic Duty 987
Classic Park 1182
Classical Dancer 1149
Claxon 479
Clepsydra 245
Clincher Club 887
Clipper 1000
Clochette 295
Cloud Castle 170
Cloud Hill 1028
Clunie 1261
Coeur de la Mer 1591
Coh Sho No 527
Collected 535
Colonella 1487
Columbine 104
Colza 233
Comeraincomeshine 1094
Common Knowledge 1021
Complimentary Pass 1574
Compose 877
Compradore 857
Compton Astoria 215
Condoleezza 640
Confidante 600
Congress 1524
Conspiracy 499
Cookie Cutter 969
Cool Clarity 1610
Coolrain Lady 211
Copy Cat 1122
Coquette Rouge 231
Corinium 813
Corn Futures 558
Corndavon 916
Corrine 296
Cosmic Countess 642
Council Rock 649
Country Spirit 1105
Court Lane 937
Courtier 938
Coventina 1464
Coy 688
Coyote 1316
Cozy Maria 455
Cozzene's Affair 717
Cozzene's Angel 131
Cradle Of Love 1196
Cradle Rock 80
Craigmill 1405
Cribella 526
Crooked Wood 310
Crossbreeze 754
Crown Of Light 983
Cruinn A Bhord 457

Crystal Valkyrie 811
Crystal View 615
Cultered Pearl 721
Cut The Red Tape 782
Cybinka 779

Dafariyna 26
Daily Double 753
Dakhla Oasis 1069
Dalawara 1197
Daltak 1125
Dame Alicia 815
Dame Jude 1010
Danaskaya 477
Dance For Fun 454
Dance Solo 377
Dancing Steps 778
Dangle 1556
Dani Ridge 732
Danielli 1540
Danilova 1225
Dans La Ville 115
Danseuse du Bois 1074
Danzante 332
Danzig Island 485
Dapprima 1209
Darabaka 1343
Darabela 228
Daring Aim 727
Dark Eyed Lady 542
Dark Hyacinth 1160
Dark Rosaleen 66
Darling 1344
Dash To The Top 1211
Dashiba 511
Date Mate 1365
Dawn Chorus 1339
Dawn Raid 1346
Day Is Dawning 1099
Dayville 1266
Delicieuse Lady 888
Delisha 1102
Delta 616
Demeter 72
Denice 665
Desert Lynx 939
Desert Order 722
Desert Tigress 345
Devil's Imp 1132
Dhelaal 1572
Diabaig 1264
Diamond Lodge 764
Diamonds For Lil 143
Diary 1106
Diddymu 270
Diese 617
Dime Bag 1226
Diner De Lune 267
Discoed 1278
Discreet Brief 1128
Distant Music 471
Divine Grace 502
Dixie Favor 1262

Doctrine 814
Dollysister 1063
Dolma 344
Dolores 576
Donna Vita 482
Doohulla 75
Dorrati 889
Doula 335
Dowager 1370
Downland 1029
Dowry 467
Dragnet 1065
Drama Class 1466
Dream Lady 725
Dream Quest 480
Dress Code 746
Dry Lightning 541
Dubai Surprise 940
Dubious 1550
Dublino 1191
Duelling 1016
Dundel 773
Dunloskin 904
Dusty Answer 673
Duty Paid 512
Dwingeloo 1129
Dyna Flyer 1320

Easter Heroine 506
Easy Mover 37
Easy Sunshine 171
Easy To Love 1543
Ebadiyla 1291
Ebatana 1304
Echo River 941
Ecoutila 1473
Edetana 297
Elasouna 1305
Elite Guest 357
Eliza 1095
Elizabethan Age 1479
Ellebanna 1036
Elrehaan 476
Elshamms 1568
Embassy Belle 48
Emerald Fire 172
Emma's Star 824
Emplane 246
Empress Anna 173
En Garde 1198
Enchant 79
Encore My Love 483
Endless Peace 651
Endure 786
Enlisted 1101
Entente Cordiale 1388
Entwine 205
Epiphany 317
Epistoliere 24
Epping 1173
Ermine 790
Erreur 1616
Escrow Agent 1419

INDEX OF DAMS 363

Esplanade 825
Esteemed Lady 1043
Eternity 1381
Eternity Ring 652
Etizaaz 490
Eva Luna 839
Evangeline 1219
Eve 65
Eveningperformance 218
Exciting Times 1190
Exorcet 2
Exotic Forest 1337
Exponent 417
Extreme Beauty 988

Fair Settlement 618
Fairy Godmother 1475
Fallen Star 578
Family At War 1445
Fanofadiga 378
Fantaisiste 358
Fapindy 977
Faraway Waters 910
Farda Amiga 1227
Farrfesheena 97
Fatefully 1420
Fatwa 1607
Fear And Greed 1457
Feather Boa 298
Feet Of Flame 1103
Fickle 619
Fictitious 760
Fifty Five 735
Final Favour 905
Final Pursuit 53
Final Shot 1150
Finity 1104
Fire Flower 844
Firesteed 402
First Fantasy 845
First Musical 197
Firth of Lorne 1502
Fivefive 1011
Flames 1538
Flames Last 638
Flaming Song 620
Flavian 219
Fleet Hill 1563
Fleeting Rainbow 305
Flirtation 93
Flower Market 1020
Fly For Fame 975
Fly Like The Wind 643
Flying Squaw 1497
Follow That Dream 230
Foofaraw 92
For Dixie 135
Forest Call 1560
Forest Lady 475
Forest Prize 50
Forest Storm 277
Formal Approval 1118
Forty Gran 1407

Fragrant Cloud 1009
Fragrant Oasis 846
Franglais 1263
Frappe 372
Frascati 601
Fresh Look 777
Friendlier 621
Frilly Front 39
Fritta Mista 1359
Frizzante 1058
Frosty Welcome 69
Fruit Punch 734
Fudge 989
Funny Girl 280
Funsie 564

Gaily Lady 1596
Gallivant 1170
Gay Gallanta 1167
Geminiani 890
Generous Gesture 957
Generous Option 1421
Genetta 1279
Get Lucky 1228
Gift Of Spring 1171
Gipsy Moth 1530
Gleam Of Light 562
Glenarcy 1412
Glinting Desert 1206
Glittering Image 6
Global Trend 622
Glorious 82
Gold And Blue 1636
Gold Bar 1482
Gold Field 1090
Gold Queen 1062
Golden Anthem 419
Golden Cat 593
Golden Crown 116
Golden Dew 1366
Golden Flyer 198
Golden Opinion 545
Golden Silca 623
Goldendale 146
Good Enough 55
Good Mood 650
Goodness Gracious 147
Gothic Dream 1325
Gracious Gretclo 106
Grail 1013
Grain Of Gold 330
Granny Kelly 1442
Grazia 1376
Great Verdict 1127
Greeba 283
Green Noon 464
Green Room 1158
Green Rosy 495
Green Swallow 309
Greta d'Argent 418
Gronchi Rosa 1140
Gryada 1229
Guana 1162

Guignol 624
Gwyneth 1096

Hagwah 1558
Handaza 1292
Handsome Anna 774
Hannda 568
Harayir 659
Harmonist 318
Hasten 625
Hathrah 491
Have Faith 990
Hawala 1205
Hazariya 1306
Headrest 459
Healing Music 1230
Heart Lake 117
Heart Stopping 1448
Her Ladyship 206
Hidden Agenda 712
Hidden Meaning 1363
High Reserve 385
High Straits 682
Highbrook 1555
Highest Dream 781
Hill Welcome 1440
Hit It Here Cafe 1280
Hoity Toity 1213
Homeward 1397
Honest Lady 247
Honey Storm 522
Honfleur 1559
Horatia 917
Houdini's Honey 1156
Hsi Wang Mu 1052
Humble Fifteen 891
Hushaby 998
Hydro Calido 856
Hymn Of Love 1624
Hyperspectra 382
Hypnotize 54

I'm A Caution 1178
Ibtihal 1111
Ibtikar 1187
Imagine 1231
Imperial Bailiwick 700
Imperial Graf 978
Imperialist 1434
Imroz 248
In Anticipation 1620
In The Limelight 1481
In The Pink 281
Inchberry 1322
Incheni 1561
Inchiri 1186
Inchyre 1314
Independence 656
Ingeburg 319
Injaaz 174
Interim 249
Intriguing 1611
Inya Lake 729

Ionian Sea 847
Irina 963
Iris May 1386
Irresistible 598
Isana 698
Isla Azul 566
Islandagore 1336
Isle Of Flame
Israar 1409
Issa 449
Isticanna 1281
It Takes Two 626
It's A Secret 1188
It's On The Air 1452
Ithaca 1488
Its All Relative 810
Itsibitsi 30
Ivory Bride 156

Jabali 395
Jakarta Jade 1353
Jalissa 351
Janayen 279
Jawaher 1135
Jeed 451
Jeweled Lady 1581
Jinsiyah 1137
Jinx Johnson 507
Jode 1364
Jojeema 25
Jouet 1463
Journey Of Hope 51
Joyfullness 445
Julie Jalouse 1293
Jumaireyah 373
Juno Madonna 73
Jupiter Inlet 20
Just A Bird 35
Just In Love 201

Kafayef 311
Kahlua Bay 1422
Kalamba 1294
Kalima 250
Kamareyah 107
Kangra Valley 663
Kapria 7
Karliyna 1517
Karsiyaka 546
Kassiyra 376
Kastaway 195
Katariya 13
Katayeb 1570
Katherine Seymour 1413
Katiba 428
Katrina 251
Kawn 690
Keepers Dawn 714
Keepers Hill 816
Kelang 149
Kelly Nicole 140
Kenema 110
Kerataka 1296

364 TWO YEAR OLDS OF 2009

Kermiyana 1295
Key Academy 1573
Khubza 1360
Khulood 486
Kilbride Lass 955
Kildare Lady 581
Kind 252
Kinetic Force 347
Kinnaird 780
Kissogram 1232
Kite Mark 160
Kithanga 380
Kitty O'Shea 1233
Known Class 1549
Kotdiji 1458
Krissante 1234
Kriva 733
Krynica 1183
Kylemore 667
Kythia 291

L'Ancresse 1236
La Belga 683
La Belle Katherine 1024
La Meillure 136
La Persiana 900
Labrusca 547
Ladeena 1500
Lady Angola 289
Lady Donatella 15
Lady Elysees 865
Lady Georgina 741
Lady Karr 1235
Lady Lahar 89
Lady Liberty 1163
Lady Liesel 1423
Lady Luck 1598
Lady Moranbon 200
Lady Nicholas 555
Lady Oriande 689
Lady Salsa 783
Lady Wells 1282
Lady Windermere 1214
Lady Zonda 175
Lakabi 928
Lake Nipigon 1505
Lake Poopo 1544
Lamanka Lass 28
Landmark 396
Last Second 1379
Lasting Chance 976
Latest Chapter 653
Laurel Delight 1237
Lay A Whisper 213
Le Montrachet 403
Lead Story 942
Leaping Water 1238
Legend Has It 1627
Leominda 508
Leopard Hunt 1161
Let Alone 40
Licence To Thrill 943
Licorne 739

Lidakiya 1297
Lidanna 881
Light Jig 1489
Lilyfoot 14
Limanora 686
Limpopo 1536
Line Ahead 425
Lishaway 1615
Liska 742
Lizanne 1107
Lochangel 27
Locharia 299
Londonnet 1547
Lonely Ahead 826
Look For Good 794
Look Here's Carol 1026
Lorien Hill 796
Lorientaise 349
Louella 1391
Love And Affection 964
Love And Laughter 95
Love Everlasting 98
Love Excelling 1037
Loveleaves 918
Lovely Later 944
Lovely Lyca 1121
Low Tolerance 176
Lowrianna 320
Luce 448
Lucky 1587
Lucky Norwegian 954
Lucky Oakwood 408
Lumber Jill 1350
Luminaria 127
Lunar Colony 627
Lunda 177
Lupulina 788
Lurina 1512
Lyca Ballerina 759
Lyrical Dance 348

Ma N'ieme Biche 207
Macademia 583
Madam Ninette 809
Madamaa 307
Madame Boulangere 1510
Madame Cerito 1185
Madame Dubois 452
Madeira Mist 1239
Magic Sister 360
Magick Top 434
Magnificient Style 1097
Magnolia Lane 836
Maharani 84
Maid For The Hills 587
Maid Of Killeen 77
Maid To Matter 41
Maid To Perfection 478
Maid To Treasure 494
Mail The Desert 657
Maine Lobster 567
Majestic Desert 268
Majestical 118

Majesty's Dancer 552
Majudel 1455
Makara 991
Mambo Mistress 740
Mambo Slew 921
Mambodorga 331
Mamounia 803
Man Eater 672
Mardavilla 1218
Mango Groove 981
Mania 868
Mantesera 178
Marain 718
Marajuana 31
Marani 352
March Star 194
Mare Nostrum 945
Margay 1100
Marie de Blois 898
Marimar 1545
Marisa 163, 262
Market Slide 1614
Marlene-D 554
Maroochydore 49
Martinique 806
Mary Jane 423
Marynsky 1240
Masaader 433
Masakala 1307
Massada 67
Massarra 1290
Masskana 1241
Maugusta 1283
Maura's Guest 368
Maycocks Bay 605
Mayenne 639
Mazuna 179
Melikah 1504
Mellow Jazz 180
Menhoubah 181
Merewood 182
Mexican Hawk 1172
Mezzo Soprano 1514
Michelle Hicks 894
Michelle Ma Belle 967
Midnight Shift 654
Milagra 1313
Mill Line 906
Mille 1180
Millefiori 45
Millie's Choice 1068
Milly Fleur 321
Millyant 655
Min Asl Wafi 288
Minerwa 290
Minister's Melody 1519
Minnie Habit 1378
Mint Royale 426
Miriana 765
Mirina 1215
Mise 543
Miss Assertive 1199
Miss Corinne 1396

Miss Corniche 81
Miss Coronado 1509
Miss Hawai 876
Miss Honorine 992
Miss Indigo 334
Miss Katmandu 85
Miss Langkawi 420
Miss Megs 1075
Miss Meltemi 1
Miss Mirasol 5
Miss Moore 1447
Miss Moses 397
Miss Party Line 871
Miss Rimex 458
Miss Riviera Golf 83
Miss Trish 1428
Miss Universe 366
Misterah 1569
Mistic Sun 364
Mithl Al Hawa 1110
Mitraillette 647
Miznapp 261
Mo Stopher 982
Model Queen 867
Moet 1355
Molly Moon 1441
Mona Em 1436
Montana Lady 1005
Mood Swings 946
Moon Dazzle 676
Moon West 730
Moonlight Dance 1242
Morale 413
Morning Queen 108
Moselle 819
Moss 1076
Most Precious 1459
Mothers Footprints 257
Motto 848
Mrs Gray 1435
Mrs Marsh 715
Mt Kobla 1356
Mubkera 701
Muja Farewell 1430
Multicolour Wave 1004
Mumbo Jumbo 151
Music Lane 1168
Musical Key 1565
Musical Treat 1507
Musical Twist 1117
Mustique Dream 208
Muwajaha 1562
Muwakleh 812
Muwali 1056
My Boston Gal 1506
My Dubai 892
My Emma 1243
My First Romance 1051
My Potters 1317
My Reem 407
My Sweet Heart 1534
Mysterial 1511
Mystery Play 424

INDEX OF DAMS 365

Mystic Belle 300
Mythie 1477

Naazeq 1284
Nafisah 1628
Najah 880
Najayeb 500
Namaste 628
Name OF Love 336
Nasaieb 183
Nasij 450
National Swagger 126
Native Force 1077
Nausicaa 1352
Naval Affair 1044
Nawaji 503
Necklace 1244
Nesting 540
Never Away 793
Nevis Peak 265
New Deal 855
New Orchid 827
Next Time 1018
Night Mirage 848
Night Rhapsody 42
Night Scent 71
Night Spirit 1285
Nini Princesse 1605
Ninotchka 1389
Nishan 636
Noble Desert 301
Noble Destiny 276
Noble Peregrine 1404
Nofa's Magic 469
Norfolk Lavender 920
North Sea 384
Not Before Time 1490
Notjustaprettyface 62
Nousairya 901
Noushkey 1032
Nouveau Riche 468
Novelette 414
Now That's Jazz 808
Nufoos 919
Nuit Sans Fn 1035
Numidie 1245

Oatey 363
Obsessive 557
Occhi Verdi 1057
Odalisque 1398
Odette 1392
Oh Bej Oh Bej 144
Oman Sea 266
Onda Nova 1478
One So Wonderful 387
Onereuse 1246
Only In Dreams 406
Opening Ceremony 536
Opera Glass 18
Opera Ridge 1321
Orford Ness 1491
Oriental Fashion 1348

Orinoco 1311
Orlena 902
Our Queen Of Kings 805
Out Like Magic 1450
Out Of Thanks 999
Overboard 960
Overcome 284
Owdbetts 1335

Painted Moon 99
Palace Affair 1124
Palatial 599
Paola Maria 1136
Papabile 747
Park Approach 818
Park Ave Princess 1019
Park Crystal 1345
Park Romance 993
Part With Pride 466
Party Doll 443
Pat Or Else 646
Patacake Patacake 702
Peace Time 1217
Pearl Bright 787
Pearl Dance 597
Peep Show 842
Pelagia 263
Penelewey 528
Penmayne 287
Penny Cross 86
Perfect Partner 1119
Performing Arts 184
Pericardia 453
Persian Fantasy 493
Personal Love 259
Petite Epaulette 1151
Petite Spectre 1061
Petonellajill 1064
Petra Nova 1577
Phariseek 1532
Philadelphie 1087
Photo Flash 460
Picolette 282
Pie High 46
Pilgrim Of Grace 772
Pina Colada 1078
Pink Cashmere 551
Pink Cristal 1247
Pink Supreme 216
Pioneer Bride 947
Pious 668
Pipalong 1454
Pippa's Dancer 1133
Pitcroy 1390
Placement 1586
Play With Fire 33
Playful Act 1468
Playgirl 221
Plead 415
Pleine Lune 492
Poised 12
Polar Storm 757
Polish Affair 1592

Polish Romance 565
Polish Spring 1269
Politesse 678
Polly Perkins 1593
Polygueza 1411
Portelet 438
Portrait Of A Lady 1298
Powder Blue 375
Prakara 1613
Preference 579
Premier Prize 515
Presto Vento 1416
Pretty Poppy 224
Princess Kris 1357
Princess Luna 596
Princess Manila 64
Princess Mood 63
Princess Speedfit 1006
Private Life 338
Private Line 1328
Prodigal Daughter 716
Proflare 1329
Promenade 1358
Proud Myth 105
Pudding Lane 911
Pure Gold 802
Purepleasureseeker 1552
Purple Tiger 693
Pussie Willow 1551

Quandary 353
Queen Of Palms 1621
Queen Sceptre 1527
Queen Titi 1207
Queen's Logic 1049
Questina 979
Quickstyx 269
Quiet Weekend 590
Quiff 1492
Quiz Time 1640

Race The Wild Wind 322
Radioactivity 697
Rag Top 762
Raheefa 679
Rainbow City 1050
Rainbow Queen 383
Rainbows For All 70
Raindancing 185
Ramona 1564
Rampage 56
Raphaela 379
Rasana 161
Ratukidul 232
Ravine 1431
Read Federica 1437
Reasonably Devout 323
Rebecca Sharp 595
Reborn 1554
Red Affair 1319
Red Azalea 398
Red Beach 821
Red Flame 1166

Red Fuschia 763
Red Peony 1176
Red Piano 1401
Red Shareef 57
Red Slipper 1553
Red Trance 1091
Reem One 838
Reematna 713
Regal Darcey 807
Regal Rose 1138
Regina 691
Regina Maria 629
Remediate 1493
Renowned Cat 186
Reunion 588
Reve d'Iman 1602
Reveuse de Jour 1539
Revival 389
Rhondaling 134
Ribbons And Bows 799
Ricadonna 1079
Ringmoor Down 1334
Ripalong 1415
Ripple Of Pride 111
Rise 324
Rise 'N Shine 422
River Belle 1518
River Cara 36
Rock Salt 1367
Roman Love 872
Romantic Drama 214
Romea 1578
Roodeye 913
Roofer 1130
Ros The Boss 1340
Rosapenna 840
Rose Of Zollern 924
Roseau 1402
Roshani 641
Rosie's Posy 199
Rosina May 1007
Rosy Outlook 530
Rouge Noir 775
Rouwaki 828
Rowaasi 879
Royal Fizz 1465
Royal Flame 766
Royal Lady 1112
Royal Orchid 1088
Royal Passion 1054
Rubies From Burma 548
Ruby Affair 1629
Ruby Rocket 586
Rule Britannia 388
Rumansy 1599
Runs In The Family 971
Rush Hour 212
Russian Dance 1164
Rye 1286

Saabga 873
Sabaah 1625
Sabreon 302

366 TWO YEAR OLDS OF 2009

Sacred Love 1169
Sadalsud 1113
Sadie Thompson 523
Safeen 1053
Sagamartha 399
Saganeca 1460
Sahara Rose 645
Sahara Star 630
Sahool 1571
Saibhreas 736
Sail By Night 1030
Saint Ann 1152
Saint Boom 325
Sakhya 308
Salagama 897
Samriah 1630
Samut 1248
Sanpa Fan 456
Santolina 631
Santorini 1143
Sao Gabriel 843
Sara Moon 1508
Saraa Ree 359
Saramacca 829
Saratoga Sugar 155
Sarayir 1566
Sarcita 1014
Sarifa 1384
Sarina's Princess 1349
Saristar 362
Sateen 142
Satin Bell 1385
Satin Flower 948
Sauterne 594
Savieres 260
Saxon Maid 632
Sayyedati 830
Scandalette 1387
Scottish Exile 680
Scottish Spice 958
Scribonia 130
Scrooby Baby 1015
Sea Of Showers 229
Seamstress 1351
Search Party 278
Seattle Ribbon 517
Sebastene 1031
Security Interest 1080
See You Later 949
Seek Easy 1040
Sefemm 1131
Sejm's Lunar Star 416
Selebela 145
Sena Desert 703
Sentimental Value 591
Sequoyah 1249
Serene Nobility 1403
Serene View 831
Seven Moons 237
Seven Of Nine 1153
Shaanara 1287
Shabby Chic 1528
Shades Of Rosegold 724

Shadow Dancing 1575
Shadow Roll 100
Shahalo 1081
Shakalaka Baby 1377
Shalwell 1109
Shambodia 749
Shannon Dore 549
Shapely 463
Sharakawa 1200
Sharesha 1299
Sharp Minister 560
Sharplaw Star 1001
Shbakni 1414
She's The Tops 1085
Sheepscot 1250
Sheer Reason 1424
Sheesha 220
Sheppard's Cross 671
Shimna 1501
Shining Bright 1635
Shining Desert 1444
Shiva 241
Shivaree 240
Shohrah 1576
Shoogle 633
Short Shadow 1288
Shortfall 866
Shouk 1251
Show Off 896
Showbiz 1038
Shuruk 694
Shy Lady 392
Sierra Madre 442
Siksikawa 959
Silent 292
Silent Eskimo 950
Silent Heir 187
Silk Law 1023
Silver Bracelet 1594
Silver Kestrel 440
Silver Queen 1184
Silver Rhapsody 11
Silvereine 1092
Silvia Diletta 1082
Simianna 101
Singed 235
Sinnariya 1308
Sinntara 1309
Sintra 1060
Ski Run 912
Sky Galaxy 1268
Slap Shot 951
Sleepytime 94
Snow Peak 731
Snow Polina 952
Snowdrops 481
So Discreet 10
So Spirited 634
Solar Crystal 1582
Solvig 687
Somaggia 209
Someone Special 674
Someone's Angel 421

Sometime 361
Sometime Never 441
Song Of Hope 604
Song Of Skye 572
Song Track 1516
Sophielu 326
Sophisticat 1252
Sosumi 1546
Sound Asleep 1330
Soundwave 439
Source Of Life 859
South Bay Cove 129
Southern Swing 1066
Souvenir Souvenir 743
Spacecraft 253
Spanish Gold 1338
Sparkle Of Stones 1469
Special Dancer 1541
Special Oasis 1253
Speciale 744
Specifically 1480
Speech Room 1083
Speedy Sonata 1522
Spice Island 192
Spinner 1201
Spinning The Yarn 575
Spirit Of Tara 365
Splendid 1254
Splice 1382
Spot Prize 514
Spotlight 497
Spout 342
Spritzeria 677
Spry 285
Staploy 752
Star Express 985
Star Queen 804
Star Tulip 29
Starchy 1467
Stark Passage 849
Starlight Dreams 1212
Starry Ice 637
Starstone 1583
State Secret 994
Staylily 980
Storm Dove 832
Streetcar 1202
Strike Lightly 354
String Quartet 995
Strings 532
Stroke Of Six 1637
Stylist 202
Subtle Affair 1394
Subya 850
Success Story 162
Succinct 556
Sudenlylastsummer 550
Sulitelma 427
Summer Breeze 1494
Summer Crush 1003
Summer Dreams 1425
Summer Spice 1622
Summer Trysting 1618

Sumora 122
Sun On The Sea 1641
Sun Seasons 1606
Sun Silk 769
Sunblush 1059
Sunley Stars 771
Sunny Davis 592
Sunset Café 1175
Super Crusty 738
Super Gift 1623
Superlove 461
Supersonic 563
Superstar Leo 685
Surprise Me 1449
Surval 188
Susi Wong 851
Susun Kelapa 340
Sweet Firebird 1098
Sweet Home Alabama 1383
Sweet Pea 1503
Sweeten Up 1255
Swift Baba 431
Swilly 1042
Swingsky 767
Swiss Roll 1461

Tafseer 236
Tahrir 817
Takarna 272
Takarouna 1310
Takrice 150
Talah 1426
Talighta 1084
Tamalain 1331
Tammany Hall 1256
Tanaghum 501
Tantina 355
Tap Dance 1361
Tarbela 709
Tarfshi 860
Tariysha 1034
Tasha Yar 1406
Tashrya 524
Tatora 327
Tee Cee 1429
Tee Kay 1257
Teeba 496
Tell Me Now 553
Temple Street 711
Tempting Fate 165
Ten Carats 462
Tencarola 1093
Tender Is Thenight 582
Tenpence 1557
Tentative 1332
Tentpole 381
Tequise 895
Testament 658
The In Laws 559
The Jotter 505
Theatrical Pause 405
Thorntoun Piccolo 707
Thracian 519

INDEX OF DAMS 367

Three Days In May 273
Three Wishes 907
Thunder Kitten 1520
Tia Lea 1326
Tidie France 1595
Timber Tops 1123
Time Crystal 390
Timed Saved 189
Tincture 1535
Titchwell Lass 275
Tobaranama 525
Tochar Ban 862
Toffee Nosed 1165
Token Grsture 1604
Top Forty 333
Top Table 909
Topiary 74
Topkamp 90
Tosca 264
Total Aloof 908
Totally Yours 1142
Touch Of Truth 1626
Traou Mad 1380
Traude 899
Treble Seven 1126
Treca 242
Tree Peony 341
Trempjane 1617
Trew Class 1548
Tribal Lady 1120
Trick 930
Triple Green 965
Triple Zee 996
Trois Heures Apres 1483
Troubling 141
True Crystal 1048
True Joy 893
True Love 120
Truly Generous 852
Trump Street 1027
Trust Your Heart 1525
Try To Catch Me 8

Trying For Gold 337
Tu Eres Mi Amore 1631
Tulipe Noire 751
Tutu Much 1362
Twenty Eight Carat 926
Twiggy's Sister 1603
Twilight Mistress 222
Two Clubs 869
Two Halos 1585
Tyranny 1181

Umniya 1154
Unfortunate 102
Unique Pose 1608
Untimely 584
Upend 696
Upperville 1474
Uptown 152
Urgent Liaison 346
Ushindi 17

Vagary 124
Valandraud 1033
Valentine Band 1258
Valley Lights 190
Vanishing Prairie 1259
Vanitycase 785
Varenka 589
Velouette 853
Velvet Appeal 1368
Velvet Queen 400
Velvet Slipper 968
Velvet Waters 531
Ventura 9
Ventura Highway 861
Venturi 1159
Verasina 254
Via Borghese 60
Victoria Lodge 854
Vida 1012
Villa Carlotta 44
Villa Deste 1395

Vinicky 1443
Volvoreta 148

Waafiah 312
Wadud 922
Walayef 1354
Waldmark 1531
Walkamia 1193
Walnut Lady 1108
Wandesta 255
Waratah 833
Waroonga 570
Wars 1134
Waterfall One 1067
Way For Life 1318
Wedding Morn 1046
Weekend In Seattle 1498
Weiner Wald 47
Well Warned 256
Welsh Valley 837
Weqaar 473
Westerly Air 602
Westerly Gale 303
Westlife 1312
Westwood 210
What A Picture 489
Whats Doin 708
Whazzat 32
Wheeler's Wonder 537
Where's Charlotte 1203
Whirly Bird 243
Whitby 745
White Palace 1375
White Rose 791
Whittle Woods Girl 669
Whole Grain 370
Widescreen 356
Wild Catseye 748
Wild Planet 984
Willisa 1638
Willowbridge 509
Wimple 191

Wince 1495
Windomen 914
Winning Colors 1204
Winning Season 929
Wish 1116
Wish List 409
Wissal 488
Witch Of Fife 1208
With A Wink 927
Withorwithoutyou 569
Wolf Cleugh 953
Woodland Orchid 465
Woodmaven 719
Words Of War 1260
Wosaita 704
Wrong Key 1369
Wunderbra 68
Wunders Dream 1174

Ya Hajar 258
Yabint El Sham 1022
Yanomami 328
Yding 737

Zabadani 329
Zaghruta 834
Zanna 776
Zavaleta 128
Zeeba 374
Zenda 635
Zietory 1216
Ziffany 391
Zina La Belle 728
Zither 1471
Zoftig 1410
Zonic 770
Zoom Lens 974
Zuleika Dobson 304
Zuri 164
Zvezda 1393